Harold Macmillan, Prime Minister of Great Britain for nearly seven years until his retirement in 1963, is, on the evidence of this volume, one of the most winning and complex of contemporary figures. Half-Scottish and half-American by birth, wholly English by upbringing, he emerges from these pages as a man of deep sensitivity and feeling, with a strong vein of underplayed sardonic humor and an impassioned sense of justice. His memoirs present the history of our times through the personal experience of a participant long involved with great events.

Mr. Macmillan tells in his opening volume the story of the stark onset of the winds of change: the fifty-year revolution that began with the convulsive death of the old world in the horrors of the First World War. The world of his childhood and adolescence was, indeed, the old, split-down-the-middle world—on one side, wealth and privilege; on the other, poverty and frustration—and much of the emotional drama and many outward events reported here reflect his increasing involvement with the victims of social injustice.

Macmillan was twenty, and still at Oxford, when the Great War began. As an officer in the Grenadier Guards, he saw active colleagues. Despite his party label, he was a friend and admirer of Lloyd George, subscribed to many of Keynes's economic theories and took the lead in promoting social legislation.

Then, as the thirties darkened, he allied himself with Churchill and Eden in their futile stand against the Government's appeasement of Hitler. The chapters in which he recalls what it felt like to watch the drift to war are vivid with emotion. Through the Sudeten crisis, through Munich, through impassioned battles in the House of Commons, the volume moves to its end on September 3, 1939, when, after twenty years of social and economic upheaval, Britain, almost totally unprepared, once more went to war.

Written with intensity, directness and grace, *Winds of Change* is seasoned with Macmillan's unexpected and utterly frank appraisals of his great contemporaries and with scenes of unforgettable immediacy—some disarming in their intimacy, others epic in drama.

WINDS
OF CHANGE

1914-1939

HAROLD MACMILLAN

*

B

HARPER & ROW, PUBLISHERS

New York and Evanston

Contents

Illustrations

*The following are grouped in a separate
section after page 248.*

Harold Macmillan at Loos
Daniel Macmillan
Alexander Macmillan
Dr. J. Tarleton Belles
Mrs. J. Tarleton Belles
Harold Macmillan, aged four
Harold Macmillan, aged twelve
Maurice Crawford Macmillan
Helen Macmillan
The Oxford Union, 1912
Lady Dorothy Cavendish
The author and his son, Maurice Macmillan
Christmas at Chatsworth
Harold and Lady Dorothy Macmillan and their children
Coal strike poster
Bus leaving garage during the General Strike
Electioneering in Stockton, 1929
The unemployed being fed in Hyde Park, 1931
First cabinet meeting of the National Government
Harold Macmillan at Stockton, 1935
Stanley Baldwin
The War Cabinet, November 1939
Sir Oswald Mosley
Neville Chamberlain
Harold and Lady Dorothy Macmillan with nursery-school children

Acknowledgements

I wish to express my thanks to the writers of personal letters, or their representatives, who have allowed me to publish extracts in the text.

Also I have to record my debt to a number of histories, biographies, and autobiographies, which I have consulted, especially to those specified in the footnotes.

I am deeply grateful to Miss Anne Glyn-Jones, who has carried out all the necessary research into my own papers and other relevant books and documents, as well as to Miss Mary Manus, Miss Anne Macpherson, and Miss Susie Mercer, who have typed and retyped with exemplary care and patience.

Finally, I have to thank Mr. David Dilks, who has put at my disposal his unrivalled knowledge of this period.

H.M.

February 1966

Prologue

I HAVE started to write this book on 4 August 1964, the fiftieth anniversary of the outbreak of the First World War. This fearful conflict, to be followed within a single generation by a second, of even greater magnitude and duration, set in motion forces, in every part of the globe, which have led to the most far-reaching revolution in recorded history. We are still too near to these events to grasp their full implications. Yet, in these convulsions, the old world has perished and a new world has been born.

Fifty years ago, the great European nations still enjoyed the traditions or cherished the hopes of imperial power.

For myself, I can just recall what was the zenith of our imperial fabric, and of the structure of which the Queen-Empress was the apex. It was the Jubilee of 1897. If my recollection of the Queen is dim, even although fortified by constant repetition in the nursery, I have a clear picture in my mind of the endless procession of troops, of all races, with an infinite variety of uniform, led by Captain Ames, the tallest officer in the British Army. In 1914 all these diverse forces were available, without question, to the support of British power and interests.

Perhaps, in the inter-war period, there was a growing realisation of the inevitability of a process of transformation in due course. Yet we still used to sing, without embarrassment, the hymn of the ever-widening Empire, on whose bounds the sun never set.

Today, when the major European Powers have either shed their responsibilities or merged them in a wider and looser association, these dreams have vanished and these concepts seem to the modern generation either incomprehensible, or distasteful.

Meanwhile, throughout the world, another revolution has been occurring, to which the two wars gave tremendous impetus—a revolution of which I am reminded, as I write these words, by the great jet airliners roaring overhead to Gatwick Airport, or by the stream of cars on the country roads, replacing the clop and jingle of the horse-drawn traffic of my childhood. The vast changes wrought by the development of science and technology have permeated every aspect of life. The lights that were going out all over Europe in August 1914 had flickered in dark slums as well as shone in brilliant assemblies. Today, the rays of applied science have brought to the humblest homes an illumination of widespread comforts and conveniences, undreamt-of in the first decade of the century. Yet they have also brought new and terrible fears, with soulless means of mass destruction from which our fathers would have shrunk in horror as well as amazement.

Though technology has greatly facilitated the social revolution which is one of the most striking features of the last fifty years, it has not been the only agent. In contrast to the excessive individualism, the 'devil take the hindmost' philosophy of the nineteenth century, there has developed a sense of collective responsibility, of caring for the human family, in some ways more akin to medieval ideals. When an archbishop could speak of Communism as a 'Christian heresy', he revealed how far we had come from a generation that was content to sing of 'the rich man in his castle, the poor man at his gate', and complacently ascribe to the Almighty sole responsibility for their respective estates. To most people in Britain, because it affects their lives so closely, the coming of the Welfare State is perhaps the most marked of all the changes that the last fifty years have brought. Yet in this new growth of collectivism, the finer aspects of the individualism of the Reformation, the freedom of personal decision, initiative, and responsibility, have not been forgotten. Indeed, much of the controversy in domestic politics has been generated by the fruitful interaction between these two philosophies.

With this change in social attitudes has come a new era in economic thinking. The years between the wars saw the decay of the old Liberal doctrine of *laissez-faire*. There began to grow in most impartial minds the idea that some form of effective partnership must be formed between the State and those concerned in production, distribution, and even exchange. The most extreme form of reaction from orthodox theory—that is, Marxist Socialism—was not seriously put forward even by the Labour Party. Yet to those Tories who had delved into their party's history and brooded over its philosophy, it was clear that the traditional principles, fiscal and economic, of Toryism had been weakened since 1886 by Whig and Liberal recruits. In the Liberal Party, Asquith and his more 'moderate' followers were faithful to the classical economic doctrines; yet the vital force and strength which Lloyd George brought into play before the First War had left their mark. As the international situation darkened in the thirties and rearmament became essential, these problems of the relations between Government and industry became more acute and more urgent.

For Britain, two world wars have meant the outpouring of her wealth on such a scale that from the leading creditor nation of the capitalist world, she has become, at least in the short term, a constant and embarrassed debtor. Nothing has altered more since my youth than the relative strength of the British economy. In those days, the mysteries of exchange, balance of payments, inflation or deflation, the size of reserves, the rate of growth, were carefully hidden from the vulgar gaze. They played little or no part in the political controversies of the day. They were scarcely referred to even by the serious part of the Press, and altogether neglected by the popular journals. Most businessmen spent their lives without thinking about them at all. If they exported their products, they did so for profit and not under the impulse of an officially inspired export drive.

Already before the Second World War, the emergence into public discussion of the question of money, which was fiercely debated with almost theological fervour by economists and politicians in the twenties and thirties, marked a profound departure from the prevailing atmosphere of the years before 1914, when the business community, broadly speaking, did not concern itself with the workings of the monetary system. But in the inter-war years, especially after the effects on Britain of a return to gold with an overvalued pound, and on all the capitalist world of the general collapse of the credit structure in 1929–31, problems which had long been regarded as academic became cruelly practical. Men began to question the sanctity of a monetary faith which appeared to condemn them to poverty and unemployment, when the unused resources were so great and so apparent. 'Starvation in the midst of plenty' became a popular slogan to describe this paradox.[1]

All these are still lively issues. The question of the proper relationship between the State and industry and commerce is still debated, sometimes on a theoretical and sometimes on a practical basis. In spite of the great achievements of the various international systems for the improvement of credit, and the arrangements to prevent the recurrence of a general slump being precipitated by the difficulties of particular countries, we are all aware that the question has not been finally resolved. The debate continues; plan after plan is still being put forward. Although up to now the world has escaped disaster—partly, perhaps, because of the general acceptance that capitalist society must expand or die—yet we live with our fingers crossed, and if we are honest are forced to admit that we have not yet found the true answer. The basis of credit still does not match the potentialities of production. The risk remains.

My first volume carries the story through one war to the beginning of another. For most of us, the greater part of this period appeared full of hope and confidence. In spite of difficulties, we did not doubt that knowledge, inspired by enthusiasm, would lead us to the right solutions. It was only in the last few years that we seemed to be drifting, as in a Greek tragedy, to a catastrophe that we could foresee, but could do little either to forestall or to prevent. I was elected to Parliament in 1924, and with two short intervals remained a Member until the dissolution of 1964. During the vital years, therefore, that this first volume will describe, I was able to watch the development of events from the back-benches of the House of Commons. Although I was never a member of any administration until that formed by Churchill in 1940, I knew many of the leading figures and took some part in most of the great controversies. Subsequent volumes will cover the Second War and the post-war years until my resignation from the office of Prime Minister in October 1963.

My personal entanglement in the unfolding of this great drama

---

[1] This phrase was curiously anticipated in a letter from Dundas (later Lord Melville) to Lord Spencer, written on 28 October 1800. He refers to 'The fallacy that the people are by artificial means obliged to starve in the midst of plenty'.

began by being small and ended by being substantial. Although it will be necessary to describe in some detail, especially in the later volumes, many events in which I had increasing responsibility, it is not my purpose to make this book an apologia; but rather, as one of the few old enough to have been born before the great cataclysm and to have survived into this strange new world, at once so distracting and so exhilarating, to tell a story which may be of interest not only to my contemporaries—of whom, alas, few now survive—but also to those young and middle-aged men and women who have lived through certain acts and scenes but have not been witnesses of the whole.

Horace Walpole, in one of his letters, makes the complaint about the difficulty of contemporary reporting:

> It is one of the bad effects of living in one's own time that one never knows the truth of it till one is dead.

Nevertheless, the spectator does see something, even of the current game. Churchill, in the preface to the first volume of his history of the Second World War, uses these words:

> I have followed, as in previous volumes, the method of Defoe's *Memoirs of a Cavalier*, as far as I am able, in which the author hangs the chronicle and discussion of great military and political events upon the thread of the personal experiences of an individual.[1]

This is a system equally suited to one who does not aspire to be an historian, but who is engaged on the humbler task of recording his own period. My chief purpose has been to describe events as they struck me or as they affected my life. At the same time I have tried to paint my limited picture against the tremendous background of the Fifty Years Revolution.

The years of my childhood, boyhood, and even adolescence, were years in which the imperial authority of Britain based on sea power was still unchallenged—or, at any rate, unshaken. Our own parents and teachers had their roots in a century in which the British Navy had for a hundred years kept the peace of the world; in which, with

[1] Winston Churchill, *The Second World War*, vol. i: *The Gathering Storm* (London, 1948), p. vii.

the exception of the Crimean War, which made but small impact on
the lives of great nations, there had been no European war involving
Britain; in which the Concert of Europe had operated, in spite of
many minor and some major difficulties, in preserving peace and
allowing adjustments to take place in the relative strength of nations,
including their colonial ambitions, without serious conflict. It was a
period in which the great majority of intelligent people, whether
Conservative or Liberal, felt that gratifying progress was being
made in the solution of internal political and social problems, and
that such progress would continue without serious upheavals. It was
an age in which, with certain temporary set-backs, then as afterwards considered inevitable in any economy, there had been a
remarkable increase in the production and even distribution of
wealth, both at home and overseas. After the first fluctuations and
confusions which followed the Napoleonic Wars, the international
gold standard had been successfully established and maintained.
Neither excessive deflation nor excessive inflation had proved serious
menaces. Unemployment in periods of depression, though harsh in
its effect, was normally remedied in periods of expansion. In any
event, the general view was that a certain measure of human suffering was, like poverty or sickness, inevitable. The stirrings of the
social conscience had of course made considerable effect upon
thinking people. The Liberal Government of 1905, under the dynamic influence of Lloyd George, the true successor to Joseph Chamberlain, the Radical reformer of the eighties, gave what seemed to
many a somewhat strident expression to these feelings. Yet only a
few reactionaries regarded this as heralding revolution. Reform,
even what seemed radical reform, never shook the confidence of the
capitalist structure of society. In general, most of us young men at
school or university felt that both as regards external and internal
policies, the world would probably go on more or less as before. If
we were optimists, we expected a steady advance towards the greater
happiness of mankind. Even if we were more sceptical and perhaps
increasingly alarmed by various examples of German chauvinism,
none of us had any inkling of the nightmare world into which we
were soon to be plunged. Alas! this was not to be true of our children, a generation later.

The First World War rudely shook, if it did not yet altogether overthrow, the undisputed leadership of Europe and European nations. A civilisation based originally upon the Mediterranean had spread out from century to century until, in their own minds at any rate, and largely accepted by the rest of the world, the predominance of Europeans was taken for granted. The First World War did for Europe what, on a minor scale, the Peloponnesian War did for ancient Greece. The civilised nations, or those who claimed superior civilisation by virtue of which they ruled a large part of the rest, tore themselves apart in a bitter and prolonged internecine struggle. With a certain insensibility, the Allies (the Central Powers would no doubt have done the same had they possessed the means) recruited very large numbers, running into hundreds of thousands, of Africans and Asians, including Chinese, to watch this operation. At the end of the war, the economies of almost every country in Europe were partially destroyed. They had suffered casualties amounting to many millions of dead and maimed. The ancient monarchies were overthrown; Russia, with its vast population and huge potential, had undergone complete revolution in its social order and structure; Austria was dismembered and sinking; France, Italy, Belgium, had all undergone heavy losses, and internal weaknesses soon manifested themselves. Germany itself, although spared the horrors of invasion, had suffered in manpower, in wealth, and in cohesion. Towards the end of the war the United States had—at least temporarily—abandoned the policy of isolationism, pursued for so many generations, and entered the conflict with decisive result. The predominance of Europe seemed, therefore, gravely threatened, if not altogether at an end.

From the economic point of view, Europe, with its vast inflation of money and its huge debts, found itself in a desperate position; and from that entangling net few nations could extricate themselves except by repudiation. The old automatic self-balancing system of international finance seemed to be hopelessly shaken. Many prophesied that the centre of all financial and economic authority would soon pass to the United States.

So far as Britain's overseas Empire was concerned, the colonial system emerged comparatively unimpaired. The armies of the vast subcontinent of India played a great part in support of Britain. In spite of difficulties inherent in the development of India's self-consciousness and gradual progress towards self-government, there seemed no cause for immediate alarm. The great Dominions—Canada, Australia, New Zealand, South Africa—under notable leaders, were able to establish their full independence, an indication of which was their separate signing of the peace treaties.

In Britain, the war-time slogan, 'Fit to fight, fit to vote', enabled the most radical Reform Bill of all those in history to be passed without opposition. There thus came into being something approaching universal suffrage, which had been demanded so vehemently over a hundred years before, but resisted through three Reform Bills. This change, hardly noticed at the moment, brought with it for the first time women's suffrage, and although the final stages were not completed until 1928 or even 1948, yet for practical purposes, after the First War Parliamentary democracy took the place of the Parliamentary aristocracy or oligarchy which had been dominant in the eighteenth century and for most of the nineteenth.

But people still thought of 'pre-war' as 'normal'. It was the main effort of Whitehall, the City, the business world, and the trade unions to return to the well-trodden ways. Even in the purely political world, moderation prevailed. The mood of the Right was traditional; that of the Left, even under pressure, constitutional. Large-scale and continuous unemployment, with the poverty and distress entailed, and the bitterness and despair engendered, was confined to certain areas of the country. There was much talk about Russia's example and much comradely exchange of messages; but in fact there was no real danger of the British people of whatever social class being attracted by the Russian example. Communists, then as now, were generally to be found among the higher intelligentsia.

Thus, while the people were almost stunned by the magnitude of their war experiences, huge social and political changes went through almost unperceived. In Britain, as indeed in Europe as a whole, the first years after the war did not wholly reveal what had taken place. Everything on the outside seemed to be much the same. The decision of the United States, by the refusal to join the League of Nations, to revert to isolationism caused satisfaction rather than alarm to many people. Although the League was gravely weakened, and perhaps—had we known it—doomed by this action, its work went on with moderate success and high hopes. In this country, as in many, the active supporters of the League comprised all parties, and certainly the most intelligent members of all parties. Partly by the efforts of the League machinery, partly by the restoration of international trade and money, and partly, no doubt, as a result of large-scale American loans, the first half of the post-war period was actually one of remarkable recovery throughout Europe as a whole in the face of grave difficulties. This fact is often forgotten or overlooked today. We think and speak of the terrible conditions of the inter-war years; but, in fact, up to the collapse of 1929, the first ten years after the war showed a notable resilience in the Old World, coupled of course with boom conditions in the New. But the catastrophe could not be delayed beyond a few years; and from the financial and trade collapse of the late 1920s and early 1930s there followed ineluctably the series of events which paved the way to the Second World War. When the economic and financial crash came, with total repudiation of internal debt by countries like Germany and Italy, Europe began to move along the road which led to ruin. Yet to many in Britain and France, the rise of Mussolini and even the triumph of Hitler were overshadowed by fear of Russia, still in the early mood of aggressive Communism.

From 1924, when I first entered the House of Commons, up to 1935, the year of Mussolini's invasion of Abyssinia, my chief interests and those of my closest friends were in internal problems. In the Parliament of 1924 to 1929, before unemployment had developed on a massive scale, it was rather with the symptoms of distress and economic maladjustment—the human aspects—that we concerned ourselves. But as the Depression deepened and the unemployment situation worsened, we became increasingly concerned in the promotion of some radical cure. Our inspiration in the study of the first was Disraeli, whose appeal to youth is still irresistible; for the second we were naturally excited by the Keynesian doctrine, which was beginning to spread outside the ranks of economists to all those interested in practical policies.

Later, the rise of Hitler and the growing insolence of the Nazi

and Fascist dictatorships caused me to turn more and more to foreign affairs, and brought me into closer sympathy and contact with
Churchill and corresponding distrust of the official leaders of my
party. On the declaration of war, on 3 September 1939, Churchill
and Eden joined the Government. But they could not preserve it.
When the full blast of the storm burst over Europe in May 1940,
Chamberlain fell and gave way to Churchill. When Churchill
offered me, and I accepted, a junior post in his Ministry, my sixteen
years as a back-bencher came to an end. Some years later, at the end
of a tiring day, Churchill kept me up late in desultory conversation,
largely consisting of denunciation of Hitler. I suppose I showed lack
of interest and a desire to go to bed. 'What's the matter with you,' he
demanded, 'do you approve of Hitler?' 'No, Prime Minister,' I
replied, 'but at any rate you and I owe him something. He made you
Prime Minister and me an Under-Secretary. No power on earth,
except Hitler, could have done either.' I thought he would explode
with rage; but after a moment or two, that wonderful smile we all so
loved came over his face. 'Well,' he admitted, 'there's something in
that.'

Naturally, during the war years the minds and energies of all of us,
whether in humble or more responsible posts, were occupied by the
tremendous struggle—first for survival; then for victory. The daily
round of duty kept us so fully occupied with our immediate tasks
that it was difficult to trace the larger issues that were emerging.
Nevertheless, some of the essential features of what I have called the
Great Revolution of these fifty years were beginning to show themselves. At the Ministry of Supply we had hurriedly to organise the
whole of British production for a single purpose. How profoundly I
wished that some of the plans for the better organisation of production
and the more effective relationship between Government and industry had matured during the wasted years. Yet, by improvisation and
co-operation, in spite of baffling and frustrating delays, the task was
effectively achieved within two or three years. Even in the midst of
the daily pressure I could not but see that the relations between
Government and industry must take a new turn after the war. The
old detachment must be replaced (as I believed), not by 'the nationalisation of all the means of production, distribution, and exchange',

but by a true and effective partnership. I learnt, too, another lesson: the British financial system could not have stood the strain, standing alone without allies, by dependence only on its own resources and those of the British Empire, vast as these were. The provision of American aid in the shape of Lend-Lease saved us from something like disaster. Even before the Americans entered the war, Anglo-American co-operation was the pivot on which immediate military resistance and eventual recovery depended. The Prime Minister, Churchill, grasped this from the very first. It was largely by his personal efforts that America, while officially neutral, gave us all the assistance possible short of war. I shared at any rate one great advantage with Churchill of having an American mother; so I also could rejoice as our two countries were drawn ever closer to each other.

My first period, therefore, in the Ministry of Supply underlined lessons which I had been trying to learn in the inter-war years. First, the necessity for a sound national economy based on full partnership between Government, management, and labour. Secondly, the need for any country, however strong, to rest in times of crisis upon the aid of others. Independence and interdependence—two sides of the same coin. The Americans, wisely remembering the injury done by the burden of war debts after the First War, instituted the Lend-Lease system, which was in fact a loan which would never claim repayment. But the third lesson grew stronger in my mind as the months went on. The reversion of America into isolation after the First War, coupled with the economic and social effects of wild devaluation throughout Europe, brought about those movements which, even had the democratic countries shown greater courage and prevision, might still have led to the Second World War. On Anglo-American co-operation, since for the time being Europe was down and out, the winning of victory and the construction of peace must primarily depend.

I was given the opportunity of testing this faith and applying it in practice in the two and a half years that I served as Minister Resident at Allied Force Headquarters, starting in Algiers and ending at Naples. As the war proceeded, I was inevitably conscious of a change in status between the two Allies. Britain had stood alone, and alone had borne the whole weight of the Nazi and Fascist attack.

We had raised and deployed immense forces. We had fought and lost many battles, but won some decisive victories. Nevertheless, I could not but realise the growing disparity between our countries in terms of wealth and military power. The partnership which must win the war and preserve the peace could not be based upon equality of strength. It must be founded on deep respect and understanding, the memory of trials and tribulations shared and a determination to work closely together in the years of peace in support of the ideals which we held in common. Nothing that has happened since, in spite of difficulties and disappointments, has changed my view on this prime objective of British policy.

These years following the Second War were dominated by the emergence of the deep division between Russia and the countries under her control and the Western Powers. Unlike the aftermath of the First War there was no great Peace Congress, no Versailles Treaty, no comprehensive effort on the part of the victorious Powers to settle the outstanding problems of the world. The East–West rupture precluded any such procedure. The second rape of Czechoslovakia–unhappy country, destined to be seized first by the Nazis and then by the Communists–led to the formation of a defensive military alliance, including the United States and almost all the countries of Western Europe.

Of all the manifold changes that have taken place in the last two generations, the story of Russia is the most arresting. I remember the summer of 1914, when the hearts of many were stirred by the mysterious rumour that ran through Britain: 'The Russians are coming. They have been seen in Scotland, with snow on their boots!' Strange, if heartening, illusion! Then, three years later, the fall of the ancient Tsarist system; the tragic interlude of Kerensky; the struggle for power ending in Lenin's domination; the Russian military collapse with its effect upon the Western Front, allowing the transference of Germany's eastern armies to France and Belgium to launch the offensive of March 1918, which came within an ace of achieving victory before American forces could become effectively deployed. In these few years Russia was destined to pass violently from childhood to manhood. She has had no adolescence.

After the war, and during the years before the Second War, our policies towards Russia were hesitant and ambivalent. First came the phase of active but ineffective armed intervention on behalf of the White Russians, a policy violently disputed in the Coalition Cabinet, where it was warmly opposed by Lloyd George and strenuously advocated by Churchill. Gradually Britain accepted the fact of the Communist Revolution, and unofficial agents were interchanged. MacDonald followed this in 1924 with *de jure* recognition of the Communist régime, and the exchange of Ambassadors. But his attempts to achieve a further *rapprochement*, by negotiating a trade treaty and a loan agreement, were unpopular and contributed to the downfall of the first Labour Government. In the election of 1924, the episode of the Zinoviev Letter,[1] revealing the subversive activities of Russian propaganda in Britain, proved embarrassing to the Labour Party and of corresponding benefit to the Conservatives. In 1927, in the Parliament that followed, the Home Secretary, Joynson-Hicks, authorised a police raid on the London offices of Arcos, the Russian State trading organisation. Nothing very much came of it; in Lord Vansittart's words, 'We discovered what we already knew—that Russians were engaged in espionage and sub-version'.[2] But there was sufficient indignation to lead to the rupture of diplomatic relations. These were, however, restored by the Labour Government in 1929.

In 1934—an event of major significance—Russia joined the League of Nations, of which she remained a member until 1939, when she was expelled for aggression against Finland. While represented by Litvinov, Russia acted, or, thanks to his skilful diplomacy, appeared to act, as a convinced supporter of the principles of the League. 'Peace is indivisible'—this famous phrase found a ready response, not least in Britain.

'The more Russia is made a European rather than an Asiatic power, the better for everybody.'[3] This observation, although made by Balfour in a different context and before the Revolution, is still relevant and should be the fixed purpose of all Western diplomacy. But the men who held power in Britain during the vital years from the rise of Hitler in 1933 to the outbreak of the Second World War

---

[1] See below, p. 152.   [2] Lord Vansittart, *The Mist Procession* (London, 1958), p. 344.
[3] Blanche Dugdale, *Arthur James Balfour*, vol. ii (London, 1936), p. 437.

were obsessed by a deep suspicion, not altogether undeserved, of Russian policy. One can only speculate to what extent a more forthcoming attitude on the part of the British Government, during Litvinov's term of authority, might have changed the course of history. But with the fatal hesitations of those years, Britain discouraged France at a time when a combination of Britain, France, and Russia might have served to deter Hitler and his gang. Even after Munich, when there was still a chance, the negotiations with Russia were pursued feebly and without any real sense of urgency.

Then came war, and later the sudden turn of events when the Germans, flushed with their conquests of France, Holland, and Belgium or, perhaps, in disappointment at their failure to crown these by the defeat of Britain, turned eastwards. Churchill did not hesitate a moment. From that day until the end of the war, every possible help was given from the West to Russia. Yet the alliance for waging war, and the generous assistance which we and the Americans provided, could not bring our fundamental policies much closer. The Americans, whose politics are more affected by emotions than those of more sophisticated peoples, certainly became ardent Russophiles. At the Yalta meeting, Churchill was almost left out in the cold through Roosevelt's mixture of weakness and vanity. Roosevelt flattered himself that he could outmanœuvre Stalin by his skill or make him a victim of his charm. With the growing increase in the material power of America and its contribution to the war effort compared with our own, Churchill found himself in a weakened and unhappy position. I remember an episode at the Cairo Conference in 1943, some fourteen months before Yalta, which left a great impression on my mind. The Prime Minister and I had been dining with the President at his villa. We drove back rather late to the house lent by Mr. Chester Beatty to the British Government. As we sat over a last drink before going to bed, Churchill suddenly looked at me and said, 'Cromwell was a great man, wasn't he?' I replied, 'Yes, sir, a very great man.' 'Ah,' he said, 'but he made one terrible mistake. Obsessed in his youth by fear of the power of Spain, he failed to observe the rise of France. Will that be said of me?' This thought dominated his strategic purpose and led to the compilation of the greatest of all his appeals to the President, in June 1944 – in a vain attempt to stop the futile move into southern France of troops that could as easily have landed in south-east Europe and reached a point hundreds of miles east of the line on which the Iron Curtain was soon fatally to descend. Nor did Churchill abandon his efforts in the concluding stages of the campaign.

In the early years after the war, while the United States and Britain were the sole possessors first of atomic and then of nuclear power, there was overwhelming strength on the Western side. When the Russians themselves developed nuclear power on a massive scale, the situation was radically changed. The altered balance of power in the world; the new and terrible armaments; and the long-term obligations into which sovereign States have entered, the complete reversal of the policies followed by British Governments during generations: these indeed constitute revolutionary changes. It would have been inconceivable to anyone in the days before the First War that we should join a twenty years' alliance and, as a result, institutionalise our defence policy, as we have done in N.A.T.O. Many wise heads were shaken in alarm, even on the conclusion of Lord Lansdowne's pact with France in 1904, culminating in the 'Entente Cordiale'. Statesmen like Lord Rosebery felt that this entanglement would lead inevitably to conflict with Germany. The staff talks in which we subsequently engaged bound us morally in 1914. But they were not known to Parliament or the public. They were only communicated to the Cabinet in 1912. What a vast revolution to find ourselves no longer in full command of our foreign and defence policies in relation to the threat from the East! It has sometimes amused me to hear the arguments of those who objected to closer political and economic association with Western Europe, yet seemed to forget that we had already pledged our lives and our very being in the field of mutual defence. The reversal of the traditional policy of the United States was equally complete.

In the period of the two Labour Governments – 1945 to 1950 and 1950 to 1951 – there was a large measure of agreement between the two main parties on the major questions of foreign policy, but on internal issues there was naturally strenuous debate. On what might be called social questions there was general acceptance of the policies as regards the Health Service and other developments of improvement, which were clearly necessary for the new democracy to enjoy. Even in the stress of war, during the Coalition Government, preparations had been made for some of these advances, for instance by Butler's Education Act, as well as by Lord Beveridge's famous Report, the herald of the Welfare State. It was rather in the field of economic and financial policy that the political battle was fought. The Labour Government seemed wedded to a policy of controls, harassing and no longer necessary. A siege economy is essential in a siege, but it ought, in the Conservative view, to be relaxed after the siege is raised. Expansion; the release of the energies of individuals; the emergence of enterprise and effort, whether private or public; the determination to allow the whole strength of the nation to be put behind the creation of wealth and its distribution: all these seemed much more worthy themes than the prevailing restrictionism. Moreover, a handling of our financial affairs which resulted in a series of crises, including devaluation, in spite of immense dollar loans, seemed to us indefensible. No doubt, like all Oppositions, we pressed our points hard and sometimes unfairly hard. When historians deliver judgement at leisure, it will be possible to strike the balance. At any rate, here again we were all, in all parties, moving in a world that would have seemed incredible before the First World War and even between the wars. Wider distribution of wealth; the raising of the standard of the people in material comforts and opportunities; the determination to satisfy their spiritual ambitions by the provision of ever-increasing educational facilities; the ready acceptance of the care of the old and those who had fallen by the wayside, by humanising the pre-war systems of relief: all these radical developments, not merely of purpose but of performance, were approved by both parties. Politicians might differ on the means and methods, but they shared common aims. Unlike the period between the wars, especially the periods after the great slump, there have been none of the bitter feelings which massive unemployment and poverty created. Disraeli's 'Two Nations' have grown gradually but steadily into one.

On the formation of his last administration in October 1951, Churchill asked me to take the department charged with the housing of the people. It was my task to fulfil the pledges which he and his colleagues had given at the preceding election. I held this post until October 1954–about three years. In October 1954, in a reshuffle of the Cabinet, I was appointed Minister of Defence, and held that office until April 1955, when, on Churchill's retirement and on the formation of Eden's pre-election Government, I became Foreign Secretary. My tenure of the Foreign Office was short, not more than eight months, but it covered the period in which the Austrian Peace Treaty was signed and the first summit meeting was held. These months gave me my first opportunity to see the leading Soviet figures, Bulganin, Khrushchev, and Molotov, at close quarters. It was also during this period that the Burgess–Maclean incident broke out to a glare of publicity, and it was my duty as Foreign Secretary to discuss in the House of Commons the problem of how far security could be used to override the liberties of citizens in a free society, a subject to which I was to revert as Prime Minister in still more painful circumstances. Yet even these troubles have their humorous side. I remember, for instance, the head of one of the security departments coming to me one morning, his face wreathed in smiles. 'I've got him, sir. I've got him. I've been after him for months; now I've got him.' I looked particularly gloomy, at which he said, 'Aren't you pleased, sir?' I answered, 'Not at all. When a good keeper kills a fox, he buries it quietly and tells his master nothing about it. He certainly doesn't hang it up outside the kennels. Your spy', I continued, 'will have to be paraded before the Courts, Parliament, and the Press. There will probably be a Special Tribunal to review the efficiency of your service, and your success will lead to the Government's embarrassment and perhaps its downfall.' Such are the strange contradictions of security in a democratic system.

In December 1955 I became Chancellor of the Exchequer and introduced in 1956 my only Budget, which included plans for the first Premium Bonds. Before the time came for the Budget of 1957 I found myself transferred, by a series of wholly unexpected accidents, from No. 11 to No. 10 Downing Street.

It was in the summer of 1956 that Nasser's seizure of the Suez Canal brought about a situation of intense crisis. I remember well the mood in which the House of Commons, regardless of party, met this dictatorial threat. In Mr. Gaitskell's words, 'It is all very familiar. It is exactly the same that we encountered from Mussolini and Hitler in those years before the war.' The Prime Minister kept me in close touch with his plans throughout those anxious months. I shared to the fullest extent responsibility for all the decisions, all the more because I was one of the circle of colleagues whom the Prime Minister particularly consulted. I still feel that, had it not been for the injury caused by lack of understanding between the British and American Governments, we could have got through without undue difficulty. The threat to stability in the Middle East was no illusion, and when, during my Premiership, it became necessary for Britain to give military assistance to the political security of Jordan, American troops, by a strange new twist in the Eisenhower–Dulles foreign policy, were landing in the Lebanon.

Eden's ill health, to the sorrow and almost despair of his colleagues, forced him to resign on 9 January 1957. I succeeded him as Prime Minister four days later. The early months were a period of great anxiety in and out of Parliament. There was little opportunity to do more than try to analyse the major issues which confronted us as a nation. In my different offices I had dealt with specific aspects, but not with the whole complex. I recognised the great revolution which the two wars and their aftermath had caused. I realised that the old society had passed away and a new order, with all its dangers but with all its hopes, was painfully emerging. As soon as I felt the Government reasonably secure, I began to study, with the help of my own staff and with my closest colleagues, the whole vast problem of how best to grasp the opportunities and counter the dangers that this new world afforded. For the rest of my period as Prime Minister, with the occasional interruptions of minor if troublesome issues, these fundamental questions occupied my thoughts and energies. The greater part of the last volume of this book will be devoted to the degree of success and failure which we met in trying to cut our way through an intricate and often baffling tangle.

First, there was the British economy. Britain's overseas investments were largely disposed of in the First War. To the extent that they had been rebuilt between the wars they had once more to be sacrificed. Britain, so long a creditor country, had become largely a debtor country. Meanwhile, the situation of America was correspondingly reversed. Moreover, within six years, the huge American loan to Britain of £1,000 million had been spent, leaving the interest and redemption to be met by future generations. One devaluation had become necessary, and towards the end of 1951 another was threatening. Of course, this did not in any way weaken the fundamental power of the British people to produce, to work, to invent, to strive. Indeed, as a result of two wars, the labour force had been significantly increased by the great expansion in the employment of women. If hours were shortened and holidays increased—and very properly so—enormous technological progress had placed machine-power at the disposal of industry and agriculture, on a scale undreamt-of hitherto. The capacity to produce wealth had therefore been multiplied many times; but so had the need for imports of all kinds to feed the rapacious demands of modern production and consumption. The revival of agriculture, the victim of nineteenth-century industrialisation, certainly alleviated the position from the exchange point of view. Nevertheless, an island very highly populated in relation to its size, possessing few raw materials, and ambitious to achieve an ever-rising standard of living, can only do so by a combination of exertion and restraint.

Above all, the rise in costs and prices and very heavy demands for capital, both at home and in the overseas countries for which we have a traditional and moral responsibility, have emphasised the insufficiency of the reserves which were left to us at the end of the Second War. Even the most strenuous efforts cannot result in an accumulation of reserves at a sufficient rate to match the increasing volume of business. In a word, post-war Britain has been and is 'trading beyond its means'. This situation, familiar through many generations to individual businessmen, can be remedied by a successful entrepreneur through recourse to banking accommodation or by raising fresh capital on the market. A nation cannot readily do the same.

The dilemma, therefore, that has faced us since the war, and will continue to face us, is persistent and haunting. If, on the one hand, we go forward at the maximum speed which the resources of machinery and manpower available are able to sustain, this almost inevitably leads to larger imports and a growing divergence between exports and imports—in other words, an unfavourable trade balance. If, on the other hand, we reduce the speed of advance, we risk under-employment of our resources, both of men and material. In this dilemma lies the origin of what was contemptuously termed the 'Stop–Go' system. I remember one Member of Parliament accusing me of using alternately the brake and the accelerator. I was tempted to inquire how else anyone could be expected to drive on a crowded road. A policy of using both at the same time, which has since found some favour, seems somewhat bizarre.

Nevertheless, in spite of some irregularity in the rate of progress in the economic field, the almost incredible improvement in the life enjoyed by the British people cannot be challenged. Indeed, it is now difficult to cast one's mind back to the period immediately following the war, still more to the inter-war period. In every item that goes to make up the national standard of living—food, clothing, housing, health, holidays, educational facilities, and all the rest— there is so great a gap between the conditions of people today and those of past days that the young are unconscious of it and even the old can scarcely grasp it. If there have been occasional fluctuations and set-backs, we must not exaggerate them. To use a famous phrase of Macaulay's, 'Now and then there has been a stoppage, now and then a short retrogression; but as to the general tendency, there can be no doubt. A single breaker may recede; but the tide is evidently coming in.' Indeed, so successful was our policy that a new line of attack was begun by the Opposition and taken up by some armchair critics, generally in well-to-do circumstances themselves. It was said that by the 'Affluent Society' we had debauched our population; by making them prosperous, it was claimed, we had undermined their moral fibre. Remembering the passionate debates of thirty or forty years before, I could not help being somewhat surprised by the novelty and unexpectedness of these accusations. Of course, material prosperity can be used or misused. It can be the foundation of a fuller life, opening up new prospects to every individual in the country; or it can be temptation to wantonness and folly. But, recalling the old days—the slums and the poverty, and the unemployment, or the state of my constituency in Stockton when the works were closed and men, willing and able to work, walked aimlessly up and down the streets, to the tune of 30 or 40 per cent of the population, hopelessly looking for a job—I did not sympathise with these peevish complaints. On the contrary, I felt sincerely grateful to have been spared to see so great a change and, under Providence, to have been allowed to play some minor part in bringing it about.

One of the products of the technological revolution has been immensely to complicate the practical problems of defence. Even in the so-called 'conventional' weapons, the progress of science and technology moves with such inconvenient rapidity that it is very hard to devise and stand by consistent programmes. In the sphere of unconventional weapons, the problems are multiplied. The passing of the McMahon Act in the United States was a grievous blow to the development of the independent British deterrent, and I took up with President Eisenhower the question of its amendment. By his efforts, the Act was amended, thus allowing interchange of information to be resumed, saving us an incalculable amount both of money and of time and enabling us to produce an effective deterrent weapon on our own account, with all its implications on the strategic and political strength of our country. The problems associated with 'Blue Steel' and 'Blue Streak', with 'Skybolt' and 'Polaris'—to name only the most important—all of them requiring difficult decisions of economic and strategic importance, are further examples of the intricacy and costliness of defence in the twentieth century.

Startling as have been the changes in our financial and economic position and in the needs of our national defence and the means of meeting them, there has been no more remarkable development in any sphere than in the story of the British Empire and Commonwealth. Pessimists would describe it as the liquidation of the British Empire; optimists might view it as the transformation of a colonial and imperialist system into a Commonwealth of free and independent nations. Certainly, we can roll up the old maps of my youth in which a quarter or more of the globe was painted red, covering not merely the countries of British descent like Canada and Australia and the Crown Colonies governed by direct colonial rule, but also the territories like Egypt and the Sudan under *de facto* if not *de jure*

British control. Perhaps the most dramatic way of describing the rapidity of these changes is to be found in the membership of the Conference of Commonwealth Prime Ministers. The first over which I presided was in 1957; the last in 1962. At the first there were ten Prime Ministers or their representatives present; at the last, sixteen. In 1965 no fewer than twenty-one nations had a claim to be represented. The 'winds of change' had indeed blown to some effect.

The process began in 1925, when the Dominions Office came into being and, as a result, the channels of communication between the Governments of Canada and the other Dominions ceased to be through the Governors-General and were transferred to the respective High Commissioners. Further changes were given legal and constitutional sanction by the Statute of Westminster. By the time the Second War broke out, the old Commonwealth (to use a convenient term)–Canada, Australia, New Zealand, South Africa– were in fact independent nations, though closely bound together with each other and Britain by blood, tradition, and sentiment, and above all by a common allegiance to the Crown. Between the wars the process of constitutional development was steadily pursued in India, Burma, and Ceylon, and the first steps were taken in many if not all of the Crown Colonies. Some of these, like the West Indian territories, enjoyed ancient constitutions concentrating power on the white populations. The process of enlargement of the franchise was, however, already at work. The India Act of 1935 marked a further stage forward. In all of the controversies of the time, it was generally agreed that the ultimate end to be reached must be Dominion status or virtual independence. Argument was concentrated not so much on the final purpose as on the means and pace of its achievement.

After the Second War independence was granted to India, not alas to the unified subcontinent over which Britain had presided for so many generations, but to each part of a divided India. It was accompanied by tragic loss of life on a hideous scale, and has left behind it many unsettled problems between the two emergent nations, India and Pakistan. But it was done; and it could not in the view of most informed opinion have been much further delayed, although the change could perhaps have been brought about with less confusion and suffering.

The next and decisive alteration in the old conception of Empire or Commonwealth followed rapidly. For the direct allegiance to the Crown was substituted recognition of the Monarch as Head of the Commonwealth. It was agreed also as a consequence that the emergent nations could if they wished adopt a republican form of constitution. This concession having been made—and, in my view, rightly so—to India and Pakistan, it could hardly be denied to other countries as they reached independence.

The next question which commanded our attention was that of the relations of Britain and Europe. During our period of Opposition from 1945 to 1951, Churchill had launched at The Hague the European Movement, which resulted in the creation of the Council of Europe and thus helped to restore Western Germany to the family of democratic and peaceful countries. Ernest Bevin, the Labour Foreign Secretary, was not unfavourable to the main purposes that lay behind the unity of Europe, although it would not be unfair to say that neither he nor the Foreign Office were enthusiastic about its new institutions. At Churchill's request I took a considerable part in the European Movement at its foundation; but the Conservative Party, like the country, had its anxieties and reservations. I shall never cease to blame myself that I did not, even from my comparatively junior position in the Cabinet, raise as a matter of high principle the question of Britain joining actively at least in the preliminary talks which ultimately led to the Treaty of Rome. It was of course discussed; but the views both of the Foreign Office and the Treasury, as well as the Board of Trade, were all hostile, largely on technical grounds. The Foreign Secretary, Eden, was doubtful, if not opposed to the concept. Churchill was Prime Minister. But either from age or unwillingness to precipitate what might have caused a major conflict in the Government and thus put at risk the urgent problems of internal reconstruction which it fell to us to carry out with a slender majority, he accepted without much resistance the general verdict. Moreover, in launching the European Movement, Churchill always had in mind the moral renaissance of Europe rather than any clear organisational system. Certainly, he gave his full support to Eden's efforts to rescue the European Defence Community, and thus to allow the rearmament of Germany with

French approval. It is strange to remember, in view of what has happened since under de Gaulle's leadership of France, that Britain felt obliged to undertake heavy military obligations in Europe, in order to satisfy French opinion, still suspicious of Germany as a military partner in the Alliance. These obligations we have since been able somewhat to reduce, but they are treaty undertakings, and both onerous and long-dated. Once again, as so often in her history, Britain has given much and received little in return. About Europe, regrets still haunt me. I was so fully occupied with my own office, which combined the conduct of complicated legislation with the largest administrative job I had ever undertaken, that although I wrote to Churchill to protest, I did not press the issue. The considerations I have stated are, alas, excuses, not valid reasons. I can only comfort myself that I could not, even with the help of the few colleagues who shared my view, have had any hope of getting my way. I could only have contented myself with the sense of rectitude following a resignation on a matter of principle.

When I became Prime Minister, the first months were heavily engaged in other matters, but I soon decided, with the approval of the Cabinet, that we must undertake a negotiation to see how far a plan could be made by which Britain and other Powers in Western Europe not included in the Six could co-operate with the European Economic Community, by the creation of an industrial free-trade area for Western Europe. At one time it looked as if we should succeed, but the French Government finally prevented this, although their colleagues in the Six would probably have proved agreeable. We therefore set about the organisation of the European Free Trade Association—that is the seven countries of Western Europe outside the Six. This has been of great value of itself, and much progress has been and is being made for the increase of trade between the countries concerned. Our next step, with the approval of our E.F.T.A. colleagues, and in full consultation with the Commonwealth, was a formal application for the United Kingdom to join the Six. Long negotiations in Brussels followed. Finally, at the beginning of 1963, the French Government imposed their veto. This was a cruel blow. But neither my colleagues nor I should regret that we set out upon this adventure. Nor do I feel that the events of

January 1963 are the end of the story. They are, perhaps, only the end of a chapter.

When the Conservatives returned to power in 1951, the East–West split dominated all foreign politics. The Iron Curtain seemed impenetrable. During the years of the last Churchill administration, my friendship with the Prime Minister made me not infrequently a confidant of new ideas forming in his mind, and I knew how unwilling he was to rest content with the complete deadlock that had settled down between East and West. This outlook was not only creating a grim and dangerous division between the two sets of nations, including the allies or satellites of the principals of the two groups, but its evil effects spread to every country of the world. The so-called neutrals, or those who tried to keep themselves (in the jargon of the day) 'non-aligned', were subject to the pressure of propaganda of the active contestants. Sometimes, it is true, they could obtain positive advantages by setting off one group against the other. But as a whole the life of the world was either paralysed or poisoned; nor did there seem any way of breaking through this wall of steel. All this made Churchill anxious and restless. He had a strong desire to begin at least some probing operation, and I remember that in the spring of 1953, not long before his illness, he was anxious that some initiative should be taken. His famous speech in May of that year gave public utterance to his hopes. Although it was somewhat coldly received in official quarters, here and overseas, yet it made a deep impression on public opinion all over the world. Churchill was thus the author of the concept of the 'summit meeting'. It fell to Eden to bring about the first of these, which was held at Geneva in the spring of 1955. Although, in a sense, the meeting of Heads of Government and the subsequent conference of Foreign Secretaries were disappointing, yet I felt that they had at least achieved some useful contacts. I attended both of these, as Foreign Secretary, and although the formal discussions were fruitless, our long unofficial conversations seemed to me not altogether barren.

Soon after I became Prime Minister, I made up my mind that Churchill's initiative, which Eden had followed up, must, when the occasion seemed more promising, be renewed. In the summer of 1958 I had an opportunity to ventilate some of my thoughts in talks at Washington and Paris, and in the autumn of the same year at Bonn. At that time, Moscow had moved from a purely negative to a threatening position over the question of Berlin. In the late months of 1958 I determined on visiting Moscow, and arrangements were made for an invitation to be extended to me. I informed, although I cannot honestly say that I consulted, our allies. President Eisenhower did not much like it, but wished me good luck; President de Gaulle was sceptical; Chancellor Adenauer was offended. But this British initiative was certainly widely welcomed by the smaller Powers and by neutral opinion. As soon as the visit was over I went again to Paris, Bonn, and Washington, my chief purpose being to bring all the pressure I could upon the Heads of these States to agree or acquiesce to a new summit meeting. After many months, I succeeded. Alas ! the U2 incident resulted in the total failure of this conference almost before it began, and the hopes of the world were cruelly dashed.

In following years, in spite of some improvement in East–West relations, there hung over the whole world, like a dark cloud, the unresolved threat to Berlin. To this was to be added the Cuba crisis, in 1962. For one hectic week, the provocative action of the Russians in introducing nuclear missiles into Cuba seemed dangerously near provoking a fatal conflict. President Kennedy spoke on our special telephone every day—sometimes two or three times a day—and I had no hesitation in giving him full encouragement and support. He and I were both convinced that the Russians would not force the issue in Cuba. But what about Berlin ? In the event, the world passed unscathed through a dark and perilous period, short but agonising. Indeed, we were soon able to take up again, with some hope of success, the question of nuclear tests.

After the Russians had broken in the summer of 1961 with a massive and spectacular series of explosions the unofficial moratorium which had lasted two years, it was imperative for the West to maintain the equilibrium of nuclear technique and power. Accordingly, an Anglo-American series took place on Christmas Island.

But I did not abandon the idea of reaching an agreement to ban the tests. In the end, fortified by the growing acceptance of the fact that underground tests were not of major importance, either from the point of view of any injury to the health of the inhabitants of the earth or from that of a major breakthrough in the nuclear art, both the President and I accepted, although with reluctance, the Russian willingness to discuss an agreement confined to banning atmospheric tests. Even then there were many pitfalls. Up to the last moment I feared there would be a fatal 'slip 'twixt the cup and the lip'. It so happened that the first news of the agreement having been finally signed reached me from Washington. President Kennedy rang me up himself on our private telephone at five o'clock on the afternoon of 25 July 1963. Here at last was something achieved on the long road to peace and better understanding.

I have set out the main issues which dominated my thoughts and those of my colleagues during all these years. All resulted in one form or another from the fundamental changes brought about in the world and in Britain's position by the two wars and their consequences. I now come to the last—our relations with the United States. This formed a thread running through all the others, since in all the United States was involved for good or ill. In the economic field, American policies at home and overseas affected us at every point. An American recession had corresponding ill effects upon our exports to America; a boom helped us. Their tariff arrangements were vital to us, both as applied to their own tariffs and to the influence they had upon the tariffs of other countries. Their credit policies and the contributions that they made to the recovery of the world, first through the Marshall Plan and then through various forms of aid, coupled with their membership and support of the various international organisations for widening the basis of credit, were of supreme importance. In defence, apart from the question of the exchange of nuclear information, which we were able to resolve, we were broadly agreed. The United States was involved in all the alliances, N.A.T.O., C.E.N.T.O., and S.E.A.T.O. Their practical aid was shown by the large number of American troops serving overseas. In Europe, their sympathy with our plans for European unity was important, since any form of free-trade organisation, whether E.E.C. or E.F.T.A., must have its effect upon American interests. In our policies towards Russia, the Americans of course played the major part in defence through their nuclear strength. In plans towards a *détente* or a test agreement, they held the key, and similarly in the long, dreary, and hitherto ineffective struggle for disarmament.

Partly from my own birth, partly from my sympathy and close connections with Americans throughout my life, in war and peace, I firmly believed that the peace and prosperity of the world depended upon close co-operation between Britain and the United States. That is still my view; but I have never thought that this should involve any abandonment of vital British interests or undue deference to American opinion. Nevertheless, on the occasions when Britain and America have let themselves, for whatever reason, be separated, disaster has generally followed. For example, the Suez tangle was largely due to the devious and obstructive policies followed by Secretary of State Dulles. Happily, after that date, when new and menacing issues arose, as over Jordan and the Lebanon, or the off-shore islands and Formosa, or in South-east Asia, our relations with America were so good that our influence could during my term of office be exerted to the full.

The American people, very much like the British people, are torn between two emotions. One part of their heart and mind looks back to the past; the other is always straining forward to the future. The old isolationism has died hard. The Russian and now the Chinese menace, like the German aggression in two wars, has helped to make it out of date. None the less, there is always the tendency to slip back. Similarly, the generous and noble sentiments which have taken the form of Marshall Aid and widespread assistance to all the countries of the world, are paralleled by the tradition of protection, the power of pressure-groups, the shipping policy with its subsidies and restrictions, and the sometimes discreditable treatment of foreign tenders for important contracts nominally open to the world. In the same way, American anti-colonial sentiment, often embarrassingly pressed on countries like Britain, who were already following their own well-thought-out plans for creating by stages a free Commonwealth of self-governing nations, was often very hard to submit to, especially when it took the form of an unhelpful attitude in the United Nations. One sometimes felt tempted to remind our ally that they were only just beginning to face their own racial problem, growing daily more acute. Nevertheless, I have always found it very easy to deal with my American friends, whether officially or unofficially, on the basis of absolute candour. I was fortunate in my relations with two Presidents. For Eisenhower I had a sincere affection and deep respect, based on experience of his fairness and generosity throughout the Mediterranean campaign. He treated me, in our many meetings, as an old and trusted colleague. With President Kennedy, I formed an immediate and intimate friendship. We met frequently, and were in constant touch by letter, telegram, and telephone. His death only a few months after his visit to my Sussex home was to me a grievous personal loss. It was a disaster for the whole world.

To sum up, as my story unfolds, it will be found that Anglo-American co-operation was an essential thread running through the whole tangled skein.

There will be many other incidents and crises at home and overseas that I shall have to deal with in the course of these volumes. My Premiership ended suddenly, and unexpectedly, as it had begun. It began with Eden's serious illness. It ended with my own. Churchill, during the period of our Opposition from 1945 to 1951, was in the habit of entertaining his colleagues in the Shadow Cabinet to fortnightly luncheons at the Savoy Hotel. At one of these there was brought in a rather equivocal and shapeless pudding, which he viewed with some distaste. He called the waiter, 'Pray take away this pudding. It has no theme.' I have always remembered this incident—a warning to authors as well as to cooks. This Prologue—if I may so term it—attempts to set out my theme.

CHAPTER ONE

Childhood and Adolescence

IWAS born in London on 10 February 1894 at 52 Cadogan Place, which was the home of my parents for nearly fifty years. Like most of the houses of its type and period, it was tall and thin. The distance from the nursery to the kitchen and basement seemed an infinity. There were, of course, no lifts, nor (in our house) any back stairs. Everything, including our food and coal, was carried up daily from the bottom to the top. The day nursery looked out over 'the gardens'. These ran between our street and Sloane Street and were a great boon, particularly on hot summer days. Opposite our house was an acacia tree which I liked; also a lamp-post, with the nightly activities of the lamp-lighter. The night nursery faced the mews and immediately behind us was a blacksmith's shop. Among my earliest memories is the noise of the hammer on the anvil which seemed to go on from early morning till late at night—the making of shoes and the shoeing of horses. When we were half-asleep, we could still hear the rumble of the carriages returning from a party, with the ring of the horses' hooves on the cobbles. In our mews there were a few small shops, to which we were not allowed to go, but access to which we sometimes obtained with the help of our cook, who let us out through the back garden. Mrs. Cameron was with my mother for many years. She was stern but kind. Of course the traditional warfare raged between the nursery and the kitchen.

Both at the back of the house, because of the mews, and in the front of the house, because of the daily passing and stopping of carts and carriages, there remains very strongly in my memory the peculiar smell of London in those days. London was in a sense still a country town. Carriages, drays, wagons, omnibuses, four-wheel cabs, hansoms, milk-carts, butcher's carts, and all the rest were horse-drawn. Dung, straw, and sparrows were everywhere. From time to time, large quantities of straw were put down outside one of the houses in the street to deaden the noise. This meant that either a dowager was dying or an important lady about to give birth to a child. London has now lost all the old country odour. The new reek of petrol and diesel oil has taken its place.

At the top of our street was a large mansion, Chelsea House. Readers of Edward Cadogan's charming book of reminiscences[1] will remember his description of life there. To us humbler neighbours, Chelsea House was a kind of baronial castle only outmatched in importance by Buckingham Palace, to which we were occasionally taken to see the Changing of the Guard. On the steps outside there could generally be seen as we passed a splendid figure, with powdered hair or wig, blue coat, red velvet waistcoat, blue velvet knee-breeches, white or yellow stockings, and silver-buckled shoes. This person, who commanded our deepest respect, we firmly believed to be Earl Cadogan himself, proudly surveying his tenants and his properties.

At the top of Cadogan Place you turn left; sometimes you may be going by perambulator, sometimes trotting along the pavement. I forget what sort of dress I wore. I only remember with a particular sense of grievance one which was copied from that of the hero of a famous and successful story, and was called a 'Little Lord Fauntleroy' suit. This hateful outfit consisted of brown velveteen coat and shorts, with a large lace collar. But it may have been that this horror was only for indoor use. If you are specially fortunate, and it is a morning walk (that is, if the ordeal of 'lessons' which I did with my mother after breakfast, in the library, has been successfully negotiated), there is a chance that you may meet 'the Guards' on their way to or from morning drill in Hyde Park: the men in short white pea-jackets; the non-commissioned officers in red tunics and sashes; the officers in black frock-coats, white gloves, sabretaches, and gold-peaked caps. If lessons were still going on, this delight had to be forgone. All the same, even from our house, you could hear the drum-and-fife band, as the column marched down Sloane Street with only the gardens intervening. But even without the Guards—a

[1] The Hon. Sir Edward Cadogan, *Before the Deluge: Memories and Reflections, 1880–1914* (London, 1961).

special and exceptional excitement and therefore not, in this world of sin and sorrow, to be expected more than as an occasional 'treat'— plenty of romance lies ahead, especially if Nanny is in a good mood and inclined to linger over the shops. Along the top of Cadogan Place, and then turn right into the pleasures of Sloane Street. A few yards up the street was Mr. Vigo's fish-shop. I can still see the great marble slab covered with all kinds of fish: some large, some small; some flat, spotted, and shapeless, others neat and elegant. Mr. Vigo himself, a commanding figure, was always dressed the same, summer and winter: straw hat and a great blue-and-white apron that covered him from head to foot. In his hand was a formidable instrument, like a great dagger, to be used upon vast blocks of ice. Occasionally, as a great treat, he would show me some lobsters or crabs. Then, half-way up the street, was the post-office at which for some reason there seemed always occasion to call. I remember well the iron cage, the dim and repellent counter—my earliest contact with bureaucracy. Opposite was Mr. Macpherson's Gymnasium and Dancing Academy. Here, I suppose at the age of five or six, I paraded once or twice a week with a number of other children, and first experienced my distaste for any form of joint performance. This extreme dislike of doing things in public, especially things which I thought foolish in themselves, haunted me all through my youth—at school, university, and later (at least at first) in the Army. There was an exercise called 'Indian Clubs' which was particularly distressing, and in which I showed extreme lack of agility. Climbing a rope I could never do, and scrambling up wooden bars fixed to the side of the wall filled me with disgust. The only thing I enjoyed was something called the 'Giant Stride'. You seized a rope, and with a lot of other children ran round in a circle, while the mechanism from which the ropes hung was gently rotated. There was some fun in this; it was more like a circus or a fair than a drill, and was performed to the enchanting notes of the popular tune of the day:

> Daisy, Daisy,
>   Give me your answer do.
> I'm half crazy,
>   All for the love of you!

At the top of Sloane Street, turn to the right. Here some wonderful new shops were being erected, Harvey Nichols, Woollands, and the like, replacing the old buildings dating, no doubt, from the days when Knightsbridge was little more than a village. Then the crossing —a skilled and dangerous undertaking—as the carriages and omnibuses swooped by, at what seemed a breakneck pace. Or else you had to thread your way through one of the great traffic blocks. It is curious to think that people in those days put up with this inconvenience without demur. In the summer a traffic jam could last two hours or more. Into the park at Albert Gate and then a choice of paths. The one we loved best was at the bottom of the Serpentine to see the rabbits play in their enclosure, and so at last to the great lake itself, vast in size beyond any stretch of water that we had seen or conceived of. Then back to nursery tea; in the summer, to play in the garden after tea; in the winter, to enjoy the cosy heat of the nursery fire and the reading of favourite books. Our horizon then was bounded by the nursery and Nanny was the presiding genius. Since my eldest brother was eight years and my second brother four years older than I, and there were no sisters, my childhood was rather solitary. Later, there was almost a plethora of French governesses, tutors, and so forth, in holidays as well as in term-time; for learning and improvement of the mind were never to be neglected.

This was the even tenor of my life until I went from home at the age of nine to a preparatory school, Summerfields, in Oxford. Compared to the lives of my children and grandchildren, ours was dull and drab. Now children seem to rush wildly about all over Europe—France, Spain, Italy—or, when in England, from one house to another. With us it was not so. In my case, we had no relations with country houses to which we would naturally go. We followed a simple and regular routine, week by week and month by month. Nor did school change it much. In the summer holidays, we went away, either to Hunstanton, where my father took for the holidays a small private school and some of our MacLehose cousins generally joined us, or to a house—Holland House it was called—at Kingsgate in Kent. One year at Hunstanton there was a circus. I was allowed to watch its progress through the town, though I was judged too young to go to the actual performance. But the procession was entrancing and unforgettable. At both these resorts there was paddling, bathing, riding, and searching the cliffs for fossils. In 1906 my father bought a house and small property in Sussex. Then my whole life changed. I roamed all over our small acreage, half farm, half woodland. I trespassed in all our neighbours' woods. I learnt to watch and love country things, and this has been a source of great happiness and relief to me ever since.

Up to then we were London children. My two brothers lived in a world different from my own—more advanced, with all kinds of interests which I could not share. They were very kind to me, and I think spoilt me. But I was rather a lonely child and the way in which we lived then did not encourage many outside friends.

In my recollection of those first years, a few things stand out, chiefly public events. As I have said, I remember well the Queen's Diamond Jubilee and Captain Ames—the whole six feet eight inches of him—leading the procession. We watched it from Mr. Bain's bookshop in the Haymarket. I remember, too, being taken to see the lights in the evening. My father carried me most of the way—down Piccadilly and St. James's Street—and somehow home. I was a few months over three years old, but I recall it vividly. Then there was Mafeking Day (19 May 1900). I was in the park with our French governess when, towards three or four o'clock, we were conscious of immense crowds gathering. We followed their direction, since our way home took us either through Albert Gate or Hyde Park Corner. I can see now the vast multitude outside Lady Baden-Powell's house, which was near St. George's Hospital. Of course, we did not witness the wild celebrations of that night, but it was the first crowd that I had ever seen. It made a deep impression on me. I remember, too, Queen Victoria's funeral, in February 1901. Even I could realise something of what the Great Queen's death signified. We watched the procession from a house at the corner of Park Lane and South Street. The vast blackness of it all—black clothes, black ties, black crêpe; the slow march of the soldiers; the muffled bands; King Edward VII; the Kaiser. To my delight we saw later, from the top of a bus at Hyde Park Corner, the troops marching back from Paddington, this time in quick time.

The Boer War had meanwhile been a source of continual emotion, so far as this was allowed in our placid life. Nanny was a tremendous partisan, with a fierce hatred of pro-Boers, and some quite unjustified suspicions of the French governess. There were maps, with little flags to be stuck in. There were pictures from the *Illustrated London News* to be pasted into scrap-books. There were shiny buttons, to be worn in one's lapel, with portraits of Roberts and Kitchener; it was my first introduction to the latter's grim features, afterwards to be so compelling and so familiar. There was —a possession beyond price—the uniform of a British regiment (mounted infantry, I think), with slouch hat and carbine all complete. This was a present, birthday or Christmas, from my godfather 'Cousin George' and, with sword as well, came dangerously near 'spoiling'.

Another public event was the Russo-Japanese War in 1904, and the great naval battles so wonderfully illustrated by the artists in the papers of the day. We shared the general pro-Japanese feeling; I think we liked them because they were believed to be small. Gallant little Japs !

Later—when I was twelve years old—there took place the General Election of 1906. It was during the Christmas holidays. Elections, in those days, stretched over a period of three weeks or more. We used to go to see outside Harrods the agreeable sight of effigies of Balfour and Campbell-Bannerman climbing up their respective ladders, as the results were announced day by day. I was a keen supporter of Campbell-Bannerman—I think because the general opinion in the family was Balfourian.

Some of the other rare but outstanding pleasures of childhood are still vivid. Sundays at the Zoo—with green tickets, which admitted only the Fellows and their friends; rides in hansom cabs—a tremendous thrill; the Sunday military band in Hyde Park, recently allowed, after prolonged Sabbatarian opposition in Parliament, and heard either free at a distance, or—for 2d.—on a green iron seat within a railinged enclosure. But perhaps the best of all was a journey by railway. This, with us, was in effect confined to the family move for the summer holidays, and was a tremendous affair. Father; mother; three boys; a French governess; Nanny; a nursery-maid; a cook; and a vast quantity of luggage, including the brown nursery bath, of tin, with its cover, strapped and corded, and filled with various impedimenta. The day of the journey was unforgettable. I was always ready an hour or more before the jobbed carriage, or sometimes the 'brake', hired for the occasion, in which we were all to go to the station. Mrs. Cameron had great supplies of food prepared which we consumed on the train. There was usually a reserved carriage and, if I remember right, we travelled second class—at that time a kind of middle course much favoured by families of modest means, between the expense of travelling first and the discomfort of going third. Once, at the age of six or seven, I was taken by my mother to stay with some friends in Norfolk. This journey was less boisterous, but enthralling. We travelled first class, and were provided (for the train was not heated) with a foot-warmer —an oblong iron container, filled with hot water. I had a cap—my first cap—and my mother a great quantity of wraps and rugs. It was not so exciting as the great family journeys, but it had a refined charm of its own. A little later, there was the still greater thrill of a journey to Scotland—by train to Glasgow, and then by boat to Arran.

Apart from Nanny and the nursery—the true centre of life and the only secure world—my childish memories are mainly connected with my mother. My father was shy and reserved, and always at work. On weekdays, he would never be home till late. On Sundays, he would sometimes take me out, to row on the Serpentine, to the Zoo, or even, on a tram, to Hampton Court. After bicycles came in and I had learnt to ride, we would make the circuit of Battersea Park. (My father had given up horseback riding, which he used to like, after a bad accident.) But otherwise I scarcely saw him. In his brief summer holidays we had a short and happy experience of his charm and good nature, playing games with us. Then I think of him in white flannels, with the inevitable straw hat of the day. Otherwise, my memory of him at this time is in London, leaving the house early and returning late, in tailcoat and top-hat, which was the normal uniform of every respectable man in those days. My mother was passionately devoted to her children. She was, nevertheless, somewhat alarming and even forbidding. She believed in the highest standards of work and behaviour. I learnt from her the multiplication tables, and the dates of the Kings and Queens of England. These I could manage. But there was a terrible trial called 'mental arithmetic'. She meant to be kind, but was very concerned over my inability to make the appropriate calculations accurately and rapidly.

Downstairs we always spoke French until I went away to school. Since we had a series of French nursery-maids and afterwards, or in addition, a French governess—who became a lifelong friend—and since my mother spoke French perfectly, I found myself excelling most of my contemporaries at school in this subject. I could speak French fluently and read French books. This, it seemed, was only half the business. I had been taught nothing of the grammar—those terrible subjunctives and those peculiar accents—and here I had to start again.

When I was about six or seven, and till the age of nine, I went to Mr. Gladstone's day-school near Sloane Square. He was an admirable teacher, both of Latin and Greek. The school was connected, through Mr. Morton, its founder, with Summerfields, and the same teaching methods were followed. My chief friend was a boy called Gwynn, the son of Stephen Gwynn, author and critic. I do not remember his Christian name. We stuck to surnames in those days.

Until my father's purchase of the small property in Sussex, all Christmas and Easter holidays were spent in London. For summer holidays we went to the seaside. In London we were not without treats, but they were few in number and looked forward to with corresponding enthusiasm. The best of all was the Drury Lane Pantomime. Through my mother's friendship with Lady Arthur Russell (who was my godmother), we were sometimes lent the Duke of Bedford's box. This, with the great room behind it and the magnificent flunkey to lead us into it, was a sort of introduction to fairyland. Then the drama! I thought I had never seen nor could conceive anything so beautiful as the Transformation scene. But I have one memory better still: that is, of Dan Leno and Herbert Campbell in *The Babes in the Wood*. I do not know how old I was, but I did not forget Dan Leno's power to hold and enthral that vast audience.

Perhaps our family life was a little more austere than that of most of my mother's friends and neighbours. Certainly we were brought up in a tradition of hard work and application. Since my eldest brother, Daniel, was a brilliant scholar, I suffered in comparison with him. I slightly resented this. He was the First Scholar at Eton; I was only the Third. He was the Senior Classical Scholar of his year at Balliol; I only achieved an Exhibition. His First in Classic Moderations was of a very high standard; I just managed to scrape a First with some difficulty. In addition, until I fortunately outgrew him, I normally inherited his clothes.

My next brother, Arthur, was musical, and really understood and loved music. I am ashamed to say that I was—and remain—wholly unmusical. But we were fond of each other, and quarrelled incessantly.

The theatre or the pantomime was not—as the cinema or the television is today—something to be enjoyed every day of the week. There was one theatre or pantomime for each holiday. Sometimes we were taken to the Natural History Museum, which, on the whole, I disliked, for the skeletons rather frightened me. There was, however, a splendid instrument with a pendulum which somehow proved that the earth really went round the sun—a proposition that I felt no inclination to deny.

One of the quiet pleasures of our simple life was my father reading to us, which he did on Sunday evenings. He read beautifully; and I always sat in the corner of his big armchair. He read mostly poetry— Shakespeare, Milton, Keats, and a good deal of Tennyson. I once tried to start a similar tradition with my family, but it was ill received.

Our own private reading was very varied. We were never prevented from reading or encouraged to read any particular book. There were always lots of books around and we were provided with plenty of material. Scott and Dickens I loved at a very early age; but of course we equally enjoyed Henty, Rider Haggard, and Conan Doyle. In those days, each Sherlock Holmes story was a new excitement. Nor have I forgotten, when I was at Summerfields, the Wodehouse school stories which came out in a magazine called *Captain*. They were of a pre-Jeeves vintage but, in their way, of good body and quality.

Looking back upon this typical Victorian or Edwardian home, it is curious to note the mixture of what would now seem comfort and austerity. Even in our small house we had, I suppose, apart from Nanny and a nursery-maid, six or seven servants. In London, my father kept no carriage. But when we went to the country, we had a dog-cart, chiefly for station use. We had no luxuries. I remember a bath being put into our London house when I suppose I was about four or five. It occupied the inevitable half-landing in the London house of that date. Its installation caused much enthusiasm. Normally we had our tin bath in front of the nursery fire; but when the Great Bath came, we were allowed to use it on Saturday nights. It was long and deep, with mahogany sides, polished brass taps, and a long brass handle, like the tiller of a ship, to keep the water in or let it out. There were three steps up, and a rope. It was a splendid kind of minor Serpentine for sailing little ships.

About religion my father spoke very little, partly, no doubt, from his natural reticence. Even at the end of his life I scarcely knew his real opinions. He had been brought up in the traditions of F. D. Maurice and Charles Kingsley, my grandfather's intimate friends. I know of no man who lived a life of greater unselfishness or rectitude, but I think he had discarded dogma. The Bible and 'Scripture', of course, we were taught, both at home and at school, as part of our education.

My mother was 'raised' in the Methodist Church in America, and retained strong Protestant feelings, not to say prejudices. The most powerful criticism she could make of any argument was that it was 'Jesuitical'. We were, however, members of the Church of England, to which my grandfather adhered when he settled permanently in England. But our church-going was without marked fervour or even great regularity. When we were in London, we went to Holy Trinity, Sloane Street. When we moved to Sussex, we attended the parish church. Every Sunday night my father read the Evening Service, in the winter before, in the summer after, supper.

There were certain days when committees of ladies met at our house. They were, I believe, of the Women's Liberal Unionist Association, or of the Victoria League, or of the Ladies' Working Guild, for of these institutions my mother was either Honorary Secretary or Honorary Treasurer. The ladies who came generally arrived in carriages which much impressed me, especially the coachmen and the footmen. The ladies themselves appeared very large and billowing; their furs and hats and cloaks seemed to fill our hall. I used to stand on the stairs and watch them come. They assembled, for some reason, in the dining-room.

There were other strange customs which have now wholly disappeared. One was connected with visiting-cards. As we went in and out, we watched with interest a platter on the hall-table which contained the last additions. There was a mysterious but important set of rules which governed this ritual. Sometimes there appeared to be three or four cards and only one name; or the husband's card was left in addition to the wife's; or one or two young ladies, presumably just 'out', were included on the mother's cards. There was a particularly esoteric custom of turning up the corner, which apparently meant that the card had been left in person and not merely sent round by a servant. All these conventions have disappeared except, I believe, in diplomatic society.

Finally, there was 'calling'. Saturday or Sunday afternoon was the great time for this. We would often pass on the stairs or in the hall the addicts, chiefly male, of this habit. Occasionally, I was introduced into the drawing-room as an exhibit, and was rewarded by the fascinating spectacle of the caller's hat and gloves placed on a table or on the floor. It was obligatory to bring these articles upstairs and not to leave them in the hall.

All this jumble of memories of my life until I went away to school remains with me. I cannot frankly say that I was as happy as I think children are now, certainly as my children and grandchildren have seemed to be. I was always anxious lest I might do something wrong or commit some solecism. I was oppressed by some kind of mysterious power which would be sure to get me in the end. One felt that something unpleasant was more likely to happen than anything pleasant. This was not because my parents were not affectionate; on the contrary, they were devoted. They had scarcely any other interest than the welfare and success of their children. In addition, our nurse, Mrs. Last, who lived with us all her life, ending as my housekeeper when I married, was kind and loving. (Incidentally, all my mother's servants seemed to stay on almost indefinitely, although she treated them with stern severity.) Nevertheless, there was always a feeling of unease. Talleyrand said that anyone who had not known France before the Revolution had never known 'la douceur de vivre'. This may have equally been true of the life of some people before the First War. But there was not much douceur about the nurseries of the upper middle classes in my childhood. But perhaps we were different. We had, of course, times of great happiness and enjoyment. Yet I always felt that, on the whole, the world was something alarming, and people of all ages would be more likely to be troublesome than agreeable. Hence I grew up shy and sensitive. It is only by a long self-training that I have, to some extent, overcome these inhibitions. I have hardly ever had to make an important speech without feeling violently sick most of the day before. The House of Commons or the platform were equally bad; and even at the end of seven years of Premiership I had the same painful anticipation about Parliamentary Questions as men feel before a race or a battle. I always made it a rule on Question Days, Tuesdays and Thursdays, to lunch alone. Perhaps the reason that I was able to conceal if not overcome this nervousness was because I had learnt from childhood that these anxieties were natural, inevitable, and must somehow be endured.

I went to Summerfields in 1903, at the age of nine, well-grounded in the classics at Mr. Gladstone's school. I succeeded, through the admirable teaching of Dr. Williams, in obtaining the Third Scholarship to Eton in 1906. To be in College at Eton, with its chapel, college buildings, cloisters, and the sweet memory of Henry VI, our founder, as well as all its proud traditions, is a unique privilege. It was plain living and high thinking—at least in those days. But I was brought up to both. My earliest recollection, apart from ordinary schoolboy events, common to all generations, was Founder's Day, where I learnt, unwittingly, my first lesson in applied economics. We seventy Scholars were each in turn presented by the Provost with a 'peculium' or gift in memory of the King. It was a threepenny bit. My brother Daniel—either from his own knowledge or from his friendship with Maynard Keynes, a Scholar of his time—later explained to me that this sum, which would have been a very decent tip in the fifteenth century, now seemed meagre

only because of the continual depreciation in the value of money. I
have often remembered this in later years. Although I was not good
at games, I enjoyed cricket and played for College at the strange
'Wall Game'. I was a member of the team when a goal was scored—a
memorable event.

But ill health injured my school life. I was always a delicate child,
or at least supposed to be so; although in view of the many injuries
which I have sustained, and illnesses which I have surmounted in
later life, I must have inherited a fundamentally sound constitution.
At Summerfields I was always sent to bed early, instead of sitting up
with the other boys to do preparation. During my first half at Eton
I had a serious attack of pneumonia, which I only just survived.
Some years later, I suffered from growing too fast, and a bad state of
the heart was diagnosed. This led to my leaving Eton prematurely
and spending many months in bed or as an invalid. I had a series of
tutors to instruct me, and retained the supreme advantage of the
help and interest of my classical tutor, Mr. A. B. Ramsay (afterwards Master of Magdalene College, Cambridge), who came up
once or twice a week to London to correct my Latin and Greek
compositions. I owe him in every way a great debt, and I kept up a
close friendship with him until his death. Naturally, during this
period my life was somewhat solitary. Apart from my classical work,
I read greedily in English.

I retained during this time many of my Eton friendships, and
renewed them during my university years. Of these, the most
intimate were Julian Lambart (subsequently Lower Master and
Vice-Provost of Eton), Harry Willink (later Minister of Health,
Master of Magdalene College, Cambridge, and Vice-Chancellor),
and Harry Crookshank, who held many Ministerial posts before
and after the war. After my defeat at Stockton in 1945 and my
re-election at a by-election at Bromley, I had to be introduced into
the House with the usual formality. It is customary for an ex-
Minister to be introduced by the Chief Whip and another Whip. I
chose to make my bow between Crookshank and Willink, both
ex-Ministers. We had been Scholars elected in the same year at
Eton in 1906 and had sat as fellow Ministers in Churchill's Government. Similarly, when Willink had himself been elected at a by-

election at Croydon North in October 1940, and we were all three Ministers in Churchill's Government, he had been introduced by Crookshank and myself. This, I think, must be unique in Parliamentary history.

Among my tutors was Ronald Knox, who afterwards became one of my closest friends. He had a profound influence upon me, both then and afterwards. I shall never forget his coming to spend a day or two at No. 10 Downing Street, shortly before he died. Though I had not followed him, as I was at one time much tempted to do, when he left the Anglican for the Roman Church, our friendship continued unimpaired. During those last days at Downing Street, both he and I knew his life was nearing its end. I took him in my car to Paddington, to go by train to Mells, where he died a few weeks later. I said to him, perhaps without thinking, 'I hope you will have a good journey'. He replied, 'It will be a very long one'. To which I said, 'But Ronnie, you are very well prepared for it'. These were the last words we spoke together. Among my other tutors in the interval between Eton and Oxford was his brother, Dilwyn. He was perhaps an even more accomplished scholar than Ronnie, but of a very different outlook and temperament. With all this help, I succeeded, not indeed in obtaining a classical scholarship at Balliol, but at least in being elected to an Exhibition.

When I went to Oxford, my eldest brother, Daniel, had already gone into the business. My second brother, Arthur, had also left Balliol and been called to the Bar. I was the youngest, with long gaps between us. We were then all living a great deal in our country home in Sussex. Although we argued incessantly and quarrelled correspondingly, we were a very united family. My father enjoyed our debates, although he took very little part in them himself. We could discuss anything—religion, politics, history, literature, economics. The only subjects of which he disapproved were references either to food or money, which he thought vulgar and unworthy of serious consideration. What bound our family together was a sense of unity, based largely upon the business which my grandfather had founded, which played a great role in all our lives.

From early schoolboy days I saw the name 'Macmillan' on many of our class-books. At home we had the current publications of the

firm, as well as other books of interest coming out at the time. My
grandfather's achievement was something of which we were intensely proud. He had set us a high standard. The fact that the
firm remained a family business added to our sense of being bound
up with it and the world of publishing and letters. My father's
partners were his brother, Frederick, and his cousin, George
Macmillan. Afterwards my brother Daniel and I succeeded them.
I am glad to think that my son, Maurice, has carried on the tradition.

My grandfather's life was always in our minds. Daniel was born
in a croft at Upper Corrie, in Arran, his grandfather having himself
lived at the Cock Farm at the extreme north of the island. The
kirkyard at Lochranza was full of tombstones of Macmillans. To
visit these—to us hallowed—spots was a solemn pilgrimage. I was
first taken there at the age of eight.

The two years of my Oxford life did at last justify for me the
application of Talleyrand's saying; for life was indeed sweet. A
young man then seemed suddenly to grow up, especially coming
from a home where the discipline was severe and a mother's love
almost too restraining. After home and school life, it was an in-
toxicating feeling to be on one's own, in a society of countless
friends, old and new. In term-time I pursued every kind of activity,
joined every available society, and took part in every possible discussion. My politics were confused. I was a Liberal-Radical, a Tory-
Democrat, and a Fabian Socialist. At the Union I generally supported
the Liberal Government of the day, especially in its more radical
efforts. But I read every book that I could obtain about Disraeli, who
was my hero.

It would be tedious (though tempting) to recall the names of
many friends who were kind to me, and for whom I had formed
deep affection. Alas, few survived the next few years. Others have
gone since. Among lifelong friends were Geoffrey Madan, Victor
Mallet, Alan Herbert, Cranborne, Vincent Massey, and countless
others. For being a little starved of society at home I revelled in
friendships at Oxford. Walter Monckton, who was President of the
Union when I was a freshman, gave me my first chance in that
assembly, and was always kind then and afterwards. Gilbert Talbot,
to be killed in 1915 at Hooge, was another staunch ally. Of the dons

at Balliol, Urquhart ('Sligger' to everyone) was then and ever patient and understanding. Cyril Bailey and Pickard-Cambridge were inspiring and devoted teachers. It was by the help of these last two—both outstanding classical scholars—that I managed to get a First in Honour Moderations in the Easter term of 1914. Apart from Ronald Knox, my dearest and most intimate friend was Humphrey Sumner, Brackenbury Scholar of my year, who survived the war but not middle age. He was afterwards Warden of All Souls. He had the most refined and penetrating mind of any man I have ever known. He and I were the sole survivors, when the war ended, of the Scholars and Exhibitioners of our year.

Visits to Italy (second class on the train, first class on the boat) in the company of a few Oxford friends; reading-parties at Urquhart's Savoyard chalet; hard steady work in the vacations and, in term-time, an orgy of pleasurable social life: to all these I look back with nostalgic regret but with deep gratitude.

Best of all was the summer term of 1914, more than two years before Greats (the final school) had to be faced; a term, therefore, devoted almost wholly to enjoyment. It was, as so often again in a year of dramatic events, a perfect English summer. Oxford, not yet an industrial town or crowded with the buildings which science has brought in its train, was hardly changed from the Oxford of past centuries. The only concession to modernity (apart from the railway, which was some way from the town) were the trams. But these were horse-drawn. All that summer we punted on the river, bathed, sat in the quad, dined and argued with our friends, debated in the Union, danced at the Commemoration Balls. When term ended we made our plans for our reading-parties abroad or at home. A few of us —although so young (for in those days young men of twenty were not asked to formal London entertainments)—had the occasional invitation to a great house in London. I remember one such on the night of 28 June. It was a grand ball, in the old style—carnations and smilax up the stairs, and Mr. Cassani's string band, with one waltz succeeding another. At first there was little room to dance; but when the old and the great had gone away, then the young could enjoy themselves. I was rather shy and awkward, for, having no sisters, I had lived in almost entirely male society except for the few

Oxford dances. In those days, the waltz was rapid and exhausting. It was the habit of young men to bring two or three additional collars, which they left in the cloakroom, and by which they replaced each in its turn as it withered. I remember coming out into the street in the early hours of the morning, after making such an adjustment, and hearing a paper-boy calling out the news—for in those days late editions were sold all through the night. Raucously he cried out the words: 'Murder of Archduke'. To me, as no doubt to nearly all my fellow guests, this news had no particular implication.

So I approach the date on which my story of the Fifty Years Revolution begins. The old world ended, with its strange mixture of beauty and ugliness, happiness and sorrow, good and evil—so much to be proud of; so much, looking back, of which perhaps to be ashamed. Yet the most rabid radical or the most caustic critic of the Britain that had fought and won a twenty-year battle for freedom a century before, that for a hundred years had helped to keep the peace of the world, and spread civilisation to its distant corners, cannot but feel that if, in this sequence of rapid change, much has been gained, something, too, has been lost.

CHAPTER TWO

Family Background

IN childhood, and even in adolescence, we are almost wholly obsessed by the daily drama of our own lives, with their rapid alternations of pain and pleasure, sorrow and happiness. As the years pass, our stage becomes crowded with an increasing and often bewildering number of players. We are so taken up with adapting ourselves to the present, or dreaming about the future, that we have little inclination to concern ourselves with the past.

So, inside our own family, we accept the grown-up element— father, mother, uncles, aunts, and cousins—as inevitable and static figures. We rarely know, or want to know, much about their lives and characters. It is only later that we learn to understand them, or their predecessors.

The exception to this, in my early years, was the figure of my paternal grandfather, Daniel. He was the founder of our family and our fortunes. He, and my great-uncle Alexander, were of the heroic age. Their portraits—or engravings of them—hung in our nursery, conspicuous and revered. Of the others we knew little. Yet, if I am to tell my own story, interwoven with that of the tremendous period of history through which I have lived, it is right that I should give some account of my family and its background.

A short biography of my grandfather, Daniel, by Thomas Hughes, the author of *Tom Brown's Schooldays*, was published in 1882. This little book gives a finely drawn picture of a man of remarkable charm and character. 'Many young Scotchmen', writes the author in his preface, 'have come south, and made fortunes, and founded great houses of business. . . .' But he adds that it is not for that reason that, a quarter of a century after my grandfather's death, he was urged by many friends to make some permanent memorial to him, and he gives the reason: 'Whoever glances at these pages cannot fail, I think, to admit that there was something in this man's personal qualities and character, apart from his great business ability, which takes him out of the ordinary category—a touch, in fact, of the rare quality which we call heroism.'

Daniel Macmillan was born in 1813 on the Island of Arran. His grandfather, Malcolm, was 'tacksman' of a farm called 'The Cock', at the extreme north of the island. The tacksman in those days was a kind of 'chief peasant', with a certain responsibility for the welfare of the smaller cottars in his neighbourhood. Malcolm was an Elder of the Established Church; a man of stern character, but tender to those suffering from illness or misfortune. His son, Duncan, was drawn away from the stricter tradition of his father and the conservative rules of doctrine and discipline. When the Haldanes, the great revivalists of the day, sent missions to Arran, Malcolm looked upon them with disfavour; but he allowed his children to attend their meetings. William Crawford, Malcolm's neighbour, friend, and fellow Elder, was of a more impressionable and less austere temperament. The younger people were attracted to the new movement, including Duncan Macmillan, who had married Katherine Crawford, William's daughter. Of this marriage, Daniel was the tenth child and third son. Hughes says of him: 'From his earliest years he seems to have combined in a striking manner the characteristics of his two grandfathers; of Elder Malcolm, the man of order and duty, of Elder William, the man of progress.' But, much as he owed to his father and grandfather, it was his mother who had the greatest influence upon Daniel. Reverence, affection, tenderness, and devotion—these were their mutual relations. Moreover, from her Lowland blood—the Crawfords were Ayrshire folk who had migrated to Arran—he inherited a strain of caution and perseverance to balance his Highland impetuosity.

My grandfather was one of twelve children. Four were carried off in early life by what is described as an epidemic, but no doubt was tuberculosis; and he himself was struck by this dread disease before he was twenty. All his life he suffered from recurrent bouts of illness, hampering his work and sometimes involving prolonged absences for recuperation. Nevertheless, by the time of his death at the age of forty-four, he had laid the foundations of the publishing business and set it on its path. It would be inappropriate to describe here in any detail my grandfather's life and achievements, which are fully set out in Thomas Hughes's memorial volume. Moreover, the story of the firm has been written, to mark the centenary of its foundation, by Charles Morgan, in his book *The House of Macmillan, 1843–1943*. Thomas Hughes's biography was given to me by my father when I was still a child. I treasured it, and read it over and over again. Certain passages comforted me in my secret ambitions, which, even before I went to Oxford, were definitely bound up with a determination somehow or other to play a part in politics. I knew there would be difficulties about this because of other ties, but I was determined to overcome them.

My grandfather was bound apprentice to a bookseller in Irvine on 1 January 1824, for a term of seven years, at a wage of 1s. 6d. a week for the first year, with a rise of 1s. a week for each of the succeeding six years. At the end of this period, being now eighteen years old, he obtained employment with a bookseller in Glasgow. In spite of ill health, he was soon determined to try his fortune in England, if possible in London. In 1833, when a young man of twenty, his restless ambition was reproved by his elder brother, Malcolm, now a schoolmaster in Stirling. He replied as follows:

You seem rather to like twitting me about being ambitious, and this is the third or fourth time you have said, 'What are you, or your father's house, that you should be ambitious?' I have once or twice thought of giving you an answer. I shall do so now. You must not think me angry though I speak warmly. I have too much respect for you to speak disrespectfully. So you must not mistake me.

What am I? A very humble person who had no objection to raise himself if he could do it honourably. If all my relations were slaves, I should not feel that I was bound *therefore* to be a slave, that is, if I could purchase my freedom. I do not feel bound to follow in the footsteps of any of my relations. I am here to act for myself. None of them can stand in my stead in any very important matter. The most important things must be done by myself—alone.

This was a passage which particularly appealed to me. He goes on to describe his upbringing, after a reference to his brother's question, 'What is my father's house?'

Well, to begin with father; though I was very young, only ten, when he died, I have the deepest reverence for him. He was a hard-working man, a most devout man, and as I have heard mother say, cared for nothing but his family, that is, did not care what toil he endured for their sakes.

This is not a bad description of my own father, especially as regards his devotion to his family. He goes on:

You knew him better than I did, you can value him more highly. I now remember with pleasure, and with something better than pleasure, the manner in which he conducted family worship. Though I did not understand a word of his prayer, the very act of bowing down on my knees did me good, at least I think so.

He continues in the same strain:

Of my mother I can speak what I do know. I know her as well as ever a son knew a parent, and my persuasion is that she is the most perfect lady in all Scotland. With so little knowledge derived from books, with so very little inter-course with the higher ranks of society, with so little care or thought on what is most pleasing in external conduct, was there ever a lady who, so instinctively, so naturally, did what was right, acted with so much propriety in all cases? She has such high and noble notions that no one ever heard her say, or knew her do, a mean thing, no one could ever venture to say an impudent thing to her, or talk scandal in her presence. If any one did so once, it never was repeated; some quietly spoken but most bitter and biting saying put an end to such garbage.

Later in the book there is a description, drawn from his letters home, of his going to London in search of a post. He tried, in vain, one bookseller after another, for he was determined to stick to the book trade. Then, while awaiting the result of another application, there is a poignant account of his feelings during this discouraging search for employment.

I now had nothing to do but wait. My mind was in the most restless state. I could not tell what made it so. Old sins kept stalking before me. I was miserable. I walked about the streets, but saw nothing. I was jostled on the streets, yet I saw no face that I cared about, scarcely noticed those who pressed on me. The strangeness of everything increased my misery. I prayed. I tried to pray. I thought. I tried to think, my mind was a strange whirlpool. I could look at nothing. I could only weep, and try to pray. I do hope that these things will leave some powerful and permanent impression on my mind and heart. What a wonder the world is, what a mystery man is!

His efforts in London failed, and he went to Cambridge, where he was lucky to find employment with a bookseller named Johnson, the salary being £30 a year, the hours from 7.30 a.m. to 7 p.m.

I often thought of the experiences of this young Scotsman in 1833, when I was Member for Stockton-on-Tees in those terrible days of depression between the wars, when thousands of men, anxious and ready to work, ate out their hearts in the vain search for employment.

After Daniel's death in 1857, the business was carried on and developed by his younger brother, Alexander, whom he had brought down from Scotland to help him, and who lived till 1896. He, too, had had an adventurous life, having sailed to America before the mast almost in his childhood. Daniel and Alexander Macmillan not only founded a publishing house which was to prosper, but also gave it a character which has remained through the years. It is clear that both these young Scotsmen, although determined to succeed from the material point of view, were not prepared to succeed at any cost. Quality was to be the test. Thomas Hughes's words about Daniel applied equally to his brother, Alexander:

No man who ever sold books for a livelihood was more conscious of a vocation; more impressed with the dignity of his craft, and of its value to humanity; more anxious that it should suffer no shame or diminution through him. And his ideal did not abide in talk, a fair image to be brought out and worshipped when the shop was not full of customers. He strove faithfully to realise it amid difficulties which would have daunted any but a strong and brave man.

My father, Maurice Crawford Macmillan, the second son of Daniel, was born in 1853. Since my grandfather died when my father was four years old, he was brought up entirely under the guidance of his mother and his uncle, Alexander. He was named Maurice after Frederick Denison Maurice, one of his godfathers. The other was Charles Kingsley. Although Maurice's writings are now largely forgotten, he had a very considerable influence upon his contemporaries. The Christian Socialist movement, in spite of certain logical weaknesses, attracted many young men of generous minds in the second half of the century. Nor is the impetus which he gave to the promotion of social reform and education altogether forgotten today.

Maurice, with his two brothers and sister, was entrusted to the care of his uncle, Alexander, who himself was married and the father of several children. The two families lived together, and Alexander treated his brother's children as if they had been his own. My Uncle Frederick, being the eldest, went into the shop on my grandfather's death. A year or two later there was enough money to send my father to Uppingham, then under the rule of one of the great headmasters of the century, Dr. Thring. I have still in my possession an old-fashioned marble clock, presented to him on his leaving Uppingham, with the following inscription: 'Presented to Maurice Macmillan by the members of his house on his leaving Uppingham –September 1871'. This seems to be both an unusual and a remarkable tribute to the boy's character. From Uppingham he went to Christ's College, Cambridge, where he took a First in the Classics Tripos in 1875. My father did not go immediately into the business. For six years, from 1877 to 1883, he was classical master at St. Paul's School, of which the famous Dr. Walker was then headmaster. The position of classical master was an important one, and the tradition of the school was and remains one of a high level of scholarship. No doubt that experience was useful to him later.

My father was reserved and taciturn. It was seldom that he let himself go. I have given some childhood memories of him. As I grew up, I learnt to know him better. He died in 1936, at the age of eighty-three. His life fell into two distinct portions: his private life at home with the family, and his work as a publisher. He was a man of simple purposes, all within his grasp. As a father he was kind, considerate, and generous. He was devoted to the interests of his children, and for them was ready to make any sacrifice of money or leisure. He seldom said anything to me by way of reproach or correction, but it was always clear from his demeanour what were his feelings. He left the management of his house and everything to do with the garden or our small estate to my mother. In such matters I never heard him express in our presence any opinion, except to approve of what she proposed. Nevertheless, his influence, because so restrained, was powerful. It was a great source of sorrow to me or any of my brothers if we caused him anxiety or pain. It was a corresponding pleasure if we felt that we had earned his approbation. He took a great delight in my children—his only grand-children—and, like many shy men, got on very easily with small children. He read many books, old and new; but, as he grew older, he chiefly delighted in re-reading favourites. These were Scott, Dickens, and Thackeray.

Although there was no difficulty in which I would not be sure of my father's help, it was to my mother that I turned first. In the last resort, on a matter of real importance, his will would prevail. But he preferred to keep any expression of his decision for rare occasions. In general society my father took only a small pleasure. He liked my mother to have friends in the house, and he was pleased by her general popularity and her easy hospitality. But he had only a few intimate friends, chiefly from Cambridge days.

In the business my father was stern, eminently fair, and respected by all. I do not think it could have occurred to him to take any advantage over any man or to stoop to any action that had the slightest taint of meanness. He himself had inherited from my grandfather some of his impulsiveness, for in business matters, although generally cautious, he was sometimes surprisingly bold. But he claimed that he often found himself having to correct the much greater impulsiveness of his partners, who were apt to take, as he thought, an over-optimistic view of some particular project. It was he who strengthened and developed the educational side of the business, and was responsible for its spreading overseas. The branches in India and elsewhere were started by him and were left by his partners largely to his direction.

Children seldom have any clear picture of their parents' character or the story of their lives. This comes later. As I grew older, I realised my father's qualities, and had for him not merely the love of a son for a kind and forbearing parent, but an affectionate under-standing of the way in which he had decided to manage his life. He did not wish to impose his views or his rules of conduct on his children; but we learnt from my mother that before he was forty he decided to abandon both smoking and drinking alcohol in any form. He did not do this on any conscientious ground, but because he was afraid that the first would injure his health—he suffered from a weak throat and chest all his life—and that the second could not strengthen but might weaken the self-control which he regarded as the essential quality in every man. When my political career began, and seemed likely to conflict with my work in the business, my father did not discourage me. As it turned out, I was able for many years to do a full day's work at the office and attend the House of Commons after the business day was finished. Up till 1940 I was not tempted away by political preferment—for I was not offered it. So the two occupations could be carried on side by side. When the Second War came, my father was dead. Through my brother Daniel's generosity, I was able to join the War Government. Again, in 1951, although I had returned to business during our period in Opposition, he urged me to accept office. It will be seen, therefore, that my political career, as well as many other things, I owe to the generosity of my father and my eldest brother.

I must now write of my mother. She was born in 1856 at Spencer, a small country town in Owen county, Indiana. When I went there as Foreign Secretary and as Prime Minister I found it still a small and typically American town. The neighbouring city of Indianapolis had, of course, developed into a highly populated and thriving society. But life in Spencer seemed not very dissimilar to what it must have been a century before. My grandfather, Dr. J. Tarleton Belles (his surname was a corruption from Bellasis, one of which family had been an early emigrant to America), was the leading, perhaps the only, doctor in the town. His memory was still cherished. He had clearly been a man distinguished both by kindness of temperament and firmness of character. His house still stands, or did till a few years ago, a typical wooden house of the period. The chapel in which my mother used to sing as a girl in the choir had been destroyed by fire and rebuilt. Little else, however, seemed changed when I attended the Sunday service. My grandfather, who came originally from Kentucky, had experimented in various undertakings—one of which took him to the Far West, just being opened up—before he decided on medicine. He was one of the first students at De Pauw University, which a hundred years later conferred on me an honorary degree. From the stories which my mother told us from time to time, I gathered that he had quarrelled with his family, or rather with some members of it. Those who had stayed in

Kentucky were keen supporters of the South in the Civil War; he and others who had moved northwards took the other side. His wife—a Reid—was a Northerner, of Scottish descent. Many American books have described the bitterness of these family divisions and, although my mother's accounts of them were only based upon the memories of childhood, I later heard them confirmed by the conversation of relations or friends whose sympathies were equally divided. My mother's Christian names were Helen Artie; she was known always as Nellie. At the age of nineteen she married a musician by the name of Hill. Some six months after her marriage her husband died. I can never remember my mother, except in the last few months of her life, making any reference to her first marriage. But I found in a drawer in her bedroom some keepsakes— a watch chain, a seal, a gold cross, a small miniature—which she preserved. In those days people were reticent.

Soon after she became a widow, my mother felt an urge to leave the little town in which she doubtless found insufficient room for her energy and ambition. Perhaps the fact that after my grandmother's death my grandfather had married again may have had some influence on her decision. At any rate, she was determined to leave; and somewhere about the year 1876 she persuaded her father to let her embark on what must have then seemed a great adventure. My grandfather, for some reason, had friends of influence in Paris, where my mother decided to go. One of these was Mr. Linnear, a banker. Armed with this and other introductions, my mother set out alone on her journey in one of the best ships then available, a 4,000-ton paddle-steamer. In Paris she made many friends. She studied sculpture, and exhibited at the Salon. She cultivated her excellent voice with good teachers. Although it did not quite reach opera strength, she sang at concerts and at the Madeleine. She certainly had great talent. She treasured many photographs, portraits, and letters of her friends in those days. Among them were some of the most famous artists and singers in France.

How and when she met and fell in love with my father, I do not know. I believe it was at the house of Alexander Macmillan, my great-uncle, who had married as his second wife Emma Pignatel, a lady of Italian descent. It was probably through her that my mother became introduced to the Macmillans—whether in Paris or in London, I do not know. Here again, children are seldom well informed about the romances of their parents. Alas! I never heard my mother sing, for after my birth her voice failed; but she had a beautiful speaking voice and no trace of any but a pure English accent. She spoke French admirably, and had some knowledge of Italian.

An excellent hostess, with great skill in composing interesting and agreeable parties, whether in London or in Sussex, my mother had a very wide circle of friends, drawn from many different sections of society—authors, painters, politicians. She had many foreign friends. Her public and philanthropic activities were considerable, but concentrated upon two or three organisations to which she gave devoted service. She had none of my father's shyness, and enjoyed functions or gatherings which he only tolerated for her sake. But she was rigid in her views, indeed somewhat puritanical. She loved her adopted country, but never forgot her own.

My mother was a woman of unusually strong character. She had high standards, and demanded equally high performance from all about her. She had great ambitions, not for herself but for her children. This was sometimes embarrassing both to my father and us. But I can truthfully say that I owe everything all through my life to my mother's devotion and support. She nursed me through many illnesses and comforted me in many disappointments. In the First World War she literally saved my life. After the Battle of the Somme, I was shipped back, some weeks after I was wounded, in a very dangerous condition. The authorities were not to blame, for the overwhelming weight of casualties must have presented almost insuperable difficulties. I remember arriving at Victoria Station, with a high temperature and in a state of extreme exhaustion. I had a shrapnel wound in my right knee, and a series of machine-gun bullets had penetrated my pelvis. I persuaded the ambulance driver to go round by Cadogan Place, instead of going straight to some hospital in Essex. (No doubt he was properly rewarded for this breach of discipline.) My mother came to the door, made a quick decision, rang up a surgeon of her acquaintance, Sir William Bennett, and drove with me to a hospital in Belgrave Square, then provided and managed by Lady Ward and Lady Granard, both American by birth. Since no tube had been inserted, the wound had been allowed to heal superficially. As a result a deep abscess had formed and I was dangerously ill, almost at the point of death. I was operated on as soon as Sir William arrived—the first of a long series of operations. My life was saved by my mother's action. I gathered later that there was a good deal of trouble with the War Office authorities, but the unlucky general whom she interviewed soon collapsed. No one who has not experienced it can realise the determination of an American mother defending one of her children.

This incident is only one of many, but typical. In everything I tried to do I was apt to fail or lose heart at the first set-back. Without my mother's encouragement and the high standard of work she insisted upon in my youth, I should never have attained even the smallest academic distinction. If I failed at the first attempt, she felt certain I would succeed in the next; and so it often proved. In my disagreements with my political leaders and the indiscipline which I showed, my mother was sympathetic. She always said, 'You will win in the end'. At every important stage of my life I have felt her presence, both while she was alive and after her death.

Of course, there was a less agreeable side to this picture, at any rate in normal conditions. My mother was a formidable character, not easily deterred from anything on which she had set her mind, whether great or small. She had no sympathy for the conventional feelings of English boys. With two elder brothers it was seldom that I had a new suit of clothes. Sometimes the ones that I inherited had gone out of fashion in some small detail. This I resented. But she could not understand my concern about such trumpery objections. Worse still, when I was a little boy, low down in the school, she would speak to 'swells' in sixth form or the eleven, if she happened to know their parents. This caused me much agitation and confusion. She would even tackle the headmaster, if she happened to see him, generally with not unmerited criticisms of the sanitary or other arrangements. Apart from these minor troubles, there were other causes of irritation. My mother tried to enter into every aspect of her children's lives; she wished to know our friends, our amusements, and almost our daily doings. This, which naturally seemed to us interference, was in reality based on love and care. Nevertheless, we resented it, and sometimes resorted to appropriate evasive action. I have now learnt as a father of a family, and still more as a grandfather, how dangerous it is to ask questions and how little you will be told if you do. But these defects were insignificant compared with the sense of strength and confidence which she gave me, and the knowledge that in any trouble—whether due to my own folly or not—she would, once the truth was known, uphold me to the end.

My mother died in August 1937, less than eighteen months after my father. They are both buried in the same grave in our parish church at Horsted Keynes in Sussex. In their different ways, my father and mother contributed to any success I have won in any field. I live in the home they made, daily surrounded with memories of them both. Happily, there are some still alive who remember them and are grateful to them. The debt which I owe them is beyond description and, alas, beyond repayment.

CHAPTER THREE

The First War

T HE First War, in contrast to the Second, burst like a bomb-
shell upon ordinary people. It came suddenly and unexpectedly—a real 'bolt from the blue'. It is true that the large
expansion of the German Navy was regarded by many informed
observers as a serious portent. But the German retreat at Agadir and
the somewhat better relations that followed seemed reassuring.
Indeed, in the summer of 1914, there was far more anxiety about a
civil war in Ireland than about a world war in Europe. Certainly,
had we been told, when we were enjoying the carefree life of Oxford
in the summer term of 1914, that in a few weeks all our little band of
friends would abandon for ever academic life and rush to take up
arms, still more, that only a few were destined to survive a four
years' conflict, we should have thought such prophecies the ravings
of a maniac. The occasional outbursts of the Kaiser were treated
as pardonable indiscretions; Germany, after all, appeared to be
governed by men of solid reputation and a civilised background.
Her rulers were not in any way comparable to the ruffians led by
Hitler who were to seize power in the next generation.

Even those in the inner circles of Whitehall did not foresee that,
within six weeks of the Archduke's murder,[1] the grim and apparently
inevitable processes of threat and counter-threat, mobilisation and
counter-mobilisation, would lead to the launching of the greatest
war in human history. It was thus not to be expected that my young
friends and I, who were looking forward to our various plans for the
summer vacation, could have any inkling of our fate. Even when
war came, the general view was that it would be over by Christmas.
Our major anxiety was by hook or by crook not to miss it.

[1] Archduke Franz Ferdinand and his wife were assassinated at Sarajevo on 28 June
1914.

Unluckily for me, I had undergone an operation for appendicitis a few days before the outbreak of war. At that time this was considered quite a serious matter, and demanded a considerable period of convalescence. I had therefore to submit to the heart-breaking experience of hearing from all my friends who were hurriedly getting themselves into this or that regiment, while I had to remain inactive.

Some of us were members of Territorial regiments or yeomanry. Others had joined the Officers' Training Corps. I, alas, had not had the energy or the inclination to do either. In that bitter period of anxiety lest one should miss the whole affair, I envied them and cursed my own remissness. By a strange chance many of these found themselves victims of Kitchener's contempt for amateur soldiers. To their disgust, they were moved to India and other overseas stations, and thought themselves cheated of the opportunities of joining in the real show. Thus it must have seemed to them that 'the foolish virgins' had the best of it. However, before the end, they too were drawn into the all-devouring maelstrom.

During the first weeks of war I was at home waiting for news. The movement of the Expeditionary Force to France was a secret well kept, and we heard very little of what was going on. The retreat from Mons, the battle on the Aisne, and the final halting of the German onslaught on the Marne formed a tremendous and dramatic sequence. But it was very difficult for our unmilitary minds to grasp its significance. We followed the story as best we could from the official communiqués and the rather meagre accounts which the censorship allowed the Press to publish. There was, of course, no radio or television. It is strange to remember that at that time and indeed until the early twenties, a Government had no method of communication with the public except through the Press. There were no broadcasts from No. 10. The most stirring appeal was that of the famous Kitchener poster—'Your country needs you'—with the pointing finger and the accusing eyes. There were also recruiting meetings all over the country, following and inspired by a sonorous speech by Asquith, the Prime Minister, at the Albert Hall. But there was nothing except the communiqués, which were uninformative, to guide the public mind. The articles and diagrams of Mr. Hilaire Belloc in *Land and Water* were our chief recourse. In these weeks of waiting, I was naturally at a loss as to what to do; to continue the reading of Herodotus or Plato seemed inappropriate and likely in the long run to be a waste of time. Soon, however, I was allowed to join the Artists' Rifles, and began to drill in the Inns of Court, without uniform or rifles. At last, I was able to 'pass out', and found myself—how or why I do not recall—a second lieutenant in a new army battalion of the King's Royal Rifle Corps. One further obstacle had to be overcome—the medical examination. My body, I believed, was now sound, but I knew that my eyesight would be a serious hurdle. Fortunately, the pressure of men going through was very great, and made the medical officers correspondingly lenient. Actually, I suffered no serious difficulty from my need to wear (and carry spare) spectacles. The gas-mask was a bit of a problem. But I do not believe anybody could see much out of gas-masks, with or without spectacles.

In the late autumn of 1914 I found myself directed to join my battalion, the 19th I think it was, of this famous regiment, stationed at Southend-on-Sea. This, at any rate, was better than nothing; but there was still the fear that the war would be all over long before I could play any effective part. Over by Christmas—even after the early defeats and the stagnation that had settled on the Front—was still the common delusion. Kitchener, however, was known to have said it would last three years and, as members of Kitchener's Army, we put our hopes in him. But, without rifles, with little equipment, and with a state of readiness which even I could understand made our battalion quite unfit for operations, would the war last long enough for us?

Meanwhile, I heard from my friends, by correspondence and occasional meetings on leave. Most of them, in one way or another, were employed much as I was. Some had been lucky and had got into the Regular Army. Some had got to France already. Naturally, the heavy casualties suffered by the Regular Army in these months were chiefly felt by the families that had traditionally contributed to the Services. There were some of course, among my Eton and Oxford friends, whose names had already appeared in that inexorable list which, as the war went on, every household in the country began to fear more and more. But, for most of us, it was in the years that lay ahead that the great swathes would be cut.

Our battalion was commanded by a retired officer of the old type, with Boer War and other medals, named Sir Thomas Pilkington. With his white hair, rubicund complexion, and aquiline nose, he was a figure from the past. He treated us with kindness, but seemed somewhat surprised at the strange collection of officers, non-commissioned officers, and men of which he found himself the chief. The Adjutant had been a Regular soldier; but no one else, with the exception of one or two sergeants, seemed to have any military experience. However, what we lacked in knowledge, we made up in enthusiasm.

The officers occupied one or two hotels, typical seaside establishments of the time. The men were mostly billeted in lodging-houses. We shared with troops of other formations a small hall, where elementary instruction was given in the theory of musketry. But if we had no weapons, at least we could drill. This took place on an open field on the cliffs outside the town. The theory of drill fascinated us, and I remember spending long evenings with my comrades trying to reproduce by matchsticks the proper methods of 'forming platoon' on the right, and similar evolutions. In those days, we fell in two deep on parade. The first thing we learnt was to form fours. This involved numbering off each man in the front rank, with the usual absurdities and confusions. Finally, the men being numbered off, the command was given, after the preliminary or precautionary words had been duly spoken, 'Form fours!' Odd numbers stood still, even numbers took one pace to the rear and one to the right. Then, if all was well, the command was given, 'Right turn!', and there was a body of troops in proper formation, ready to march. Of course, some stepped to the left instead of the right, while others forgot their numbers. Others on the command 'Right turn!' could not, somehow, fail to turn to the left. I still remember our lovable and bewildered Colonel, watching us, with mingled sympathy and astonishment, all anxious to do it right, but all very liable to do it wrong. I can see him now, with well-cut uniform, smart polished boots, and spurs, gazing mournfully at a number of men—some of whom had tunics but civilian trousers, others with khaki trousers but civilian coats—all constituting a formation of troops which must have struck him as singularly unlikely ever to become soldiers. Now, of course, it is all much easier. The modern battalion falls in in threes, and is spared some of the old difficulties.

Since it appears to be a rule of war that it always rains, during those winter months there was a perpetual and pitiless deluge. The grass field turned to mud; the men were soaked through every day; the officers and sergeants discouraged. Yet we struggled on. We had no proper parade-ground. But we learnt and practised the various complexities of drill. At first I disliked it in practice as much as I had anything of the kind when I was a child. But I soon learnt to understand the merits and even the satisfaction to be obtained if we did occasionally do something reasonably well. At any rate we tried. In the evenings we studied various textbooks. *Infantry Training, Field Service Regulations, Manual of Military Law*, took the place of ancient history and philosophy. Occasionally these researches revealed nuggets of pure gold. For instance, 'Officers of Field rank on entering Balloons are not expected to wear spurs'. Actually this gem was first discovered and set to music by Alan Herbert; but the good news somehow drifted down to Southend. Nevertheless, as the weeks passed, and after Christmas was over and my twenty-first birthday approaching, I began to lose heart. It seemed to me that we were so low down in the list of battalions in this vast Kitchener's Army that we must be forgotten. Our hope of getting overseas seemed more and more remote. I felt I must do something about it, and effect an exchange into some other regiment where there would be a better chance.

Naturally I turned to my mother, and by her help and the recommendation of one or two of my Oxford friends I was sent for and interviewed by the Lieutenant-Colonel of the Grenadier Guards, Sir Henry Streatfeild. I could not help feeling the contrast when I went to see him at the Regimental Headquarters in Buckingham Gate. The smart saluting of the sentry and of the sergeant put me to shame. I was conscious that when I went in to see the Lieutenant-Colonel my bearing would be ignominiously unsoldierly. However, he asked only a few questions and put me at my ease. After a few weeks, I heard that my application had been successful. I was gazetted to the Reserve Battalion of the Grenadier Guards in March 1915. Of course, readers today will exclaim that this was all wrong. It was all done by influence. It was privilege of the worst kind—and so it was. It was truly shocking. But, after all, was it so very reprehensible? The only privilege I, and many others like me, sought was that of getting ourselves killed or wounded as soon as possible.

In a sense, of course, I was sorry to leave my Kitchener's Army battalion. Had I known how long the war would last and how, in fact, it would be possible for organisations of our kind to be armed and trained and take their place in combat, I should perhaps have waited patiently. Eighteen months later, at the Battle of the Somme, I saw the New Army—Kitchener's Army—in the full glory of its manly pride. Both in the First and Second War, Britain has put great armies into the field. It should never be forgotten that in the First War, by voluntary recruitment, nearly five million men were raised to fight for King and country. No doubt the system was inefficient; it was unfair; it was unscientific. But it was splendid. Naturally, as the war dragged on, the gaps had to be made good by compulsory service. Nevertheless, it was Kitchener's men who fought the great battles of '16 and '17. If, as many feel, the bloody sacrifices of the Somme and Passchendaele were indefensible, those heroic struggles stand for ever in the record of our country as the triumph of the spirit of the patriot and the volunteer.

However, I could not see the future, and was impatient for the change. And it *was* a great change. The square at Chelsea Barracks was a long way from the muddy field on the outskirts of Southend. The drill sergeants, sergeant-majors, sergeants, corporals, and even guardsmen, were all smart, all with spotless uniforms, creased trousers, and shining buttons. The fact that there was no such rank as lance-corporal struck me as significant. It was two stripes or nothing. The Orderly Room was almost as alarming to the novice as a headmaster's study. The mysteries of the regiment and of the wider clan of the Brigade of Guards were obscure and required careful study. I, together with other 'young officers' (and this term applied to anyone between the age of eighteen and forty-five who had no previous military experience), was initiated into some of these under the kindly guidance of Major George Powell (many years afterwards a colleague in the House of Commons). Some of these applied to regimental traditions, others to rules of behaviour, especially of civilian costume. All these conventions were outside formal regulations, and depended for their authority only on the sanction of pride and custom. Naturally, I had to discard my uniform and purchase another, at an approved tailor; also a sword. The uniform has gone; I have the sword still, for by the time I went to France in the summer of 1915, these weapons had been regretfully discarded. Until the new uniform was ready we drilled on the square in 'plain clothes', not 'mufti'. (The latter expression was a frightful solecism.) The correct style was a bowler, a blue suit, and a stick. Before the parade started we marched smartly up and down for five minutes. Then, when the Adjutant or other officer commanding the parade appeared, we halted, removed our hats, and stood to attention. I have preserved the habit of being five minutes early for appointments.

It is, or was, one of the healthy experiences in the life of many young men to go through a series of periodical changes of status. A boy would go to a preparatory school and be the most miserable little creature at the bottom of the school. Three years passed and, with luck, he found himself at the top—respected by the boys, and treated as more or less grown up by the masters. Then, to a public school; from the top he drops—as in a game of Snakes and Ladders—to the bottom again. Laboriously, he climbs up to eminence, either scholastically or athletically. But this is transitory; he goes as a freshman to a university or a cadet to a regiment—once more, back to square one. From the moral point of view, much is learnt by this continual rise or fall of fortune.

But from the technical point of view, much has to be unlearnt. I realised at once when on the square that I could not turn to the right or to the left correctly; that I could not salute correctly; that I had never even tried to 'slow march'; that I was ignorant of the niceties of giving a command, either 'Forward' from marking time or 'Halt' when on the march, at exactly the moment when it could be executed with precision. The further complication that the time of giving the command has to be varied with the distance of the officer from the squad he is drilling, was a refinement naturally quite unknown to me. So I began all over again; and I am bound to say I began also to realise the delight that can be taken in drill properly executed, or indeed in any movement of men, singly or in groups, smartly, efficiently, and proudly carried out.

When I became Prime Minister, one of my great pleasures was to watch from my bedroom windows, overlooking Horse Guards, the rehearsals for the Birthday Parade. In the Trooping, drill has been developed to something like the beauty of a ballet. Although my wife and I became a little tired of the *Figaro* slow march, three mornings out of four, for seven or eight weeks, I used to delight in this exercise. As the full rehearsals drew nearer I would often go out and watch them from a closer vantage-point. They brought back, year by year, many memories.

At the same time, I must confess that on my first arrival at Chelsea I was made to feel a little despondent. When I went into the Ante-Room (as the mess-room is called in the Brigade of Guards) on the second or third day of my joining, I sat down unobtrusively in a corner. There were a number of officers in the Reserve Battalion, who seemed to me to be very old men. They all had Boer War medals. In the Ante-Room they wore their caps but not their belts. To wear a hat indoors was an old custom, which also survived both in clubs and in Parliament. I suppose, in fact, they were men of forty or forty-five, but to me they appeared veterans. One of these officers growled out to me, 'I suppose you are very glad to join the regiment?' I said, rather nervously, 'Well, I am very proud to be allowed to do so.' 'Oh, I don't know,' said another old boy, 'there's not much in it nowadays. When I joined, my battalion was run by the Sergeant-Major, and it was damned good. When I left, it was run by the Adjutant, and wasn't too bad. Now, they tell me, the Commanding Officer is trying to run this battalion. All I can say is, God help us!' As I seemed a little surprised and perhaps disappointed, the first speaker good-naturedly offered me a glass of port.

The drills went on, but I had the great advantage during this period of living at home, at Cadogan Place. Friends were easier to meet and keep touch with when I was in London. Old Eton and Oxford friends were continually passing through London on leave, in some cases going out to the Front, or in others already back wounded. Within our own Reserve Battalion, the officers came and went. Some Regular officers in particular, after a period of recuperation from wounds suffered in the early months of the war, came back to the Reserve Battalion before setting out again to take the place of fresh casualties arising from trench warfare. Life went on in this strenuous, but pleasant, way for several months. I hoped to be sufficiently approved by authority to be soon regarded as available for a draft to one of our battalions in France. As I had committed no serious fault, either inside or outside barracks, my hopes seemed well-founded.

Then came the news that a new battalion—a fourth battalion—was to be formed. All the Guards battalions were to be grouped together in a single Guards Division—twelve battalions in three brigades. It was certain that either I should be chosen for this fourth battalion, or sent to fill a place in one of the other three. In the event I was posted to the 4th Battalion. It was the first time in history that the regiment had formed a fourth battalion. Soon after we were formed we moved from London to camp.

The decision to form the 4th Battalion was taken in July 1915. By the middle of the month, the battalion had completed its establishment and moved to Bovingdon Camp, near Marlow in the Thames Valley. Our Commanding Officer was Colonel G. C. Hamilton, our Second-in-Command Major Myles Ponsonby, our Adjutant Tommy Thorne, our Sergeant-Major E. Ludlow. To look through the list now is indeed tragic. Even the first engagement at Loos was to prove fatal to many of our comrades.

Our camp at Marlow was on or near the property of the greatest living Grenadier, General Sir George Higginson. Later, between the wars, I was to attend a dinner on his one-hundredth birthday. Meanwhile, he was a kind host to us all. While we had a fair number of drills and some field exercises, it was really like a perpetual garden-party. Glorious weather; lots of friends from London; plenty of visits to London; and, in both places, agreeable female society. Among the leading spirits was a young man of singular charm and attraction, Edward Tennant ('Bimbo' to all). Born of talented parents, he seemed to illustrate in his person all the Elizabethan ardour that still gave some enchantment and excitement

to war. His life was not destined to be long; but he has left to all
those who knew him a lasting memory. Of the many volumes
written about the young men of those days, none is more moving
than Lady Glenconner's tribute to her son.[1]

In due course, the day came for which we were all waiting. The
3rd Battalion was sent out to take part in the new Guards Division,
and sailed at the end of July from Southampton to Le Havre. Our
battalion, just a month after our arrival at Bovingdon Camp,
followed them on 15 August. I remember one striking incident on
our crossing, which might have taken place, perhaps more ap-
propriately, in earlier campaigns, when uniformity of practice was
less observed. It was none the less welcome and agreeable. After we
had embarked and seen to the comfort of all 'other ranks' and
ensured that their food and quarters were suitable, we were ushered
into the saloon where the officers were to take their refreshments. To
our amazement, we found ready a full luncheon—with napery,
crockery, silver, and all the rest—in the style of a peace-time party.
The *maître d'hôtel* was Charles, the presiding genius of the Ritz. A
posse of waiters from the same establishment accompanied him. A
full meal was served during the crossing, with a fine selection of
food and wine. 'We ate it in a kind of rapturous silence from 1.30–
3.30.'[2] All this was provided by Captain J. A. Morrison, commanding No. 1 Company, a man of equal wealth and generosity. How he
arranged it, I don't know. But this splendid send-off put us in very
good heart. We little thought then that within a month Captain
Morrison would find himself commanding the battalion at the
Battle of Loos, after the loss of four officers killed, two gassed, five
wounded, and casualties in other ranks amounting to over 350. We
disembarked in fine fettle at Le Havre where we received an
enthusiastic reception from the French. *'Assurément, ils feront bien
peur aux Boches!'*[3] was the comment as we marched through the
town. We entrained—'proceeded' as military parlance has it—to St.-
Omer. Here we detrained and marched to a village called Blendecques. There we remained for over a month.

[1] Pamela Glenconner, *Edward Wyndham Tennant: A Memoir by his Mother Pamela
Glenconner* (London, 1919).
[2] Letter to my mother, 16 August 1915.   [3] 17 August 1915.

I was in billets in the house of a typical French *bourgeois*, with Captain Aubrey Fletcher, our Company Commander, Lieutenants Hoare, Layton, and Tennant. We stayed at Blendecques until the division was fully formed in September. The battalion was inspected by our Brigadier, General Heyworth, and by the Divisional Commander, Lord Cavan. As the days went on, we knew that we were preparing for operations on a great scale. Meanwhile, the time passed pleasantly enough, in fine weather, some training, a little bridge, and much chaff. A few incidents of this period stand out in my memory. One of them was my first experience of a company entertainment behind the lines.

The concert which we had in our company was a great success. Imagine an old, draughty barn, about 100 ft. long and 30 wide—with straw on the brick floor of it, and for all illumination 3 oil lamps, hung round the wall, burning rather gloomily, moody, ill-omened.

Into this barn (where 3 platoons would ordinarily be asleep) 5 strong men introduce a cottage piano. This is gala night. On the piano 5 bottles stand, a candle in each. Then a sturdy corporal, with more bottles and more candles—and soon the place is (to our eyes) as well lit as any West End theatre.

So the evening begins. A recitation, very pathetic this, about the poor lad who slept at his post, and how the colonel sentenced him to death, and how his widowed mother pleaded for him, her only son, and how his pal, a hero of some 17 years, did so noble a deed in battle as to win the Victoria Cross—and the 'pal' chooses to refuse his decoration and asks instead a favour of the colonel. 'And what my lad is this, I pray?' 'Pardon Bill Williams, Sir' the hero said. (Bill is the delinquent.) 'He is but young. Give him his head! So Bill's alive whom all gave up for dead!'

And then wild and vociferous applause—almost tears in some eyes. Quite wonderful. Then a 'sketch' by an erstwhile music-hall comedian, now enlisted. A few rousing choruses follow, and then the Sergeant-Major (by request) gives 'Old King Cole' (a great favourite, which appears at every sing-song):

> 'What's the next command?
>> said the Major—
> 'I want six months' leave—
>> said the Captain—
> 'We do all the work,
>> said the subalterns—

'Put him in the book,
                    said the sergeant-major—
(i.e. take his name and report him)

'Move to the right in fours
                    said the sergeant.

'Left, right, left, right, left
                    said the corporal.

'We want jam for tea,
                    said the privates.

'Tum-tiddle-um, tiddle-um
                    said the drummers—

      For there's no one here
      That can compare
      With the men of the Grenadier Guard.'

Then more songs and recitations and the like, till at last bed-time comes. But before we go, 'The British Grenadiers' and 'God save the King' worthily finish a not unenjoyable evening. And not unimpressive either. For in a barn like this 250 voices make a fine 'Grenadierly' noise.[1]

Just before we moved a curious episode took place. All the officers of the division were assembled in the square of a small village near Blendecques to be addressed by the Corps Commander. He made us a speech in which he described at some length and in some detail the battle which was about to be launched. Since the civilian population were freely admitted to this open-air lecture, from the security point of view this seemed a somewhat odd procedure. Indeed, it was alleged by some of the more cynical of our officers that smiling matrons, leaning out of the windows of the houses, could be seen releasing pigeons at a frightening rate. In the course of his address the General assured us of his full support. 'Behind you, gentlemen, in your companies and battalions, will be your Brigadier; behind him your Divisional Commander, and behind you all—I shall be there.' I had absorbed enough of the typical regimental officer's attitude towards the staff to be unable to conceal my amusement at hearing one of my fellow-officers say in a loud stage whisper, 'Yes. And a long way behind too!' Another

[1] Letter to my mother, 25 August 1915.

incident is of the same disrespectful character. Before marching off to the battle, we were all instructed to read a message of encouragement from, I think, the Commander-in-Chief. Generals are, broadly speaking, better at plain statements than when they attempt rhetorical appeals. All I can remember of the message are the opening words, 'On the eve of this, the greatest battle in history . . .'. I was a new and raw recruit; but as I read these words out I heard a soldier in my platoon, who had been through it all—Mons, Le Cateau, Ypres, Festubert—exclaim, 'Now we're for it, boys!' I was too young and too amused to attempt any reprimand of this breach of discipline.

It is not my intention to give a general account of the Battle of Loos. This has been written in many histories. It started on 25 September with the attack by I Corps on the line between La Bassée Canal and Vermelles, and by IV Corps from Vermelles to Grenay. The attack was partially successful, but casualties were heavy, and certain positions could not be held, although the 15th—the splendid Highland—Division had pushed on to Loos and even over Hill 70, but only after terrible losses. On the afternoon of 26 September XI Corps, consisting of the Guards Division and the 21st and 24th Divisions, was transferred by Sir John French to Sir Douglas Haig's command. Throughout that day—it was a Sunday—violent fighting took place, the 21st and 24th Divisions being used to reinforce the battle. There were heavy losses, and serious counter-attacks by the Germans. Hill 70 had to be abandoned, leaving Loos exposed. The Guards Division, the third division in XI Corps, did not reach Haillicourt, nearly ten miles off, until early Sunday morning, and marched through Nœux-les-Mines to Vermelles. It was the first time the Guards Division had been in action since its creation. But, as our regimental historian says, 'All element of surprise had disappeared, and the Germans had had time to recover from the effects of the first blow and to collect reinforcements. It is doubtful whether the Guards Division ever had any real chance of succeeding in its attack. It had to start from old German trenches, the range of which the German artillery knew to an inch, while the effect of our own original artillery bombardment had died away.' It was, however, decided to put in the Guards Division and try to regain as much of the lost ground as possible. The battle continued through 26 and 27 September. By the 28th it was in effect over. Lord Kitchener subsequently described it as a substantial success. Actually, what was achieved was a gain of something under a mile at a cost of 45,000 casualties. It is true that 3,000 prisoners and a number of guns were taken, and the official estimates—but only estimates—of German casualties were put at 50,000. How far all this may have justified Lord Kitchener's description must be left for individual judgement.

However, of all these grand designs, whether failures or successes, my comrades and I knew little at the time. Our 4th Battalion, one of the four battalions of the 3rd Guards Brigade, set out for its place of concentration—on foot, no lorries then—and arrived at Haillicourt on Sunday morning, the 26th. One episode is significant. At a place called Marles-les-Mines we had to halt for a period of six hours because of the crowded condition of the road. But we were not allowed to break off for refreshment or repose. All the men could do was to sit down on the muddy road and wait, hoping every moment that a passage would be cleared.

We waited from 3.30 p.m.–9.30 p.m. We were kept standing almost all the time; but every time we were about to move on, fresh orders came for us to wait. The line of troops passing in front of us seemed never-ending. To add to our discomfort it poured steadily all those six hours. We got a cup of tea while waiting, but otherwise no food, except chocolate.

A stream of motor-ambulances kept passing us, back from the firing line. Some of the wounded were very cheerful. One fellow I saw sitting up, nursing gleefully a German officer's helmet. 'They're running!' he shouted. The wildest rumours were afloat—I do not yet know whether there was any truth in them. I fear not. But our men were much encouraged, and we stood on that road from 3.30–9.30 and sang almost ceaselessly, 'Rag-time'—and music-hall ditties, sentimental love-songs—anything and everything. It was really rather wonderful. At last, at 9.30 p.m. we were able to move. The rest of the Brigade had gone ahead of us, with six hours start, and we were temporarily without any communication with them at all. This of course means shocking staff work and we were all most indignant. We had no idea where we were supposed to get to or what to do. The C.O. sent out signallers and bicyclists all over the place to find the rest of the Brigade, and we marched on in the direction which seemed most probably right. At 11 p.m. we halted in a field. Luckily the rain had now stopped. The stars were shining in a clear sky, and the full moon gave us a splendid and most encouraging light. We halted then, in this field. The 'cookers' had been cooking the tea on the march, and we all got hot tea and bread and cheese. At 11.45 p.m. we set off again, having established communication meanwhile with our Brigadier. We marched till 1.15 a.m. to the village where we now are. We found billets in some fine barns with plenty of straw. At 1.30 a.m. we sank into a blissful and well-deserved sleep. . . .

We were woken up again at 4.30 a.m. this morning and breakfasted at 5 a.m. expecting to move immediately. But it is now 7.15 a.m. and no orders have yet arrived.[1]

The reason for this disturbance was curious: it was to allow a cavalry corps to pass. The young and optimistic regarded this inconvenience as a good sign: the famous breakthrough must be at hand. The more sophisticated were not so credulous. This strange concept of a cavalry breakthrough and the return of a war of movement dominated the minds of the cavalry generals who commanded the British armies almost to the end of the war.

We moved off again on the afternoon of Sunday, the 26th. We marched to Vermelles, where we spent the night. It so happened that my company were allotted some old trenches for this purpose, where we slept in comparative safety, but under somewhat macabre conditions. Our bit of the trench ran through an old French church-yard and, in the course of the bombardment, the coffins and bodies of the dead had received rather rough treatment. Here a skeleton, more or less entire; there a hand or head or leg. I thought, naturally, that this might have some effect upon morale. But quite the opposite. Our guardsmen thought this a most amusing coincidence, and there was much joking about it. 'That's where you'll be tomorrow, mate!', 'Lor! It's all got ready for us!' and other exclamations showed that this strange *memento mori* was regarded as a sly joke of the higher command.

On the morning of 27 September the brigade was ordered to attack Hill 70. Our Commanding Officer, Colonel Hamilton, sent for the Company Commanders to explain to them what our battalion was to do. Since he was ordered by the Brigadier to accompany him into Loos, he handed over the command of his battalion to Major

[1] Letter to my mother, 26 September 1915.

Ponsonby. At the same time, my Company Commander was told to go forward to reconnoitre the best road to Loos. In the confusion of the subsequent battle, I do not think that I or any of my fellow subalterns ever received any information as to what was expected of us. However, we set off gaily along the road in column of fours, at about 2.30 on the afternoon of the 27th. Ours was the leading battalion of the brigade, with No. 1 Company leading and mine, No. 4, at the rear. The Welsh Guards, the 2nd Battalion Scots Guards, and the 1st Battalion Grenadier Guards followed in that order. We advanced along the road under very heavy artillery fire—not only shrapnel, but plenty of high explosive. This was my first experience of shelling. It soon became apparent that to stick to the road would be folly. The order was, therefore, given to deploy and advance in 'artillery formation'. (This was a system by which a battalion broke up into platoons irregularly spaced, each still marching in fours.) The whole brigade went forward in this formation for something between one and a half and two miles. We were in full view of the Germans on the high ground, and heavily shelled throughout the whole of this manœuvre. Our historian says, 'Perfect order was maintained.' He goes on to say, 'Nothing more splendid has ever been recorded in the annals of the Guards than the manner in which every battalion in the Brigade faced this trying ordeal.' I have been told that the Germans watched the performance with amazement.

Our battalion being on the right had the additional disadvantage of coming under heavy machine-gun fire. I can still remember vividly this march from Vermelles to Loos. I must confess that for many months and even years I would dream of it. It is perfectly true that the exercise was carried out as if on a parade-ground. We naturally had a certain number of casualties, but these were not so severe as later. The only time I can remember any men showing any tendency to break ranks was when a hare got up between my platoon and the next. There were sufficient countrymen among our guardsmen for this incident to cause the same excitement as it invariably does during a shoot at home. 'There she goes! There she goes! After her!' and so forth. This little episode was surprising but comforting.

What was distressing for our men was that the whole ground that we covered in our march was filled, or seemed to be filled, with the remnants of troops who had attacked in the earlier days of the battle. Apart from the killed and wounded of the gallant Highland Division, there were the men of the 21st and 24th. Some were dead, some wounded, some broken and having lost all discipline or order. I have often wondered since why the decision was made to put in these divisions, who had never seen a shot fired and come straight from England, ahead of the Guards Division. It seemed a fatal error.

When we got to Loos our battalion was met by my Captain, Aubrey Fletcher, and was ordered to double down the slope and get into a trench which ran through some ruined houses. Loos was being heavily shelled, and a lot of gas shells were falling. When we had gone some way down the trench, the Brigadier was seen gallantly and somewhat unexpectedly galloping down the road. He ordered No. 3 Company and No. 4 Company not to go into the trench any further, but to follow him. From then on our battalion was separated into two parts. At the time, of course, we had no idea that this was happening, but much trouble followed from it. In the general confusion of the rest of the day, I recall only my own experiences and those of my company. What happened to the other half of our battalion I was of course unaware of until much later. Layton and I (commanding the two rear platoons)—the Commanding Officer having been gassed, the Second-in-Command and the Adjutant killed, and our own Captain Aubrey Fletcher having been separated from half his company—placed ourselves under the command of Captain J. A. Morrison. He then had his own company—one platoon of No. 2 Company, two platoons of No. 3 Company, and two of No. 4 Company, the only two officers in my company (No. 4) being Layton and myself. Bimbo Tennant had been left behind. Since Captain Morrison had received no orders and had no idea of what had become of the rest of the battalion, he took a very sensible decision. He placed himself in command of all the men he could collect. Since he had been told, at the beginning of the march, that the brigade was to take Hill 70 and that our battalion was to take part in the attack, he decided that it would be wrong for us to wait for orders which would be unlikely to reach us. The rest of our battalion having disappeared and any orderlies that he had sent to obtain instructions having failed to return, he thought he had better join in where he could.

Captain Morrison knew that the 2nd Brigade was to attack Puits 14. So on his own responsibility, he decided to join on to this brigade. We therefore extended in the correct manner on the right of the 1st Battalion Scots Guards, who were starting the attack. Unhappily, their advance was most fiercely contested, and they were forced by heavy machine-gun fire to retire. Of the meaning of all this, while it was going on, I had of course the dimmest idea. All that I knew was that we were advancing to attack in the conventional open-order formation, under considerable fire from shells and bullets. At the time, however, one does not notice these things. There is a kind of daze that makes one impervious to emotion. Anyway, it was my first experience of a battle, and I could not suppose that this was any worse than usual. Our half-battalion under Captain Morrison, when the Scots Guards were driven back from Puits 14, found itself completely isolated. There seemed to be no one on our left and no one on our right. Captain Morrison ordered us to stop the advance and lie down, which indeed was the best thing we could do. We were then told to crawl back and dig in a little further back on the Hulluch road. Captain Morrison ('Jummie' as he was known to us) behaved throughout these proceedings with complete calm. (He was a Reserve officer, who had left the regiment after the Boer War, which accounted for his modest rank; for had he remained a Regular officer, he would have reached the high command that his intelligence and courage justified.) The orders were for the men to crawl back, but since Jummie could not crawl (he was proud and corpulent), I did not see that I could very well do so either. I therefore walked about, trying to look as self-possessed as possible under a heavy fire. We succeeded in getting back to the road and began at once to dig in.

Later in the evening, almost as darkness fell, I received a bullet through my right hand. I had received earlier in the day an insignificant but painful wound in the head. We were ultimately relieved by the 2nd Battalion Scots Guards. I have very little recollection of the next days because I had, apart from the wound in my hand which was very painful and the arm much swollen, some concussion from the injury to my head. I have a vague recollection of Captain Morrison telling me at some point in the evening or the next morning to go away, and finding myself in a field dressing-station. So ended my first battle. It was one in which, at any rate, I learnt the lesson of what was meant by the phrase 'the fog of war'.

The confusion of the day had one curious consequence. When I got back to England I was sent to a hospital in Lennox Gardens, in the house of a friend of my mother, Lady Mary Meynell. I assume—but I do not remember—that my mother had somehow 'fixed' this, as it was a good hospital, near where she lived. The Lieutenant-Colonel of the Regiment, Sir Henry Streatfeild, came to see me in the ward. He was full of admiration for the wonderful work of the 4th Battalion in capturing and holding Hill 70. Being young, in-experienced, and slightly feverish, I protested that we never captured Hill 70 or got anywhere near it. I even said that I thought the whole affair had been frightfully mismanaged. He expressed, in his courteous way, some surprise, and maintained his version of our exploits. I was continuing to argue, when I suddenly realised that if I went on maintaining my point, he might very likely regard me as either ill-disciplined, shell-shocked, or even mad. I therefore gracefully accepted my share in his praise. It was only long after that I discovered the true history of the battle, and both the Lieutenant-Colonel and I were right. It was this unlucky division of our battalion at the very start which had made me maintain my account vigorously and, so far as my moiety of the battalion was concerned, accurately.

Shortly before Christmas I was discharged from hospital and given leave. In the New Year I was posted to the Reserve Battalion at Chelsea Barracks, and was engaged on routine duties. My wounds were fully healed; but I have never recovered the full strength of my right hand. The work was not onerous, and some of it was novel. I particularly enjoyed going on King's Guard. At that time, it was the custom of the Guard to 'mount' at St. James's Palace. The fact that the monarch had thought fit to go and live at Buckingham Palace more than one hundred years before did not seem to the Brigade of Guards any reason for altering their own habits. Even the recent change by which the Guard now mounts at Buckingham Palace was made chiefly to please the visiting public, British and foreign, and to benefit the traffic. In those days, after the mounting ceremony a small detachment was marched to 'Buck House'; but the officers and the main body remained in the old Palace. The quarters were good, and the day spent on guard by no means disagreeable. Apart from periodical 'going the rounds', there was nothing to do but read and lounge. Women guests were allowed at luncheon and men guests at dinner. The food and wine were excellent. The old waiter, Pierre, was a great character. The Guards Club, then in Pall Mall, was only a few yards from the Palace, and in the afternoons officers on guard were allowed to use the Club. I have often since dined on guard as a guest, and always enjoyed it. I believe I was the first Prime Minister to dine on guard since the Duke of Wellington.

These months of convalescence and 'light duty' afforded a chance of seeing some old friends. I went to Oxford and Eton, and saw other friends in London. But already the shadow of death had begun to darken all our young lives. Among the most grievous to me of the losses in 1915 was that of Gilbert Talbot. I had known him well at Oxford. I had stayed with him at Farnham, where his father the Bishop of Winchester and Mrs. Talbot lived, and savoured the rare quality of that atmosphere. I feel certain that if he had been spared he would have made a great mark in our politics. Politics were his dream and delight. As President of the Union he was a commanding figure. He was killed at Hooge at the end of July 1915. Whatever might have happened to others, I am sure that Gilbert would have fulfilled his early promise. I was also saddened by the death of many of my fellow-officers, among them Ivo Charteris, a young man of singular promise and charm.

By the spring of 1916, the early hopes of a rapid conclusion to the war had begun to fade. The dreary trench warfare seemed to be settling down into a siege, only occasionally varied by bloody attacks and counter-attacks on both sides, which failed to produce any marked result. For the young, time began to drag. I remember beginning to feel a sense of despair and disillusionment. Life at home, although not without its pleasures and gaieties, was becoming intolerable. When, by the spring of 1916, I was fit to go abroad again, I greatly welcomed the chance.

In April 1916 I went out in charge of a draft, and was posted to the 2nd Battalion. This battalion was commanded by a man of remarkable character, Colonel C. R. C. de Crespigny. He had already proved himself one of those fearless officers who had become a legend. Although suffering much pain from internal ulcers, he refused to go sick. This, and his gay and easy manner, made him adored by his men and popular among his fellow-officers. Indeed, he exercised an unconscious attraction on all men with whom he came in contact. My own upbringing, training, interests, and background were about as different from his as it was possible to imagine. Hunting, steeplechasing, gambling, and fighting were 'Crawley's' chief if not only interests. I never saw him read a book, or even refer to one. To all intents and purposes, he was illiterate; but he was a magnificent regimental officer, unequalled by any that I have known, except perhaps by Colonel G. D. Jeffreys (later General Lord Jeffreys). 'Crawley' maintained a strict discipline on duty; off parade he pushed almost to extremes that traditional freedom of behaviour in which we took a great pride. His sense of discipline, however, did not extend upwards. Indeed, he expressed the greatest contempt for any officer senior to him. He had a particular dislike of the Brigadier, who was a harmless enough person. This subversive spirit found expression in various ways, especially in the kind of simple jokes that gave great pleasure to all his battalion. For instance, there came down from Brigade Headquarters an order, doubtless emanating from G.H.Q., on the subject of rats. Whether there had been a correspondence in *The Times* or whether some inquiring M.P. had asked a Parliamentary Question, I do not know. At any rate, the rat problem as it reached us when we were in the line between Poperinghe and Ypres took the form of requiring a 'return of rats' in our trenches. 'Crawley' organised a three- or four-day shoot on a great scale. Sandbags were filled with rats, left a day or two to mellow, and then, in the dead of night, carried down and piled up outside Brigade Headquarters. This was *our* return.

Another instance of 'Crawley's' disregard of any orders of which he disapproved was in the matter of uniform. By the spring of 1916, the 'powers that be' had decided rather belatedly that officers' uniform was too conspicuous. In the first months of the war, officers in the Brigade had worn gold-peaked caps and swords. Both these were discarded by the time of Loos, but we wore Sam Browne belts and carried sticks, which still made us a good mark. Later on, officers in the front line or in any serious engagement not only discarded their Sam Browne belts, but wore the same webbing equipment as other ranks, and even carried rifles in an attack. 'Crawley', however, did not approve of this plan, which he thought degrading. He always wore a gold-peaked cap, belt, boots, and gold spurs—a perfect mark for the enemy. But he had a charmed life, and survived the whole war from the beginning to the end.

In the short time I served under Colonel de Crespigny I received many kindnesses from him. He treated me as a strange animal from another world, who read books and argued about philosophy and politics with any of my fellow-officers whom I could get to listen. But since I also enjoyed our friendly and even boisterous social life when we were behind the lines, he bore me no grudge; rather the opposite. Sometimes, I felt that I had earned his approbation, not from any words he spoke but from a particularly pleasant grin. Strangely enough, such was this man's attraction that if, at any time after the war, he had asked me to undertake some service—however disagreeable or however interfering with my own plans—I should unhesitatingly have accepted. In a word, he was a leader of men.

In rejoining the battalion I found some old friends. In June there joined us Harry Crookshank, one of my dearest friends for a whole lifetime. As children we were neighbours. Our mothers were both American. We went in the same year to the same preparatory school. We won scholarships at Eton at the same election. We were at Oxford together. By chance we found ourselves in the same regiment. Now we were in the same battalion. Harry was a painstaking and accurate classical scholar; when he was made Machine-Gun Officer he treated the 'stoppages' of the Vickers gun like Greek irregular verbs, and soon mastered them. After the war our comradeship continued. We were both elected to Parliament at the same time, in 1924. Although he took office as Minister of Mines and afterwards as Financial Secretary in the Baldwin and Chamberlain administrations, he retained his independence of mind, and never reproached me for mine. After the Second War, in which we had both served in Churchill's Government, we worked closely together in Opposition. Subsequently, he became Leader of the House, and proved one of the most successful that there has ever been. He could respond to all its moods. He could repel attacks or deflect inquiry with a deadpan calm. For winding up a debate, I have seldom heard a more gifted Parliamentarian. But his real strength lay in his character. From childhood till the day of his death in 1961 he was always the same: truthful, diligent, humorous, honourable, loyal. With him, a mean thought, or a mean action, were inconceivable.

Harry Crookshank had been wounded earlier in the war in somewhat unusual circumstances. As a result he always bore the regimental nickname of 'Lazarus'. When the Germans blew a mine in front of his trenches one morning in August 1915, he and his Company Commander were out with a working party. Harry was completely buried in about four feet or more of earth. He could breathe, but could not make himself heard. There he remained all day. When night fell, his Company Commander, who, though wounded, had got back to our line, sent out some men to try to find him and dig him out. Harry could hear them talking, and once or twice they seemed about to abandon the search. 'Only a poor bloody officer.' 'Oh well, he's not a bad bloke. Let's have another go.' And so on. Finally he was extricated, and sent down to a dressing-station. No one expected him back. However, after remaining there during the next day, in the evening he rejoined his company in the trenches. Hence his nickname.

We used sometimes to discuss this incident in later years. Harry would insist that he had been very fortunate. Had this happened to him in the Second War, he would have been kept back in hospital, fallen into the hands of a psychiatrist, sent to a mental home, and been insane for the rest of his life. 'Fortunately,' he would say, 'these new refinements had not been thought of in our day.'

We spent the next three months in or around the Ypres salient. We followed the routine so well known to thousands of men in those years: front line, support, reserve, a short rest, then front line again —and so the sequence went on. On one occasion, we had taken over some very bad trenches, the worst of any we had ever seen. They had apparently been constructed by indolent pigmies. The parapets were only waist high, and nowhere bullet-proof. There were no communication trenches, and nobody seemed to have done anything about drainage and sanitation. However, we set to work, and got them into quite a decent state. The trouble was that once we had finished this kind of job, we were sent somewhere else.

No one who fought at Ypres can ever forget the road from Poperinghe to Ypres. Sometimes, when in reserve, we occupied cellars at Ypres, dug-outs in the ramparts, or held the line between Railway Wood and the Menin road. Once we were accommodated in the prison at Ypres, which caused a good deal of merriment. 'Today we are living in—a Prison! I slept last night in a prisoner's cell; not for the last time, either, as we shall be back here after our first 4 days in the trenches. . . . Naturally, to have a company housed in a prison gives rise to a deal of persiflage among the men. But it is a good strong place, with fine cellars as well as the cells above ground. And with all the windows sandbagged up the place is fairly shell-proof.'[1] And then the trenches. The mud, the duck-boards, the darkness, the shell-holes, the sniping from a fixed point, the shelling. How vividly all these stand out in one's memory! Then, in the line, the daily 'strafe'; sometimes heavy, sometimes light; sometimes a few casualties, sometimes many. Perhaps the most tedious, although not the most dangerous, of all we had to do was the relief. But the next day, even in the front line, there was some sleep and rest; at any rate if things were fairly quiet. This routine continued more or less uninterrupted until the end of July. It was certainly a strange kind of war.

Perhaps the most extraordinary thing about a modern battlefield is the desolation and emptiness of it all. I think I have tried to describe this to you before. One cannot emphasise this point too much. Nothing is to be seen of war or soldiers—only the split and shattered trees and the burst of an occasional shell reveal anything of the truth. One can look for miles and see no human being. But in those miles of country lurk (like moles or rats, it seems) thousands, even hundreds of thousands of men, planning against each other perpetually some new device of death. Never showing themselves, they launch at each other

[1] Letter to my mother, 5 May 1916.

bullet, bomb, aerial torpedo, and shell. And somewhere too (on the German side we know of their existence opposite us) are the little cylinders of gas, waiting only for the moment to spit forth their nauseous and destroying fumes. And yet the landscape shows nothing of all this—nothing but a few shattered trees and 3 or 4 thin lines of earth and sandbags; these and the ruins of towns and villages are the only signs of war anywhere visible. The glamour of red coats—the martial tunes of fife and drum—aide-de-camps scurrying hither and thither on splendid chargers—lances glittering and swords flashing—how different the old wars must have been. The thrill of battle comes now only once or twice in a twelvemonth. We need not so much the gallantry of our fathers; we need (and in our army at any rate I think you will find it) that indomitable and patient determination which has saved England over and over again. If any one at home thinks or talks of peace, you can truthfully say that the army is weary enough of war but prepared to fight for another 50 years if necessary, until the final object is attained.

I don't know why I write such solemn stuff. But the daily newspapers are so full of nonsense about our 'exhaustion' and people at home seem to be so bent on petty personal quarrels, that the great issues (one feels) are becoming obscured and forgotten.[1]

The last sentence reflected the disgust which we felt at a certain wave of despondency which, according to the newspapers and private letters, seemed to be sweeping over the country at home during this period.

There is one incident which I should perhaps recall. To use the words of our regimental historian, 'The monotony of trench life was relieved by the exciting but dangerous ventures of patrols.' This is certainly one way of putting it. There were two views about the patrol mania which seized the staff during this summer. According to one theory it was to keep up the fighting spirit of the troops. According to another—probably more correct—it was to try to get the identification of German regiments for intelligence purposes. Anyway, one day I was sent for by the Commanding Officer, and told what I had to do. I was to go out that night with a corporal and a guardsman, and our object was to seize a German, either in his own trench or one who happened to be working or patrolling out-side. There were many difficulties in this small exercise. First there was our own wire; secondly, in the continual firing of Very lights, a

[1] Letter to my mother, 13 May 1916.

German sniper or machine-gunner might take a shot at us; thirdly,
if we ever got near the German trenches, we had to get through their
wire. We were successful in the first part of our enterprise, but we
soon ran into either a German sentry or a patrol. There was a
scuffle and a few ineffective shots on both sides. Then a German
threw a bomb, which hit me on the head. It exploded on the side of
my tin helmet, but somehow I escaped any serious injury. My
Corporal struck my assailant with one of the clubs with which we
had been served out. His helmet fell off, and Corporal Williams
struck him again. In the affray another German was killed or
wounded. We succeeded in getting back to our line, but without a
live prisoner. In the morning we made our report. I was suffering
from severe concussion and had the worst 'hangover' that I can ever
remember. Otherwise I was unscathed, apart from one or two minor
wounds in the face. However, I was not in a very good condition to
give a succinct account of the night's work. The Commanding
Officer gave me up as clearly rather confused. He turned to Corporal
Williams, and said, 'What happened? What did you do when Mr.
Macmillan was wounded?' 'Well, sir,' he replied, 'I saw the German
trying to run away. So I 'it 'im, and 'is 'elmet came off. Then I 'it 'im
again and the back of 'is 'ead came off.' I received three rewards for
this not very successful effort: first, another wound stripe which I
prized; secondly, a friendly compliment from 'Crawley' which I
prized still more; thirdly, the following message from the Brigadier:
'The Brigadier wishes Lieutenant Macmillan and his patrol on the
19th inst. to be congratulated on their excellent report and the most
useful information which they brought in.' I think the Brigadier
was trying to be nice, for I do not recall that we brought back any
special information. But perhaps our little escapade afforded some
satisfaction to someone at some distant château at Army or General
Headquarters, who would be able to regard it as a further proof of
the usefulness of patrols in 'reducing the monotony of trench life'.

The Medical Officer was prepared to send me back to hospital,
but since all the hospitals were being cleared in view of impending
operations, this would have meant going back home. My wounds
were certainly not grave enough to justify this and after some discussion with the Medical Officer and Colonel de Crespigny, I

decided to stay. I was very kindly treated and by the time our next rest out of the trenches was completed, I had recovered.

Meanwhile, the great Battle of the Somme was about to begin. In its opening gains we were not included, nor in its opening losses. But at the end of July we left Ypres and began to concentrate for a movement to the south. Then we knew that we were going into the battle. After long marches and a short period of rest, we reached Bertrancourt on 10 August. The Guards Division was now approaching the Somme area. Our battalion moved into the right sub-sector of the Beaumont-Hamel line. We were greeted with some pretty heavy shelling, and suffered a number of casualties. After a few days we were relieved and marched to Courcelles. From there we came to Méaulte. This was the base from which we should soon deploy into one of the fiercest actions in the long history of the Brigade of Guards.

The Battle of the Somme has been the subject of countless articles and books in the last fifty years. Debate still rages as to the gains or losses to the Allied cause which flowed from that tremendous conflict. Never before in history had there been such vast forces massed on both sides. Never had such a volume of shells been launched from guns of all calibres. Never had rifles and machine-guns poured out such a hail of bullets. Never had there been casualties on such a scale. It is not my purpose to join in this argument. I will only try to sketch my tiny share of this huge canvas.

On the night of 12 September our battalion took over part of the line which had been occupied by the 3rd Guards Brigade. We knew that the Guards Division was about to be launched into the great and consuming battle. We were told that it was likely that our brigade and the 2nd Brigade would lead the advances, the 3rd Brigade being in reserve. The usual encouraging messages were circulated, including one from Lord Cavan, who commanded our corps. But there was a preliminary operation which fell to our battalion. In order to have what was called 'a good jumping-off place' for 'D-Day', it was essential to gain certain ground, small in area but strongly held. We had to drive out a German machine-gun stronghold on the Ginchy–Flers road. Two platoons, under Second Lieutenant Minchin, were detailed for this task. I was ordered to bring up two platoons in support. I remember that it was a bright moonlit night, and the attacking party in front of us showed up distinctly. However, the leading platoons were very successful; the orchard was cleared of all the enemy in spite of heavy fire. Although the leading troops pressed forward in their enthusiasm beyond their objective, Minchin wisely decided to halt and dig in. This he did successfully before daylight. My small body joined up for this purpose, expecting a counter-attack which did not materialise. All the next day, our battalion remained in the front line, where we were heavily shelled, losing among other casualties one captain and two company sergeant-majors. We were relieved on the evening of the 14th, and bivouacked just behind Ginchy. Rations and rum were produced, with his usual punctuality, by our admirable Quartermaster.

That night I was instructed to go up with an orderly to make contact with the battalion of Coldstream who were to lead the attack in front of us, and to note the line of approach. I do not remember whether I was to act for the whole battalion or whether officers of other companies did the same. We passed a dead German lying in our path with his arm held out in a gesture of greeting. My orderly, who had a sardonic humour, shook him warmly by the hand as we went by. I don't know why this particular incident has remained so strongly in my memory, but it is so. I certainly took some moral comfort from it. The corpse was also a good landmark for the return journey. In the course of the night we were told that zero hour would be 6.20 a.m. the next morning. The 2nd and 3rd Battalions Coldstream were to assault the first, second, and third objectives. We were to follow in support. The third objective was within a few hundred yards of Lesbœufs. In fact, when nightfall came, only the first objective had been captured.

For many days past, rumours had been going about regarding some mysterious engines of war, which were said to be likely to take part in the attack. Nobody had actually seen them, and every kind of distorted account was given of these portentous monsters. They were in fact the tanks, in action on this day for the first time. Whether or not it was wise for the High Command to disclose their existence in this battle, which their number could not vitally influence, was subsequently much disputed. In the course of the day I can remember seeing one or two of these strange objects moving about, and one definitely bogged down in a huge shell-hole. They were useful, but not decisive.

In accordance with our orders we moved off—just after dawn—advancing in platoons in artillery formation, about three to four hundred yards behind the Coldstreamers. Colonel de Crespigny marched along in front, in his usual smart but irregular dress. All the rest of us had our steel helmets and our webbing equipment. When we got to Ginchy, a very heavy barrage came down; we were almost blinded by the noise and confusion. Most of the bombardment was directed a little to the south of the village, but the effect was none the less distracting. We were also worried by heavy rifle fire from our right, and some apparently from the rear. This was the dangerous point of juncture between our division and the next, the 6th. Fortunately, the ground was so boggy that many of the shells did not explode. But we had a number of casualties. Captain Lloyd of No. 2 Company was killed, but I did not see this. A young officer of my company, No. 3, named Arbuthnott, was wounded in the stomach, as it proved, fatally. As we were going along I was wounded, with a piece of shell in the right knee, just below the knee-cap. But I managed to continue and did not feel much inconvenience until later.

As I learnt afterwards, Colonel de Crespigny realised that something had gone wrong. We were going forward in accordance with our orders, with our right on the Ginchy–Lesbœufs road. But the two Coldstream battalions were nowhere to be seen. What actually happened was that the whole of the leading attack had swerved to the left, and the Coldstream battalions were no longer in front of us. We were supposed to be in support of them, but they had mysteriously disappeared. I remember that we halted for what seemed a long time (it was in fact only twenty minutes), and then the order was given to move on. We advanced hopefully towards what we believed to be the first objective, which we confidently expected to be in the hands of our friends. But it was still held by the Germans, the attacking troops having swerved away from them. Our creeping barrage had naturally ceased, and we had no support of any kind from the artillery. All we could do was to deploy and attack. We captured the line of trenches after fairly heavy fighting, but without great difficulty. The Germans were perhaps as surprised as we were. We also managed to make some contact with our own 3rd Battalion on our immediate right. Meanwhile, we cleaned up the position we had captured, and awaited further orders. Our companies and platoons had got a bit mixed up, but we were in good heart. There was some tiresome machine-gun fire annoying us from a position on our left flank, and I went out with a party of men to try to silence it. Unluckily, although the enemy gunners were successfully dealt with, I was shot at short range while half crawling, half crouching. The machine-gun bullets penetrated my left thigh just below the hip. I afterwards discovered that they had stuck in my pelvis. The experience of a severe wound like this is curious. Quite unlike the far less dangerous wound in my hand which I had received at Loos and which was excruciatingly painful, this body blow knocked me out, but did not hurt. I rolled down into a large shell-hole, where I lay dazed, but not—at first at least—unconscious.

The trench we had captured was behind me. The next objective was in front of me. I speculated on what was likely to be the course of the battle. As it turned out, no further advance was possible by our battalion, partly owing to the failure of the attack of the 6th Division on our right, and partly because of the heavy casualties suffered by the two Coldstream battalions and ourselves. There was fierce fighting on the left of the trench which we had occupied, and some dangerous moments. But of all this I, naturally, knew nothing. I lay in my hole. Even if I had known of a 'better 'ole' I could not have gone to it. I had in my pocket Aeschylus's *Prometheus* in Greek. It was a play I knew very well, and seemed not inappropriate to my position. So, as there seemed nothing better to do, and I could not move in any direction, I read it intermittently. The shelling went on from both sides with tremendous uproar, but since I was between the trenches I felt I was perhaps in a good position from this point of view. Only the 'shorts' would hit me. But, looking up from my deep hole, I saw two or three times in the day enemy counter-attacks. The German soldiers ran round the lip of my shell-hole. But I lay 'doggo' and feigned to be dead. Nor did any German have the curiosity to interfere with me. Had I moved, I might no doubt have tempted one to dispatch me finally. Although these counter-attacks gave me some anxious moments, they were beaten off; and occasionally I saw Germans running back. I lay out all day, indeed for over twelve hours, thinking of many things and nothing. My chief worry was the fear that I had been hit in a vital place, for everything seemed numbed. I bled very little, at least externally. I had no water, for my water-bottle had been destroyed by the machine-gun bullets which had entered my side. However, I was comforted by the thought that either our troops would advance or that, if they consolidated their position behind me, somebody would come and look for me in due course.

This is just what happened. When darkness fell, Company Sergeant-Major Norton, a splendid man, came out with a search party. I think he knew more or less where I was. At any rate, he found me. I was brought back to the trench which we were holding, and was taken to the point at which our Commanding Officer made his headquarters. My right knee was stiff and unusable—and painful. The wound in my thigh made me equally unable to use my left leg. I was dazed but quite conscious. After a little conversation, 'Crawley' observed, 'Well, I think you'd better be off.' The stretcher-bearers were formed up—one party carrying me and another party an officer by the name of Ritchie, commonly known as 'Dog' Ritchie, who subsequently became a distinguished game-warden in Kenya. When we were going through Ginchy the shelling was terrific. According to the orders before the battle, there was to be a dressing-station established at Ginchy. But since the advance had not been sufficient, and since the bombardment was on such a heavy scale, the dressing-station had clearly been abandoned. Ritchie and I conferred together. We felt it would be quite wrong to risk the lives of four able-bodied guardsmen to carry us any further. We therefore told them to go back to the battalion and we would make what progress we could. In the darkness, and the confusion of the bombardment, we became separated. At that point, fear, not to say panic, seized me. I suppose that courage is mainly, if not wholly, the result of vanity or pride. When one is in action—especially if one is respon-sible for men under one's command—proper behaviour, even acts of gallantry, are part of the show. One moves and behaves almost automatically as a member of a team or an actor on the stage. But now it was all over; I was alone and nobody could see me. There was no need to keep up appearances, and I was very frightened. The shelling was tremendous, and I was determined to get out of it. Although, in theory, I could not move, I remember very well running or at least stumbling through the village, and out at the southern end, to get away from the bombardment. How far I actually succeeded in going, I do not know. But I do remember the sense of comparative security when I got out of Ginchy, on which the enemy shelling was concentrated. I must have been on some kind of road, for I was able to roll myself down into a ditch on one side. There I was later picked up by the transport of a battalion of the Sherwood Foresters. Whether it was that day or the next, I am not sure. I am conscious of lying in a dressing-station, where I saw Neville Talbot (Gilbert's brother, and our chaplain at Balliol), who spoke to me. I remember nothing more until I reached hospital at Abbeville. It seems to me that at some point we went by canal in some kind of barge. At Abbeville we were put in a French military hospital, designed and appointed in the usual French style. Here I began to get better, but owing to the pressure of casualties, my wound was not drained but allowed gradually to close up, with the natural consequence of abscesses forming inside and a general poisoning of my whole body. Finally, I was sent to England. I have a dim memory of the hospital ship; then the train to Victoria. I was told that I was to be sent off to some distant hospital. Then I rebelled. I was determined—although very weak—to have my own way for once. I had had enough of being messed about by friend and foe. I have already described how I persuaded the driver of the ambulance to go to my home in Cadogan Place, and my mother's prompt and effective action.

There is a curious incident connected with this battle. In the summer of 1943, when I was Minister-Resident in the North African campaign, I had to make a journey from Algiers to Cairo. The plane in which we started crashed, and I got out with great difficulty, badly burned by the flames of the engine and suffering from shock. We had left about midnight, and I was taken in the early hours of the morning to a hospital not far from the airfield. It was a

French hospital, with white tiles, long corridors, and high vaulted rooms, which evoked a memory. At Abbeville in 1916, I had begged that a message be sent to my mother to say that I was all right. Somehow this got through by the kindness of some medical officer or chaplain. Now, in Algiers, I demanded that a similar message should be sent. Alas, my mother had been dead some seven years. I am ashamed to admit that I had forgotten my marriage, my children, and everything else. For a day or two, I was persuaded that I was a wounded officer from a battle nearly thirty years before. When I recovered, I felt that this lapse was pardonable. For everybody and everything seemed much the same—the efficient sister, the pretty nurse, the good-looking subaltern, the grumpy major, the *Sketch* and the *Tatler* and the novels of Philip Oppenheim. There was even a gramophone, wound up by hand, with few but often-repeated tunes. I felt more than ever certain of victory.

The casualties suffered by the 2nd Battalion of the Grenadier Guards in the operations of 13, 14, and 15 September were severe. They amounted to three officers killed or died of wounds, nine officers wounded; of other ranks there were 108 killed or died of wounds, 235 wounded, and 12 missing. But that was not the end. After receiving fresh drafts, both of officers and men, the battalion was sent into battle again only ten days later. On 25 September, still under the same Commanding Officer and Adjutant who had both survived the early engagement—Colonel de Crespigny and Captain Bailey—they were launched into the assault on Lesbœufs, which was carried out with courage and success. They captured the strong German positions at Lesbœufs and then pushed further on to a line which they were able to consolidate. In this second action there were once more heavy losses. Officer casualties were four killed and five wounded; other ranks, 108 killed, 122 wounded, and 12 missing. The usual congratulatory messages were sent. They had indeed been earned.

With the Battle of the Somme, my experience of actual operations in war came to an end. It was sharp. But it was short. I suffered none of the long-drawn-out pressures which weighed so heavily on officers who had to undergo, without relief, long periods of trench warfare. It is not to be wondered at that in those days to get wounded, 'to get a Blighty', was regarded as a piece of good luck rather than a misfortune. I well remember individual officers who had been through many battles and very long periods of service in the trenches, without sickness or wounds. Gallant as they were, they began eventually to show signs of deterioration. It is true that later in the war periods of posting to home units were arranged in certain cases. But a more flexible and imaginative management would have regarded relief in these cases as normal. There were others in the Reserve Battalion ready to go out in their place. A few days of battle had at least its excitements and satisfactions, as well as its dangers and hardships. But the dreary round of trench life was a much greater trial. Of course, this war presented completely novel problems, human as well as technical. Nothing of the kind had ever been encountered before.

The generals of the First War were very different from their successors in the Second. A story which went the rounds – perhaps apocryphal but certainly typical – was of a well-known general to whom at dinner a staff officer, with more sympathy than prudence, observed, 'I feel sorry for the troops in this frightful weather. It hasn't stopped raining for days.' To which the general is said to have replied, 'Well, they've got their macintosh sheets, haven't they? Pass the port, please.' Nor, except on the rarest occasions, did these great figures appear in the line. Had they done so, they could not have authorised the continuous and useless operations at Passchendaele, where 400,000 casualties were incurred to little purpose. The Second War was fought by great generals from their caravans. The First War was conducted by men of lesser quality from their châteaux.

These feelings about the command were widespread throughout the Army, even before the Somme. It is quite true that such sentiments were partly stimulated by the pride of the fighting Army. They were also due to a change in the whole conditions of war from the days of the Peninsula and Waterloo, or even of the Crimea. The aide-de-camp in those campaigns held the post of honour; his was the most dangerous task in battle. The commander of the small forces of those days took part in the battle, just as much as an admiral in naval combat today. His staff officers galloped to and fro with his orders,

in the very centre of the fray. One has only to read the casualties
suffered by the staff in the old campaigns to realise that these were
positions of danger as well as of distinction. But, in the First War,
all this was changed. The post of A.D.C. had not infrequently
become the refuge for men who preferred safety and comfort to
honour. The same seemed to apply to other staff posts. According
to a current story, either at the first or second Battle of Ypres,
Colonel de Crespigny (then a captain) had with impish mischief
collected all the first-class tickets he could from the ruined railway
station. These were printed 'Bruges to Ypres', 'Brussels to Ypres',
and so forth. He crossed out 'Bruges' or 'Brussels' and substituted
'War Office', 'G.H.Q., Cairo', 'G.H.Q., B.E.F.', etc. He then sent
the amended tickets to various officers who, in his view, might well
come and take some part in the fighting.

The spirit of animosity between the regimental officers and the
staff was therefore strong—often quite unfairly strong. Nor did many
of us realise how much we owed to the efficiency of a trained staff for
our comfort and our safety. Perhaps we understood it best (and I am
speaking more of the experience of my comrades than of my own)
when we moved from any of the other armies into General Plumer's
army. Here everything was invariably well arranged and well
ordered. One of the reasons for this growing ill feeling was trivial
but important. The brass hat and the red tab of the staff gave
offence. To many of us, red tabs were 'like a red rag to a bull'. One
of our most popular songs was one composed by Captain 'Jummie'
Morrison. I can only remember the chorus :

> The Army Corps Commander
>   had a hundred thousand men;
> The Army Corps Commander
>   had a hundred thousand men;
> The Army Corps Commander
>   had a hundred thousand men;
> But the 'Red Tabs' frittered them away!
> Glory! Glory! Alleluia!
>   The 'Red Tabs' frittered them away!

Later on, of course, I realised that there was another side to this
story. Meanwhile, like many other young officers—whether at the

Front or in the hospitals at home—I gloried in the combination of the high sense of discipline within the Brigade of Guards and the attitude of rebellion against all authority outside. This mood corresponded well enough with my own inclinations.

I was fortunate in watching the greater part of the North African campaign through what I might call 'the other end of the telescope'. I got the feeling that the armies of the Second War, the High Command, the staff, and the fighting troops were bound together by respect and affection. This was largely due to the fact that many of the leading generals had served as regimental officers in the First War and had not forgotten their experiences. They also appeared constantly in the front line and were well known to the troops. In this respect, the armies of the Second War were luckier.

There was one other difference which struck me. The First War was a singing war; compared to it the Second War was mute. In the First War there were countless songs. It was ushered in by 'Tipperary', a song destined to become famous in every part of the world. 'Tipperary' was similar to the 'Lilliburlero' of the seventeenth or 'Malbrouk s'en va-t-en guerre' of the early eighteenth century. With the exception of 'Lili Marlene' and one or two others, there were few great songs of the Second War. The reason is perhaps twofold. In 1914–18 the music-hall was still in its prime. At the beginning of the war there was Basil Hallam with 'Gilbert the Filbert'; George Robey and Violet Lorraine in a famous song, 'If You Were the Only Girl in the World and I Were the Only Boy'; and countless others. All this gaiety was supported in a metropolis free of air attack and crowded with officers and men on leave. Perhaps the second reason is that the First War was a marching war: three miles in fifty minutes; ten minutes' rest; and then on again; twelve to fifteen miles of full day's marching with, of course, equipment; rifle, ammunition, pack, and afterwards steel helmets to be carried. There were no lorries to carry the men's kit until right at the end of the war. March, march, march. Tramp of feet, sometimes on the cobbled French roads, with the iron-shod boots of the soldiery ringing on those ancient stones; sometimes shuffling along the duck-boards through the long communication trenches. The infantry fought upon their feet. In the Second War, so far as I could observe it, it was a ride by lorry, jeep, armoured car, tank, and many other forms of transport. In the First War, at any rate until I had left France, all our battalion transport was horse-drawn. It was indeed a marching war. So perhaps it was naturally a singing war; for soldiers sing when they are marching, into or out of battle.

I was put into hospital at Bathurst House in Belgrave Square at the end of September 1916. I left it for the last time a few weeks after the Armistice, in December 1918. I was not in hospital continuously. After about nine months I recovered enough to go on sick-leave. I was later able to do light duty at Chelsea Barracks and, for a short time, as adjutant at a school of drill for young N.C.O.s and officers, drawn from the ever-expanding ranks of the new armies. I could not do the 'duties' such as King's Guard, because I could not carry a sword owing to the wound in my left thigh. From time to time I returned to the hospital for a fresh opening of the wound and the removal either of bits of metal or of bone. I became naturally very impatient with this slow recovery. After the first months, when I began to mend, I was anxious for some more drastic treatment. But the accomplished surgeon who looked after me, Sir William Bennett, was insistent on his own methods. He believed that, given time, my injuries would mend. Those pieces of metal not easily extracted would be covered over by nature. Eventually the wound would heal from the bottom without the danger of poison. All that he promised came true. But it took a long time. Early in 1919 the tube was removed, and I was able to deal with the minor suppuration of the wound by a daily dressing which I applied myself. The wound was not finally healed until the beginning of 1920.

This long and compulsory sojourn in and out of hospital—mostly in—was a wearisome experience. When out, on sick-leave or light duty, there were, of course, the pleasures or at least the distractions of life in London. Yet, somehow, as the months dragged on, these became in a sense more and more superficial. One was haunted by memories and fears. By that time, the list of dead piled up, month by month and year by year, to a frightful sum. There were the great names of those whom I had looked up to in my childhood—Raymond Asquith, the Grenfells, Patrick Shaw-Stewart, and many others. Then there were those whom I had met in my short Oxford life, like

Rupert Brooke, who came often as Urquhart's guest. Then there were Eton friends, Oxford friends, and regimental friends, friends of my own age and now, alas, friends even younger than I. Day by day the list grew. One scarcely dared to read the newspapers, especially if a new battle had begun to rage. The communiqués claimed constant and unbroken success; but the casualty list revealed the cost. There were some who, being at home either on leave or wounded, tried to escape from this nightmare by continuous and even hectic amusement. They certainly had every right to 'drink and be merry'. Some had escaped death yesterday; others would die tomorrow. But I had neither the health, strength, nor inclination to join to any great extent even in harmless pleasures, still less in any more ambitious dissipations.

For the last months of 1916 and early months of 1917 I was very weak, and did not pay much attention to the news. I remember reading in the newspapers the headline announcing the resignation of Asquith and the formation of the Lloyd George Government. There had been much talk in the summer before I was wounded about the possibility of a change of Government. I remember seeing 'Bimbo' Tennant for the last time before he was killed, who told me some of the gossip that he had had from home. 'He told me a nice saying of F.E.'s (or attributed to him) apropos of Lord Milner as a candidate for the succession to 'Squith. "Why should a man who started one war be considered necessarily capable of ending another?" '[1] Had I been in ordinary health, this political drama would have excited me greatly. I had always admired Asquith. He treated me with great kindness when I had stayed on one or two occasions at No. 10 Downing Street at the invitation of his youngest son, Cys, who was a friend at Balliol and for many years afterwards. I had realised what a frightful blow Raymond's death in the Somme battle must have been to his father. But my sympathies were also with Lloyd George, to whom I had only spoken once in my life, that is when he came to the Oxford Union at Gilbert Talbot's invitation. For me—much as I admired Asquith's intellectual sincerity and moral nobility—Lloyd George was the rebel, the revolutionary; and, above all, the man who would get things done. Asquith represented,

[1] Letter to my mother, 12 May 1916.

as it seemed to me, the qualities but also the faults of the old world. Above all, he had tolerated too long the mistakes of the High Command. So, after the turn of the year, when I began to feel better and understand more what was happening, I was a strong supporter of the new Government in all the discussions, either in the hospital ward or in messes and clubs. It is true that Lloyd George disappointed me by his agreement to such battles as Passchendaele and his apparent inability to control the generals in high places.

In these years I read a great deal, chiefly history but also some classics. In Greek I read the *Odyssey* and *Iliad*; in Latin the *Aeneid*. I read also Gibbon. I read a great many political memoirs and biographies. My hero, Disraeli, had said, 'Read biography. There you have history without theory.' When I was on leave I got home whenever possible to Sussex. I made many acquaintances who were kind to me, among them Osbert Sitwell, who became and remained a lifelong friend. But the weeks and months dragged intolerably slowly, and the news seemed to hold no promises of the end. Ronnie Knox seldom came to London. One of his and my greatest friends, Guy Lawrence, who had been invalided from the Dardanelles, had then gone to France. Alas ! he was killed a few weeks before the Armistice.

The long-drawn-out battles of the autumn of 1917 oppressed me with their futility. I had at least enough knowledge to read between the lines of the official statements. I and many others felt bitterly over all this; perhaps more bitterly, because we were at home, than had we been in the field—or rather, in the mud.

Then came the spring of 1918 and the German breakthrough. I remember that I was back in hospital at that time, and could only get intermittent news from friends who came to see me. Finally then the tide began to turn. Unity of command was established. The Germans had clearly exhausted their effort, and we watched—through July, August, and September—the final reversal of all our ill fortune of four years. At last—at long last—came Victory and the Armistice.

It so happened that when the Armistice was announced I was back in hospital for some minor treatment, but able to walk with sticks. I remember well going out from Belgrave Square and watching the crowds converging on Hyde Park Corner. It was a scene of ecstatic relief and delight. Yet, among all those cheering men and women, there must have been many sad hearts.

The four years of war seemed an age, for time passes slowly in youth. I was twenty when it started; twenty-four when it ended. Perhaps because of my enforced inaction during the last two years, I brooded more over these dire events than had I been at the Front. Moreover, men of whatever age are not often confronted with death —certainly not violent death. Now we lived with death, day by day.

I found afterwards that few of the survivors of my own age felt able to shake off the memory of these years. We were haunted by them. We almost began to feel a sense of guilt for not having shared the fate of our friends and comrades. We certainly felt an obligation to make some decent use of the life that had been spared to us. When the war finally ended most of us were at a loss as to how to take up our lives again. I could not face going back to Oxford. Whenever I went there, it seemed to be a 'city of ghosts'. A certain bitterness began to eat into our hearts at the easy way in which many of our elders seemed to take up again, and play with undiminished zest, the game of politics. 'Old men lived; the young men died.'

At the same time, for many of us, our Army experience brought certain satisfactions. Apart from the good fellowship, soldiering had unexpected but undoubted charm. For me and the family in which I was brought up, the fighting Services had been something rather apart. I had very few friends or connections in the Regular Army or the Navy. It would not have occurred to the great majority of my school or university friends to enter upon the career of a Regular soldier. At first, the unfamiliar routine and surroundings were somewhat disturbing. But there was a novelty which was at once strange and inspiring. Particularly after I joined the Grenadiers, I began to take genuine pleasure in the high standards of discipline, in contrast with the rather sloppy way in which I had lived in school and university. Smartness and the beauty of drill itself, well performed, began to exert their influence. A sense that, if a thing is done at all it ought to be well done, is a very important element in any efficient military formation; but it also makes a good working rule for civilian life. I owe a great deal to what I learnt in the Brigade of Guards.

Another aspect of my fellow-officers, especially of some of the Regular officers, which I gradually realised, was their breadth of view and generosity as well as their simplicity. One might at first regard a fellow-officer as of limited outlook, interested only in sport, horses, and perhaps women. It was not until after a considerable period that one might find him to be a talented organist or an expert on miniatures. I learnt, therefore, to be a little ashamed of the intolerance and impudence with which the intellectual classes (to which I belonged) were apt to sweep on one side as of no account men who had not learnt their particular jargon or been brought up with their prejudices.

Next to that, and of even greater importance, I learnt the meaning of courage. War is a terrible disaster for a nation, even the old wars of pre-nuclear days. They reveal dark forces and bring into play brutal passions; and, as we have now learnt, victory brings almost as many dangers as defeat. This is no doubt true of whole peoples. But it cannot be denied that to the individual war may and does bring an extraordinary thrill—a sense of comradeship—a sense of teamship and a sense of triumph. Everything that the King said so nobly to his men before Agincourt was as true in 1914 as it had been in 1415. Any man who, of his own choice, misses or shirks such an opportunity is not a complete man. I have always felt a certain contempt for those 'gentlemen in England now abed', whether in the First War or the Second, who voluntarily missed their chance or chose to avoid danger by seeking positions of security.

Soldiering, in addition—and perhaps this was its most important contribution to the development of my own thoughts and ideals—brought to many young men of my own background and class an experience which in ordinary life they could seldom, at any rate in those days, have obtained. One of the advantages which the landed gentry and those who take delight in rural sports and popular amusements have always had over scholarly types and men to whom it has not fallen to move much outside of their own circles, is the power to get on with all types of people. Educated by grooms, gardeners, and keepers, as well as by schoolmasters, afterwards sharing their pleasures with the mass of the people and constantly mixing with all kinds of men, whether in the Army or the racecourse, they learn from earliest days how to consort with and how to treat, without either familiarity or shyness, the wide circle with whom they are brought into contact. To me this did not apply. The family business, except for a few of my father's clerks, was too remote. Our country estate was too small. I found a letter to my mother which describes this in words that I would not wish to alter now.

> I am very happy; it is a great experience, psychologically so interesting as to fill one's thoughts. . . . Indeed, of all the war, I think the most interesting (and humbling too) experience is the knowledge one gets of the poorer classes. They have big hearts, these soldiers, and it is a very pathetic task to have to read all their letters home. Some of the older men, with wives and families, who write every day, have in their style a wonderful simplicity which is almost great literature. And the comic intermixture of official or journalistic phrases—the kisses for baby or little Anne; or the 'tell Georgie from his daddy to be a good boy and not forget him'—it is all very touching. They love to buy little things to send home—postcards, or little pieces of silk, or ornamental sewing work—And then there comes occasionally a grim sentence or two, which reveals in a flash a sordid family drama. 'Mother, are you going ever to write to me. I have written you quite ten times and had no answer. Are you on the drink again, that Uncle George writes me the children are in a shocking state?' . . . There is much to be learnt from soldiers' letters.[1]

The great liberator, Bolívar, said that mankind is divided into swordsmen and gownsmen. The latter comprise the 'clerks' (in the medieval sense), the Civil Servants, the merchants and so forth. The former are the men of action and leadership. Every man, he declared, is born into one or other of these groups. I was certainly born a gownsman. Scholarship was the highest of all pursuits, in which the greatest honour was to be gained. Amusement was to be found in intellectual argument and debate. But the war made me, at least by adoption, a swordsman, living for the first time with men of this type, and watching and admiring their qualities. But it did much more. By the daily life, working in close contact with the men in one's platoon or company, we learnt for the first time how to understand, talk with, and feel at home with a whole class of men with whom we could not have come into contact in any other way. Thus we learnt to admire their steadfastness, enjoy their humour, and be touched by their sentiment. Even to censor letters was an experience; to be consulted by one's men on their personal troubles opened a

[1] 30 August 1915.

whole new picture of their lives. Afterwards, I found this one of the most rewarding aspects of constituency life. The 'surgery', as it came to be called, was not so very different from the relations between a company officer and his men.

Four years of war, while it brought me both suffering and sorrow, gave me, by widening and deepening my experience, both a confidence and a humility which I lacked in adolescence. By nature and training a 'gownsman', and ever grateful for all that the happy days of my youth had given me, I had acquired, although in a grim school, a little of the 'swordsman's' qualities.

If the First War caused a sudden and drastic change in my life and that of my friends, it marked the beginning of that revolution which, spread over fifty years, is the subject of my story. How far was the public conscious of the vast impending changes? How far were they grasped even by the Cabinet and the governing figures in British life? How far were they understood by Parliament? One thing at least the survivors of the war were spared. Had we foreseen in 1918 that all the labours of these four years would prove in vain and that, within another generation, partly by the wickedness of the masters of Germany, partly by the readiness of the German people to follow a teaching even blacker than that of the Kaiser and his friends, partly by the weakness and folly of those in charge of British policy, all this would have to be endured again, then indeed the cup of bitterness would have overflowed. Happily the curtain was closed upon the distant future. What then did we feel about things more immediate?

Of course, the vast battles, the great drama of life and death, the huge dislocation of the whole nation, dedicated either to the fighting of war or to the manufacture of munitions, made a tremendous upheaval. Would anything be the same again? How far could anything like the pre-war life be restored? These questions many people evaded; some devoted themselves as far as possible to the reconstruction of the old world; some dreamed of building a new one. At any rate, the Parliament that was elected in 1918 did not seem likely to make a very hopeful start in grappling with these problems. It was once cheerfully described by Lloyd George as 'the Trades Union Congress facing the Associated Chambers of Commerce'.

Of one great fact we were certainly conscious. While empires had rocked and monarchs been cast off their thrones all through Europe, the British monarchy stood firmer than ever. The British Empire had rallied to the cause of the old country, unsparing of its resources of men or wealth. The self-governing Dominions, India, and the Colonial Empire had all made their full contribution. At that time, the problem of imperialism or colonialism had scarcely emerged. While the future might bring changes, the present structure of the British Empire seemed firm and solid, strengthened rather than undermined by the experience of war.

Perhaps the most obvious changes were in the realm of technical advance. Before the war I had been a conscientious and devoted reader of H. G. Wells, who appeared to me the prophet of the new scientific age. But during the war a great revolution had already come about. The motor-car, which before the war was a luxury of the few, was in ever-increasing private and commercial use. In the Army, horse transport began to be replaced by the motor-lorry. The horse was ultimately to become an animal for pleasure or sport, but not for work. Even in the countryside the transition had begun. The aeroplane, which was a toy before the war, had become a powerful military instrument on both sides. It was soon to become a normal method of civilian transport.

The economic changes were obscure, and I had not yet begun to study economic questions. War naturally produced an inflationary boom, and the tide was still in full flow when the war ended and for a year or two later. I of course did not understand the reason, but enjoyed the result. I do remember wondering how it was that, in spite of all the squandering of treasure on so vast a scale (money was always 'treasure' when the politicians were speaking), everybody seemed to be so much better off. Certainly on this score I had nothing to grumble about. Instead of the very modest allowance which my father gave me in pre-war days, I found myself with generous pay, supplemented in those days with what was called 'Guards pay'; and, whether at the Front or at the hospital or at home, living more or less for nothing.

Nevertheless, though I certainly cannot claim to have foreseen the problems which would eventually emerge, there was a general feeling throughout the country that the old conditions of labour must be improved. The politicians called this 'homes fit for heroes'. Thoughtful people felt that the time had come to close the gap between the 'Two Nations'. Others, more sceptical, did not see where the money was to come from.

Already the most striking changes had taken place in the franchise. The Speaker's Conference, at which all parties were represented and all in agreement, more than doubled the electorate. The necessary legislation was passed before the end of the war. The size of the constituencies was bound to alter the whole character of elections. For the first time something like real democracy had come into being. For the franchise for women had been granted, if not yet on a universal basis, at least on a large scale. Thus had come to an end one of the strange features of pre-war England, the 'Suffragette' revolt. At the same time, apart from women's admission to the vote, the old position of women, in all classes, had greatly changed. Women were admitted to trades in which they had never participated before. Previously women's labour had been mainly in the textile and allied industries. Now they were brought into engineering on a wide basis. They played their part on the land, and they were recruited in very large numbers into the Forces. Offices, which had never admitted any but male clerks, were now largely staffed by women. At the same time a change in manners was taking place. It is difficult to recall that fifty years ago a young lady of good position could not walk in the street alone, without damage to her reputation. To walk down St. James's Street was to put her beyond the pale. All those conventions were already relaxed in 1918, and were about to disappear altogether in the twenties.

Turning to the wider field, Russia was then, as it was destined to remain so long, an unplumbed mystery. At the end of the First War we knew little about what was happening. All we knew was that Tsarism had fallen and that the Communists had seized power. The civil war and the much-disputed intervention were hotly debated, but little real information was available. If Russia was far away, we were certainly fully aware of the change in relations between ourselves and America. America 'had arrived' in full force, pushing, self-confident, but none the less welcome. To me, with my American descent, the first years of the war had been painful. President Wilson's famous phrase 'too proud to fight' had caused only contempt. Nor were matters much improved by his statements in December 1916 about the similarity between our war aims and those of the enemy, or his demand in January 1917 for 'Peace without Victory'. At that time Mr. Pélissier's 'Follies' were helping to distract a war-weary public with their inimitable entertainment. I remember a famous turn in which the singer began each verse with the words, 'I takes off my hat to . . .', going through a list of notabilities. The salute to President Wilson sticks in my mind:

> I takes off my hat to Mr. President Wilson.
> And why do I do it?
> Because,
> Tho' he's too proud to fight,
> He got married all right!
> So give him your kind applause!

This combination of pacifism and matrimony had much amused the British people. We were ignorant, of course, of the financial assistance and the many other methods by which America had favoured the side of the Allies. The American Ambassador, Walter Hines Page, was an intimate friend of my father and mother, and I therefore heard something of the problems and the diplomatic difficulties caused by the British blockade and the interference with neutral shipping. Lord Robert Cecil, who lived near us in Sussex, would tell us a little of the story too. I shudder to feel how near these disputes had sometimes brought us to open conflict. When, therefore, America at last entered the war it was a great day for my family. I remember my mother's delight and excitement when the first American division marched through London, led by the massed band of the Brigade of Guards. However modest the part which the Americans were actually able to play before the German collapse, once America came into the war the end was certain. Ludendorff's last offensive in the early months of 1918 was a desperate and final throw. It was the knowledge of the almost limitless support which American power would inevitably bring the Allies that sustained through 1917 and early 1918 the British and

French will and determination. President Wilson, although by no means a genial figure, was accordingly received with enthusiasm and gratitude when he came to London. There was hidden from us the great disaster that lay ahead, through the Senate's repudiation of Wilson's pledges and treaties. In the mood in which the war ended, America seemed to have abandoned isolationism for ever, and to be ready to play a leading role in the maintenance of peace.

Meanwhile, the most remarkable feature of the immediate post-war years was the strength and resistance of the old traditions of civilisation. Europe had been shaken, but not fatally. In spite of the fall of monarchs and violent changes in régime in many countries; in spite of the break-up of great empires; in spite of the triumph of Communism in Russia; much remained of the fundamental basis of European civilisation. It is true that the New World had come to the rescue of the Old, first through the splendid contribution of the British Colonies and Dominions, and later through the decisive intervention of the United States. Yet even after the repudiation of the Treaty and the abandonment of the League of Nations, the countries of the Old World made a remarkable effort towards recovery, and almost reached their goal. All this, however, lay in the future.

After the Armistice, all these thoughts and reflections, which I had turned over in the long months of illness and convalescence, were put in the background of my mind. To a young man of twenty-four, scarred but not disfigured, and with all the quick mental and moral recovery of which youth is capable, life at the end of 1918 seemed to offer an attractive, not to say exciting, prospect. I was more than ready to have done with one chapter and open the pages of another.

CHAPTER FOUR

Interlude

THE end of the First War—whatever may have been the less reassuring features which lay unrevealed beneath the surface —left Britain in a splendid position. As Churchill has pointed out, the fourth victory in four successive centuries over those who had attempted to set up a military tyranny in Europe constitutes 'a record of persistency and achievement without parallel in the history of ancient or modern times'.[1] We little suspected that all this would be lost within a single generation.

In the winter following the Armistice, although I was in no condition to take part in any very active celebrations, I was conscious of a great sense of deliverance and triumph. Those Christmas months were indeed months of rejoicing and thanksgiving; even though so many families had so much reason to mourn. Nevertheless, within a few weeks, and regardless of the effect upon the power of the victors to impose their will upon a troubled world, the ordinary man in the Services was intent only upon one thing—to go home. Demobilisation was the word which summed up this demand. It became irresistible, and before it could be satisfied threatened the discipline of an Army that had never wavered in war, even under the most intense strains and unparalleled casualties.

The progress of demobilisation was one which gave me my first insight into the dangers as well as the merits of planning. This is especially true of planning on a theoretical basis without due regard for the human aspect. During the closing years of the war a most elaborate scheme had been worked out, by which demobilisation could be made an effective instrument of industrial reconstruction. The plan was keyed to the needs of industry. It was logical. It was

[1] Winston Churchill, *The World Crisis*, vol. iv: *The Aftermath* (London, 1929), p. 17.

ingenious. But it took very little account of the feelings of the men involved. It was a beautiful design and, had it been possible to apply it, it would have had admirable results. The basis of it was that 'key' men were to be released first. They were sometimes called 'key' men and sometimes 'pivotal' men; and the assumption was that by their immediate return to work they would facilitate the restarting of industry and commerce. But the trouble was that the 'key' men were not the first, but in most cases the last, to have been recruited. If they were really 'key' men, they had been dissuaded from joining even during the period of voluntary enlistment. When conscription came in, they were only gradually released from civilian employment. Thus the demobilisation system, though in principle sound from a national point of view, came into violent conflict with the sense of justice of individual men. It was good planning; but it was grossly unfair. Moreover, it was tremendously abused. A man who wanted to be demobilised tried to produce a letter from his employer, claiming his services. The employer might in fact be an engineering firm; but he might be running a fish-and-chip shop. It was hard to check. All this had to be sorted out by the unfortunate company officers or the battalion headquarters.

Soon after Christmas, I returned for light duty to Chelsea Barracks, where I found the Reserve Battalion wrestling with this problem. Even the high state of discipline of the Brigade of Guards was threatened, though it never yielded, by the genuine indignation which was felt. Over the Army as a whole the sense of justice came into collision with the sense of duty, and several troublesome and even dangerous incidents took place at home and abroad. There were riots at Dover, Folkestone, and Calais, as well as at Luton. At Grove Park—a transport depot—there was even an attempt to form a soldiers' council.

I well remember one of these incidents early in February 1919. A large number of men—two or three thousand—from a great variety of units, were due to return to France from leave. When they got to Victoria Station there was some breakdown in the arrangements made for their comfort, and they refused to take their places in the trains. They drifted off to Horse Guards in considerable disorder, and demanded that their grievances should be met. They even appointed a 'leader' to prescribe the conditions to the staff of London Command. Our Reserve Battalion was accordingly instructed to send out a number of companies and to co-operate with two troops of the Household Cavalry to round up the 'mutineers'. I did not take part in the encircling operation, but was in charge of a company somewhere in Green Park in reserve, waiting to be called upon if necessary. Actually everything passed off very well, and the men concerned were shepherded back to Wellington Barracks, given a good breakfast, and put into the trains. Although the action of these troops was reprehensible, as were similar disorders elsewhere, yet one could not but have a good deal of sympathy for their complaints.

One of the many debts that the nation owes Churchill is not now remembered, except by a few. As soon as he was appointed to the War Office, he devised a completely new plan. When it was promulgated it was universally accepted as reasonable and equitable. It was broadly based upon the principle of 'first in, first out'; it gave some weight to wounds in the application for a discharge; it raised the pay of the army that was needed for the occupation of Germany and other duties overseas. There was, however, a dangerous interval between Churchill's ready grasp of the situation and the machinery for getting Cabinet and Parliamentary approval. However, this awkward period was somehow overcome, and order and contentment restored. Had there not been a change at the War Office early in 1919 and had not the new Secretary of State been a man of vision and courage, we might easily have been landed with the complete disintegration of the military forces. These incidents made a deep impression on me. The inquiry made from Whitehall as to whether the Reserve Battalion of Grenadiers 'could be depended on' seemed to us insulting. But it was somewhat of a shock to hear that such a question had even been posed.

Great then as was the military glory which Britain had won, imposing as were the responsibilities and dangers of enforcing peace, the minds of ninety-nine out of a hundred of my contemporaries, including myself, were concentrated on the sole question, 'What do I do next?' Most of us, amateur soldiers, regarded the war as a contest of will and strength, the mere winning of which would bring the fruits of victory. If we had been asked, we would have been surprised to be told that there was anything more to be done, except perhaps to 'hang the Kaiser' and 'squeeze the Germans until the pips squeaked'. Anyway, the great majority had had enough of soldiering, and wanted to be home. Let the boys, or the latest-joined of the conscripts, do what work was necessary. Let the rest get out and start again.

These were certainly my sentiments as regards myself. I did not want to stay as a Regular officer, even had I been fit enough to apply for a Regular commission. Yet I was not anxious to go immediately into business, although my father and his partners had invited me to do so. I fully expected to spend the rest of my life at an office desk, and shrank from starting unnecessarily soon. In the course of the winter, a new idea was put into my head. Could I not use my temporary commission as an instrument for seeing something of the world? In my Oxford days I had got to know fairly well George Lloyd.[1] I met him once or twice when I was in London in the winter of 1918, before he took up his appointment as Governor of Bombay. He invited me to go as an A.D.C. on his staff, and this seemed a splendid opportunity. It would give me a year or two of an easy and agreeable existence, seeing a country where I had never been, and learning something of a world about which I knew nothing. It would postpone at least for a time the routine of London office life. It would give me a chance to convalesce, in body and mind. I therefore accepted with alacrity his proposal, to which the regimental authorities agreed. I was to have gone out sometime in February or March. However, when it came to the medical examination, to my great disappointment, the doctors were firm in refusing me the necessary certificate. My wound was still not healed and I was assured that it would have been foolish to go out to India in that state. What, then, was I to do? I could apply for demobilisation like anyone else. I could not claim that I had anyone working under me, or that I was in any sense a 'key' man. But I have no doubt that the authorities, who had not got much value out of my intermittent service during the last two years, would have been glad to let me go. But I did not want to go; at least not then. I wanted, if possible, to be away from England, to be away from home, to be on my own, to

[1] Later Lord Lloyd of Dolobran.

see a new part of the world and new faces, and to enjoy new experiences. Bombay would have given me this, as well as the advantage
of serving a man whom I already knew and much admired. Happily,
at this moment, recruits were needed for the staff of the Duke of
Devonshire, the Governor-General of Canada. During the war he
had taken on older men, badly wounded, who naturally wanted to
get back to their own avocations; so young A.D.C.s were required.
My mother, who was a long-standing friend of Lady Edward
Cavendish, the Duke's mother, heard of this. It was suggested that
I might do. The Duchess of Devonshire, on leave in England, was
consulted. I still preferred India and made a final effort to get
medical agreement; but this again failed. So it was to be Canada, not
India. In Canada I found, in due course, health and a wife. On such
small chances does the romance of life depend.

I arrived in Ottawa at the end of March 1919 and remained there
until the end of January the following year. These ten months were
in many ways the happiest in my life. The duties were interesting
though not arduous. The atmosphere of Government House was
that of a large and cheerful house-party, with the family, a continuous flow of guests, young and old, and our own very congenial staff.
The opportunities for making friends, especially in Ottawa, Montreal, and Toronto, were considerable; and we all took full advantage
of Canadian hospitality. I was able to travel on duty from coast to
coast, both upon the Canadian Pacific and the Canadian National
systems. In addition, the autumn visit of the Prince of Wales made
this a memorable year. In the summer there was plenty of relaxation.
Often at weekends we motored to the house which the Duke had
built on Blue Sea Lake in the Gatineau Hills. There were several
tours of interest, including one from Quebec to the Saguenay river.
There was fishing; there was boating; there was swimming; there
was flirting. And there was also a little serious work.

We have got so accustomed to the new concept of the Commonwealth that it is difficult to remember how rapid and how recent have
been the changes in the relationship between Britain and what we
now call the 'old' Commonwealth countries. In 1919 the functions
and duties of a Governor-General were more than ceremonial. As
Sir Harold Nicolson has pointed out, the old colonial theory did not

collapse with the death of Queen Victoria, but lasted unchanged until after the First World War.[1] It was the impact of the war which hastened developments which no doubt would have become in due course inevitable. Nevertheless, when I went to Canada, the Governor-General was still appointed by the King on the sole advice of the British Prime Minister. He and his office were the chief if not the only method of communication between the Canadian and the British Governments. Everything of importance passed through him, and was reported by him to the Colonial Secretary. The Governor-General, especially if he was a man of political experience, was freely consulted by Ministers and his advice was welcome. Nobody then challenged the sovereignty of the British Crown and Parliament over the whole Empire. The Privy Council at home was accepted as the ultimate Court of Appeal. Two demands by the Canadian Government had caused considerable strain just before my arrival. The first of these was Sir Robert Borden's insistence that Canada should have separate representation at the Peace Conference. It is curious to recall that William Fielding, for many years Sir Wilfrid Laurier's chief lieutenant and still a leading Liberal, although he had become an independent supporter of Borden's War Government, strongly criticised this claim. He issued a solemn warning against a step which might lead to the danger of making Canada a separate nation. This was rebutted by Arthur Meighen, acting for the Prime Minister, in words at the time thought almost revolutionary. 'I affirm here', he said, 'as a Canadian citizen that as a distinct entity within the British Empire, and as a distinct self-governing entity, we are entitled to a voice in the attitude assumed by Great Britain in the disposal of every question that pertains to the terms of peace.' A second significant step had been taken by the Canadian Government in October 1918, when they announced their intention of appointing a Canadian Minister in Washington.[2] This, however, could be regarded as a special case, owing to the close economic and geographical contacts between

---

[1] Harold Nicolson, *King George V: His Life and Reign* (London, 1952), p. 470.

[2] This was agreed by the U.K. Government in 1920, although the post was not filled until 1926, when Vincent Massey was appointed the first Canadian Minister in Washington by Mackenzie King.

Canada and the United States. Few expected it to lead to a wide extension of diplomatic representation.

Looking back, it is interesting to see the development of the independence of the old Commonwealth countries, and the difficulty of finding a logical foundation for the continued unity of the Empire. Naturally enough, the First War resulted in a complete change of status for Canada, as for other Dominions. The Dominions were given their place at the Peace Conference. The Dominion countries joined the League of Nations as separate entities. From 1927 onwards, they exercised the right of appointing diplomatic missions overseas. This problem was faced in the 1926 Imperial Conference, which adopted the Balfour Formula. At the next conference of 1930 it was agreed that the Balfour Formula should be given statutory effect, and this was done by the Statute of Westminster at the end of 1931, with corresponding legislation in the Dominion Parliaments. It is perhaps worth recalling the precise words of this characteristically ingenious definition:

The Dominions are autonomous communities within the British Empire, equal in status, in no way subordinate one to another in any aspect of their domestic or internal affairs, though united by a common allegiance to the Crown, and freely associated as members of the British Commonwealth of Nations.

All this, however, lay in the future. The experience which I gained at Ottawa made me realise later how far-reaching but necessary were the changes introduced and approved by Parliament during the next few years.

The Duke of Devonshire, who was appointed Governor-General in 1916, was a man singularly well suited to command both the respect and affection of Canadians. His combination of dignity and simplicity appealed to them. Some years later his genial and sunny temperament was overshadowed by the sad effects of a paralytic stroke. Those who only knew him as a querulous and suffering invalid in the last years of his life could scarcely imagine the charm of this essentially kind, wise, and modest man. Some of his Canadian Ministers used to tell me that when they first knew him they underestimated his knowledge, and the strength and shrewdness of his character. Nor was it uncommon for a vain or foolish man to leave an interview with a very false idea of the impression he had made upon His Excellency. But the leading Ministers found in the Governor-General not merely a friend, but a useful political adviser. He had long experience of the House of Commons, in which he sat for nearly twenty years. He had been Financial Secretary in Balfour's Government and Civil Lord of the Admiralty in Asquith's War Coalition. From us, of course, in the A.D.C.s' room, much of this was hidden, although something of our chief's work and influence was revealed. It was then the practice of the Governor-General to go every day that he was in Ottawa to his office in the Parliament Building. One of the A.D.C.s would accompany him. It was there that he saw Ministers and transacted official business. When the Duke found that I was interested in political problems, he would discuss them freely with me. I learnt much from him in this way.

Indeed, the problems of Canada in that summer were serious and perplexing. The country was still shaken by the imposition of conscription, especially in Quebec. The death of Sir Wilfrid Laurier, the old and respected Liberal leader, in February 1919, was a severe blow, as much deplored by the Conservatives as by the Liberals. For Laurier's influence, although to some extent diminished, had always been on the side of the unity of the country.

Soon after I arrived, social unrest, culminating in the Winnipeg strike in May, caused much alarm. Meighen, however, in the absence of Sir Robert Borden in Paris at the Peace Conference, handled the situation firmly and effectively. Apart from the usual timid group of alarmists, many serious people were genuinely anxious about the difficulties both in the Prairie Provinces and in Vancouver. The 'one big Union' movement and the inter-provincial Labour Conferences were inspired by the example of Soviet Russia and the Spartacist revolution in Germany, to the leaders of which they sent fraternal greetings. The death of Sir Wilfrid Laurier had left the Liberal Party without a head. Sir Robert Borden was still away. This imposed upon Meighen heavy responsibilities without the full authority of a Prime Minister. Although the appointment of Mackenzie King as Leader of the Opposition was the beginning of what proved to be a long tenure of power, at that time King's leadership was regarded as ineffective and unpromising. I was fortunate to make his acquaintance at this time, and so began a friendship which lasted over many years.

In this situation Borden, on his return to Canada in the summer, was deeply immersed in the problem of the reconstruction of his party and of his Government. A substantial number of the Liberals had given support to the War Government, accepting the necessity of conscription. Might it not be possible to found a wider Union Party, based upon the Coalition which had won the war? If the more moderate of the French-Canadian leaders could be won over from the Liberal Party, this would give solidity to the administration, and peace and quiet to the country. The key figure in this was Sir Lomer Gouin, and I remember having to arrange—when the Governor-General's yacht was at Murray Bay—a meeting between him and Borden, of which even then I appreciated the significance. The Duke gave me full details of all that was going on. Curiously enough, almost the same problem was facing Lloyd George and the Coalition Government in England. Here, too, the Liberal Party had split under the hard pressure of war.

Borden's July 'Odyssey' had involved meeting not only with Gouin but with other French-Canadian leaders, Bureau, Lapointe, and finally Lemieux. In spite of all these discussions, no real progress was made, even with the skilful help of Sir Charles Fitzpatrick, the Lieutenant-Governor of Quebec. However, it was my first introduction to politics at the top level, and I thoroughly enjoyed it.

In addition to picking up the gossip in Parliament Building, from the Ministers and others who came to see His Excellency or by lunching at the Rideau Club, I used to follow the discussions in Parliament as closely as opportunity allowed. I often went into the Gallery to hear the debates and remember being impressed particularly by Meighen's ability. I only heard Mackenzie King once or twice. His style was old-fashioned from our point of view, and his language rather pompous. Meighen had much more of the 'cut and thrust' in debate, as I was afterwards to hear it called. Indeed, Canadian speeches were then, and I think still are, much longer and more formal than is now customary in the British House of Commons. They generally followed a nineteenth-century style. But I always enjoyed listening and was fascinated by what I saw of the Parliamentary scene.

Later in the year, it became apparent that none of the efforts to form a permanent Coalition, or to detach the French-Canadian leaders from the official Liberal Party, would succeed. Although at the time Mackenzie King had little following in Quebec, he finally inherited a situation which gave him control in that province and, therefore, for many years in Ottawa.

The summer and autumn of 1919 were largely taken up from the political angle by the question of railway amalgamations from which, whatever the rights and wrongs, the Government did not gain strength. Finally, Sir Robert Borden decided that his health would not allow him to continue as Prime Minister. After much discussion, about which the Duke told me, he announced his decision to his colleagues towards the end of 1919, but yielded to their pressure that he should take a year's holiday without resigning. This he did, and left for a foreign tour early in January 1920. I well remember his last visit at Government House, and the deep impression that he made upon us all. Apart from his magnificent voice and splendid presence, the sincerity and firmness of his character were apparent. He was a truly great man. As it turned out, the plan of a Prime Minister on a year's sabbatical leave broke down, as it was bound to do; and Borden's resignation followed in July. But by that time I had left Canada, and had no further personal experience of the intricacies of Canadian politics. Nevertheless, I was fortunate to retain many contacts, which in some cases ripened into friendship. There were some outstanding figures—Drayton, White, Burrell and, in his own way, Crerar. With Vincent Massey (afterwards Governor-General), an old friend from Balliol days, I renewed a close intimacy, which has lasted all through the years.

However, the greater part of our life in Canada was not concerned with politics. To be quite frank, it was one of almost unalloyed enjoyment. The senior staff was headed by Colonel Henderson, Military Secretary, and Lord Richard Nevill, Comptroller, both friendly and congenial figures. Lord Richard had a great knowledge of Canada, having served with the Duke of Connaught, the previous Governor-General. The A.D.C.s, Harry

Cator, Hugh Molyneux,[1] Geordie Haddington,[2] and, later, Larry Minto,[3] were all pleasant young men, who have remained lifelong friends. We had somehow or other all managed to survive the war, and were determined to get as much pleasure as possible out of the first year of peace. The house was always full—partly of the family and partly of a constant flow of guests. Although there were a number of formal duties, chiefly acting attendance to one or other of Their Excellencies at various functions, there was a great deal of informal entertaining. Trips to Toronto and Montreal were frequent. Perhaps the most memorable visit of all was to the Citadel of Quebec, where we received the Prince of Wales on his arrival. I also went with the Duke to see the Prince leave at Halifax at the end of his tour. Here the Prince entertained all the mayors and other functionaries to a great farewell dinner. Whether because of the excellence of the fare, or for some other reason, one of them fell into the sea, but was soon fished out amid considerable merriment.

Although at that time Ontario was 'dry', and this included Ottawa, prohibition happily did not apply to Government House. As a result, our official entertainments were popular and gay. The Country Club in Hull was also 'wet', being across the river in the Province of Quebec. We were all frequent visitors. When I came many years later to Ottawa as Prime Minister, I was entertained by Mr. Diefenbaker at the Club, a place of happy memories.

The months passed rapidly. I suppose that every young man, when he falls in love, is unconscious that anyone else is aware of what is going on. At any rate, when Dorothy Cavendish accepted me as her future husband, the fact seemed to cause little surprise either to her parents or to the rest of the staff. Many years later, I became Minister of Housing and Local Government. One of my duties was concerned with the National Parks of England. I have always had a great affection for National Parks, for it was amidst the wonderful scenery of Jasper Park in Canada that I first knew that my affections were returned.

In the first month of 1920, Dorothy and I came home; later followed by her father and mother on leave. We were married on 21 April in St. Margaret's Church, Westminster. Bishop Temple, a

[1] Later Lord Sefton.   [2] Lord Haddington.   [3] Lord Minto.

cousin of the Cavendishes, and John Macmillan, my own cousin (later Bishop of Guildford), performed the ceremony. In those days it was the fashion to have large congregations, including every conceivable relation, old and young. On my wife's side, these were very numerous as she came from a family with a large range of cousinship. Mine were fewer in number. I have among my records a copy of the marriage register. The Church, State, and Literature were suitably represented; among the signatories being Bishop Temple, the Bishop of Derby, Queen Alexandra, the Duke of Connaught, the Duke of York (afterwards George VI), Lord Morley, Lord Bryce, and Thomas Hardy; the last three being amongst my father's oldest friends.

So eighteen months after the war we began our life together, which as I write has lasted forty-four years. My wife has sometimes reproached me that she thought she was to marry a publisher, with the prospect of the quiet world of literature and art. Instead, she has been drawn into the hurly-burly of politics, which she has had to endure for more than forty years. However, she accepted with zest what was after all, on her side, almost a hereditary profession. For my part, I could not have sustained the excitements and frequent disappointments of the early years, or the heavy burdens of the later, without her wise advice and loyal support.

CHAPTER FIVE

Apprenticeship

T HE next three years were years of apprenticeship, in publishing and politics. Soon after my marriage I came into the family firm to learn the trade. In 1923 I became a Parliamentary candidate. In spite of the great issues which had already begun to disengage themselves, the prospect was anything but dark. In the summer of 1920 the boom was still at its height. It was only as winter approached that the first menacing signs of unemployment began to appear. We were young; we were happy; everything smiled upon us. The first thing was to get a house. My parents still lived in Cadogan Place, which Dickens described in *Nicholas Nickleby* as 'the one slight bond that joins two great extremes; it is the connecting link between the aristocratic pavements of Belgrave Square and the barbarism of Chelsea'. Of Chester Square where we settled the same might perhaps be said. It was the frontier between Belgravia and Pimlico. In those days we obtained the lease of a house on very modest terms, and lived there for the next sixteen years. My four children were born there. Now, with the steady migration westwards that has for centuries characterised the development of London, Chester Square has become both smart and expensive. In our day it was neither; it suited us very well.

The head of the business was then Sir Frederick Macmillan, my father's elder brother. The other partners were my father, Maurice, and his first cousin, George, the son of Alexander, one of the founders. The juniors were Will, George's son, and my brother Daniel, who had been invalided out of the Army and afterwards served with distinction at the Admiralty, and in Paris during the making of the Treaty. I was the last to join. In those days there was a delightfully Victorian atmosphere. For the partners, like the Forsytes, whom they in many ways resembled, were true Victorians.

Each family had its special characteristics. My uncle loved the country and rode to hounds. He must have had almost the widest circle of friends and acquaintances among writers, actors, artists, business and professional men of any man of his time. For many years he was chairman of the Beefsteak Club, where some will still remember him. He took a great part in county work in Hertfordshire, where he had lived for a long time and was Deputy Lieutenant. He was equally devoted to hospital work—he was chairman for many years of the National Hospital for Paralysis—and served on other public bodies. George was serious, and his spiritual home was the Athenaeum. He had a house in Yorkshire, to which he was passionately devoted. He took a great part in developing the theological, classical, and higher technical side of our publications. My father, who allowed himself very few holidays—not more than a fortnight or three weeks in a year—gave his whole energies to the business. He concerned himself especially with the educational side and overseas developments. He was responsible for our expansion and the institution of our branches throughout the Empire. The partners met daily. Although close relations and lifelong partners, they shook hands with each other in the morning with due solemnity. Every day we lunched together, and much business was then done. Sometimes there was a guest. To miss luncheon was permissible but rather frowned on. Our seniors treated us not merely with kindness but with generosity. Gradually the minor details, and then the major problems, fell into our hands. All our three senior partners died at advanced ages in 1936. But some years before that time my brother Daniel and I had become in effect the managing directors.

Although I had lived all my life in the atmosphere of books, and heard much about the publishing business, these first years were of enthralling interest. My uncle handed over to me the duty of looking after the affairs of some of our leading authors, including Thomas Hardy, Rudyard Kipling, Hugh Walpole, and many others. As things turned out, I worked for twenty years at the daily grind of management. I returned to the business for six years from 1945 to 1951. Since my retirement as Prime Minister, I have not been able to do much more than try to give a guiding hand. These three years then, from 1920 to 1923, were a fascinating apprentice-ship to a fine craft.

Before our home was ready for us, we lived with Lady Edward Cavendish, my wife's grandmother, in her house in Carlos Place. She was a most remarkable character, brought up in the Whig and Liberal circles of the second half of the nineteenth century. She remembered every detail of the great crises and conflicts: the murder of her brother-in-law Lord Frederick by Irish terrorists in Phoenix Park; Mr. Gladstone's conversion to Home Rule; and the bitter feelings which followed the great schism in the Liberal Party. The Cavendish and Gladstone families were closely connected through the great complexes of Lytteltons, Glyns, and Talbots. The old lady had a sharp tongue, as well as a clear memory. Mrs. Drew, Mr. Gladstone's daughter, used to stay often and devoted much of the end of her life to the care of Lady Edward. She used to read to her by the hour. In the summer of 1920 the last two volumes of Buckle's *Life of Disraeli* were published. Lady Edward insisted that Mrs. Drew should read these to her in full. She listened attentively, interjecting every now and then with a purposeful and wicked air, 'Why, he was the greatest man of the century, after all, wasn't he, my dear?' Mrs. Drew shook her head sadly, and read on.

By the turn of the year and the spring of 1921 the boom was over. The hardships and miseries of unemployment began to appear. Although the South suffered less than Scotland and the North of England with their exporting industries, there were many manifes-tations of poverty and distress which were beginning to appear even in the centre of London. In those days provisions for the unemployed and the poor, although novel and effective in preventing overt trouble, were on a modest scale. We therefore saw appearing in the streets considerable numbers of beggars, ex-soldiers' bands, and other mendicants, whose pitiful condition—even if some were not genuine—was disturbing. Marches and demonstrations of unem-ployed began to take place. Disappointment, which is the shadow that haunts victory, began to be widespread. Happily, we were spared the tragedy of unemployment after the Second War.

I remember having seen something of this when I was a boy at school. In the spring of 1907 or 1908 there was a march of unemployed to Windsor, led by Victor Grayson, a well-known agitator of the times. It was to pass through Eton. The headmaster, Edward Lyttelton, invited Mr. Grayson to address the boys, which he did in School Yard to some effect. This gesture seemed at the time quite natural. Yet I think there are many critics of public schools who would be surprised to know that such an incident occurred nearly sixty years ago.

The Government elected immediately after the war, at the General Election of 1918, in spite of the overwhelming support which it had received at the polls, resulting in an unprecedented Parliamentary majority, had within it the seeds of instability and even of decay.

At a grim period, following the failure of the Dardanelles expedition and growing concern about the conduct of the war, as well as the alleged shortage of munitions, Asquith had been forced in the summer of 1915 to abandon the management of the war by a single party. He therefore invited the Conservative leaders, Bonar Law and Lord Lansdowne, to join with him in a Coalition Government. Eighteen months later, after the failure of the Somme battles and with a mounting sense of the inadequacy of Asquith as a War Prime Minister, a coup was staged against him which resulted, after some confused manœuvring, in the formation, in December 1916, of the second War Coalition under Lloyd George. Although the new Prime Minister was, next to Asquith himself, the most notable Liberal leader, few of his Liberal colleagues consented to join his administration. Indeed, they resented both the supersession of Asquith and the methods by which it had been accomplished. As a result, while all the Conservative leaders joined the Lloyd George Government, with the approval of the whole Conservative Party in the House of Commons and in the country, the Liberal Party was bitterly and, as it was to prove, fatally divided. About half the Liberal back-benchers and only one or two of the front-bench figures joined or supported the new administration.[1]

Immediately after the war—indeed a few days after the Armistice

[1] 'On the formation of Lloyd George's Government in 1916, 126 Liberal M.P.'s or almost half of the Parliamentary Liberal party pledged their support.' (Frank Owen, *Tempestuous Journey*, London, 1954, p. 347.)

–a dissolution of Parliament was announced. The election took place on 14 December 1918. Lloyd George, as the victor in the Great War, asked and received an overwhelming vote of confidence from the electors. But since those Liberals who supported Asquith were opposed by Lloyd George Liberals or by Conservatives with the support of Lloyd George, official Liberals suffered a humiliating defeat. Asquith himself lost his seat at East Fife. The National Liberals, as the supporters of Lloyd George came to be called, generally held their seats. But they were, in a sense, the prisoners of the large Conservative majority. Asquith retained the official machine and the affection of traditional Liberals throughout the country. But the Liberal Party was shattered, and the first step was taken in the descent from a Parliamentary party to a small group.

Not unnaturally, as the months passed, the Government's initial popularity was not maintained. Moreover, the political future, with one of the traditional parties in the State divided beyond repair, was obscure and disquieting. In 1920 there was much discussion in political circles of an amalgamation of the Conservatives and the National Liberals. My father, who followed politics with a mixture of shrewdness and detachment, thought this ought to be done. I remember him saying to me that if it were not done quickly it would never be done at all. Curiously enough, the opposition to 'fusion', as it came to be called, came from the Liberal rather than from the Tory section in the Coalition. Lord Derby, who wielded great influence in Conservative circles, seems to have shared my father's view and to have warned his friends in 1920 that it must be done 'now or never'. Bonar Law's retirement (due to ill health) in March 1921 was, of course, a serious blow to the stability of the Government. So long as Lloyd George and Bonar Law worked together, they made a wonderfully effective and complementary pair. Bonar Law could exercise a restraining hand over Lloyd George's impetuosity. When he left, there was no one to replace him. I remember hearing the rumour before the summer of 1921 that Lloyd George was desperately trying to get Bonar Law back. But he still maintained that he was too ill and too exhausted to do anything but rest. He had indeed had a hard war. Five years of the greatest responsibility, with a position next to and almost equal to that of the head of the Government, and the loss in action of two out of his three sons, had worn him out.

By the summer of 1921 the sense of disillusion had begun to grow. Unemployment rose to the alarming figure of two million; trade was stagnant. The provisions of the peace treaties were bitterly attacked by some and weakly supported by others. Nobody bothered about hanging the Kaiser. The Dutch Government saved the Allies a lot of trouble by giving him asylum. But what about reparations? The publication of Keynes's *The Economic Consequences of the Peace* at the end of 1919 and its wide circulation had serious effects. It did much to injure the authority of Lloyd George, and weaken rather than strengthen his efforts to deal with the reparations question by stages. Its account of the way in which President Wilson had been outmanœuvred in Paris seriously undermined his position in America at a crucial time. Finally, it did much to create throughout Britain and the Commonwealth—and even the United States—a kind of guilt complex about the Germans, which has never been wholly effaced and which was to prove the source of disaster. The legend of the 'Carthaginian Peace' did infinite harm both in Germany and in Britain. When all is said and done about reparations and the folly of the promises given by some politicians and the estimates made by leading bankers and 'experts', it is almost comical to recall the facts. Over the years Germany actually paid £1,000 million. To meet this she borrowed from the outside world £1,500 million. In a word, it was Germany who received the indemnity, largely from America.

Meanwhile, after a bitter period of civil war, with all its attendant cruelties, the centuries-long conflict between Britain and Ireland was brought to an end by the treaty of 6 December 1921. All members of the Coalition Cabinet, Conservative and Liberal, took equal responsibility for this tremendous decision. Lloyd George and Churchill were Liberals. Lord Birkenhead, a lifelong Conservative and stalwart defender of the Union before the war, took a prominent part in the negotiations. The northern counties were preserved as part of the United Kingdom and the old liberties of Ulster thus safeguarded. But Southern Ireland, or Eire as it was now to be called, became independent and was later to decide to repudiate her nominal membership of the Commonwealth.

So tremendous a revolution could hardly take place without arousing bitter cries of betrayal and accusations of cowardice, especially from the Unionists of Southern Ireland. Indeed it has often been said that the anger of Conservative Members was the main cause of the decision of the Parliamentary Party to leave the Coalition a year later. This is by no means clearly established. My father-in-law, the Duke of Devonshire, on his return from Canada, was offered by Lloyd George the India Office; this was in March 1922. After much reflection he refused, as did Lord Derby. Lord Derby's diary is perhaps worth quoting:

> Victor I think hit the nail on the head when he said that probably we had less fault to find with the actual Government work as the way in which they did it and the complete want of unity of command.[1]

The diary goes on to say, and these words are of some importance:

> He is strongly for the Irish Bill and means to support it in every way....[1]

This is quite significant. It is interesting to note that the Duke, who was a large Irish landowner himself and whose father-in-law, Lord Lansdowne, had extensive Irish properties, approved of the treaty. I never heard him change his view. Perhaps I might allow myself another quotation from Lord Crawford's diary, which refers to these approaches:

> Derby refused and talked about it. Victor Cav[endish – Duke of Devonshire] didn't want the post either, but has not been chattering.[2]

Diaries are notoriously dangerous sources for historians. But this rings true.

In fact, apart from the normal unpopularity from which every Government suffers as the end of a Parliament approaches, the reasons for the Government's difficulties as the summer of 1922 ended were more complex and more immediate than regrets over the loss of Ireland. At home, the farmers were disgruntled by the repeal of the Corn Production Act, which had guaranteed them a high price for cereal crops. In the industrial parts of the country, the widespread slump and consequential unemployment were by no

[1] Randolph Churchill, *Lord Derby: 'King of Lancashire'* (London, 1960), p. 430.
[2] Lord Beaverbrook, *The Decline and Fall of Lloyd George* (London, 1963), p. 156.

means compensated by the fall in the cost of living. Low prices are of little benefit to men with no wages.

Abroad, the high hopes of a reconstituted Europe had been falsified. One international conference followed another with bewildering rapidity, in the hope of resolving the reparations problem and laying the foundations of a recovery in the economic life of Europe. German default in March 1921 had led the French to impose sanctions, including the seizure of important German cities and the imposition of levies on German imports and exports. After the Cannes Conference in January, where Briand adopted a more conciliatory attitude, and obtained in return a promise of an Anglo-French pact of security, the French Chamber was suspicious and accused the French Prime Minister of weakness. He was succeeded by Poincaré, a narrow, legalistic Lorrainer, who was unsympathetic towards the subtle Celtic Lloyd George and drove him almost to despair. The British Prime Minister made a last effort at the Genoa Conference in April 1922. On this he had pinned all his hopes. It was one of the greatest international gatherings in history with more than thirty nations represented, including—for the first time since the war—Germany and Russia. Not only did the conference fail to make any progress in the political and economic issues, but the separate treaty negotiated at Rapallo by Germany and Russia, behind the backs of all the other nations and during the course of the main conference, brought discredit on the Allies and particularly on the main promoter of the Genoa Conference, the British Prime Minister. Yet never in his life did Lloyd George put up a more splendid fight in order, in his own words, to bring about 'the reconstruction of Europe'. He never gave up his efforts and displayed every aspect of his extraordinary virtuosity. But he failed, and with it failed much more than we knew at the time—the hope of peace and prosperity in Europe. As Sir James Grigg—no mean or inexperienced commentator—has written, had Genoa succeeded, there might perhaps have been no Ruhr, no Hitler, no Second World War.[1]

Lloyd George gained no credit for his gallant endeavours. He had failed, and failure brought discredit upon him and his Government.

Finally, and perhaps more damaging than any other set-back in the

[1] P. J. Grigg, *Prejudice and Judgment* (London, 1948), p. 82.

field of foreign affairs, was the flare-up between Greece and Turkey, which seemed to threaten an involvement of Britain in a new war with Turkey. Lloyd George had certainly encouraged the Greeks to make their imprudent incursion in Asia Minor. While a settlement was ultimately reached at Chanak, opinion at home was thoroughly alarmed. Both Balfour and Lord Curzon, the Foreign Secretary, supported the Prime Minister in his determination not to let the Turks back into Europe. Moreover, in spite of the protests of the official Liberal Party, he could certainly claim that he was following the Gladstonian tradition. Yet the Chanak affair shook the confidence of both the Conservative and Liberal sections of the Coalition. Both Churchill and Birkenhead were thought to have been rash and imprudent.

Apart from these anxieties and disappointments at home and abroad, there were two other causes of Lloyd George's diminished estimation in the public mind. First, his growing arrogance which seemed to increase as his difficulties became greater. Some Ministers were treated almost with insolence. His habit of dealing with juniors behind the backs of their superiors became more and more marked. The whole entourage seemed more appropriate to a dictator than to a Parliamentary leader. Yet he had none of the power necessary to support a dictatorship. The second thing which stuck in people's throats was the traffic in Honours. One incident followed another. The Honours system changed from the mild abuse it had been in former days into a real scandal. While all established parties through the nineteenth century had always collected funds from individual supporters and often given Honours in return, the matter was then more delicately handled and the recipients of Honours were generally men of good standing and high character. Lloyd George's agents operated on a basis quite different from that well known and long established. Certain recipients were so disreputable that the Honours had to be cancelled or surrendered. It was commonly reported that in the last stages, when the fountain was running dry, Honours could be purchased on the basis of so much down and a few yearly instalments. The whole truth will probably never be known, but what mattered to Lloyd George's prestige was that these stories were generally believed.

But perhaps the chief cause of Lloyd George's political weakness, when the test came, was that he was a Prime Minister without a party. Churchill followed a prudent course in 1940 when, after Neville Chamberlain's death, he insisted, against the advice of some pedantic critics, on making himself leader of the Conservative Party. He had seen enough twenty years before of a man trying to operate without a firm base.

Meanwhile, as the political situation worsened, it was believed that Lloyd George himself wanted to resign. Lord Curzon, attracted by the glittering prize of the Premiership, was preparing to abandon the ship. Nevertheless, he continued to affirm his loyalty. With the conventional term of the Parliament's life approaching, some decision had to be taken. Broadly speaking, the Conservative leaders wanted the Coalition to continue. The under-secretaries and rank and file were not so sure. As the weeks passed, they began to be openly mutinous.

It was finally agreed that the Parliamentary Party—that is, the Conservative M.P.s—should be asked to decide whether they wished to fight the approaching election as a separate party, with a Conservative Prime Minister, or in alliance with the National Liberals, under Lloyd George's banner. For this purpose, a meeting was summoned at the Carlton Club on 19 October 1922. The Conservative leaders—Austen Chamberlain, Balfour, Birkenhead—were confident that they could secure a majority for continuing the Coalition. But they had reckoned without two important personal factors—and they had a piece of bad luck.

First, Stanley Baldwin, President of the Board of Trade, came out against Lloyd George, for whom he had a violent, almost pathological, hatred. He was a little-known figure among the public, but he was respected by his fellow Members.

Secondly, Bonar Law, who was the only man who could possibly head a purely Conservative Government, if the Coalition broke up, decided to return to politics and make a bid for power. His retirement through illness had at least preserved him from the recent unpopularity. Under the strong influence of his friend Lord Beaverbrook, he made up his mind, after much hesitation, to throw his hat into the ring. He signified this in two ways. On 7 October, two weeks before the Carlton Club meeting, he wrote a letter to *The Times*, strongly criticising the Government's handling of the Chanak crisis. It was, in effect, a plea for an abandonment of adventurous policies. We could not be 'the policeman of the world'. After eighteen months' absence, he thus formally re-entered the political arena. His next step was even more important. He spoke at the Carlton Club meeting. He made it clear that he was in favour of ending the Coalition and that he was ready to resume the leadership and form an independent Conservative Government. Baldwin's speech was important. Bonar Law's was decisive.

One piece of bad luck was somewhat bizarre. The Conservative Ministers who supported Lloyd George had arranged for the meeting to take place the day after a by-election at Newport (Mon.). Here, an Independent Conservative was standing against both Labour and the official Coalition Liberal. It was confidently expected that the official candidate, having received the Government 'ticket', would be victorious. In the event, the Independent Conservative was returned by a majority of over 2,000, with Labour second and the Coalition Liberal a bad third. Mr. Clarry, the successful candidate, did not achieve any further renown. He did not need to. Like single-speech Hamilton, he could stand on one burst of fame. He had helped to destroy a Government which had been returned to power four years before with 526 seats out of 707 – almost the largest majority in history.

At the Carlton Club the actual vote for leaving the Coalition was 187 to 87. Nine Ministers voted in the minority. They immediately resigned from the Government, and Lloyd George, as soon as he heard the news, offered the resignation of himself and his Government to the King. There was no need to await a Parliamentary debate or vote. The forces ordinarily supporting the Government had withdrawn their confidence. The great War Coalition was at an end. Lloyd George, the greatest War Minister since Chatham, left Downing Street, never to return. He never held office again.

Bonar Law at once accepted the King's Commission and set about his task as soon as he had been re-elected to the leadership. In his new Government, my father-in-law became Colonial Secretary. Being both shrewd and modest, he did not take a very hopeful view of the strength of the new Government. It consisted largely of noblemen of good reputation, but not spectacular achievement. Lord Birkenhead, a leading Conservative Minister in the Coalition, remained loyal to Lloyd George. He declared, with some bitterness but much truth, that the new Conservative Government was an administration of second-class brains. The Duke, who liked to consult me on political matters, asked me to call on him while Bonar Law's Government was being formed. I found Lord Derby in conference with him. The Duke took rather a poor view of their chances of survival, and pointed out the extreme weakness of the front bench in the House of Commons. This great array of peers might be all right. But what was to happen in the Commons' house? 'Ah,' said Lord Derby, 'you are too pessimistic. They have found a wonderful little man. One of those attorney fellows, you know. He will do all the work.' 'What's his name?' said the Duke. 'Pig,' said Lord Derby. Turning to me, the Duke replied, 'Do you know Pig? I know James Pigg [he was a great reader of Surtees]. I don't know any other Pig.' It turned out to be Sir Douglas Hogg! This was a truly Trollopian scene.[1]

As soon as Bonar Law formed his Government, purely Conservative in character, he asked for a dissolution. Voting took place on 15 November. I took no part in the election. Although I had hoped one day to try for Parliament, I did not venture at so early a stage to approach my business partners for their permission. But I watched it with interest and, since some of my friends were involved, with growing excitement. But I was deeply torn. I was then, as I have always remained, a great admirer of Lloyd George. I was not close enough to affairs to be conscious of his faults; but I recognised his greatness.

During this summer two curious incidents took place, in which my wife and I were to a small extent concerned. In the last months of Lord Northcliffe's life, he fell victim to an illness which amounted to megalomania. He was then living at No. 1 Carlton Gardens. No. 2 had been purchased by my father-in-law after the sale of Devonshire House. One afternoon my wife and I were in the house,

[1] Randolph Churchill has given a version of this story in his biography of Lord Derby, which is broadly correct.

looking at the various alterations that were being made and the
moving-in of pictures and furniture. The Clerk of Works, in a state
of considerable excitement, informed us that those who were looking
after Lord Northcliffe wished him to be moved to the roof of the
Duke's new house. It seems that in his morbid condition he insisted
that there should be nothing between him and the heavens. No. 1
had a sloping, No. 2 a flat roof. The Duke and Duchess were away;
my brother-in-law could not be found. What was to be done? It
seemed to us that the only thing to do was to assent to the request.
But it was a strange and tragic story.

When Lord Northcliffe's life was despaired of, there was already
keen interest as to what would happen to *The Times* newspaper. Lord
Beaverbrook has described how a plan was put forward by Sir
Campbell Stuart for the formation of a group of reliable people who
might purchase the controlling interest, and that one of the objects
was to offer the editorship to Lloyd George. It seems that this had
some attraction for him. It also appears that even the King's help
was sought, but naturally in vain. None of this was known to me at
the time. It was feared also that Lord Rothermere would buy the
shares, and many people felt that his political views would be almost
as unreliable as his brother's. Meanwhile, of course, Wickham
Steed remained in full control, and was a strong opponent of Lloyd
George. At one time he was in daily, if not hourly, touch with Bonar
Law. The Duke of Devonshire was approached to see whether he
would purchase, either separately or jointly, the shares which gave
control. The sum was large, but the sale of Devonshire House had
no doubt provided him with a good deal of ready cash. I remember
his discussing the project with me at various stages and, at the
critical point, by telephone to a house in Scotland where I was
staying. Eventually he turned down the plan; partly, I think,
because he had a hope of re-entering British politics under more
favourable conditions than in March, when he had refused Lloyd
George's offer of the India Office. He would certainly not have
thought it right to be a Cabinet Minister and a newspaper proprietor. He was also satisfied that the shares would pass into respectable
hands. For after all these comings and goings, the shares were
ultimately purchased by Colonel John Astor against Lord Rother-

mere's high bid. Colonel Astor did this with the best possible intentions, to preserve the independence of the paper and to allow the policy to be a matter for the editor rather than for the proprietor. Alas for good intentions! The editorial policy before the Second War was disastrous; there were no worse 'appeasers' than *The Times* editorial board. Even during the Second War, as I shall come to describe in my account of the Communist revolution in Athens, *The Times* was pitifully ignorant and dangerously pedantic at a moment of great peril and decisive importance for the future of the Eastern Mediterranean. It is amusing to reflect what the course of *The Times*' history might have been had the Duke made an effective bid.[1]

Some people, including Bonar Law himself, were not very hopeful as to the outcome of the election of 1922 and thought that the Conservatives on their own would, at best, have a majority of 25. It turned out to be a majority of over 70. The election was fought upon a strange cry, 'Tranquillity'! It did not seem very inspiring, and when Baldwin repeated it in 1929, under the title of 'Safety First', it proved a great flop. But after all the emotions of war and the uncertainties and anxieties of the post-war years, tranquillity proved to be just what the people wanted. Lloyd George had an apt description of it, which amused but did not convince the electorate: 'Tranquillity!' he exclaimed, 'it's not a policy, it's a yawn.' But tranquillity triumphed. The Liberal Party was divided into two almost equal parts. Lloyd George had 62 followers; Asquith 54. The Labour Party gained, and returned 142 Members as against 76.[2] Churchill lost his seat at Dundee, but Asquith regained a place in the House of Commons.

The Parliament of 1922 was confidently expected to run its normal course. Unhampered by any great legislative programme, it was to concentrate on a gradual restoration of sound government at home, and steady progress towards the solution of difficulties abroad.

[1] A detailed account of these negotiations is to be found in *The History of The Times*, pt. ii: *1921–1948* (London, 1952). It is clear that there were a number of schemes, some separate and some interlocking.

[2] These and subsequent General Election statistics are based on David Butler and Jennie Freeman, *British Political Facts, 1900–1960* (London, 1964).

In fact, it lasted only a year. Bonar Law retired from office within seven months through serious illness. He died five months later. His successor, Baldwin, who came thus unexpectedly to the Premiership, advised the dissolution of Parliament before the end of the year. But the story of this short Parliament must be briefly told.

The fall of the Coalition had brought no relief. Indeed, the major problems seemed rather aggravated than alleviated.

At home, in spite of 'Tranquillity', in spite of the disappearance of Lloyd George, now become the villain of the Peace instead of the hero of the War—so mercurial and often ungenerous is public opinion—trade did not recover. Unemployment remained at well over a million, and at one point nearly a million and a half. Prices continued to fall and business to decline. Deflationary policies were pursued, and Bonar Law rejected with orthodox rigidity any question of borrowing or deficiency budgeting. Although at the time I had not begun to study these economic problems which were destined to engross my thoughts during the next fifteen years or more with increasing urgency, all we young men who had survived the war began to feel a growing uneasiness at a situation so unsatisfactory, and so disappointing. For some of us, it was to prove intolerable.

On the foreign front, the new Government did not seem more successful than the old. Bonar Law and Lord Curzon (who had rapidly changed one leader for another) altogether failed to deter Poincaré and the new French Government from their plans. The occupation of the Ruhr by the French Army began in January 1923, with all that followed from it.

If the problems of the British economy and the dangers besetting Europe revealed themselves in that year, even to the most superficial student, a significant and pregnant decision was taken in the sphere of colonial policy. The Duke of Devonshire, although normally a reticent man, used to speak to me freely about affairs. He took his post at the Colonial Office very seriously and, although not a quick brain, had generous and sound principles. He has thus left a permanent mark on British colonial development, by a declaration of policy which brought upon him severe criticism from many quarters. This was in regard to British East Africa—or Kenya, as it was now called. After much thought and full consideration of the hostile reaction which would be caused among the settlers and the Right wing of the Conservative Party, the Duke laid down the principle of 'paramountcy'. It was formally declared that on any question which might arise where the interests of the settlers and native inhabitants were in conflict, those of the latter must be regarded as 'paramount'. In 1923 this doctrine, if not revolutionary, was certainly unexpected. Great pressure was brought upon the Duke to withdraw or amend it. But he remained quite firm and, for good or ill, this decision set the pattern of events which culminated in some of the decisions which Governments had to take many years later.

Meanwhile, a serious dispute arose between Britain and America. The story of the American debt settlement is one of the most remarkable in diplomatic history. Detailed accounts have been written, both from the point of view of Bonar Law and that of Baldwin. The Balfour Note of August 1922, suggesting that common sense and justice required an all-round settlement of debts, was ill received in the United States. In the spirit of Coolidge's famous declaration, 'They hired the money, didn't they?', the authorities in Washington were pressing for an immediate and an onerous settlement. They dismissed altogether the argument that so large a portion of the British debt had been incurred on behalf of the Allies. There was an urgent demand to agree the terms between our two Governments before the rising of Congress in early March. The dualism between the executive and legislative branches of the United States system has certain inconveniences. But it has corresponding diplomatic advantages. Although I did not fully understand it at the time, this was one of many occasions on which the Executive would call in aid their weakness in Congress, in order to defend otherwise doubtful policies. As is well known, Baldwin—then Chancellor of the Exchequer—suddenly and unexpectedly, without reference to the Cabinet, and in spite of Bonar Law's telegraphic warnings, closed with an offer which imposed upon Britain an annual payment of £34 million for ten years, and after that of £40 million. These sums had to be paid largely in gold or the equivalent of gold, since the United States' high tariff policy made it almost impossible to pay in goods.

Bonar Law wished either to reject Baldwin's settlement or to resign. We know now that he was supported by two colleagues of very different temperaments—Lord Novar[1] and Philip Lloyd-Greame (later Lord Swinton).[2] I saw the Duke at the end of a long day's discussion when all this was still unsettled, and he told me of the concern which he felt about Bonar Law's announcement that he would rather resign than be party to such disastrous terms. This was on 30 January 1923. The Cabinet had adjourned in some confusion. It seemed as if the 'second-class brains' had their weaknesses, and that the 'first-class' would soon be able to point the moral to some effect. A Government, it would be said, that was brought in to clear up the confusion and lack of central control of the Lloyd George system, had broken up within three months in utter disorder. This was, indeed, a gloomy prospect. The Cabinet met the next day without Bonar Law being present, and it was finally agreed that, in the circumstances, bad as the terms were, they must be accepted. It was impossible to repudiate an agreement entered into by the Chancellor of the Exchequer, however unwisely.

I remember the Duke coming to Chester Square that evening. He and Lord Cave were appointed to call upon Bonar Law to urge him to accept the situation. To this the Prime Minister reluctantly agreed; but this episode certainly did not give Baldwin's colleagues a very high opinion of his skill or determination. However, the general view in the country as a whole was in favour of the settlement. The bankers and businessmen were not disposed to cavil too much about the difference between the £20 million which Bonar Law was prepared to concede, and the £34 million and subsequently £40 million which Baldwin gave away. The only two experts who were strongly opposed to the debt agreement were Maynard Keynes and McKenna.[3]

The contest for the Premiership after the retirement of Bonar Law in May 1923 has been described in detail from many sources. It has also been the subject of wide controversy. It lay between

[1] Secretary of State for Scotland.   [2] President of the Board of Trade.
[3] The Rt. Hon. Reginald McKenna (1863–1943), former Liberal M.P., and successively First Lord of the Admiralty, Home Secretary, and Chancellor of the Exchequer in Asquith's Cabinet, was then Chairman of the Midland Bank.

Baldwin and Curzon. It is, however, clear that the general opinion of the party, both in the Lords and the Commons, was against Curzon's claims. I remember the Duke telling me that he felt a Prime Minister in the Lords quite impossible, certainly with a Government with such a large membership of peers. He went so far as to say that he felt there could never be a Prime Minister in the Lords again. It is true that the Duke was a Liberal by tradition, and in many ways more sensitive to changing conditions than his Tory friends. Apart from this, in spite of his modesty and apparent unconcern over small matters, I think he had found Lord Curzon a somewhat patronising friend and neighbour for a great many years. He used to tell me a story of Lord Curzon's delight in getting the Garter. Curzon explained to him at great length that this was a signal honour for himself. No Curzon had ever had the Garter. He had won it by his own unaided efforts and his triumphant career. He went on: 'You, Victor, of course, have got the Garter as the head of a Garter family. Dukes of Devonshire always get the Garter. It is no credit to you at all. But for me it is a personal honour.' The Duke tried feebly to protest that he had had a long political career in both Houses of Parliament, and had done his best to serve at home and overseas. This was waved aside. 'No. No, Victor,' Lord Curzon kept on saying. 'It means nothing to you. I have earned it myself.' Curzon's superior attitude, as well as the strangely insensitive side of his nature, did not make him very fit to be a Prime Minister in modern conditions. At any rate, the matter was soon settled during a Parliamentary recess and, with few changes, the Government went on.

McKenna—strangely enough, in view of events to follow in a few months—was pressed to go to the Treasury. After some hesitation he refused and Neville Chamberlain was appointed. McKenna was a free-trader. Chamberlain was not.

Within a few months, apparently forgetful of his offer of the key financial post in his Government to a convinced free-trader, Baldwin reached the sudden conclusion that he could not face the unemployment problem through the coming winter except upon a basis of protection. But the Government had been elected at the end of 1922 on a basis of free trade. What then was to be done?

It is difficult for a reader today to realise the almost theological fervour with which the fiscal question was debated in those days. This fanaticism concerning what is today more objectively regarded as a matter to be settled pragmatically had its roots in history. Since Peel had shattered the Tory Party on this issue in 1847 and was then himself destroyed in revenge, the question had been put to rest for many years. In those days, protection meant, of course, protection for British farmers against imported food. Free imports meant, in effect, free food and raw materials. The import of manufactured goods so as seriously to threaten the textile industry, still more the heavy iron and steel industry, was in those days of British industrial supremacy 'unthinkable'.

When Joseph Chamberlain raised, in 1902, the whole question of tariff reform, it was in circumstances very different from those in which Peel had sacrificed the farmer and farm labourer to the manu-facturer. Yet Chamberlain's main purpose was external, not domes-tic. The radical imperialist conceived a structure from which the Old Country and the Colonies should both be beneficiaries. Since the main exports from the Empire into the United Kingdom were food and foodstuffs, a moderate duty should be imposed on foreign and remitted on imperial trade in these categories. In return, the Empire would agree to a substantial preference on British manufactures, which formed the bulk of colonial imports. This complementary system, called the preferential system, was regarded as mortal sin— sin against the very foundations of the free-trade faith—by its ortho-dox opponents, whether Liberal or Conservative. Joseph Chamber-lain's campaign split the Unionist Party in the early years of the century, and resulted in 1906 in the greatest—and last—of Liberal electoral triumphs. In the years immediately before the war, the Conservative Party was bitterly divided by this question, raised out of oblivion by Joseph Chamberlain, in the fervour of his imperialist zeal. For Chamberlain—the first Chamberlain—had been and re-mained at heart something of a revolutionary. But his policy had failed, not because of the intellectual disapproval of the pundits, but because of the practical objections of the people. For preference for colonial imports involved, inescapably, taxes on food—the hated 'stomach tax'—the Tory Little Loaf in place of the Liberal Big Loaf.

Anyone who attempted to set this proposed tax on imported wheat in some reasonable perspective was savagely denounced as a kind of resurgent Marie-Antoinette. Yet without food taxes there could be no effective preference, since food was what the Empire had to send us. Without this benefit to their food exports to our market, they could not be expected to give British manufacturers a correspondingly privileged position in their own.

A new factor, however, had now begun to appear. The nineteenth-century free-traders had cheerfully sacrificed the British farmer to secure free food and thus avoid a wage structure in British industry related to an artificially high cost of living. Free imports meant, in their eyes, free imports of food and materials. But now, in the opening decades of the twentieth century, it was the British manufacturer who was beginning to cry out against free imports of manufactured goods, produced in foreign factories with low wages and long hours of work. Even in the heavy industries the 'unthinkable' had happened. In the iron and steel trade, cheap bars, billets, and angles were flowing into the harbours of Britain—on the Clyde, the Tyne, the Tees, and all the rest of the rivers intended by Providence for the export, not the import, of iron and steel and engineering products—and this under the eyes of the great stalwarts of free trade and Liberalism, who saw their principles preserved but their profits melting away, their works idle, and their men trudging the streets, out of a job.

This was the picture that presented itself to Baldwin and his intimate colleagues in the summer months of 1923. A radical change in the tariff system appeared the only solution. But there was this difficulty. At the General Election of the previous year (1922) Bonar Law had definitely pledged his Government and his party, if elected, to do no such thing. There were to be no adventurous policies, at home or abroad. There was to be tranquillity—even if, to the growing number of unemployed, it meant the tranquillity of enforced and unrewarded leisure.

Baldwin determined at least to be free to act. To be free involved another election, at which this liberty of action could be won from the electors. In no other way could he face what the next few months might bring of unemployment and misery. The logic of this was, of course, to ask for absolute freedom—in the realm of food taxes, of imperial preference (a two-way traffic), and of industrial protection against foreign competition. In the war, to save tonnage space and to raise revenue, the McKenna Duties had been imposed by a Liberal Chancellor of the Exchequer of irreproachable free-trade purity. They covered motor-cars, pianos, and watches. The devotees on both sides, free-traders and protectionists, had regarded these war tariffs with resignation or triumph, according to their predilections. At least, said ordinary folk, they will be an experiment. The experiment had now lasted several years and, as might have been supposed, no particular lesson seemed clearly to have emerged.

One other, less respectable, reason for the Prime Minister's sudden and unexpected decision was freely circulated in the clubs and in political circles. It was said that he had information that Lloyd George, who was touring the United States and Canada in triumph, intended to return and promulgate his conversion to protection as a cure for unemployment. It was somewhat cynically assumed that a Conservative Prime Minister should be more concerned to forestall a rival than to welcome a convert.

Under pressure, Baldwin quickly made an important concession. Partly because of Lancashire's strong objection to food taxes in any form (and Conservatism in Lancashire at that time meant Lord Derby, and seventy seats were involved), and partly because of the danger of offering too easy an opportunity for both sections of the Liberal Party to reunite in the 'battle for the people's food', Baldwin restricted his programme to a mandate for industrial protection.

Baldwin's decision was disagreeable to two groups of Conservatives. Austen Chamberlain and his friends still outside the Government, and those Ministers in the Government who had been devoted followers of Joseph Chamberlain's crusade, deplored the curtailment of the full programme. On the other hand, the free-traders in his Government, Derby, Salisbury, and Devonshire, felt naturally aggrieved at the way in which Baldwin had reached his decision without consultation with his colleagues. The Duke took this rather philosophically, because he was by no means bigoted on these questions. He inclined to free trade more from tradition than from conviction. He had the minor embarrassment of being a trustee for a fund founded by his uncle, the 8th Duke, for arranging prize essays and other encouragements to the principles of free trade. However, this was not an obstacle which need prove serious. Other Ministers would have preferred a period when an educative and propaganda campaign could have been launched. From what I have learnt by later experience, I do not think that such a plan was really practicable. Once a policy is decided, and is known to have been decided, the best course is to pursue it boldly. At any rate, the die was cast and Parliament was dissolved at the end of November 1923.

All this year my interest in politics had been growing. My close connection with a Cabinet Minister; the friendship that I had developed with my brother-in-law, Lord Hartington, who had been an unsuccessful candidate in 1922, but had been invited to stand again and was a keen politician; contacts with many friends from school and Army days, who in one way or another were starting on political life: all these excited me. I was tempted and fell. But my position was difficult. I could not easily so early in my business career hope to persuade my father and his partners that I ought to spend in fighting elections the time that should be devoted to learning my trade. Yet I very much wanted to be a candidate, if only as a trial run. But it was essential that I should not win. In this mood, therefore, I went to the Conservative Central Office—then in Palace Chambers—where I was introduced to a gentleman who dealt with these matters. I told him I wanted to stand somewhere; I realised that I could not expect to get, so late in the day, a winnable seat, still less a good seat. Nor did I really want that; I wanted the experience. The gentleman concerned seemed to agree with this, because I was very callow and experience was what I clearly needed. Various constituencies were passed in review. Finally, somebody came along and said, 'We've got the very thing for you. Come this afternoon. They want a candidate at Stockton-on-Tees, and the Chairman will be here. You can't possibly win it.' In this way my political career was launched.

The Chairman duly arrived and proved to be a man of considerable charm, but whose ideas of political campaigning were almost as indeterminate as my own. I remember that he wore a coat with an astrakhan collar and a jewelled pin in his tie, which gave him a vaguely theatrical appearance. In fact, he was a shipowner, who had made a good deal of money in the war and had now sold out. He was very insistent that in Stockton I should find all that I needed for my experiment. The tradition of the seat was Liberal, not to say Radical. It was true that it had twice been won by a Conservative—a Ropner and a Wrightson. But both these figures had been leading local industrialists, and their victories had taken place at the time of a strong swing to the Tories. A Mr. Samuel had held the seat in the Radical interest for a long time. His widow still carried great influence. The Chairman thought that we would have a good fight; but in view of the distress in the town and the general swing to the Left which had followed, we had very little chance of doing more than making a sporting demonstration. 'It will be a fine thing for you, my boy,' he said, 'and you will thoroughly enjoy it.' I asked him why they had come to me. He was quite frank about it. The Committee had invited both him and other local gentlemen to stand, but no one had felt inclined to waste his time or his money. It did not take much to persuade me. I agreed to set off for Stockton as soon as possible.

It is a strange experience for any young man to be launched in this way into a political campaign. Sometimes, perhaps usually, a candidate has had some training in constituency work. Under our modern system of highly organised parties he would not be selected without some previous record. He has probably canvassed, belonged to the Young Conservatives' movement (if he is a Tory), attended political schools and area gatherings. He has perhaps taken some part in local government. To be chosen, therefore, as a candidate comes generally at the end of a certain period of service and preparation. But owing to the war and the circumstances of my life immediately after the war, I had none of this background. I had not the faintest idea what a party association was supposed to be. I had never canvassed. The politics that I had learnt had been from my own contemporaries or from the lips of the philosophising politicians like John Morley, James Bryce, and Lord Robert Cecil, friends of my father. Of course, I had picked up something at Oxford. My time there, however, had been short and hardly got beyond the

ambitions of the Oxford Union. My closest contact with actual
political problems had been, in the last year, through my father-in-
law. But all this was high-level stuff—the politics of the council
chamber. I had never joined in the rough and tumble of the market-
place and the street.

Now I was suddenly to enter the fray. But what made my position
at once exhilarating and perplexing was that I had no practical
knowledge of the world into which I was to move. I had never been
to Tees-side or even Tyneside. I knew nothing at all about any
mechanical or industrial processes, except, to a minor degree,
printing and binding. Apart from Glasgow, where my printer
cousins lived, I had scarcely been to an industrial town. I had never
seen the great ironworks, steelworks, engineering works, shipyards,
which had been built up on the banks of the rivers of the North of
England and of Scotland. Nor, except for the war, had I any actual
experience of living among an industrial population. In the regiment, N.C.O.s and Guardsmen had been drawn largely from South
Wales, the Midlands and, to some extent, Newcastle. I had begun
to understand them as comrades; but, except from reading their
letters and talking to them, I knew little of their real way of life. I
had been persuaded by a friend to help with a troop of Boy Scouts in
East London. This had given me some small insight into the world
of working-class boys and their parents. But it was very limited.
Perhaps the most valuable thing which Stockton gave me over the
next twenty years was the sympathy and humility that comes from
understanding.

I set out the next day on the long journey, and found myself at
once involved in the confusions of the railway system of Tees-side.
In order to go to Stockton, it seemed to be necessary to go to
Thornaby; changing, of course, at Darlington. I arrived on a dark,
wet night, and was met by the local Chairman. We motored some
miles to a house belonging to him, which had been let to Colonel
George Pollitt, the genial and—as I learnt afterwards—brilliant
organiser of the Billingham Works which Imperial Chemical Industries were beginning to plan.

For the next few days I was to find a condition of complete
confusion in the organisation, which I thought then to be unique,

but subsequently learnt to be more or less common form—at least at that time. Ours may, perhaps, have been a little more distracted than usual. There was an agent, a women's organiser, something of a men's organisation, and rather more of a women's organisation. The Chairman himself was baffled by the situation, and when appealed to retired into his fur collar. However, we did not lack advice. I was urged to dismiss the agent and appoint another in his place. Nobody seemed to know quite why this should be done, but there was clearly a party that wished to substitute a local favourite. Happily, I refused. The agent, who had been appointed a few months before, proved to be a fine man—pure Cockney, ignorant, illiterate, but loyal and, in his own way, efficient. He served me for five elections before he retired, and I never had a better friend. Well, if I would not get rid of the agent, what about the women's organiser? She should be joint or at least deputy agent. The agent took a very poor view of the women's organiser—and rightly. She subsequently proved to be better at backbiting than organising. Was there a headquarters? Were committee-rooms to be taken? When would nomination be? Who would nominate me? What about the Liberals? Everything would be all right if I would see Alderman X; for he was supposed to control that part of the Liberal vote that had favoured the Coalition. I went to see Alderman X. He proved to be reticent, although not without a certain non-committal geniality. And so it went on.

My wife, who was still nursing her second child, soon made the necessary arrangements and arrived a few days after the campaign began. For convenience, we moved to another house, in the town, where we were looked after by a dear and kind host, Mr. Kirk, who was to spoil us for many years between and during elections. My wife had some political experience, because she had been brought up almost from the nursery in the atmosphere of elections. But these had been rural contests, where the chief hardships had been ice and snow. Our troubles were different. However, a routine soon established itself. By day you went round any works that were still open and spoke to as many men as possible. In the afternoons, women's gatherings; in the evenings, the round of meetings in the schools— two or three a night. Familiar as it all is now to hundreds of candidates who have taken part in these almost ritual ceremonies, to me it all seemed very strange. We particularly liked going round the works, especially at night, after the meetings, when the flames leaped up to the sky or the casting of a great ingot seemed like the labour of a giant's forge. The meetings in the schoolrooms I found at first very difficult. I made a lifelong friendship with a man—alas, now dead—who worked all day for his living, and all night for the party, to which he was devoted. Billy Ellis said to me once, 'You are no speaker; but you're a good lad'. Twenty-five years later he said the same to my son. When he made the second criticism, he said I had gradually improved; and the same might be hoped for in another generation. One reply, at any rate, was well received. At the adoption meeting, I was recommended, among other things, as a businessman and a publisher. A young man got up at the back of the hall, who clearly had had a secondary-school education. He said, 'Your name is Macmillan. Do you publish Hall and Knight's *Algebra*?' I answered, 'Yes, we do.' 'In that case,' he said, 'my vote's not for you!' To which I replied, 'Ah, but you must have got the wrong edition. You should have had the one *with* answers, not the one *without* answers!'

Whether from malignance or stupidity, the meetings always seemed to be arranged in the Infant School. I can still see the massive bulk of the listeners trying to squeeze into those puny forms. I soon began to learn the importance, and danger, of the Chairman. Any hope of keeping things reasonably quiet might easily be thrown away by his opening remarks. If he was a local employer, and started with the words 'You men', it was hopeless. My speeches were at first written out in polished form, more suitable to the Oxford Union than to Tilery, or Portrack, or Paradise Row. (Such were the names of the slums, long since cleared away.) They were occasionally listened to with the kind of awed respect which is sometimes shown to a preacher or a lecturer. More often they were shouted down. I soon realised that what the people came for, if at all, was 'questions'. Even by the end of my first campaign, I had developed a technique in a rowdy area of not trying to make a speech, but devoting the whole hour to questions. In that way one made the speech without seeming to and, incidentally, dealt with the topics that interested the audience. In those days, long before the radio or the television, the meetings were vastly important, even decisive.

So the days passed on. The time seemed interminable—as at school—and then, suddenly, we were at polling day. There were the usual alarms and excursions, all of which were new to me and would have caused me some anxiety if it had not been for the imperturbable good sense of my agent, Joe Cooke. 'Somebody's opened a committee-room above a licensed premises!' 'Even if we get in we shall be unseated—perhaps sent to prison!' 'What licensed premises; a pub?' 'Oh no, a gin-shop just off something Street.' 'Somebody has stood somebody else a drink and asked for his vote.' 'Who?' 'One of the paid men of the committee-rooms.' 'Breach of the criminal law!' 'None of the pamphlets have been reaching Hartburn.' 'Why not?' 'There are no canvassing-cards in Thornaby.' 'They were sent over last night.' 'Yes, but that fool Johnny left them in the tram!' and so on and so forth.

I devoted much energy to composing an elegant election address, which I was told would be read with attention by every constituent. In the event, whether from political bias or boredom, far the greater part of them were thrown by the postman into the Tees from the bridge which links Stockton with Thornaby. Later, we heard that this gesture was pretty impartial, all the candidates having suffered alike.

Then at last, at the end of it all, polling day. The candidates can do nothing but parade from committee-room to committee-room, wearing vast favours on their persons and ribbons on their cars. Our colours were red, the Liberal blue, the Labour yellow and green.

My wife quickly acquired the art of canvassing which, after all, is merely the art of being natural, simple, and a little humble. The middle-class ladies tried to dissuade her from going into what were called 'the bad streets'. At this election, and at five subsequent elections, as well as on many occasions in between elections, there was hardly a house in Stockton or Thornaby in which my wife's face was not familiar. She was always received with courtesy and has long been remembered with affection.

At last polling day is over, and the count comes. The Town Clerk is a masterful man who allows no expression of opinion at any time within the council chamber, where the count is held, but demands absolute silence, as if in church. It had become apparent, during the week or so of the election, that we were getting more support than we had believed likely. But, of course, we could not tell what would be the division between the Liberal and Labour vote. The count was efficiently done, because the Town Clerk only employed selected men and women of his own choice who worked rapidly and well. My wife was exhausted and slept a good deal of the time, which won much approval as being a sign of inherited phlegm and self-control.

Finally, that terrible moment—the worst thing in any election for a candidate—when the count is completed. For quite a long period nothing seems to emerge; then suddenly the little streams of hundreds, next of thousands, of ballot papers flow into their appropriate piles. It is finishing. It is all over. I had no idea, nor had my supporters, how close the fight would prove. At one moment it looked as if I had won. Had I been more experienced, I would certainly have asked for a re-count. Perhaps there was a little packet of a hundred somewhere, with ninety-nine of my votes and one Labour or Liberal vote on the top. But I knew nothing of these mysteries. The Mayor announced the result. The candidates were pretty level: Liberal 11,734, Conservative 11,661, Labour 10,619. We were out—but, in a sense, we had triumphed.

What was the future? Until the next election—probably at least four years distant—my work would be at St. Martin's Street with my partners, and not at Westminster. This was what I wanted—or was supposed to have wanted. Later in the night, and in the course of the next day, we learnt that Baldwin's gamble had failed, and that Bonar Law's 1922 majority had disappeared. In the new House there would be 258 Conservatives, 191 Socialists, and 159 Liberals. Who had won? This seemed rather obscure. Who had lost? This was clear enough. In the circumstances, seeing the substantial losses of seats which the Conservatives had suffered, to be beaten by only 73 at Tees-side was thought a mild success. We returned to London—excited, exhilarated, not disappointed, and looking forward to another fight. Of course, with such a tiny margin, we must come back to Stockton.

Yet all the time at the back of my mind was the thought of how much I had learnt. It seemed almost impudence for me, without experience of industrial life, without close contact with the suffering of unemployment or poverty, without technical knowledge of the problems besetting industry, to come before these people and solicit their suffrages. Of one thing I was glad. It was not an election fought on 'Tranquillity'; it was an election fought upon a positive plan—protection against cheap industrial imports threatening British wage standards and jobs. Baldwin's message was easy to explain to those already unemployed or in fear of unemployment. Cheap imports were beginning to flood into the country, even of billets and bars, still more of manufactured iron and steel products. Surely we needed a tariff, if only for bargaining with other countries. Thus it was not difficult to preach protection with sincerity. I felt all the time that our policy attracted many trade unionists who would only not vote for us because of pressure or a false sense of solidarity. After all, before the rise of the Labour Party, the working class had traditionally been Tory; the tradesmen, the shopkeepers, and the middle classes had generally been Liberal. At any rate, it was a policy for which we could canvass by day, talk in the schoolrooms by night, or preach in the afternoon from the Market Cross in Stockton or the Five Lamps in Thornaby, to an audience mostly out of work themselves. Conditions were destined soon to get worse, even catastrophic. Meanwhile, the memory of massive unemployment began to haunt me then and for many years to come.

CHAPTER SIX

Election to Parliament:
First Impressions and Personalities

THE Parliament of 1923–4 was one of the shortest but one of the most dramatic in our history. The results of the election were declared on 8 December 1923. The Conservative membership of the House of Commons was reduced from 344 to 258; the Labour rose from 144 to 191. The Liberals, temporarily reunited in the defence of free trade, increased their numbers from 117 to 159. Asquith and Lloyd George were nominally reconciled almost for the last time, although they worked together on a healthy basis of mutual distrust. The Conservatives were thus the largest party; but they had lost the clear majority over all parties which they had won in 1922. Labour could form a Government with the acquiescence of the Liberals, but only if the Liberals first voted out the Conservative Government. The Conservatives could remain in power if they could make an agreement with the Liberals to maintain them against the Labour Party. In the last resort, if it was thought vital to prevent a Socialist administration, the Conservatives might offer to keep a Liberal Government in power. All these permutations and combinations were hotly debated during the weeks after the election. The clubs were filled with a tremendous amount of activity. Tapers and Tadpoles were in their element. As was to be expected, the Conservative Ministers who had supported the Coalition and remained faithful to it were the chief critics of Baldwin and the protagonists of the movement to prevent a Labour Government at all costs. Austen Chamberlain, Birkenhead, and even Balfour canvassed actively for this view. The Conservative Party managers, led by Lord Younger, also argued in favour of a Liberal–Conservative Coalition under Asquith. The editor of the *Spectator*, with that strange aberration which seems to attack editors, normally reliable, at moments of crisis, thought McKenna ought to be Prime Minister. It is extraordinary how McKenna kept on cropping up all through these years. First Bonar Law and then Baldwin offered him the Treasury; then Mr. St. Loe Strachey—in the columns of the *Spectator*—drafted him to the Premiership. As he was not even a Member of Parliament and declined to offer himself for any seat more hazardous or onerous than the City of London (which the sitting Member obstinately refused to surrender), all this came to nothing.

Baldwin in this predicament kept his head admirably. Having demanded a dissolution on the ground that only effective protection of industry could solve the problem of unemployment, he would indeed have been foolish as well as dishonourable if he had formed a free-trade Government for the sole purpose of keeping out Labour. It is true that a year later he fell partially into this trap, by diluting the firm word 'protection' into the woolly term 'safeguarding'. Meanwhile, as might have been expected, Asquith remained calm and resolute; he was under no illusion. If the Conservative Prime Minister chose to meet Parliament and if, as seemed proper after the failure of his electoral gamble, he was defeated on a vote of censure, the only constitutional procedure open to the Monarch was to send for the leader of the next largest party, that is to say, Ramsay MacDonald. This is what, in fact, happened. Baldwin rightly decided not to resign, but to meet Parliament. He was defeated on a motion in which the Liberals and the Socialists went into the same lobby. Whether or not he calculated what the ultimate result would be, nothing could have turned out more to his advantage. The excitement and even alarm caused by the Labour Party actually forming a Government for the first time in history distracted attention from his electoral miscalculations. Moreover, although Asquith acted patriotically and constitutionally, what he did was fatal for the future of the Liberal Party. Austen Chamberlain foresaw this with great acuteness. In the debate on 21 January 1924 he used these words about the Liberal leader :

He has taken his choice, and he has by that choice constituted his own immortality. He will go down to history as the last Prime Minister of a Liberal

Administration. He has sung the swan song of the Liberal Party. When next the country is called upon for a decision, if it wants a Socialist Government it will vote for a Socialist; if it does not want a Socialist Government it will vote for a Unionist.

It was perhaps hard on the Liberals. But this prophecy proved true, and what Chamberlain predicted has lasted for more than forty years.

But the Liberal vote did more than sow the seeds for the collapse of the Liberal Party. It helped to reunite the Conservative Party. The Coalition Ministers—Balfour, Austen Chamberlain, Birkenhead, Worthington-Evans—who had been engaged in a rather hesitating negotiation with Baldwin just before the election, were, by the march of events, divided from Lloyd George, their old leader, and reconciled to the main body of the Conservative Party. Churchill, it is true, took two bites at this particular cherry. At the Abbey, Westminster, by-election he had stood as a 'Constitutionalist', with a great deal of Conservative support, against an official Conservative. He was defeated by a mere handful of votes. After that the transition became easy and was generally welcomed. In the General Election of 1924 he was adopted as a 'Constitutionalist' candidate for Epping and enjoying full Conservative support was elected by an overwhelming majority. The wheel had come full circle. The apostate of twenty years before was welcomed as the 'prodigal son'. The actual size and quality of the 'fatted calf' proved something of a surprise when Baldwin made him Chancellor of the Exchequer after the General Election of 1924.

I naturally watched the development of the 1923–4 Parliament with keen interest. I was back at business. But it soon became probable that it would not be so very long before a new crisis would arrive in my life. If the Parliament had lasted four years or more my decision could have been postponed. But I began to see that I should have to break the news to my partners earlier than that. In a word, I would soon have to go back to Stockton and fight again, and with every prospect of success.

For, as the months passed, the position of the Socialist Government got gradually weaker. In foreign affairs, the Prime Minister, who combined with his post that of Foreign Secretary, had indeed achieved considerable success. He was respected abroad and to foreign Ministers seemed an agreeable change from the pomposities of Lord Curzon. Yet, in the end, his sensitiveness was his undoing.

Many people have supposed that Asquith had the idea in January 1924 that if he put in a Labour Government by voting out the Conservatives, and if such a Government should subsequently be defeated in the House of Commons, the old doctrine of a Parliament not yet having exhausted its usefulness would hold force. In this event, the King might send for Asquith, and a Government be formed which the Conservatives would be forced willy-nilly to support. This would not result from any agreement or bargain but from the force of circumstances. Many people at the time assumed that this was Asquith's plan; but it is very difficult to find any support for this in documents published or unpublished. Asquith did in January what he conceived to be his plain duty. It seems probable that, being a man of great integrity, he acted solely on the grounds of constitutional propriety and the national interest. If ever there was to be a Labour Government, now was the time when the experiment could be made in conditions of comparative safety. Asquith would, no doubt, have maintained the first Socialist Government in power for several years if MacDonald and his friends had made any response in return. On the contrary, they treated the Liberals with rudeness and contempt. The Liberals got tired of being regarded, in the phrase of the day, as 'patient oxen'. When, therefore, the equivocations of the Prime Minister over both the Campbell case and the Russian Treaty began to disgust the Liberals beyond what was tolerable, Asquith was bound to react.

But of all these twists and turns of Parliamentary fortunes I was only a spectator at a distance. I heard much about them from my friends and relations, especially from my brothers-in-law, Hartington and James Stuart, who had been more fortunate than I in the 1923 election. As the summer progressed, my hopes and anxieties began to increase. When, finally, MacDonald rejected Asquith's proposal for a Select Committee on the Campbell case and was defeated in the House of Commons by a combination of Liberals and Conservatives on 8 October, I knew that the moment of decision had clearly come. On the next day, MacDonald saw the King and asked for a dissolution. We now know that the King was very un-willing to grant this request—three General Elections in three years seemed to be imposing an intolerable burden upon the country, with all its dislocation of trade and the possible adverse effect upon employment. Nor was there any certainty that the political difficul-ties would necessarily be resolved. Some authorities have since criticised the King's action. Asquith had stated publicly only a few months before that the King was under no obligation to grant a dissolution to a Prime Minister who did not normally command the majority in Parliament. In his biography of King George V, Harold Nicolson tells us—what we did not know at the time—that the King did not accept the Prime Minister's advice without asking both the leaders of the Conservative and Liberal Parties separately whether either of them was able or willing to form an administration.[1]

So, less than a year after my first adventure as a candidate, I found myself setting out upon the second. This time the situation, from a purely electoral point of view, was much improved. The weakness and vacillations of MacDonald had aggravated ordinary folk. He appeared to men of moderate views to be unduly influenced by the extreme Left. The story of the Russian Treaty, where nego-tiations were first broken off and then apparently restarted under Left-wing pressure, and, for similar reasons, the Prime Minister first refusing a loan to Russia and then granting it, was an incident on the high plain of international politics. That of the Campbell case, where a prosecution was first instituted against a Communist agitator by the Attorney-General and then withdrawn, apparently at the request of the Prime Minister—again under Left-wing pressure—was on a lower level of importance, but equally significant. Nor had the Government much to show—at any rate in terms of home politics—on the other side.

I had been defeated in 1923 by a Liberal; but my most dangerous opponent at Stockton was now likely to be the Labour and not the Liberal candidate. It was even possible that some Conservatives had voted Liberal last time to keep out the Socialists. The cry against the Liberals was therefore easy and effective. 'You put them in—now we'll put you out!' Towards the end of the campaign we were

[1] Harold Nicolson, *King George V: His Life and Reign*, p. 400.

given an unexpected bonus in the strange affair of the Zinoviev Letter (or 'Red Letter' as it came to be called). The text of a confidential communication from Zinoviev, as President of the Third International, to the British Communist Party had fallen into the hands of the Foreign Office. It was the usual inflammatory and subversive stuff. Perhaps the most dangerous passages were those referring to the creation of revolutionary cells in the fighting Services. In view of the recent and friendly negotiations between the British and Russian Governments, a Note of protest seemed called for. The Foreign Office advised MacDonald in favour of publication of the text of the letter, all the more because the *Daily Mail* was known to have obtained a copy and would undoubtedly publish it before the end of the election. But here again poor MacDonald's luck was out. Whether the letter was genuine or a fake we shall perhaps never know. At least he seemed to regard it as genuine, and made some fumbling excuses about it in the last days of the election. Added to other examples of maladroitness and muddle, the Red Letter came in at the end as the final piece of testimony of the unfitness to govern of MacDonald and his friends. Certainly no Conservative candidate could ask for more.[1]

Yet there was one aspect of the campaign which distressed me. Baldwin, who a year before had protested with deep sincerity that he could not face the problem of unemployment until he was relieved of the Bonar Law pledge against protection of British industry, proceeded a year later to bind on himself the same or very similar shackles as his predecessor. Leo Amery has explained in his reminiscences how the first draft of the election address left Baldwin in a fairly free position by adopting those ambiguities so familiar in election manifestos. However, at a later stage, when Amery's guiding and persistent hand was temporarily removed from him, Baldwin was led into a statement which could only be interpreted as a promise not to adopt a general system of tariffs. It is true that the concept of 'safeguarding' industry was put forward in its place. But

---

[1] The authenticity of the Zinoviev Letter was much disputed. According to Lord Strang (*Home and Abroad*, London, 1956, p. 56), Sir Eyre Crowe, Permanent Under-Secretary at the Foreign Office, 'satisfied himself that the letter was authentic' and so advised MacDonald. An inquiry after the General Election confirmed this.

this was to be an individual and not a general mechanism. Each industry would have to show that it was suffering from 'unfair competition'. Although at the election those of us who believed, as I did, in protection tried to represent 'safeguarding' as only like a rose—smelling as sweet under its new name—yet I confess that I was a little shaken. I remember consulting with various local notabilities as to whether I could make the same moving speeches about foreign imports as I had made last time. As none of those whom I consulted seemed to have any recollection of what it was that I had said, and as all seemed to think these niceties unimportant incidents in an election campaign, I stuck to my argument for protecting the iron and steel industry. This at least gave some variation to the campaign, which was chiefly concentrated on attacking the Labour Government for their incompetence and on the Liberals for having put them into power.

One of the most melancholy occupations of old age is to re-read election addresses. But on examining my own in these two elections I can take credit for having put the tariff issue fairly. In my election address of 1923, I said that I wanted 'to safeguard, to defend, to protect', and to use the new duties as 'a bargaining weapon'. In 1924 I said that I was in favour of safeguarding any industry that could show that through no fault of its own it was suffering from unfair competition. This formula, I argued, certainly included our local industries. So I seem to have stuck pretty well to the party line, although in my heart I regretted the change of emphasis and the muting of the protectionist theme.

The campaign proved lively. Many of the meetings were rowdy, although few were actually broken up. As the days went on it became more and more apparent that the contest would be between the Conservative and Labour candidates. Many of the moderate Liberal voters, and some of those Conservatives who had supported the Liberal at the previous election on the ground that he would be the most likely candidate to beat the Socialist, were clearly coming over to our side. Once more, I was persuaded to visit certain Liberal notables—generally respected members of various chapels and temperance associations—whose support, if it could be obtained, would command considerable following in their own circles. But the main job as before was the solid canvassing, house by house and street by street. I began to realise that the personal approach was as important as the public meetings and more likely to win votes. My wife became a very skilled exponent of this art. By now we had with us our two children, and the final appeal—a most moving picture of the family— was circulated with some nauseating caption like 'Vote for Daddy!' As the years passed, we became hardened to these methods, which are traditional and I hope effective.

During the year we had made many visits to Stockton, and the organisation both on the men's and the women's side had been considerably strengthened. We had a good working committee in every ward. In the twelve months, I had attended many smoking-concerts to encourage the men, and my wife an equal number of tea-parties to inspire the women. There are some Members of Parliament who dislike all this machinery of electioneering and find it rather degrading. Baldwin himself with his sensitive nature was one of these and has expressed himself on this topic.[1] For my part, I enjoyed it all. It was new to me, and brought me in touch with a very large number of people whom I would not ordinarily have met, and about whose difficulties and ambitions I was interested to learn. Conditions in the town were still very bad; the rate of unemployment was desperately high and destined to rise still higher. But there was a feeling of hope in the air, which inspired me and all those who worked for me. I was young and enthusiastic and perhaps was able to impart some of my own keenness to the people whom I met, and whose suffrages I was seeking.

It was a fine rousing campaign, ending with a vast progress of my supporters through the streets on the eve of the poll. This served, at any rate, to show that we were not frightened by opposition. I regret to say that I rather encouraged this demonstration, by leading the procession, and a good deal of mild fighting took place—happily without any serious result. I never shall forget the declaration of the poll. The Town Clerk, with the same severity as the year before, prevented any expression of opinion within the council chamber. Even after the Returning Officer had disclosed the result to those in the hall, not a sound was allowed. But when we walked out on to

[1] G. M. Young, *Stanley Baldwin* (London, 1952), p. 24.

the platform erected outside the old Borough Hall, the scene was overwhelming. Since my wife and I came out first, the people knew the result before the figures were actually made known. The great broad High Street—characteristic of northern towns—was filled as far as the eye could see. It seemed as if the whole population were out that night. I well remember the mass of upturned faces. For the first time in my life I heard the roar from thousands of throats, acclaiming victory. This was not made any less agreeable by the opposition cries of anger or disgust. It was impossible for us to get away through the surging crowd. The police wanted us to leave by the back of the hall through a street that ran parallel with the High Street. This I refused to do. Finally, as a compromise, I agreed to walk out of the front of the hall, where a gangway was kept by the police, and mounted with my wife to the top of a tram which had somehow been halted not far away. On this, after considerable delay, we rode triumphantly away.

There can hardly be any thrill so great for a young man as his first successful election. The sense of gratitude to one's supporters; the determination to earn the confidence of all—whether on your side or against you; the emotion at having achieved a long ambition: all these are tremendous moments in life. In addition, there was the feeling of responsibility towards the great community so harshly struck by poverty and unemployment—so ready to grasp at any straw of hope.

When the national figures were examined it was found that the great Conservative majority had not made, at any rate in the industrial seats, any great inroad into the Labour vote. Indeed, in Stockton the Socialist polled 11,948 as against 10,619 a year before. My poll had risen from 11,661 to 15,163. The Liberal had fallen from 11,734 to 8,751. On cool reflection, therefore, it was evident that it was not the skill of our campaign, the magnetism of the candidate, or the charm of his wife—or any of the reasons which vanity might suggest—which were responsible for our success. As Austen Chamberlain had predicted, the failures and confusions of the first Socialist administration made little effect upon the Labour vote, but proved fatal to the Liberal Party. Over the country as a whole, 419 Conservatives were returned to Parliament, 151 Labour, and only

40 Liberals. Asquith again lost his seat and never re-entered the House of Commons. The two-party system of political life in Britain became dominant, and has broadly remained so to this day.

Parliament met on 2 December 1924. I can recall, even at this distance of time, the sense of exhilaration with which I joined my fellow Members in the taking of my seat. In this Chamber, where I had so often listened to debates from the Gallery, I now had the right to a seat as a Member. Here I could, at least for the period of one Parliament, observe the great figures, so well known to me by name and reputation, watch important issues develop, listen to enthralling debates, begin to take some minor part in these high matters, and see unwinding itself before my eyes the great political drama—no longer as a spectator, but to a small degree as a participant.

For a young Member, coming for the first time to the House of Commons is very like going to school, and the atmosphere of the place is very similar. There are the top boys of the sixth form, who sit on the front benches and hold the great positions either as Ministers or leaders of the Opposition. Even in the attenuated Liberal benches there were the notable personalities of Lloyd George, the hero of the war; of Samuel, Simon, Alfred Mond, and other ex-Ministers. On the Opposition side there was the late Cabinet, led by MacDonald, flanked by Snowden and Arthur Henderson. On our side, there was Baldwin, Churchill, and the two Chamberlains. All these front-bench figures constitute a society of prefects who rule the school under the general guidance of the headmaster or Speaker. Junior Ministers are like boys half-way up the school or who have just got some distinction in games or work, subservient to the older boys and condescending to the new. We, the general ruck, with varying degrees of humility, ambition, and sometimes cheekiness, were like the lower boys of the school, who suffer their present indignities in the hope of reaching in due course the gaudy splendours of the sixth form. Naturally I did not know, when the Parliament of 1924 began, that it would be some sixteen years before I left the back-benches for a junior post in a Ministry. It was a long spell. But I must be fair. Lack of promotion was my own fault and the result of my deliberate determination, as the years

passed, to pursue my own plans and purposes. This long and sometimes frustrating exclusion from the centre of power did not prove
in the end a bad training. For the moment I was enthralled by the
sense of being a member of this historic assembly. I would wait and
watch and learn.

There was certainly much to learn. To the newcomer one of the
most confusing things about the House of Commons is the complexity of its procedure. Apart from the traditional formalities surrounding the Opening of Parliament, the summoning of the
Commons to the bar of the House of Lords, the reading of the
King's Speech, the election of the Speaker, and so forth, the day-to-
day machinery by which business is conducted requires a lifelong
study to be completely mastered. I must admit that at the end of
forty years I should find it very difficult to pass even an elementary
examination on some of its niceties. It is true that the private
Member can depend upon the most sympathetic assistance of the
'table'; that is to say, the Clerks who serve the House. They are
always ready to advise on the form which questions should take in
order to comply with the rules of order, and with the drafting of
amendments in the committee stages of Bills, whether on the floor
of the House or in Standing Committee. The form of all these is
governed by traditional regulations, which are the product of many
years of experience. They derive partly from printed Standing
Orders, partly from case-law—that is, the rulings of various Speakers
through many generations—and partly from Erskine May, the
accepted authority, almost the 'Bible' of the House of Commons.
Some new Members and many outside are inclined to regard all this
elaborate procedure as unnecessary and obsolete. Indeed, it is very
easy to attack it. But these criticisms may spring, not from ignorance
or inexperience, but from sinister motives. The rights of Opposition
parties and the protection of minorities are essential to any form of
democratic government. These are secured by our traditional
Parliamentary methods. In Speaker Onslow's words, 'Even Pedan-
try may be the last barrier against Tyranny'. It is quite true that
Ministers sometimes become impatient at the delays imposed. Yet I
found the same men, when out of office, rejoice in the defensive
machinery provided. Moreover, having had at the end of my

political life experience of assemblies which appeared to operate without any effective procedural rules, I have been horrified at the contrast. For instance, in the Security Council of the United Nations, the lack of any effective system frequently leads to dangerous confusions. It often happens that in the course of long day-and-night sittings of the Security Council, resolutions are moved, the terms of which have never been 'put on the Order Paper' in time for them to be properly considered by the Governments most concerned. Frantic messages pass between their representatives in New York and the capitals of the great nations. Manuscript amendments are sometimes moved without notice. The difference in the time-factor adds a further complication which nobody seems to remember. I have known the Foreign Secretary or Prime Minister to be rung up at two or three in the morning (it then being nine or ten p.m. in New York), to ask how the British representative is to cast his vote on a motion of which no one has seen the original and to which amendments are being proposed. Yet great matters of policy may be at stake; and the British Government may be taking responsibility for important decisions which they have had no proper time to consider. It is only when one has seen some of the trouble caused by all this laxity of procedure that one appreciates the value of our Parliamentary tradition, apparently somewhat cumbrous, but in its present form, with the modifications introduced during the last hundred years, effective both to prevent obstruction and to secure legitimate criticism and discussion.

In 1924 the House met at 2.45 p.m. and adjourned normally at 11 p.m. The earlier and shorter hours which now prevail (2.30 to 10 p.m.) were introduced after the Second War and were adhered to afterwards. In my first Parliament, since I was fully employed in my business, I seldom got to the House, except for some special reason, until between four and five o'clock in the afternoon. Consequently, I generally missed 'Question Time', attending only on the rare occasions when I had some question of my own on the paper. For a new Member to miss Questions is unfortunate, for it is by this means that you most readily learn the names of your fellow Members. However, in one way or another, chiefly by assiduous attendance at the debates, I became acquainted with the names and appearance of most of the personalities on both sides. I tried also to study the art of Parliamentary debating, which can only be learnt on the floor of the House itself. Following the advice of some of my older friends, I did not attempt to make a maiden speech until I had sat in the House for some five months.

Of recent years, the Chamber has been less full and debates less well attended, except on the great occasions. This is partly due to the large number of meetings held by Members outside the Chamber during the afternoon and evening. On the Conservative side this practice began in the 1923–4 Parliament. After Baldwin's defeat in the autumn of 1923 the party was in rather a nervous state. Eyres-Monsell (the Chief Whip), after discussion with Lord Crawford, one of his predecessors, decided to set up an organisation by which better liaison could be maintained between the party leaders and private Members. Obviously private Members had complained that the leaders were out of touch with the rank and file. These committees were set up at first under different headings : finance, defence, home affairs, overseas affairs, and so forth. The Chief Whip thus restricted them to a fairly small number. After the Conservative victory of 1924 the situation was different. The party was triumphant, but it had so large a majority that Eyres-Monsell decided to develop the system to involve a large number of committees covering almost every Ministry. His purpose in this was partly to keep Ministers in touch with the party but largely to occupy Members in an agreeable and harmless manner. But attendance at these committees has had a bad effect on the House of Commons. It may have suited the Whips but it injured Parliamentary institutions.

The 1922 Committee[1] continued as before and still goes on. When the party is in power, Ministers do not attend, except by invitation. When it is in Opposition, ex-Ministers may attend. It is a committee of the whole party and, in moments of difficulty, can play an important role.

But attendance at Westminster is by no means all a Member's work. I had not fully realised the heavy burden of local affairs. This

---

[1] This committee, to which any Conservative Member can go, was started during the Coalition. It still retains the original name.

was especially so in a large industrial constituency, suffering from all the individual problems arising from four years of war and several years of unemployment and distress. I have preserved all this correspondence, running into scores of files. Even a cursory glance through them today recalls many individual hardships and tragedies. Alas! in most cases, there was little practical aid that one could bring. Yet sympathy seemed always to be welcome, and sometimes one could give useful advice. The 'cases', as we called them at that time, fell largely into three categories. The arrangements for war pensions were on the whole satisfactory, but they were operated by a number of complicated rules, the application of which sometimes led to real hardship. Here, protracted correspondence was often involved between the Member and the Minister. Sometimes, to bring matters to a head, the threat of a Parliamentary Question (to which Civil Servants are curiously allergic) was a useful instrument. A frequent cause of dispute was the argument as to whether a man's present state of health was due wholly to war service, or partly to physical conditions previous to his engagement. This often seemed a rather cruel distinction. For instance, how could it be known whether a man was suffering from the effects of a gas attack or whether he had had weak lungs as a boy? Gradually a set of precedents, interpretations, and alleviations of the rules brought the system into increasing conformity with a reasonable code. Nevertheless, the system of continual medical examinations and boards of appeal, although in principle correct, was often tedious in its operation. I soon found, however, that it was important for a Member to try himself to distinguish between the 'scrimshanker' and the genuine case. If he did so, and the Minister of Pensions began to feel confidence in his cases, the results would be likely to prove satisfactory.

The second group of individual problems turned on unemployment, at that time very high throughout the North-east Coast. In the years 1924–9, the rate in Durham and Northumberland varied from 20 per cent to 25 per cent. The cases fell into two classes. There were the men who came to the office at the stated times, generally once a week, in the hope that I might be able, by some influence with this or that employer, to help them towards a job. Unhappily, during this time, many of the industries were contracting if not closing altogether. The shipyards were under particular pressure. The only industry that brought a new sense of life and hope to our area was the Brunner Mond business, soon to be known as I.C.I., and ambitious plans of this progressive firm were developing at Billingham. This has turned out to be a vast industrial enterprise, giving considerable direct and even greater indirect employment. Of course, during the construction period, much of the work involved was not suitable to more than a fraction of our unemployed engineers and shipwrights. It even entailed the temporary invasion of the town by imported navvy labour, as I was to learn to my cost in 1929 (since it was these voters who were largely responsible for my defeat).

The third class of cases dealt with the regulations covering the drawing of unemployment benefit. This whole subject dominated our discussions in Parliament for many years, and incidentally led to the final collapse of the Labour Government that took office in 1929 and broke up in 1931. Every great piece of social legislation, however progressive, brings with it its own difficulties. It is hard now to realise that before the First War, apart from any funds to which a man might be entitled from his union or friendly society, there was nothing for an unemployed workman after his savings were spent except the Poor Law. The introduction after the First War by Lloyd George's Government of a national system of unemployment relief, however circumscribed by various rules and conditions, undoubtedly saved us from something like revolution when the great Depression came.

Under the first unemployment insurance plan, the weekly payment to unemployed men had a definite relation to an insurance principle. Such a system, however well suited to a period of low general unemployment evenly spread throughout the country, was quite inapplicable to a period of high unemployment with outstanding peaks in what soon became called the 'distressed areas'. Here it was necessary to introduce some form of extra benefit, not wholly justified by the contribution made by a man and his employer in respect of him. This 'extended' or 'uncovenanted' or 'transitional' benefit, called by the opprobrious name of 'dole', was itself subject to limitations. When these rights became exhausted, there was no recourse except to the Poor Law – hateful to a family of good record and pride and, being financed from local rates, increasingly onerous on an area already carrying the heavy burdens resulting from widespread distress.

A large part of my work was in trying to deal with the many border-line cases, and to appeal for special treatment in view of special circumstances. The more general problem was also destined to occupy much of my Parliamentary activities. The lack of understanding in Whitehall and the South of England of the human problems involved; the legal and pedantic arguments, based on mathematical concepts of insurance which were in fact illusory; the actuarial rather than the human approach: all these were the first causes of my disillusionment. I found the correspondence and the individual interviews interesting, but depressingly frustrating. The war years had given me in regimental life my first insight into and contact with the rank and file. These years, 1924–9, gave me a similar contact with men and women of a typically working-class industrial town. It was, of course, necessary to remember that one only saw the hard cases. Men who had successfully drawn their war pensions, or who had found employment, did not call at my office. But, alas, the state of affairs meant that suffering and hardship were not confined to individuals who through their own fault or some inherent weakness of character had fallen on evil days. These calamities struck many of the finest workmen in our country, with long traditions of craftsmanship, skill, and loyalty to their established firms, to whom the very thought of receiving charity was abhorrent.

In later years I was to find economists and newspaper editors arguing against the principle of full employment, to which after the Second War all political parties attached so much importance. While I recognise the dangers of 'over-employment', I have little sympathy with those who, writing from pleasant suburban retreats or comfortable editorial chairs, dilate upon the disciplinary values of pre-war conditions. It was my fate to live with the problems of heavy unemployment for fifteen years. They were not substantially eased by any conscious effort either in the industrial or economic field. Rearmament under Hitler's pressure and ultimately under war brought their own grim solution.

In addition to the individual men and women who called at our offices and wrote to me, there were of course the normal duties of a Member to support the interests of his constituents, and to be present on occasions of local importance. The first brought me into contact with all the leading industrial figures, in our efforts to try and help the area by all possible means. This led, of course, to the arguments about protection and 'safeguarding industry', which filled a great deal of this Parliament, the problems of export credit, rationalisation, and so forth. It involved also attendance at the popular festivals and amusements, from a football match to the Mayor's dinner.

There was, in addition, a great deal to be done to our Conservative organisation through all the usual methods. Into all this my wife threw herself with the greatest energy and devotion. As a result it was a fairly strenuous life. Normally, we would go north two or three times a month—sometimes more. The 1.20 p.m. from King's Cross on Thursday or Friday; then back on the night train on Saturday or Sunday. There is no station so cold and so windy as Darlington in the early hours of the morning. However, the stationmaster was very kind to us, and took us to his room with its comforting fire.

This development of a Member of Parliament into a kind of local welfare officer certainly has its disadvantages. It takes up a great deal of his time, is very fatiguing, and, combined with full attendance in the House of Commons, allows very little opportunity for serious thought. One sometimes envies the Members of the nineteenth century, who only thought it necessary to visit their constituents once or twice a year. Typical of this was an election address, said to have been issued at successive elections by one of my wife's family, which ran as follows:

My views are well known to the electors. I do not therefore think it necessary to repeat them.

Even Disraeli contented himself with addressing an occasional farmers' dinner at Aylesbury.

Another disadvantage of the system that has grown up is the pressure on front-benchers, whether in or out of office. This has led to Ministers or ex-Ministers drifting inevitably into the safer seats of their party. Yet it is just the unsafe seats which are the most interesting. We know only too well the views and arguments of our keen supporters. It is a valuable and correcting experience to be in constant contact with our critics and opponents. In spite of the disadvantages, I look back with gratitude to the twenty-odd years of my association with Stockton and the North-east Coast. I learnt there lessons which I have never forgotten. If, in some respects, they may have left too deep an impression on my mind, the gain was greater than the loss.

The Parliament of 1924–9 was dominated by a few leading personalities, of whom by far the most exciting to a new Member like myself was Lloyd George. I had first heard him speak at the Oxford Union in 1913, when he accepted an invitation from the President, Gilbert Talbot. His visit caused an immense stir in the university. It was at a time when Lloyd George, as the leading radical, almost revolutionary, politician, was a highly controversial figure. He was regarded by rival parties with hatred on the one side, and devotion on the other. There was a good deal of apprehension among the authorities lest an undergraduate rag might develop into something like a riot. The police were out in full force. Although I have now forgotten the content of Lloyd George's speech, I remember how he held the very crowded debating-hall with a display of extraordinary virtuosity. All were charmed, delighted, and impressed, not least those who had come to scoff and jeer. The next morning Gilbert asked me to breakfast to meet the great man; and this indeed was the only time that I had seen him to speak to.

There have been so many descriptions written of Lloyd George— by those who knew him in his youth and in the supreme period of his authority—that I can add but little. I remember him only during the long decline—a tragic period—in which he bore his disappointments with unfailing good humour. In later years, as I shall describe, I had some fairly close relations with him, but in this Parliament I could only watch him from a distance.

Only two or three years had passed since the zenith of his power. No one in this House believed that he would never return to office. He was still the great hero of the war. When he rose to speak, the House filled up, Members hurrying in from smoking-room, tea-room, dining-rooms, committee-rooms, library. To us young Members, who had never or seldom heard him, it was a stirring experience. Since he was no longer on either of the front benches, the exact time at which he would speak could not be known precisely in advance. He had, therefore, to fill the House before embarking upon his theme. I noticed, after one or two such occasions, that the method he adopted was ingeniously chosen to meet the situation. He would begin quietly in a low voice, with some passing references of no great significance to previous speakers, and a word or two of praise or criticism. He rather encouraged Members to cry, 'Speak up!' Then, when the audience was collected, he embarked upon the full flow of his magnificent stream of argument, imagery, and rhetoric. If he could not convince the House of Commons, in which he and his party formed such a small minority, he could keep us all enthralled. I can see him now: the wonderful head, the great mane of white hair (turned from raven black to pure white during the few years of the war); the expressive features, changing rapidly from fierce anger to that enchanting smile, not confined to the mouth, but spreading to his cheeks and eyes; above all, the beautiful hands, an actor's or an artist's hands, by the smallest movement of which he could make you see the picture he was trying to paint.

In February 1928, the Liberals obtained a day on the Debate on the Address for a discussion of the 'Yellow Book'—the famous pamphlet on unemployment and reconstruction—which had been compiled under his leadership by many distinguished writers and thinkers. I found myself in sympathy with most of the proposals—or at any rate with the general line of approach. Some of these very ideas a number of my friends and I had tried to put forward ourselves in an amateurish but sincere way. I spoke during the debate, but did not attack these imaginative plans as the Socialists had done, but rather welcomed them. Nevertheless, I had to tread warily, for I knew that the views we were developing were by no means popular with my own party. I tried, therefore, to temper my support with some partisan banter. I expressed my pleasure at the Yellow Book's 'repudiation of the more cruelly calculated crudities of the Cobdenite creed', and welcomed the new recruits which Progressive Toryism was gaining from the thinning ranks of the Liberal Party.

All this was poor stuff of which I am now ashamed. I added that it seemed to me a strange irony that the heavy expenses of preparing this treatise had been defrayed by the famous Lloyd George Fund. One wondered what the noblemen who had subscribed to it would think at this result of their generosity? This was in doubtful taste, although well received on my own benches; and Lloyd George in his reply quite rightly rebuked these observations as 'cheap jeers'. It so happened that shortly afterwards I met him for the first time since those Oxford days, at a small party given by one of my friends, to which he consented to come. I felt anxious lest he would remember and resent my puny darts, so impudently launched at so great a man. He had not forgotten. But he was not at all resentful. With the most charming and disarming smile he said, 'I saw very well what you were doing the other day. You were trying to disguise your revolt against your Tory front bench by a side-attack on me. It is an old trick and I have done it many times. But you are a born rebel!' So an evening to which I had looked forward with some apprehension proved to be both delightful and memorable.

Lloyd George had a quality sometimes denied to great men. He was a very good listener. He liked to draw out other people's talk, especially that of young men. That night he made all of our little group feel that we had something important to contribute that he was genuinely keen to hear. Some great men are like beech trees and nothing grows under them. Lloyd George was like an oak under which the wild flowers and plants of the forest flourish freely. This was my only contact with him in this Parliament. But I have never forgotten the enchantment of his talk and presence.

It was the fashion among many Conservative leaders, with some notable exceptions, to denigrate Lloyd George throughout this and later Parliaments. This was partly because many of them, both in the Cabinet and among junior Ministers, had been the instigators of the downfall of the Coalition in 1922. They therefore felt it necessary to justify their action by an attitude of moral disapproval of the man under whom they had been happy to serve, until they decided to overthrow him. Moreover, Lloyd George's line in the General Strike, which on a study of the complex story—based on knowledge now available—seems to have had some ground, was much resented in our party and indeed throughout the country. It led, incidentally, to a final break with Asquith. Baldwin, who had almost a physical loathing of Lloyd George, used his powerful influence to warn young Members against falling under his spell. Although the leading figures of the War Coalition, Austen Chamberlain, Birkenhead, and, of course, Churchill, remained on close terms of personal friendship with Lloyd George, lesser fry affected disapproval and dislike. As the Parliament wore on, for many Members the thrill of seeing Lloyd George's name go up on the board began to fade. For me, the charm and interest remained. In any event, the generous tribute paid by the greatest national leader in our long history still stands: 'When the English history of the first quarter of the twentieth century is written, it will be seen that the greater part of our fortunes in peace and in war were shaped by this one man.'

The uniqueness and to some extent loneliness of Lloyd George was emphasised by the little team of Liberal leaders. Asquith had gone to the Upper House. The only others of importance were Samuel and Simon. It was pretty clear that Lloyd George disliked Samuel and despised Simon. It was equally clear what their feelings were for him. Samuel always spoke well, but never superlatively well. When in office, he had always been efficient but never brilliant. In debate his arguments were clearly marshalled but the tone was rather low—there was something of the governess about him. John Simon, no doubt because of his antipathy to Lloyd George, paid scant attention to the House during this Parliament. He did emerge, however, during the General Strike into great prominence. His speech on 6 May 1926, which maintained the view that the General Strike was illegal and that its promoters could not claim the protection of the Trade Disputes Act of 1906, had an important effect in bringing the Strike to an end. He implied that the trade union funds would not be immune; he said that every trade union leader involved would be 'liable in damages to the uttermost farthing of his personal possessions'. Whether this was good law or not is still disputed. But it was certainly good politics. It had a dramatic and devastating effect on the morale of the T.U.C. leaders.

On the Opposition side, two or three stand out. First Mac-Donald, then in his prime, or at any rate showing no perceptible sign of the physical and mental decay which afterwards overcame him. He spoke best on foreign affairs, in which at the time I took only a detached interest, on several occasions, therefore, missing the debates. But he was dignified and statesmanlike in general, although like everyone when in Opposition, capable of rather weak and even silly interventions. Next to him sat Philip Snowden, the Snowden of the Socialist movement, not the Snowden of the later National Government. His gibes and jeers he kept then for his enemies; in a few years he was to turn them on his old friends. The most exciting debating displays were Snowden versus Churchill; each in his different way giving a splendid exhibition. Snowden was acid and pitiless, Churchill gay and bantering. Of the other Labour leaders, I retain a vivid memory of Arthur Henderson. He did not take much part in debate, but when he did, spoke effectively and sincerely. I can see him now, standing benignly at the bar of the House, watching his flock, the supreme organiser of the Labour Party, whom they all looked up to and trusted. Everyone knew him as 'Uncle Arthur'.

Below the gangway, on the Opposition side of the House, were grouped the famous Clydesiders. First and weightiest was Wheatley, who combined extreme, almost revolutionary, views with great administrative capacity. His early death was a great loss to his party. David Kirkwood was a natural insurgent, but time and experience had already begun to mellow him. His outbursts were splendid; and he could usually be relied on for starting a good row. Campbell Stephen was a copious and indeed an almost unending speaker, once on his feet. At first one was apt to feel that he had nothing to say except verbiage; but, in fact, his argument, although prolix, was clear and logical. He was one of the best obstructors that I can remember—always just 'in order'. Geordie Buchanan, a pacifist and a rebel, looked like an agreeable schoolboy out on a spree. We all liked him, although we feared his tongue. When he afterwards left politics to preside over the Assistance Board, the appointment was generally welcomed. But, of course, the commanding figure was that of James Maxton. Many descriptions of him have been written, but none can quite depict the strange and ominous appearance of this man. His long black hair, his sunken cheeks, his deep-set eyes, combined to make him look a true revolutionary. He seemed to have stepped straight out of 1789. Listening to him denouncing the aristocrats—or their successors, the bourgeois classes—one felt that he would happily condemn us to the lamp-post or guillotine. But he had one fatal weakness; he was born with or developed in the House of Commons—I know not which—a sense of humour. After a terrifying attack upon us all, he would join us in the smoking-room in friendly conversation. I remember one of the stories that he told against himself. When he was in prison in the war, he had managed to converse, during the dreary tramp of the prisoners round the yard, with one or two of his fellow convicts. He asked what they were in for. One for housebreaking; one for manslaughter ('hit the old woman on the head with a bottle'); another for burglary with assault. When they found out, however, that Maxton was in for sedition, they made a formal protest to the Governor against having to associate with a man who was a traitor to his country. When he spoke, the House filled up. However much many of our respectable and solid Members disapproved of him, they could not help being fascinated. I can remember many of his speeches, but they all showed the same flaw. In the first twenty minutes he would describe all that was wrong with the world—the unemployment, the poverty, the slums, the terrible condition to which capitalism had reduced half the inhabitants of Scotland and the North. Listening to these vivid passages, you could almost see the starved children, the worn mothers, the hopeless, unemployed fathers. But the second half of the speech, to which all this should have been the preliminary, drifted out like some great river into the sands and never reached the sea. He had nothing practical to suggest. He had no useful contribution to make. We were gripped by the questions posed. But we never got the answer.

Among the less exotic members of the Labour Party I also made many friends; chiefly in the tea-room or the smoking-room, where we chatted and drank together. Those we most respected were the solid trade union leaders—many of them experienced and earnest men.

On the Conservative side, Baldwin, the Prime Minister, was undoubtedly looked up to with something like affection by Members in every part of the House. The young and progressive wing of his party had a special regard for him. His speeches, particularly on industrial problems, struck just the note which we thought appropriate and illuminating. The fact that the Right wing and especially the so-called 'Industrials' had little love for him, confirmed our feelings. Later on, I shall try to give a coherent picture of Baldwin as I saw him. In these early days, I knew him only as the man who had led us to a great electoral victory and who had made it possible, through his reputation for decency and fair-mindedness, to win the support of working men and women throughout the country.

It is true that certain aspects of his policy in the immediate past puzzled us. Was he a free-trader or a protectionist? The continual changes of programme, as between 1922, 1923, and 1924, may have been justified by political exigencies, but were scarcely consistent. His settlement of the American debt on the other hand had been forgotten and Bonar Law's protest now seemed exaggerated. As was subsequently pointed out by Arthur Salter, the real harm which the debt settlement did was to hamper future negotiations over the whole field of inter-governmental obligations. It was a decision which was at once premature and unilateral. Nevertheless, it was a closed episode. At the same time, the years ahead, when the danger of European war would loom up again, were far away. In 1924 the great peril that seemed to threaten our country was the class war. Baldwin was out to end it. He seemed to have inherited the true Disraelian tradition. The fact that he had played only a minor role in Lloyd George's great Coalition rather put people on his side. For the mood of the day—certainly at the beginning of the Parliament—was to be a little tired of the brilliant figures who had emerged during the war. If Bonar Law had preached 'Tranquillity', Baldwin practised 'Peace in our Time'. He sat almost continuously in the House. Unkind people said later that it was the only way that he could avoid being troubled. But I do not think that this was fair. He liked to watch and study his fellow Members. He often came into the smoking-room. It is true that he seldom spoke to anyone, but he would give one a friendly nod and we had a sense that he cared about us, like the father of a young and growing family.

Baldwin had made a deep impression, upon all those who heard it, by his broadcast in the previous election. The radio broadcast (happily for politicians the torture of the television had not yet been invented) was used effectively for the first time in 1924. Neither MacDonald nor even Lloyd George ever mastered this technique. MacDonald had made the mistake of having part of a platform speech put over the programme, with all the interruptions and confusions of a great meeting, where his style of rhetoric—admirable for a large and living audience—was not effective to small family groups of listeners. Baldwin had adopted a method—afterwards perfected by President Roosevelt—of what was to be called 'the fireside chat'. He was simple, clear, moderate, and seemed to remember the vital point that in a radio speech—as indeed in a television broadcast—the audience is confined to two or three people in their own homes. They want a talk, not a speech.

Baldwin's leadership of the Conservative Party was certainly firmly established in this Parliament. At the time of the General Strike his wisdom and sympathy impressed us all, as had his famous speech on the Political Levy Bill the year before. When this was in the offing, our little group, under Noel Skelton's leadership, went in a deputation to him, asking him to oppose the Bill. He received us kindly, and the fact that he appeared to follow our advice was naturally a source of gratification to us. It was only as the Parliament proceeded that some of us began to feel some doubts, not as to his desire, but as to his power and determination to influence events. After the General Strike he had an overwhelmingly strong position but he did not use it as he might have done—and, as we now know, some of his colleagues, including Neville Chamberlain, wished him to do. His intense and bitter dislike of Lloyd George struck us as exaggerated. But it was based, he would insist, on moral grounds. He felt that the later days of the Coalition had dirtied the waters of politics and he was determined to clean them. He affected to dislike 'intellectuals'. But that is a common pose of men of high intellectual qualifications; and Baldwin was certainly much more of a sensitive artist than of a rugged countryman. For he was half Celt. His father was a Worcestershire ironmaster, but his mother the daughter of a famous Highland preacher. Even in those days he disliked the Press lords, but as I knew none of them this did not worry me.

Even to the most superficial observer it was clear that Baldwin operated at his best in a crisis, and this was followed by a need for rest and recuperation. He was highly strung, nervous, and indeed the opposite in almost every way to the 'image'—to use the modern expression—which the party machine built up of him. It was said of Lord Liverpool that the secret of his policy was that he had none. To some extent, this was true of Baldwin also. Protection, 'safe-guarding', defence, above all European problems, did not excite him unduly. He was not a great administrator. He was an influence, and an influence for good. The fact that he commanded the respect and even affection of the Labour Opposition confirmed our admiration for our leader. Nor should it be forgotten that, although marred by the troubles of the coal dispute, leading to the General Strike, and long drawn out after the General Strike was over, the Parliament of 1924–9 was a great constructive Parliament. It marked some of the greatest advances in social and administrative reforms that have ever been made. For these, Baldwin relied on Neville Chamberlain and on Churchill. To both he gave loyal and ungrudging support.

Although I only knew Neville Chamberlain from the back-benches, and scarcely ever had any but the slightest conversation with him, I realised the strength of his convictions and the deter-mination with which he pursued his policies. It is said that when he took over the Ministry of Health in 1924, he wrote down a list of twenty-five Bills which he intended to pass into law during the four or five years that the Parliament might last. Actually he achieved twenty-one of these. He moved firmly along a clearly marked course. He was associated, above all, with the Widows, Orphans and Old Age Pensions Act—one of the foundations of the modern Welfare State—and with the great reforms of local government. He was sympathetic to the demand that local rates should be relieved of some of the heavy burdens which oppressed above all the distressed areas, and in the derating proposals and the block-grant system embodied in the 1929 Local Government Act, he made a spectacu-lar advance towards what are now accepted concepts.

To those who, like myself, did not know him personally, he was a rather forbidding figure. He had a sardonic, not to say con-temptuous, look; his voice was harsh and rasping. Now that I have read the lives that have been written of him, and especially the quotations from his diaries, I realise that underneath this stern exterior was a warm, sympathetic, and sensitive heart. But this was not apparent then to me, or indeed to any but his most intimate friends. One act of real kindness I much valued. In the spring of 1927, some of my friends and I published a little book called *Industry and the State*. It was an unpretentious effort, and I think written with modesty. My co-authors were Bob Boothby, Oliver Stanley, and John Loder. The book was regarded as a manifesto of the progressive wing of our party. It received courteous reviews from all but the Right-wing Press, but caused a good deal of commotion among the die-hards. Very unexpectedly I received a letter from Neville Chamberlain, dated 26 April 1927, of which I will quote the first paragraph:

During the Easter Recess I have been reading *Industry and the State*, and I cannot resist the pleasure of congratulating you and your co-adjutors upon a very suggestive and interesting bit of work. I had observed some reviews which were not very friendly, and I feel, therefore, the more impelled to say that, although I do not profess to agree with everything that you put forward, I see nothing to be shocked at in your suggestions, and a good deal that is, or ought to be, stimulating to Members of the Conservative Party.

He went on to send three pages of closely typed foolscap, dealing one by one with all our proposals. This was a very gracious action, and I naturally expressed my gratitude. But, characteristically, he never sent for me or spoke to me during the rest of the Parliament. As I shall describe, I had one interview which I sought myself, where I was rather coldly received. Neville Chamberlain in this Parliament, as in previous ones, proved himself a true successor to the reforming tradition of England. Some of his ideas went back to those of Disraeli; others to the unauthorised programme of his great father, Joseph Chamberlain. Others followed naturally on the work of social reform which made the Liberal Governments of 1906 onwards so outstanding. His heart was in all this work, which he thoroughly understood. But he did not wear his heart upon his sleeve; on the contrary, he kept it so closely buttoned up behind his formal morning-coat that he was not suspected of anything except a desire for efficiency. In fact, he was inspired by a deep sentiment and feeling for the poor and suffering. Neither the Opposition who disliked him, nor those of our party who admired him, could see behind the mask. Yet in this Parliament he stood out. If Baldwin was by nature indolent, Neville Chamberlain was the most hard-working of men. The troubles of later years should never be allowed to obscure the great achievements of this period.

In the formation of the 1924 Government, Baldwin was able to build an administration rather less lop-sided than that of 1922. There were more commoners and fewer peers. This meant the dropping of some individuals who had stood well by him, such as the Duke of Devonshire, Lord Derby, and Lord Peel. Lord Curzon left the Foreign Office for the honorific post of Lord President. As a result of these changes, three important members of the old Coalition came back—Austen Chamberlain, who became Foreign Secretary, Birkenhead, who went to the India Office, and, most notable of all, Churchill, who was unexpectedly appointed to the Exchequer. In the House of Commons, Austen Chamberlain rarely appeared except for foreign affairs debates. I did not get to know him at all in these years, although I became friendly with him later, when the European scene was dark and threatening. It was cruelly said of Austen Chamberlain that he always played the game and always lost it. But that is really a tribute to his deep sense of honour and loyalty. More than once he could have seized the Premiership had he chosen the road of self-advancement.

Since Baldwin always advised young Members to take a particular group of problems and concentrate on these, and since the situation in my own constituency naturally led me to the study of social, economic, and industrial matters, I excluded foreign affairs from the range of my interest. Two of my friends, Eden and Duff Cooper, on the other hand, 'specialised' on foreign questions, and soon established a high reputation in this field. This meant that I was not brought into contact with Austen Chamberlain. He was, nevertheless, a great House of Commons figure, and we looked up to him as such. In many ways, he recalled the spacious pre-war days. In appearance, costume, method of speech, he seemed almost a survival. His top-hat, his eyeglass, his exquisite courtesy, and his rotund oratory, marked him out from his colleagues. Incidentally, he is the last man whom I have seen to sit in the Speaker's chair as a convenient place from which to listen to a debate. The benches everywhere were crowded, and he could not find a seat. Since, when the House is in Committee, the Speaker's chair is nominally out of the House, it was permissible – and I suppose still is – for anyone to occupy it. But I have never seen anyone try to do so, except Austen. Nor do I think anyone else could have got away with it.

The second important recruit from the eminent Conservatives who had served in the Coalition was Birkenhead. I had a slight acquaintance with him from Oxford days. He had always shown me the greatest kindness whenever I chanced to meet him. If many people expressed disapproval of his dramatic and somewhat flamboyant personality, none could withhold their admiration of his supreme gifts. It was Austen Chamberlain, I think, who said of him that 'he paraded his few defects, but kept hidden his many virtues'. To us young men in the House of Commons, although he occasionally came into the smoking-room, he was rather a distant though notable character. We only heard by rumour the accounts of his special virtue in Cabinet; his wisdom; his moderation; his search for conciliation. This latter quality became well known at the time of the General Strike. But when we were told that a speech from F.E. in the House of Lords was likely to take place, we used to troop along to hear it. I can well remember the still youthful figure, slightly bent, the mellifluous voice, the ease with which – without a note and without a fault – a complicated argument, illuminated by occasional flashes of wit, was unrolled before us. Yet, in this Parliament, his fire was largely spent and his decline was soon to begin. He was to die within a year of its dissolution.

The third, and to us by far the most dramatic of the three old Coalitionists, was of course Churchill – or Winston, as he was universally called by all, friend or foe. It is difficult, with the later knowledge of Churchill's extraordinary life, to put one's mind back to see him as he was in 1924. He was fifty. He had already had a remarkable record, in peace and war. The versatility of his career had shocked some morose critics, who could not bring themselves to believe that in modern times a man could do so many things so well. He had been before the war a most unpopular figure with the party that he had left, and treated with some suspicion by the party that he had joined. The truth is that Churchill never was and never had been, in the true sense, a party man. He would fight the party battle *con amore*, when necessary. But behind these ephemeral struggles, he saw always the vision of the nation. He was proud of its great past and was determined that its future should be no less glorious. Some of the older Members of the party were surprised and even disturbed at his being given the high post of Chancellor of the Exchequer immediately after his return to the party fold. The ardent protectionists were dismayed to find an unrelenting free-trader installed in the inner sanctuary of Treasury Chambers. But as the Parliament proceeded, no one could withhold admiration for the wit, humour, ingenuity, and oratorical skill which he deployed. The Budget speeches were a work of art. None of us had ever heard anything of the kind—such mastery of language, such careful deployment of the arguments, such dexterous covering of any weak point. If, as sometimes happened, a flaw developed and in the later stages of the Finance Bill a retreat had to be made, as for instance in the case of the kerosene tax in 1928, the tactical retirement was brilliantly carried out under cover of a spirited counter-attack.

I had only once met Churchill before this Parliament began. I recall the grace and courtesy with which he spoke to me about my uncle and the kindness which he had shown to him over the publication in 1906 of his first important book, *Lord Randolph Churchill*. As the Parliament proceeded, I was included among his friends. He cultivated the Young Conservatives, whom he regarded as the inheritors of 'Tory Democracy'. One of our number, Boothby, became his Parliamentary Private Secretary. At the later stages of the Parliament, he gave me his confidence in connection with the great derating scheme. As my story unfolds and the years pass, Churchill becomes an increasingly dominating figure. I kept in close touch with him during the long years when he was out of office, and from 1940 I served him in and out of office until his retirement. But I am trying to picture the Churchill of 1924–9: unique, wayward, exciting, a man with a peculiar glamour of his own, that brought a sense of colour into our rather drab political life. Asquith recorded in his diary of October 1915 a conversation with Churchill:

For about a quarter of an hour he poured forth a ceaseless cataract of invective and appeal, and I much regretted that there was no shorthand writer within hearing, as some of his unpremeditated phrases were quite priceless.[1]

How much the world missed over his long life that there was no such automatic Boswell. Many of Churchill's sayings are, of course, repeated and recorded. But it is impossible to describe the effect of the continual flow of his talk. The arresting thoughts were invariably clothed in equally striking phraseology. It is in these years that I had my first taste of a banquet which I was fortunate enough to enjoy for many years on a generous scale.

With Austen Chamberlain as Foreign Secretary, somewhat remote from the House of Commons, with Birkenhead in the Lords, the Conservative Party and Government was dominated by a trio—Baldwin, Neville Chamberlain, Churchill. At that time it seemed likely that if Baldwin were to retire, Churchill would take his place. In that event, history might indeed have been different. Churchill and Chamberlain were known to work closely and harmoniously together in the great programme of social and administrative reform. Yet, as I shall describe, Churchill's dominant position at the Treasury, and his continued faith in free-trade doctrine, ensured that the pledges given by Baldwin at the election were scrupulously maintained. A full tariff policy was to come—but only after something like total economic collapse.

Apart from these, the Ministry included a number of men of importance and ability. Cunliffe-Lister (formerly Lloyd-Greame and afterwards Lord Swinton) was undoubtedly the ablest. I began then with him a friendship which has increased as the years passed. Edward Wood (later Lord Halifax) was sympathetic and charming. Ormsby-Gore (later Lord Harlech), Walter Elliot, Eustace Percy, all had comprehensive and receptive minds. The last two we looked to as specially favourable to the views we were trying to develop.

In the early months of the first session I joined a group of young Members, most of whom had entered Parliament for the first time. They were known as the Young Conservatives and given the nickname of 'Y.M.C.A.'. In fact, like all these groups, it had no

[1] The Earl of Oxford and Asquith, *Memories and Reflections*, vol. ii (London, 1928), p. 46.

strict membership nor any specially defined doctrine. Duff Cooper, like Eden, confined himself mainly to foreign affairs. Perhaps those who worked most consistently together were Noel Skelton, Oliver Stanley, John Loder, Rob Hudson, Boothby, and later Terence O'Connor. These were the core; but others came and went, or were vaguely attached. Undoubtedly, the most striking mind and real intellectual leader of our little company was Noel Skelton. It was he who developed and occasionally published in short but intensely interesting pamphlets the philosophy of the new Toryism.[1] A little older than most of us, he commanded not only our affection but our respect. His early death was a grievous loss. Had he lived, it is hard to say what would have been his career in politics. But his influence on politics and political thinking must have grown steadily year by year. Of all the friends of those years whom I most admired, and whom I missed most afterwards, Noel Skelton is the chief.

In strong opposition to us and to all our ideas were some of the older Members, largely survivors of the 1918 Coalitionists, whom we irreverently dubbed 'the Forty Thieves'. The kinder commentators in the Press referred to them as 'the Industrials'. Among them were some very agreeable characters, as well as some very intelligent and distinguished men. But to our young and enthusiastic minds they represented the forces of reaction.

Connected with, but not part of, the Industrials were the political die-hards, survivors from the great pre-war struggles, and destined to be Baldwin's chief opponents in the fight over the leadership in 1930. The leader of these was Colonel Gretton, a man of real kindliness but a somewhat forbidding aspect. His drooping moustache, his heavy spectacles, and his rather sinister appearance made some lover of Sherlock Holmes christen him Professor Moriarty. The name stuck.

Another group to which I belonged was mainly social in character; it was led by Colonel Spender-Clay, a man of moderate and reasonable opinions, and a general favourite. We dined together, sometimes by ourselves, sometimes with a guest to speak to us—a Minister, a Civil Servant, or an economist. This group had no

[1] The earliest of these, *Constructive Conservatism*, was published in September 1924 and had a great effect on all the younger Members of the party.

specially political character. It was neither Right nor Left. It nevertheless had a considerable importance. It could be relied on in general terms to stand in favour of a moderate approach to any problem, personal or political.

Presiding over this House of Commons, with the mixture of individuals and groupings that I have described, was our genial 'headmaster', Mr. Speaker Whitley. I have sat under five Speakers. Captain Fitzroy ruled the House with a severe discipline which was accepted because he was absolutely fair. But he was rather frightening. Colonel Clifton-Brown charmed the House and managed with remarkable skill the difficult Parliament that followed the Second War. 'Shakes' Morrison, with his splendid presence and deep Scottish voice—which all Englishmen love—governed by wit as well as dignity. Hylton-Foster displayed while I served under him similar qualities. For Whitley, my first Speaker, I had the affectionate regard which any young Member feels for a Speaker who treats him with sympathy and understanding. He seemed always to enter into the anxieties of unimportant back-benchers sitting through long hours of debate waiting hopefully to be called. If, at last, five or ten minutes could be spared during the dinner-hour, with not more than a dozen Members in the House, Mr. Speaker, whether in the chair himself or perhaps later on his return, would somehow make one feel that he had been glad to help. Some said he was a weak Speaker. But all Government Whips say that about Speakers, who very properly protect the Opposition and the minorities in the House. Mr. Whitley was a kindly Speaker. It was characteristic of him that he devoted so much of his time in the period following the First War to the cause of industrial peace. He has left his memorial in the joint industrial councils which were instituted under his chairmanship and, in popular parlance, still bear his name.

CHAPTER SEVEN

Life in the Twenties

THE twenties were a period in which we could look with some confidence to stability and progress. If the conditions in the depressed areas were worsening, yet in these same areas the war years had been boom years, with high wages and high savings. In the rest of the country business was on the whole good. New industries were rapidly coming into being. This was the beginning of the great drift of population, reversing that of the previous century. Many of the unemployed, especially young men and women, moved from the North into the Midlands and the South. The great trek had begun. But since unemployment and depression were largely limited to certain areas, throughout the country in general in every class actual standards of life were rising. Although taxation seemed, and was, high by pre-war standards, we should think it low today. Income tax, 6s. in the pound in 1920, was steadily reduced and for the last five years of the decade was at 4s. in the pound. Surtax never rose, even in the higher-income groups, to the confiscatory level established during the Second War and still largely effective. If wages and salaries were modest, so was the cost of living. All through this period commodity prices were falling. But as the cost of living fell, so the rate of unemployment rose. Nevertheless, to those in employment or living on fixed incomes the low cost of living was a real benefit. For the upper and upper middle classes the comfort of living, if not quite so high as in the Edwardian and early Georgian times, was still considerable. Personal service, now almost unobtainable by those of moderate means and gradually becoming so even for those with large incomes, was part of the common way of life. There were over a million people, mostly women, in domestic service. A very high proportion, certainly three-quarters, perhaps more, were engaged as the only servant employed, and therefore working in quite simple households. Those of a little larger income might have two or three domestic servants. Even in homes which would now seem of modest pretensions, there might be five or six. Richer people, but still by no means in the highest income group, would employ more. In the great houses, there would be, of course, any number up to twenty or thirty. Wages were low, in terms of money; but in terms of actual earnings, including board, food, and so forth, the rewards were sufficient to attract among the general body of domestic servants a continuous supply and, among the élite, an almost hereditary recruitment.

In the life of a normal family of the upper and upper middle classes, the centre of the household was undoubtedly 'Nanny'. Our Nanny, Mrs. Last, had come soon after my eldest brother was born. When I married more than thirty years later she was housekeeper to my mother. By her decision and with my mother's agreement, she took charge of our affairs. For the first few years of our married life she managed us with a strict rigidity and relentless economy. I can see her now, unchanging in appearance or in dress, tiny but domineering, affectionate but firm. When I was a child, our first visit on coming home from school was always to her room. She exercised the same attraction over my children. After some years of living with us she retired, but remained a loved and respected friend. Happily for us, in my own family the same story of devotion has been repeated. Our Nanny, Mrs. West, came to us in 1921 when our eldest child, Maurice, was born. Though retired, she still lives with us in a cottage at the end of the garden, which is the centre of the life of many children and grandchildren.

Long service, therefore, was a rule rather than an exception in most houses. Nor did this appear to depend necessarily either upon pay or conditions. There was a personal tie between the 'master' or 'mistress' and the servants, which was more than the economic link which modern writers would have us believe. It was based upon a real intimacy and much private talk, fortified no doubt by a great deal of gossip and scandal, delightful morsels, shared equally and generously.

My mother kept both indoor and outdoor servants, in spite of the high standards she demanded, for many years. We had, for instance, the same head gardener from 1906 till 1935, when he died and was replaced by the second gardener. Since gardeners' wages were low, five or six men would cost scarcely more than one today. The coachmen had, of course, in the twenties made way for the 'chauffeurs'—strange gallicism that had crept into our language. These fell into two distinct classes: the 'Henry Strakers', that is to say, the young modern and up-to-date mechanics, usually in a blue suit with only a cap as a concession to uniform; then the other class, the fat ex-coachmen who dressed themselves as nearly as possible to look like liveried servants with leather leggings and long coats, who sat at the wheel of a car very much as on the box of a carriage, urging on a recalcitrant and sometimes refractory machine with encouraging cries. I almost believe that when they cleaned the car in the mews they still had a straw in their mouths, and hissed as they rubbed it down.

The houses these families lived in were large by modern standards —often rambling and inconvenient. Nevertheless, when there were many children, they were admirably suited to the stresses of family life. It is true that they had few of the comforts that are now regarded as essential. In the great houses the bath was steadily, but by no means universally, making its way. When my father-in-law inherited Chatsworth in 1909 there was only one bathroom in that vast palace. Where greater progress had been possible or insisted upon, the bathroom had not yet been elevated to the high position which it now occupies. Nor did every guest expect a bathroom under his own control. You stood in the passage, and waited your turn. But the great advantage of the houses in which we and our friends lived was, broadly speaking, the possibility of escape. Even in our old house, before my father rebuilt it, there were always separate rooms for me and my brothers to work in. In those days, whether at school or university, the hardest and most continuous study was done in the holidays or vacations. I remember well a schedule of seven or even eight hours a day's reading at home. This would have been impossible unless one had a room, however small, away from the main stream of family life. I am sometimes lost in admiration for the way in which young people now seem to have learnt the art of concentration against all the competitive noises of television, radio, gramophone, or a rowdy game among the smaller children. It must be a cause of great strain. However, in the twenties we still had 'a room of our own'.

The fall in the price-level and the moderate taxes made it possible, in this period, for the rich to think in terms of restoring, with certain modifications, more or less pre-war life. It was equally practicable for those of moderate incomes to think in terms of substantial comfort. For the employed, in every class, it was reasonable to hope to raise their standards progressively and meanwhile to live well enough in terms of real wages and earnings. In an epoch in which the whole situation has been reversed, it is difficult to realise that the great industrial disputes of these years were concerned not with the raising of wages, but with their reduction. The coal stoppage, which led to the General Strike and was continued for many months after the General Strike, was dominated by the economic need to reduce the cost of production (of which wages were the most important item), in order to meet the conditions of a falling market. Many similar readjustments had to be made, sometimes by agreement and sometimes only after great and painful conflicts. Indeed, the economists of the day recognised the need for what was called 'readjustment'. The great argument against the return to gold at parity, which was put forward by the unorthodox economists, was that it would be a much simpler readjustment to alter the value of money than to try and reduce everybody's wages, industry by industry. That real wages had to be reduced was accepted. The only question was: should it be done by detailed negotiation or by a single act of currency depreciation? Nevertheless, in these years, for those employed, whether wage- or salary-earners, for those enjoying incomes, whether earned or unearned, there seemed no reason to look with anything except a quiet confidence, in spite of some anxieties and dangers, to a prospect of increasing stability.

The educational system remained on familiar lines. In popular education, advances were made as the older schools were pulled down and better schools substituted. Secondary education became steadily, though not dramatically, extended. Among our own friends and relations, boys normally went, as they still do, to residential preparatory schools and then to public schools. In the 1920s, girls from similar homes began to go to school, except perhaps among the families of the 'grandees' where the 'schoolroom' or the sharing of lessons was still thought more appropriate. Broadly speaking, all upper- and upper-middle-class boys were sent away for their education. Certain great families, by tradition, opted out of this opportunity—the Russells, perhaps, being the most notable. Whether the result was good or bad, I would not care to judge. In general, however, all of what I suppose would now be called 'the Establishment' went to public schools. I have never thought this was really a dangerous class distinction. No doubt, the 'old school tie' has done a lot of harm by the suspicion that it has become an instrument of nepotism. Yet many of those who are now strongly anti-public-school have been themselves the beneficiaries—or victims—of the system. From time to time, the ruling classes in any democratic country are invaded by a sort of political 'Buchmanism'. They think it necessary to get up and explain to the world how useless and sinful they are and how anti-social are the institutions which have nurtured them. In fact, the chief difference between boys who have gone away to school and those who have remained at home is the effect of separation from their parents. A boy who has left home at the age of eight or nine, and from that age onwards until he leaves university is not at home for more than a few weeks at Christmas, Easter, and the summer, is forced into a certain independence of spirit. He is thrown into the stream at a tender age, to sink or swim. Some undoubtedly sink, either disappearing altogether or destined to turn up from time to time either in the police courts or as members of extreme and subversive movements. But on the whole the great majority in one way or another manage to strike out for themselves. This early development of self-reliance is the main difference between the boy living at home during his education and the boy who has the chance to leave at a very early age, escaping thereby the indifference of selfish or the devotion of affectionate parents, both of which can be equally disturbing. Whether this distinction, not of class but of experience, should remain will, no doubt, soon be decided. At the time of which I was speaking, the general mood would have favoured extending this privilege rather than destroying it.

These reflections may seem disappointing to my readers who would believe English life in the twenties to have been both hectic and vicious. There were, of course, a number of different groups or cliques. There was a section fostered largely by the illustrated papers, claiming to constitute something that, in the old language of snobs, was called 'Society'. Their membership was indeterminate, and included men and women of high distinction on one hand and the 'hangers-on' and 'tuft-hunters' (heirs to Thackeray's favourite butts) on the other. Then there was a group whose method of living appears to have been accurately and dramatically described in the novels of Evelyn Waugh. But younger critics and historians would be unwise to take these characters as typical, if indeed any of them ever existed. There were certainly what were called 'the Bright Young Things', who seemed only to be putting into effect new variations on a very old theme. This fashion had begun many centuries before, and was called 'beating up the watch'. Now its chief purpose was to shock respectable people, especially parents. Success was assured if some brawl drew down the rebuke of a magistrate or an editor. Then there was the racing world—as indeed there is still—and the show world, the political world, and the literary and artistic world. These groups often intermingled; yet, broadly, the social life of the twenties did not differ very substantially from the pre-war structure.

My own family and background I have tried to describe in an earlier chapter. It continued along the same lines. In publishing, apart from the purely mechanical and business problems, with which my brother and I found ourselves dealing more and more as the older partners began to withdraw from active management, there was also the interest of personal contact with our chief authors. Rudyard Kipling I met from time to time, either at a club or by his calling in at the office to see me on some point. Two or three times I went to Bateman's, his house in Sussex. He did no business in the strict sense of the word. All this was done for him by Mrs. Kipling or his literary agent, Mr. Watt. But he would occasionally like to get advice about such things as illustrations and format. He was very reserved, and always seemed to me a somewhat sad figure. Partly, this was due to the death of his only son in the war. I remember the devotion which he gave to his history of the Irish

Guards, as a tribute to his son's memory. But by the time I knew Kipling, he had retired from the world. Occasionally, he would lunch at the Beefsteak or dine at Grillions, where he would sometimes talk freely. He was still the supreme journalist, always interested in the master of any craft or the hero of an exciting adventure. He treated me with kindness and courtesy; but he did not unbutton himself.

Of Thomas Hardy I have only one or two memories. I went occasionally to call on him at his house in Dorset on some minor matter. He was rosy-cheeked like an apple; and one felt he had the slight acidity of a good Cox's Pippin. My uncle, Sir Frederick Macmillan, was fond of telling a story of going to lunch with him during these years. At the end of his life Hardy, who in his youth and middle age had been neglected by the general public and only appealed to selected readers, by becoming old had also become fashionable. The occupants of some of the great houses round the humble home where he lived tried to 'take him up'. This was encouraged by Mrs. Hardy for one reason, and not altogether discouraged by Thomas Hardy for another. He had a sly humour of his own. On one such occasion, there was a small party to lunch in his little dining-room at Max Gate, including one or two ladies of high rank. One of these, sitting next to Hardy, leant over and said to him in rather a gushing way, 'Oh, Mr. Hardy, dear Mr. Hardy, tell us about Tess. Tell us what Tess meant to you.' Hardy called across to my uncle at the other end of the table: 'Lady Blank wants to know about Tess. What shall I say? Anyway, Tess has been a good milch cow to you and me, Fred!'

With Hugh Walpole I formed an intimate friendship. I looked after the publication of his highly successful novels, and saw him frequently. He is out of fashion now; but he wrote a good story in a good sound style. He was very sensitive, especially to criticism from his fellow authors; but beneath this strange jealousy and lack of confidence, he was kind and thoughtful of others, a delightful companion and a loyal friend.

Charles Morgan was a close friend of my brother, Daniel, but I saw a good deal of him too. I found his grave dignity and delicacy attractive. His writing has always appealed to French even more than to British critics and readers. The French have also been more loyal to his memory.

Yeats used to come in unannounced to my room in St. Martin's Street. I can recall his splendid figure, his tie flowing through a fine ring, his somewhat dramatised appearance of the poet and dreamer. But he was also a practical man, and by no means despised the mundane problems of publishing.

The Irish school was well represented in our list. The older ones included George Russell ('Æ'), who often headed his letters with a charming water-colour drawing, some of which I now have. James Stephens, the author of *The Crock of Gold*, was himself like a leprechaun. He was fond of stealing unannounced into the room in which I sat. He would half open the door, put his head round the corner, and only if suitably encouraged could be persuaded to follow it with his body. It is a sad thing that the ease with which he could earn a living on the radio and journalism discouraged him in his later years from serious writing. When I used to urge him to do another book, he would reply, 'Why should I write when I can be paid for talking?' Among my greatest friends in this group was Sean O'Casey. He and his talented wife used to come to stay with us in Sussex, and I watched with growing delight his rise to fame. Although he claimed to be a Communist and, I think, an atheist, his was a truly Christian nature; one of the kindest and most genuine men that I have known. He and Ronald Knox—in their very different ways—were saintly men.

Our life then, whether at Chester Square or at Birch Grove House —where my wife and I and our children would stay for long periods with my parents and which we sometimes borrowed from them when they returned to Cadogan Place—were years of a varied and agreeable social life, as well as very hard work at business and politics. We had many political and literary friends, and I went a good deal to Eton and Oxford. At Oxford especially I had the links of intimacy with Urquhart and Humphrey Sumner. But naturally, with our growing family, with my wife's deep love of children, and with the pressure of other calls upon us, we took no very active part in entertaining or being entertained for its own sake. This rather withdrawn attitude presented no difficulty to us. Her family tradition has never been what is called 'smart'. Successive Dukes, according to their own temperament, had had varied interests, but all had centred upon the life of the countryside or industry, and in general the duties of great proprietors. Politics also was in their blood, and they and their children took almost automatically an active part in political life. They had too, as a family, a sincere respect for learning. The same was true of the Duchess's family. I remember a visit soon after we were married to Bowood, where my wife's grandfather, old Lord Lansdowne, was spending his declining years. He had served in and resigned from Gladstone's administration in the 1880s. He had been Governor-General of Canada and Viceroy of India. He had been Secretary of State for War and Foreign Secretary in the Unionist Governments of the early 1900s, and the chief designer of the 'Entente Cordiale' with France. He had held office in Asquith's first Coalition Government in the war. He had been subjected to bitter criticism for the Lansdowne Letter, published in 1917, raising, if not definitely advocating, the possibilities of peace before Europe destroyed itself. Now he was an old man. I can see him still, sitting in his famous library, turning over the leaves of a beautifully printed and bound edition of one of the classics. Living very quietly with one or two guests, mostly of his own family, he retained to the end the appearance and character of a *grand seigneur*. In accordance with the Whig tradition he was ready to grasp new and radical ideas. But they were still cast in ancient forms. One custom particularly delighted us at Bowood. It was a sort of survival of the former *fêtes champêtres*. Lady Lansdowne ('Granny Maud' as she was called by her grandchildren) would ask the guests after breakfast whether they would like a picnic lunch as a change if 'Daddy Clan' (Lord Lansdowne) thought it would be fine enough. On his approval being given, the arrangements were made. On the first occasion I assumed that this would entail a walk or drive, by car or carriage, and perhaps an uncomfortable but agreeable lunch in a wood or on the side of a hill. As the hours of morning passed I began to wonder what was going to happen. At one o'clock we were ready to start, and the little company walked about two or three hundred yards from the house to the lake. At the lakeside was a boat-house, and a kind of chalet or summer-house, built in rustic style. The luncheon had been carried down; the tables were arranged with the same silver and glass and napery as would have been used in the house. The butler and one or two footmen were there to serve. In fact, the 'picnic' was no different from an ordinary lunch, except that we had ventured a few hundred yards from the mansion and sat above the boat-house. After luncheon and all the suitable wines had been served and coffee drunk, we processed back to the house. The great expedition had taken place. This was not to say that Lord Lansdowne had not been a most adventurous sportsman, both in youth and middle age. But this old man's substitute for an outing I found rather touching.

Perhaps in all the year the great period to which we most looked forward was Christmas. At first we spent these alternately with my parents at Birch Grove House or with my wife's family at Chatsworth. But as our children grew in number and age, and my parents saw how much my wife looked forward to the yearly reunion with her scattered family, my father and mother unselfishly pressed us to go to Chatsworth for Christmas, and come to them at other times. The Chatsworth Christmas parties were certainly memorable. To remember them now is to recall another world, almost as remote from present-day England as the descriptions of Count Rostov's family in *War and Peace*.

Christmas at Chatsworth was conducted on traditional lines. Every year was the same, except for the increasing number of children. By the end of the decade these had become a formidable array. The Devonshires' own family consisted, in addition to the Duke and Duchess, of two sons and five daughters, all married. A day or two before the festival, these began to arrive from different parts of the country. The average number of children in each family was about four. These, with their attendant nurses and nursery-maids, amounted therefore to something like fifty souls. Then there were the lady's-maids and valets, bringing the total to at least sixty. In addition there were other guests; sometimes my father and mother or other grandparents; sometimes 'Great-Granny Maud'—the Dowager Lady Lansdowne. There were others, too, who came year after year, by long-established custom. There were generally two or three cousins of the Duke's or Duchess's. In addition, there

was Mr. Erskine, Deputy Serjeant at Arms, the son of the great
Serjeant at Arms who had been a lifelong friend of the Cavendishes;
and Mr. Mansfield. These two last had been Christmas guests from
the times before the Duke succeeded, when he lived at Holker Hall,
in Lancashire. They always called the Duchess 'Lady Evie', as a
kind of hallmark of long-established friendship. They were reputed
intimate cronies of the Duke; he certainly treated them with more
than his usual taciturnity. 'Hello Jim', 'Hello Walter', he would say
when they arrived and 'Goodbye Jim' and 'Goodbye Walter' when
they left. So far as I know, no other conversation passed between
them. My much-loved sister-in-law, now Mary, Dowager Duchess,
came from a very different home and background. At first, I think,
she found the long silences of the Cavendishes somewhat trying; for
she was a Cecil and Cecils talk all the time about everything under
the sun, with animated and fiercely contested verbal combats. The
Duke did not like argument.

With all these Christmas visitors and their attendants, together
with the permanent and temporary servants in the household, the
number gathered under that vast roof must have been something
like one hundred and fifty people. The children, of course, delighted
in this strange and exciting world. They were spoilt and pampered
by the servants and made many long friendships with them. It was
always a new pleasure to be conducted through the great kitchens,
the huge pantries, the larders with their stone floors and vaulted
roofs; above all, the great building, larger than many butchers'
shops, where hung rows of carcasses of oxen and sheep, and game of
every kind. Many of the families, including my own, arrived with
their ponies. So the stables were a continual source of interest to be
visited, each string of animals being accompanied by their attendant
grooms. One special treat was to be taken through the plate-rooms.
Here was kept, in the care of an old retired under-butler, a great
collection, much of it dating from the seventeenth and eighteenth
centuries. The beautiful William and Mary dressing-sets were there;
and in addition, the gold plate. On certain occasions, at Christmas or
at other great parties, the best of the plate was shown in the dining-
room. But for the most part, except for the pieces in daily use, these
treasures were kept in the vigilant care of their devoted guardian.

The ritual did not differ from year to year. All assembled the day before. As each family arrived, 'Granny Evie' received them at the top of the stairs where the Outer Hall led into the passage leading to the great Painted Hall. My children still remember her greeting each family in turn—always in her place, as the cars passed the lodge—a gracious and dignified figure, dressed in dark colours and long flowing dresses, never changing. Shy and reserved as she was, with the children, like the Duke, she had no inhibitions. The sons-in-law, of course, soon learnt the desirability of sending their families by the early train, and ensuring sufficient important business in London to make it necessary for them to follow later and more comfortably.

Christmas Eve in this, as in every other home throughout the land, was a flurry of mothers filling and hanging stockings, decorating nurseries, and getting to bed very late themselves. All this is still carried on in a modified form in my own home as, happily, in many other houses. Children and grandchildren gather yearly for the great festival.

Christmas Day. Early to church at eight o'clock across the park in the darkness; then breakfast and the morning with the enjoyment of minor presents. Balloons to be inflated, trumpets to be blown, and roller-skates to be tried out. No house is better fitted for roller-skating. The whole course is good, with particularly fast going on the stone floor of the Statue Gallery and the Orangery. Then Matins at the parish church in the park, with a full and overflowing congregation; all the familiar hymns; and a mercifully short sermon. The clergyman likes to be asked to shoot, and the Duke, though he says little, has a good memory. Christmas lunch, to which children over a certain age were allowed—the rules strictly enforced—and then the photograph. In those days the ingenious methods by which these can be taken indoors had not been invented. We all trooped out to a particularly cold and draughty part of the garden—by Flora's Temple, outside the Orangery. When at last all the generations could be brought into some kind of order, the yearly photograph was taken. Each year showed a steady increase and, happily, no casualties—not yet. A walk in the garden followed, which was supposed to be healthy and after the Christmas cheer was no doubt salutary.

One of the old traditions of Chatsworth scrupulously maintained was Evensong every Sunday in the house chapel. Those who know Chatsworth will remember the great beauty of this masterpiece of late seventeenth-century work, with its lovely altar and the fine ceiling. The village organist and choir came up for the service. Two rows of straight Jacobean chairs stood facing each other. On one side were the men; on the other the women. When the house was full, with all the guests, servants, and visiting servants, there was a goodly company. The service always ended with the same hymn, called the Benediction hymn, sung kneeling:

> Father give us now Thy Blessing,
> Take us now beneath Thy care;
> May we all enjoy Thy presence,
> And Thy tender mercies share.
>
> .   .   .
>
> Guard us through this night from danger,
> Keep us in Thy heavenly love;
> Through our life do Thou be near us,
> Then receive us all above.

Its origin is unknown.

The weather at Chatsworth was of two kinds and both in an extreme form. Sometimes the glass was low and the temperature mild. Then it was dark, rainy, foggy, and uninviting. Or there could be a high glass, with snow and ice and tobogganing and skating. These were the Christmases I remember with the keenest pleasure— the beauty of the great trees in the garden and park, and the house shining with a strangely golden glow in the rays of the low winter sun. The weather played an important part in the daily routine. Following a custom of many generations, every day at breakfast there was placed on one of the splendid Kent side-tables a book recording the temperature, the hours of sunshine, and the rainfall, compiled by one of the gardeners. The Duke studied this every morning, carefully, but without emotion.

After tea on Christmas Day came the ceremony of presents given and received. This took place in the Statue Gallery, where stood the huge tree. First, all the presents to the servants, taken round by the children; then presents from children to grown-ups; then, at last, the childrens' own presents from all their different relations. They were perhaps not so expensive or so elaborate as they are today, but with the enormous family interchange, they were very numerous.

Boxing Day. Children who survived (there were always some casualties to colds or over-excitement) went off to the meet of the High Peak Harriers at Bakewell. At this time my sister-in-law Maud Baillie and her husband Evan were the Joint Masters. It was a great gathering of local sportsmen, including many children, coming from far and wide. There was no shooting on Boxing Day so that all the men on the place could enjoy their holiday. For those who did not hunt it was, therefore, a day of sleep, or bridge, or reading. During the next few days there was shooting—and good shooting—and then some of the older members of the party began to disperse. But the mothers and children generally stayed on for two or three weeks, the fathers returning each weekend for more shooting. At last, reluctantly, but with a sense of great achievement, this large family party came to an end until the next year.

In one year, as my wife reminds me, what she regards as the highest peak of felicity was reached—there were fourteen children under four in the nursery. Cavendishes have always liked children. The old Duke, after his illness, became, except on rare occasions, gruff, unapproachable, even morose. But with children, especially little children, he was just the same as in old days. They were not afraid of him, and teased him, and took no notice of his disabilities. In return, he loved them dearly and spoilt them all. He even forgave them when they tripped over his gouty foot.

To go home to London or Sussex was almost as great an undertaking as to set out upon the Christmas journey. In addition to the quantities of luggage which everyone took about in those days, there were all the presents. One year, with rare unselfishness, I had agreed to travel back with my family. In addition to everything else— children; nurses; servants; ponies; dogs; toys (mechanical and otherwise); luggage—we brought back with us a gift to my eldest daughter —a little pig. It was the runt of a litter on the home farm and had been given her by her dear friend, Mr. Shimwell, who managed almost everything at Chatsworth. It lived a long time in our nursery in Sussex where it proved a clean, intelligent, and in every way desirable pet. It followed its mistress about everywhere with dog-like devotion. It once fell into the bathing-pool and I acquired a high reputation among the children for courage, by jumping in and saving its life. Alas, it grew at last too big; and one day, when the children were away, it disappeared—I hope to an honoured grave.

I have given this picture, by no means unique, of the old family life. It continues no doubt today, with the same happy mixture of a religious and a family festival every succeeding Christmas throughout the land. But its celebration, on this patriarchal scale, is necessarily a thing of the past and so perhaps worth recalling.

These Chatsworth gatherings lasted throughout all this decade and well into the next—indeed, until after the Duke's death in 1938. Chatsworth is still, happily, a private home and if anything more beautiful in my niece's hands than even my mother-in-law was able to make it. Some of its treasures have, alas, been swallowed into the insatiable jaws of the death-duties. But much remains. Indeed, by the closing of the great houses at Hardwick and Compton Place, and by the sale of Devonshire House, in Piccadilly, Chatsworth has gained; for many of the best pictures and furniture from these collections are now concentrated there. Many people suppose that it is only since the last war that these historic houses have been on view to visitors. This is an error. As readers of *Pride and Prejudice* will remember, Chatsworth Park has always been open to the public. Chatsworth House was equally open to visitors three or four days a week through all the spring, summer, and early autumn months. Indeed, according to records, it is remarkable how many visitors came even before the days of motor-cars and motor-coaches. For instance, in one year in the nineteenth century, nearly 80,000 came. Now well over a quarter of a million people come each year, and admirable provision is made, not merely for casual tourists, but for the care and comfort of scholars who may wish to study in detail the pictures, the drawings, the books, and the manuscripts. As I write, Chatsworth lives on under the loving care of its present owners. Nevertheless, with all its beauty, it has changed from the Chatsworth I remember. It is, necessarily, more of a museum, though it is still a home.

A particular feature of political life in this period, and indeed extending right up to the Second War, was entertainment both on a large and on a small scale. This took place in London continuously during the Parliamentary sessions, sometimes in the large houses like Lady Salisbury's, Lady Londonderry's, Lady Astor's, Lord Derby's, and the like; but sometimes in small houses such as ours. We all lunched and dined a great deal together. Today this is much more difficult, and the restaurant or club has had to be substituted for the home. Or that abomination, the cocktail party, which allows of no real conversation, has—necessarily—become the substitute for the great evening assemblies. These changes are more important than they would seem at first sight, for the leaders of the party and other political hostesses, as well as many Members, regarded it as a duty as well as a pleasure to entertain their colleagues and their wives either upon a large or a small scale. In this way we all got to know each other; and the life of a Member, and especially a Member's wife, was both agreeable and interesting. Moreover, these continual meetings for talk and argument went on in a less formal manner than is now possible. In addition, the country houses —Hatfield, Cliveden, and many others—were the almost weekly scene of gatherings of all kinds of people—politicians, artists, authors, bankers, diplomats—who could meet in easy circumstances without formality. Indeed, there was nothing so agreeable as the country-house party in a large English house. There were no rules except the necessity of appearing at dinner and a certain bias in favour of turning up at lunch. Otherwise, in a large company the groups organised themselves for golf, tennis, walking, talking, or quiet reading.

A great deal of harsh criticism has been written about the so-called 'Cliveden Set'. Although this belongs really to the next period of which I am to write, much that has been alleged by ignorant writers is exaggerated or untrue. My wife and I were frequent guests at Cliveden and at St. James's Square, and received much kindness from Nancy Astor. She had two sides to her character. She was a deeply religious woman of the highest principles and genuine love for all her fellow-creatures. She was also the most loyal of friends, always ready to help, with warmth and affection. At the same time, she was ardent to support any cause which she thought might benefit humanity. On the other side, she was a great hostess, although perhaps too indiscriminate in her invitations. At her house in St. James's Square, or at Cliveden, one might meet, and did meet, every conceivable kind of person. Like many others before and after, she pursued, perhaps too fervently, the notabilities of the day. Nevertheless, she contributed much to the amusement and entertainment of her guests. Most of them argued; some were argued at. Certainly, in the years immediately before the Second War, men like Lord Lothian, Neville Chamberlain, Geoffrey Dawson (editor of *The Times*), and Tom Jones, who were frequent visitors, were 'appeasers'. Readers of Tom Jones's diaries will realise the significance of their activities. They, no doubt, had the sympathy of the Astors for their policies at this critical time. Nevertheless, their houses were an open forum, and bitter arguments, for and against, were encouraged, and all kinds of divergent views were freely expressed.

One other family I must recall for their special kindness to us. Wynyard is but five miles from Stockton-on-Tees. All the years that I was Member for Stockton, Lord and Lady Londonderry made us feel that it was a second home. We used it as we liked, and we seemed always to be welcome. There, too, there were often great parties of all kinds of people representing every walk of life. Edie Londonderry ('Circe' as she was to the special group of friends, of which I was proud to be one, whom she admitted to her Ark) had greater vitality than anyone I have ever known. She had, no doubt, faults; but I prefer to remember only her great qualities. Perhaps the greatest of all was her loyalty. Her friendship and confidence, once given, were lasting and immutable. In the normal ups and downs of life, one gets accustomed to the fact that there are some people—even some 'great people'—who unconsciously act as convenient barometers of one's political fortunes. When one's stock is low, one is conscious of not being altogether welcome. As it rises, so does the warmth of one's reception. That was not true of the Londonderrys. All through the long years that I sat on the back-benches, although I found myself in growing opposition to the policy of the leaders of the party and even renounced the Whip, Charlie and Edie Londonderry remained absolutely the same to me. She was a good and staunch friend throughout. When I became Prime Minister, she told me that she was pleased but not surprised. But I did not forget her friendship during the bad times.

The outward conditions of life have changed so rapidly in recent times that is has seemed worth while recalling some of these memories of the past. I frankly enjoyed, in the short holidays that I could take from business and politics, all the pleasures and amusements of the period. I confess that very often the transition from a few days at Stockton among my poor unemployed, to the various degrees of comfort and wealth which we all either commanded or enjoyed, left me with a growing sense of the great gulf. If much that was good and generous in the old way of life has passed away, it is comforting to reflect that these wide differences have been so largely closed in my lifetime. But the gap is surely better bridged by liberal and fertile acts of statesmanship to raise the level of the many, than by jealous and malicious policies that concentrate on pulling down the few.

CHAPTER EIGHT

The Parliament of 1924–9

THE nineteen-twenties were a time of general optimism, and rightly so. In spite of the many baffling problems at home and abroad, there seemed no reason to doubt that the evolutionary processes which had served us so well in the past would continue to operate in the future. At home a Coalition had fallen; a Conservative Government had followed; a Labour Government had come into power for the first time. The advent of the last had been dreaded by many. But it turned out to be anything but a revolutionary affair. If it had made some executive muddles for which it was rightly punished, it had by no means reduced the stature or reputation of Britain overseas. The Prime Minister, who acted also as Foreign Secretary, was respected and admired in Europe. Even the underlying economic and industrial problems weighed on different parts of the country with varying degrees of intensity. Apart from shipbuilding and the heavy industries, which had been so rapidly expanded in war and were now in serious difficulties, there was much activity and a high rate of employment and profit in many new and developing enterprises. The adverse trade balance, though not altogether satisfactory, was not yet seriously amiss. We were entering the last stages of the long journey of the return of Britain to the gold standard, to which orthodox bankers and economists had looked forward so long. Other countries had taken or were about to take the same step.

Members like myself, who were brought into close contact with the areas of depression, were not unnaturally led into rather a jaundiced view of the whole scene. But more balanced observers were conscious of the feeling of confidence which prevailed. Changes, of course, there had been, and must be, since the Great War. There would never be a return to the pre-war life in its old form.

But these changes, whether of social custom or of the balance of political power, did not seem any greater than those which had been cheerfully and successfully surmounted by the nation in the hundred years since the first Reform Bill. The fundamental and almost revolutionary alterations of which I must trace the course over a period of fifty years were still obscured. America, politically and militarily, had retired from the world, or certainly from Europe. She was, nevertheless, playing an important, if often vacillating, part in the various efforts to resolve, or at least ameliorate, the evils which followed from the Peace and, above all, from the tangle of reparations and inter-governmental debts. Russia was still an enigma. The Labour Government had a kind of sentimental feeling for the Soviets which led them first to *de jure* recognition and then to proposals for a loan. But this policy had led to rather discouraging results. Great as was the part that Russia was destined to play, her future, to ordinary folk at any rate, was still wrapped in mystery.

The Empire seemed rather strengthened than weakened. Although the independent status of each self-governing nation accepted in the Imperial Conference of 1926 would soon be formally defined in legislation, yet the great structure remained firm. The task of devising a constitution for India would be difficult but not unmanageable. The Colonial Empire was moving quietly but calmly on its evolutionary path. As for defence, it was a period of strict economy. Churchill, as Chancellor of the Exchequer, in effect reverted to the attitude he had adopted in 1908–11 when, in company with Lloyd George, he vehemently opposed McKenna's determination to lay down the extra Dreadnoughts. In this Parliament, Churchill's motive was the same as it had been sixteen years before. But because it is a policy not commonly associated with him, it is worth, perhaps, recalling his arguments. On each occasion he felt that armaments were wasteful of public money better spent on social reform. Long afterwards, Churchill had the candour to admit that McKenna had been entirely right about the Dreadnoughts before the First War. But it may reasonably have appeared to him in 1924 that the situation was wholly different. As I have described, the foreign position abroad seemed greatly improved. With Italy friendly, France co-operative, and Germany apparently in a state of impotence, the only potential enemy at the time seemed to be Japan. Churchill had not been in office more than a month before seeking from the Foreign Secretary, on 15 December 1924, a declaration to the Cabinet ruling out a war with Japan among the reasonable possibilities to be taken into account in the next ten, fifteen, or twenty years. He sent Austen Chamberlain a copy of a letter which he had addressed to Baldwin, in which he expressed his anxiety at the rise in the Naval Estimates, which looked like going up from £55 million in 1924–5 to £80 million in 1927–8. There would also have to be considered the rise of some £5 million in the Air Estimates. All this, in Churchill's view, made any relief of taxation impossible and blotted out any hope of social schemes. As usual, his thesis was set out with weighty and powerful argumentation. It resulted in the doctrine 'No war for ten years' being agreed and carried forward as an overriding instruction from year to year. Churchill was therefore able to fight the cause for economy with greater energy than any Chancellor of the Exchequer since Lord Randolph—but without the same disastrous results to himself.

Indeed, the European situation had steadily improved. The acceptance of the Dawes Plan in 1924 was followed by a period of real recovery in Europe. The fall of Poincaré and the rise of Herriot led to the French evacuation of the Ruhr. So little in the years immediately following the war was Germany's future military power a matter of alarm, that many leading British statesmen looked with greater suspicion to the French superiority. In February 1923, for instance, Lord Birkenhead called attention in the House of Lords to the 2,000 or more first-line aircraft that the French could boast, against our miserable 400 or 500. All through these years, up to the Second War, both friends and critics of France were apt to over-emphasise her strength. In truth, the terrible catastrophe with which France began the First War and her frightful losses in the attacks on the southern part of the Front, followed by the casualties suffered at Verdun, had really destroyed for ever the spirit of military aggression in France. All that France needed was security. Yet of security she felt that she had been cheated at the time of the Treaty. She had abandoned the claim to the Rhine frontier in the Paris negotiations, on the clear understanding that she would have in exchange the Anglo-American guarantee. It is commonly but wrongly said that President Wilson was beaten in Paris. He was beaten in Washington. It was America that refused the guarantee to France, as a result of which the British guarantee fell by the way-side. It was Washington that rejected the League of Nations. It was Washington that rejected the Treaty and by so doing sowed the dragon's seed of the Second World War.

Nevertheless, during these years much good work had been done. In Baldwin's time, in 1923, the Reparations Commission had set up the expert committees which led to the Dawes Report. In June 1924 MacDonald and Herriot accepted its terms and summoned the London Conference which met in July. In August, Germany came to the Conference and agreement was reached, not only to imple-ment the Dawes Committee but for the evacuation of the Ruhr. This was indeed a constructive period. It is true that by 1929 it was necessary to make some changes in the reparations arrangements because American investment was beginning to slow down, and therefore Germany was unable to meet her obligations. Nevertheless, the Young Plan made the appropriate adjustments in 1929.

In another field, in October 1924, the Protocol for the Pacific Settlement of International Disputes had been accepted at the Assembly. The Conservatives, soon after taking office, rejected the Protocol. Some still feel that this was a serious if not fatal mistake, and that the last and best attempt to strengthen the League had thereby failed. On the other hand, it was clear that the great Do-minion nations would not be bound by such arrangement—they would not even accept any responsibilities under Locarno—and there were doubts as to whether many other countries would finally accept. Moreover, this instrument, had it become binding on all the nations, did not, in fact, except as regards the undertaking to submit all justiciable disputes to the Court of International Justice, impose any obligations not already borne by all members of the League under Article 16 of the Covenant.[1]

In any event, the Locarno Pact, which followed this disappoint-ment, seemed a real landmark in the search for peace. The meeting in London, where Austen Chamberlain welcomed Briand, Strese-

[1] C. L. Mowat, *Britain Between the Wars, 1918–1940* (London, 1955), p. 181.

mann, and other statesmen, including Mussolini and Beneš, was a
historic occasion. Apart from the points agreed, such as the mutual
guarantee of France and Germany's western frontiers and the
definite commitment of Britain, the signing of the Locarno treaty
was a real gain, and welcomed as something like a triumph for
British diplomacy. Although the eastern frontiers of Germany were
not similarly guaranteed, it was agreed that reliance in this case
should be placed on the League Covenant. Following the Locarno
treaty, Germany was in 1926 admitted to the League. In 1928 a
Disarmament Conference, for which a preparatory commission had
been appointed in 1925, began its work. Although the Anglo-
French compromise reached in 1928 was to prove ineffective, yet
the general feeling was still one of optimism. The failure of the
Three-Power Naval Conference between the United States, Great
Britain, and Japan in 1927 did not appear to be a great disaster, and
the public were somewhat mystified when Lord Cecil resigned from
the Government in protest. Finally, the Kellogg–Briand Pact in
1928 for the renunciation of war as an instrument of national policy
seemed to all but the most sceptical a definite turning-point in the
history of human endeavour and the search for peace.

Abroad, we felt reasonably secure. The world was moving along
the right path. There were many set-backs and obstacles; but the
general movement seemed to be forward. The more extreme figures
had disappeared from French politics and more 'European' personalities like Herriot and Briand had taken their place. There seemed
no reason to look beyond the present German leaders or to question
their good faith. The British Foreign Secretary, with all his long
experience and with the deep sincerity which made him a trusted
statesman, assured us that the spirit of Locarno would spread over
Europe.

In these circumstances, the main attention of the House and the
country was concentrated on home affairs. Here the area had been
circumscribed by two important decisions taken by Baldwin; the
first immediately before the election, and the second on the formation of the Government. By his election pledges he was precluded
from putting forward any general system of protection. Nor was
this promise limited to foodstuffs. It applied equally to a general

revenue tariff or to protective measures over industry as a whole. Any changes, therefore, in these parts of our fiscal system, were limited to the reimposition of the so-called 'McKenna Duties' which Snowden had taken off the year before, together with the imperial preference arrangements; to the return to preferences in relation to any existing duties, which covered mainly the small field of dried fruits and other similar commodities; and, finally, to whatever might emerge under the heading of 'safeguarding'.

Had there been any temptation to give a less scrupulous interpretation to these pledges, the appointment of Churchill, who was a lifelong free-trader, to the Treasury made this impossible. By a strange paradox, Churchill and Snowden, although in frequent and sometimes bitter conflict in debate, were fundamentally agreed on the main principles of financial and economic policy. They were both convinced free-traders. They were also both agreed on the need for continuing a deflationary and classical financial system. The Sinking Fund was rigorously maintained by Churchill with Snowden's full approval. The return to the gold standard in 1925, which was a feature of Churchill's first Budget, was welcomed by Snowden and had the general support of all parties in the House. Although there were doubts expressed in Churchill's private circle, I do not remember that there were more than two or three Members, notably Sir Robert Horne and Boothby, who spoke against this decision. Outside the House, in the City as well as in commercial circles, this culmination of many years of effort was generally acclaimed. The one notable exception was Mr. Vincent Vickers, V.C., who resigned from the Board of the Bank of England in protest. Keynes was the only important critic among economists. Looking back it is easy to be wise. Yet it was not so much the re-establishment of a gold standard which is open to criticism. For this there were cogent arguments. It was a step in conformity with the general policy of other countries and helped to promote the re-establishment of an orderly exchange system in Europe and the world. But fixing the rate at $4.86 to the pound, the pre-war parity, was more doubtful. Making the 'pound look the dollar in the face' proved an expensive act of faith.

Although the deflationary policies of successive Governments, implicit in and assisted by the return to gold, helped to reduce internal costs and to that extent were an aid to exports, yet the effort to reduce wages correspondingly led to long and bitter struggles which culminated in the coal dispute and the General Strike. The return to gold at pre-war parity more than counteracted the benefits of falling internal prices, and did nothing to assist in the process of readjustment. It is hard to blame Churchill for his decision. He felt, no doubt, an instinctive reluctance to follow blindly the advice of all the experts. Such was certainly not his nature at any period of his life, as he was to show in even graver decisions in his War Government. But after exhausting every argument and probing every aspect of a problem, it was seldom, if ever, that he would reject the tested and sustained positions adopted by his technical advisers. So it was in this case.

Nevertheless, within these limits of financial orthodoxy on the one hand and general free trade and the maintenance of free imports on the other, Government policy was active and imaginative. Its first manifestation was shown in the Budget of 1925. Apart from the announcement of the return to the gold standard and the maintenance of a high Sinking Fund, it contained three main proposals. The first was the reduction of income tax by 6d., accompanied by substantial reduction in the tax liability of those enjoying the smaller range of incomes. The second was the reimposition of the McKenna Duties. The third was the outline of the bold plan for the creation of a pension system for the benefit of widows, orphans, and old people. This was to be both compulsory and contributary. It was linked with the existing National Health Insurance and Workmen's Compensation and Unemployment Insurance schemes. It thus provided the first move towards a comprehensive system of protection against all the major risks to which the mass of the working classes were subject.

Churchill's Budget speech created great enthusiasm in the Conservative Party. Apart from the substance, the method in which the whole scheme was announced was striking and impressive. Any qualms that there may have been among some of the older members of the party at Churchill's appointment were removed. For the

younger ones, it seemed the inauguration of a period of constructive
reform. On 30 April 1925, in the debate on the Budget resolutions,
I took the opportunity to make my maiden speech. Except for 'going
over the top' in war, there is hardly any experience so alarming as
this. Indeed, in many ways, the two are very similar. There is the
long period of waiting, when nerves are wrought up to a high pitch.
There is then the irrevocable act of 'moving into battle'. Through
the kindliness of the Whips and the Speaker, it is usually arranged
for a young Member to be informed at what time he is likely to
be called; yet when this moment actually arrives there is a sense
of dazed confusion. You stand up with a dozen or more other
Members. The Speaker calls out a name. You can hardly distinguish whether it is yours. You hesitate, not knowing what to do.
But as everybody else sits down, you conclude you must now go on.
Perhaps you have written out the text of the speech, in which case
you read it clumsily and in breach of the strict traditions of the
House. Or you try to memorise it, in which case you probably forget
it completely. The safest method is to have a number of notes
containing the salient points, and one or two of what you conceive to
be the more striking sentences. The furniture of the House is so
arranged that when you stand up to speak the bench in front of you
seems to catch you just below the knee and gives you the impression
that you are about to fall headlong over. However, if you survive all
these difficulties you can make a start.

There is probably no more unrewarding occupation than to read
old speeches, especially one's own. Often they are unintelligible, or
the points that seemed so striking have disappeared into the limbo
of past controversies, and the jokes seem as flat as the forgotten
music-hall quips of the last generation. A maiden speech, however,
commands a certain interest and has the advantage, unless it be
flagrantly contrary to the customs of the House, of being listened
to without interruptions and being given generous praise afterwards.
In re-reading mine, I find that I was more controversial than
convention normally expects or allows. But I wished to answer the
rather violent attacks which the Opposition had made on the main
Budget proposals, and to show the Government how welcome they

were, especially to the younger Members of the party. After the proper request for the indulgence of the House, I proceeded as follows:

We have had from the late Chancellor of the Exchequer [Snowden] a speech full of his usual skill and with a full amount of the acerbity with which he is wont to speak. I am not blaming him for that, because I think it is not unnatural that, under the circumstances in which this Budget was introduced, he should feel a little bitterness in the matter. While the Chancellor of the Exchequer was unfolding his proposals, one of the most interesting things was to see the expression upon the faces of some of the hon. Members opposite. First of all, they had to listen, of course, with interest to what the Chancellor was going to say, but the interest turned rapidly to surprise at the audacity and the magnitude of his proposals, and finally, I think, to horror and disappointment when they thought of the way in which these proposals would be received in this country. Possibly it added a little to the bitterness of this disillusionment to think that all this, from their point of view, miserable state of affairs is very largely their own fault.[1]

This, of course, referred to the new pensions proposals, the finance for which it was the main purpose of the Budget to provide. I then went on to say, with a touch of impudence:

We should expect from the late Chancellor of the Exchequer rather more bitterness than he usually shows, because after all, poison always irritates more in a wound which is self-inflicted . . .[1]

He really had the temerity to say that this was a rich man's Budget. When you think of the remissions of taxation, remissions which he supported, affecting most of all the poorer classes of Income Tax payers, I think that is a monstrous statement to have been made in this House. . . . The late Chancellor said, with regard to the remissions on the lower scale of Income Tax, that it was a proposal which had always been made by members of the party sitting behind him, and he was sure that they would not be in a position to oppose the proposal, which had their sympathy while in office. That is where the shoe pinches. If these proposals had been made by the members of the party sitting behind him when they were still in office, all would have been well.[1]

As all this seemed to be going off quite well, I ventured upon a passage which I had prepared but not quite decided to use. During the recess, I had noticed that Ramsay MacDonald, as Leader of the

[1]*Hansard*, 30 April 1925.

Opposition, had made a speech in which he had referred to the so-called 'Young Conservatives' and had appealed to them to cross the floor of the House, and join the really progressive party, the Labour Party. It naturally flattered us that our existence should have been even noticed, and I thought it was an opportunity not to be missed.

I well understand that the General of an Army, half of which is reputed to be in mutiny, and the other half in a state more or less of passive despair, should wish to find some new recruits, but I can assure him . . . that, if he thinks that we are either so young or so inexperienced as to be caught by a trap so clumsy as his, it shows that he totally misunderstands the moral principles and ideals of democratic Toryism. He has no conception of what those ideals and principles mean to us. If he thinks that he and his party have only to offer us as the true socialism a kind of mixture, a sort of horrible political cocktail, consisting partly of the dregs of exploded economic views of Karl Marx, mixed up with a little flavour of Cobdenism, well iced by the late Chancellor of the Exchequer, and with a little ginger from the Member for the Gorbals (Mr. Buchanan)—if he thinks that this is to be the draught given to our parched throats and that we are ready to accept it, he is very much mistaken.[1]

I then reverted to the main issue—the great Pensions Bill and the Budget proposals to support it—with these words:

Hon. Gentlemen opposite are . . . not quite certain whether to take the line that we have been stealing their clothing while they very incontinently went to bathe in the muddy waters of Russian intrigue, or whether they are to say the clothes are no good anyway. They have not made up their minds, but the people of this country have made up their minds that these proposals are to their benefit, and I am quite certain of this, that for myself, and for many others who have the same views as I have, although we are but young, newly arrived, and inexperienced members of the party, it has been, to have a Budget like this, an immense encouragement, and we claim it as a sign of what Conservatism can do and has always done, when it is true to itself.[1]

When I concluded there was a generous degree of applause, and the usual compliments from the speakers who followed. The national Press was both complimentary and friendly—from *The Times* to the *Daily Mirror*. The local Press was enthusiastic. My friends were generous in their praise. I had waited five months; I had got it over and in this, 'my first engagement', unlike some of those in the past, I had reached my objective unwounded.

[1]*Hansard*, 30 April 1925.

My maiden speech brought me a certain notoriety. I began to contribute articles on housing and on rating reform, which were syndicated in various provincial newspapers. Those on housing dealt with many of the questions which were to become so familiar to me a quarter of a century later—including slum clearance and quicker and unconventional building methods. One of my statements, which appeared in a local paper in September 1925, was my slogan in 1951: 'Housing is not a question of Conservatism or Socialism. It is a question of humanity.'

The Rating and Valuation Bill, which Chamberlain introduced and carried through the House at the same time as the Widows, Orphans and Old Age Pensions Bill, turned my mind to the whole rating question. In this bold reform lay the foundations on which a new structure might be built. It was the key to the Government's future work, for without it there could be no reform of local government, nor could there be any effective housing policy or a proper method of spreading the cost of unemployment and pauperism over the country as a whole. My articles, therefore, which were widely published, concentrated on the unfairness by which the heaviest burdens fell upon the areas least able to bear them, as well as upon the need to remodel a valuation system which was antiquated in its form and arbitrary in its results. Nevertheless, this was not a popular line either in the party or generally throughout the country. The reduction of rating authorities from over 15,000 to under 2,000 caused a lot of ill feeling locally, although it was an essential change if uniformity of rating was to come about.

Apart from these activities, I was asked to go to a by-election at Eastbourne in June 1925, where I made a speech upon the principles of Conservatism which made a certain stir. For some reason, it was given an unusually long report in *The Times*. In addition, their correspondent, commenting on the speech, observed:

Eastbourne's imagination has been touched by a remarkable speech from Captain Macmillan, one of the band of young Conservatives who have already made the present House of Commons memorable by a series of maiden speeches of rare ability and freshness. I am disposed to think that the revival of what he calls the real and fundamental principles of Conservatism may prove the outstanding issue in this election.

There was, I fear, nothing very remarkable in what I said. It was a mixture of Disraeli's 'Young England', Shaftesbury, Joe Chamberlain, and all the rest. But it seemed, surprisingly, to strike a respondent note in that agreeable watering-place. *The Times* correspondent added:

Eastbourne is at this season and in this weather a seething South Coast pleasure town, but even so its comments on Captain Macmillan's speech show that it is not averse from political speculation and experiment.

This writing and speechifying, in addition to frequent visits to Stockton, my own daily work in the publishing business and the normal interests of family life, kept me happily employed during this summer. Nevertheless, the clouds of unrest were gathering. The 1925 Budget, like all Budgets which give remissions of taxation and other benefits to the people, was popular at first but soon began to wear thin. As I have learnt since, people do not reject benefits but soon forget them. The Pensions Bill was applauded as a fine piece of reform; but nobody was to get anything out of it for another two years. Meanwhile, the unemployment figures continued to rise, and by the end of the summer session a coal strike was threatening. A large subsidy bought time for an inquiry, but the crisis was only postponed. At the end of November there were debates on unemployment. Tom Shaw opened a vote of censure on the Government. I played my part in attacking the former occupant of the Ministry of Labour but I was not content with a mere debating speech. I put forward for the first time a policy for which I continued to fight throughout the rest of the Parliament. It was this: insurance should be restricted to cases which come under a true insurance system, and the Fund should not be asked to carry indefinitely able-bodied employees long after they had exhausted any actuarial right to benefit arising from contributions made by them and by their employers. Neither employer nor employee should be asked to make additional contributions to this burden. It should not be placed on the Poor Law, still locally administered and supported. There must be a new measure of national relief, carried nationally. I maintained that until this was done there was no alternative except to relax the strict rules of insurance. But it was a bad alternative.

It was properly a national burden and should be carried nationally.

The coal industry, as so often in the past, became once more the centre of economic and political conflict. For the first years after the war, both the internal and external demands for coal were satisfactory. But with the beginning of the slump, especially affecting the heavy industries, the home demand began to decline. At the same time, the French and Belgian mines gradually started to recover their output. However, the French occupation of the Ruhr and the sit-down strike that followed meant a sudden windfall for British mining, and large tonnages were sold abroad. This factor alone supported the three-year wage settlement made in 1921. In 1924 a new agreement more beneficial to the men was accepted by the owners, but by a strange irony the political success of MacDonald in persuading the French to evacuate the Ruhr took away the advantage which British coal-mining had enjoyed during the occupation. Moreover, the return to gold at parity in the summer of 1925 imposed a further handicap on coal exports. The new wage structure could not be maintained, and in the middle of 1925 the owners gave notice of its termination. The stage seemed set for a strike which would probably be supported by other important unions and develop into something like a general strike. After long negotiations, when the miners stuck resolutely to their slogan, 'Not a penny off the pay, not a minute on the day', the Government finally agreed to pay the necessary subsidy during the period in which a new inquiry would consider the whole future of the industry. On this basis, the miners' representatives agreed to co-operate with the proposed commission. The subsidy was expected to be of the order of £10 million. In fact, it reached the sum of £23 million. This was itself a symptom of the deteriorating situation and the falling demand for coal at home and abroad. The strike was averted at the last minute—on 31 July 1925. The inquiry was entrusted to a Royal Commission. Sir Herbert Samuel agreed to act as chairman. His colleagues were men of parts and distinction: Sir Herbert Lawrence, a banker and formerly Chief of Staff to Sir Douglas Haig; Sir William Beveridge, already famous as an administrator and an economist; and Mr. Kenneth Lee, a cotton magnate.

Their Report was published in April 1926. On a great part of the issues which had been emphasised by the Miners' Federation they favoured the trade union argument. They supported the nationalisation of coal royalties which had already been recommended by the Sankey Commission but still not been implemented, even by the Labour Government of 1923–24. They argued strongly for a wide-scale reorganisation of the industry, but under private ownership, and without any general measure of compulsion. The amalgamation of mining undertakings, in order to get rid of hopelessly uneconomic units and to secure a general improvement in the structure of the industry, was powerfully urged. There were other points dealing with research and distribution, and aid from the Government in these fields was suggested. In addition, they proposed a number of measures which it was hoped would improve relations between employer and employee; for instance, pit committees, family allowances, profit-sharing, more pithead baths, holidays with pay (when the economic conditions allowed), and various other methods to encourage productivity.[1] The owners disliked all this and stuck obstinately to their own position of general immobility—except for wages, which must be reduced. Still the immediate problem remained. If the subsidy was ruled out, and the Samuel Commission was strongly against any repetition of the subsidy, how was the industry to continue? Nobody denied that the margin of profit had disappeared or was disappearing, and that losses were now being incurred in every coal-field, except possibly in parts of Yorkshire and in Nottinghamshire. Some sacrifice of wages, therefore, had to be made to bridge the gap. Even here the Commission did what they could to help the unions. They were against the increase of the working day; they were in favour of national and not local agreements; and they recommended that before actual wage reductions were put into effect, there should be a real agreement as to the reorganisation of the industry and the improvement of its efficiency.

Unmoved by the Report, both owners and unions remained stubborn to the point of obtuseness. The president of the Miners' Federation, Herbert Smith, could only repeat the same slogan over and over again. The organising secretary, Cook, more intelligent

[1] C. L. Mowat, *Britain Between the Wars, 1918–1940*, p. 298.

but more extreme, took up the same inflexible posture. We back-
benchers could only read the accounts in the Press and pick up
the rumours that were going round the lobbies. Even after the
deadlock towards the end of April, we were told there was every
hope of a formula being found on which negotiations could be
resumed under Government auspices. It was believed that Baldwin
and Birkenhead in particular were working hard for a settlement.

The intransigence of the Miners' Federation forced the other
trade union leaders to issue directions for a general strike in support of the miners. This had always been understood to be the
necessary, indeed unavoidable, consequence of a failure to settle
the mining dispute. It came about after the breakdown of final
talks at Downing Street on Sunday night, 2 May, in circumstances
which were then and still remain somewhat obscure.

When we met in the House of Commons on Monday the 3rd, the
atmosphere was tense. Baldwin explained the situation in a moderate
and balanced speech. J. H. Thomas, the well-known and remarkable secretary of the National Union of Railwaymen, was also
careful to strike a reasonable note. Lloyd George did not please the
House by what seemed a rather casuistical distinction between a
sympathetic industrial strike and a general strike, intended to coerce
the Government. Since everyone agreed that the only possible way
that the General Strike could have been avoided short of a reduction
in wages was by a continuation of the subsidy, this seemed rather
special pleading. The next day, Baldwin spoke to a large meeting
of Conservative Members in one of the committee-rooms, in the
course of which he suggested that Members for industrial constituencies might do well to go there at the end of the week and see
how things were going. On the Wednesday, there was a debate
upon the Emergency Regulations, in which Thomas rather upset
many Conservative Members by his revelation as to the actual
conditions in which negotiations were ended on the Sunday night.
He alleged that the Government took the opportunity of a strike
in the *Daily Mail* offices to declare war, while he and his colleagues
were still trying to find a formula for peace. Later in the debate,
Baldwin explained that the direct action of the printers' union

marked the beginning of the General Strike, and showed that the General Council had lost control. The Government had gone to the furthest limit in negotiating under the threat of a general strike. Moreover, the miners had made it perfectly clear that the Trades Union Council had no power to do anything but talk. They could negotiate. But they could not settle.

The next day Simon made his famous speech, asserting the illegality of the General Strike. It had a profound effect, both inside and outside the House of Commons, and the fact that it was supported shortly afterwards by Mr. Justice Astbury in a case which came before him in the High Court added to its impact.

These days were ones of almost continuous debate—either on the Emergency Regulations or on the Adjournment. The general tone and temper of the House of Commons was responsible and impressive. Except for the extreme Left wing of the Labour Party, speakers tried hard to be fair and moderate. Whatever might be the view of some of the trade unionists engaged in the conflict, it was clear that the leaders were deeply disturbed and as anxious for a settlement as everyone else. Many years later I have read much of the material which has been published, but still no very clear picture emerges. There was, no doubt, a difference, if not of opinion, at least of mood inside the Cabinet, just as there was inside the trade union movement. Some Ministers may have welcomed the *Daily Mail* incident as bringing to an end a position into which the Government was steadily drifting, and which was becoming more and more dangerous. The Government were in danger of being accused of yielding to the threat of an ultimatum and showing indecision, if not impotence. After all, the strike was to start within a few hours and measures had to be taken to keep the life of the nation in being. Nevertheless, Baldwin, supported by Birkenhead, undoubtedly strove up to the last moment to find a formula. Others, of which the most important were probably Neville Chamberlain and Hogg, perhaps thought that the game had been played long enough, and that the best thing to do was to bring the uncertainty to an end and face the issue. On the trade union side, Thomas, Pugh, and all the rest strove hard to get some concession, however small and however guarded, from the miners' leaders. They failed altogether to do so.

The Government, of course, had utilised the period gained by the subsidy to considerable effect. A nation-wide organisation had been set up, based on a well-devised regional structure. With the help of volunteers who were readily forthcoming, the people could be fed and life carried on with reasonable comfort. The date chosen, the beginning of May, could not have been more fortunate from this point of view. The weather was fine; there was a kind of holiday atmosphere, at least at the beginning; and many people thoroughly enjoyed undertaking new and rather exciting jobs. Members of Parliament became porters and guards; some even drove locomotives. Very large numbers of men and women of all classes acted as bus-conductors, drivers of lorries, helpers in canteens, and so forth. The essential services were thus carried on. It was commonly believed that many men on strike in one industry were volunteering in another.

Following Baldwin's advice, I went off on the Friday to Teesside. My friend and neighbour, Leonard Ropner, Member for Sedgefield, drove me up in an open car at great speed. I found in Stockton the Mayor and the voluntary organisations hard at work and no untoward events. In the surrounding mining villages there was, however, a rather more tense atmosphere, and a number of minor 'incidents' took place and were exaggerated by rumour. Some people naturally were very 'windy' and thought that the revolution was about to begin. I drove with the Mayor to Newcastle, which was the headquarters of the regional commission, for a talk with Kingsley Wood, who was in charge. Electricity was in difficulties, but the crew of a submarine was arriving. Otherwise, things seemed reasonably calm throughout the North Eastern area. I did not feel any serious anxiety but rather sorrow and shame that there should be strife on such a scale between two sections of our own people. War is bad enough; anything like civil war is a thousand times worse. I remember, however, being specially comforted by the good relations clearly existing between the Stockton police and even the most excitable of the strikers, which was reflected in the calmness of the former. I went in to see the Superintendent in his office, as I often made a practice of doing, to ask how he was getting on. He was a huge man, well over six foot in height, with vast limbs and great powerful hands which gripped your own in a friendly handshake but left considerable damage behind. When I came in, he was speaking on the telephone to his colleague in Durham and asked to be excused for a moment. I remember his side of the conversation, which went roughly like this: 'Oh, they have stopped a train, at ——, and thrown some carriages over the embankment. Now about the police concert next Thursday. I am very anxious that that girl who was put at No. 2 last time should have a better place–in the second half I would say–she's very good. Oh, they have overturned a tram and stopped some buses at ——. Yes, I expect we will deal with that all right. But about the concert. I've sold nearly all our tickets and could do with some more if you can spare them.' I listened to their conversation with growing admiration. It gave me great confidence.

I have another memory of the Superintendent. At a large public meeting, when my wife and I were going in through a crowded entrance, a man shouted an insulting and very obscene remark. I saw the 'Super', who was hovering near, flick him in the face with his glove. Some months later, I had occasion to see him and recalled the incident. I asked who the man was, what was his trouble. 'Funny you should mention that, sir,' he replied. 'You'd hardly believe it, sir, but the chap came round to complain to me next day; said I'd knocked some of his teeth out.' 'What did you answer, Superintendent?' 'What did I answer, sir? Why, I said to 'im, I said, "Lucky for you, me lad, that me 'and wasn't in the glove."'

Before leaving for the North and in the few days that the Strike lasted after my return, I went each night after the House had risen to Printing House Square, to help in packing and dispatching the edition of *The Times*, which was being produced by volunteer labour. I do not know that any of us achieved a great deal, but we were treated with great hospitality and kindness by the management, and picked up all the late news. Other Members, with more militant views, went to perform the same services at the *Morning Post* office, which Churchill had taken over for the production of the *British Gazette*. Churchill deplored the situation which led to the Strike as much as any of us. He had been ready enough as Chancellor of the Exchequer to provide for the original subsidy, in the hope of avoiding the dispute. When the General Strike was over, he was to be a keen advocate of peace during the tragic months, lasting till December, that the coal strike dragged on. Nevertheless, during the actual days of the General Strike he was, in accordance with his temperament, an active and confident participator in the fray. Some of the statements published by the *British Gazette* were considered unwise and provocative. But Churchill's character was such that while he did not like the fight, being in it he thought the Government had better win, and as soon as possible. There is something to be said for this point of view.

The General Strike was called off on 12 May. The leaders of the T.U.C. went to Downing Street and agreed that the General Strike should be terminated forthwith, 'in order that negotiations might proceed'. Baldwin, in reply, made it clear to them, and subsequently to the House of Commons, that he would do everything possible to reach a satisfactory solution of the coal problem. I was present when he came into the House, where he was given a tremendous and well-deserved reception. He said only a few words, but they were well suited to the occasion, quiet and impressive. His hopes of an early coal settlement were, however, to be disappointed.

In so far as the General Strike was an attempt to coerce Parliament, it was doomed to failure in a country so long accustomed to constitutional government. Nevertheless, the credit for the response of the public as a whole belongs largely to Baldwin. The T.U.C. leaders had—and rightly—trust in Baldwin's honesty of purpose. Most of them were genuinely anxious lest a prolongation of the General Strike might let loose forces beyond their control. In the same spirit, when a troublesome position began to develop on 13 May—the very next day—it was Baldwin who helped to calm the situation. Many men going back to work found themselves refused work or offered terms different from those obtaining when they had gone out on strike. A kind of second General Strike therefore started, and all sides of the House of Commons were united in disgust at what was alleged to be widespread victimisation. Once more, Baldwin took a firm stand against any attempt to use the re-engagement of strikers as an occasion for reducing wages, lengthening hours, or worsening conditions. This comforted the House and on the next day we were told that agreements were now being reached with the dockers, the railways, and other industries, by which work was being generally resumed. So ended the General Strike—a thoroughly unhappy story.

Lloyd George once observed that Baldwin was a miser of power; he collected it, hoarded it, but never spent it. Certainly this is a fair criticism of Baldwin's inaction after the collapse of the General Strike. His position in the country was overwhelmingly strong. He was trusted on all sides by men and women of very different sympathies and background. He could without difficulty have imposed his will upon his party and on Parliament, had he put forward a clear and simple programme for bringing the coal dispute to an end. He was deeply pledged by the words that he had used both during and after the General Strike. He had been equally definite in Parliament and on the radio. But now, as at other times, a strange lethargy seemed to overcome him as the almost physical consequence of special mental and moral strain. In accordance with his promise, he certainly brought both sides together without delay and submitted proposals which included a national agreement—a reduction of wages by negotiation, while leaving the subsistence wage intact—and a National Wage Board under an independent chairman. He offered a grant of £3 million to tide over the difficult period while the new arrangements were being made. As regards the other recommendations of the Samuel Report, he undertook to introduce legislation in regard to almost all the main points, omitting altogether the nationalisation of royalties. The immediate response of both owners and miners was disappointing, as he might have expected. But Baldwin contented himself with a stern reproof. He made no attempt to take any effective action. On the contrary, so far as the Government undertook any legislation, it was to suspend the Seven-Hour Act and merely to facilitate, not in any way to impose, the various proposals for the amalgamation and better management of the mines. Suspension of the Seven-Hour Act involved raising legal hours of work in the pits from seven hours to eight, and was bitterly resented, all the more since it had not been recommended by Sir Herbert Samuel and his colleagues.

I ventured to circulate to a number of Conservative Members, including Ministers, a short memorandum giving my views as to what should be done. I have this memorandum still. Its major proposals were that the amalgamations should be made compulsory and the right to work coal in certain circumstances could be compulsorily acquired by a colliery undertaking. I urged that the Government should now make its own proposals, broadly based on the Samuel Report, but not slavishly adhering to it in every detail. This was a somewhat bold step for a private Member, but I received considerable support in the party and from certain Ministers. However, the Government contented itself with legislation—both as to hours and as to reorganisation—which could not lead to an agreed solution. The owners behaved with more than their usual obstinacy and truculence, and even objected to the Government interfering at all with industry, especially with the coal industry.

As the summer months passed by, the Government relapsed into a mood of apparent indifference towards bringing the dispute to an end, or building up a healthier condition of affairs. Some of us put down an amendment to the Committee stage of the Mining Industry Bill which, although not going so far as the official Labour amendment, proposed a workable plan of compulsory unification through an appeal to the Railway and Canal Commission, after careful and independent examination. It was, however, rejected in Committee and this opportunity was allowed to slide out of our hands, with evil consequences for the reputation of the Government and of the party. This weakness especially disgusted those moderate voters who had supported us in 1924 and whose sympathy was vital for success at the next election. The miners became more and more stubborn and so did the owners. The miners sullenly drifted back to work; a great opportunity was missed.

All this made me and my friends turn our minds once more to the problem of the proper relations between industry and the State in modern conditions. The Conservative Party as a whole seemed to have absorbed the old Liberal *laissez-faire* concepts. There was, however, a large and growing number, especially in the younger sections of the party, who were becoming impatient of this doctrinaire attitude. In September of this year (1926), I made a speech on the role of Government towards industry, and an appeal for a new interpretation. This caused a considerable amount of interest. The speech was described in the Press as being listened to by Lloyd George with manifest approval. But approval was by no means confined to him. The object of our movement was, of course, to try to get a more constructive approach to the whole question of the relations between the Government, the owners, and the trade unions. It was a plea for recognition of the importance of the trade unions and for the development of a sense of partnership in industry. We recognised that there might be other undertakings besides electricity which had become ripe for some form of public control. We pleaded also for the progress of statutory schemes for arbitration and conciliation. The *New Statesman* reported that our views had 'some sympathisers in the Cabinet. Mr. Baldwin's mind is supposed to be in the balance'. But these efforts proved, at the time at any rate, unsuccessful. The Press was mostly hostile. The *Evening Standard* attacked us and criticised equally those who had written in support as expressing opinions 'indistinguishable in substance from the effusions of Mr. William Graham, late Financial Secretary to the Labour Government'.

As a result of these controversies a small group of us began during this winter to work further on these questions, culminating in the production of a little book called *Industry and the State*, which was published in April 1927.[1] It would be tedious now to try to set out the main arguments of this small and unassuming volume. In effect, it was a first attempt at working out some coherent system, lying in between unadulterated private enterprise and collectivism. It was a policy which I afterwards called 'The Middle Way'; an industrial structure with the broad strategic control in the hands of the State and the tactical operation in the hands of private management, with public and private ownership operating side by side. We pleaded for some form of collective bargaining to be given, at any rate in certain industries, statutory authority, on the lines adopted by the railways in the Act of 1921.

[1]For list of signatories see above, p. 173.

We advocated an extension of joint industrial councils with increased powers and, where suitable, of trade boards. Other matters dealt with an economic general staff and with transference of certain burdens from the rates to the National Exchequer.

Thus the unhappy year of the General Strike stimulated us to try to find some constructive alternative to Socialism. In the next ten years, in one way and another, I tried with various groups of friends and differing organisations and movements to promote this theme by books, pamphlets, speeches. After a lapse of forty years, it appears that what then seemed so visionary has now become commonplace and generally accepted. The tide has indeed flowed on; and although we are still struggling with the problem of what is now termed 'the mixed economy', all parties in the State have, in effect, accepted this concept as a necessary practical basis for a nation such as ours. Many of the solutions adopted have followed the general lines that we tried tentatively, and no doubt amateurishly, to explore.

All through the winter the Cabinet was known to be discussing the details of the Trade Disputes Bill which had become necessary as a result of the General Strike. Some were believed to be in favour of a limited Bill, confined to declaring the illegality of a general strike; others wished to see the inclusion of a number of provisions dealing with various aspects of the growing power of trade unionism. Still others, as we now know from Neville Chamberlain's diaries, wished to introduce a Bill not wholly negative in character, but including some more constructive elements. The party was much divided. The only thing upon which there was agreement was that there must be a Bill of some kind.

In the first days of May 1927 the Trade Disputes Bill was finally introduced. Its main provisions were as follows. It declared illegal any strike or lock-out other than in connection with a trade dispute in which the strikers were employed, or which was designed or calculated to coerce the Government by inflicting hardship on the community. This was designed to prevent any repetition of the General Strike, but it seemed to extend the ban to any form of sympathetic strike. It declared intimidation to be illegal. It substituted 'contracting in' for 'contracting out' in any political levy raised by the unions. It prevented established Civil Servants in future from joining any but their own unions, reserved to Crown employees.[1]

The terms put me and those who felt with me into a difficult position. It was unquestionable that some form of legislation was required. I spoke on the Second Reading and took the general line that the Bill must be given broad support, but that it should not stand upon its own. It must be accompanied by a progressive programme of social reform and industrial reorganisation carried out in a constructive spirit. I concluded:

... the public, in the long run, the moderate men who belong to no definite party, will not, in my opinion, declare that the Clauses of this Bill are wrong or unjust. But its secondary results will depend not so much on the Bill itself, but on the temper in which it is passed, on the programme of the policy which is pursued by the party in power. . . . If this Bill is to be the prelude to a general swing to the right, if it means the beginning of reactionary policy, then I am bound to admit it means the beginning of the end of this party of which I have the honour to be a member, and it means also the end of all the members of the moderate party opposite. It means that the parties . . . are captured by the extremists. But if the Conservative party proceeds with its programme, passes this Bill into law, carries on in the spirit in which it was returned to office, the spirit which has dominated its leadership during the period it has been in office; if it proceeds undisturbed with its programme; . . . if it is not unwilling to adopt a bold policy with regard to many questions of taxation, finance, social and moral questions, questions on international reform, Washington Conventions and the like; if it goes steadily on in that spirit, when the electorate have to judge whether this Bill is a revengeful Bill passed in a spirit of reaction, or whether it is a wise Bill passed with the genuine desire to put right a real wrong, then I have no doubt that the electors will decide that this Bill is justified, and that its passage into law has been wise.[2]

In the Committee stages I took some part in trying to improve the drafting, and we secured from the Government a number of amendments which were helpful in making quite clear that a

[1] C. L. Mowat, *Britain Between the Wars, 1918–1940*, p. 336.
[2] *Hansard*, 2 May 1927.

sympathetic strike was not in itself illegal, and that the full rights of trade union leaders should be preserved. There was one important amendment which was moved by Sir Leslie Scott, and widely supported by moderate speakers. It was even welcomed in principle by the Opposition. The Bill made certain provisions regarding strikes in essential industries. Our amendment was to provide a system of delay and conciliation before strikes in public utility services could take place. Sir Alfred Mond put his name to the amendment and spoke strongly in support. Lloyd George, while deploring the Bill as a whole, made a powerful speech imploring the Government to accept our new clause. In speaking for the amendment, I asked my usual question. Having dealt with negative legislation, when would the Government proceed with the positive suggestion for the improvement of economic and industrial conditions? The Minister of Labour, while sympathetic in general, devoted his speech to the technical difficulties and promised a Committee of Inquiry—a device to which Ministers of all parties resort when they are in a tight corner. Nothing very practical resulted from this effort of ours; but undoubtedly the debate did some good and helped to bring a better atmosphere into the discussions. Twenty years later, the Trade Disputes Act was repealed by the triumphant Labour Government of 1945. But many other things had changed too, and just as no great good was done by the passing of the Act, no great harm was done by its repeal.

By a strange irony, I read many years later in Sir Keith Feiling's *Life of Neville Chamberlain* this quotation from his diary (of 16 June 1927):

Among the few clauses was one put down by Leslie Scott, backed by Mond, which was in effect the same as the one I so nearly got adopted . . . the debate showed how much we had lost by not adopting my proposal; Lloyd George for instance complained that the bill was nothing but an attack, the government ought to have made a survey of the industrial situation, and put in some constructive proposal. This was, of course, precisely my point of view.[1]

It was sad we did not know at the time that we had so strong a supporter in the Cabinet.

[1] Keith Feiling, *Life of Neville Chamberlain* (London, 1946), p, 159.

Meanwhile, the evil effects of the long coal dispute had already shown themselves. Unemployment, which in April 1926 had been a little over a million—one of the lowest figures since early in 1921—rose sharply.[1] Baldwin seemed to be losing his grip on the situation, and the party was distracted by all kinds of minor or at least irrelevant issues. The die-hards were putting up resistance to many of Neville Chamberlain's reforming plans, and much of our time was spent on abortive proposals for the reform of the House of Lords, on which the party was more or less equally divided—for and against. The Betting Tax and the Prayer Book controversy occupied the minds of many Members, while the great economic problems of the nation remained unresolved. This was all the more galling because during these years Europe and the world in general were making marked progress towards recovery.

The Labour Party, of course, were in the happy position of declaring, without regard to the situation overseas, that our troubles were all due to 'the system'; the only cure was Socialism. The Conservative Party believed in protection for the home market with a corresponding extension of imperial preference. But they were precluded from applying this cure by the pledges given in the 1924 election. At various stages in the Parliament there were strong movements in favour of a use of the 'safeguarding' method on a wide basis, but Baldwin regarded this as a breach of the spirit if not of the letter of his pledge. The test case was iron and steel; and in spite of many powerful advocates within the party and the demand both of employers and employed in the industry, he stuck firmly by this decision. The only other plans to deal with unemployment within the limits of a general system of free trade were various schemes for internal development to be supported by the Exchequer. In spite of the formidable case built up by Lloyd George and others, little was done on these lines. Moreover, such plans had to be kept within very modest bounds, in view of the orthodox monetary policy upon which the seal was set by the return to the gold standard.

[1] Unless otherwise stated, unemployment figures throughout refer to insured men and women, and are taken from the *Statistical Abstract for the United Kingdom* (after 1935–36 the *Annual Abstract of Statistics*).

We were therefore caught in a trap of our own making. All that remained was to concentrate attention upon the various methods of dealing not with unemployment but with the support of the unemployed. Naturally, so long as the figures remained at this high level, the original insurance scheme, developed from a modified form introduced before the war, came under great financial pressure. Yet humanity demanded that some alleviation of the strictly actuarial rules should be made from time to time. This threw the Fund increasingly into deficit.

I was deeply involved in the attempt to legislate measures effecting a change in this very distressing situation, arguing, among other things, that the Exchequer and not the local rates should shoulder responsibility for long-term unemployment. One part of the bill, rigidly enforcing the insurance rule requiring thirty contributions in the two years previous to the year of claim, was particularly resisted by our group, and this qualification was postponed. But in the end, Parliamentary action avoided any radical reform. It merely continued the unsatisfactory system of extended or transitional benefits which fell upon the Fund, and even at current rates of unemployment were bound to lead it into further deficit. When, in the next Parliament, the country was struck by the economic blizzard which attacked the whole world, and unemployment rose to the staggering figure of over two and a half million, the Socialist Chancellor was to find in the insolvency of the Fund one of the main causes of the undermining of British credit abroad.

Nevertheless, this Parliament was destined to end as it had begun, in a reforming spirit. In the spring of 1929, a comprehensive plan took its final form, incorporating Chamberlain's measures for local Government reform and Churchill's bold scheme for derating the tax burden on industry and agriculture and replacing the losses of local authorities by direct subsidies from the Exchequer. The two streams of policy, Chamberlain's and Churchill's, although in some senses parallel, took nearly two years' discussion before they reached their confluence.

In spite of all these complications and the long period of gestation, Churchill's plan was, in essence, simple. Some £29 to £30 million, a large sum for those days, was to be made available. Like the armies of reserve, it was to be a mass of manœuvre. It would be deployed wherever the line was hard pressed. The weak part of the line was clearly the heavy industries and agriculture. £17 million therefore would go to reduce rates paid by industry to one-quarter. To finance complete remission of rates on land and agricultural buildings would require a further £4¾ million. The railways and docks, and the like, would benefit to the tune of £4 million, but it was a condition that these should be wholly passed on in the form of reduction of freight charges. I had pressed strongly for this condition, knowing how much help could be given by these means to the transport of coal, iron, and steel. Finally, some £3 million were necessary in order to float off the local government reforms. All this ambitious plan was magnificently described in the Budget speech of 1928, one of Churchill's triumphs. To the young men who were his ardent followers it was a great occasion.

I spoke in the Budget debates and spent a good deal of time in the next few months in trying to publicise the scheme, I wrote in various journals and local newspapers and took part in the Parliamentary debates. I also spoke on the scheme in various constituencies.

The necessary measure to make the derating plan effective, coupled with the reform of local government, was introduced in November, in a comprehensive and persuasive speech, by Neville Chamberlain. The Bill finally reached its Third Reading in February 1929. In spite of many changes and upheavals in the years to come, nobody sought to reverse the broad structure of local government which the Minister created in this massive Bill. It would have given Chamberlain pleasure to reflect, had he survived to do so, that this part of his scheme, which occupied so much of his energies during these two years, has stood the test of time and experience. Neither Churchill, nor those who worked with him, would have claimed industrial derating as more than an immediate and temporary piece of rescue work in a political and economic situation which ruled out almost every other contrivance. The organisation of local government, on the other hand, has been of permanent value. The main principles upon which Chamberlain based his great work are unchanged. Whatever alterations or adaptations have been made since are in conformity with his broad design. On the completion of the last phase, in the spring of 1929, *The Times* used these words: 'The great scheme of rating reform which has been the principal Government measure during the present session ... is one of which its authors may justly be proud. ... It will take its place as one of the outstanding legislative achievements of the twentieth century.'

CHAPTER NINE

The Great Divide: 1929–31

THE Parliament elected in October 1924 was dissolved on 10 May 1929. Polling took place on 30 May. The Conservative record in the four and a half years was by no means contemptible. In the field of foreign affairs the Treaty of Locarno had been generally welcomed as a considerable achievement, although the fact that it was negotiated outside the League of Nations allowed an imputation of coldness towards the League, which some Conservatives undoubtedly felt, to be pinned upon the party as a whole. At home substantial reforms and advances had been made. 'Safeguarding' duties had at least begun on a moderate scale and further advance was not ruled out where a case could be made. Schools and houses were going up at an increasing rate; and the cost of living, which was considered of prime political importance, had fallen substantially over the period. In spite of some million unemployed there were more men at work; and the foundations of 'modernisation', as it would now be called, had been effectively laid, both in the electricity supply scheme and in the local government reforms. The latter, when effective, would lead to the fairer sharing of burdens and substantial relief to productive industry. *The Times* summed up this record in these words:

> In the Parliaments of the last fifty years only two or three will be found to rival in quality and quantity the output of the past four and a half years.[1]

Nevertheless, the Conservatives were handicapped by some minor and some major difficulties. It so happened that the increased valuations for rating, though not in poundage, which were a necessary by-product of the local government reform scheme, were published shortly before the General Election. Indeed, ratepayers, who of

[1] *The Times*, leading article, 5 June 1929.

course were also voters, actually received their increased assessment only a few days before the poll. This resulted in widespread discontent, especially among house-owners and middle-class voters. At the same time, after nearly five years of office, the shadow of unemployment still lay over a great part of the country. Although the figures were no worse, they were very little better than when we began. The long coal dispute, which had been allowed to drag on for months and months—Baldwin's most fatal and tragic error, where he made no effort to support Churchill's initiative for a settlement— had left its mark over the country, at any rate north of the Trent. Finally, although we were able to put forward a respectable programme, it was not inspiring. It reflected a tired and rather defeatist mood. There was no call to positive or creative action.

I am amused, on looking at my own election address, to see that I put as an important feature the modernisation of industry, and especially of the railway system. I was soon to be elected to the board of the Great Western Railway,[1] and this enabled me to study the problem in some detail. But I cannot claim that I foresaw the Beeching Age. Any glamour or romance with which our programme might have been clothed was made impossible by the election cry which Baldwin chose. Strange and unaccountable man! After a Parliament in which he had added some millions to the total electorate by the so-called 'flapper' vote, in an election in which youth played a larger part than ever before, he decided to appeal to the people with a singularly uninspiring slogan—'Safety First'. I shall never forget the placards plastered all over the country, with Baldwin's great head, smoking his pipe, and underneath in huge letters, 'Safety First'. Yet this man, who seemed so often to hit the nail on the head without ever driving it in any further, and who was on the whole, as Lord Eustace Percy has reminded us, 'content to regard himself as the mouthpiece of his government, rather than as its directing brain',[2] could at the same time show not merely genuine emotion in a crisis, but political sagacity of a high order. He outmanœuvred Lloyd George time after time. In the struggle to maintain his leadership, he defied and

---

[1] I was a director from 1929 to 1940 and again from 1945 to 1947.
[2] Lord Percy of Newcastle, *Some Memories* (London, 1958), p. 128.

completely defeated the Press barons, Rothermere and Beaverbrook. According to his biographer, G. M. Young, he said, 'My worst enemy could never say that I do not understand the people of England.' There is a great truth in this. But there was a curious hesitation to strike a continuous and a bold note. His manœuvres were tactical and defensive. He disliked the great offensive and strategic design. Perhaps the 1923 decision—the sudden and unsuccessful appeal on protection—and its results had shaken his confidence. 'Safety First' at any rate revealed a temperament which would not be able to face the terrible dangers soon about to threaten the life of the civilised world. Within two years, however, Baldwin would reasonably be able to claim that this very slogan, on which he lost the election of 1929, had proved the successful rallying-cry of a Coalition in which the Conservatives were the dominating element and had won the greatest political victory in our history. The Labour Party, which in 1929 was returned as the strongest party in the House, with 288 Members elected, was to be reduced by this appeal in a little over two years to a membership in the House of Commons of only 52. Such are the paradoxes of politics.

In the 1929 election, if the Conservative programme was uninspiring, the Labour policy was conventional. They depended upon their normal appeal—the unemployment figures, the lack of any Government policy, the alleged regressive taxation, and a general insistence upon a cry which has done good service for both sides before and since: 'It's time for a change'. The Liberal Party, now united under the full control of Lloyd George, could attack both Right and Left. The Tories had gone to sleep. After all it was a Tory Member, Colonel Moore-Brabazon, who had made a characteristic outburst, after resigning his office as Under-Secretary to the Minister of Transport in 1927 as a protest against the hopeless inefficiency of his immediate chief, in these bitter words, 'The snores of the Treasury bench resound throughout the country'.

For some years, a series of arresting reports had been brought out under Lloyd George's aegis: *Land and the Nation* (1925), *Coal and Power* (1927), *Towns and the Land* (1927), and, most important of all, *Britain's Industrial Future* (1928), the so-called 'Yellow Book'. This was summarised as a popular pamphlet entitled *We Can*

Conquer Unemployment. Its motto was simple: 'We Mobilised for War—Let us Mobilise for Prosperity'. Its long-term policy went back to the Genoa Conference, which Arthur Salter always described as the turning-point in Lloyd George's fortunes and perhaps the last chance for Europe. Now it was an appeal, externally for the stabilisation of gold prices and the expansion of trade; and, internally, for easier finance for industry and the improvement of industrial efficiency. He proposed also the redistribution of workers on a large scale and the development of new industries. On the gold standard he was cautious. He recommended 'a currency and banking policy which, consistently with the maintenance of the gold standard, will secure a greater measure of stability in British prices and easier money conditions for British industry'.[1] But Lloyd George's main efforts and those of the Liberal Party were concentrated on the short term. Broadly speaking, the proposals amounted to large and ambitious measures for roads, houses, telephones, electrical supply, drainage, railway development, and other projects, which would secure the maximum of employment and 'compensate for the frozen savings which the community is not choosing to invest'. This latter phrase is, of course, the first instance of the Keynesian policy brought into practical politics, and the recognition that one of the causes of the slump might well be that the rate of investment no longer equalled the rate of savings.

In a General Election in which all the Press commented on the apathy and listlessness of the electors, the Liberal Party in this major effort under the greatest of its leaders certainly did not lack enthusiasm. Five hundred Liberal candidates were put into the field. Lloyd George himself spoke all over the country, and the Liberal leaders temporarily disguised their deep dislike for each other in a spirited condemnation of the other two parties. Owing to the working of our electoral system, although the Liberal Party polled five million votes, they obtained only 59 Members in the House of Commons, one of whom, Mr. William Jowitt, K.C., immediately defected to the Labour benches. Many Members expressed indignation at this sudden conversion and Lloyd George attacked him in a vigorous speech. Using the jargon of the day, he declared that no

[1] David Lloyd George, *We Can Conquer Unemployment* (London, 1929), p. 7.

one could accuse him of 'not genuinely seeking work'. Churchill was more generous and is said to have observed in the smoking-room, 'He did it in the wrong way. If he had come to me I could have explained to him the technique of tergiversation.'

I became a victim of the general movement against the Government and the tide swept me away. The Labour candidate led the poll with 18,961 votes. I was second with 16,572. The Liberal polled 10,407. At the previous election I had had a majority of 3,215; now Labour was 2,389 ahead. The electorate had certainly been en-larged, partly by an influx of navvies on the I.C.I. development at Billingham. But the chief reason for my defeat was that whereas in 1924 I had gained a good deal of Liberal support, this time the old Liberals returned to the official Liberal candidate, who also no doubt gathered in behind Lloyd George's appeal a good many waverers. After the declaration, there were the usual emotional scenes, the victors triumphant, the defeated in tears. As the news of the polls began to reach us from all over the country I realised that I was not alone in my disappointment. Of our little group, Duff Cooper, Hudson, Loder, Terence O'Connor, as well as other progressives like Lord Henry Bentinck, were out. Only Oliver Stanley, Boothby, and Ralph Glyn remained. The next day was occupied with the usual visits of thanks and condolence among our supporters. We left in the afternoon. On the train were a large number of Labour M.P.s for Durham, justifiably celebrating their restoration after the defeats of 1924. Not the least boisterous was Dalton. When they were all met at King's Cross by an excited party of sympathisers, led by Oswald and Cynthia Mosley, my wife and I tried to raise a rather feeble counter-demonstration. I could not help reminding Dalton of this two years later, when we travelled back on the same train after the election of 1931. Then his position and mine were exactly reversed, and Mosley had left both the Labour Government and the Labour Party.

So far as the national vote was concerned, the Conservatives had not done at all badly. Their popular vote was well over $8\frac{1}{2}$ million and the Labour vote under $8\frac{1}{2}$ million. That they only got 260 seats against Labour's 288 was part of the way the cards fell. It was largely due to the very high Liberal vote; for the Liberals were operating as a united party with a dynamic programme. While the triangular system in previous years had tended to favour the Conservatives, from now on, and indeed to this day, it has proved a handicap to them over the country as a whole.

As always after defeat, there soon began a flow of explanations and recriminations, both in the Press and outside. While the disappearance of the young and progressive Conservatives was deplored by such papers as *The Times*, the *Daily Telegraph*, the *Observer*, the *Spectator*, and most of the provincial Press, other commentators took exactly the opposite line. The *Daily Mail* complained that 'Conservatism as it was led before the General Election was not Conservatism. It was the semi-Socialist policy that went down in the great defeat'.[1] It went on to protest against the provision of any vacant seats for 'semi-Socialists such as Captain Harold Macmillan'. This note was echoed in the *Saturday Review*, which pilloried Duff Cooper and myself as 'only Socialists in disguise'.[2]

In the autumn, discussions on the future of Conservative policy continued. A major speech was made by Neville Chamberlain towards the end of October on the subject of the tariff. He drew an important moral from the election. One of its results had been to free the Conservative Party from all the pledges and all the conditions which it imposed upon itself in the past. The slate had been cleaned and they were free to write upon it whatsoever might seem to them after due consideration and due consultation desirable to put thereon. This important declaration meant, of course, that the party was now without inhibitions, and able to consider new policies such as a general tariff (as opposed to 'safeguarding') and a wide extension of imperial preference. On the very same day I made a speech in London on the same lines, in which I welcomed the impetus which Lord Beaverbrook's papers were giving to this theme. At that time, of course, the great conflict over Empire free trade had not emerged, and Chamberlain and Beaverbrook were on good terms. Unfortunately, as is the habit of young men, I allowed myself the luxury of some sentences which were more highly publicised than the serious arguments which I deployed. In reference to the lack of constructive policy on unemployment, on the heavy industries, on

[1] *Daily Mail*, 22 June 1929.   [2] *Saturday Review*, 29 June 1929.

industrial reorganisation, and the like, I observed that we must avoid a situation where the people of Britain at the next election would find 'the same old shadow Cabinet still shadowing away until it is worn to a shadow by its exertions'. At that time I was at the pushing end of the movements which are common in political parties for change at the top and for the removal of older leaders, in order to make way for the promotion of more vital figures. It did not occur to me that some thirty years later I should find myself at the receiving end of such agitations.

Nevertheless, both before and after the election, I recognised and applauded the unique contribution which Baldwin had made to the strengthening of moderate forces in the country and to the reduction of extreme and violent emotion:

This steady process of moderation has profoundly affected party politics. The whole temper of the nation is cooler than it was five years ago. Passions, then excited to breaking point, are now calmed and soothed. The fortunes of the Socialist party, from the narrow party point of view, may be greatly favoured by this change; the interest of the nation must be greatly served by it. Perhaps, when the history of these times comes to be written, this steadying process may prove to be at once Mr. Baldwin's political grave and his political monument.[1]

In one way it was a bad prophecy, for the fortunes of the Socialist Party were soon to fall very low and not recover for the next fourteen years. This was largely by their own fault. But it was a fair and deserved tribute to Baldwin's most important achievement.

Controversy continued during the winter of 1929-30 between the various wings of the party. Some attributed our failure to too radical a policy and the abandonment of high Tory principles; others, of whom I was one, demanded a more positive policy for the future. I wrote some articles in the *Saturday Review* in November, in which I tried to develop a theme which seems still strangely familiar. In the first article I asserted with the confidence of youth what seemed to me the weakness of the present leadership:

The fundamental weakness of the Unionist Party to-day lies in its present confusion of thought. It has no clear policy on immediate problems; it has no clear goal towards which it feels itself to be striving. It has too many 'open

[1] *The Round Table*, 19 June 1929.

questions' and too many closed minds. It is at once Protectionist and Cobdenite; imperialist and internationalist; reforming and static. At some moments it favours State interference with the conditions of industry, at others it embraces *laissez-faire*. According to the varying amount of pressure exerted from varying quarters, it now follows one policy, now another. Sometimes dominated by the memories of Shaftesbury and Disraeli, it seems about to revive Young England; at other times it appears far more nearly a twentieth-century edition of nine-teenth-century Liberalism. Now almost cheese-paring, now almost prodigal, its financial policy presents a series of baffling contradictions.[1]

In the second article I set out the principles which I thought should guide us:

It seems to me that there are three chief classes of problem which await solution. First, we require a more efficient and a more economic organisation of our industrial system from the purely technical aspect. Secondly, we need to recognise the fundamental causes of the unrest and lack of cohesion among the personnel of the system. Thirdly, we must at all costs devise a means of ex-panding the markets available and securing to our own industry the greatest possible share of those markets.[2]

This policy I summarised as follows:

... There are three great aims upon which Unionism must concentrate—modernisation of our economic methods, the humanisation of our industrial relations, and the expansion of our foreign, and primarily of our imperial, markets.

I now had to consider my own future. The Labour Government in its first months was doing pretty well; certainly in the field of foreign affairs. The moderate wing of the Labour Party was clearly dominant in the Government, and this created a feeling of relief, if not of confidence, throughout the country. Although the American slump had begun, its world-wide effects had not yet become apparent. There seemed no reason, therefore, why the new Parlia-ment should not run its full course. I was naturally anxious to return to the House of Commons and enjoy the experience, so far denied to me, of being in Opposition, where a greater degree of freedom is allowed and even encouraged among back-bench Members. In December I accepted an invitation from the Hitchin Conservative

[1] *Saturday Review*, 2 November 1929.   [2] *Saturday Review*, 9 November 1929.

Association to stand for the constituency. Major Guy Kindersley, the sitting Member, was anxious to retire for business reasons and it was agreed that the by-election should take place as soon as practicable. What both he and I had in mind was sometime in the spring of 1930. However, in May 1930 he felt it would be unwise to have a by-election in existing conditions. There was danger that with the Beaverbrook campaign and the movement against the leader of the party there would be confusion and division. The president of the National Farmers' Union resided in the constituency, and it was possible that they would run a candidate. If there was no Liberal candidate, the Liberals might on this occasion, in view of the importance of the tariff issue, vote for the Socialists. In the sitting Member's view, 'the seat might easily be lost'. Although disappointed, I yielded to his arguments. In fact, during this period I suffered from a good deal of trouble with my old wounds, which caused me great pain and lameness. I was forced later on, in the summer of 1931, to go abroad to try to get the necessary treatment and rest. In February 1931 Major Kindersley informed me that he had definitely reached the conclusion that a by-election might be disastrous. I had no alternative but to accept his sincere view – all the more because I knew him to be a man of the most scrupulous honour. About the same time Mr. Leonard Ropner (uncle of the M.P.), who had been adopted in Stockton in my place, was led by family bereavement and ill health to resign as prospective candidate. I had been very happy in handing over Stockton to his care. He was a man universally respected locally, both for his generosity and for his character. He had served successfully as Mayor and seemed more likely than any other candidate we could find to win back the seat.

In March 1931 I received an appeal from the Stockton Committee, signed by a large number of my old supporters, urging me to return. After some negotiation everything was arranged. Hitchin Conservatives were good enough to express their regret but their full understanding of my motives. I made it plain that the only consideration which had led me to abandon Stockton was the opportunity of entering Parliament as soon as possible. This had been the agreed plan; but for various reasons it had not been thought practicable to put it into effect. It seemed now too late to ask for a by-election with the uncertainties of how long this Parliament would last. I felt, therefore, that it was in the interests of the party that I should return to Stockton. I was given a very friendly and helpful send-off by the Hitchin Conservatives, who praised me for my 'public spirit' in returning to my former constituency.

So it was settled. I shall never forget the scenes of welcome when we came back for our adoption meeting at Stockton in May 1931. We had a wonderful reception at the station and big crowds in the streets. Grateful as I was for the kindness I had received at Hitchin, I was frankly glad to be back in the North where my affections lay. I had not more than a few months to wait.

The two years from 1929 to 1931 had been a period of increasing political confusion and complexity. The salient features were on the one hand the struggle for the Conservative leadership and on the other the gradual disintegration of the Labour Government. Baldwin's long fight against the forces demanding his deposition was finally won in March 1931 by the outcome of the famous by-election at St. George's, Westminster. For more than eighteen months the battle had swayed backwards and forwards. Lord Beaverbrook began in July 1929 his campaign for Empire free trade. Although most Conservatives recognised that in their crude form his policies were impracticable, yet the raising of Joseph Chamberlain's old standard naturally attracted a large measure of support. Early in 1930 Baldwin met the pressure by his acceptance in the programme of full protection and imperial preference on manufactured goods, but rejected taxes on food. Naturally this did not satisfy Beaverbrook and the agitation continued unabated. In June 1930 Baldwin called a meeting of Conservative M.P.s and candidates. He demanded and obtained a vote of confidence. In this, he was much assisted by a letter from Rothermere to a Conservative Member which he was able to quote with considerable effect. The great newspaper magnate impudently demanded not only to know what the policy was to be but the names of Baldwin's most prominent colleagues in the next Ministry. Baldwin was able to make a devastating reply to what he rightly called an 'insolent demand'. Neville Chamberlain then came upon the scene, and with great loyalty accepted at the end of June the difficult and unrewarding task of party chairman, with full control of the research department. Baldwin gained much strength from Chamberlain's authority. There was a general confidence that with his clear and logical mind he would be able to develop a more constructive and positive policy.

Nevertheless, the unrest in the party did not diminish. Churchill still remained a convinced free-trader. He was taking a leading part in fierce opposition to the Government in the House of Commons, where it was known that he favoured an arrangement with Lloyd George and the Liberals to turn out the Government and fight an election on the basis of Conservative–Liberal collaboration; in other words, the old Coalition. This was as distasteful to Baldwin and to Chamberlain as almost any plan could be. Both these men had a deep distrust of and dislike for Lloyd George. The loss of South Paddington to an Independent candidate supported by Beaverbrook in the autumn of 1930 shook, but did not destroy, Baldwin's position. By February 1931, however, the leadership was again in question. Chamberlain records in his diary that he was 'getting letters and communications from all over the country'.[1] Yet there was little he could do without appearing to stab his friend and leader in the back. Churchill had resigned from the Shadow Cabinet on the question of constitutional advance in India, to which he was strongly opposed, although his speeches in the House of Commons, attacking the Government with extraordinary verve and skill, delighted the party. On 26 February Neville Chamberlain received a memorandum from the principal agent of a most gloomy and defeatist character. After consultation with Austen Chamberlain, Hoare, Cunliffe-Lister, Hailsham, the Chief Whip, and Bridgeman, it was agreed that Neville Chamberlain should show this document to Baldwin.[1] It is interesting, having regard to the many years of office and power that still lay before Baldwin, to recall the actual words of Chamberlain's diary: 'Everyone I think except Willie Bridgeman was of the opinion that S.B. would have to resign.'[1]

Nevertheless, once more the Press lords came to Baldwin's rescue. The St. George's by-election marked the end of the struggle. It was one of the most extraordinary episodes in recent political

[1] Keith Feiling, *Life of Neville Chamberlain*, p. 185.

history. The sitting Member, Sir Laming Worthington-Evans, had died. The seat was offered to Colonel Moore-Brabazon, who refused it on the grounds that he could not support Baldwin. This was damaging enough. Sir Ernest Petter, supported by Beaverbrook and Rothermere, then announced his intention to stand as an Independent. On the afternoon of 1 March Baldwin decided on immediate resignation. It was Bridgeman who urged him to hold on, at least for a few weeks. It was clear that the St. George's by-election, whichever way it went, would decide the issue. So Baldwin stayed.[1]

Never since the famous Westminster election, when Fox was triumphantly returned with the combined support of high Whig society and the London mob, has there been anything to equal this dramatic contest. Duff Cooper stepped into the breach with admirable courage, and fought a skilful campaign. In spite of a personal friendship with Beaverbrook, Duff Cooper attacked both him and Rothermere mercilessly and effectively. The constituency was partly composed of large fashionable houses. Their owners and the many servants who inhabited them in those days constituted an important proportion of voters. All 'Society' rallied to Duff Cooper. Lady Diana was already a famous and popular figure; even Georgiana, Duchess of Devonshire, cannot have surpassed her in charm and beauty. Meetings were held in every drawing-room, as well as in every local hall and school. Excitement grew daily to a fever pitch. Baldwin, who had a remarkable power of rising to a real crisis, soon recovered from his mood of a few weeks before. At a great meeting in the Queen's Hall he came out with a direct challenge to the Press lords. He attacked their personalities and their methods. For once in his life he was angry. The culminating point of his speech was a sentence which will live in political history: 'What the proprietorship of these papers is aiming at is power, but power without responsibility—the prerogative of the harlot throughout the ages.'[2] Duff Cooper won the election with a majority of nearly 6,000. The campaign against Baldwin began to die down and soon ended altogether as the national situation moved

---

[1] Keith Feiling, *Life of Neville Chamberlain*, p. 186.

[2] It was generally believed that these words were given to Baldwin by his cousin, Rudyard Kipling. They are certainly worthy of him.

to a crisis. There was a further result, not without importance. The Press lords lost their power and never regained it.

Of equal significance for the future was Churchill's withdrawal from the Shadow Cabinet in January 1931. He was strongly opposed to any policy in India which would inevitably end in self-government. He was therefore highly critical of the line which his colleagues were taking in support of the Labour Government on this issue. Although, when the National Government was formed later in the year, with characteristic generosity he moved the vote of confidence in Baldwin at the meeting of Conservative M.P.s, yet he was destined to remain out of office and without any control over the main stream of events for ten years. History might indeed have been different had it been otherwise. When Churchill returned to office Britain was once again at war.

Looking back upon his fight to retain the leadership, it seems clear that Baldwin was in fact protected by the multiplicity of his opponents. The progressive elements of the party, however dis-satisfied with his apparent inability to design or expound in public a reformist policy, could not but admire his attitude over the Indian problem. On this issue Churchill could command the support of the Right but not the Centre or the Left. In the same way, those who were attracted by the general purpose of the Empire free-trade crusade, so actively pursued by Beaverbrook, could not accept his plans in detail. Moreover, they became more and more disinclined to join in a movement promoted by such violent and such personal attacks upon their leader. Here again, Beaverbrook was by no means assisted by his uneasy alliance with Rothermere. Beaverbrook had an aim, chimerical as it might seem to many, which he pursued steadily and consistently throughout his whole life. Rothermere was both unstable and unfair. When Baldwin therefore roused himself to counter-attack, he was able to rally the party without difficulty. His fine speech on India and his withering attack upon the Press lords added greatly to his stature. As so often in his life, he was able to command the sympathy not only of Conservatives, in and out of Parliament, but of the mass of his fellow-countrymen.

During this period, the inner history of which has now been partially revealed, most of us, especially those like myself no longer in the House of Commons, were largely in the dark as to what was happening. I did my best by occasional speeches or articles to keep alive some of the ideas which we had put forward in the last Parliament. In this I had the particular sympathy and help of Noel Skelton. But he warned me in November 1929, 'you will get no response for thought and sacrifice from the present Unionist Party. The harrow will have to go over their backs again and again before they accept the necessity of thinking.' This was perhaps written in an unusually despondent mood, by a man who had given more constructive thought to politics than almost any other member of the party in or out of the House of Commons. Little did we know then how soon our purely party difficulties were to be resolved by political developments which lay only two years ahead. Meanwhile, in the meetings in my new constituency, I maintained my views but began to move more firmly towards the need for tariffs and protection: tariffs as a means of retaliation and protection as a means to help our much-distressed heavy industry. At the same time I had some tentative discussions with Beaverbrook. Being young and inexperienced, I was at one time tempted to come out in open support of his movement to change the leadership. Beaverbrook was both wiser and more considerate than many people have given him credit for. He urged me to keep out of any situation which was likely to embarrass me and not to appear on any platform which would compromise my position. I was then still hoping to have an early by-election, and he went so far as to offer to do his best to prevent any independent opposition from the farmers or from any other quarter. As things turned out, our courses were not destined to meet again for many years. Indeed, I do not remember having seen him, except once or twice, until the beginning of the Second War, in the early years of which I found myself at one stage acting as his Under-Secretary in the Ministry of Supply. It was then I learnt to appreciate the extraordinary gifts of this strange and wayward genius.

If the Opposition was in disorder throughout this Parliament, a similar disintegration soon began to attack the Government. They started with high hopes and achieved some success, particularly abroad. At the Hague Conference—one of an interminable series to deal with the vexed question of reparations—Snowden had almost a triumph. Although the results were wholly disproportionate to his trenchant defence of British interests—the successful claim to £2 million of the nominal Young Plan annuities was all it amounted to[1]—he won the approval of the British people, who were beginning to be wearied by the continual sacrifices demanded from them. Henderson, as Foreign Secretary, was responsible for the signing of the 'Optional Clause', as it was called, by which Britain bound herself to submit all disputes to the Court of International Justice. This appealed to the large body of opinion which saw in the League of Nations and in an international system for the peaceful settlement of national conflicts the best hope for the future. The resumption of diplomatic relations with Russia in October 1929 was broadly acceptable, not least to the business community. The death of Stresemann threw a shadow on the future; but the rise of Hitler to actual power was still some years ahead, although the increase of the Nazi Party seats in the Reichstag, from 12 to 107, in September 1930 was a disagreeable foretaste of what was to come.

The long-drawn-out discussions in the Naval Conference, in spite of the dissent of France and Italy, led at least to an agreement between three Powers—the United States, Japan, and Britain. It was true that restriction of the number of cruisers to fifty in no way corresponded to the real needs of the British Navy and its vital task of protecting merchant shipping in time of war. It was bitterly attacked by Churchill on this ground. But the public felt that at least some agreement was better than none. The final evacuation of the Rhineland by French troops in June 1930, long before the date specified in the Treaty of Versailles, marked further progress in international reconciliation. Henderson's conduct of affairs at Geneva won approval, both at home and abroad. He was a most popular Foreign Secretary, and his international reputation became an asset for the Government. MacDonald's visit to the United States in the autumn of 1929 was a success; and Anglo-American relations, which had not been very happy during recent years, were correspondingly improved. Finally, the firm advance towards a constitution for India and the summoning of the Round Table Conference provided MacDonald with an opportunity, which he was not slow to take, of

[1] C. L. Mowat, *Britain Between the Wars, 1918–1940*, p. 374.

displaying his conciliatory talents. Baldwin gave generous help. It was, therefore, not in the field of foreign or imperial affairs that the Labour Government found itself in difficulties. On the contrary, in spite of criticism on this or that aspect from the Conservative Opposition, the Government could count on a wide degree of general support. Indeed, it was rather in the ranks of the Opposition than on the Government side that fissures were disclosed.

Unhappily for MacDonald and his colleagues, as so often before and since, the public paid more attention to internal than to external affairs. The real test came at home. At the General Election the Socialist Party had made bold claims. They and they alone would be able to deal with the problem of unemployment. They had no very clear plans, but they made very fine promises. Miss Margaret Bondfield, who was in general respected as a serious politician, was even unwise enough to assert that unemployment could be cured in three weeks. Not for the first time and not for the last, the successful party at the General Election found itself confronted with the disagreeable task of redeeming its pledges. So far as the purely Socialist aspects of the Labour policy were concerned, MacDonald's difficulties were in a sense simplified by two factors. In the first place, the composition of the House of Commons, in which there was no clear majority, meant that the Government must rely on Liberal support. This was an adequate excuse for keeping in the background Socialist experiments, the desirability of which was becoming in his mind more and more remote. 'Evolutionary' was the word he now used to describe his brand of Socialism. Secondly, the inner Cabinet consisted of moderates. The Left-wing leaders, like Wheatley, had been conspicuously excluded. If MacDonald's Socialism was wearing pretty thin, Snowden's had almost disappeared under the pressure of events. His views, in fact, scarcely differed from those of the leading nineteenth-century Radicals. He was even keener on retrenchment than on reform. He was equally determined to agree to nothing that savoured of Lloyd George's bold expansionist concepts. It is true that he agreed to the appointment of J. H. Thomas to be in charge of schemes for employment, in which he was to be assisted by George Lansbury, the veteran of the party, Thomas Johnston, Under-Secretary for Scotland, and Oswald

Mosley. But Snowden made it quite clear that this body was not to be allowed to do anything effective. A few minor concessions might be made here and there, and a little window-dressing. Consequently, the Development Act and the Colonial Development Act, which were now hurriedly passed through Parliament, were only 'enabling'. The Treasury 'watch-dog' would see to it that their permissive character should be strictly maintained. Snowden, speaking in the House of Commons about plans for the relief of unemployment, used these ominous words:

Schemes involving heavy expenditure will have to wait till prosperity returns.

It would hardly be possible to state more succinctly the contrary to what is now the accepted antidote to a period of depression.

In these circumstances, although MacDonald tried to share some of his responsibilities with Parliament as a whole, by his solemn proposal that the House should act as a Council of State, more sceptical Members recognised this declaration as meaning that he did not know what to do. At the time of the election in June 1929 unemployment stood at 1,164,000. This was denounced by the Labour Party as an intolerable figure. By June 1930 it reached 1,911,000; and by the summer of 1931 it stood at 2,707,000. This was the brutal answer of events to the high hopes held out by the Socialists at the General Election. Of course, it was not the Government's fault. But it was their misfortune 'to take office just as the unsound structure of the post-war international economy began to crumble'.[1] By now, we know—or think we know—what happened and why. But just as Governments take the credit for good fortune, so in the harsh political world in which we live they have to bear the burden of ill luck. Opposition Members would indeed have shown unprecedented restraint if they had not retaliated for all the accusations made against them during the four and a half years of the previous administration. For four and a half years they had suffered almost monthly votes of censure on unemployment. Much as they deplored the worsening of the situation, they could not be expected to refrain from exploiting it.

If unemployment could not be reduced, the unemployed had still

[1] C. L. Mowat, *Britain Between the Wars, 1918-1940*, p. 357.

somehow or other to be maintained. Soon after the election of 1929, Neville Chamberlain asked me to call upon him to discuss the future of unemployment insurance. This was a compliment which I appreciated and I recall a conversation in which he showed an unexpected sympathy for the line that I had been taking in the previous Parliament. At the same time he felt that this question would be the 'Achilles' heel' of the Labour Government, and that we should work out some policy of our own for the future. Accordingly, I sent him a memorandum summarising my ideas, some of which later took shape in the National Assistance Board.

Meanwhile, by a bitter irony it fell to Miss Bondfield as Minister of Labour to introduce a series of measures not to cure unemployment in three weeks but to increase the Treasury's contribution to the Unemployment Fund. The first of these became necessary shortly after Parliament met; a further sum was required in the autumn and at the same time some rearrangements were made, which would allow transitional benefits to a number of persons, even though they were lacking the minimum number of contributions. She also introduced a new condition in respect of the onus of proof hitherto lying upon the applicant that he was 'genuinely seeking work'. The obligation of proving the contrary passed to the officials of the Labour Exchange. In the course of the discussions on the Bill the Government was forced to appoint a Royal Commission to examine the whole working of the system.

In the spring of 1930 the proposals of Lansbury, Mosley, and Johnston for the reduction of unemployment were submitted to the Cabinet. They were embodied in a document which soon became known, and indeed notorious, as the 'Mosley Memorandum'. The Cabinet rejected these bold plans in May. A month later Mosley resigned his office. His main ideas, although largely in accord with the Labour election promises, included some novelties: earlier retirement from industry; the protection of the home market by tariffs; import restrictions and bulk purchase agreements with foreign and especially Empire producers; the development of British agriculture; the rationalisation of industry under public control; and an improved system of credit for industrial development. These ideas, at least as a basis for action, commended themselves to a number of non-partisan critics. Mosley won much sympathy at a special meeting of the Labour Party to consider the situation. But at this point he made a fatal mistake. Not only did he insist upon a vote, where he naturally could rally only limited support, but he carried on the fight, in a somewhat truculent mood, at the Labour Party's conference of 1930. With this demonstration he ought, from his own point of view, to have been content. But in December of the same year he published a manifesto, supported by A. J. Cook and seventeen other Members, including Strachey, Bevan, and W. J. Brown.[1] Then early in 1931 he took the decisive step of announcing the formation of his New Party. It is easy to see that whatever the merits of his proposals—and they were considerable—he made a serious error in tactics. All young men (as I learnt from experience) find it difficult to exercise patience. But looking back, it is clear that if he had accepted his temporary defeat and continued his agitation, while remaining inside the Labour Party, his position would have been a strong one. When the crash came six months later, and the party found itself divided and shattered, Mosley would have been welcomed into the inner circles. Had he been able to secure re-election, with the leading members of the old Labour Government out of Parliament, he would have found his only rivals in Lansbury, an ineffective and ageing figure, and Attlee, at that time a rather dim one. The leadership of the party might easily have fallen to him. All this, of course, it is easy to see with hindsight; yet the lesson remains for others to ponder over and digest. A certain arrogance and impatience brought an end to his Parliamentary career. When he later took refuge in an extra-Parliamentary movement, and tried to bring Fascism into England, he was doomed. Nevertheless, at the early stages, in the spring of 1930, he had many sympathisers in all parties. Whether wisely or not, probably unwisely, I could not resist the temptation to write a letter to *The Times* which caused a certain stir. It was published on 27 May 1930 and its most important passages were as follows:

The position ... is fairly simple. As the result of the General Election of 1929, a Socialist Government was formed and Sir Oswald Mosley was given,

[1] C. L. Mowat, *Britain Between the Wars, 1918–1940*, pp. 359 ff.

if not the leading, at least a most important role in the task of carrying into effect those of the Socialist promises to the people which had particularly to do with the cure or the alleviation of unemployment. Actually, in the course of the 12 months during which the Socialist Government has been responsible for the conduct of our affairs, this problem has been gravely accentuated and the pressure of unemployment has almost doubled. Faced with this startling and even spectacular calamity, Sir Oswald seems to have conceived a novel, and no doubt according to the accepted political standards of what are called 'responsible statesmen', incredibly naive, idea. He drew up and actually went so far as to present to his chief a memorandum which suggested that an attempt should be made to carry out at least some, if not all, of the pledges and promises by the exploitation of which the Socialist Party obtained power.

Regarded as a genial academic exercise, the famous memorandum no doubt excited among the more experienced Ministers emotions varying from patronising appreciation to mild disapproval. But when this document was elevated ... to the ... status of an ultimatum, it was met at first, indeed, with incredulity; then with horror and indignation.

Had these feelings been confined to the 'Elder Statesmen' of the Socialist Party, I should have felt no surprise and certainly no alarm. But I confess, Sir, that I do not understand the reasons which have led you and non-Socialist commentators generally to such an unappreciative attitude towards Sir Oswald Mosley's position. Is it to be the accepted rule in our politics that a political programme is to be discarded as soon as it has served its electoral purpose? Are we to accept the cynical view that a statesman is to be applauded in inverse ratio to the extent to which he carries out in office what he has promised in Opposition? ... Your Parliamentary Correspondent remarks this morning that Sir Oswald's speech (at the Socialist Party meeting) 'contained little in the way of new proposals, most of the suggestions having already been made public in *Labour and the Nation*'. That is exactly my point. Had these proposals been novel, a Socialist Cabinet might properly have resisted them. In point of fact they are part of their own official prospectus. ...

The mere suggestion that election promises ought to be implemented seems to have fluttered the dovecotes of more than one political party. It has deeply shocked what are called 'moderate men' of all parties. It is a novel and dangerous experiment, which might, if it were allowed to pass unchallenged, spread later on into a fantastic precedent, with serious and even devastating effects. An example must be made at once. We must stop the rot. Whoever has so far broken the rules of the political game as to suggest that a politician ought to say what he means and mean what he says, must receive immediate and severe castigation 'in order to discourage the others'.

The letter went on to make some comments, of a critical kind, on the Conservative leadership and expressed the hope that the practice of fighting elections on the basis of a programme which is either self-contradictory or obscure should be brought to an end. One paper described my letter as 'brilliantly indiscreet'. It was certainly indiscreet.

I had only a slight acquaintance with Sir Oswald, although his wife was an old friend of my wife and her family. As a result of this incident, I had many conversations with him during the next few months, and was struck both by his acute intelligence and his energy. There was a moment later in the year when I was myself tempted to work with his New Party, for there were many of the points of his programme which seemed to me at once reasonable and constructive. But it became clear on reflection that the traditional political parties are far too strongly entrenched for any separatist movement of the kind he had launched to be successful, even to deal with so great a crisis as was now impending. It is a deep and, no doubt, a sound political instinct in our country, that men do better to stick to their own parties and try to influence their policies and their character from within. This may often be tedious and disappointing; but it is more likely to lead to results than breaking away in a mood of disillusionment. I deeply regretted the course that Sir Oswald Mosley later took. Even his loyal friends, such as Strachey and Bevan, left him when they saw his movement beginning to develop into a form of Fascism, with everything which that implied. This whole story was something of a tragedy. Great talents and great strength of character were thrown away in vain. Among those who left Mosley was Allan Young, who had been his assistant and a Labour candidate in Birmingham on more than one occasion. He was a true democrat, and found the drift towards Fascism altogether abhorrent. We made a deep and lasting friendship. I was able to make use of Young's experience and keen intelligence in some of the undertakings in which I was later to become connected.

Mosley's resignation from the Government, and the joint Conservative and Liberal attacks on the Government's policies, led to a new attempt by Lloyd George to come to terms with Mac-Donald. But this in turn produced a disintegration of the Liberal

Party similar to those which had attacked the other two. Lloyd George found the new unity which the Liberals had achieved in the election of 1929 essentially hollow. Liberals soon acquired a habit (which, incidentally, they have often followed since) of not operating as a single body when the test of voting was applied. When Lloyd George tried to move towards the Right, he would lose the sympathy of the more Left-wing Members. When he tried to move towards the Left, he was opposed by the Right. Liberals began to vote in different lobbies. Sometimes their small group broke into three streams: the first for the Government, the second against, and the third abstaining. The fissure which later resulted in the two main groups, Simonites and Samuelites, now began.

While all the political parties were in a state of some uncertainty and confusion, the Government somehow staggered on. Its own weakness was matched by that of its opponents. In the Budget of 1931 Snowden did not really face the coming storm. A Conservative vote of censure had recently been staved off by his acceptance of a Liberal proposal for a special committee to recommend economies on the lines of the famous Geddes Committee.[1] In appointing the committee under Sir George May,[2] whose Report afterwards obtained great notoriety, Snowden must have known that he was riding for a fall—or perhaps setting a mine. According to Dalton,[3] the Cabinet, contrary to his wishes, vetoed in this month any reduction of the insurance benefit. Yet it was the growing expenditure of the Fund which would prove the ultimate cause of the break-up of the Government. It is possible that he felt that the Report of the May Committee would bring his party to its senses. He therefore balanced his Budget with only minor adjustments and a small increase of taxation. He threw in a future tax on land values as a sop to the Liberals. But the Budget made no real attempt to meet the difficulties ahead, at least on the orthodox lines which Snowden was known to favour.

[1] A committee under Sir Eric Geddes which in 1922 recommended drastic economies.
[2] In February, as a result of a Parliamentary debate, a committee was appointed under the chairmanship of Sir George May, formerly Secretary of the Prudential Assurance Co. Ltd., to make recommendations for economies.
[3] Hugh Dalton, *Memoirs*, vol. i: *Call Back Yesterday* (London, 1953), pp. 264–5.

...ther at 'Vermelles' nr. Loos, at
...bout 2.30 p.m. Monday. Sept. 28th 1915
...st before the attack on Hill 70.

Harold Macmillan at Loos, 1915.

Daniel Macmillan, the author's grandfather, founder of Macmillan & Co., Ltd.

Alexander Macmillan, the auth[?] great-uncle.

Dr. J. Tarleton Belles, the author's maternal grandfather, who practised medicine in Spencer, Indiana.

rs. J. Tarleton Belles, the author's maternal grandmother.

Harold Macmillan, aged four.

Harold Macmillan, aged twelve

Maurice Crawford Macmillan, the
author's father.

:len Macmillan, the author's mother.

The Oxford Union, 1912. *Back row*: G. W. Talbot, E. H. G. Roberts, H. G. Strauss, Mr. Wedderburn, M. W. Gill, A. F. H. Wiggin, V. A. L. Mallet. *Middle row*: Sidney Ball, Rt. Hon. Austen Chamberlain, A. H. M. Wedderburn (*President*), Sir William Anson, W. H. Moberley, From row:

Lady Dorothy Cavendish, who
became Harold Macmillan's wife.
Portrait by Philip de Laszlo.

The author with his son, Maurice
Macmillan, 1922.

Christmas between the wars at Chatsworth, country seat of the Duke of Devonshire, the author's father-in-law.

Harold and Lady Dorothy Macmillan and their children, Catherine, Maurice, and Carol, 1929.

Coal strike poster.

Bus leaving garage under escort during the General Strike, 1926.

Harold Macmillan campaigning at Stockton, 1929.

The unemployed being fed from a food wagon in Hyde Park, 1931.

First cabinet meeting of the National Government at 10 Downing Street, 1931. *Foreground:* Ramsay MacDonald, J. H. Thomas. *Center, on steps:* Lord Reading, Stanley Baldwin, Philip Snowden. *Rear:* Sir Herbert Samuel, Neville Chamberlain, Sir Samuel Hoare, Sir Philip Cunliffe-Lister, Lord Sankey.

Harold Macmillan at Stockton, 1935.

Stanley Baldwin leaving 10 Downing
Street during the abdication crisis,
1936.

The War Cabinet, November 1939. *Standing*: Sir John Anderson, Lord Hankey, Leslie Hore-Belisha, Winston Churchill, Sir Kingsley Wood, Anthony Eden, Sir Edward Bridges. *Sitting*: Lord Halifax, Sir John Simon, Neville Chamberlain, Sir Samuel Hoare, Lord Chatfield.

Sir Oswald Mosley, leader of the
British Fascists.

Neville Chamberlain when he returned from Munich, 1938.

Munich week, 1938. Harold and Lady Dorothy Macmillan at Birch Grove House with children from Rachel McMillan Nursery School.

The summer passed by without the storm which had broken over Europe apparently reaching Britain. Although, in a debate just before Parliament adjourned, Snowden and Chamberlain by previous agreement both gave grave warnings, no action was taken. Members separated in the ordinary way for their summer holidays. They were unconscious of the tense days which lay immediately ahead. When they returned, it was to find a new Government, with MacDonald presiding over an administration drawn from all parties, and with the bulk of the Labour Party in Opposition. This was the National Government, destined to survive at least in form until it was replaced in 1940 by Churchill's War Coalition.

Many thousands of words have been written on the economic and political aspects of the 1931 crisis. Some of the chief actors— including Snowden and Herbert Samuel—have given their own accounts. In other cases, such as Baldwin and Neville Chamberlain, their biographers have published considerable extracts from their own diaries and records. Some of the minor figures, who stood only on the fringe of events, such as Dalton, have recorded their own impressions. MacDonald has remained silent; nor has any account based on his papers become available. King George V's part has been described in some detail by his biographer, Sir Harold Nicolson. A careful analysis of the whole story is contained in R. Bassett's *Nineteen Thirty-One*. He has weighed all the evidence with scrupulous care and it is difficult to differ from his main conclusions. Yet the action and reaction of individuals on any such situation is always obscure. Even at this distance of time, the 1931 drama can profitably be studied as a matter of interest, both from the human and the technical points of view.

Whatever may have been the failures of his closing years, due primarily to physical and intellectual fatigue, there is no doubt that MacDonald was a very considerable man. He was the main founder of the Labour-Socialist movement. He built it up from a handful of Members in the House of Commons to a strength where it was twice able, under his authority, to take office as a Government. He brought to the Labour Government dignity and credit. He was admired abroad and, until he made the break with the main body of his party in 1931, venerated by his supporters at home. He had a charm of manner and a natural courtesy which were both genuine and endearing. When he took his decision to form the National Government, he did so with his eyes open. He knew that he would be covered with abuse and denounced as a Judas. His position was far more poignant than that of Joseph Chamberlain in 1886. The latter divided an ancient party of which he had been a keen and active Member. The former temporarily destroyed a party of which he was one of the actual founders. But it is clear from all the accounts that MacDonald, although he had come to dislike the pettiness of many of his colleagues, was careful of their interests. He made no real effort to bring with him the main body, either of the Cabinet or of the junior Ministers. Those whose careers were coming to an end he was glad to have with him—Snowden, Sankey (the Lord Chancellor), J. H. Thomas, and the like. But younger men, such as Herbert Morrison, whose sympathies were certainly with MacDonald, he seems to have dissuaded. In other words, he was enough of a statesman to think not merely of the immediate needs of his country, as he saw them, in what he and others confidently believed to be a short-term, temporary, and manageable crisis. He also thought of the future. He realised that it would be a grave injury to the nation if the Labour movement were to be deprived of all its moderate elements. Under the immediate pressure of events it might be shattered. But it would revive, and remain the constitutional expression of the aspirations of the Left. Judged in this way, much is explicable and indeed admirable in MacDonald's conduct.

There is some evidence which supports the view that MacDonald's mind was turning to the possibilities of a National Government some months before the actual event. For instance, it appears from Neville Chamberlain's diary of 6 July 1931 that MacDonald had sounded Lord Stonehaven, the chairman of the Conservative Party, although he adds that on referring this to Baldwin they both agreed 'that our [the Conservative] party would not stand it for a moment'.[1] Dalton, in his memoirs, maintains that there had been earlier meetings between Baldwin and MacDonald. There is other evidence of the same kind, which points to friendly talks between MacDonald and Baldwin during the spring. From

[1] Keith Feiling, *Life of Neville Chamberlain*, p. 189.

MacDonald's point of view this seems a wise precaution. Similarly, his various conversations with Lloyd George, during the same period, were essential in his position. He was, after all, the leader of a party which had no clear majority in the House, and it is natural that he should have been in touch with the leaders of the two other parties. Baldwin, however, did not agree to join in 'official' talks, and refused a public offer of consultation on the unemployment situation which Lloyd George accepted.

I was in touch with Mosley after his resignation and held discussions with him from time to time. He also approached, in the spring of 1931, others of the so-called 'Young Conservatives', as well as Liberals and Socialists, to see how far a combination could be made to promote a constructive plan. As Lord Boothby recounts in his memoirs, this was discovered by Baldwin, who accused Boothby and his friends of hunting with packs other than their own.[1] As Baldwin was soon to amalgamate his own pack of hounds with two others, there is a certain amount of humour in this. In any case, MacDonald cannot be convicted of any deep-laid plot, or of taking action that was not normal in the circumstances. Snowden's real position throughout seems more obscure. The Government's agreement to appoint the May Committee was under the pressure of the Liberal amendment some months before. Some commentators have thought it suspicious that the Report of the Committee was timed to be published on 31 July, the day after the House of Commons adjourned for the summer holidays. But the wish to avoid Parliamentary debate might equally be due to the desire to preserve the Labour Government as to destroy it during the recess.

There is no evidence of any carefully hatched plot. The crisis itself got out of the control of the politicians. The course of events was as follows. On 11 May the Credit-Anstalt, the most important bank in Austria, failed, threatening the collapse of the German banking system. On 20 June President Hoover's proposal for a one-year moratorium, although a helpful and genuine attempt to meet the situation, was not enough to stop the rot. The Bank of England, and the British banking system in general, did their best to meet the impending collapse of the German economy. It is true that they took

[1] Robert Boothby, *I Fight to Live* (London, 1947), p. 92.

great risks in so doing, for they were borrowing short and lending long. But that after all is the function of a central bank. It is now accepted as the duty of the great financial organisations of the world to help each other. Perhaps the most serious error made by the British authorities was to agree to a 'standstill' agreement not to call in advances made to Germany, without any similar arrangement to protect Britain. In fact, the French immediately began to withdraw gold in London in large quantities and with great rapidity.

Meanwhile, certain events in England added to the internal difficulties. The Royal Commission on Unemployment Insurance reported at the end of June, recommending reductions in benefits and increases in contributions. This the Government, for understandable political reasons, could not accept. Early in July the long-awaited Report of Lord Macmillan's Committee on Finance and Industry was published. It was not exactly a document of limpid clarity and gave little practical assistance to a distracted administration. Even the minority Report, signed by Keynes and others, was of no immediate help. The whole was the result of years of work by the greatest experts, and it was irrelevant. On 30 July Parliament adjourned for the summer holiday. Ministers and Members were scattered all over Britain and the Continent. Baldwin, as usual, went to Aix-les-Bains. On 31 July the Report of the May Committee came out. It was sensational indeed. It shook confidence everywhere. It demanded cuts of £120 million in expenditure, some of which must obviously fall upon the unemployment insurance system. A few days later, two loans of £25 million each, made by New York and Paris, rapidly went down the sink. As fast as money was being put into this country by one method it was being drained out by another. It was with this situation that Ministers had to deal. Ministers did not dispute the need for drastic action. Nor did they differ from the orthodox solutions put forward by the authorities.

Historians and economists, writing in the light of experience, have described with varying emphasis the impact of the world economic crisis on Britain. While there is still controversy as to the remedies which should have been applied, there can be little dispute as to the sequence of events which led to the situation which MacDonald and his colleagues had to face in August. What was perhaps not understood at the time was the extent to which the return to the gold standard, not only by Britain but by some twenty other countries, had resulted in both a serious shortage and an even more serious maldistribution of gold. Gold was now required by the reserves of many countries, and this pull on gold was itself deflationary and the cause of a steady fall in prices over the whole period. The annual production of gold was insufficient to keep up with the increase in population and trade. Gold sent to America and France was not used as the basis of as much money or credit as it had been in the countries from which it was exported. Indeed, the additional flow of gold from 1926 to 1931 to France alone was equal to all the new gold mined in the world. Moreover, Britain's return to gold at the old parity required as its complement a corresponding adjustment of wages, salaries, and costs, which it had not been possible to achieve. As the crisis approached, not only was the whole world in difficulties but British exports had become more expensive in terms of money. In Salter's words: 'In the last analysis the fall of sterling in 1931 represents the victory of economic forces over monetary action.'[1]

But the real charge against the Labour Cabinet as a whole is not that they differed in principle with the Treasury view but that they did not follow out the logical sequence of the principles which they accepted. It was true that there were bolder spirits, such as Leo Amery or Keynes, who might, if they had been in charge, have followed a different course. But the Labour Ministers, whatever they may have protested later, cannot claim to have been anything except obedient devotees of the classical creed. In a word, they accepted the diagnosis but refused to apply the cure. They agreed to large economies. They only hesitated and finally broke up on the question of any reduction in insurance benefits. This was the 'sacred cow' of Labour and it could not be touched. It can, of course, be argued that the payments were already insufficient. Nevertheless, in comparison with the lower rates of wages, and having regard to their recent increase, they were by no means contemptible. Moreover, their real value was substantially higher than a few years before, owing to the continual fall in prices and the consequent reduction of the cost of

[1] Sir Arthur Salter, *Recovery: The Second Effort* (London, 1932), pp. 67 ff.

living. The hesitant Ministers might have demanded, as an alternative to the insurance cuts, the immediate imposition of some control over imports. They would have gained considerable support for such action; for the real reason of the crisis was not fundamentally that of an unbalanced Budget. Snowden made great use in the Cabinet meetings and outside of the fact that the Budget deficit would be higher even than that already anticipated—£170 million, not £120 million. But this was on the basis of the maintenance of the full Sinking Fund at £50 million, itself deflationary. The difference could have been met, as it ultimately was, by additional taxation, both direct and indirect. The unbalanced Budget was no doubt the cause of the lack of confidence all over the world in the strength of sterling. But the real cause, as we have now all realised, was the increasing gap in the balance of payments. The majority of Ministers were in favour of a 10 per cent revenue tariff. But they did not dare to press it against Snowden's flat opposition. They might have proposed special measures to reduce imports such as were in fact to be introduced in the autumn by the National Government through the Abnormal Importations Act. They could have instituted, and this would have been in strict accordance with their own doctrine, quotas, import controls, bulk buying, and all the rest. But all the arguments in the fateful Cabinets were apparently restricted to the details of how to make the necessary economies to reduce the Budget deficit. No larger questions were even considered, still less pressed to an issue.

The proposals of MacDonald and Snowden were therefore based upon a diagnosis of the situation which was accepted by everyone, certainly by all the members of the Labour Cabinet. In other words, when the political crisis broke, it appeared to the ordinary outsider that the Labour Government were agreed as to what ought to be done but had shrunk from doing it. Many of them made no bones about their motive. 'If it's got to be done, leave it to the Tories' was their somewhat uninspiring cry. Despite, therefore, the unpopularity of the cuts themselves, this was the fatal weakness in the official Labour position; and the public soon realised the truth.

In these critical days, the public saw the hurried comings and goings of Ministers, bankers, and—very soon—leaders of other parties. They did not yet know the internal wrangles that led to the disruption of the Cabinet. Subsequently, in the Parliamentary session which followed, far more of the intimate discussions of the Cabinet and the views of various Ministers were allowed to be known than on any previous occasion. Indeed, the debates are unique in this respect. Few of the Ministers seemed to pay any regard to the customary reticence. As the Parliamentary discussions continued, more and more was revealed and often disputed. Indeed, public opinion became somewhat sickened by all this recrimination. The facts spoke for themselves. In the space of two days, Mac-Donald had ceased to be head of a Labour Government and had become head of a National Government. The new administration was rapidly constituted. The Cabinet consisted of ten members: four from the Labour Party, four from the Conservatives, and two from the Liberals. Snowden, Lord Sankey, and Thomas alone of his Cabinet colleagues remained with MacDonald, and retained their existing offices as Chancellor of the Exchequer, Lord Chancellor, and Dominions Secretary. Baldwin became Lord President of the Council, a sinecure post, but in the circumstances a very strong position. Hoare went to the India Office. Neville Chamberlain became Minister of Health, and Cunliffe-Lister President of the Board of Trade. Herbert Samuel, the Liberal deputy leader, became Home Secretary, and Lord Reading went to the Foreign Office. The rest of the Government was filled up from Conservative-Liberal notabilities. Only a few Ministers outside the Cabinet and one or two junior Ministers came from the Labour Party.

This imposing team, when it was announced, had a good reception at home and abroad. It was another 'Ministry of all the talents' or, as Churchill is said to have observed, 'a Ministry of nearly all the talents'; for there were two major omissions. Churchill was excluded, no doubt because of his views on India. But he was not given the opportunity of considering how far he would be prepared to modify or waive them in a national emergency. Lloyd George, by one of those chances which have so often altered history before and since, was seriously ill. He had been struck down suddenly and compelled to undergo a most drastic operation, which kept him immobile and unable to act. To some of his followers it may be surmised that this untimely illness may not have been altogether disagreeable. Another omission was John Simon, or any representative of the group of Liberals who had been moving to the Right over recent months. His turn was soon to come.

Of course, it was not a Coalition in the old and discredited sense of the word—like Lloyd George's. It was a National Government. It was formed, not as a Coalition for an indefinite term, but for a short period and limited purpose. (It actually went on for the next nine years.) It is said that England does not like coalitions, but as Feiling has pointed out, 'England does not object to coalitions if they avoid the name'.[1] Indeed, MacDonald's achievement was something quite unique and even outrivalled Peel's; for when Sir Robert Peel carried free trade in a similar crisis, against the wishes of the Conservative Party, he was soon forced from office and never came back to power. MacDonald was able to remain for another four years. It is true that the National Labour Party, as it was called, played no role comparable with that of the Peelites. There were too many groups of Peelites already.

The National Government laboured at their task with courage and determination. They imposed fresh taxation, direct and indirect, to sustain the Budget. They introduced the necessary economies, including cuts in the salaries of all Crown servants and reductions in unemployment benefits, which they justified by the substantial fall in the cost of living. Payments from the Unemployment Insurance Fund were limited to twenty-six weeks, provided the applicant had made sufficient contributions—a not ungenerous provision, since the benefits thus available almost certainly exceeded the strict actuarial value of the contributions. But at the termination of the twenty-six weeks, further benefit (the 'dole', financed not by contributions to the Fund but by the taxpayer) would be paid not as of right, but in accordance with the applicant's needs. These were to be assessed by the Public Assistance Committees of the local authorities. The principle of this means test was not unfair; but the investigation of individual means and the variations across the country in interpreting the rules were to be a source of great bitterness.

The Government were able to command a small but adequate

[1] Keith Feiling, *Life of Neville Chamberlain*, p. 93.

majority with which to fight their proposals through the House of Commons. It is no criticism, either of their sincerity or of their efficiency, that they were not in fact able to 'save the pound'. Pressure on sterling continued, in spite of the action taken. Whether or not the mutiny of units of the Fleet at Invergordon on 15 September was the cause of the further run on gold, which led to the final decision to stop gold payments, cannot be proved one way or another.[1] In fact the pound was overvalued and could not be maintained at the old parity. But this is by no means a condemnation of the men in all parties who genuinely and honourably strove together to defend the probity of British credit. If the cuts had not been made, if the fresh taxation had not been imposed, there can be little doubt that there would have been a panic fall of the pound, with a corresponding effect both on imports and exports, and something like a general collapse. It was then fresh in the memory of all of us that other countries had suffered from similar catastrophes. It was the moral effort involved in an act of national unity that brought with it many material advantages. Nevertheless, as the weeks began to pass by, the practical problem presented itself. What was to be the Government's future? The statement of MacDonald on 25 August, that a National Government had been formed only to deal with the immediate emergency and would be dissolved as soon as this had been done, was made in all good faith. But it was to prove impracticable. Baldwin repeated this pledge at his own party meeting on 28 August amid great applause. Hailsham had added a rider giving two months as the right period of duration. But Amery at once pointed out the difficulty of this idea in a letter to *The Times*:

We are told this is to be for a few weeks only, and that then the members of the new Government will 'bow to partners' and rejoin their respective parties for the battle on the main issue. Experience shows how difficult it is for a Cabinet to deal with one issue only. New issues arise which must be dealt with,

---

[1] Two groups made difficulties about the cuts to be imposed upon all servants of the Crown. The judges, while ready to offer a voluntary reduction, took their stand on the high constitutional principle that their salaries could not be altered by an act of the Executive. The naval ratings, on whom the cuts bore particularly harshly, had a more practical objection.

and which each tend to justify the prolongation of a Government's existence and to consolidate it.[1]

This difficulty was satisfactorily resolved after a few weeks of stately manœuvring.

No party held a clear majority in the House of Commons. A new Labour Government obviously could not be formed, since its Parliamentary situation, without MacDonald and his friends, was even weaker than before. A Conservative Government would have no independent majority and could not introduce any of the measures, such as a general tariff, which it thought necessary to deal with the fundamental issues. A Liberal Government was out of the question. Nevertheless, the pledge had been given and it was on this understanding that the National Government had come into being.

The House had met on 8 September. It must have been a poignant moment when MacDonald and Henderson faced each other across the table. These lifelong friends had together created the Labour Party and together made two Labour Governments. Now they were parted for ever. Churchill's contribution, according to Amery, was audacious and rollicking.[2] But the main significance of Churchill's speech was that he accepted the inevitability of tariffs and appealed to the Liberals to join in supporting them. He also said that the sooner the election came the better. All this, as so often with Churchill's speeches at this time, was thought by the pundits to be true and therefore in rather bad taste. But of course he was right. It was inconceivable that Parliament should carry on for the rest of its term as if nothing had happened. Moreover, after the Bank of England had stopped gold payments on 21 September, a new situation had arisen. The Conservatives became more and more insistent on an election. The Liberals developed the ingenious argument that since we had gone off gold, and the fall in the value of the pound had resulted in an automatic encouragement to exports and discouragement to imports, there was now no need for tariffs, whatever might have been the arguments before. If there was no need for tariffs, there was equally no need for an election. This seemed to

[1] L. S. Amery, *My Political Life*, vol. iii: *The Unforgiving Years, 1929–1940* (London, 1955), p. 62.
[2] Ibid., p. 64.

be supported by a letter to Samuel in which MacDonald stated: 'Obviously there is not even a theoretical justification for an election now'.[1] Within a fortnight the Parliament was to be dissolved.

The Conservatives were strongly placed and they continued to force the pace. They were prepared to continue the coalition but 'only on terms which would force Samuel and the intransigent free traders to resign'.[2] MacDonald wavered. First he would agree to an election with a joint manifesto; then, under pressure from the Liberals, he swung back again. Finally, Neville Chamberlain produced a formula for what was to be called the 'Doctor's Mandate'. The National Government would go to the country as a joint Government but leave policy to be settled after their return to power. A good deal of discussion took place about the formula, and Lloyd George brought the greatest pressure upon the Liberals to refuse to take part on the basis proposed. He was beside himself with rage at what he called Samuel's betrayal.[3] Finally, the Liberals accepted a modification of the formula, which seemed to everybody a happy solution.

It was agreed that the Government would go to the country as a National Government, leaving each party leader free to advocate any policy he pleased. This somewhat bizarre basis for political co-operation seemed to suit all concerned. MacDonald could issue a general manifesto in favour of national unity; Samuel could advocate free trade; and Baldwin could argue for protection. In less critical times, for a Government to appeal for support on such a programme would have been laughed out of court. Yet, curiously enough, what seemed absurd to the politicians appeared quite sensible to ordinary folk. The Labour Government had failed. What the people wanted was that all men of goodwill should keep together and make the best of it. They were not much interested in the protectionist–free-trade argument as such. Being as usual ahead of the keen party men, they were beginning to feel the tariff controversy somewhat outdated.

All this coming and going came to an end on 5 October and the

[1] Robert Boothby, *I Fight to Live*, p. 94.
[2] L. S. Amery, *My Political Life*, vol. iii: *The Unforgiving Years, 1929–1940*, p. 67.
[3] Frank Owen, *Tempestuous Journey*, p. 720.

Parliament was immediately dissolved and the election fixed for 27 October.

During the greater part of August and September I was trying to recover from my bad state of health in a clinic in Germany. Not only was I having a great deal of trouble with my old wounds but, as a result, I was suffering from a form of neurasthenia which had brought me to a very low condition. However, I soon began to improve and to watch with intense interest the news that was coming from home. Relations and friends were good enough to send me almost daily reports. These gave a vivid picture of the general confusion. My brother-in-law, Lord Hartington, wrote to me on 16 September an interesting account of Simon's speech, which he ironically dubbed 'a masterpiece'.

There was a most effective phrase in which he explained how he and his friends had in all honesty conclusively proved at hundreds of meetings the proposition that exports pay for imports, and how disconcerting it was to find out that the proposition was untrue.

The letter goes on:

Snowden was really grand in his peroration when, in a hissing voice, he explained that for the last two or three days he had been able for the first time to see the faces of his old associates. . . .

Nancy Astor, writing on 25 September, gave a very sad account of the return of the Fleet to Plymouth:

I went to Plymouth last week-end, hoping to get a little quiet and found myself involved in the Navy affair. It really was pathetic to see the great Atlantic Squadron come to in Plymouth Sound with not a cheer to receive them. A great many people refused to go out to watch them and old sailors stood there with tears flowing down their faces. As a matter of fact it was not so serious as it seemed. The men felt that they had a grievance and knew that it would take weeks to get it through the ordinary channels and that the cuts were to operate from October 1st; so they took the only course they thought would be effective.

My wife wrote continually with all the news that she could collect, urging me to stay away as long as possible to finish my treatment, since it was still uncertain whether or not there would be an election. My sister-in-law, Lady Hartington, describes a talk with one of her Liberal friends who said that:

... as Samuel really does feel strongly about Free Trade he made it complicated about the election. I told her what you told me about his having advocated Tariffs in Palestine but she waved this airily aside!

On 21 September she wrote me a letter which gives an interesting picture of the decision to abandon the gold standard. She says that a City friend, 'who I suppose knows quite a lot, says that if we keep our heads it may be the best thing for trade'. Later, writing from Derbyshire, she says:

> Mr. and Mrs. Baldwin were here till this afternoon when he had to go up to a Cabinet.
> He looked worried but was very calm on the whole I thought. He licked and smelt a good many things but that was his only sign of inward strain!

Perhaps the most amusing of the large correspondence which I received was from Lord Cranborne. His letter was written just before the final decision of the Liberals to hold together in spite of Lloyd George:

> At the present rate of progress, the two and a half years which this Parliament still has to run will be over long before the national leaders make up their minds what a free hand means. Next time there is a crisis, it must be arranged for Ll.G. to move his sick bed a day's march nearer home. It takes the Cabinet all day long getting to and from Churt. Neither their offices nor the House of Commons sees them. I'm told that last Tuesday, at the end of the Cabinet, Ramsay said: 'Well, shall we meet again tomorrow afternoon?' 'I'm afraid I can't', said Samuel, 'I've got to go down and see Lloyd George at Churt'. 'Well, what about Thursday?' 'I am afraid I can't', said Reading, 'I've got to go down and see Lloyd George at Churt'. 'Well, I'm afraid *I* shan't be available on Friday', said Ramsay. '*I've* got to go to Seaham'. 'What!', said Snowdon, 'Have you got to go and see him too?' 'I said S-E-A-H-A-M'. However, he has been to see him today. No one knows as yet why he went or what is the result. But I can't believe they can put off deciding any longer. We ought to get the announcement tomorrow or the next day.

Although all this playing for position may be thought unworthy of the difficulties with which the country had to grapple, it would not be fair to underestimate the strong views sincerely held by many leading politicians on the free-trade issue. The older ones had been brought up in this controversy, which had been argued with almost theological fervour for more than a generation. What now seems to almost all of us a matter to be resolved on pragmatic lines was to many of the older statesmen the 'Ark of the Covenant'. Even Churchill was not able at this time to disentangle himself from the historic debate which had dominated his younger days. Although he had very wisely admitted in Parliament that a general tariff was now necessary, he did so on the basis of the practical situation and not because he was intellectually convinced. Very soon, this question on which he had stood so firm for so long was to become relatively unimportant (for him at any rate), in view of the deterioration of the foreign situation and the emergence of new and formidable dangers.

It was commonly believed that Lloyd George's antagonism to the National Government was rather on personal than on theoretical grounds. It was certainly a piece of bad luck for him to find himself incapacitated by illness at one of the most critical moments since his fall from power. He must have felt that had he not been laid low, he would have been able to exert an important and perhaps dominating influence on the handling of the crisis. He knew that an early election must mean a great Conservative triumph. Although he could take little part in the election, he made a broadcast in which he used some bitter phrases. He called the National Government 'a partisan intrigue under the guise of a patriotic appeal'.[1] He had perhaps forgotten the criticisms of his own election in the autumn of 1918.

As soon as the dissolution was formally announced, my wife sent me a telegram, leaving it for me to decide whether I was well enough to come back and fight the election. I had no doubt at all. Health of course had to be regained; but so had Stockton. Of the two, the Parliamentary borough was the more urgent. I was still rather weak and walking with sticks; but I managed to arrive a few days after the beginning of the campaign. My wife had been at work for a fort-night or more, and the organisation was getting into good shape. I found the same kind of manœuvring going on locally as had been so eagerly carried on nationally. First, what would the sitting Labour Member, Mr. Riley, do? I thought it prudent to issue a statement

[1] Frank Owen, *Tempestuous Journey*, p. 720.

that if he would stand as a supporter of MacDonald and the Government, I would stand down. I held my breath. There was a terrible moment of anxiety. What if he should turn out a patriot? Happily, he proved a loyal partisan and I was not called upon to make this great sacrifice. It would certainly have been a bitter pill to swallow if, after having abandoned the safe seat at Hitchin, I had felt obliged to support my former opponent at Stockton. I have never ceased to be grateful to him for his staunchness. Next, what would the Liberals do? On this, perhaps, everything might turn. A prospective Liberal candidate was in the constituency. He certainly could not win, but he might prevent my doing so. There was a great deal of coming and going and in the end a kind of unofficial arrangement was arrived at. The two Liberals in Middlesbrough were given a straight run without Conservative opponents, and the Liberal stood down at Stockton. Kingsley Griffith, an able Parliamentarian, was then Member for West Middlesbrough. If there had been any future in the Liberal Party, he would have had a distinguished political career.

Our propaganda was simple and very easy to put over. All we had to do was to concentrate on what the various Labour Ministers and ex-Ministers had said about each other. County Durham had up to now been a Labour stronghold. Naturally, the whole force of the official Labour Party was concentrated against MacDonald. It seemed impossible that he could hold his seat at Seaham; but as the days went on we began to hear hopeful news of the state of feeling even there. MacDonald had a strong personal hold upon the people, and the bitterness and unfairness of the attacks on him were ill judged. Snowden's broadcast and newspaper articles were bitter too; but they were so brilliant in their satire that their effect was overwhelming. He was proved a veritable Swift in controversy, with an almost equal command of irony. Towards the end of the election, Runciman produced a very damaging story about Post Office Savings. Most people felt this to be rather unfair. He alleged that the people's savings had been lent to the Insurance Fund, and were at risk. Actually there was nothing unusual in the procedure followed. What Runciman no doubt meant to argue was that if there was runaway inflation, the people's savings, whether in the

Post Office or in any other form of gilt-edged security, would in the end prove valueless. Still, we were not sorry that this particular hare had been started by a Liberal of the highest respectability.

I do not remember any contest in Stockton which was more violent. I can see now the crowded schoolrooms and hear the excited cries and counter-cries of the audience, inside and outside the building. At most of these ward meetings it was impossible to speak at all; but there was usually a certain amount of order given for question and answer. Old hands had always told me that a rowdy election is a good sign. When things are quiet it means that the opposition are confident. As they had no particular objection to me personally, they did not think it necessary to shout me down if they were sure of winning. But if they thought they were going to lose, then the row began. This certainly proved true over the six elections I fought in Stockton over a period of twenty-two years.

Locally, as nationally, the gravamen of the charge against the Labour ex-Ministers was that of cowardice—they had run away from the job. The means test and the cuts in unemployment benefit were, of course, very unpopular in a community where so large a number had by this time become dependent on the so-called 'dole'. Yet it is remarkable that throughout the country as a whole a sense of the nation's needs outweighed individual interest. Moreover, their broad common sense led the unemployed to believe that there was more hope of work coming back to the industrial towns if the National Government was returned.

By the time polling day came we were confident of victory. But when the figures were actually announced, both sides seemed to be dazed. We had expected a majority of 3,000 or 4,000. As it turned out, we got one of just over 11,000. I polled 29,199 votes, and my Labour opponent 18,168. Yet, on examining the figures, the Labour vote had remained pretty steady—only 800 less than two years before. What had happened was that 10,000 Liberals must have voted pretty solidly for me. Considering the dramatic circumstances in which the election took place—the abandonment of the party by their own leaders, the sudden break-up of the Government, the sense of confusion and betrayal—the Labour vote remained remarkably loyal. The real reason for the overwhelming majority for the

National Government was the staging of straight fights in so many seats.[1]

Taking the nation as a whole, the vote for the Government candidates in 1931 was 14½ million, as against 6½ million for Labour. Five hundred and fifty-four Members were returned supporting the Government: 473 Conservatives, 35 Simonite Liberals, 33 Samuelite Liberals, and 13 National Labour. The Prime Minister, MacDonald, was returned triumphantly in Seaham by a majority of 5,951. In County Durham, as in Yorkshire and Lancashire, seat after seat, which had always been solidly Radical or Socialist, went down. It was perhaps the greatest landslide in our history. I doubt whether there will ever be anything to equal or rival the result of the General Election of 27 October 1931. On 2 November, Baldwin, in an interview with the King, 'intimated that there would be plenty for him to do, as the Prime Minister knew nothing of his new Party, especially the Conservatives—many of them young, impetuous and ambitious men—who had no chance of making reputations with no Opposition to speak against'.[2] In the next decade this difficulty was, in some degree, overcome. Sufficient issues arose in which there could be no difficulty in speaking against the Government.

[1] Hugh Dalton, *Memoirs*, vol. i: *Call Back Yesterday*, p. 297.
[2] Harold Nicolson, *King George V : His Life and Reign*, p. 494.

CHAPTER TEN

Salvage

THE events of the years 1929–31 made many of us realise, or half realise, that we had reached a climacteric in history. The prestige of the new Government was sufficient to avoid a catastrophic collapse of sterling, yet we seemed to be moving into new and uncharted seas. At the same time, the great American slump involved the calling-in of America's existing short-term loans to Germany and the suspension of all foreign lending. The increasing weakness of the Weimar Republic was a source of general anxiety. All the foundations on which the strength of Europe and the prestige and power of Europeans throughout the world had been based were almost in ruins. As a result, many of the assumptions on which our social, economic, and political life had been founded began to be questioned. Even to conventional minds, new problems seemed to require new solutions.

Of course we had all known that there must be great changes resulting from the war: changes in economic and financial methods; still more, changes in concepts of social justice. But up to 1931 there was no reason to suppose that these would not, or could not, follow the same evolutionary pattern which had resulted from the increased creation and distribution of wealth throughout the nineteenth century. We had only to remove the hindrances to trade which the war and the peace had artificially created. The rest would follow. Now, after 1931, many of us felt that the disease was more deep-rooted. It had become evident that the structure of capitalist society in its old form had broken down, not only in Britain but all over Europe and even in the United States. The whole system, therefore, had to be reassessed. Perhaps it could not survive at all; it certainly could not survive without radical change. It was in this mood and within this framework of ideas that many of my friends and I acted during the next period. Something like a revolutionary situation had developed, not only at home but overseas, and it was bound to lead to novel manifestations of political as well as economic experiments, which were not, indeed, slow to show themselves in the rise of new, and the increasing arrogance of old, dictatorships. As for our own country, traditionally so dependent on exports, the situation had become catastrophic. In 1929 British exports by value were something like £839 million; by 1931 they had sunk to £461 million. Here was a grave sickness. How far was it epidemic? How far had it become endemic?

The collapse of the gold standard and the failure of our banking system, even though sustained with substantial foreign loans, to overcome the crisis may have been due to a premature attempt to re-establish the old monetary supremacy of London. But if this was so, even those who accused the bankers of mismanagement or imprudence by their policy of generous short-term loans overseas had to admit that this was another proof of the failure, after ten years of effort, to restore normal conditions. It was true that the policy of tariffs had still to be tried. But even when the Conservative forces in the National Government were able to implement what had long been their main ambition, few of us thought that in themselves, and by themselves, tariffs could produce the cure to troubles as deep-rooted as ours now seemed to be. Whereas, therefore, in the first Parliament of which I was a Member—that of 1924-9—the greater part of my time was devoted to trying to alleviate the hardships of unemployment, particularly as they affected the depressed areas and my own constituents, I now began to feel that something more was needed; a more radical and a more imaginative approach was necessary. We must examine again the structure of British industry and its place in a world which seemed now, economically speaking, to have fallen apart. Meanwhile, with the staggering figures of unemployment, the methods of alleviation could not be neglected. By June 1931 unemployment had reached a total of 2,707,000, or 21 per cent of the working population. It was destined to rise still further and reach almost 3 million before the tide began to turn. In the 'special areas', as the 'distressed areas' were soon to be renamed by one of those euphemisms which so appeal to the official mind, the long period of depression had certainly brought with it special problems. Many men, and indeed whole families, had been without work and wages for long periods, with corresponding difficulties and hardships. Their clothes were worn out; their furniture in disrepair; their savings gone; their homes dilapidated. Weekly sums of money, drawn from whatever source, which might have been adequate for a man out of work for a few weeks, were cruelly insufficient for men involved in what had become almost permanent unemployment. This, of course, especially affected the older men, who found it more difficult to move to more hopeful areas or adapt themselves to new skills.

I shall never forget those despairing faces, as the men tramped up and down the High Street in Stockton or gathered round the Five Lamps in Thornaby. Nor can any tribute be too great to the loyal, unflinching courage of the wives and mothers, who somehow continued, often on a base pittance, to provide for husband and children and keep a decent home in being. Even in the South of England, the sight of wounded or unemployed ex-Servicemen begging in the street was now too common to be remarkable. Sometimes these demonstrations of misery took a more organised but none the less distressing form, such as the 'hunger marches', as they came to be called. Of these, the march of the Jarrow unemployed was the most poignant; for with the closing of Palmers shipyard, almost the sole means of employment in the town had come to an end. There was of course national, local, and individual relief and assistance, on a scale unequalled in the history of this or any other country. But charity, whether of the nation as a whole or from their neighbours, was not what the men wanted. They wanted work. The British economy was indeed sick, almost mortally sick, with a great part of its capital of machinery and manpower unused, and, in some areas, rotting away.

These grim conditions filled the background of my life and thoughts until the years immediately before the Second War, when rearmament and the substantial degree of recovery, which followed the efforts of the National Government, brought some alleviation. In those days I had neither authority nor responsibility. I watched from the back-benches and did my best with those I could gather round me to discover and promote both short-term and long-term solutions. I little dreamt that it would fall to me many years later to have to deal with wholly different troubles which from time to time attacked the British economy. These arose not from unemployment but from over-employment; not from unused machinery but from resources strained too hard; not from great supplies of men and women and machines waiting to be put into the economic battle, but from no reserves at all, all being fully employed in the front line. At that time, neither to me nor indeed to any of the leading economists and political thinkers, did such dangers present themselves. We lived through years when national unemployment was often 15 or 20 per cent, and in certain areas reached 40 per cent or more. Had we been told that overall unemployment would fall to something like 2 per cent, with a still lower figure in some areas, and that these almost Utopian conditions would bring with them novel and perplexing problems, we would have been incredulous. But we should unhesitatingly have closed with any offer on these lines.

At the same time, some of the other issues with which British statesmen have had to grapple during the fifty years of my active life, although not yet developed to the point of acute danger, or requiring an immediate readjustment of the basic concepts with which we had been brought up, were beginning to develop.

In defence, for the guidance of the Treasury and of the Service Ministers, the principle had been laid down, soon after the war, that no major war need be expected for at least ten years. This 'rule' had for long been and was still the governing policy. It is true that in 1932, as the Disarmament Conference dragged wearily along its ineffective life, it was rescinded. But no serious question of British rearmament was entertained until the closing years of the 1931–5 Parliament.

The imperial system had been regulated by the Statute of Westminster in 1931. This formally recognised the end of the old colonial system in respect of the white Dominions and the establishment of a group of independent nations. The self-governing Dominions were joined together, indeed, through a common allegiance to the Crown. But they in no sense constituted a single or closely-knit unit for the purposes either of defence or of foreign policy. On the economic side, the Ottawa Conference in the summer of 1932, from which much had been hoped, was in essentials a disappointment. The vision which Joseph Chamberlain had seen nearly thirty years before proved to be unrealisable, largely because of our unwillingness to face substantial taxes on foodstuffs. Preferences were established which were of value, both to the Old Country and to the Dominions, and agreement was reached that existing industrial tariffs should not be increased. British exports to the Empire thus began to expand; but the concept of an imperial *Zollverein* faded away.

Europe, which had made so remarkable an economic recovery in the years immediately following the war, had been thrown back into chaos by the events of 1929–31. The British Government, fortified by the overwhelming majority which it had obtained at the 1931 election, had increased the credit of Britain and confidence in its moral strength. For in their determination to defend stability and sound finance, the people had accepted with a good grace the cuts in pay and benefits. At the same time, there was general agreement that the world-wide crisis could only be resolved by international action. The conference at Lausanne in 1932 at last marked the virtual termination of reparations. The hopes built upon the World Economic Conference to be held in London in 1933 were destined to be destroyed, chiefly by the action of the American Government. All the economists and statesmen of all the leading countries of the world were assembled, by a strange choice, in the Geological Museum. But any hope of restoring an international banking system on the basis of fixed currencies, attached to gold in some form or another, proved illusory. The refusal of President Roosevelt to join in any such plan and his clear determination to start a process of devaluation of the dollar must have made all those learned gentlemen seem almost as out of date as the curious collection of prehistoric animals in the mute presence of which they held their ineffective meetings, under the presidency of MacDonald. Thus the New World had rudely intervened to destroy the nostalgic hopes of the Old.[1]

[1] Between September and December 1933 the U.S. Treasury, by buying gold at steadily increasing prices, depreciated the value of the paper dollar by some 50 per cent.

The President's action, which had the effect of sabotaging the World Conference, was not a purely wanton act. He had realised that the underlying cause of the Depression and consequent unemployment was the fact that prices had fallen below costs. There could be no incentive to production unless this could be reversed. But in America, as in Britain, the reduction of wage-rates necessary to reduce costs would be slow and difficult. He therefore decided that prices must be raised by radical action. To rely on orthodox methods—'open-market' operations and the like—would be a long process and, in view of the large gap to be bridged, not necessarily successful. So he chose the direct method of devaluation. Since the main purpose of the international conference was to bring some stability into a state of widely fluctuating exchange values between the different currencies, the President's action was a mortal blow. Any chance of agreement between the countries concerned was destroyed. In point of fact, the resulting increase in American dollar prices was considerably smaller than the amount by which the dollar had been devalued. The reason for this unexpected result was that the American devaluation tended to drive down gold prices all over the world. This in turn resulted in a new wave of deflation and serious damage to the countries who had been trying to restore their currencies on a gold basis and bring stability between them, by linking them once more to gold. The lesson is twofold. First, any action of this kind, to be effective, must be taken internationally and not nationally. This still applies. Secondly, if a small country devalues, the effect is small; but if a large country, which has a dominating influence upon the economy of the world, does so, the resulting consequences must be widespread.[1]

If the long-term questions had to be studied and, if possible, resolved, the short-term difficulties had also to be dealt with. At the very opening of the new Parliament, the Government found itself faced with the urgent problem of dealing with the vast—and still growing—army of unemployed. Under the Economy Act of 1931 and under the Orders in Council that followed it, in addition to the means test, cuts had been imposed in the rate of 'standard benefit'— that is to say, the benefit an insured worker drew as of right in

[1] Sir Arthur Salter, *Personality in Politics* (London, 1947), pp. 180–2.

respect of both his own contributions and those made by the other two partners, the employer and the State. Similar cuts were made in what had been previously called 'uncovenanted benefit', but now came to be known as 'transitional benefit'. These were payments made to those who had exhausted their 'rights'. Until these cuts could be restored, and while unemployment remained in certain areas so heavy and so prolonged, a corresponding burden necessarily fell upon the Poor Law. Although this was now, under Chamberlain's reforms in the Parliament of 1924–9, operated by the counties and county boroughs and no longer by the old Guardians, yet it was still a local and not a national responsibility.

It would be tedious to recall the details of these past controversies. Gradually, the administration of relief became at once more uniform and more humane. At last, the Government produced a permanent plan to replace the temporary and emergency system. I have now learnt what was, of course, unknown to me then, that Neville Chamberlain had as early as October 1932 put before his colleagues a comprehensive scheme, by which the whole relief of the able-bodied unemployed should be taken away from local authorities and Ministers, and entrusted to a statutory body. He had thus already become a convert to the view that some of my friends and I had argued for several years, that unemployment must be a wholly national charge. Nor, as he saw it, should provision be restricted to the mere payment of money. There should be opportunities for education, training, voluntary occupation, recreation, overseas migration, and transference to more prosperous areas at home. His ideas were contested with considerable animation in the Cabinet. The final plan was to some extent a compromise.[1]

The broad acceptance of national responsibility and the inauguration of the Unemployment Assistance Board almost completed the liquidation of the old Poor Law. It left only the aged and the sick to be cared for out of local funds. The system was perfected after a shaky start, due to some of the terms of relief having been fixed unduly low. It has steadily grown in strength and public support. It has taken its final form in the National Assistance

[1] Keith Feiling, *Life of Neville Chamberlain*, p. 231.

Board which, while retaining the principle of ascertaining the re-sources available and the need to supplement them, has, by general consent, succeeded in administering very large funds efficiently and humanely. One of the ulcers which poisoned our national life in the years between the wars has thus been successfully lanced.

The next problem to occupy the 'National' Members represent-ing industrial seats, especially in the North of England, was that of the so-called 'distressed areas'. It is hard for us today, as indeed it was hard for some of those who lived in the more prosperous parts of the country, to grasp the full gravity of the disaster that had befallen whole counties and even regions. It was therefore only from 1932 onwards, largely as the result of continuous pressure and agitation in Parliament, that attention began to be focused on the distressed areas and their special needs. The localities concerned were well, or reasonably well, defined. They covered the industrial parts of Scotland; the North-east of England, from Tyne to Tees; South Wales; and West Cumberland. Northern Ireland, of course, had its own particular and almost endemic troubles, although it was not actually scheduled as a distressed area under the Govern-ment's later proposals. The same was true of the textile districts of Lancashire. But, whatever the precise geographical definition, the symptoms were similar. Broadly, their condition was due to the collapse of the heavy industries and of the old exporting industries. In shipbuilding, steel, and textiles, it was the same story—empty or declining order-books; weak selling; potential overproduction; and lack of effective organisation to win and hold what markets might become available.

The winter of 1932–3 was the worst that I can remember. The rate of unemployment in South Wales reached over 36 per cent. In the North-east it was something of the order of 27 per cent. But particular towns were even worse hit. In Jarrow the unemployment was 67 per cent, in Gateshead 44 per cent, in Abertillery nearly 50 per cent, in Merthyr Tydfil nearly 62 per cent.[1] Even in the pros-perous towns and districts, unemployment might range from 4 per cent to 8 per cent. In those days such a figure was almost a mark

[1]C. L. Mowat, *Britain Between the Wars, 1918–1940*, pp. 464, 465.

of 'full employment'. Naturally, there was a considerable migration of younger men. But this only made the situation worse for those who remained. When Chamberlain, with a somewhat brutal frankness, declared that the unemployment problem would remain with us for another ten years, there was an explosion. Forty northern M.P.s supporting the Government immediately demanded that the Prime Minister, MacDonald, should receive a deputation. Among other proposals, the Northern Group called upon the Government 'to embark on a well-thought-out policy of employment expansion, both public and private'. As the *Manchester Guardian* observed on 18 February 1933:

> It might be amusing if the times were not so serious to see a Tory deputation entreating a Socialist Prime Minister to adopt state action in the interests of the unemployed.

The agitation continued to grow inside and outside Parliament. But the Government seemed to have no particular ideas or, if they had, did not reveal them. Finally, in March 1934, three well-argued and moving articles appeared in *The Times* on conditions in County Durham. These revelations coming from so loyal a quarter had their effect. Neville Chamberlain discloses in his diary a certain anxiety about the opposition developing on the Government side. He resents any criticism as disloyal:

> Opposition who oppose for the sake of opposing; fellows who think they ought to have had office and want to show the government what a mistake was made in leaving them out, fellows who want to show how clever they are in detecting weak points.[1]

He especially deplores

> the frightfully sudden slump in the government's stock, and the continual nagging and carping by the young Tory intellectuals.[2]

Nevertheless, some gesture had become necessary, if only on political grounds. Consequently, at the end of March, four commissioners were appointed to investigate conditions in Scotland, West Cumberland, County Durham, Tyneside, and South Wales.

---

[1] Keith Feiling, *Life of Neville Chamberlain*, p. 233.   [2] Ibid., p. 239.

The appointment of commissioners to discover Scotland, Durham, or South Wales had a somewhat ludicrous aspect. After all, this island was neither so large nor so unexplored as to require intrepid Livingstones and Stanleys. However, some good might well come of it and it was something, in those days, even to be noticed by Whitehall. Moreover, with the Prime Minister a Durham Member (he had held Seaham triumphantly in 1931), we felt we could look to sympathy at the top. Naturally I welcomed this decision, although there was much local feeling at the omission of Tees-side from the commissioners' field of inquiry. We were reassured by the statement that these 'investigations' were to be merely tests, and did not necessarily govern the precise areas to which any remedies would be applied. In the House of Commons I argued that there could not be an easy or purely local solution to the problems of the distressed areas.

We shall have to take great powers in the hands of the State to direct in what localities and areas fresh industrial development will be allowed.[1]

This was then frowned on as revolutionary and subversive doctrine. However, it was later to be accepted as mere common sense.

I was not too hopeful that the report would lead to any large or comprehensive plan. In spite of the improvement in the financial situation, the Government seemed very unwilling to embark upon any ambitious measures. After the publication of the report in the autumn of 1934, I had an opportunity to speak in the Debate on the Address. I appealed to the Government to take a broader and more imaginative course, and to deal with the fundamental problems. The period of salvage for which the National Government had been formed was ending. The period of reconstruction should now begin. The reorganisation of industry and the increase of employment by capital investment—these were the urgent needs. If private investment was not forthcoming, public investment must take its place. The last passages of the speech were somewhat rhetorical, but well received by the House. Perhaps unwisely, I allowed myself one crack, which was naturally picked out from all the rest of the speech by some of the popular Press. There had been reference

[1] *Hansard*, 22 March 1934.

in the commissioners' report to one of the useful jobs that might be done by the clearing away of the old slag-heaps which defaced the countryside in many of the mining areas. A good deal of attention had been attracted and interest shown in this idea. So I used these words:

> Mr. Disraeli once said that he saw before him a bench of extinct volcanoes. I would not be so rude but there are a few disused slag heaps which might well be tidied up.[1]

Some of my friends, who were now on the front bench, were amused; but by no means all.

When we came to the Second Reading of the Bill, which was originally named the 'Depressed Areas Bill' and subsequently renamed in the House of Lords the 'Special Areas Bill', there was little scope for much discussion. The financial resolution had been very tightly drawn; and the opportunity for amendments, either to widen the areas or increase the functions of the commissioners appointed under the Bill, was correspondingly restricted. Naturally, there was a row about this; but it was ineffective. The Third Reading, therefore, was more important than usual and the debate was well attended. There was one last chance for me to deploy my case:

> We can now see the Bill in its true perspective on this last stage of the Measure. When the commissioners were sent to the distressed areas high hopes were raised. It was the official recognition by the Government of the importance of this problem, and, when the reports were published, there was a general sense that the commissioners had more than fulfilled their task and had produced reports of real value because of the depth of thought which they had shown in compiling them. . . . There has, of course, been some sense of disappointment at the apparent dashing of those hopes to the ground. . . . *Parturiunt montes; nascetur ridiculus mus.* The mountains have been in labour and there has been born a mouse. My right hon. Friend the Minister for Labour appealed to us, in the first stages of the Debate on the report of the commissioners, not to belittle the importance of the provisions of this Bill. I think I can say for myself and hon. Friends of mine who have spoken during the Debates that we have lived up to that appeal. At no stage have I attempted to minimise the importance, which I believe to be great, of this Bill, but in com-

[1] *Hansard*, 22 November 1934.

parison with the problems before us this is a mouse–a nice mouse, a good little mouse, a profitable and helpful little mouse, but a ridiculous, microscopic Lilliputian mouse.[1]

Towards the end of this Parliament, on 9 July 1935, there was another discussion on the same melancholy subject. It was equally inconclusive. By that time it had become more and more clear that the question of the special areas was not one which could be treated separately. Our debates and arguments, during the last few years, had become increasingly discussions of general economic and political policy. In July 1935 MacDonald had recently faded out as Prime Minister and Baldwin, as it were, faded in. There was no perceptible change of method or approach, for these two men had long worked together in great harmony and with increasing respect and sympathy for each other. Both eschewed action, and preferred atmosphere. In this debate, the new Prime Minister repeated all the old hopes and assurances. He was, of course, conscious of his political strength. In the approaching election, which must take place this year or the next, while some seats would be lost and the Labour membership of the House substantially increased (which he probably welcomed), his Government would almost certainly be returned by a substantial margin. So he told us, rather wearily, that while he realised that the need of attracting new industries to the old areas was undoubted, he had no particular ideas or positive plan to suggest. He added that he thought he must rely largely on the continuation of his policy of transfer of population. In a word, I exclaimed in reply, we are to go to our people and say 'You are now depressed–you must become derelict'.

Once more, I went through the plans for action which were by then the result of several years' thought and co-operation with many men and women of all parties. Most of these–new industrial estates; the use of planning permissions; the wider distribution of electric power; monetary expansion; schools, universities, hospitals, and public works of all kinds–have long been adopted. Perhaps the chief political interest of that debate was the position of Lloyd George, who was planning new incursions into this field.

[1]*Hansard*, 13 December 1934.

After a passage advocating public works, I thought it fair to say:

I know it is said—and I want just to strike a personal note—that anyone who puts forward a policy of this kind is in some way in league with the right hon. Member for Carnarvon Boroughs (Mr. Lloyd George). We are all very glad that the right hon. Gentleman has returned to active politics, but perhaps I may, without, I hope, saying anything to which he might object, say that the northern group of our party, and friends who are associated with me in all kinds of activities, men of all parties and all groups—economists, thinkers, and people of all kinds who are studying these questions—have been preaching this policy for four years; and, even if we have fallen under the wiles of the wizard, he has not been able to ante-date his magic by that time; we have done this on our own account. I welcome, however, the right hon. Gentleman's return to politics. More than that, there is the new feeling that is growing up all over the country among all kinds of groups that a much more active policy is now possible, and I think any reasonably impartial man would say that it is possible largely because of what the Government have done. Whatever one may say of the past, with regard to the future we have now possibilities of wealth and power that were undreamed of before.[1]

Meanwhile, I earned many rebukes for my advocacy of public works, which was all the more curious because the Government had at last embarked on this policy with at least modest ardour. Considerable capital sums were being made available for London Transport and for telephone development. In spite of all his caution, Chamberlain was a mild expansionist at heart. Perhaps it was the form in which I put forward the argument which shocked the orthodox. I confess I thought it a not unreasonable appeal. It was as follows:

Public works, so far, have only dealt with the necessities of life. Are there no amenities of life upon which the expenditure of money is required? Are there no recreational facilities, no open spaces, no national parks that would preserve at once the threatened beauties of the countryside, and be a lasting joy-giving possession to a great people? Are there not splendid public buildings to be erected? When was this gloomy, dismal view invented that a legitimate public work must always earn its exact amount of revenue? On that basis Pericles would not have built the Parthenon unless he could have shown to his colleagues on the front bench that the revenue from tourists who would come to look at it would pay interest and sinking fund on it for all time. Even

[1] *Hansard*, 9 July 1935.

our medieval ancestors–obscurantists, as I suppose the complete commercialist to-day would call them–built for us their abbeys, their cathedrals, their schools, their foundations, which we still regard as among the greatest of our architectural glories, and among which our youth are brought up and inspired and educated. Even the tyrants, old and new, Caesar and Mussolini, have followed this tradition.[1]

It is curious to reflect how this cruel problem of the distressed areas, which so occupied our minds and hearts through nearly ten years, has now virtually disappeared. It is true that from time to time, even with a very high level of employment throughout the country, some of these same areas–Scotland, Merseyside, and the North-east Coast–have suffered from relative lack of prosperity. To correct this, full use has been made of all the negative powers of planning, as well as the positive methods of attracting industry into the areas where it is in the national advantage that they should go. At the worst, unemployment in these districts has been of the order of 4, 5, or sometimes 6 per cent, when in the rest of the country it has been negligible. When I became Prime Minister I devoted great and continuing attention to these difficulties. For I will confess that I was always troubled by the re-emergence, even in a modified form, of this old problem, with all its bitter recollections. I knew well that a rate of unemployment which, a generation ago, would have seemed mercifully low, would nevertheless, if substantially higher than the national rate, create a sense of real grievance. The old memories and fears were not yet altogether dispelled. The underlying anxieties, in these parts of the country, persisted. It was for this reason that, when power came to me, I gave what seemed to many, even of my colleagues, undue attention to these problems. I was determined, even in the fifties and sixties, not to forget the lessons of the twenties and thirties.

A report by Sir Malcolm Stewart, one of the commissioners appointed under the Act, reverted to the suggestions which had been adumbrated by Captain Wallace a year before; proposed earlier by the Northern Group; and lately incorporated in the policies of the Next Five Years Group (with which I shall deal); and advocated by Lloyd George, now returned to active politics.

[1] *Hansard*, 9 July 1935.

Every suggestion which Sir Malcolm had put forward–the raising of the school age, retirement at sixty-five, shorter hours, works of national utility and development–was received by the same formula. The Government will give 'careful consideration'. Even the final debate in the House of Commons ended farcically. The Minister of Labour–Ernest Brown–was put up to answer a Socialist vote of censure with a stonewalling speech. This is an assignment which requires a certain finesse–or at any rate lightness of touch–quite alien to the sturdy and simple nature of the new Minister. He was a man of considerable character and charm, known to his friends, of whom I was one, for the notable library which he had collected and studied, and to the House at large for his tremendous, barrack-square voice. On this occasion it was so obviously His Master's (the Treasury's) voice that his speech was a flop. So was the end of the debate. In the last few minutes, after the 'wind-up' from the front bench, I rose to make a few final criticisms. The Labour Chief Whip failed to move the closure, so this vote of censure was 'talked out'.

Thus ended this long agitation, in which my friends and I had received favourable and sympathetic attention and support both from the Press and the House of Commons. Some progress was made–perhaps more than we realised at the time. In addition, seeds were sown which have grown into vigorous and fruitful plants in later years.

Indeed, modern criticism has not been altogether fair to the achievement of this period. The National Government came into office after a crisis of confidence, in which Britain's credit had sunk to a low level. In the four years of the Parliament our national position had been largely restored. Justice has scarcely been done either to the magnitude of the task or the measure of success. Yet even unsympathetic historians have lately admitted the facts. 'Recovery, despaired of in 1931, was in the air by 1933, obvious by 1935.'[1]

By all the ordinary signs, the change was indeed remarkable. From an unfavourable trade balance of £104 million at the beginning of the period, by the end a surplus of £32 million had been

[1] C. L. Mowat, *Britain Between the Wars, 1918–1940*, p. 432.

earned.[1] The index of production showed that not only had production risen to the 1929 (or pre-crisis) figure, but had passed it by
something like 10 per cent. The figure of unemployed had been
reduced by a million. The total of 2 million in 1935 was still terrifying, but the movement was in the right direction. Within another
year, that is to say in July 1936, it had fallen to 1,600,000. Meanwhile, employment rose steadily and at a greater rate than the
increase of population.

On the financial and monetary side, the Government used its
authority and the confidence which had been created in the world
for a mildly expansionist policy. The various cuts in salaries and
relief were gradually restored. While Chamberlain resisted the
pressure for an unbalanced Budget in 1933, the deficit of 1932
was met by borrowing and the Budget of 1933 did not in fact provide for a Sinking Fund. In his Budget speech, Chamberlain
covered his position by referring to the arguments in favour of a
deliberately unbalanced Budget, which had been supported 'by
eminent economists, powerful journalists, and, if my information
is correct, by some hon. Members of this House'.

In 1934 there was a surplus of £29 million; the unemployment
benefit was restored in full; the cuts in State and local government
salaries by a half; the emergency increase of 6d. on the standard
rate of income tax was removed, and concessions were made to the
smaller income-taxpayer. In the second half of 1935 all the pay
cuts were restored. Meanwhile, there had been an important series
of measures in the economic field.

In 1932 the general tariff had been introduced by Chamberlain
in a moving speech, in which he declared his pride in being able
at last to implement the policy that had been put forward more
than a generation before by his father, Joseph Chamberlain. The
tariff had been expected to lead to the resignation of the free-trade
members of the National Government, especially Snowden on the
National Labour side and Samuel and his friends among the official
Liberals. However, this was avoided by a curious device, unpre-

[1]C. L. Mowat, *Britain Between the Wars, 1918–1940*, p. 435, based on A. E.
Kahn, *Great Britain in the World Economy* (New York, 1946; London, 1947), p. 126.

cedented in politics, which was called 'the agreement to differ'. It is true that this formula had been used in many Cabinets in the first quarter of the nineteenth century to deal with the vexed question of Catholic emancipation. But in that case it was an agreement to hold different views upon a question on which legislation was not proposed. In this case we witnessed the unusual scene of Herbert Samuel not being content merely with registering his disapproval of a measure put forward on behalf of the Cabinet, but making a violent and extremely forceful attack upon the folly of his colleagues. This episode could hardly have been possible in any Parliament brought into being in normal times, or to which ordinary rules applied.

The tariffs were expected to bring in £35 million, enough to meet the deficit. At the same time, the successful conversion of the 5 per cent War Loan to 3½ per cent made an immediate saving of £23 million and ultimately £40 million. Although the Lausanne Conference did not accept the complete cancellation of war debts and reparations, it marked—by the acceptance of the lump sum which Germany agreed to pay—the effective end of reparations. The Ottawa Conference was in a sense a disappointment, although at least some agreement was reached. But the acceptance of imperial preference was too much for the free-traders, Snowden, Samuel, and Archibald Sinclair resigned in September 1932. I doubt whether this was a source of much regret to Baldwin and Chamberlain. They must have felt ample compensation in the corresponding relaxation of Lord Beaverbrook's pressure. From the House of Commons point of view, if the Samuelites moved into Opposition, the Simonites remained, equal both in numbers and in debating strength.

In addition, the Government was responsible for a number of experiments. The increase to £350 million of the Exchange Equalisation Fund, which was initiated in 1932, was widely welcomed. In agriculture, much was done under the energetic leadership of Walter Elliot, and various measures taken, from the quota system on the one side to the subsidy of beet-sugar on the other, to reestablish some degree of prosperity in the countryside. The Wheat Act of 1932 in effect gave the farmer a guaranteed price. Acreage subsidies were also given for barley and oats. The land under the plough began to increase rapidly, and the foundations were laid for an agricultural policy which has been followed ever since.

As regards the basic industries, some degree of reorganisation began in iron and steel, which was to be followed up in the next Parliament. A subsidy was granted to tramp shipping, and the tonnage launched from British shipyards began slowly to rise. The building of the Cunarder No. 534, which ultimately became the *Queen Mary*, with Government aid was another unorthodox experiment, which met with considerable opposition among some of the more traditional Members of the Conservative Party, but was strongly supported by the progressive wing. In coal, the story was less good. Reorganisation and amalgamations, which were supposed to have been encouraged by the Act of 1930, hung fire, and no step was taken in this Parliament to deal with the problem. Even the nationalisation of royalties was postponed.

Taken as a whole, both in administration and legislation, these were four years of solid progress. Nevertheless, as the Parliament proceeded, I found myself, with many of my friends, increasingly convinced that more radical remedies were required for the basic weaknesses of our economic system. To that purpose, in these years and over the opening years of the next Parliament, I devoted all my energies.

Before embarking upon this story, it would be right to give some picture of the House of Commons—one of the strangest in our history—in these years.

This House of Commons presented, even in the seating of its Members, an unusual scene. The Labour Party had been reduced to about 50. They occupied—but did not fill—the Opposition benches. The Samuelite Liberals, after Ottawa increasingly hostile to the Government, amounted to some 35 and sat in the two benches below the gangway—the second and third. The Simonites, about the same in number, were mingled with the general body of Government supporters. The Conservatives, 470-odd, occupied the whole of the Government side and overflowed into two benches behind the Liberals, below the gangway on the Opposition side. Early in the Parliament, some of us took up our position on one of those benches, which gave us the advantage of facing the solid ranks of the Conservative Party and the Government front bench. It became a kind of Tory 'mountain'.

The life of Members was easy and agreeable. The Government majority was so large that no great stress was placed upon regular attendance except for an occasional three-line whip. When there were likely to be long sittings, the Whips worked out a shift system, which was thought by some rather improper, but proved highly convenient. As a result of the unbalanced position of parties, the character of our debates was sensibly affected. With so small a Labour representation, supporters of the Government felt much more free to suggest, propose, and even criticise than is possible where an administration enjoys only a small majority. This in its turn had a somewhat loosening effect on party ties. Many debates took on an unaccustomed tone of non-partisanship.

The leader of the Labour Party was George Lansbury. He carried out a difficult task ably and courageously. Baldwin, who was Leader of the House during MacDonald's Premiership, showed him characteristic courtesy and kindness. But Lansbury was not truly representative of the Labour movement. His pacifist views, which afterwards caused much indignation among his more robust colleagues, were by no means shared by all his followers. Although they consistently voted in this Parliament, as in the next, against any increase of armaments, they were not pacifists. They put their trust, as did many of us, in collective security to be provided by the League. But they were not disposed to any nice calculation as to how this security was going to be provided or what should be a fair British contribution.

Next to Lansbury was Attlee, the deputy leader. He attained this post at the expense of Herbert Morrison, who lost his seat at South Hackney at the election by a few hundred votes. Morrison was indeed unfortunate, for if he had just scraped in, he would undoubtedly have been either the leader or the deputy leader of the party. He thus would have become by a natural sequence of events deputy Prime Minister to Churchill in 1940. He would consequently have been Prime Minister in 1945. I always felt that he had very bad luck, for he was a man of notable Parliamentary and administrative gifts, as well as considerable political courage. By the chance of Morrison's defeat in 1931, Attlee took the place which would in all probability have been his. When Attlee resigned many years later it was too late.

The Labour Members who survived 1931 were drawn mainly from the mining seats, or from some of the oldest and most highly industrialised areas. They did their best, and put up a staunch fight. They certainly had plenty of opportunities for speaking, and many thoroughly enjoyed themselves. On contentious Bills they provided a resolute opposition and on several occasions forced us to the guillotine or all-night sittings. It was a gallant performance and we respected them. Some of the survivors belonged to the Independent Labour Party, led now by Maxton, as formidable in debate and as impressive as ever.

The Prime Minister, Ramsay MacDonald, at the beginning of the Parliament commanded not only our affection but our respect. The Opposition always treated him fiercely, often unfairly. But he rose successfully above even the most violent attacks and noisy interruptions. As in previous Parliaments, when he spoke on foreign affairs he was interesting and persuasive. But more and more, as the Parliament proceeded, he became vague and even incoherent on other matters. His eyes had begun to fail him. Generous as was the support which was given to him by Baldwin, he became more and more isolated. Some of his speeches were so tortuous and so mystifying as to seem to have no meaning. He began to lose his nerve. Always high-minded, he became woolly-minded. Yet he was, even in his decay, a noble and almost romantic figure. It is hard even now to form a clear picture of his life as a whole. It became the fashion, partly because of the almost brutal criticisms of his erstwhile friends, and partly because of the impatience which his rambling style created among the rank and file of our party, greatly to underrate this man's character and career. Some day the balance must be restored.

Baldwin held the second place to MacDonald. From the very first, the true power lay more and more in Baldwin's hands. He was head of by far the strongest party in the House and in the country. He had survived successfully the attacks made upon his leadership in the previous year. He had challenged and overcome the Press lords. On more than one occasion, while in Opposition, he had demanded and received by a comfortable majority the support of his followers. Nor had he anything to fear in the new situation. Churchill had not been included in the National Government when it was first formed and was now devoting himself almost entirely to his opposition to Indian constitutional advance. Austen Chamberlain had voluntarily 'made way for younger men'. Neville Chamberlain was clearly marked out as Baldwin's heir; but he was quite content with his prospects and showed no sign of being anxious for the actual succession. Baldwin held a sinecure office, which suited him very well, for, as Lord President of the Council, he had neither the risk nor the trouble of departmental duties. He attended the House with great regularity and got to know all the Members of both sides. He was in no hurry to take MacDonald's place. Indeed, it was only after MacDonald had become clearly unfitted for his work that Baldwin consented to step into the first position. This was in June 1935, when the Parliament was nearly four years old. In theory, Baldwin was by way of favouring the progressive wing of the party, and he certainly arranged for the promotion of some of them. But in practice, as Lord Percy says, he always had 'a doubt whether (so to speak) they would sing in tune'.[1] At the same time, he had a unique hold on all sections of his party and the House as a whole. He was rarely attacked with any vigour, and if the House was excited or unruly he could usually and without difficulty reduce the temperature. His fairness in debate, the width and generosity of his approach to life, the charm of his manner, and even the skilful way in which he could avoid a difficult argument or awkward situation by a few minutes of reminiscence or philosophising: all these qualities made him a supreme Parliamentarian.

Next to Baldwin, the most effective force in the Government was Neville Chamberlain. Sometimes he complained in private, as his diaries and letters reveal, that he had two *rois fainéants* to deal with. Nevertheless, he was in a true sense Mayor of the Palace. What he said in Cabinet or in Council was in the end accepted. So great was

[1] Lord Percy of Newcastle, *Some Memories*, p. 130.

his activity that he did not hesitate to give help and advice to his colleagues in other departments. Many of the plans which were ultimately presented by other Ministers had their origin in his tireless zeal. He was sometimes, as his diary shows, tempted into the field of foreign affairs. There is an entry under the date July 1934, when Hitler first threatened and then shrank from the seizure of Austria:

I was glad to hear of Mussolini's movement of troops. It's the only thing Germans understand. . . . What does not satisfy me is that we do not shape our foreign policy accordingly.[1]

It is a pity that this sentiment did not continue to influence his action and that he did not realise how much military force would be needed and how soon.

Chamberlain was not a favourite of the House, and he never obtained that attention from the Opposition which it is necessary for a leading Minister to secure. This was a defect partly of manner and partly of feeling. He had a certain intellectual contempt for people whose views he thought ridiculous; and most of the Labour Party he put into that category. He was not able to conceal this, and his tone revealed a degree of sarcasm and even rudeness towards his opponents, which is contrary to the true House of Commons tradition, at least at the top. Hard blows can be taken and given in our Parliamentary system. They are not long remembered. But superciliousness and arrogance are much more wounding. Nevertheless, he was a commanding personality. His speeches were admirably prepared and argued. If his voice was rasping and often weak, his Parliamentary style was good. He marshalled facts and statistics with ease. His slim figure, conventionally dressed (he usually wore a tail coat and stiff wing-collar), his well-groomed appearance, his corvine physiognomy, his perfect self-control: all these made him an outstanding Parliamentarian. I can still see him standing at the box, erect and confident. But he was respected and feared, rather than loved, except by the few who were his intimates and knew the kindliness that lay behind his bleak exterior.

The heads of both wings of the Liberal Party were originally

[1]Keith Feiling, *Life of Neville Chamberlain*, p. 253.

included in the Government. John Simon became Foreign Secretary—a disastrous choice. His clear intellect fitted him for almost any task except the one which he was given. It is often said that a lawyer does not make a good Foreign Secretary. Whether this is true or not, Simon's legal training made him appear more anxious to put forward both sides of a question clearly and accurately, and even judicially, than to take any particular line. Admirable as this may be for the professional advisers of the Government, it is a serious defect in a Minister. I remember many years later Churchill used to say that a Foreign Office brief was printed like the Psalms, in alternate verses, giving the arguments for or against a particular course. Unhappily, they were always even numbers; so you were left at the end without any clear guidance on which side you should come down. Simon's speeches were much the same and so was his conduct.

Herbert Samuel was the day-to-day leader of the official Liberals. The impression that I formed of him in the first Parliament of which I was a Member was not changed later. His speeches were always admirably and even persuasively argued, but they had no fire. Two main visions inspired his life—Cromwell and teetotalism. It was rarely indeed that he could make a speech without mentioning one or both of them, whatever might be the topic formally under discussion. They were like King Charles's head in Mr. Dick's memorial. I sat on one of the Conservative benches immediately behind him and could not resist the temptation whenever he mentioned Cromwell to say in clear but not penetrating tones, calculated to be heard only by him, 'You mean Williams, the old brewer'. This was teasing but irresistible. It always got a rise. But he was a fine man.

In my first Parliament, the greatest figure of the day, although out of office, had been Lloyd George. In the first year of this Parliament, Lloyd George, still recovering from his very serious illness, played but a small role. He was angered by the agreement of Samuel and his other followers to the holding of the election. He never forgave Samuel. The overwhelming majority enjoyed by the Government gave him no opportunity for any form of political or Parliamentary manoeuvring. It was an unhappy period in his life. Towards the end of the Parliament, however, he made a dramatic reappearance. He put forward his plans for national development and for the cure of unemployment, modelled on his 1929 programme and supported by a great wealth of expert opinion. It was a 'New Deal' for Britain. In the summer of 1935 the Government undertook to examine his ideas, and long conferences and discussions took place. It was widely supposed that Lloyd George might be about to join the administration. This was urged more especially by Austen Chamberlain, then out of office.[1] Baldwin certainly played with the idea and there was a good deal of pressure in the Press in favour. In the end, nothing came of it. I think the reasons were matters of personality rather than of policy. For the Government at that time, as they widely claimed, had embarked, at least to some extent, upon an expansionist programme. But Baldwin hated Lloyd George, whom he both distrusted and feared. One of the go-betweens in this matter was Tom Jones, one of the most queer and almost sinister figures of the period, who moved with equal freedom between Baldwin, Lloyd George, and the Astors. According to Jones, Lloyd George felt that the Cabinet Committee had treated him 'with patience and courtesy'. Indeed, Jones informed Baldwin that, in his view, Lloyd George was more anxious for the adoption of his programme than for office.[2] On the policy itself, Baldwin had no very strong views. But he became daily more and more adverse to any union with Lloyd George. Neville Chamberlain had an equal antipathy towards Lloyd George, based upon his experience as a Minister under him during the war. There is a revealing entry in his diary in the February of 1935, describing his reaction to Austen's account of his conversations with Lloyd George:

I explained that I was not prepared to sit in a Cabinet with L.G. Austen at once interrupted me, saying 'I think you are wrong', but I continued that my motives were not personal dislike, but profound conviction that our ideas were incompatible.[3]

[1] Sir Charles Petrie, *The Life and Letters of Sir Austen Chamberlain*, vol. 2 (London, 1940), p. 399.
[2] Thomas Jones, *A Diary with Letters, 1931–1950* (London, 1954), p. 146.
[3] Keith Feiling, *Life of Neville Chamberlain*, p. 242.

Whatever Neville may have said to his brother, personal dislike
was unconsciously stronger than incompatibility of ideas.

Perhaps one of the reasons why leading Ministers and the Conservative Party as a whole distrusted Lloyd George was the very
quality which made him so conspicuous. Lloyd George liked
action. He liked doing things. Sometimes he did the wrong things,
but he could not bear inactivity. If he wanted power, it was not to
hoard it but to make use of it.

If Lloyd George's public life was virtually over, the greatest
period of Churchill's still lay in the future. In the Parliament of
1924–9 he had held a powerful position. As Chancellor of the
Exchequer, he had been for four years the second man in the
Government. Although still distrusted by certain sections of the
Conservative Party and of the public, he was regarded at that time
as the likely successor to Baldwin. During the second Labour
Government, his almost daily duels with Snowden delighted the
whole House. His brilliant Parliamentary gifts were never more
effectively displayed. Bolinbroke once wrote about the House of
Commons: 'You know the nature of that assembly; they grow, like
hounds, fond of the man who shows them game, and by whose
halloo they are used to be encouraged.' But Churchill had separated
himself from the main stream of Conservative opinion on an important issue. He wholly disapproved of Baldwin's support of
the Labour Government's Indian policy and the actions of the
Viceroy, Lord Irwin.[1] In January 1931, therefore, he had retired
from the Shadow Cabinet. This breach widened during the next
few years. Nor was Churchill content with formal opposition. He
threw himself whole-heartedly into the task of opposing at every
stage the plans for India's progress to self-government. In this he
obtained the support of a substantial number of Conservative
Members, amounting to nearly a hundred. He formed the India
Defence League, and during the next four years put up a most
determined opposition to the Government's measures, including an
abortive attempt to call in aid the privileges of the House against
Lord Derby and his friends. This agitation was transferred with

[1]Later Lord Halifax.

characteristic energy from the House of Commons to the Conservative Party conferences, to use his own words, 'with a considerable measure of support, sometimes running very close, but
always in a minority'.[1]

The majority of the party regarded his attitude as reactionary
and unrealistic. We remembered that for more than a hundred years
British policy towards India had been directed to the evolution of a
system of self-government, which must logically lead to her ultimately obtaining the same status as the independent Dominions of
Australia, Canada, and the rest. Baldwin's declarations seemed to
most of us to be both imaginative and sound. There is a passage
from one of his speeches in December 1934, which made a deep
impression:

> Remember: what have we taught India for a century? We have preached
> English institutions and democracy and all the rest of it. We have taught her
> the lesson and she wants us to pay the bill. There is a wind of nationalism and
> freedom blowing round the world and blowing as strongly in Asia as anywhere
> in the world. And are we less true Conservatives because we say: 'the time has
> now come'? Are those who say 'the time may come—some day', are they the
> truer Conservatives?[2]

The isolation of Churchill at this time had tragic results. His
reliance upon the extreme Right injured his position with the party
as a whole, as well as with Liberal and non-party feeling in the
country. During the years when the German threat was developing
and the rise of Nazism was beginning, all Churchill's warnings,
as he has himself described, were in vain. It is true that the Western
Allies still retained a great superiority of power, and there was no
point till after 1936 or even later when Hitler's aggression could
not have been checked had the necessary risks been taken. But in
this Parliament, where the seeds of evil were sown, Churchill's
speeches and demands for rearmament, however effective in themselves, were injured because of the general doubt as to the soundness
of his judgement. On Indian and on imperial affairs he appeared to
hold impractical and reactionary views. The mass of the party felt

[1] Winston Churchill, *The Second World War*, vol. i: *The Gathering Storm*, p. 62.
[2] G. M. Young, *Stanley Baldwin*, p. 188.

that on this issue Baldwin and Halifax and the rest of the Cabinet were right and Churchill wrong. Thus they found it difficult to realise how on the questions of foreign affairs and rearmament the position could be so entirely reversed.

It was Churchill's fortune, good or evil, to be out of office for the ten of what are normally regarded as the best years of a man's life—from fifty-five to sixty-five. In the middle of 1935, before MacDonald's retirement, there was talk of inviting him to join the Government. The India Bill had been passed; the barrier had been removed. The question was much discussed by Baldwin with his cronies, Geoffrey Dawson (editor of *The Times*), and Tom Jones. The same kind of objections were found against Churchill as against Lloyd George. There is a most revealing account of a discussion between Baldwin and Dawson in May 1935:

... contrary to some statements that had been made, he felt no personal objection; but Winston would be a disruptive force especially since foreign relations and defence would be uppermost.[1]

Nevertheless, throughout this Parliament Churchill's speeches were always events of importance. With only a small group of devoted followers, he carried on through these years a campaign of outstanding vigour and resilience. There is a letter to Lloyd George, written in 1921, in which Churchill observes, 'Most men sink into insignificance when they quit office'.[2] This was certainly not true of either of these men. The two outstanding figures in the House of Commons were still Lloyd George and Churchill.

Of our old group in the 1924 Parliament, some were now leaving the back-benches. By far the most prominent of these was Anthony Eden. In 1926 he had become Parliamentary Private Secretary to Sir Austen Chamberlain, then Foreign Secretary. His maiden speech made a deep impression, as did his subsequent contributions to foreign affairs debates. He was appointed Under-Secretary of the Foreign Office in September 1931. On 1 January 1934 he was made Lord Privy Seal, without a seat in the Cabinet. He was to continue his general work at the Foreign Office, but to concen-

[1] *The History of The Times*, vol. iv, pt. ii: *1921–1948* (London, 1952), p. 893.
[2] Lord Beaverbrook, *The Decline and Fall of Lloyd George*, p. 114.

trate on Geneva and attendance at meetings of the League. As he
later pointed out to Baldwin, Geneva affairs were in fact foreign
affairs and separation was impossible. I had not forgotten this when
many years later I appointed Edward Heath as Lord Privy Seal,
in order to carry out the Brussels negotiations with the six countries
of the European Economic Community. But of course there was
a great difference. The Foreign Secretary at that time, Lord Home,
was in the House of Lords, and although Heath represented the
Foreign Office in the House of Commons, the prime purpose of
his appointment was to carry out the complicated and difficult
negotiations which it was hoped would lead to the entry of Britain
into the Common Market. This was his absorbing task. Moreover,
there was a complete sympathy on all general issues between Home
and Heath. This could not be said of Eden's relations with either
Simon or Hoare.

Eden's rise was the most spectacular among the young men who
entered Parliament just after the war. I never heard any criticism of
him; he was universally popular. Others followed in his wake: Duff
Cooper, Oliver Stanley, Rob Hudson, Terence O'Connor. These
all gradually took their places in the Ministerial ranks. This left our
little group rather bare, but we recruited without difficulty new
adherents.

Naturally, in a Parliament where the Government commanded so
large a majority, Members had time for a great deal of discussion in
various unofficial committees both inside and outside the House.
Apart from the 1922 Committee, which was open to all Members of
the party and constituted something like a weekly meeting of back-
benchers, there were the various party committees on special subjects—foreign affairs, finance, housing, and so forth. I regularly
attended those which interested me particularly. In addition, there
were a number of groups which formed themselves on an altogether
informal basis. It was in these that we worked the hardest. At the
very beginning of the Parliament there was formed the Northern
Group, consisting of all Members supporting the Government who
held seats in the North of England—some forty in all. Its chairman
was the senior Member for the area, Sir Nicholas Grattan-Doyle.
Naturally, since it was formed upon a local basis, it represented a

number of different and sometimes divergent views on major problems. What we tried to do was to concentrate upon those matters which most affected the life and future of our areas. This sometimes led to disagreement or compromise where our proposals impinged upon the realm of high policy. Nevertheless, as the Parliament proceeded we were able to exercise a not inconsiderable influence in the party. Our activities were of course well known to the Whips, and no doubt always looked upon with favour. But neither in this Parliament nor in the greater part of the next can I remember any interference with the amenities of social life being caused by the views which I began more and more forcibly to express in the House. I was careful, and so were those who worked with me, to stick closely to the subjects which we had tried to make our own. If we were critical on these, on all other matters we gave consistent support to the Government. It was only very rarely that any of us voted in the Opposition lobby, nor did we indulge in carping criticism on a whole variety of topics. In this way we were not put into the category of disloyal and contumacious rebels. Fellow Members, and even party machines, are generous to views strongly held and honestly expressed. But if a Member or a group of Members makes a habit of attacking the Government on every point—big or small, connected or unconnected with their main theme—they are rightly put down as peevish and cantankerous. Even what may seem to many 'crankiness' is pardoned, if it is sincere.

It was not till the time of Munich that deep and wounding fissures divided the party and spread into ordinary social relations. Until then, I do not recall any sense of ill feeling—as a result of my activities—expressed by fellow Members, by the Whip's office, or even, with few exceptions, by Ministers themselves.

CHAPTER ELEVEN

Visit to Russia

WHILE the capitalist world seemed, to many observers, in decay if not in mortal agony, the Bolsheviks had apparently consolidated their power and stability. In the early years of my political life, Bolshevism was regarded in Britain with feelings ranging between contempt and fear. But by 1932 many British people were beginning to wonder whether, after all, this régime which had imposed itself over a vast part of the world's territory might not be worth careful, and if possible objective, study. Unhappily, however, objectivity was rare among the visitors who began to take advantage of the facilities for travel which were now becoming available. Lord Strang, who spent three years at our Embassy in Moscow, has given a good picture of the usual reaction of British travellers. He describes how their views on Russia tended to reflect their own faith, whether of the Right or the Left. Intellectuals like the Webbs were specially prone to be deceived. He sums up this common reaction in a striking phrase: 'In the 'thirties, the truth about the Soviet Union was still a subjective phenomenon.'[1]

In 1932, however, few of my countrymen were able or anxious to undertake such a journey. A number of businessmen and technicians went there for shorter or longer periods; some trade union leaders; a few Members of Parliament; and some economists or Socialist sympathisers. There were also one or two specially well-known personalities such as Bernard Shaw and Lady Astor, whose journey together received wide publicity, although it seemed that they went more with the purpose of talking than of listening. Now, of course, all roads lead to Moscow. There is a continual stream of pilgrims, friendly or hostile, on business, politics, and even on pleasure bent who make this journey. In addition, artists, scientists, authors, come

[1] Lord Strang, *Home and Abroad*, p. 61.

and go across the Iron Curtain. All this interchange is valuable and healthy. In the early thirties this was not the case. In the autumn of 1932, therefore, I decided on at least a short visit. I was fully aware that I should gain no specialised knowledge in a few weeks, and that I should only see what I was shown and only be given information which I was expected to absorb. Nevertheless, I thought it would be an interesting experience and even rather fun. I was determined to put aside preconceived notions of my own. But I hoped, as a result, to be able to read and study more intelligently in future what might be the developments in that bewildering scene. My friend Allan Young went with me. Except on the boat, we travelled 'second class', and sometimes 'hard', which we thought would give us a better chance of seeing ordinary people.

Detailed accounts of a traveller's experiences are notoriously tedious, but I print here extracts from some of the letters which I sent to my mother, because they may give a picture worth recording as to how the Russian scene appeared to an unbiased observer more than thirty years ago.[1]

S.S. Cooperazia

September 1st, 1932.
Aug. 30th

Whatever may be true of the Russian 5 years' plan, our 5 weeks' plan does not appear to be working absolutely according to arrangement. We were to have left on August 31st, in a ship called the *Drenjinsky*. In fact, yielding to almost pathetic appeals from the Intourist agency, we have sailed on August 30th in the *Cooperazia*.

She is small—not more, I should say, than 2,000–3,000 tons. She is clean and apparently well kept. She was built in Russia.

We have quite a nice 2-berth cabin. The general sanitary arrangements are adequate. But the bathroom is a failure as it seems impossible to get hot water, in spite of several hot water taps.

After wandering round the ship, and having a few words with the only officer—I think the mate—who knew any English, we were

---

[1] Purely personal and family references have been omitted. Some repetitions have been excluded. Otherwise no major changes have been made in the text.

summoned by a nice old steward, with a bald head and a real Tartar face, to supper. This consisted of tea, smoked salmon, cold ham, and cheese. There seems to be plenty of bread and also butter—at least for us.

Aug. 31st

There are only two first-class passengers besides ourselves—a German engineer, living in Leningrad, and his wife. Among the 5 or 6 third-class passengers (the ship is very empty) are two Americans. One—a Russian—is paying a short visit to his old home near Dvinsk. Although he has a kind of sentimental admiration for the new Russia, this little man is a real New Yorker. The other American is rather a pathetic old gentleman. He is a "sociologist". I think he must hold some position at some university. He has come to Russia to form an independent judgment. "My mind", he keeps saying proudly, "is a complete blank." As he has no books about Russia, intends not to employ a guide, has no letters of introduction, and knows no other language except American, I cannot help thinking that his mind will remain in this calm and virgin state for a good long time.

If there are few passengers on this ship, there is a large enough crew. The crew consists, in about equal proportions, of men and women. Curiously enough, the stewards are all men, as far as I can make out. Certainly all the waiters at the meals are men. But women are employed really as sailors. One has been sitting aloft all the morning, in what seemed to me a most precarious position, trying to paint the mast. She did it, I thought, very well. Women also do most of the swabbing of decks, polishing brass-work, etc. The crew all seem well fed and happy. None speak English. They are pleasant and smile at one.

As the crew seem to work on an 8-hour day basis, there are a great number of them. In addition, according to our German engineer, every Russian undertaking ordinarily employs about 20% more people than is really necessary. Neither is there any lack of wireless sets and gramophones. These play continuously from different parts of the ship; moreover, the German engineer plays the piano and most of the crew sing a good deal. Altogether, it is very jolly.

S.S. Cooperazia

September 3rd, 1932.

The 'plan' is certainly not going with a swing. Instead of being well on our way to Leningrad, we are still in Hamburg. Most of yesterday was spent in unloading a cargo, chiefly of hides; and then they began to take on a very large amount of stuff, steel bars, billets, machinery of all kinds. This loading will probably go on till tonight, when we hope to leave for Russia.

It annoys me to see this immense purchase of iron, steel, and machinery from Germany. Germany is giving Russia the longer credits which we refuse. But Germany is doing it out of the immense loans which our bankers have made to her of English money, and which (since the standstill agreement of August 1931) she refuses to repay. Hence, we are in fact financing Russia and risking our money indirectly in all this cargo which is being loaded today—only, instead of it being at least manufactured in Middlesbrough or Stockton, it is coming from Stuttgart and Essen.

On board S.S. Cooperazia

Sunday, Sept. 4th, 1932.

The food is quite good, if rather monotonous. We have plenty of bread and butter; eggs are given us fairly often, but they are not fresh. The meat is not too bad, but they have produced a goose and some chickens which I think must have survived from the Tsarist régime. The ship's doctor is certainly the most intelligent and the most forthcoming of the crew. Most Russians seem very reluctant to talk politics at all.

The crew's quarters on this ship are excellent. They all have cabins—2 or 4 to a cabin—with proper bunks, not hammocks. They have also a very good recreation and reading room, where they have games and also lectures. They seem very keen on education of all sorts, whether vocational (on nautical matters) or general (mainly political and economic). The crew elect a soviet or committee of their own, and this committee discusses questions affecting the crew with the ship's officers. As far as I can make out, the soviet cannot overrule the captain, but it can make a complaint to a higher soviet if it wishes.

Leading out of the recreation room is the Lenin room. This is a little room with table and chairs where the ship's soviet meets. Above the president's chair hangs a huge photograph of Lenin, and on the wall is a rifle and the various parts of a rifle, to be used for instruction, with the legend "All true workers must learn the use of this weapon against capitalists and counter-revolutionaries!" There was a great meeting of all the crew the other night, followed by songs, etc., to celebrate some anniversary in the revolutionary calendar. It is all very queer, but they seem to take it very seriously.

On the Volga (between Samara and Saratov)
September 16th, 1932.

I hope the postcards have arrived, but do not feel quite confident of this. The Russian postal service is notoriously inefficient, and has just incurred the wrath of the highest authorities—Stalin etc.—who have demanded early reform.

We landed at Leningrad on the morning of the 7th. On arrival, we were at once met by our guide—a certain Mme. Kinderfreund. This lady was to look after us during our stay in Leningrad, and a large motor-car (a Lincoln) was placed at our disposal.

Mme. K. proved to be a lady of considerable knowledge, intelligence, and character. We have not had as good or efficient a guide since. She was, of course, really of "bourgeois" origin (as the phrase is here). I should say her father was probably a doctor or something of the kind. Her husband (of German birth) was an accountant, and employed in the costing side of production and in economic research.

After a snack at the hotel (which was quite adequate, although deficient in what Americans call "plumbing") we started out to see the city. Everyone knows the general plan of Peter's grand design. The actual physical achievement of building so large and imposing a collection of edifices on a water-logged marsh is in itself remarkable. Still more so, is the series of broad streets and boulevards (the Nevski Prospect etc.), the fine public offices, the great cathedrals, churches, etc., and of course, most characteristic of all, the Fortress of Peter and Paul. Of course, a great number of the most striking buildings are the work of his successors. Indeed, the city has developed in a different direction from his intention, and even on the other side of the River Neva. Nevertheless, the city owes its general character to its founder. He has left his stamp upon it. Even Revolution has respected it, and the magnificent equestrian statue of the great Emperor has been allowed to remain undisturbed.

After a general drive round the town, which gave us a good idea of its form, we went to the Hermitage Museum. During our drive, the thing which one chiefly noticed (apart from architecture etc.) was the fact that the streets presented such a strange appearance. The pavements everywhere were crowded to overflowing. (The population of Leningrad has almost doubled of late years and is now nearly 3 million.) In the middle of the broad "prospects" run the trams—equally crowded or rather swarming with humanity, clinging precariously like bees to these antiquated and clattering machines. But the streets themselves—i.e. the space on either side between the pavement and the trams (which run through the middle)—are completely deserted. Except for our "Intourist" motors, I saw hardly a car. A very few of the old "droshkis" are left. Hardly even a cart could be seen. Accustomed as we are to the traffic of English roads and streets, it was a strange sight.

The Hermitage is a fine collection which I need not describe. I wanted chiefly to see the Rembrandts, which are specially good. But as we have come to see the New rather than the Old, we did not spend an unduly long time in the museum. We went next to one of the queerest exhibitions I have ever seen. It is called the "Anti-Religious Museum". It is situated in the old Cathedral of St. Isaac, which has been taken over for this purpose. It consists of a series of exhibits designed to show the folly of the old superstitious beliefs in God, held by successive generations and races of mankind. Contrasted with these are shown (with a good deal of skill from the propagandist point of view) the certainties of Science. If you can imagine H. G. Wells using *The Golden Bough* to produce a popular skit on religion suited to the intelligence of the junior classes of an English elementary school, you get an idea of this unique museum.

At 5 o'clock we dined. The meal system in Russia is as follows.

You have 3 meals a day, breakfast, dinner and supper. The first can be any time between 8 a.m. and noon; the second from 3–6, the third from 9–midnight.

After dinner, we went motoring again, to see particularly the poorer quarters of the town and some of the new buildings (huge apartment houses in concrete) which are being erected to deal with the acute housing shortage. We also visited a "Home of Culture"—a sort of working man's club or institute. These clubs are a great feature—and one of the best features—of the new régime, and supply a real demand for adult education as well as for recreation.

At eight o'clock we went to the opera, which was *Prince Igor*. It was very well performed, although not (I believe) quite up to Moscow standards. The orchestra seemed to me very good and the *mise en scène* was excellent. The opera house is a magnificent building (old régime, of course) and about the size of Drury Lane. It was strange to see the audience in this very ornate and typically "capitalist" opera house. The Imperial box (in the centre) is reserved for officials, as are the two main side boxes (once reserved for members of the Imperial family). The partitions have been taken out of the other boxes, so that the 3 rows of boxes are now 3 galleries. The house was absolutely packed. We were in the parterre. The audience seemed to be half proletariat, and half office workers or skilled workers. They were intensely enthusiastic and they seemed really to appreciate the performance. I think the Trade Unions organise parties who get specially cheap tickets. Otherwise the price ranged from 3 to about 12 roubles.

I ought to say a word about the food. It is adequate, but badly cooked and unappetising. In Leningrad there is definitely a shortage of butter, eggs, and to some extent meat. We are, of course, travelling 2nd class, but even so we are given more (naturally) than ordinary people. The fish (mainly sturgeon) is quite good, and so is the cheese. There is one first-class hotel, where I am told the food is as in any cosmopolitan hotel, but here the prices are terrific.

Sept. 8th

After breakfast, and some arrangements at the Intourist office, we went off to see a maternity home and children's welfare centre. This

was the main experimental and teaching centre which was responsible for the work of other clinics in the city and district. According
to the lady doctor at the head, they have now reached a stage (with
over 300 maternity hospitals in the city) where no child is born
except in hospital in the whole city (except, I suppose, children of
the unfortunate remnants of the "bourgeoisie"). All children at
school are given free milk by the educational authorities. Children
up till 7 years (when they go to school) are given milk etc. through
the child welfare clinics. We saw the mothers and children coming
for their bottles. Each factory has a doctor or doctors attached, and
they are supposed to get in touch with expectant mothers, who come
to the clinics for medical advice. Of course it is difficult to tell how
far what we are told is actually in existence and how far it is merely
"planned" for the future. Actually, the clinic we saw seemed very
well managed, though I should say that it did not approach in
cleanliness and care one of our best welfare centres.

A peculiar—and perhaps less attractive—side of this work follows
from the legalisation of abortion. This is now allowed by law;
moreover, any pregnant woman who does not wish to have a child is
by law entitled to have the operation performed in a State hospital.
About 20,000 such operations were performed last year in Leningrad.

At 2 p.m. we went to a telephone factory. This factory was
originally operated by the Swedish firm of Ericsson, and of course
confiscated at the Revolution. As the old owners had, during a
course of years, trained up a force of 2,000 skilled workers, it was
perhaps natural that the new régime could make a success of it.
Perhaps that is why we were taken to see it. Nevertheless, it was an
interesting visit. The factory (working 2 shifts) now employs 7,000
workers of both sexes. The manager—who was extremely friendly—
explained to us the organisation both on the technical and on the
labour side.

At 5.30 we dined. At 8 p.m. we went to a cinema—again very
crowded. The film was (as most of the films are) propagandist in
character. It described the advantages of the 'collective' farms over
the old system of individual holdings and the greater productivity of
new scientific over the traditional methods of cultivation.

At 10.30 we had supper. At 12.30 a.m. we caught the train to Moscow, after 2 crowded and interesting days at Leningrad. We travelled "hard", 4 berths (or wooden shelves) in each compartment. A mattress and blanket provided. No undressing. After a liberal application of Keatings (to prove not altogether effectual) we got into our bunks and went to sleep.

On the Volga
Sept. 9th, Moscow

We arrived at about 10.30 (only 1½ hours after the advertised time). We were met at the station by a guide from Intourist. She was middle-aged, swarthy, and very ugly. She spoke English only moderately, but proved to be pretty efficient and very willing. She was a keen and energetic Communist.

Our hotel—the Hotel New Moscow—was decidedly second-class. But then we are second-class travellers! There are two very good hotels in Moscow, but they are, I am told, outrageously expensive. We had no bathrooms or hot water. The food was poor—worse than Leningrad—but sufficient in quantity. What is really good everywhere is the tea, which you have with every meal. The soup also is good; but the fish and meat is beastly.

At about 12 (noon) a car (provided by Intourist) arrived (together with our guide) and we had a general drive round the town. This gave us our first view of the Kremlin (the ancient walled city), the Chinese or Tartar City (also surrounded by a wall) and the modern town. We were taken to see an enormous stadium and recreation ground for workers (post-Revolution) and a colossal aerodrome, filled with new machines. Everywhere great military activity and heaps of soldiers.

There is a much more prosperous look about Moscow than you see in Leningrad. Being once more the capital has of course bene-fited it. The people seemed better dressed; there are more cars etc.; and naturally, since it is Whitehall, the City, Victoria Street etc. all rolled into one, there is a greater proportion of higher-paid officials and office-workers. There has been a great deal of new building—mostly in the American sky-scraper style, as modified by German and Swedish influences. It is very good, I think, of its kind in design, although it seemed rather shoddy in execution. In the poorer quarters, there is vast activity in building huge apartment houses, adding new stories to old mansions (of course all the Park Lane and Mayfair is now divided into workers' flats) and clubs, "culture houses", etc. etc. Most of the streets are being repaired. New drainage systems are being put down. Everywhere there is upheaval, disorder, reconstruction, turmoil. The police are excellent—as courteous in helping stranded foreigners as ours. Everyone seems interested in foreigners and very friendly, at least on the surface.

From 2–4 daily Lenin's mausoleum is open to the public. There is a daily queue of 1,000–3,000 awaiting admittance. It is a handsome structure of red and black marble—quite low, in a rather Egyptian style—and stands in the Red Square, just below the Kremlin. We were taken in (out of turn) and a strange sight it is. Lenin lies embalmed—the pale wax-like look that embalming gives is rather unpleasant—in a glass coffin. The head is a fine one—very high forehead, delicately-chiselled features—thin, aristocratic nose, small and fine aristocratic hands. The people file reverently by, just as formerly they visited the relics of some saint. From the propaganda point of view it is very effective. Even under Communism, human nature reasserts itself. Man longs to adore something or somebody. Christ has been taken away, and Lenin put in His place.

We were also taken to see—among other things—a prison. The guide insisted on this and we agreed reluctantly. It was apparently a prison for the worst offenders and apparently the Government is very proud of its success in prison reform. All the prisoners worked at a textile factory in the prison and earned some small wage. The prisoners elected their own committee or soviet, to discuss questions affecting them with the Governor. They seemed to come and go as much as they liked and they were allowed a week's holiday (if earned by good conduct) once a year. Most had long sentences but they could earn very big reductions so that the maximum sentence for a well-behaved man became (in fact) about 3 years. Apparently only 2 men had ever failed to return from their holiday. Perhaps this does not speak very favourably for conditions outside as compared with those inside the prison. But I suppose that in reality a man who escaped would have no chance. The police system is much more rigid and efficient than in old Russia. Moreover, he would not be able to go from one place to another without his passport. He could not obtain work in a State undertaking without his papers and especially his Trade Union card. He could not obtain work elsewhere, since there are no private employers. He would have no ration card, and could therefore obtain no food. He could only live by stealing or crime.

I went to pay my respects to the Ambassador. Sir Esmond Ovey, to whom I had a letter of introduction, was away on leave. But the Embassy had been informed by the Foreign Office of my visit, and Mr. Strang, the First Secretary, received me with the greatest courtesy and kindness. I had a very interesting conversation with him for some time, and left at about 7.30. He gave me a very acceptable cocktail and sent me in his car to the opera. The opera was *The Snow Maiden*—a typical Russian opera, very well staged and (as far as I could judge) excellently performed in every way. The performance was delightful, but portentously long, since there are considerable intervals for food and talk between the acts. We had some excellent smoked salmon and beer. We got back to the hotel about midnight. We had to walk and rather lost the way. There are no taxis and the few remaining "droshkis" are exorbitant in their demands.

Sept. 10th

By the courtesy of some official, who knew me to be an M.P., I was given a car for myself today, a privilege which ordinarily cannot be claimed by tourists, at least by those who travel 2nd class. We spent the morning going round various government offices, delivering the letters of introduction which I had obtained in England. I had a very interesting interview (conducted in French) with a certain M. Dvolatsky, of the Foreign Trade Department. He was the second in command; his chief, whom I hope to see on my return to Moscow, was away on holiday. We had a long discussion of the Anglo-Russian trade position; the balance of trade; imports and exports etc. I obtained the figures which I required, and (by letting him do all the talking, which indeed he was very ready to do) a very good idea of the official Russian attitude on this question.

At 2 p.m. we went to see one of the new factory kitchens. This huge "cafeteria", employing 3,000 people, supplies cheap meals to workers, men and women, on a mass production basis. It served about 18,000 meals a day and the organisation seemed admirable. (All these privileges, of course, are confined to the Trade Union proletariat.)

After dinner, and a short rest, we set out for a cinema, where we saw another propagandist film, excellently produced. It was called *The Road to Life*. Its subject was the method by which the thousands of homeless and degenerate children (products of the Civil War) were taken by the Government and trained in labour colonies etc. to be useful citizens. Like all the propaganda, there is a little too much of it. But it was an artistic and interesting performance.

Sept. 11th

In the morning we visited the Kremlin. The palaces have been turned into historical museums, and the churches (of which there are 3 within the walls) are also museums of religious art, etc. The collections in the palace are interesting, but I did not see anything supremely good. I believe that many of the best things are not shown. The collection of vestments, richly and rather barbarically encrusted with jewels of all kinds, was good. There is a good exhibition of costumes etc. of all periods; also of coaches, coronation coaches, carriages, footmen's liveries, etc. etc. of all periods.

The churches or cathedrals are intensely interesting. The Government is looking after these churches excellently from an antiquarian point of view, and a lot of restoration, removal of over-painting and whitewash etc. is going on.

At 1.30 I lunched (at one of the smart hotels!) as the guest of a party of 4 young Conservative M.P.s, who are on a visit here. Their names: Manley, Mitchell, Anstruther-Gray, and Maclay. They gave me a wonderful luncheon—caviare; poulet. I hope they are rich.

From 3.30–4.30, I had an interview with M. Litvinoff, Commissar for Foreign Affairs, who corresponds to our Secretary of State. He speaks excellent English and made himself very agreeable.

At 11 p.m. we left Moscow by train, for Nizhni-Novgorod, on the Volga. This town is on the confluence of the rivers Oka and

Volga and was in old days famous for its annual fair (since the collectivisation of agriculture, the fair is no longer held). This journey was unspeakably foul. We were in a long open carriage (like an Underground carriage) with I think about 26–30 people. Boards folded out from the sides (at queer angles) and formed beds. Mattresses (of a kind) were provided, but it was extremely difficult not to fall off the board-berths. Luckily the train never went more than some 20 miles per hour. The people (of every class, workers, officials, peasants etc.) were charming. A loudspeaker roared most of the time classical music (jazz is luckily forbidden by Communism) and every sort of food and drink noisily consumed throughout the night. I'm sorry to say that Keatings proved to be of little avail ! (I wish the Government would 'liquidate' the bugs as well as the 'kulaks'.) We arrived (exhausted) at Nizhni-Novgorod on the morning of

Sept. 12th at about 10 a.m.

Here we were met by a charming young guide (a girl of about 22) who took us to the hotel. The railway station lies on the east side of the river, and to reach the main town and the Kremlin or upper town, you have to cross the River Oka. The road is on a pontoon bridge, which has to be taken away and re-laid every year, as the river freezes in winter. A new high level bridge is in course of construction. Naturally, the river level of all these rivers varies enormously—as much as 20–30 feet or more. Now the rivers are low; but in April and May, after the snow and ice has melted, there must be a terrific volume of water.

The hotel is so-so. Still no bath, but a kind of sickly shower is provided (cold) which is better than nothing. By soaping oneself all over first, and then standing under the shower, at least reasonable cleanliness can be obtained.

After breakfast (about 11.30) which consisted of the usual cold fish, cheese, etc., we sallied out to see the sights of Nizhni-Novgorod.

On the Volga (between Saratov and Stalingrad—formerly Tsaritsin)
September 17th, 1932.

The old town of Nizhni-Novgorod, as is usual with all these old strongholds, is built on the top of a hill overlooking a river. This citadel, or kremlin, consists of a space, about the size of a Roman camp, surrounded by a high brick wall—a beautiful old pinkish brick—with the usual complement of towers, gates, machicolations etc. Most of these kremlins were built in the 15th century or earlier, and represent the long struggle for supremacy between the Muscovites and the Tartars. In later days, of course, the kremlin naturally becomes the seat of government. Here, for instance, there is a very beautiful 18th century house, formerly the residence of the governor of the province, built in the classical style. It is now, of course, the seat of government, but occupied by the local soviet. Alongside of this building, there has been erected, since the Revolution, a very fine town hall, with offices etc. and a good hall; this is in the modern style, all straight lines and glass, not without distinction and beauty.

We went next to see the market. Here was a picturesque crowd of industrial workers, peasants, etc., of every race and kind, ranging from the purely Slavonic type to the Tartar and Mongolian. The costumes were just those that one has always associated with the peasantry—blouses, padded coats, high leather boots, bark and bandage leggings, kaftans, fur caps and coats of every possible description. The women all still wear the kerchief over their heads. The noise and tumult was indescribable—also the various odours—unwashed humanity, meat, fruit, vegetables, sunflower seeds, cattle, etc.; there were also more flies than one can conceive possible. The market was of 3 kinds—first, the stalls belonging to the cooperatives; second, those belonging to the collective farms; third, a free market of the few remaining small traders. The last sold often rather better quality goods, but at very high prices. They are gradually being taxed out of existence, and can only maintain themselves at all by having some speciality, not perhaps available at the socialised booths, and charging exorbitant prices for their wares.

After seeing the market, we drove out in a car (provided for our use by Intourist together with a guide) to the motor-truck factory, which lies about 10 kilometres from the town.

The road like all roads in "pioneer" countries (and Russia today *is* a pioneer country, reminding one in many ways of Canada) was very bad. After a hot, dusty, and jolting drive we at last reached the site of the factory. This town—for such it is—has been built in the middle of the forest. The trees have been cut and utilised; but all round is an apparently endless jungle of fir, birch, and poplar. I did not gather the exact population, and of course many of the workers are brought from Nizhni-Novgorod. But you can judge of the size of the undertaking when you know that the projected output of the factory is 140,000 trucks per annum. Huge factory buildings, kitchens, apartment houses, clubs, theatres, etc., have been hastily erected within the last 2 years. Army detachments, housed in tents and huts, are helping with the work. Everything is still in a state of considerable disorder, and (like many things in Russia) the "plan" is certainly not yet in working order. Much to our disappointment, we were not allowed *inside* any of the workshops. The official figures of output are only about 40–50 trucks a day (say 20,000 a year) and doubtless some hitch has occurred. But the effort on so large a scale is certainly impressive, and one imagines that the difficulties–mainly that of training skilled workers–will gradually be surmounted. A large number of foreign workmen are being employed–American, German and English, as well as the foreign technicians of a higher grade. Since the change of policy as regards wages, allowing different wage scales according to the skill of the worker and substituting piece for time work, good workmen can earn up to 500 or even 1,000 roubles a month.

We went back to the hotel and after dinner we walked in the town and on the ramparts. It was a beautiful evening, followed by a lovely clear and moonlit night. In the course of our peregrinations, we had a great stroke of luck. Noticing that all the lights were on in the assembly room of the town hall, we asked our guide if there would be any opportunity of going in. She volunteered to make the attempt, and after a good deal of parleying with the men at the door, we were admitted and given seats on the platform. The audience, consisting of about 200 persons of both sexes, were seated in a horse-shoe auditorium, built with rising tiers, like a theatre. On the platform were about 20 or 30–the praesidium or managing committee–and at each end of the platform was a rostrum, shaped like a pulpit. From one of these a speaker was addressing the meeting. We found, on enquiry, that we had been admitted to a meeting of delegates, representing the Communist party of the whole district of which Nizhni-Novgorod is the capital, who were attending a special conference organised by the party to discuss the question of education in its various aspects, both of children and adults. The speaker was the secretary of the Communist party for the district, and was engaged in delivering the speech opening the conference. The delegates were of all types—mainly working class and peasantry, with a good sprinkling of apparently more educated persons, probably technicians and office workers. (I wonder, by the way, if any Tory member of Parliament has ever before attended a meeting of the Communist party!) The speaker dealt first with the problem of teachers; more must be trained; their status must be raised and better wages paid; they must have more adequate training; they must have better provision for study, by the organisation of special reading rooms etc. in the local clubs. Then he dealt with books and newspapers. Village libraries must be increased in number and more newspapers must be printed and circulated. A greater knowledge of Communist principles and "economic materialism" must be spread (this now takes the place of religious teaching in the schools). These and cognate matters were the main theme of his speech, which was delivered with great enthusiasm and astonishing fluency. The audience seemed fairly interested, although some seemed to find the speech rather long and went out to smoke quietly in the lobbies, just as they might do in any Capitalist country. After the speech, there was an interval, before the conference proper began. At this stage we were told to leave.

Sept. 13th, 14th, 15th, 16th, 17th

We went on board the river steamer at about 11 a.m. and sailed about noon on the 13th. The distance from Nizhni-Novgorod to Stalingrad is about 1,200 miles, but progress is very slow as the boat has to steer a most difficult zig-zagging course in order to avoid the sandbanks which are such a feature of the Volga. The river at this time of year is very shallow; I should imagine the difficulties of navigation to be somewhat like those attending a trip up the Nile. The steamer is a flat-bottomed screw steamer, of very little draught; there are four classes. For the purpose of this trip, we are first-class passengers. We each have a very small cabin, with a basin which works imperfectly. There is, however, a bathroom, where hot water can occasionally be obtained after long discussions with the engineer. Class 1 has its saloon, with great plate glass windows, and quite comfortable chairs at the front; Class 2 at the stern of the ship. Class 3 and 4 are below deck, and indescribably horrible are the conditions here. The ship is absolutely crowded out. Everyone seems always to be travelling in Russia. Enormous numbers of peasants land or come aboard at the various stops, peasants of every type and nationality, carrying with them huge loads containing, presumably, all their worldly possessions. The consumption of water melons and sunflower seeds and tea is never ending.

In the first class there are mostly officers of the Red Army or engineers travelling to some new place or on holiday. They are all charming and courteous. They play the piano and sing bits out of Russian operas; they play draughts with us and ask innumerable questions about England. The peasants also sing a great deal—delightful part-singing is a regular feature of the evening. Last night the crew held a soviet meeting to protest against their inadequate clothing and victuals. The captain was sent for and cross-examined and finally agreed to do better in future and buy them some new overalls at Stalingrad.

The river is wide in most places ($\frac{3}{4}$ mile to $\frac{1}{4}$ mile would be about the variation, I should say), but the channel is very narrow. We pass several villages and stop at some large towns. Here we can get off and go for a walk and see the sights. The most notable of these are Kazan, Samara, Volsk, and Saratov. They are mainly towns from which cement (made from the chalk and limestone range of hills that runs along the right bank most of the way) is exported—also fruit, grain, timber. Great rafts of timber are floating down to Astrakhan; fishing seems an active occupation of many.

It has been a very peaceful trip and (except for the insect life) I have enjoyed it very much. Our conversations with our fellow passengers give us a lot of information. Everyone says that things are better than in old days; some are intensely enthusiastic, with a kind of "crusading" spirit (if one can use that word of communism), and, of course, all the younger generation take the system as a matter of course, just as we accept capitalism, because they have never known any other. The intensive propaganda in the schools; the abolition of all religious teaching, which cannot even be given on a voluntary basis; the 6-day week, which abolishes Sunday and leads the younger people to reckon always by the date and never to use the name of the day (Monday, Tuesday, Wednesday, etc. are almost obsolete); the pride in the material achievements of Communism— all this for the moment satisfies or seems to satisfy the average mind. What will happen when they begin to solve the material problems and the "war spirit" begins to flag, one cannot tell.

Moscow

September 25th, 1932.

Sept. 18th. Stalingrad.

This town was originally called Tsaritsin. Its present name is, of course, due to a desire to remove all memories of the old régime and to honour the present secretary of the Communist party and *de facto* dictator of Russia—namely, Stalin, the successor to Lenin. It was a small provincial trading town, of some importance owing to its position on the Volga. It is now rapidly becoming a great industrial centre. In the morning, from 11–3, we visited the great tractor factory which has been erected just outside the town. Unfortunately, it was a holiday; but we were none the less able to see the general lay-out of the works (which are on a vast scale) and the various dwelling houses, clubs, factory kitchens, recreation rooms, schools, clinics, etc., which have been erected for the workers. About 18,000 people are employed; the annual output is supposed to be 50,000 tractors. That figure (like many others in "the plan") has not yet been reached. Nevertheless, it is clear that a great output does exist. We had some interesting conversation with some Americans who were working as instructors. They considered the Russian peasant quick and adaptable, and a keen and energetic pupil. But, naturally, having no mechanical experience, a great deal of work is spoiled and valuable machines are frequently damaged by inexpert use.

This visit took a long time; but it was intensely interesting and we had a particularly intelligent guide, who had been employed at the tractor plant since it started. After dining at about 4 p.m. (meals are at all times in Russia) we went to a local cinema, where we saw a propagandist film about the Civil War in the Crimea, contrasting those bad times with the present happy conditions. The Crimea, formerly the Riviera of Russia, is now used as a place for workers who need special cures, and the old hotels and villas have been converted into rest-houses and sanatoria.

At 11.30 p.m. we left for Rostov.

Sept. 20th. Rostov.

At 9 a.m. we left by car to visit one of the great State farms or Sovkhoz, as they are called. This means a farm where the State is the employer, and the peasants are the hired labourers. It is in contradiction to the Kolkhoz or *collective* farm, where the peasants combine together, pooling their land and stocks to form a unit which they operate themselves, dividing the proceeds of the harvest after paying a proportion to the State.

This State farm, called Verblud, was organised about 2 years ago. It occupies what was largely deserted or uncultivated land, in the Black Soil area, belonging to the Don Cossacks. These used the land for ranching and horse-breeding and very little of it was under the plough. The acreage is enormous—250,000 acres. It is divided into units of about 20,000 acres each, with a manager of each unit. The chief headquarters of this farm is a little colony where most of the experts and many of the workers live. About 3,000 people are employed and the farm is almost wholly mechanised. It produces only grain—wheat, maize, barley, etc. We saw the autumn sowing in operation—great American machines, drawn by tractors.

The village which forms the centre seemed well arranged and quite good housing. As usual, the housing accommodation takes the form of blocks of flats, not separate houses. There were the usual clinics and crèches; but here, unlike the factory conditions, only about 20% of the women are employed.

We were given a most excellent meal on the farm, and treated with more genuine hospitality and kindness than anywhere else. Our guide was a charming young man, who had lived in one of the middle-western provinces of America and spoke English well. The countryside is just like the prairie provinces of Canada—except that the soil is blacker and richer. No kind of manure is ever put upon it;

but it seems (for the present at any rate) inexhaustible. Of course the yield per acre is very low according to English standards—but then the acreage is so enormous. As we were driving from Rostov to the farm, we had a curious and thrilling experience. We turned a sharp corner in the road (about half way from Rostov to the farm) and suddenly saw, not more than 20 yards from the roadside, standing quite still, two huge eagles. We stopped the car; the birds were not at all frightened and we had time to see them quite closely for several minutes. They were a magnificent sight. At last, after taking a good look at us, they slowly took to flight and sailed majestically away.

In the evening, after dinner, we went to a kind of open air amusement park and saw quite a good performance of Circassian dancers, male and female. The dances were picturesque rather than beautiful; the music quite barbaric.

Rostov and the south generally seems much more prosperous than the north of Russia. There is more food about; the people looked happier and less strained (Leningrad was the worst place we have been to in this respect) and generally there was a bourgeois and jolly look about Rostov which contrasted strangely with some of the other towns. I do not know the reason for this, unless it is purely climatic.

Moscow.

September 26th, 1932.

Sept. 21st. Rostov.

In the morning (11–2) we were taken over a great factory for making various forms of agricultural machinery (not combines—but sowing machines, ploughs etc.) which has just been completed. I thought this plant a good deal the best which we had seen. The foundry was a wonderful shop—automatic mould-making (which I have never seen even at Dorman Long and have only heard about as a new American device); a belt which carried the moulds to the place where the metal is poured into the cast—and in general a very fine equipment. The forge was an excellent shop, but I thought not so efficiently organised and a good deal here was done by hand which in modern plants should be done by machine. Perhaps the machines had not arrived or were too expensive. The wood-working shop was very good, but the workers did not appear very expert. One of the novelties of this shop was a system by which all sawdust was sucked up through pipes and carried to the furnace of the power-plant, where it is consumed. This factory, called Selmash, employs about 18,000 people. We have a lot of figures regarding categories of workers and rates of pay. The workers are divided into 8 categories, according to skill. In the highest are only 168; in the lowest are 778. The main body are in the bottom but one and bottom but two—(6th and 7th. About 8,000 in these two classes). The pay is by piece rate. The guaranteed minimum of the lowest class is 75 roubles per month; of the highest 278. From this you will see how far the new non-equalitarian policy is going. The whole pressure now is to pay the best workers the best wages and piece work (now universal wherever technically practicable) has immensely helped to strengthen this tendency.

Sept. 23rd. Kharkov.

Kharkov is now the capital of the Ukraine Republic, and is really a remarkable city. Kiev (the old capital) is (I believe) a beautiful and picturesque riot of towers, domes, minarets, campaniles—the old world of religious fervour and colourful life. Kharkov is a sort of imitation Chicago—grey, efficient—or fairly efficient—with huge public offices in the grand sky-scraper style and colossal industrial plants in the outlying districts. Like all the towns which we have visited, the population has been trebled and almost quadrupled since the Revolution. Hordes of peasants are attracted by the better conditions and higher wages of the industrial worker. Kharkov—for instance—had a population 15 years ago of just over 200,000. Today it is over ¾ million. The huge tractor plant employs already 23,000 people; the special suburb surrounding the works houses over 50,000 persons. In addition, the largest electrical turbine plant in the world is in course of erection. Altogether, a surprising, even staggering, city. Everyone is wildly enthusiastic about the future. The atmosphere is that of a Canadian or American city during a boom. I wonder if there will be a slump!

Sept. 23rd. Moscow.

Our train was rather late from Kharkov, and by the time we had reached the hotel, washed and eaten, it was nearly 2 p.m. I went round to the office of Voks (Society for Cultural Relations) and had a long and interesting talk with M. Amdur, the director. I found that he had received instructions from M. Litvinoff (Foreign Affairs) to arrange for me the various interviews etc. which I wanted.

At about 5 p.m. we went to see a Mr. Duranty, to whom we had a letter of introduction and stayed talking to him till nearly 8. He is the talented correspondent of the *New York Times*, and he has been in Russia since 1921. He is generally supposed to know more about Russia than any other foreigner, except perhaps Chamberlain, the representative of the *Christian Science Monitor* and *Manchester Guardian*, whom I am to meet later. It is, incidentally, a strange thing that none of our great English newspapers is represented here (in Moscow). Only the German and American Press are really properly represented.

Duranty takes a hopeful long-term view of Russia, but he thinks this will be a bad winter. Owing to industrial inefficiency and undue pressure on the peasant, output and production are low. The immense investment in capital goods (i.e. the *means* of production) has resulted in a very great shortage of *consumption* goods. This means that the peasant cannot be tempted to work really hard at agricultural production, since he can only get paper roubles and not commodities in return for his labour. Meanwhile, the fall in world prices has made it necessary to increase the *volume* of exports, in order to raise the same amount of foreign currency. Hence a shortage of food etc. in the towns. But, in the long run, if the pressure is not too great, the production of consumption goods must rise enormously and with it the production of the peasant, whether working as an individual or in collective farms.

Sept. 24th

1 p.m. Saw M. Rosengoltz, the Commissar or Minister for Foreign Trade, and several of his colleagues. The most intelligent of these was M. Ozenky, who is shortly coming to London. We had a general discussion on trade, the balance of trade, Russia's commitments, the credit position, loan possibilities etc. M. Rosengoltz unfortunately speaks no English, but M. Ozenky spoke well and so

the conversation was fairly easy. This talk lasted till about 3.30 when we left for the hotel and dinner.

Moscow.

September 27th, 1932.

Sept. 25th.

At 11 o'clock we went, by appointment, to see M. Broido, who is the head of an organisation called Partizdat—that is, the publishing business of the Communist party. This worthy, who is an old-time revolutionary, is none the less a man of considerable charm. I expect his hands are red with blood; but he is very amiable and jolly all the same. He received us with great hospitality, and assembled in his room were the heads of all his departments.

An enormous spread of butter, cheese, caviare and bread, with delicious tea and sugar, was produced—the best meal we have had in Russia! He then proceeded to explain in great detail and with no little pride his business and how he conducted it.

Partizdat is an organ of the Party, not of the Government. But of course the two are, in this country, inextricably intermingled. Partizdat produces all the innumerable books, brochures, or pamphlets of a propaganda character. It has its own book-stores for the circulation of these and of course it uses the machinery of the Party in the various localities in addition. The output and sale is prodigious. For instance, for Stalin's last book they had advance orders for 3½ million copies. Actually, owing to the acute paper shortage, they only circulated 1 million.

Besides pure propaganda, Partizdat publishes all the books into which tendentious matters can be introduced, e.g. History, Economics, Logic, Philosophy etc. All these school and university books are produced with a Marxist bias and therefore come within the scope of Partizdat, not of Orgiz, the State publishing monopoly which deals with ordinary books where no question of Communism or Anti-Communism can arise. Partizdat also produces the anti-religious textbooks. Instead of the hour set aside in our schools for religious teaching, there is a daily lesson in anti-religion—a most important part of the educational system.

After dealing with the subject matter of his publications, we discussed technical questions—paper, printing, binding, etc. He also explained his relations with his own book stores and with those owned by the State publishing company, and the rates of discount, etc. Altogether, our discussion lasted till nearly 2.30; the latter part being taken up with my answering a large number of questions about book publishing in England and the nature and extent of our business.

My next appointment was with a M. Nagler, the second man to Grinko, who is Minister of Finance. He was a man of very different character—not a revolutionary leader but a typical public official. Charming, intelligent, a good linguist and very well-informed. We had a most interesting discussion on Russia's financial position and foreign trade and the possibilities of increasing trade with England. We also discussed in great detail the possibilities of an Anglo-Russian loan, from the point of view of both countries.

Russians seem to like talking to us and never appear too busy to do so. How they manage to get their work done, I don't know.

At 7 p.m. we went to a great demonstration in honour of Maxim Gorki.

Leningrad.

September 28th, 1932.

The particular ceremony which we saw—this has been a regular Gorki week—was the official function. It took place in the great Opera House. The stage was occupied by the leading figures of the Soviet State. Kalinin—the nominal head of the State, i.e. the Chairman of the All-Union Soviet—presided. And at a long table—draped of course in red—sat many of the well-known commissars or ministers and other figures prominent either in the Government or (which is more important) in the Party. After a little delay, there entered at last Gorki. Great applause. Then Henri Barbusse. More applause. Then (very modestly) there came in Stalin. The whole audience rose to greet him with vociferous applause. (The ambassadors remained calm and seated.) Stalin, of course, holds no office or only a very minor one in the Government. But he is the secretary of the Party—and therefore *de facto* dictator of Russia. The diplomats present their credentials to Kalinin (who is a sort of Mr. Clynes) but they know who really rules and that the party machine is far more important than the nominal constitutional organs of government. Then followed speeches—of interminable length—in praise of Gorki. First, a literary critic spoke for an hour. Then an author, called Ivanoff, who fortunately lost his head and broke down. Then the Minister of Education for $\frac{3}{4}$ hour; then Henri Barbusse; then a poet, who recited a long poem of his own in praise of Gorki—then various members of the Government, who made various announcements— these, all in honour of Gorki, were received with thunderous applause. (1) Gorki has been awarded the Order of Lenin—like our O.M. (2) Nizhni-Novgorod is to be called in future Gorkigrad. (3) A theatre in Moscow is to be named after him. (4) One of the main streets in Moscow is to be re-named in his honour etc. etc.

After all this and some more speaking, adjournment for refreshments. (All this speechifying took place without a word from Stalin, who sat inconspicuously in the second row chatting to a young man on the platform. And so Bonapartist is the régime becoming, that all the evening the one subject of discussion was the identity and prospects of the youth who had been thus singled out by the quasi-royal favour.) The speeches seemed to please the audience vastly, as well as the announcements about the honours to Gorki, although we are told that among the intelligentsia there is some grumbling and a good deal of talk about Gorki's villa in Italy, his four motor-cars, his idle and pretentious family and all supported—I suppose—out of his royalties earned in Russia as well as in capitalist countries. It is (incidentally) rather curious, as an example of the gradual movement to the right which is very noticeable here, that Henri Barbusse (so gossip says) was reproved by very high quarters for the tone of his speech. It was said to have been too extreme and to have laid too much stress on "World Revolution". This was regarded as dangerous and "bad form".

After the speeches etc., there was an interval. We retired to the great room behind the old Imperial box, where was a supper table richly supplied with every conceivable delicacy—all in the old Russian style. There followed an excellent concert, played by the orchestra of the opera, from Tchaikovsky, Borodin, Rimsky-

Korsakov, etc., with some renderings of parts of various operas by the chorus of the opera house. We also had a recitation of an extract from Gorki by the leading tragedienne now on the Russian stage. After this, another interval, and more food. Then there began (about 11.30 or 12) a play of Gorki's called (I think) *The Underworld*, played by an all-star cast of the best Russian actors and actresses from Moscow and Leningrad. After the first act, which ended just before 1 a.m., we went back to bed.

Sept. 26th

The chief thing which occupied today was a visit to M. Luppol, of the State publishing company. The actual head of this concern is M. Tomsky, but I fancy he is mainly there as an old party leader and revolutionary and that M. Luppol is the chief brains of the show. I had a most interesting discussion with him, lasting 11–1.30, on every detail of his business, and he supplied me with a lot of details (balance sheet etc.) and a special memorandum which he had caused to be written for me. Unfortunately, he spoke no English or French, and the interpreter was not very good. But I had, none the less, a most delightful talk with a man of a very engaging and attractive personality. He gave me copies of various documents, including his agreement form with authors! I must say that, from the point of view of the publishers, there is something to be said for this system. There are certainly no literary agents to bother about!

Sept. 27th

We spent the morning doing some sightseeing. We went to the Central Anti-Religious Museum, which was quite interesting, but not so cleverly done as the one in Leningrad. It was still more crude. But it gives a good idea of the propaganda, which is (in reality) an attack not so much on religion as on superstition.

We also visited the Tolstoy museum, which is quite interesting and a place called the "House of Handicrafts", where modern handicraft work from the villages is on sale. I thought the stuff ugly and very badly made. There was scarcely anything one could want to buy.

I met today a young man on his way back from the task of erecting some machinery in Siberia, which had been purchased from an

English firm. This youth gave a pretty bad account of conditions at this particular spot—the worst thing, I thought, being the fact that a lot of the labour is forced labour from the dispossessed "kulaks" (richer peasants) of Astrakhan, who were working at 50 roubles a month—about one third the ordinary rate—and treated so badly that their only hopes and thoughts were resting on the chances of a Japanese invasion of Russia !

Sept. 28th

We arrived in Leningrad at about 9 a.m. After washing and eating, we set off with the same excellent guide who looked after us before (Mme. Kinderfreund) to Tsarkoe Selo—about half an hour by train from Leningrad. The Catherine Palace—a sort of Versailles—is really wonderful. It was built at various periods, but mostly in competition with French standards of luxury. Often the decoration is in bad taste, though there are some beautiful rooms. The ballroom is wonderful—much finer, I think, than the Galerie des Glaces. But even where the taste is questionable—as in the Agate room or the Lapis Lazuli room—the effect, richly and even barbarically splendid, is overwhelming. One of the nicest rooms is a Chinese lacquer room, with some exquisite screens and cabinets.

The other palace—the Alexander Palace—is an ordinary classical building, of no particular architectural, but of intense human, interest. Nicholas and his wife lived here ever since the revolution of 1905 (they never came to the Winter Palace in Petrograd after that). Their private apartments are shown; even the rooms and playthings of the children. The private apartments were all specially decorated for the Tsar. They are indescribably banal—like an English provincial bourgeois home in the 1880's. But there is a strange pathos in it all. The Empress's bedroom (furnished in the worst possible Maple style) has still 300 ikons on its walls. Charms, crucifixes, and every sort of relic of mediaeval times—and then the blue and white flowered wallpaper, the innumerable photographs in brass frames—the whole effect is quite extraordinary.

On the whole, these palaces are well kept by the new régime. But propaganda is nowhere neglected. In all the splendid rooms of the Catherine Palace, there are reminders of how the peasantry were starved and bullied amid all this splendour. In one room, where there are set out a lot of robes etc., there is a great announcement saying that these ridiculous dressings-up still go on in Capitalist countries; then there is a picture of the King opening Parliament (taken from the *Illustrated London News*) and also a photograph of George V at the Coronation. I was looking at this with a little amusement, when my eye was suddenly attracted by a familiar physiognomy—it was a drawing (by Byam Shaw) of the Duke (of Devonshire) in his robes (I suppose at the Coronation) and holding the Queen's crown on a cushion. I don't know how it got into Bolshevik hands, but above was this delightful inscription "Typical Boyar of the old régime in Capitalist countries, living on the exploitation of the working classes."

*   *   *

The period that I chose was, unknown to me when I set out, one of supreme importance in the development of the Communist system. It has been well described by Lord Strang in the following words:

My three years and a few months in Moscow fell within the period of the first Five-Year Plan; the period of Stalin's consolidation of his personal rule; of the urgent steps for the massive industrialisation of the Soviet Union; of the collectivisation of agriculture, the liquidation of the *kulaks* and the famine which followed; of the beginning of the evolution of Soviet foreign policy towards co-operation with the non-aggressive Powers in the face of the threat from Germany and Japan.[1]

I well remember Strang, who showed me the greatest kindness in Moscow where he was then Chargé d'Affaires, giving me this picture almost as he has set it out in his book.

It was a strange feeling to have passed, like Alice, into a kind of looking-glass world where everything was the opposite to what one would expect. Three instances occur to me which have remained in my memory. First, the Customs arrangements seemed very easy and perfunctory; and this was sensible, since Russia lacked almost everything. The general view appeared to be that if anybody brought

[1] Lord Strang, *Home and Abroad*, p. 60.

in anything of value to Russia, they were doing the country a benefit rather than an injury. The only exception was books. These were jealously scrutinised. I had with me a volume of Homer in Greek, which seemed to the official a kind of bastard Russian and might perhaps be the language of some distant territory, and the *Odyssey* a weapon of propaganda. The second was the degree to which Communist faith had become as respectable as its opposite in Western countries. I remember being taken into a school, where I was courteously received by a rather formidable-looking head-mistress, indistinguishable in appearance from a typical schoolmarm at home—short hair, pince-nez, and a rather disapproving expression. I raised some points about the curriculum, which she answered clearly and with obvious pride in the progress of her school. I ventured to ask how they began the school day. She looked at me with amazement, as if I had asked an impudent question, and replied: 'Why of course, we begin the day with the anti-religious lesson.' The way in which she said this was just as if I had asked such a question in a Church school in England, and received an appropriate rebuke: 'Why of course, with Prayers.'

The third example was a long discussion with the ship's doctor on the Russian ship on which I travelled. This, like all Russian conversations, lasted for many hours. He spoke good English; his father, he told me, had been a clerk. He had been in the volunteer army during the Intervention and the Civil War and severely wounded. I remember him as a most intelligent and, to some extent, discriminating supporter of the régime. He was not a member of the Party but perhaps might some day aspire to membership. He talked more freely than I expected, perhaps because of the privacy of the small saloon, where we were alone. He said about us almost all the things which we were continually saying about them. He complained of the lying British propaganda, of the many agents employed by the Capitalist countries in subversive and counter-revolutionary work, of Imperialist plots to encircle Russia and finally to attack her. His final appeal was obviously sincere: 'If you would only leave us alone and not go on with your continual spying and propaganda, things would be better.'

One thing in particular delighted me. In spite of the unwillingness to talk freely, at any rate where others could overhear, Russians apparently were still allowed, as a kind of safety-valve, to make and enjoy what jokes they liked. These were very popular. I will give one example. There was a shortage of everything; crowds besieging every shop and every tram, aggravated by the vast populations which had flowed in from the countryside to the cities, mainly in the hope of better food. Everyone was on the move, but the train service was hopelessly insufficient. Scenes in the railway stations were like those one sees in India. The people waited patiently in the station yard in hundreds and even thousands. There was a queue for everything. (I was not destined to see queues at home until some years later.) But of course in the very hierarchical society which was already developing, there were all kinds of different advantages given to the higher ranks—the functionaries, the officers, and so forth. One of the most popular jokes in circulation was about a man who, seeing a long queue waiting outside either a shop or a booking-office, pushed his way past to the front, with angry gesticulations, shouting: 'Out of the way, out of the way. I have a permit here not to stand in the queue.' One of the affronted crowd replied: 'You silly fool. This is the queue of people who have a permit not to stand in the queue.' In 1940 I remembered, and made use of, this story when I was in the Ministry of Supply and the great battle of priorities was on. Army, Navy, Air Force—each wanted their particular demands marked A1. The result was that everything became Priority 1 and confusion for a time was worse confounded.

In the course of a few weeks we saw great stretches of country from Leningrad to Rostov. I had a number of conversations, not with the highest but with officials of some standing in Moscow. But I did not attach much importance to them. They said, no doubt, the same things to everybody and I had nothing new to hear or to report. One of my purposes was, of course, to learn how far something might be done, if credits were available, to increase the sale of our exports, particularly from the heavy industries. It was clear that Russia was going through an immense economic revolution, with everything devoted to building up as rapidly as possible a high productive capacity. The people were deprived of consumption goods in order to concentrate upon capital goods. I also formed the view, rightly or wrongly, that Russia's main difficulty was that she had scarcely emerged from feudalism, and was trying to pass to Communism, or at least State Capitalism, without going through the ordinary course of development which the Industrial Revolution had brought about in most Western countries. They were, therefore, working at frantic speed, trying to do in five years what in other countries had taken several generations. This, of course, meant many sacrifices. It also involved a certain shoddiness, especially in buildings and other projects, and great waste through ignorance and inexperience in handling the precious machines which they had bought so dearly. There were also grievous errors in calculation by the high authorities. Perhaps the most obvious deficiency was in transport. The railway system seemed to be just as in Tsarist times. Trucks were few and motor-cars practically non-existent. Nevertheless, it was a mighty effort.

I could not, of course, see below the surface, although I suspected the brutalities and tyrannies of a police State. On the other hand, I was deeply impressed, especially as we moved away from the great cities to the south, by the good nature and kindness of ordinary, especially peasant, people. All these are now commonplaces. We know so much more of Russia and they, happily, are learning to know more of us.

When I returned to England I contented myself with one lecture of a very objective kind to my constituents and did not try to pose as an expert on Russian affairs. But I had learnt much which was useful to me. I must confess that when I crossed the frontier and came back into the Western world, I seemed to be stepping back from a kind of nightmare world into the world of reality. But then I reflected that perhaps Russians would feel the same. The problem is still unresolved. Who are the lunatics in the world? Those in the asylum or those outside?

CHAPTER TWELVE

Reconstruction

AFTER the crisis of 1931 the same questions were being asked
all over the world. Can the old system survive? Can it be
saved and, if so, how? Russia had already made her reply
by the establishment of Communism, or at any rate of State Capitalism. Italy had adopted a highly controlled economy, although the
Fascist regime embodied, at least in theory, a mixed system. Germany, still in the throes of utter collapse, was soon to move into the
centralised structure of National Socialism. The United States remained loyal to free enterprise and competition; yet in spite of its
vast resources and its modest requirements of imports, was in a
hopeless state of confusion and almost of despair.

In Britain, by a great act of national self-restraint, the classic
remedies had been taken to deal with the immediate situation. In
accepting these, at the expense of their own comfort and standard of
living, the British people had displayed their customary sense of
discipline in an emergency. Nevertheless, the gold standard could
not be sustained. Whether we liked it or not, we were now in a
period of a managed currency. We had somehow, if not to insulate
ourselves, at least to protect ourselves from the economic hurricane
that was sweeping across the world. Our immediate crisis was over;
the firmness of the Government and of the people had demonstrated
that, although the pound was devalued, it was not out of all control.
There was no question of anything like the German inflation of
1923, with all its devastating social effects.

Yet an answer must be given to the question, what do we do now?
The Government's policy, apart from the drastic economies, which
were deflationary, seemed confined to the introduction of a tariff
system. This in itself, it was believed, would lay the basis of recovery. Many of us could not accept this diagnosis. How was the

price-level to be raised to a level of profitability which would induce greater business activity? How was employment to be provided? How was idle money to be guided into investment? We believed that a much wider and more imaginative design was required. We welcomed the imposition of protective tariffs as the first step, or at any rate as part of a wider programme. Within the security of tariffs, a measure of reflation became feasible. But we must decide by what machinery tariffs should be operated and what aims they should serve. The early months of 1932 were much taken up with this controversy. Three articles were published in *The Times* on 'A True Tariff Policy', and the question was there posed as to the sort of tariff commission which should be set up. I contributed (on 18 January 1931) to this discussion by a letter to *The Times* on the constructive use of tariffs to provide an opportunity for the increase of industrial efficiency. I strongly urged that tariffs would not of themselves achieve the purpose which we all had as our real objective. Indeed, if by the protection of inefficient and old-fashioned methods prices were raised to the consumer industries and especially to the exporting industries, there might be more harm done than good. This was especially true of the iron and steel industry, with all its complications and ramifications. Surely, the only way was to make sure that the tariff became an instrument for industrial reorganisation? This view was shared by Neville Chamberlain. In a speech in the House of Commons on 4 February, he emphasised the duty of a tariff commission to encourage increased industrial efficiency, and not merely to provide shelter. This was the debate in which Chamberlain announced so eloquently the final triumph of his father's policy.

In the same debate, Herbert Samuel, while an unrepentant free-trader, put forward a plan of reorganisation through an industrial commission. My plea was for a combination of the two approaches. Let the tariff be used to bring about reorganisation and rationalisation. I urged that a tariff commission should be something more than a mere judicial body.[1] It should be on the lines of a development or industrial commission, planning the growth of the nation's economic life, and helping industries to reorganise themselves in the

[1] The official name was Import Duties Advisory Committee, known as I.D.A.C.

changed conditions. This might involve interference by the State with private interests. But protectionists could not attack it on that score, for the abandonment of free trade surely meant the end of *laissez-faire*. In this connection, I circulated privately in March a short sixteen-page pamphlet under the title *The State and Industry*. Its argument was simple. The passing of the Import Duties Act would mark the end of a period in Britain, both in economics and in politics. From now on, protection, not free trade, would be on trial. Had the right administrative machinery been chosen for the implementation of the new policy, if tariffs were to be anything but a system of log-rolling or a shelter for inefficiency or a device to exploit the consumer? For tariffs must be made to play a creative role in the reconstruction of British industry. The Import Duties Advisory Committee—the tariff commission set up under the Import Duties Bill—would therefore be the keystone of the structure. But it would be overwhelmed with work. It would be insufficiently specialised. It would not set up a vast bureaucratic structure of its own. If it was to work quickly and constructively, it would need advice from those with real experience of the problems, both as producers and consumers. My plan was that the Committee should be empowered to call into being representative bodies for each of the great national industries, with full representation of labour as well as management. Such councils should send their reports to a body of industrial advisors. This sub-parliament, composed of representatives both of the producing and the consuming industries, should consider the tariffs and make its recommendations.

I went on to argue that this continuous contact between the Government and its representatives and industry was an essential preliminary to an effective grappling with other policies, especially an imperial trade policy. Some form of functional representation was necessary, because the fundamental problems of the day were problems for experts as well as politicians. My paper, based on the administrative problems arising out of the Import Duties Act, therefore, went on to consider the various extensions of Government authority which had already taken place or were becoming necessary, and set out a plan to adumbrate a system of partnership between an organised industry and the new machinery which tariffs made inevitable.

The little pamphlet had a wide circulation in the Press and a good deal of friendly response, although naturally some hostile criticism. Meanwhile, the Import Duties Bill made its way through Parliament. There was certainly to be an Advisory Committee. But it was not, unhappily, charged with the responsibility or equipped with machinery for industrial consultation, both of which were imperative if protection was to be the foundation on which reconstruction could be built.

In the middle of May I circulated in the same way a longer and more ambitious document, entitled *The Next Step*. Here was an attempt, however amateurish, to form some analysis of the fundamental problems and to propose some solutions. The argument ran as follows:

Prosperity might be defined as that economic situation in which all the forces of production—capital, labour and resources—were fully utilised to supply human needs up to the limits of productive capacity.

Equilibrium was not a static balance but a continuous poise, and fluctuations were inevitable. The nineteenth-century system for dealing with these factors—to leave market demand to regulate the balance of production and to base financial policy on the gold standard which automatically regulated credit policy—worked only so long as markets were expanding, and the increasing surplus which industry produced could be channelled into new capital investment. The system had ceased to work because the world had developed on competitive, not complementary, lines, with increasing economic nationalism.

In the place of the old *laissez-faire* system, we had to create economic prosperity and provide some organisational method to maintain equilibrium. There was need for a central organisation, directing economic effort and the flow of investment. Reflation to the 1928 wholesale-price level would require a 30 per cent increase in wholesale prices. There could be no assurance that entrepreneurs would be willing to undertake such investment, even if offered cheap money. Therefore the Government had to be prepared to take up such new money as the industrialist failed to utilise.

I outlined specific proposals, many of which were then thought novel. Some have been proved impracticable. Yet the broad principles laid down and some of the methods advocated, which then seemed almost revolutionary, have become generally accepted today.

From Maynard Keynes I received a particularly interesting letter:[1]

I like the enclosed very much. My criticisms are really due I expect to the sort of middle position you occupy. But as you ask me for them, I will give you one or two for what they are worth.

1. My main feeling is that you are not nearly bold enough with your proposals for developing the investment functions of the State. You are trying it would seem to minimise the part which the State must play and you endeavour to get your results by a sort of combination of private enterprise and subsidy; and I doubt the feasibility of this, at any rate in present times.

2. You do not call attention to the extent to which the present policy of the Government is contradictory. They are still maintaining a lot of the maxims and watchwords which date back from the deflationary period. . . .

3. Are you clear that it is impossible that the rise of prices can come *first?* This can only appear as the result of a greater volume of purchasing power, brought about by increased business activity or development schemes. . . .

4. Do not you pay far too much lip-service to economy? I consider this problem of Budget economy difficult. There are enormous psychological advantages in the *appearance* of economy. It prepares the way for the conversion of the Debt and it tends to lower the long term rate of interest. The opposite would also be bad for business sentiment. But that does not prevent economy from being deflationary and probably injurious to business profits. . . .

Keynes quite naturally put the greatest stress on reflation and monetary policy generally. I, for my part, and many agreed with me, felt that this was only one part of the policy; that the efficient organisation of industry, and everything that was involved in

[1] 6 June 1932.

the term 'rationalisation', was just as vital. My constructive proposals were discussed—sometimes favourably, sometimes critically—but the diagnosis at any rate met with a wide measure of agreement. During the crisis of 1931, people had placed their hopes in ruthless economies and protective tariffs. Now purely deflationary economies seemed of a very doubtful value, certainly if pushed too far. We were also now beginning to feel the relief of no longer being tied to the gold standard. So long as we were prudent, and did not rush into extravagant schemes, we could certainly make use of this new freedom. All this was leading to the adoption of a general attitude towards political and economic problems which lay between the old *laissez-faire* and the new Socialism.

Thus was a powerful impetus given in favour of what became generally known as the policy of 'Planning'. Our group began increasingly to urge the Government to embark upon productive schemes of Government expenditure and to finance liberally similar schemes of local authorities. This question became, before the end of the Parliament, a subject of acute controversy, as indeed it had been in 1929. By 1933 I was able to speak in the House on this theme without fear of automatic opposition. In a debate in March 1933 on economic questions, it was possible, without too much difficulty, to advance arguments for increased Government expenditure:

One might almost argue that under the modern capitalist system the technique of a Government should always be to operate in exactly the contrary direction to that in which individuals are operating. In a period of boom, individuals are investing freely, and even over-investing to a speculative extent. During that time, the Government should be 'bear'. It should save, it should pull in its horns. On the other hand, a period of depression, when individuals are unwilling to invest, is the time for capital investment on the part of the Government. The trouble is that the Government, being composed of individuals, is subject to the same psychological forces as individuals. At a period when the rate for money was 7 or 8 per cent, and houses cost £1,400 to build, we built hundreds of thousands of them, and raised a great burden of debt around us ever afterwards. Now, in a period of depression, when we can borrow money cheaply and build houses cheaply, we are a little reluctant to invest capital sums from Government sources.[1]

This was good Keynesian doctrine, and some twenty years later became generally accepted in the famous White Paper on full employment, which was the product of the War Coalition. As things have turned out, it has not been easy to apply it, even when its soundness has been generally accepted. For in times of boom, the demand for increasing Government expenditure—roads, schools, universities, and the like—becomes very difficult to resist. In other words, we have learnt how to turn the tap on. To turn it off, or even reduce the flow, has not proved so easy. Towards the end of his life, Keynes recognised this difficulty of checking undue pressure on over-employed resources. It has not yet been resolved, although the need is at least now generally recognised, and various efforts have been made to find an effective machinery of co-operation between all concerned to this end.

In the course of this year I continued my efforts. I contributed to almost all the leading national and provincial journals. I wrote in other magazines and journals, wherever I could get a hearing. I spoke to Rotary Clubs. I lectured; I debated; I used every possible method to promote my views. I thus became, in a minor way, something of a national figure.

The idea of 'Planning', originally so disreputable, began gradually to acquire a certain vogue. Apart from organisations like P.E.P. (Political and Economic Planning), which were supported by various businessmen, as well as by theoreticians—by tycoons, as well as by cranks—the concept of central and local planning, properly integrated and co-ordinated, began to gain ground.

In February, and again in March 1933, I pleaded in the House of Commons for a more imaginative policy. Money was available. Bank deposits had increased in the last year by £250 million-odd. But bank advances had only increased by £130 million. Both Sir Arthur Salter, a distinguished economist, and Mr. Rupert Beckett, a leading banker, agreed that the only quick and sure way to remedy

[1]*Hansard*, 8 March 1933.

this continual deflation was to modify immediately and decisively the restrictions upon public expenditure, national and local. 'Obviously,' I declared, 'in the list of things to be done, housing comes first'.

All through 1933 I maintained—within the limits possible for a back-bench Member of Parliament and a private individual—an active campaign. I had the assistance of some of the Northern Group M.P.s and, more particularly, of my friends in Tom Martin's group. On the whole it was a lonely and unrewarding struggle. Yet I have not regretted it. Many of my ideas may have been unworkable; some may have been premature; yet, looking back on those years, I feel that in the light of the social and economic developments of today I was more in sympathy—more 'with it' (as the phrase now is)—than some of those who regarded me with so much disapproval.

My own family were very understanding during this period of my political life, which lasted till the Second War. My father was, in his quiet, rather sceptical way, suspicious of orthodoxy in any form. My mother, who was ambitious for my success, was confused by my political isolation, but loyal and devoted. My wife's family had a traditional indulgence for eccentrics. If I held odd views on politics and economics, so, many years ago, had Lord Shelburne—and more recently, his descendant, Lord Lansdowne—so had Uncle this and Cousin that. It was all in the Whig tradition.

During this year, although I worked hard in my business and in these manifold activities, my health began to improve. I planned—and completed—a more ambitious book, in which my ideas were further developed. It was published in December 1933, under the title of *Reconstruction*. This book developed at greater length the analysis which I had set out in the smaller pamphlets and the plan of action recommended. It had a good reception, both from the public who bought it and from the newspapers who reviewed it. Broadly speaking, it was clear that I was justified in my claim that 'Planning', as a political and economic concept, was winning approval in many, and some unexpected, quarters. The reception of my ideas stimulated me to persevere.

Outside Parliament, a number of bodies were coming into being, all of which interested themselves in the broad concept of planning, both central and local. I now took the lead in promoting a definite movement for industrial reorganisation. With the help of Henry Mond (the second Lord Melchett), who became vice-chairman, the Industrial Reorganisation League was launched in the summer. The small executive committee included Sir Robert Horne, Major Cyril Entwhistle, M.P. (a textile manufacturer), Sir Felix Pole, the former manager of the Great Western Railway, Sir William Firth (the steel magnate), Sir Valentine Crittall (the well-known industrialist), and Sir Malcolm Robertson (chairman of Spillers). Among the sixty members of council were a large number of businessmen and economists, with some Members of Parliament. We carried out by this organisation for the next two years considerable propaganda in favour of the improvement of the industrial system, and we studied the problems of each industry one by one.

One of our purposes was the promotion of a Bill to give, under the direction of the Government, statutory authority to any scheme of industrial reorganisation which received the support of a substantial majority of an industry. There was to be proper protection for minorities and for the interests of the workers, as well as for consumers of the industry's product. The work of popularising these ideas proceeded with great energy from the autumn of 1934 until the days when such plans for reconstruction became overcast by the dark shadows of imminent war. In order to clarify our proposals, an Enabling Act on these lines was actually introduced into the House of Lords by Lord Melchett as a Private Member's Bill in November 1934. The Bill was drawn up on a limited basis, and dealt with fifteen major industries, such as mining, iron and steel, shipbuilding, the chemical industry, and the like. The Bill made it clear that it was of a 'permissive' character, and it was for each industry to decide for itself whether or not to make use of it. Moreover, there were safeguards as to the operation of any scheme and as to the power and duty of the Board of Trade to preside over its development.

Some advance towards the practical application of these ideas was made by the Government in regard to the textile industry, when the majority decisions on wages and conditions were made obligatory upon a minority of disagreeing employers. If this principle was right in one function of industry—the fixing of wages and labour conditions—why, we asked, should it not apply to the organisation of the industry itself—research, marketing, selling, and the like?

During this year I laboured hard with many of my colleagues, both through the League and in other ways. In March 1935 fourteen Members of Parliament joined with me in the publication of a booklet called *Planning for Employment*, or *Planning for Work* as it became popularly known. It was the basis of a campaign which we carried on as energetically as we could throughout the whole of 1934 and 1935.

One of the features of this confused and difficult period was the growth of a feeling that there was much in common which might become acceptable to members of different political parties and backgrounds. Official parties naturally tended to underline differences. But was there not something to be said for trying to find and emphasise points of agreement? Could not a practical programme of action be brought into being by these means, at least to deal with immediate and urgent needs? There was still unemployment on a huge scale. There was still the problem of the ageing men and women who had lost heart through prolonged idleness. There was still the need for efficiency in every field. There was still the need for expansion. In spite of some improvement, there was a long way to go. Could not people be induced to concentrate on that part of the road on which we were travelling together?

Inspired by these sentiments, and anxious to underline short-term needs rather than long-term theories, a number of men and women of all political parties, and of none, came together in a movement known as the 'Next Five Years Group'. Its leader was Clifford Allen,[1] one of the most remarkable men whom I have known and one of the most attractive. He began life as an extreme Left-wing Socialist; a rebel; a conscientious objector; and later on,

[1] Lord Allen of Hurtwood.

an important member of the Independent Labour Party. In 1931, in the great Labour schism, he threw in his lot with Ramsay MacDonald. He became chairman of the National Labour Party and on MacDonald's advice was given a peerage. In spite of continuous ill health, his energy and enthusiasm for any cause which he took up was unbounded. In 1933 he and some of his friends were becoming more and more obsessed by the growing strength of Fascism and Communism in Europe and the danger of Britain becoming infected. In February 1934 he organised a manifesto to which I and other Conservatives willingly adhered, protesting against these tendencies. It was entitled *Liberty and Democratic Leadership*. It was, in effect, a plea for the substitution of reason and goodwill for bias and prejudice.

At the end of the summer of 1934 a meeting was held at All Souls College, Oxford, which I attended, and as a result a more or less coherent group was formed. A book was prepared, consisting of two parts: the first on economic policy and the second on international relations. Under the title *The Next Five Years* it was published in July 1935. I worked on Part I, economic policy, which was a compromise between Socialists and anti-Socialists; but it was a compromise very much to my taste. On looking through it again, it must have seemed at that time to lean rather more to the Left than to the Right, especially as regards the proposals for an increase in public or semi-public control of utilities such as transport, gas, and electricity. My Conservative colleagues and I naturally yielded on some of these questions, in order to meet the many concessions made towards our views on industrial organisation. Nevertheless, on all the other aspects—on the use of money; on expansion; on development; and above all, on the organisation of economic planning, both nationally and locally—the policies of *The Next Five Years* did not differ substantially from those which I had already promoted in my own speeches and writing, and through the organisations with which I was connected. This part of the book might fairly have been described, in political jargon, as a little Left of Centre.

Part II of the book was a plea for the sincere support of collective security through the League of Nations. Since this was, at least officially, the Government policy and was the basis on which they were soon to fight the General Election of 1935, my Conservative friends and I found no difficulty in associating ourselves with this section of the manifesto. But it was in Part I that public opinion was chiefly interested, as it was more precise and more practical. Altogether, some 150 prominent men and women of all parties signed the document. The greater part were not politicians as such, although there were some sixteen Members of Parliament, mostly supporting the Government. These included such 'respectable' Conservatives as Major Jack Hills, Terence O'Connor, and Geoffrey Ellis. Among trade union leaders we had the support of John Bromley, secretary of A.S.L.E.F. and an ex-chairman of the T.U.C., and Sir Arthur Pugh, another ex-chairman of the T.U.C. and secretary of the Iron and Steel Trades Confederation. Among the clergy, there were the Bishop of Birmingham (Barnes) and the Archbishop of York (Temple). Literature was represented by that great philosopher, Professor S. Alexander, as well as by such writers as Laurence Housman, Gilbert Murray, Desmond McCarthy, and H.G. Wells. Economists were to the fore, the most distinguished perhaps being Arthur Salter, one of the principal draftsmen. It was in the course of our work together during these months that we made what proved to be a lifelong friendship.

This project could not have been brought to a successful conclusion without Lord Allen's enthusiasm and almost apostolic fervour. The spirit of our co-operation was simple. We tried to put aside divisions about ultimates in order to concentrate upon priorities. The old arguments between individualism and Socialism seemed to us irrelevant. For it was clear that 'our actual system would in any case be a mixed one for many years to come'. In the same way we regarded the issue of free trade and protection as out of date and that a pragmatic approach was the only sensible one. We all agreed on the need for some machinery 'by which a design and plan could be substituted for improvisation and the tradition of muddling through'.

As was to be expected, *The Next Five Years* received wide

notices, both in the news columns and by the specialised critics. Moreover, in view of the catholicity of the signatories, it was regarded always with respect and sometimes with enthusiasm.

The work of our group was complicated by the approaching election and the confused political situation. Lloyd George had come back into politics with his 'New Deal' policy, put forward with all his vigour and highly organised publicity. For a time it was uncertain how far the Government would handle his re-emergence. In the end, his plans were turned down—partly, no doubt, because they were his. Actually, Lloyd George's policy was neither so carefully worked out nor so novel as our own. But once it became clear that the Government would not co-operate with Lloyd George, it seemed as if the campaign he was about to launch must be transformed from a contribution to national policy to another bid for power. However, he denied this; and in the great meeting in which he set out his new plans he claimed that his movement would also be 'non-party'. So, many Conservatives like Sir Arthur Steel-Maitland, Eustace Percy, and Londonderry welcomed it as a valuable contribution. Churchill also gave it a generous acclaim.

This situation led to some difficulty among the Next Five Years group. Certain confidential discussions were held just before publication of our book as to whether Lloyd George should become a signatory. We did not want, as Allen remarked, the 'New Deal' to turn out a 'New Game'. It was therefore decided not to ask him to sign but to let things develop. Lloyd George's next step was to form 'Councils of Action for Peace and Reconstruction' and to initiate a campaign of meetings throughout the country. For myself, I was quite prepared to appear on a non-party platform, on the understanding that it really was non-party, and I was followed in this by other Conservative Members. Consequently I attended the first meeting at the Central Hall. But with the approaching election the situation clearly became both delicate and embarrassing. Allen, Crowther, Sir Walter Layton,[1] and I, representing the group, saw Lloyd George on 12 August at Churt. Naturally this tea-party fluttered the political dovecotes and caused a great excitement in the Press. There had been much talk about the formation

[1]Later Lord Layton.

of a new Centre Party; but of course this was quite impractical, and was never at any time contemplated. As a result of our discussion, we recommended to our colleagues that we ought not to participate as a group (whatever individuals might do), because such an action would be contrary to the spirit of our original constitution. The problem came to a head in November, when the General Election was called. Some of us were standing as Labour, some as Liberals, and some as Conservatives. In Stockton, a Liberal candidate had not long ago appeared on the scene, and the result of a three-cornered fight was unpredictable. Allen made great personal efforts to persuade Samuel to withdraw the Liberal candidate. But this attempt failed, and I had to fight the election with two opponents.

The Council of Action, however, did play some role, because it sent questionnaires to all the candidates of whatever party and brought a considerable amount of pressure upon them in this way. As the election approached, candidates, as is normal, became more easily subject to suggestion and more elastic in their views. For my part, I was in no difficulty. I had already intended to fight my election on the Next Five Years programme and there was nothing that Lloyd George had to propose which made any problem for me.

All these activities belong to those strange years before the war, now largely forgotten. No doubt the tremendous events that followed make this seem to modern readers a somewhat remote and shadowy period. But it is perhaps worth at least recording my own experiences, typical of many other men of my age and time. The work that I undertook was heavy and the results often seemed disappointing. I could not have carried it through without the devotion of my friend who acted as my secretary and main assistant—Allan Young. I had got to know him during the period of the Labour Government and he remained working with me until I joined Churchill's Government in 1940. He then joined the Civil Service, where he remained to the end of his career. Although our active co-operation had to cease, my friendship and affection remained, and I would wish to pay my tribute here.

This, then, is the story of the campaign for economic reconstruction in the period from 1931 to 1935. I have described it in some detail because it was to this that my mind and efforts were almost exclusively devoted. But while we were working consistently and often hopefully for internal reform and progress, events were taking place throughout the world which were destined to make all these discussions seem trivial and all these labours puny. What Churchill has called the gathering storm was at first but a little cloud on the horizon; but in these years it began to grow. It was soon to be moving across the sky, charged with menace, threatening doom.

CHAPTER THIRTEEN

Fateful Years: 1931-5

WHEN the Conservative Government was defeated in the General Election of 1929, it had completed, in the foreign as well as in the domestic field, a not unfruitful term of office.

The Dawes Plan in 1924 began a substantial scaling-down of reparations, to be followed in 1929 by the Young Plan, the last stage before their virtual extinction at the Lausanne Conference in 1932. The Locarno Treaty in 1925, freely negotiated between Britain, France, and Germany, was hailed as a turning-point in the reconciliation of Europe and the extinction of old feuds. As a result, Germany joined the League of Nations, amid general acclaim, in the following year. In 1928 the Kellogg–Briand Pact for the renunciation of war was accepted by the majority of nations. Finally, there began in 1929 a process, to be completed in June 1930, by which all Allied troops were withdrawn from the Rhineland, many years before the date laid down in the Treaty of Versailles. In all this, there was a story of steady progress towards peace which it was confidently believed would be followed by disarmament, and the establishment of the effective authority of the League of Nations.

Yet, in the spring of 1935, when Eden paid the first visit of any Western statesman to Moscow, he and Stalin discussed a rapidly deteriorating situation. Stalin thought it worse than in 1913. Although Eden could still claim the existence of the League as an element in the struggle for peace which was absent before the war, Stalin pointed out in reply that 'In 1913 there was only one potential aggressor, Germany. Today there are two, Germany and Japan.'[1]

What then had happened, in so short a time, to bring about so

[1] The Earl of Avon, *The Eden Memoirs: Facing the Dictators* (London, 1962), p. 154.

radical a change, and to dissipate the high hopes of a few years back?

First, Japan. Her aggression was indeed not merely potential but actual. Three and a half years before, in the autumn of 1931, Japan's invasion of the Chinese mainland was launched. The Manchurian Crisis, as it was called, proved a grave blow to the whole structure of the League of Nations. It was the first instance in which the League Covenant was seriously flouted by a first-class Power. There had been minor incidents which had, in one way or another, been condoned or contained. But this was a blatant seizure of large tracts of the territory of one great country by another. It was conquest, followed by annexation.

No doubt this successful challenge by Japan of the authority of the League ought to have thrown into sharp relief the inherent defects of the Covenant, and the dangers of believing that it could provide an automatic security to 'peace-loving nations'. But there were certain considerations which seemed to place the Far Eastern crisis in a special category. Most important of these was the absence of the United States from the League, dangerous in Europe; fatal in the East. America had the power, if it had the will, to take effective action against Japan. As a result of American unwillingness to substitute deeds for words, the only member of the League which was also a first-class Far Eastern Power—Britain—must sustain alone the burden of making sanctions effective. But Britain's naval power had been seriously impaired in the preceding years. The 'No war for ten years' rule and the various naval agreements entered into had much reduced our strength in Far Eastern waters. In the course of the rigorous curtailment of expenditure on defence, which, as I have already described, was the feature of Churchill's reign at the Exchequer from the very commencement, a divergence of view had arisen between him and Austen Chamberlain, then Foreign Secretary, as to the likelihood of trouble in the Far East. Churchill, maintaining that the money could be better spent elsewhere, wanted the Cabinet to accept the principle that the possibility of war with Japan in the next ten, fifteen, or twenty years could be ruled out. The Foreign Secretary reacted strongly. There followed, as is not unusual, a sustained argument between the Treasury and the Foreign Office.

But in effect the Treasury view prevailed, at least to the extent of maintaining the ten-year rule. It might be thought that this naval weakness would not prevent economic sanctions being imposed. But if economic sanctions were declared by the League, the burden would still fall on Britain. There was no reason to believe that the threat or even the use of economic sanctions would prove enough. The Japanese might well decide to break any blockade by force and Britain, without American support, had no hope of bringing sufficient armed strength to bear upon Japan. The Admiralty were clear about this and lost no time in so informing the Foreign Secretary of the day, John Simon.[1] It was freely stated at the time, and is still widely believed in the United States, that Simon turned down a proposal by Secretary of State Stimson, which might in due course have led to the United States sharing in the imposition of economic sanctions. Even this rather shadowy prospect never, in fact, had any reality. America contemplated gestures but never action. Yet this story of Simon's refusal of Stimson's help was quickly elevated to the status of a dogma. It was based upon a complete illusion. No such proposal was made. The most that the United States suggested was some form of moral pressure. Stimson's first idea was to enunciate the doctrine of 'non-recognition' of Japanese conquests. The second proposed the invocation of the Nine-Power Pact of 1922 to respect the territorial integrity of China. Neither of these would have affected the Japanese determination to set up the puppet State of Manchukuo. Indeed, in February 1932, the Council of the League did adopt a resolution of 'non-recognition', but it proved an empty gesture, in which by that time the State Department had lost all interest. Unfortunately, however, Simon's method of handling the American Secretary's proposals was unfortunate and led to serious misunderstanding. A confused telephone conversation and muddled communications were the unhappy foundations on which a legend grew up, none the less damaging to the true interests of both countries because it was based upon a misconception. Simon, with all his extraordinary ability and intellectual power, had neither the sensitiveness nor the

[1] H.M. Foreign Office, *Documents on British Foreign Policy*, Series 2, vol. ix (London, 1965).

touch which are the necessary equipment of a Foreign Secretary. Stimson, in the event, had no difficulty in using Simon as a scapegoat.[1] Apart from the ill feeling created in the United States, another serious consequence was the alienation of many loyal supporters of the League from Simon in his own and other countries. Yet the failure to prevent Japanese aggression could not fairly be charged against Britain. It was a failure of the League, which lacked the power, and of America, which lacked the will.

Nevertheless, in view of the special circumstances, this episode did not destroy British belief in the League. There had originally been some sympathy for Japan, whose undoubted economic interests and rights had been injured by the prevailing anarchy in China. Anyway, what could the League, or even Britain, do? The scene of action was some 10,000 miles away from home waters and nearly 3,000 miles from Singapore. It was a set-back, but it was not necessarily a final defeat. The next test was destined to take place a few years later in Africa, involving a European country more easily, it would seem, controlled—with lines of communication running not through the Pacific but the Mediterranean.

For a successful foreign policy at that, or indeed at any time, two things were essential. First, there must be sufficient force of arms, either alone or in concert with allies; secondly, there must be a firm public opinion. As regards defence, Britain had carried out radical disarmament in full conformity with the spirit of the obligations which many people felt to be implied in the Treaty of Versailles. Between 1926 and 1931 our total defence expenditure actually fell, while that of every other country rose substantially. Indeed, the story of disarmament after the First War was not unlike that of free trade in the nineteenth century. Britain adopted free trade in the evident expectation that she would be imitated by other great industrial countries. In the same way, in spite of her commitments over almost every part of the globe, Britain disarmed unilaterally, hoping that other countries would follow; it was our duty to lead the way. Yet, with Britain and France acting resolutely together, the situation might still have been saved. As Churchill has emphasised, up to the end of 1934, German rearmament, in breach of her treaty

[1] Lord Vansittart, *The Mist Procession*, p. 437.

obligations, could have either been prevented by strong action of the Allies or met by rearmament on an equal scale.[1] Even in 1935, as we now know, Hitler's claim to have reached parity with Britain in the air was falsely based. It was not until after March 1936, when German armies reoccupied and began to fortify the Rhineland, that the Anglo-French position began seriously to deteriorate. All this time, the British people believed in the League of Nations, some fanatically, and others more tepidly. The League commanded general support. Certainly no party could afford to seem hesitant in its devotion to the principles of the Covenant. The serious blow to the League's strength caused by the Senate's rejection of President Wilson's treaty had not discouraged us. While the great Dominions were anxious about any special commitment under a purely regional pact such as Locarno, they accepted without demur their general responsibilities under the Covenant. The Japanese defiance made us all the more determined to cling to the League as the basis of our policy.

Germany's admission to the League in 1926 was hailed as a great step forward. It was not till Germany finally left both the Disarmament Conference and the League in 1933 that it became apparent that, in effect, the League depended upon a solid Anglo-French alliance, rallying support from what other countries could be influenced. This, indeed, became Churchill's concept of the League in the years that were to follow. It was under the aegis of the League that the strength of Britain and France might be built up to defend peace. In 1931-5 there still existed—if we acted in close concert with the French—sufficient armed force to restrain Germany. There was a public opinion to be rallied behind the concept of 'collective security' through the League, which, if necessary, might play the role of another Grand Alliance to defend at least the liberties of Europe.

During this Parliament I was absorbed by economic and social questions at home. I did not attempt to follow in any detail developments abroad. Young Members, on the back-benches, are well advised not to try to cover the whole range of public affairs. They should confine themselves to a limited field. In other words, they must, to some extent, specialise. I was certainly content in the field

[1] Winston Churchill, *The Second World War*, vol. i: *The Gathering Storm*, p. 40.

of foreign affairs to follow the guidance of the Government as a whole. Moreover, I had confidence in and respect for my brilliant contemporaries like Anthony Eden, Duff Cooper, John Loder (afterwards Lord Wakehurst), and others, who were all strong supporters of the League. Eden's position, first as Under-Secretary for Foreign Affairs and then as Lord Privy Seal, was commanding. His fine war record, his charm, his versatility, his pre-eminence in debate, his appeal to men and women of all parties: all these made him an outstanding figure.

But if effective power had not yet, although weakened, finally slipped away, neither in Britain nor in France was there any clear or determined line of policy, tenaciously and confidently pursued. This, no doubt, was partly the result of the weaknesses inherent in democratic and Parliamentary systems. In France, where Governments of the Right or Left succeeded each other with bewildering speed, no clear course was followed for any length of time. Her armaments, powerful in theory, grew obsolescent in practice. Her Army, the effectiveness of which was always exaggerated by her friends, was gripped in the enervating grasp of old and traditional concepts, tactical and strategic. France was not an aggressive Power. Far from it. She sought, above all, security. But French statesmen were too logical and too realistic to find it in the paper commitments which passed for a system of collective security. They asked, where were the arms to fulfil them? Yet, in this vain search for security, they found themselves at variance with successive British Governments, who sought in disarmament—about the effective application of which the French were sceptical—and later, in the principle of equality between Germany and France, a system which, given the difficulties of enforcement, the French instinctively distrusted.

British opinion was sadly confused. Throughout all these years, until just before the catastrophe, British people refused even to consider the possibility of another war. The last war had been so terrible in its devastations that it was 'unthinkable' that this degrading and humiliating internecine strife between civilised countries could be repeated. War was not only intolerable, it was incredible. After all, the German people, whom our occupying troops had found to be decent and respectable folk, had not really wanted war.

It was just the Kaiser and the militarists. We forgot, alas, how easily the Germans have succumbed to such leadership throughout history, and how readily they have applauded wars, so long as they were—as under Bismarck's guidance—short and successful. But modern war, it was believed, with engines of destruction even more frightful than in 1914–18, would prove the end of civilisation.

Hence 'Pacifism', in various forms, whether under the auspices of the Peace Society and Canon Sheppard, or expressed in the famous (or infamous) resolution of the Oxford Union, flourished even as the danger seemed to grow. The Parliamentary Labour Party, led in these years by Lansbury, and the Labour movement generally became pacifist in effect, if not actually in intention. The Liberal Party followed the same general line. All took refuge in a collective security to which the individual contributions seemed dangerously small.

The belief in the automatic efficiency of the League and the Covenant continued, even after the successful Japanese aggression and the rise of Hitler. The first manifestations of Hitlerism did not cause undue anxiety. After all, we had seen Mussolini and Fascist Italy, and the results had not seemed too bad. Hitler was an almost predictable reaction from the effects of the economic blizzard of 1931 onwards and its resulting unemployment, combined with the ruin of the middle class. These first excitements would calm down, as and when prosperity was re-established. Moreover, by an unlucky chance, the British people found it difficult, when they first heard of him, to take Hitler too seriously, with his Charlie Chaplin moustache and his everlasting raincoat. Naturally, nobody had bothered to read *Mein Kampf*. Nor could anybody see below the apparent insignificance of his appearance the deep, cunning, malignant brain. Here was concealed a combination of deceit and wickedness under a certain guise of plausibility, which can only now be fully grasped, when all the documents have been published and the whole evil story fully displayed to the world.

Two further beliefs were deeply engrained in popular opinion, encouraged by powerful authority. The first was the conviction that armaments were the main cause of war.[1] Had not Sir Edward Grey, than whom no man should know better, declared in 1914 that 'the

[1] John F. Kennedy, *Why England Slept* (London, 1940), p. 40.

enormous growth of armaments in Europe, the sense of insecurity and fear caused by them . . . made war inevitable'?

The causes of war, alas, go far deeper. It was not armaments that were the cause of the First War, but the determination of an aggressive Germany to use armaments to force her will in Europe. No one who reads the history of the pre-war years can fail to be struck by the genuine efforts of the peace-loving Powers to avoid the arms race and the reluctance with which they accepted the unwelcome necessity, in default of surrender to ever-growing German pressure. Nevertheless, that armaments in themselves cause war became an accepted dogma.

The second, and equally firm, belief was that any increase or even any modernisation of obsolete armaments was against the whole purpose and character of the League. Even when great powerful nations, themselves busily rearming, had left the League, this view remained strongly held throughout the country. It could be controverted, but it could not be neglected. 'Without disarmament', it was said, 'the League could have no reality.'[1] Yet with disarmament, the League proved powerless.

Amid all these hesitations and confusions, there was a still more powerful force operating on the British conscience. We were uneasy about Germany and her treatment since the end of the war. Britain had won the war and with characteristic magnanimity the British public, within a few years, began to feel sorry for the Germans. They even developed a sort of guilt complex. They were rather ashamed of the 1918 election. They regretted the vulgarity of the promise to squeeze Germany 'until the pips squeaked'. The Treaty of Versailles was no sooner framed than it came under powerful attack. Keynes and his arguments had been too readily accepted, and the phrase 'Carthaginian Peace' had stuck. There was a feeling, too, that the Allies as a whole had imposed very strict disarmament upon Germany without carrying out their side of the understanding. In several speeches, Churchill used and repeated a famous but somewhat ambivalent phrase to describe this general sentiment. 'The removal of the just grievances of the vanquished', he declared, 'ought to precede the disarmament of the victors.'

[1] John F. Kennedy, *Why England Slept*, p. 41.

But what precisely were those grievances? On the economic side, the whole reparations story is certainly a dismal one. It seems now incredible that serious economists and bankers could have advised that anything like the sums originally proposed could, by any known means, be transferred from one country to another. If they were to be paid in gold, the limit of capacity would surely be soon reached. If they were to be paid in goods and services, the effect upon the receiving countries would be disastrous. Yet, curiously enough, this same illusion governed the whole attitude of the American Government towards Allied debts during the inter-war years. They demanded to be paid; but they put up a tariff wall calculated to make payment almost impossible. In any case, reparations were, in effect, not paid by the Germans—certainly not to any unjust degree, in view of their cruel devastation of France and Belgium. In the early stages they borrowed from abroad the full amount—and more—necessary for their creditors. When foreign lending ceased, the reparations system was suspended. Even before, the sums had been reduced; and after the Lausanne Conference in 1932 reparations virtually ceased. It is true that Poincaré's policy in occupying the Ruhr in 1923 led to the wild inflation of the mark, which the German Government used to outwit the French, and this in turn had serious disruptive effects on the German economy and social structure. But all this had happened many years before; and by 1932 there were no further agreements to be made or grievances to be removed. Was it the political aspects of the Treaty of Versailles which were to be deplored? But the territorial settlements were not unreasonable. The Rhine frontier was not granted to France, although France was cheated of the security in return for which she had abandoned her claims. The return of Alsace–Lorraine was surely questioned by nobody. There were, no doubt, some grievances over frontiers which had left German minorities in some of the emerging States of Central and Eastern Europe. But this was unavoidable if these States were to have any reality. A strict application of the Wilsonian doctrine of self-determination to the many minorities scattered throughout Europe would lead to an absurdity. Some practical arrangements had to be accepted.

It was often said that the end of the Austro-Hungarian Empire,

as confirmed in the Treaties of Saint-Germain and Trianon, led to
a disastrous Balkanisation of Eastern Europe. This is perhaps true.
But it was not the fault of the statesmen in Paris. While the representatives of the victorious Allies were gathered in conference,
Austria-Hungary disintegrated. The various national groups declared themselves independent and no external authority could
conceivably have prevented them from doing so, or reintegrated
them in any acceptable political structure. From the economic point
of view this was no doubt deplorable. The failure to form any kind
of free-trade union between the groups that had constituted the old
Empire led to an outbreak of extreme economic nationalism, and a
corresponding diminution of general wealth and prosperity. But all
this did not result from the mistaken plans of the peacemakers. The
natural forces exploded and could not be contained. It is true that
this left Austria proper in a parlous position, with Vienna as an
imperial capital without an empire. Yet between the two wars the
League of Nations was able to rescue the Austrian economy; and
we have learnt since 1945, and particularly since the signing of the
Austrian Treaty in 1955, that even the reduced Austrian State can
be viable and healthy.

In effect, the German grievances, just or otherwise, turned upon
these two claims. There was also the question of the guilt clauses of
the Treaty. It is no doubt true that you cannot 'draw an indictment
against a whole people'. Yet the story of Prussian policy through
many generations is dark indeed. 'Prussia's whole policy', declared
Metternich, 'consisted in the enlargement of her territory and the
extension of her influence; to attain it, she was willing to adopt any
manner of means and pass over the law of nations and the universal
principles of morality.'[1] What Frederick the Great began was
followed by his successors at the end of the century, and continued
by Bismarck. It inspired the Kaiser and his advisers in 1914. It was
soon to be surpassed in cynicism and crime by Hitler.

It may well be that it was not an act of wise statesmanship to insist
upon the guilt clauses, or to require an imposed, rather than seek a
negotiated, treaty. It is not easy, however, for anyone who did not
live through the First World War to realise the intensity of feeling

[1] Algernon Cecil, *Metternich* (London, 1933), p. 24.

among the British and French people immediately after four years of sufferings unparalleled in history. Was it so unnatural or so inhuman to ask at least for an expression of regret? After the Second War the technical problem has not arisen, since no peace treaty with the whole of Germany has been possible. The war criminals have been punished after solemn trial. At the same time, a terrible retribution has fallen upon the German, and especially the Prussian, people; all the more bitter, because the partition, which has now lasted twenty years, divides Germany spiritually as well as politically.

Nevertheless, Churchill expressed in these famous words, more than once repeated, about the grievances of the vanquished, the confused but generous views of most people in this country at that time. There *was* a guilt complex; there *was* a feeling that Germany had had a rough time; and there *was*, above all, an irritation with the French who were held especially to have treated Germany badly. The fact that the power and efficiency of the French Army was overrated made us all the more impatient of their apparent unwillingness to disarm. Nor did we give sufficient thought to their sense of insecurity, due partly to the growing disparity of populations between Germany and France, and partly to the unwillingness of their old allies to guarantee their safety. Moreover, German propaganda was admirably carried out and German grievances grew with every attempt to find a remedy. What, unhappily, neither the public nor Parliament appreciated was the warning behind Churchill's phrase. Whether the grievances are just or unjust, if the vanquished either feel them genuinely or are made to resent them by constant repetition and out of calculated policy, it is not wise for the victors to cast aside prematurely their protective armour. Perhaps the emphasis of Churchill's words should have been differently interpreted. In the event, the grievances, true or false, soon became the main instrument of Hitler's success in undermining the confidence of his enemies abroad and rousing the frantic enthusiasm of his people at home.

Meanwhile the disarmament clauses of the Treaty had never been effectively enforced. The Army of 100,000 men soon became a cadre of officers and non-commissioned officers, ready for expansion when the time came. Other clauses were skilfully evaded. The full story of General von Seeckt's secret plans, by which, in spite of the Allied Control Commission, all the preparations were made for the moment when a new German Army, and a new German General Staff, could arise, like a new phoenix from the ashes of the old, with new arms ready to be poured out from the factories, is truly astonishing.[1] Nor was this evasion unknown to the British and French Governments, who must equally have been aware of the military help which Russia was giving to Germany.

How far all the democratic Ministers of the Weimar Republic were party to these deceptions is perhaps uncertain. It is clear, however, from his papers, that Stresemann actively abetted this process of rearmament and was guilty of making Briand his dupe. During the Locarno negotiations he knew and approved the wholesale breach of their treaty obligations by the German military authorities.

Such was the background against which the public watched, sometimes with apathy, sometimes with despair, the interminable and obscure wrangles of the Disarmament Conference.

It would be tedious to describe in detail the involutions and convolutions of this famous gathering of sixty countries. It had been long prepared; technical commissions had sat over several years at Geneva, in order to prepare a detailed agenda. The Conference met formally in February 1932, under the chairmanship of Arthur Henderson, who had agreed, after the fall of the Labour Government, to continue this work to which he devoted the remaining years of his life. He brought to this intractable problem both enthusiasm and common sense, and soon earned the confidence and respect of the delegates.

The schedule of proposals put forward by the preparatory committee included no specific limitations on the forces of any nation except Germany. The German Government immediately declared that no such discrimination was acceptable. Consequently, the original plans, the result of so much labour, had hurriedly to be abandoned. In this situation, the only hope of success would have been to have forced the pace with some alternative scheme. But

[1] Winston Churchill, *The Second World War*, vol. i: *The Gathering Storm*, pp. 36–37; J. H. Morgan, *Assize of Arms*, vol. i (London, 1945), *passim*; J. Wheeler-Bennett, *The Nemesis of Power* (London, 1953), *passim*.

Simon was cautious and even dilatory in his approach. The Germans would clearly demand equality. The French, already alarmed by the knowledge that the Germans were paying little attention to the limitations of the Versailles Treaty, would be reluctant to agree. After six months' delay, the British made a bid to break the deadlock and put forward a plan by which, as a first step, all armaments should be reduced. It has often been said that had this proposal, which involved eventual equality, been made earlier, while Brüning's Government was still in power, it might have paved the way to ultimate agreement. It is, of course, possible that a success in this field would have sustained Brüning; but it is very doubtful. Long before his fall in May, he had been reduced to governing by decree instead of by Parliamentary methods. Germany was the victim of the same financial and economic storm which had swept over the whole world, and the tender plant of democracy bent and withered under the strain. Eden has certainly expressed the view that an earlier acceptance of the principle of equality might possibly have saved Brüning. But he points out that even so, the French demand for security would have had to be met. Nor must we forget that even under the Weimar Republic many measures were being prepared to restore Germany's military power. Among them, by a bitter irony, were the first experiments, made in 1930, which eventually produced the most formidable weapons to which the British people were to be subjected in the Second War−V 1 and V 2.

During the eight months' interval before Hitler's final accession to power, Germany put forward a formal demand for equality. At this time, of course, they were in open breach of the Treaty; but public opinion in Britain was reconciled to this, and even felt inclined to the German side. In September, von Papen, who had succeeded Brüning, announced that Germany would leave the Conference. The only way out of the impasse appeared to be the initiation of Four-Power talks−Britain, France, Germany, and Italy. At a conference of these four countries, with the United States represented by an observer, an ingenious formula was agreed between MacDonald and Herriot, which, it was thought, might bridge the gap. Germany was to be conceded 'equality of rights in a system which would provide security for all nations'. On this, General von Schleicher, who had replaced von Papen in November, agreed that the German delegates should return to Geneva in December. But he proved but a transitory phantom flitting across the stage, the centre of which Hitler was about to seize. At the end of January 1933 Hitler became Chancellor, and from that time on, in spite of various and sometimes apparently hopeful discussions, no proposals, however ingenious or however generous, could have obtained Hitler's honest consent. It should not be forgotten that throughout his career Hitler never entered into an engagement by which he meant to be bound, and never made a promise which he did not intend to break. He had, of course, his anxieties, for he had to take great risks. It suited him to appear as reasonable as possible in the early stages of his rule, since he had to consolidate his position. But his wicked plans had been made and, indeed, had been published to the world for anyone who chose to read them. This, unhappily, few had done. If they had, his promises would have been dismissed as mere vote-catching. It transpired later that this extraordinary man not only had a programme but intended to carry it out scrupulously and even go beyond it. The Parliamentarians of the West were first incredulous and then indignant.

The Conference, undeterred, carried on its work with commendable perseverance. In March 1933 there was launched the MacDonald Plan, which included actual figures for the armed forces of various countries and limits on the size and types of armament. The French Army would be reduced; Germany would be able to obtain parity with the French. In support of the plan, Arthur Henderson set out on a pilgrimage round the capitals of Europe. When this scheme was debated in the House of Commons, Churchill made his famous outburst, 'Thank God for the French Army', which, to use his own words, 'was received with a look of pain and aversion'.[1] I well remember hearing the speech from the back-benches and the impression made by his formidable attack upon the MacDonald Plan, in the course of which he called the Disarmament Conference 'a solemn and prolonged farce'. But Eden's defence was powerful and effective. He was inspired by his own desperate efforts to save the Conference, in conformity with the

[1] Winston Churchill, *The Second World War*, vol. i: *The Gathering Storm*, p. 60.

almost unanimous hopes and wishes of the British people. Although at that time I made no serious effort to study the details of these perplexing international matters, I remember being deeply impressed by both speakers. But I unhesitatingly gave my support to Eden, who seemed to embody all the aspirations of the war generation. The novel feature of the British plan was that there should be a period of five years when experiments should be made in the efficacy of international control. At least, had the proposal been accepted, we should have had a test on how far such a control could be realistic or how readily, if at all, the Germans would allow it to work.

In March 1932, soon after the Conference had started its serious work, the Japanese established their puppet State of Manchukuo. A year later, in March 1933, Japan left the League. These were sinister reminders of the collapse of the principles of the Covenant, at any rate in the Far East. Hitler made a conciliatory speech on 17 May—one of many speeches intended to be soothing—in which he declared his willingness to abolish all military forces and destroy all weapons if other nations would do the same. This was the first of a series of declarations by which he tried to divide and confuse the Allies. In recent years we have been accustomed to these generalised statements in other disarmament conferences. They sound well, but have no practical significance. However, in June 1933, there was a moment of optimism, for the Germans accepted, at least in words, a proposal for two periods of supervision. But by then the French Government had begun to draw back.

After much coming and going, Simon produced in October 1933, on behalf of the British Government, yet another plan. There should be neither disarmament nor rearmament for five years, but there should be international supervision. After five years there should be disarmament devised to bring all countries to equality with Germany.[1] Hitler was quick to see the danger in view of his May speech. He immediately gave notice of Germany's withdrawal from the Conference and at the same time her determination to leave the League. This marked the end, or the effective end, of the Disarmament Conference. It lasted till June 1934, but its lingering demise

[1] C. L. Mowat, *Britain Between the Wars, 1918–1940*, p. 425.

was disastrous. So long as the Conference was sitting, the British Government did not wish to prejudice its chances of success, which were by then non-existent, by embarking upon any substantial plan of rearmament. It was not, therefore, until July 1934 that the first increases in the Royal Air Force were decided and announced.

The final collapse of any prospect of agreed disarmament was a serious blow to the British public. We had hoped against hope, for we felt that by one method or another disarmament might yet be attained. The public were not deeply impressed, by the many proofs coming forward, that the Germans had themselves ignored the provisions of the Treaty of Versailles. In this respect, as I have described, the mass of the people felt vaguely guilty about Versailles. They also felt that international justice required that Germany and France should be treated alike. Nor was this sentiment substantially diminished by Hitler's accession to power in the beginning of 1933, or by Germany's withdrawl from the Conference and the League. Even the dark story of Hitler's suppression of Röhm's alleged plot against him, with its monstrous outbreak of gangster violence, did not shake them overmuch. It is now believed that between 5,000 and 7,000 persons were 'liquidated' at the end of June 1934. Those bloody days should have given us a warning of the kind of man we had to face. I remember being at a house-party in the country when the news came through. Some of those who were present were ultimately to be the protagonists of the policy of appeasement. I recall that they were trying to find some comfort in the excuse that Röhm and his friends were guilty of immorality, as well as of treason: Hitler might be a tyrant; but at heart he was a puritan.

At the time of the Fulham East by-election in October 1933, when Germany was leaving the Conference, the mood was not one of fear of Germany, or anxiety over Britain unilaterally disarming. It was one rather of zeal for further disarmament and the opportunity for party accusations against the Government for 'warmongering'. I took little part in these arguments at that time, but I was provoked by this. It fell to me to speak at a by-election a few days afterwards at Kilmarnock, where the Labour victor of Fulham East, who had accused his Tory opponent of 'standing for armaments', was brought up to play, it was hoped, a decisive role. I made a violent attack upon him at the hustings, which was not ill received by the audience, more especially as I appealed to the superior sense of logic of the Lowlander over the Cockney. Curiously enough, although the loss at Fulham made a deep impression upon Baldwin, as he afterwards revealed in a famous speech, he appears to have disregarded the remarkable success of the Government candidate at Kilmarnock. In contrast with the general mood, Churchill's campaign for rearmament was carried on with occasional but impressive interventions during these years. I heard nearly all of them, including that in November 1933, which gave warning of the rate and magnitude of German rearmament. But he laid even more stress upon the new Nazi philosophy which was being inculcated into the German youth; 'something', he said, 'to which no parallel can be found since the days of barbarism'.[1] But Members, with few exceptions, were not ready to do more than admire his eloquence. On the Labour and Liberal side, everything that he said was regarded as malicious and dangerous. The Conservatives were shaken and unhappy, but they trusted in the Government and somehow persuaded themselves, in spite of yearly reductions in the Service Estimates, that whatever steps were necessary for Britain to defend herself and to play her part under the Covenant would not be neglected. Moreover, so long as there was any hope left of agreement on disarmament being reached, no private Member wished to do anything to hinder or obstruct any fruitful negotiation. We little knew that, behind the scenes, Eden was pleading for a strengthening of our defences in order to increase our authority. Our reticence, as we now know, was foolish on our part and perhaps weak. Yet, since all these international and inter-governmental negotiations continued in one form or another, with the perpetual comings and goings of leading Ministers from capital to capital, it was not perhaps unnatural that those who did not bear the chief responsibility should be content to follow leaders for whom they had both affection and respect.

The Disarmament Conference of 1932-4 has been followed by many others. It has fallen to me to take a personal and detailed interest in many of them. The same features are in general repeated: admirable work by the experts; preparatory expositions of all

[1] *Hansard,* 7 November 1933.

possible methods; masses of growing files, of memoranda and resolutions; committees; sub-committees; adjournments; and private discussion behind the scenes. I have learnt that in all negotiations of this kind nothing matters except the will to reach agreement. If it is not there, no proposals, however elaborate, and no plans, however ingenious, will succeed. For national armaments touch the tenderest spots in a nation's life. But if suddenly there is a general mood among the leading figures to reach at least some agreement, even in a limited field, then action is swift and sure. Such was the story in 1963 on the treaty, limited it is true, but of profound significance, by which the United States, Russia, and Britain agreed to the abolition of nuclear tests in the atmosphere. Months and even years of discussion had gone on; interminable examination of every possible loophole; continual discovery of new methods of testing, almost incapable of detection. Finally, in a few weeks, I found President Kennedy and Mr. Khrushchev ready to agree upon a simple but vitally important decision to abandon all atmospheric tests. The will to make this advance suddenly became apparent; the means of expressing it in an acceptable form was then a matter of a few days.

In the months between the German decision to leave the Conference and the League, and the collapse of the Conference in June 1934, intense diplomatic activity continued. British Ministers did their best to promote the latest British plan embodied in a memorandum published at the end of January 1934. This was one more effort to find a solution by a rearrangement of various items in what would now be called a 'package deal'. In Rome, Mussolini was not altogether unhelpful, though he warned Simon that the Germans would never agree to armed forces of less than 300,000 men. Mussolini was beginning to be worried about Austria, and was still inclined to look for Allied support. In Paris, one Government had just fallen, enveloped in the murky bog of the Stavisky scandal. Another, headed by a respected octogenarian, M. Doumergue, was acting as a stopgap. In Berlin, although the British Ambassador gave his warning that whatever happened the Germans intended to rearm in the air as well as on land, the atmosphere was not unfavourable. A distinction was drawn, not for the first or the last time, between

Versailles and Locarno, between treaties imposed and those freely negotiated. In the end, Hitler was to break the latter as lightly as the former.

Hitler now agreed that the French should keep their heavy armaments for the first five years of a ten-year pact. Germany's air defence would be 30 per cent of the total air strength of Germany's neighbours; but, as a special concession to France, not more than 50 per cent of the French. The S.S. and S.A. (that is, the para-military formations) were not armed and would not be armed; they might even be subject to inspection. This seemed not unhelpful, although no one appeared to have inquired how, for instance, Russian air strength was to be ascertained. But the French were sceptical. These so-called para-military forces were capable of mobilisation within a few weeks, and would add enormously to Germany's potential Army. The Germans had broken the Treaty by building civilian planes on a large scale. These could easily be turned into military bombers. Finally, what sanctions would there be for France's security? Eden tried to persuade the British Government to devise some form of guarantee more defined than our normal obligations under the Covenant, and even stronger than those under Locarno. But his colleagues were not forthcoming. Then in April the German Budget was published, with its enormously increased military expenditure.

In May, by way of being helpful, Mr. Norman Davis, on behalf of the United States, presented to the General Commission in Geneva an important declaration. He said that the United States, although anxious to co-operate in the preservation of peace, 'would not participate in European political negotiations . . . and would not make any commitment whatever to use armed forces for the settlement of any dispute anywhere'.[1] So that was that. Finally, at the end of May, Barthou delivered the *coup de grâce* to the Disarmament Conference in a brilliant but bitter speech.

During all these months, British public opinion was growing more and more concerned and divided. One stream of opinion followed with increasing fervour the pacifist lead. The Peace Pledge Union canvassed widely for support and enrolled in due course at

[1] The Earl of Avon, *The Eden Memoirs: Facing the Dictators*, p. 92.

least 100,000 members.[1] The Labour and Liberal parties opposed
with vigour and acerbity any strengthening of our defences. The
Conservatives, dismayed by the failure of disarmament, supported
loyally any increase in the Service Estimates proposed by the
Government and would have gladly accepted more. Churchill
continued his grave warnings. On the whole, there was more
criticism of the French than of the Germans; for the Germans had
presented their case with greater skill, although, as we now know,
with complete insincerity. But the dominant sentiment was still in
favour of the League of Nations and the Covenant, supported by
whatever strength was necessary to preserve peace and punish an
aggressor. The theme of collective security was inspiring, if imprecise. Round it could rally men of very different backgrounds and
opinions.

I was then in close collaboration on social and economic matters
with sympathisers largely of Centre or Leftist views. Neither I nor
my Conservative friends found any difficulty in associating ourselves
in the ideas that finally took shape in the second part of *The Next
Five Years* publication; that is, the paragraphs on Peace and the
League. For the theme was collective security and return to the
Covenant. In March 1934, when I was speaking in my own
constituency, I proclaimed this view. I was rebutting the attack,
already being launched by the Opposition parties, against even a
modest measure of rearmament. I used these words:

> We must either retire from our obligations and accept the policy of isolation,
> which would be mean, immoral, and dangerous, or we must go with all our
> force for the collective system, and so shoulder our responsibilities as honest
> people of a responsible nation.

As the summer of 1934 drew to an end, Russia joined the League
of Nations. This was a notable event, fraught with opportunities.
Litvinov soon began to assume an important role. So long as he
enjoyed the confidence of Stalin, there was every hope that Russia
could be counted on for firm opposition to Germany. The Russians
did not conceal the alarm which Hitler's ambitions caused. Nearly
five years later, the fall of Litvinov was the sign that the rulers of the

[1] C. L. Mowat, *Britain Between the Wars, 1918–1940*, p. 538.

Kremlin had lost confidence in the Western Allies, and thought it best to make their own terms while they could.

Meanwhile, Hitler continued skilfully to blow hot and cold. His propaganda was carried out with devilish ingenuity. We later learnt to look with scepticism at the solemn protestation that each claim was the last he had to make, and to recognise the offer of a unilateral pact of non-aggression with any country as the kiss of death. His private audiences were equally dangerous. He could present the right facet of his personality or policy to suit individual visitors. It is no mean feat to have deceived and charmed such varied and distinguished men as Lansbury, Lothian, Rothermere, Arnold Toynbee, Londonderry, Allen, Tom Jones, and Lloyd George. When one considers that some at least of these visitors must have known and deplored the racial persecutions, if no other aspect of his régime, and the tyranny of his police State, Hitler's achievement is really remarkable. One almost wishes he had not missed the opportunity of meeting Churchill in 1932, before his rise to absolute power. Unhappily, Churchill had observed to Hitler's go-between, 'Why is your chief so violent about the Jews?' Hitler, on hearing this, cancelled his request for a meeting and thus, in Churchill's words, 'lost his only chance of meeting me'.[1]

Before 1934 was out, a great calamity struck Europe. On 9 October King Alexander of Yugoslavia and Louis Barthou, the French Foreign Minister, were assassinated at Marseilles. The consequences of this were grave. The chances of a firm Balkan stand against either dictator were reduced, and the hopes of a resolute French policy were dashed. Barthou had some faults, but many redeeming qualities. If his tongue was sharp, his brain was clear and his heart sound. He had done much to restore confidence in the French Government after the name of France had been dragged in the mud in the previous winter. He was under no illusion as to Hitler's purposes and ambitions. He therefore saw no object in condoning Germany in breaches of existing treaties. Whatever happened, Hitler meant to rebuild the military power of the Reich. Barthou therefore saw little to be gained by the signing of new agreements to take the place of those which had already been broken. He

[1] Winston Churchill, *The Second World War*, vol. i: *The Gathering Storm*, p. 65.

had largely repaired the damage recently done to France's allies in the 'Little Entente', who were jealous of the Four-Power meetings and suspicious of all negotiations outside Geneva. He had done his best to forge an eastern pact of mutual guarantee against Germany. The King, too, was a powerful figure, and left no successor able to carry on his work. These brutal murders resulted in bitter feelings throughout the Balkans, and only the skilful management of the affair by Eden, when it came before the Council of the League, prevented serious trouble. But the mischief was done. An almost mortal blow was struck at those forces which might have built a firm resistance to Hitler in the years ahead. Barthou was succeeded by Laval.

The year 1935 opened hopefully. After the completion of the fifteen years provided in the Versailles Treaty, the time had come for a plebiscite to be taken in the Saar as to the future of that area. There was a good deal of anxiety lest the Germans might stage a *putsch* before the vote was taken, or, alternatively, create a general state of confusion and disorder. Largely through the efforts of Eden, an arrangement was made by the League of Nations Council for troops to be available for police purposes. The commissioner was an English diplomat named Geoffrey Knox, who behaved throughout with remarkable phlegm and courage. In the event, owing to the presence of forces provided by Britain, Italy, Sweden, and the Netherlands, the plebiscite passed off without any untoward incident. The vote in favour of returning to Germany was overwhelming. The French were disappointed of their confident expectation that there would be at any rate a substantial minority. But the fact that the Treaty had been carried out in a proper manner and without trouble was reassuring. It tended, moreover, to strengthen the authority of the League. Nevertheless, as regards general policy, the British Government was still uncertain what to do next. Should they abandon any further attempt to reach general agreement as to the level of national forces in Europe? Should they at long last turn seriously to the remodelling and rebuilding of Britain's defences? In the event they decided to follow both policies in parallel. Accordingly, some weeks after a meeting in London in February, attended by Flandin, now Prime Minister of France, and Laval, the new

Foreign Secretary, it was decided to make a fresh effort to negotiate 'on a basis of equality' with the German Government. For this purpose, it was agreed that Simon and Eden should visit Berlin and that, since the Russians, Poles, and Czechs were anxious to be in close contact with developments, Eden should subsequently visit in turn Moscow, Warsaw, and Prague.

Thus, on the one hand, the policy of conciliation was again set in motion and a new set of figures in the international quadrille was arranged. On the other, the Government's defence plans were formulated and published. On 4 March a famous White Paper was issued, signed by the Prime Minister, MacDonald. It had been a subject of much discussion in the Cabinet and many Ministers, including Neville Chamberlain, had taken part in its drafting. The White Paper was a comprehensive picture of the state of British defences and the Government's plans, both for the modernising of the equipment of the Army and Navy and for expediting the increases in the Air Force announced in July 1934. These had involved an additional forty-one squadrons to be completed in five years. Under the White Paper the period was to be shortened. In view of the situation, the proposals were certainly modest, involving an immediate rise of only some £10 million in the Service Estimates. What caught the public attention was the reference to Germany and the anxieties which her policies were producing among her neighbours, 'calculated to imperil peace'. Consequently the White Paper produced a great outburst of protest from the Opposition, who described it as 'an insult to Germany'. On the very next day after its publication Hitler reacted. He had caught a cold; he therefore could not receive the British Ministers. After that, events followed with breathless rapidity. On 9 March Hitler announced formally the creation of the Luftwaffe, the German Air Force, under the command of the flamboyant Göring. We were to learn a good deal more about the Luftwaffe five years later. On 11 March Attlee moved a vote of censure upon the Government in which, while disavowing unilateral disarmament, he violently attacked the White Paper as a reactionary and provocative declaration. At the same time he affirmed his faith in the efficacy of a system of collective security, without recognising the weakness of the League from which Germany and Japan had retired, of which the United States had never been a member, and dependent, in effect, upon any forces which France and Britain could deploy, with the doubtful assistance of Italy and some smaller nations.

It seemed to me at the time, strongly as I, too, believed in collective security, that an overwhelming case was made in the White Paper for the strengthening of Britain's contribution to that system. Austen Chamberlain, who enjoyed a more influential position as an elder statesman than perhaps he ever did in office, made a vigorous reply to Attlee which deeply impressed the House. The Government had no difficulty in securing an overwhelming majority for its proposals. The Conservative Party were relieved that at long last the necessary steps seemed about to be taken. Although rearmament was to be spread over a long period, and was devised in such a way as not to place any exceptional burden upon the economy, yet it marked a more realistic attitude towards defence problems than had hitherto prevailed.

On 16 March Hitler fired off his second barrel. He announced the introduction of conscription, and the creation of an Army of over 500,000 men, to be formed into thirty-six divisions. On 18 March the British Government entered a protest against these unilateral breaches of the Treaty, but they added, rather weakly, that they would like to know whether the visit should or should not take place; for Hitler's cold had been cured in the interval and the date fixed for 25 March. 'The wiser course', in Eden's own words, 'would have been to say that Hitler's unilateral breach of a treaty, on the eve of Simon's visit, deprived it of any usefulness and it was therefore postponed, but that I would continue with my journey to the other capitals as arranged. In other words, we ought to have returned the diplomatic cold.'[1] But we were not yet in the mood for this kind of talk.

So Simon and Eden set out on their travels. But they were to find cold comfort in Berlin. Hitler produced his usual protestations, denying any intention of doing all the things on which he was firmly decided but for which his preparations were not yet complete. He would never annex territory; annexations only led to economic

[1] The Earl of Avon, *The Eden Memoirs: Facing the Dictators*, p. 129.

difficulties. Of course, large-scale annexation in Central and Eastern Europe was part of his long-term plans. He had no desire to incorporate Austria in the Reich; in fact, having arranged for the murder of Dollfuss in the summer of 1934, a coup by which he had hoped the *Anschluss* could be accomplished, he had been forced to draw back for fear of a Franco-Italian reaction against him. He was to wait only a few years. There would never be any difficulty with Czechoslovakia; he had an arbitration treaty with Czechoslovakia. We were in due course to learn what he thought of arbitration. Germany would never declare war on Russia; that promise had to wait a little longer for its breach, in circumstances of peculiar bad faith. He could not rejoin the League, since the Covenant had its foundation in the Treaty of Versailles. When Simon meekly observed that perhaps these two—the Treaty of Versailles and the Covenant—could be juridically separated, Hitler was pleased to make a not altogether unforthcoming reply. But then there was the colonial question. Germany had been put in a position of inferiority, as unfit to administer a colony. This was intolerable. Finally, he made a proposal to Britain which was soon to become familiar. Would we not do better to offer the hand of friendship? The British Empire was large but also vulnerable. Britain and Germany in alliance could be strong enough together to face the world. As for the Eastern Locarno which Simon put forward, he would have none of it.

All these discussions, of course, amounted to nothing. There was no basis of agreement. In the course of hours of talk, some ideas emerged which Hitler affected to be willing to consider favourably: for instance, arrangements for a naval agreement, and some general understanding as to air parity, by which the French and German Air Forces should be of equal strength. In reference to the latter, he brought out a statement which had a profound effect when it became known to the world. He declared to Simon and Eden as a fact, that the German Air Force was now equal to that of Britain. It is something of a mystery why he made this assertion which has since been shown to have been almost certainly incorrect. It produced two remarkable results. The British Government believed it and in accepting it as true had to cut a sorry figure, in view of their previous statements both in Parliament and before the British public. The case for the White Paper and still further increases in the Air Force became overwhelming. Hitler may not have foreseen or intended this. But it had a second effect, and this may have been his real purpose. It led the Government to close with almost indecent haste with the Führer's offer in May to limit German naval strength to 35 per cent of the British.

The Anglo-German Naval Agreement, which was soon accepted in principle and signed in June of this year, was a serious error. The Admiralty thought they had achieved a great success. They were no doubt obsessed by their memories of Anglo-German rivalry before the war and by the experiences of the Great War. They certainly believed that any agreement fixing the numbers between the two countries should be avidly grasped. But they conceded the right of Germany to build U-boats, which she had been denied in the Versailles Treaty, and to build up to 60 per cent of British submarine strength, and in exceptional circumstances up to 100 per cent. The German Government was to be the sole judge of what were exceptional circumstances. Moreover, and this was thought a valuable concession, the Germans solemnly declared that their submarines would never be used against merchant shipping. In the course of experiences which I had many years later, I found that admirals as a class are singularly gullible when it comes to politics. No doubt they think that we politicians are equally out of our depth in discussing naval matters. But here was an agreement made with a Government which had openly and flagrantly violated its solemn treaty obligations not in minor but in major matters. Here were submarines alleged to be built for purely defence purposes, when it should have been obvious that the main, if not the sole, purpose of a German submarine fleet would be once again to threaten Britain with strangulation. Simon seems to have played little part in the negotiations, over which Hoare, as First Lord of the Admiralty, presided. Nor were the French told anything more than the probable terms. They were not asked to agree or even to acquiesce. They naturally concluded that we cared only about our own safety and the protection of our island, and the preservation of our naval superiority. Laval had every right to feel not merely suspicious but indignant. Nor had our experts taken the trouble to investigate actual conditions in Germany and their facilities for naval construction. The limitation was ineffective, for in most cases the Germans built as fast as was physically possible.[1] In certain classes of ships they built beyond the treaty terms, invoking the so-called escalator clause, and ignored British protests. But for various reasons, no doubt because of the other demands for armoured plate, they did not reach the total tonnages permitted. They concentrated naturally on the submarines, and in this alone they built to the full limits allowed. As soon as they reached the 60 per cent, they naturally claimed the advantage of the proviso and went up to the 100 per cent.[2] Finally, Hitler, as was later to be proved, regarded this treaty like every other one to which he put his name—as a scrap of paper.

The diplomatic dance went on. After the discussion with Hitler, Eden made a visit to Moscow from which he returned with the knowledge that Stalin was seriously alarmed at the German menace. Had something been done at that time to come to terms with Russia, it is possible that an alliance could have been built which would have prevented the Second War. But Russia then, as later, was thought at once too weak and too dangerous. From Moscow he went to Warsaw and to Prague. But he achieved little; as indeed was natural in the circumstances. The one positive plan which Simon had put before Hitler was an Eastern Locarno. This had been immediately rejected. But it was this—or something like this—that the countries of Eastern Europe wanted. In default, they looked for something in its place. But Eden was not empowered to make them any offer. Unhappily, he returned from his long journey in the primitive aeroplanes of the day with a seriously strained heart. He was therefore absent from the fatal meeting at Stresa, where the British, French, and Italian leaders were due to meet in a few days' time.

Eden, on his return, gave his colleagues from his sick-bed two solemn warnings. First, as a result of his visit to Germany, he declared his view, in which Simon fully concurred, that whatever might be the truth as to the precise strength of German armaments,

[1] Winston Churchill, *The Second World War*, vol. i: *The Gathering Storm*, p. 108.
[2] Ibid., pp. 108–9.

there could be no doubt as to Hitler's intentions and the enormous efforts being put into German rearmament. We should reconsider the expansion of the Air Force in particular, beyond the figures already announced.[1] Secondly, and of immediate significance, he urged both the Prime Minister and the Foreign Secretary not to miss the opportunity to confront Mussolini with the preparations which he was making for an attack on Abyssinia. For by now the Abyssinian cloud had risen well beyond the horizon. Simon assured him that he would bear this in mind and was taking with him the Foreign Office expert on Abyssinia for this very purpose.[2] In the event, the subject was never raised at all. It was naturally carefully avoided by Laval, who had other schemes in mind. Our silence was unpardonable. There was indeed some justification for Mussolini's claim that he had received, if not an assurance, at least a clear impression that there would be no trouble about Abyssinia. The very text of the communiqué, which concentrated on the agreement of the three Powers to oppose 'any unilateral repudiation of treaties which may endanger the peace of Europe', might not unreasonably be interpreted as giving him the 'all clear' for aggression in Africa.

Diplomatic events followed fast. From 15 to 17 April the League of Nations Council met and, in spite of the protests of *The Times* newspaper, censured Germany for the massive rearmament on air and land which had been announced, contrary to treaty obligations. On 2 May, as a measure of reinsurance, the Franco-Soviet Pact was agreed. Unhappily, although it bound both parties to come to each other's assistance if either were the victim of an unprovoked attack, its effect was weakened because no staff talks followed. Perhaps as a result, or merely as part of his policy of keeping the Allies guessing, Hitler delivered a speech on 21 May in which, while defending his repudiation of the disarmament clauses of the *Diktat* of Versailles, he promised to observe all the obligations of the Locarno Treaty which had been freely negotiated. He specifically included the demilitarisation of the Rhineland as one of the clauses which he would respect. He would make non-aggression pacts with all Germany's neigh-

[1] The Earl of Avon, *The Eden Memoirs: Facing the Dictators*, p. 186.
[2] Ibid., p. 179.

bours except Russia. He would be content with parity with the Western Powers in the air. He would limit his Navy to 35 per cent of the strength of Great Britain's.[1] The British Government, as already noted, was quick to accept the chance of a naval deal. But except for the Labour Party and that part of opinion led by *The Times* newspaper, this olive-branch was not taken very seriously. Baldwin, ostensibly at least, gave it some attention. But the revelations of air parity had shaken and shocked the public. Another dramatic debate followed in the House of Commons.

This series of Parliamentary discussions on the weakness of British defences, especially air defences, was indeed remarkable. I attended all of them. I had no knowledge of the subject, to which I had given no study. But I listened to them with growing interest, fascinated by the revelation of the changing moods and temper of the House of Commons, which I later learnt to know so well. Churchill, in his crusade for rearmament, struck the first blow in November 1933. Then he contented himself with a warning, mainly based upon the character of the Nazi movement of which we were then only just becoming conscious. But as the months passed, he turned to more precise arguments. In *The Gathering Storm* he has given a memorable account of how persistently he ploughed this lonely furrow. I can only add to the story, so graphically recounted by the leading actor, some recollections of the impressions of a silent member of the audience.

As Churchill himself describes, the violent attacks of the Opposition on any increase, however moderate, in defence expenditure altered his Parliamentary position. At least to a modified degree, he was now a supporter instead of an outright opponent of the Government. In the debate in July 1934 he had argued that Germany was on the way to air parity with Britain. Their force was already nearly two-thirds as strong as the British forces available for home defence. He predicted that even after the Government's new proposals were carried out, by the end of 1935 the German Air Force would be nearly equal in numbers and efficiency. In November of the same year he delivered to a packed House one of his great orations. In this he asserted that the German Air Force, illegal under

[1] C. L. Mowat, *Britain Between the Wars, 1918–1940*, p. 539.

the Treaty of Versailles and not yet openly admitted to exist by the German Government, was now actually approaching equality with our own. Baldwin followed, and denied altogether the truth of Churchill's figures. 'So far from the German military air force being at least as strong as and probably stronger than our own, we estimate that we shall still have a margin in Europe alone of nearly 50 per cent.' He maintained that this would be so for at least two years. Beyond that, he refused to look. Even as regards the future he declared Churchill's figures to be exaggerated. The House, of course, accepted this statement as authoritative. The Conservatives, who had been growing increasingly uneasy, were much relieved. Nevertheless, on 19 March 1935, when the Air Estimates were presented, Churchill repeated his challenge. Once more the Air Ministry were unshaken. The Under-Secretary, Philip Sassoon, spoke confidently and fluently from his brief. A fortnight later, on 3 April, there was published Hitler's claim, made personally to Simon and Eden, that Germany had already reached parity in the air with Great Britain. The effect was sensational.

Churchill naturally returned to the attack. He was heard with deep attention. It is true that he has himself described the sense of despair which came over him at his inability to make Parliament and the nation heed his warnings.[1] I heard the famous passage in which he recalled the effect upon the House over two hundred years before of Secretary St. John's revelation that the loss of the Battle of Almanza was due to only one-quarter of the troops which had been voted by Parliament being available. The House had sat in awed silence for half an hour, no one caring to speak. Churchill was then working on his biography of Marlborough.[2] This anecdote came, therefore, readily to his mind, filled with the history of that tremendous epoch. But he was wrong in supposing that the House of Commons of 1935 was not concerned and moved. Dramatic as was Churchill's plea, Baldwin's confession, on 22 May, was even more remarkable. Although he adhered to the estimate he had given in the previous November of British and German air strength at that time, he admitted that the figures which he had given as to

[1] Winston Churchill, *The Second World War*, vol. i: *The Gathering Storm*, p. 96.
[2] Winston Churchill, *Marlborough: His Life and Times*, 4 vols. (London, 1933–8).

the future were wrong. 'Where I was wrong was in the estimate of the future. There I was completely wrong. We were completely misled on that subject.' He then manfully took the blame upon himself and the Government as a whole. 'We are all responsible and we are all to blame.' Churchill describes his amazement at the reaction of the House of Commons.[1] Instead of demanding, as he expected, at least a Committee of Inquiry, the mood of the House was quite different. Socialists and Liberals, of course, were unconcerned, because they were already opposing even the modest additions to our armaments already decided. But even Conservatives were disarmed. The House as a whole was 'captivated by Baldwin's candour'. His frankness seemed to redeem his error and indeed produced some degree of enthusiasm for a Minister who was so straightforward. But this is a not unusual reaction in the British House of Commons. It is part of its tradition that, as in a school, Members admire a boy who owns up. There is a passage in one of Trollope's novels, *The Duke's Children*, which exactly describes it. Two men are discussing a recent scene in the House. A Member is said by an observer in the Gallery to have had the feeling of the House with him:

'Yes', was the reply, 'because he "owned up". The fact is if you "own up" in a genial sort of way the House will forgive anything. If I were to murder my grandmother, and when questioned about it were to acknowledge that I had done it. . . .' Then Lord Nidderdale stood up and made his speech as he might have made it in the House of Commons. ' "I regret to say, sir, that the old woman did get in my way when I was in a passion. Unfortunately I had a heavy stick in my hand and I did strike her over the head. Nobody can regret it so much as I do! Nobody can feel so acutely the position in which I am placed! I have sat in this House for many years, and many gentlemen know me well. I think, sir, that they will acknowledge that I am a man not deficient in filial piety or general humanity. Sir, I am sorry for what I did in a moment of heat. I have now spoken the truth, and I shall leave myself in the hands of the House." My belief is I should get such a round of applause as I certainly shall never achieve in any other way.'

So it was with Baldwin. He was to own up again, after the Hoare–Laval fiasco, and again was to 'get away with it'. Ironically enough,

[1] Winston Churchill, *The Second World War*, vol. i: *The Gathering Storm*, p. 99.

it is now almost certain that Hitler's claim was untrue and Baldwin's dramatic 'confession' unnecessary. It is difficult to agree exactly the basis of comparison. Much play was made at the time as between squadrons in formation and squadrons not yet formed, between front-line strength and machines in reserve. Hitler was probably over-claiming when he said that parity had been achieved in actual machines available. But the real comparison lay between the means of production and the possibilities of expansion in the two countries. An air force is not a static organisation. Everything depends upon how far industry has been or can be adapted to bring about large-scale manufacture. It is the lead in these essentials that is decisive.

Great efforts were made in the next three or four years. Under Lord Swinton's imaginative and energetic management, if we could not obtain at the outbreak of war a superiority in quantity, we achieved an advantage in quality. In order to do this, considerable risks had to be taken, and machines put into production straight from the drawing-board. With the simpler mechanisms of those days, this was a legitimate gamble which came off. Had it not, the Battle of Britain, after the fall of France, could not have been sustained.

All these events, which caused me increasing concern, brought me back into more frequent contact with Churchill. He did not dissuade me from pursuing my own path of economic and social reconstruction. Indeed, he always showed me the greatest kindness and consideration, at a time when I was beginning to be regarded as either a crank or a mutineer. But he impressed upon me that without greater efforts to defend ourselves and our friends, all the plans on which I was engaged would break down. Germany would reach a commanding position in the world; there would be nothing for it but a shameful surrender or a long and devastating war. He, too, was developing his position, in a way which enabled him gradually to extend his field of support. In the next two or three years he was able to rally many divergent elements in political life. His concept of collective security may have been somewhat more realistic than the imprecise slogan of the enthusiasts for the League. But he began to understand that under the aegis of the League, and by this means alone, wide-based support could be gathered for the necessary response to German aggression. With the League deprived of some of the leading Powers—America, Germany, Japan—collective security could only mean an alliance led by France and Britain, and supported within the limits of their capacity by the smaller countries. In effect, this might not differ very much from the Grand Alliances against the domination of Europe by a single Power in which Britain had taken the lead many times in her long history. But it was the only basis on which that unity and sense of dedication to high purposes could be created, which is always essential if Britain is to exert her full strength.

The spring and summer of 1935, therefore, were months of anxiety. No progress was made, in spite of restless diplomatic activity, in reaching any satisfactory arrangements with the Germans —except the Naval Agreement, which was a grievous error. The Government's plans for rearmament, violently opposed by some, regarded as insufficient by others, brought public opinion face to face, for the first time for many years, with the very disagreeable realities with which they were destined to struggle for the next terrible decade. Meanwhile, the stage was now set for another twist in the tangled tale—Italy's aggression against Abyssinia.

The story up to this date can be briefly summarised. Between Italy and Abyssinia there was an old score to be paid off. The Italians had never forgotten the defeat and shame of Adowa in 1896. In the years immediately following the Great War the Italians seemed content with the possibility of peaceful penetration and with that in mind they sponsored Abyssinia as a member of the League of Nations in 1923. Other countries, including Britain, were doubtful as to the wisdom of electing a country still living in primitive or at least medieval conditions. However, the other nations yielded to Italian pleas. In 1933, as we now know, Mussolini began to work out his plans. They amounted to either total annexation or a position of supremacy such as France enjoyed at that time in Morocco or Britain in Egypt. During 1934 military preparations were perfected. At the end of that year, the usual frontier incident was arranged at a place called Walwal. Italy sent a Note of protest to Abyssinia; and Abyssinia, in accordance with the treaty between Italy and Abyssinia of 1928, asked for arbitration. The Italians refused this request. Accordingly, at the beginning of January, Abyssinia appealed to the League under Article 11 of the Covenant, which deals with the threat of war. After some discussion, Italy agreed in principle to arbitration, but did not lose the opportunity to build up her forces in Eritrea. The arbitration arrangements broke down, as no doubt the Italians intended. Abyssinia then appealed under Article 15, which requires the Council to inquire into disputes and to try to bring the parties together or mediate between them. This was on 17 March. It was an inauspicious day; for it was the day after Hitler had announced conscription and the raising of the large German Army. The attention, therefore, of the Council was already occupied with what seemed a much more serious affair. Indeed, it was in the light of this move of Hitler's that the Stresa meeting of 11 to 14 April was arranged. Considerable delay followed, while the slow processes of the Council's negotiations were set in hand. The Italians, still building up their strength, followed a policy of procrastination, promising negotiation or arbitration but never agreeing upon the procedure. Towards the end of June, the British Government, alarmed at the increasing breach between Italy on the one side and France and Britain on the other, made a proposal of their own. They suggested to Mussolini that Abyssinia should cede a substantial part of the region of Ogaden to Italy. In return, Great Britain, in order to ease the situation, would afford Abyssinia an outlet to the sea at Zeila and a corridor through British Somaliland. Not unnaturally, Mussolini contemptuously refused this offer by which Abyssinia stood to gain. The only effect of this proposal, about which the French were given no prior warning, coupled with our deception over the Anglo-German Naval Treaty, was to add to French suspicions.

Just before this, on 7 June, MacDonald and Baldwin changed places. Baldwin became Prime Minister, MacDonald Lord President. Since the crisis of 1931 they had worked harmoniously together. If Baldwin enjoyed the reality of power, since the administration was sustained almost exclusively by Conservative votes, his exercise of it was hardly noticeable. The change at the Foreign Office was more important. Simon now went to the Home Office, for which he was indeed much more suited. With every good intention and with every desire to please, Simon had been a great failure at the Foreign Office. He did not seem to have any judgement or any instinctive ability to separate the important from the trivial. As William James once said of James Bryce, 'to him all facts are born free and equal'. In the Home Office Simon was far more at ease. Indeed, he had been a successful Home Secretary in Asquith's Government over twenty years before. Unhappily, when Lord Halifax later became Foreign Secretary in the House of Lords, Simon was brought in to support the Government in great debates on foreign affairs. Here he proved never persuasive and sometimes infuriating. It was a strange story. I always found Simon agreeable and friendly; his tragedy was that he wanted to be liked. Men, especially politicians, are like boys. They often reject those who seek their affections and look up to those who treat them with a certain negligence or even contempt. Simon was succeeded not, as many people expected, by Eden, but by Sam Hoare. Baldwin seems to have hesitated; but Neville Chamberlain was a strong supporter of Hoare and felt that Eden could wait. As it turned out, he did not have to wait more than a few months.

Meanwhile, as the Italian military preparations were proceeding openly and without any disguise, anxiety in Parliament and the country increased. The position at home was not made much clearer by the result of the famous Peace Ballot in June. This was an unofficial plebiscite of practically the whole nation, organised by the League of Nations Union under the presidency of the venerable and respected figure of Lord Cecil. A number of questions were put by the canvassers and an astonishingly large number of replies were returned. It was a kind of Gallup Poll in reverse. Instead of a small sample of one or two thousand people being consulted, over $11\frac{1}{2}$ million answers were recorded. All the questions were somewhat tendentious. For instance: 'Are you in favour of an all-round reduction in armaments by international agreement?' This, in particular, reminded one of the story of the boy who was asked by his father what the sermon had been about. After much reflection he said it had been about sin. 'Yes,' said the father, who had not himself attended the service, 'but what did the preacher say about sin?' After profound thought the boy replied, 'He was against it'. Other questions were of a similar character or else so obvious as hardly to be worth putting. For instance: 'Should Britain remain in the League?' But there were two questions which were of considerable value, although they became the subject of much misunderstanding and even misrepresentation. They were as follows:

Do you consider that, if a nation insists on attacking another, the other nations should combine to compel it to stop by

(a) Economic and non-military measures?
(b) If necessary, military measures?[1]

To the first of these two vital questions 10 million people answered in favour, and only some 600,000 against. There was, therefore, an overwhelming support for what became known as economic sanctions against the aggressor. To the second question, 6,784,000 voted 'yes' and 2,351,000 voted 'no'.[1,2] There was thus a very substantial majority in the Ballot—nearly three to one—in favour of force as a last resort.

The general feeling of the Conservative leaders was that the organisers of the Peace Ballot were open or crypto-pacifists. Neville Chamberlain, for instance, reveals in his diary impatience and indignation. He wrote contemptuously of 'the League of Nations Union cranks'.[3] I felt at the time, and I believe this feeling was shared by many of my friends, that this was a misreading of the situation. Certainly the argument that there was any clear distinction between economic sanctions and military sanctions was somewhat unrealistic. The more effective economic sanctions became, the more likely they would be to provoke war. But what was truly remarkable was the proportion of nearly 7 million out of the 9 million voters on this question who were 'willing, and indeed resolved, to go to war in a righteous cause, provided that all necessary action was taken under the auspices of the League of Nations'.[4]

It is no doubt true that many of the voters did not realise that if military sanctions had to be used (and of course at the time of the

[1] C. L. Mowat, *Britain Between the Wars, 1918–1940*, p. 542.
[2] The Earl of Avon, *The Eden Memoirs: Facing the Dictators*, p. 237.
[3] Iain Macleod, *Neville Chamberlain*, p. 181.
[4] Winston Churchill, *The Second World War*, vol. i: *The Gathering Storm*, p. 133.

Peace Ballot the case of Abyssinia was in everybody's mind), the main burden would fall on Britain. For they might well involve a naval blockade of Italy and the cutting-off of her communications to Africa. These operations, if decided upon, could only be carried out by the British, and, to a lesser extent, the French fleets.

By the time Parliament rose at the beginning of August, matters were clearly moving towards a crisis. British opinion in all parties was broadly in favour of standing by the League in a policy of sanctions, intended to force Italy to abandon her aggression. The Press, with the exception of the *Daily Mail* and the *Observer*, took this line. It was remarkable that on this issue the *Daily Express*, Lord Beaverbrook's organ, was strongly anti-Italian, also *The Times* and the *Spectator*. Dawson,[1] who was never deeply moved by any of Hitler's breaches of treaty or acts of aggression, took a quite different line about Mussolini. This was no doubt for a simple reason. Dawson was not much interested in Europe; but as a strong imperialist, brought up in the Milner tradition, he was deeply concerned with Africa. He did not like the idea of Mussolini getting control of the sources of the Nile or becoming our neighbour in the Sudan.

As the weeks passed, it was clear that the Italians, once the rains were over, would launch the attack—probably early in October. Then the die must be cast. The British Government, which was still under MacDonald and Baldwin, although the firm was now called Baldwin and MacDonald, must therefore find a policy and stick to it. The nation waited, and, in these holiday months, waited with breathless excitement. Public opinion was deeply stirred and once again, as always at moments of great crisis, there arose a situation out of which something like national unity might be created. All except the true pacifists—the followers of Lansbury or Canon Sheppard—could be rallied to a common cause. In the event, the opportunity was missed. It did not reoccur until five years later in very different conditions.

To find a policy, the Cabinet sat long hours. There were, in a sense, two Foreign Secretaries—Hoare and Eden. For Eden had now become Lord Privy Seal, a member of the Cabinet, and Minis-

---

[1] Geoffrey Dawson, editor of *The Times*.

ter for League of Nations Affairs. There was Baldwin presiding, but anxious to get away as soon as possible, and disliking foreign affairs on general grounds. There was Neville Chamberlain, at this period in a very bellicose mood. He had written in his diary in July:

> The ideal way out is to persuade Mussolini to abandon the idea of force. The only way to do this is to convince him that he has no choice. . . . We could e.g. stop the passage of his supplies through the Suez Canal. If the French would agree to play their part, the best way would be to go privately to Mussolini and warn him of our views and intentions.[1]

Even as late as the end of November he records in his diary:

> If anyone else would give the lead, well and good, but in the last resort . . . we ought to give the lead ourselves rather than let the question go by default. . . .[2]

(This was in connection with what were called 'oil sanctions'.) The younger members of the Cabinet were known to be individually supporters of the League. What would their collective decision be?

They were indeed faced with a grave dilemma. The development of events made it evident that a decision must soon be reached one way or the other. Two courses were open to Ministers, either of which, pursued with courage, might have led to the avoidance of the catastrophe which followed in a few years' time.

The first would have been to prevent at all costs the transference of Italy to the German side. In spite of the growing hostility of British opinion to Mussolini and his planned aggression, reasons could well have been found to justify the establishment of Italian authority in a great part, if not all, of Abyssinia, in the same way as other European Powers had imposed their will upon different parts of Africa in earlier times. Arguments could have been presented to show that the character of the Ethiopian Government was such as to deserve little support from civilised countries. It was a feudal country. Civil war was endemic. Slavery flourished. Moreover, the League, in its mutilated form, was clearly unable to deter Italy or to force a solution by means of sanctions. The best that could be hoped for was some form of settlement which might preserve the nominal position of the Emperor, while placing effective authority in Italian hands. This would have had the substantial, perhaps decisive,

[1] Keith Feiling, *Life of Neville Chamberlain*, p. 265.   [2] Ibid., p. 272.

advantage of keeping Italy, at that time by no means friendly to Germany, on the right side in the greater struggle which was already looming ahead. Moreover, the French Government, traditionally hostile to Italy, had lately, under great pressure from Britain, adopted a more friendly attitude. Mussolini himself, at the time of the Dollfuss murder, by moving up a number of divisions to the Brenner Pass in 1934, had effectively prevented Hitler from risking the *Anschluss* coup. At the Stresa Conference considerable progress had been made in keeping Italy on the right path, at any rate so far as Europe was concerned.

The diplomatic silence at Stresa on the problems of Africa made it easy to follow this line. By allowing Mussolini to avenge the disgrace of Adowa, and develop an African empire comparable to those of other great European countries, Britain and France would cement the alliance and prevent those dangerous developments in south-eastern Europe which Hitler was certainly meditating, even if his wider ambitions were only suspected.

Naturally, such a policy might seem cynical. But it would be realistic. It would be contrary to the strong British feelings that the League should be supported. But since no effective authority could be exercised by the League without the threat, and probably the use, of military measures, British public opinion, which—in spite of the apparent willingness shown by the Peace Ballot to face military sanctions, if collectively applied—seemed to regard peace as the prime object to be pursued, could perhaps be led to accept the end, while disliking the means. Moreover, it would not involve altogether abandoning the League. It would only be necessary to advance cautiously at the same rate as other countries were willing to do. Clearly, if France and Britain did not take the lead, smaller countries would not do much more than pass resolutions or try to apply some economic pressure. Collective action need not be openly opposed; but it could be allowed to fizzle out, and Mussolini could be told that the debates and appeals, and even perhaps minor sanctions initiated by the League, were not to be taken too seriously.

Churchill, rightly obsessed with the German danger, felt instinctively that the loss of Italian support, amounting in the long run to the likelihood of Italy joining in a war against us, was too

heavy a burden for us to carry. Vansittart, the brilliant head of the
Foreign Office, who shared Churchill's fears about Germany, took
the same line. He therefore did not urge upon the Foreign Secretary
at Stresa, or even remind him, of the need to raise the Abyssinian
question. Such a policy, of course, meant the end of the League and
the Covenant as an effective instrument for stopping aggression.
But, it could be argued, what real chance was there of the League
proving successful? Hitler was still only in the earlier stages of his
ambitious armament plans. He had been baulked in Austria, and
with Italian help could still no doubt be deterred. If Austria was
held, Czechoslovakia would be correspondingly strengthened. The
remilitarisation of the Rhineland, in spite of some sinister developments, had not yet taken place. If France and Britain remained
firmly together; if British rearmament were pushed forward with
every possible speed; if the more robust elements in France were
encouraged to do the same; then, indeed, although the League
would have failed, an alliance would have been created round which
the smaller countries could gather. If Western Europe were strongly
defended, perhaps satisfactory arrangements could be made to
contain Hitler in the east. Abyssinia would be sacrificed. But it
was a country without any powerful central Government or any
advanced civilisation. It was, in Churchill's words, a 'wild land of
tyranny, slavery and tribal war'.[1] Would this be too great a price to
pay in view of the dangers and calamities that threatened?

In the debate of 11 July, Churchill gave cautious utterance to
some of these anxieties. He recognised that we must play our part
in whatever the League might decide. But he added: 'we cannot be
asked to do more than our part in these matters'.[2] Yet it was clear
that unless Britain took the lead and, in fact, did do more than her
part, the League must fail. He ended his speech with an appeal to
the old friendships between Britain and Italy, so traditional and so
honourable to both countries. Churchill repeated these warnings,
especially the need to have a clear understanding with France, in
private conversation with Hoare early in August. These were his
words:

[1] Winston Churchill, *The Second World War*, vol. i: *The Gathering Storm*, p. 130.
[2] Ibid., p. 131.

I said I thought the Foreign Secretary was justified in going as far with the League of Nations against Italy as he could carry France; but I added that he ought not to put any pressure upon France, because of her military convention with Italy and her German preoccupation.[1]

The second course was equally clear. It would be to make this Abyssinian crisis the test case for the League and to ensure its triumph. To achieve this, Britain must take the lead. We must not hesitate to bring all possible pressure on France, and satisfy her that our rearmament plans would match the real needs of the situation. We should thus ensure that by the failure and perhaps fall of the lesser dictator all the forces of democratic freedom could be brought into action to restrain the greater. Nor were the difficulties as formidable as might appear. Germany, both for reasons of geography and in the present position of her armaments, could do little to assist Italy. Financial and economic sanctions, if promptly, vigorously, and selectively applied, could make Italy's position untenable. An oil sanction, for instance, would bring the Abyssinian campaign, when it was launched, to an early stop. Acting in the name of and under the authority of the League, the British and French fleets could blockade Italy and deprive the Italians of the use of the Suez Canal. With their forces isolated in Africa and their communications cut, the Italian Government would have no alternative but to bow to the public opinion of the world. Of course there would be risks. The British naval staffs did not fail to warn the Government of the weakness of Malta and the probable loss of capital ships. The last, in view of the Far Eastern crisis, they thought unacceptable. Of course there were risks—but they were petty in comparison with the perils we were soon to undergo.

Believing that the British Government were embarking seriously upon such a policy, Churchill tried to make clear these dangers in a conversation with the Italian Ambassador, Grandi, and impressed upon him the strength of British public opinion.[2] Earlier, in a public speech, he had conveyed a grave warning to Mussolini:

To cast an army of nearly a quarter of a million men, embodying the flower of Italian manhood, upon a barren shore two thousand miles from home,

[1] Winston Churchill, *The Second World War*, vol. i: *The Gathering Storm*, p. 132.
[2] Ibid., Appendix A, 28 September 1935, p. 533.

against the good will of the whole world and without command of the sea, and then in this position embark upon what may well be a series of campaigns against a people and in regions which no conqueror in four thousand years ever thought it worth while to subdue, is to give hostages to fortune unparalleled in all history.[1]

The Cabinet no doubt hesitated long between these alternatives, although perhaps they did not see them so clearly defined as I have set them out. By the time of the debate in the House of Commons on 1 August they seemed to have reached their decision. The new Foreign Secretary firmly declared that the Government stood by the treaties and the Covenant. We would carry out our obligations in the matter of Abyssinia. He believed the French would do the same. On the next day the House adjourned for the summer recess.

During the Parliamentary recess, any doubts as to the Government's determination—for naturally the Foreign Secretary used carefully chosen words in the debate—were dispelled by events at Geneva. Eden had been busy. Under his enthusiastic lead, opinion in the Assembly had been rallied for a policy of sanctions if the expected Italian attack on Abyssinia were launched. As we now know, but did not know at the time, Eden had considerable difficulty in keeping his French colleague, Laval, up to the mark. Laval still hoped for some way out, which would keep Italy on the right side. He was a shrewd operator and put his faith, as it turned out not without reason, in the probable unwillingness of the British Government to face the issue when it came to the point. Even the lifting of the embargo on the export of arms to Abyssinia, which had been urged for many months, had not yet been agreed. Although such embargo, applying both to Italy and Abyssinia, seemed on the surface equitable, it was, in fact, grossly unfair. Italy had been preparing for years. Abyssinia was without any modern weapons and, indeed, without artillery of any kind. Lloyd George had urged the removal of the embargo in private talks earlier in the summer. Eden equally regarded the maintenance of the embargo as a great injustice, but in his position as junior to the Foreign Secretary he was unable to get his way. Laval therefore temporised. All doubts, however, seemed to be removed by Hoare's address at Geneva on 11 September.

---

[1] Winston Churchill, *The Second World War*, vol. i: *The Gathering Storm*, p. 135.

Hoare's speech, delivered to the full Assembly of the League, had a sensational effect throughout the world. It is possible that he and his advisers did not altogether realise how great would be the reaction, and how resounding the enthusiasm. In his own words, the Foreign Secretary had decided to deliver 'a revivalist appeal to the Assembly. At best, it might start a new chapter of League recovery; at worst, it might deter Mussolini by a display of League fervour. If there was any element of bluff in it, it was a moment when bluff was not only legitimate but inescapable.'[1] It is interesting now to learn that the draft had been carefully gone through phrase by phrase, not merely with his advisers in the Foreign Office, but with Neville Chamberlain.[2] The vital sentences were as follows:

The League stands, and my country stands with it, for the collective maintenance of the Covenant in its entirety, and particularly for steady and collective resistance to all acts of unprovoked aggression. The attitude of the British nation in the last few weeks has clearly demonstrated the fact that this is no variable and unreliable sentiment, but a principle of international conduct to which they and their Government hold with firm, enduring and universal persistence.

There was indeed a proviso; 'but it seemed only to strengthen the pledge'.[3] It ran as follows:

If the burden is to be borne, it must be borne collectively. If risks for peace are to be run, they must be run by all. The security of the many cannot be ensured solely by the efforts of a few, however powerful they may be. On behalf of His Majesty's Government in the United Kingdom, I can say that, in spite of these difficulties, that Government will be second to none in its intention to fulfil, within the measure of its capacity, the obligations which the Covenant lays upon it.

It is true that a careful scrutiny of these sentences might lead to the conclusion that Britain's action would depend entirely upon the co-operation of the rest of the members. But the whole tenor of the speech made it clear that Britain intended to give a firm and positive lead. Eden records that M. Hymans, the Belgian representative,

[1] Viscount Templewood, *Nine Troubled Years* (London, 1954), p. 166.
[2] Iain Macleod, *Neville Chamberlain*, p. 186.
[3] C. L. Mowat, *Britain Between the Wars, 1918–1940*, p. 544.

summed up the effect of the speech as follows: 'The British have decided to stop Mussolini, even if that means using force.' This indeed was the only possible interpretation of this historic oration.[1] Churchill, like everyone else, was stirred when he read this speech. 'It united all those forces in Britain which stood for a fearless combination of righteousness and strength. Here at least was a policy.'[2] Nor were the British content with words. On the very next day, 12 September, action was taken, unmistakable in character. The battle cruisers *Hood* and *Renown*, accompanied by the 2nd Cruiser Squadron and a destroyer flotilla, arrived at Gibraltar.

The response in Britain, both to the speech and the naval demonstration, was immediate and impressive. That sense of national unity and pride, which is often dormant in our people, was aroused again. Since the war we had suffered from a sense of disillusionment. The 'Homes fit for Heroes'—a demagogic phrase which Lloyd George had used to describe the social revolution which was to follow victory—had come to nothing. There had followed instead a long period of depression and unemployment. All this had led in its turn to division and controversy. The gulf between poverty and wealth, all the more intolerable in those years when poverty had degenerated into something like despair, had increased the bitterness of class feeling. Yet the longing for unity was still there. It had been demonstrated in a remarkable fashion at the time of King George V's Jubilee celebrations earlier in the year. The enthusiasm of the people on this occasion was a tribute to the fine example which the King and Queen had shown through the troubled years of their reign. But it was more than this. It represented a genuine coming together of all their subjects. It was a family party; and nowhere were the celebrations more notable than in the poorer streets of every town. I remember very well driving round Stockton with my wife on that day. Flags were hung across all the streets from one side to the other. Men and women of every class and of every political complexion joined together in common rejoicing. In a similar spirit of unity, with the British Government's firm declaration, a new sense of purpose seemed to arise and a new

[1] The Earl of Avon, *The Eden Memoirs: Facing the Dictators*, p. 262.
[2] Winston Churchill, *The Second World War*, vol. i: *The Gathering Storm*, p. 135.

confidence in the future, based upon the great achievements of the past. Once more we were going to take our right place in the world. America was neutral, Germany hostile; the democratic nations now looked to us, and we would not fail them. Britain was back in the lead.

The effect upon the Labour Party was immediate. The pacifist elements, who were powerful in Parliament but by no means constituted a majority among the voters who supported the Labour Party, were in confusion. All were, at least in principle, adherents of the League. Many of those who had opposed rearmament had called for strong action against Mussolini. Ernest Bevin's robust campaign was carried on with increasing vigour. At the Labour Party meeting in Brighton at the end of September the debate was brought to a head. Lansbury and Cripps were for peace at any price. Bevin opposed them with all his strength. It was on this occasion that he used words which have become famous, accusing Lansbury of placing the movement in an absolutely hopeless position 'by hawking his conscience round from body to body asking to be told what he ought to do with it'. The resolution in favour of sanctions was carried by an overwhelming majority. On 8 October, Lansbury resigned and Attlee was elected in his place.

When the House met again on 23 October, Italy's attack on Abyssinia had been launched. The Council of the League had carried, with one dissentient, a resolution censuring Italy for having 'resorted to war in disregard of the Covenant'. A co-ordinating committee had been set up to prepare the necessary sanctions. The embargo on arms had been lifted on Abyssinia—too late, but it was nevertheless a gesture. Eden was seen to be taking the leading part in pressing forward with positive measures. His position at this moment was a remarkable one for so young a man. At that time I did not know him intimately, as I came to do later. But it was then I first understood and admired not only his skill and zeal but his sincere devotion to great causes. We did not know, of course, as we have learnt since his own story has become available, how difficult was his task during these decisive weeks. The long story of the gradual slide from the high ideals of September to the ultimate collapse of the League's efforts is admirably set out in his book: the trickiness of Laval; Eden's struggle to keep him straight in spite of his Protean elusiveness—efforts which might have been successful had it not been for London, all the time blowing hot and cold; Hoare's fickleness.[1] Hoare had soon begun to be alarmed by what he had done. After his bold words in public, he had already begun to rat in private. Nor had a very resolute line been taken by our Ambassador in Rome. Sir Eric Drummond's hesitant replies to Mussolini's threats were no doubt repeated to Paris and served to encourage Laval and those Ministers who shared his fears. All this, however, was hidden from us. At least on the surface, the mood was still resolute. Any delays in applying sanctions seemed inevitable and inherent in the League's system. Any hopes expressed for an honourable settlement did not envisage a dishonourable retreat. Whatever may have been the secret hesitations of the Cabinet, we back-benchers were convinced that this time Britain was determined to 'see it through'. Two days later, on 25 October, the decision was announced to dissolve the Parliament, and the poll fixed for 14 November. Little could we know that the House of Commons now to be elected was destined to endure four years of an uneasy peace, to be followed by six years of the most terrible war in history.

[1] The Earl of Avon, *The Eden Memoirs: Facing the Dictators*, chs. xv and xvi.

CHAPTER FOURTEEN

The General Election of 1935

AT the General Election of 1935 I contested Stockton for the fifth time in twelve years. I was by now well known in the town and had a considerable personal following. My Conservative supporters had treated me, in spite of what must have seemed to them strange aberrations, with marked patience and understanding. Facing day by day the harsh realities of a 'distressed' area, they were not so easily affected by the criticisms of my political behaviour as were some of my metropolitan friends. In the North, they rather admire a certain independence. I had taken them into my confidence all through these years. They had not objected to the policies on economic and industrial affairs, which are described earlier, or to their forcible expression. Thus they did not object to my occasional conflict with the official party view. In January 1935 Lloyd George had launched his New Deal. Although I was not able to attend his inaugural meeting at Bangor, I made it clear in a statement to the Press that many of my friends and I welcomed his proposals in general terms. When *The Next Five Years* manifesto was published in July, it was natural that there should be talk of some co-operation between Lloyd George's Council of Action and our Next Five Years group. It was made plain, however, in August that this could not take place, since the two bodies were separate in form and purpose. One was a political movement; the other was a coming together of individual men of all parties, agreeing upon a general programme and hoping to give a lead to public opinion as a whole. This did not preclude a number of us from supporting Lloyd George in our individual capacities. Accordingly, I appeared on the platform of the Council of Action meeting in London in July. Together with a number of North Country Members of all parties, I attended and spoke at a similar meeting in Newcastle on 1 October.

All these various movements were intended to galvanise the Government into a more dynamic attack upon the problem of unemployment.

I confess I had been for a moment tempted, when I received, in the course of the summer, an offer which would give me a completely safe seat in the South of England. A great friend of mine told me in June that he had definitely decided not to stand again. After consultation with his chairman, he was certain that if I allowed my name to go forward I should be nominated as prospective candidate in his place. But having gone back to Stockton after my defeat in 1929, I did not feel now that it would be right to desert. I therefore replied as follows:

> Quite frankly, I feel that I should make a mistake to leave the Stockton Seat, firstly, because one does not like giving up anything until one is beaten, and, secondly, because I now feel that I have a good chance of holding the Seat against the socialist. . . . I am now able to take a somewhat critical attitude towards the leaders of the party, which suits me in my independent position.
> . . . if I could get in at Stockton-on-Tees, I should be freer, from that position, to develop whatever line I think necessary. Between you and me, I feel more and more out of touch with the attitude of mind that is now controlling the party, and I prefer to take the risk of being beaten in the North, where I do represent a definite view. If the worst comes to the worst, I can retire from politics and devote myself to my private affairs, which I have neglected so much during recent years.

When *The Next Five Years* manifesto was published, I held a large open meeting in my constituency to explain it, and made it clear that I proposed to stand on this policy when the election came. Towards the end of September, at a meeting of the executive committee of the Association, I received their unanimous approval.

In spite of some improvement in the employment situation, things were still very bad on the North-east Coast. I knew that I should have to face a very different situation from that of 1931, when the responsibility could be put upon the Labour Government. Moreover, whereas my previous opponent had been an agreeable but undistinguished figure, I was now faced with a much more powerful contestant in the shape of Miss Susan Lawrence. She had proved herself through long service to the Labour movement to be

one of its most distinguished thinkers and one of its ablest adminis-
trators. She had been a successful Minister. She was able to rally
round her an enthusiastic band of supporters from both inside and
outside the constituency. Much, of course, would depend upon
whether a Liberal candidate would stand or not. I knew well that at
the last election I had polled a large proportion of the Liberal vote,
believed to be between 10,000 and 15,000. I had also no doubt
gained a certain number of Labour supporters. If a Liberal stood, I
might be very hard pressed. Many attempts were made by some of
my Liberal friends, including Lloyd George, to see that I should be
given a clear run. However, the local Conservatives insisted on
putting up a candidate against Kingsley Griffith, the popular Liberal
Member for Middlesbrough West–the neighbouring seat–and in
the circumstances Liberals were disinclined to stand down in my
favour in Stockton. The Council of Action did not put up candidates
at the election but sent out a questionnaire to all candidates. In
answering it, I added:

> My support of these proposals in the House of Commons, as a member of the
> Drafting Committee of the book entitled *The Next Five Years* and on the
> platform at the Conventions held by the Council of Action, is well known.
>
> As an indication of the way in which I am endeavouring to bring these
> proposals before the Electors of Stockton, I am enclosing a copy of my election
> address which, as you will see, has been drafted on independent lines.

Others of my Conservative friends–Hugh Molson, Vyvyan Adams,
Nicholas Grattan-Doyle, Denville, Robert Aske, and ten or twelve
other candidates–gave general acceptance to the Council of Action's
questions. Although my Liberal opponent also answered favourably,
Lloyd George went out of his way in the course of the campaign to
give me what assistance he could. Both in his election broadcast and
in a statement to the *Manchester Guardian* he made favourable
reference to my work in Parliament, and to the similarity of our
points of view on the vital question of unemployment. He wrote to
me privately, sending his personal good wishes. I was equally
fortunate in obtaining considerable support from leading Liberals,
both in the constituency and outside. These included two ex-
presidents of the Stockton Liberal Association, as well as Professor

Gilbert Murray and Dr. Scott-Lidgett. I cannot forbear from quoting Gilbert Murray's message:

Dear Mr. Macmillan,

Though not a member of your Party I have followed with the warmest admiration and agreement the scheme of constructive policy which you advocate and if I were an elector in Stockton and Thornaby should, without hesitation, give you my vote.

Yours sincerely,
Gilbert Murray

On the home side of my campaign I therefore felt, as the election proceeded, increasingly confident. I must also pay a tribute to the Conservative machine. Whatever their feelings as to my orthodoxy, no attempt was made to weaken my position, and all the necessary help was afforded.

As regards foreign affairs, I was comfortably placed. Although during these four years I concentrated almost entirely on economic questions, I naturally made a number of speeches, especially to my constituents, on the wider questions of European and world problems. Like all my Conservative friends, I was a convinced supporter of the League. In March 1934 I had addressed the local League of Nations Union, denouncing isolationism and advocating an active and leading role for Britain at Geneva. In March 1935 I had delivered a speech in the North of England which obtained a certain notoriety. In this I had referred to the need to face 'the new barbarism' which was coming into the world. 'It will not be overcome,' I added, 'unless we are prepared to make great sacrifices. We have got to be prepared to fight for a collective system if we want peace.' I had therefore no difficulty in supporting the second part of *The Next Five Years* manifesto dealing with foreign policy. As the Abyssinian crisis grew nearer, I became concerned as to the line which the Government would take. But Hoare's speech at Geneva relieved all my anxieties. In order to support him in the bold and, as we thought, determined line which he had taken, a number of signatories of *The Next Five Years*, of which I was one, sent a letter to *The Times* on 17 September, welcoming his firm statement. We knew that the French were showing some hesitation, and we therefore urged that it should be made clear that Britain's support of the

Covenant in its entirety applied not merely to the Abyssinian crisis but to any similar situation. The letter proceeded:

The best hope in the present situation arises from the statement made by the Foreign Secretary; the greatest difficulty arises from the fact that no such unequivocal declaration was made earlier. It may well be that the present issue will turn upon the question whether countries such as France, whose effective collaboration is now essential, feel that they can rely upon a similar policy being pursued by Great Britain in the case of a future threat to peace arising elsewhere.

Here, indeed, we had put our finger on the spot. The French doubts, apart from the internal weakness of France at the time and the innate shiftiness of Laval, as well as resentment about the Anglo-German Naval Agreement, were largely due to the traditional unwillingness of the British to commit themselves and especially to deal with hypothetical contingencies. This hesitation was one of the causes of our humiliating failure in Abyssinia and of subsequent retreats at every successive crisis.

On 27 September, again before Parliament met, I joined in a letter to M. Laval, which was signed by very many leading personalities, representing a wide field of British opinion and a large number of organisations. It included six or seven Conservative Members of Parliament, as well as representatives of the universities, the Churches, and many other sides of British life. The same point was made in this manifesto:

Not only must this collective principle be applied to arrest invasion of a weak African State: it must apply equally for the purpose of preventing or repressing aggression in Europe or in any other part of the world. Such is the determination, we know, of the vast majority of the British people.

If the Government had really decided to follow up Hoare's declaration at Geneva, such support should have given them encouragement. While the debate in October was overshadowed by the prospect of an immediate dissolution, there was nothing said from the Government front bench to damp our ardour or arouse our suspicions. The Foreign Secretary's invitation to Italy to come to honourable terms before economic sanctions were applied was not unreasonable and in no sense marked a retreat. For the Council of the League had done its best to find some acceptable compromise,

and that offer was still open. It is true that he indicated that there
had been no discussion of military sanctions with the French.
Nevertheless, we naturally assumed that the Fleet movements must
have been undertaken with French agreement and approval. It was
therefore somewhat of a shock to me, after the election had started,
to find Lloyd George not only attacking the Government for using
the international crisis to win an election and a further term of office,
but issuing a warning that the Government would not hold to the
course on which it was assumed to be set. He complained of the long
delay since Abyssinia had first appealed to the League, and of the
fact that Mussolini had been able to mass his armies for an attack on
Abyssinia without any interference. Even now, after three weeks of
war, a date had not yet been fixed for the application of sanctions.
The Liberals stood behind the Government; the Labour Party had
risked a split among their own ranks and even changed their leader
in support of the League. But the Government seemed to be falter-
ing. He added a bitter phrase on sanctions. 'They are too late to save
Abyssinia but are just in the nick of time to save the Government.'
This speech worried me; but not unduly. The Conservative mani-
festo was clear. The leaders were committed. I knew, moreover, that
Eden was working hard to stimulate the other members of the
League, and to promote effective action as rapidly as the procedure
of Geneva allowed. I could not believe the accusation that the
Government were using the crisis merely for electioneering purposes.
In any event, I decided in my own mind that whatever might occur,
I would not abandon the policy for which I was seeking the support
of the electors.

The election in Stockton ran along what were now to me familiar
lines. My election address was a summary of *The Next Five Years*
plan. I circulated a number of pamphlets and leaflets, including
letters from the various prominent Liberals, local and national.
There were the usual meetings in schoolrooms and in the few
available halls—and the usual rows. Of the outside speakers who
came to support me, Lord Allen was by far the most effective. I shall
not forget the crowded meeting in an upstairs room, packed and
overflowing, and the impressive speech which he made. He was a
great platform speaker: his fine head, with its strange ethereal look,

and a beautiful flow of well-chosen, simple phrases. To my political work he paid a very generous tribute:

He could have earned the ordinary plaudits of his party. He could have gained a career, honour and comfort; instead he has insisted in making an independent contribution to the whole of our national political life.

He has shown courage, persistency, and, above all, a gentleness in the way of expressing his opinions which is beginning to win the hearts of the people all over the country.

At the start he was interrupted with cries of 'Traitor MacDonald' and the like. But in the end he captivated and held his audience.

To a candidate, every election is a sentence of hard labour. But happily the term is short. Every evening one marks another day off the calendar with relief. By polling day one is so exhausted as scarcely to care what the result will be. It had become the custom for my supporters, after the eve-of-the-poll meeting, to organise a march through the town. This year it seemed almost more enthusiastic than ever before. Happily there was no serious clash between us and our rivals. I had only one anxiety. I had conducted the election by an appeal to the intelligence of the voters, and I was not sure whether I had been able to simplify sufficiently the complex problems with which I was trying to deal. In the event the result was good. The figures were: Conservative 23,285, Labour 19,217, Liberal 5,158. I had a majority of 4,000 over Miss Lawrence and the Liberal forfeited his deposit. It was clear, therefore, that I had not merely held the Conservative vote but obtained a large amount of Liberal and moderate support. In a statement the next day, I used these words:

I have asked from the electors a more generous mandate than is usual. It would not have contented me to have been returned merely as a supporter of the Government, much as I appreciate what it has done in the past four years to achieve recovery from the trade depression.

I want to give special thanks to the electors for the freedom they have given me.

The local Press took the same line and stressed my independent campaign. They described Miss Lawrence's defeat as 'a savage blow for the Socialists'. On the other hand, I could not help being rather amused at my victory being treated by some of the metropolitan Press as 'a signal success for the Government'. I am not sure whether that quite represented the official view. Nevertheless, it proved that the electors in the depressed areas were not so wedded to Socialism as to be unwilling to listen to reasoned argument.

The General Election resulted in a vote of confidence in Baldwin and his Government. The Conservatives and their Liberal-National and National Labour supporters won 432 seats compared with 512 before the dissolution, giving the Government a clear majority of 249. Although Labour recovered some ground and numbered 154 as against 52 in 1931, and had the satisfaction of securing the return of some important figures such as Morrison, Clynes, Alexander, and Dalton, yet they were in a hopeless minority. The official or Samuelite Liberals fell to 20. Herbert Samuel himself lost his seat at Darwen.

Whatever the effect of Lloyd George's campaign on general policy, there was little he could hope to achieve in the new House. The Government had rejected his plans and made no gesture towards any form of co-operation. On the other hand, before the election there had been much talk of Churchill coming back to the Government. The very fact that Baldwin and Neville Chamberlain had refused to contemplate bringing in Lloyd George made it seem likely that they would be ready to accept Churchill. The general view in the House was that he would be offered the Admiralty. Lloyd George was sceptical about this, and had told Tom Jones that every member of the present Government 'would vote to keep him out because of his dominating intellectual force and his experience'.[1] Baldwin had indeed discussed this question with Dawson as early as May. Churchill has himself described the strong rumours that he would be asked to join. 'But after the figures of his victory had been proclaimed, Mr. Baldwin lost no time in announcing through the Central Office that there was no intention to include me in the Government.'[2] So the two most vital figures in the House of Commons were to stay on the back-benches. The mediocrities were to reign supreme.

While fighting an election—especially in a hard contest—one has

[1] Thomas Jones, *A Diary with Letters, 1931–1950*, p. 351.
[2] Winston Churchill, *The Second World War*, vol. i: *The Gathering Storm*, p. 141.

little time to follow in detail the speeches of the leaders. Every minute is engaged in canvassing, in personal contacts, in indoor and outdoor meetings. But when the Conservative manifesto was published, I saw with pleasure that it showed no hesitation, at least on foreign affairs, and reinforced the Foreign Secretary's historic speech at Geneva. The League of Nations would 'remain ... the keystone of British foreign policy ... we shall therefore continue to do all in our power to uphold the Covenant ... in the present unhappy dispute between Italy and Abyssinia. There will be no wavering in the policy we have hitherto pursued.'

On rearmament, the country was left in no doubt—at least by the Labour speakers. Attlee ridiculed the need for a 'tremendous and costly programme'. Arthur Greenwood denounced Neville Chamberlain as 'the merest scaremonger'. Morrison called Chamberlain, Churchill, and Amery 'fire-eaters and militarists. . . . [Chamberlain] would spend on the means of death, but not on the means of life.'[1] Certainly, there seemed no doubt in the minds of the Opposition what were the Government's intentions. Baldwin made it clear that there would have to be a substantial programme. It is true that in his speech to the Peace Society, and in his broadcast, he reassured his listeners that there would be 'no great armaments'.[2] But these words did not, as I saw it, detract from his determination that there would be an armament programme appropriate to our requirements, and to the confused and dangerous situation in the world. In several speeches he emphasised the needs of the Navy and of the Air Force, and the fact that other countries had rearmed while we were disarming. We now know that Neville Chamberlain would have liked to fight the election on rearmament as the main issue, and had put this proposal to Baldwin in August. But Baldwin preferred, while making the need for a stable Government in the present international crisis the justification for the election, to stress support of the League, and to defend rearmament as necessary to make collective security effective. As to the timing of the election Eden had some doubts. He would have preferred another plan. The Prime Minister should send for the leaders of the parties, explain to them the necessity for

[1] Iain Macleod, *Neville Chamberlain*, p. 184.
[2] A. W. Baldwin, *My Father: The True Story* (London, 1956), p. 242.

rearmament in the existing situation, and appeal to them for their help. If they would give reasonable support, the election could be postponed. He went so far as to tell Hoare that he thought a 'khaki' election might seem to some people 'a dirty trick'.[1] But Baldwin had no doubt that the ground on which the Government attacked was tactically well chosen, and the result of the election proved his sagacity. Naturally, none of this was known to us at the time. I myself felt that the Government were fully justified in seeking a mandate for their policy of support for the League and their firm stand against Mussolini's aggression, as well as for a rearmament programme to allow us to play our part and to resist the growing arrogance of the dictators.

As it turned out, Baldwin's approach seemed somewhat disingenuous. His speeches were admirably devised to suit all shades of opinion. There would be no isolated action over Abyssinia. That comforted the faint-hearts. There would be no great armaments; that satisfied the anti-militarists. We would stand firmly by the League; that, and Hoare's speech at Geneva, captured the League of Nations vote. The Government must give full attention in these critical days to foreign affairs and must be assured of the nation's support; so that justified the election. Amery, who openly opposed the action of the Government over Abyssinia and thought it folly to force Mussolini into the arms of Hitler, has expressed a more cynical view of Baldwin's tactics:

. . . to outbid the combined Oppositions and sail back into office on a wave of virtuous indignation as the true champions of collective security. The temptation proved irresistible.[2]

I think this too harsh a judgement. Amery saw things clearly and objectively. Baldwin's mind worked altogether differently. No doubt he felt that he had protected his position sufficiently against any real danger of war. Like Mr. Micawber, he hoped something would turn up. In any event, it was right to see if the League would work. It was right to rearm. So it was right to seek a further term of office, with carefully chosen words, calculated to leave open what line of action might later seem appropriate.

[1] The Earl of Avon, *The Eden Memoirs: Facing the Dictators*, p. 280.
[2] L. S. Amery, *My Political Life*, vol. iii: *The Unforgiving Years, 1929–1940*, p. 170.

Meanwhile, Churchill, in spite of his doubts about the wisdom of forcing Italy on to the wrong side in the larger crisis which he saw looming ahead, had rallied to what seemed a clear and definite policy. But Amery, who had expressed similar doubts, continued to criticise the weakness of the League and had spoken quite frankly and firmly against any policy which might lead to war. His speech at Birmingham in October had been repudiated by Neville Chamberlain, who had described it as a 'mischievous distortion of realities'. 'The choice before us', he said, 'is whether we shall make one last effort at Geneva for peace and security or whether by a cowardly surrender we shall break our promise and hold ourselves up to the shame of our children and their childrens' children.'[1] These were strong words—and from Chamberlain, who chose his words carefully, silenced all doubters.

But if the Government had won a great electoral victory by a skilful timing of the election—as they were quite entitled to do—they were in honour bound to carry out what, in spite of a sentence here or there of reservation, was believed by the people to be their clear and determined intention—to stop Mussolini. When the House of Commons met in November, no one—inside or outside Parliament—doubted that this was their firm purpose.

[1] L. S. Amery, *My Political Life*, vol. iii: *The Unforgiving Years, 1929–1940*, p. 175.

CHAPTER FIFTEEN

Doubts and Distractions

WHEN Parliament assembled on 3 December 1935, Members were in a quiet, even subdued, mood. In spite of the normal acerbities of party conflict, the election had revealed an unusual measure of underlying agreement. Except for the extreme pacifists, whose views had been decisively rejected by the great majority of the Labour Party, there was general and even enthusiastic approval of the course which the Government were taking on the burning issue of the day—the Abyssinian crisis. In retrospect, it is clear that the overwhelming support which Hoare's celebrated speech of 11 September had commanded rested upon a temporary and almost fortuitous coalescence of many different opinions and motives.

The Prime Minister and his principal colleagues were anxious to gain a mandate for strengthening our defences. Nobody could deny that at least some measure of rearmament was necessary to enable Britain 'to play her full part in the collective system'. As Baldwin subsequently explained in a famous speech, he believed that the time had now come when at least national acquiescence could be obtained in a rearmament programme which was clearly overdue. No one had a more delicate finger in feeling the pulse of national opinion. As the responsible Minister, it was his duty, as he conceived it, not merely to declare the need for rearmament but to ensure that it could be effectively brought about with broad acceptance, both in Parliament and outside. Although in later years certain rather unhappily chosen phrases were turned against him to create the myth of his so-called 'confession'—that he had long concealed, for electoral purposes, the need for rearmament, although well aware of its urgency—these allegations rest upon a misinterpretation of his words. In any case, Baldwin saw, in 1935, an opportunity created by

Mussolini's brutal aggression, which was not available a year or two before. As a practical politician, therefore, whatever may have been his doubts as to the ultimate success of the League's policies, he was glad to seize the occasion to secure, without undue disruption, the expansion and improvement of the fighting Services. By combining a realistic approach to our defence requirements with the idealistic wave of enthusiasm which had been built up in support of the collective power of the League, he hoped to achieve rearmament by consent.

Others were content to follow, perhaps for somewhat different reasons. Churchill and those who thought with him saw in the League and its machinery the instrument to secure a European coalition against Hitler, whom they knew to be a far greater danger to the peace of the world than Mussolini. Once the policy of trying to keep Italy on our side in this impending struggle had proved impossible, they were content to use whatever means seemed available to obtain the essential rearmament at home, and the building-up of a strong body of nations, under Franco-British leadership, to resist the greater dangers which they foresaw ahead. Moreover, they hoped that by such a policy the sympathy, and ultimately the help, of the United States might most easily be enlisted.

At the same time, another section, which might be called the League of Nations zealots, led by Lord Cecil and the powerful League of Nations Union, and appealing to Centre and non-party opinion throughout the country, saw in the Foreign Secretary's policy a return—belated perhaps but nevertheless welcome—to the pure doctrine of the Covenant.

Next, there were those, with an overriding devotion to the Empire and less concern for or knowledge of Europe, who saw in the threatened annexation of Abyssinia a menace to British interests in Africa—Somaliland, Kenya, and the Sudan. Moreover, the growing Italian expansion was a threat to the Empire's lifeline through the Mediterranean. This group, though perhaps not large, was influential. Its leader was Geoffrey Dawson, editor of *The Times*. As a result, that newspaper, subsequently to become the most disastrous of all the devotees of 'appeasement', on this occasion gave its full support to Hoare, so long as he followed his September line, and became his fiercest critic when he abandoned it.

Finally, the Government's stand against blatant aggression appealed to the great mass of those who recognised, even dimly, that a new storm was gathering; that British hopes had long rested on the League; and that if the League could not stop a second-class dictator like Mussolini, it was futile to rely upon it to stop Hitler. Yet it was to the League, fortified, strengthened, and encouraged by British and, it was to be hoped, French leadership, that we must look in order to rally resistance to the growing German menace. The only alternatives were either isolation, which with our world-wide imperial interests could not save us; or a return to regional alliances and great armaments. Yet this was the system which, according to the received historical judgement of the time, had been the cause, not the symptom, of the strains and stresses which had resulted in the Great War.

Never, therefore, was a Government in a stronger moral and political position than that which met the Parliament of 1935. The Prime Minister's prestige was higher than it had ever been. He was universally trusted. He stood on a pinnacle. Yet such are the strange vicissitudes of politics that within a few days after the opening of the new session his position was so shaken that it seemed unlikely that he could maintain himself, still less recover. He had suddenly lost his authority in the House of Commons. He seemed to be almost afraid of it. He was feeble, apologetic, and almost unnerved. Yet before the end of his political career, he was destined to regain much of this lost ground, by his masterly handling of the grave domestic and imperial crisis that culminated in the abdication of King Edward VIII.

Parliament thus met in a calm atmosphere. The King's Speech was read on 3 December. The traditional Debate on the Address followed without excitement or emotion. That part of the debate devoted to home affairs was an opportunity for rehearsing well-worn themes and repeating speeches that had already done duty on the hustings. On 5 December, devoted to foreign affairs, there was some desultory discussion of disarmament, of China, and of Egyptian problems. After dealing with these topics, the Foreign Secretary, Hoare, contented himself with a restatement, in somewhat subdued tones, of the League policy regarding Abyssinia and described the working of sanctions up to date. Towards the end of his speech, he made an appeal to Mussolini and his fellow-countrymen to put aside the suspicion that some sinister motive lay behind our support for the League. He felt that there should still be an intensive effort to bring about a settlement and 'to reconcile the divergent aims of Italy, Abyssinia and the League'.[1] He went on to say: 'The French and we intend not only to go on trying but to redouble our efforts during the short period of time that is still open before the Geneva meeting.'[1] Austen Chamberlain spoke later with general support, but added that he hoped that it would be possible to persuade the League and its members to apply quickly an embargo on the export of oil. Here, he said, was a sanction which could act both rapidly and effectively. All this took place on 5 December without arousing any particular interest, still less suspicion. On Friday the 6th the debate continued on a variety of topics—agriculture, unemployment, and so forth. Members dispersed for the weekend, expecting to return without excitement or emotion for the closing stages on Monday and Tuesday, with the formal vote on the various Opposition amendments. Yet, when we got back, we found ourselves suddenly plunged into the most extraordinary Parliamentary drama, which was to lead within a fortnight to the Government being forced, in order to save themselves, to sacrifice their Foreign Secretary and repudiate his actions.

The strange affair of the Hoare–Laval Agreement has now passed into history. The chief actor and indeed victim, Hoare, has told his own story with dignity and persuasiveness.[2] Eden, whose position as Minister responsible for League affairs was particularly delicate, has done the same.[3] From these and other sources it is possible to frame a fairly complete picture of this fantastic episode. Naturally, at the time, those who were not behind the scenes could not know what were the reasons for Hoare's sudden change of front, involving a surrender to Laval and a betrayal of the policies to which we were all so recently and so decisively pledged. At the same time, we were almost overwhelmed by the public reaction: first stupefaction, then shame and anger. Eden tells us that before Hoare set out for Paris,

[1] *Hansard*, 5 December 1935.
[2] Viscount Templewood, *Nine Troubled Years*, chs. xiii and xiv.
[3] The Earl of Avon, *The Eden Memoirs: Facing the Dictators*, ch. xvi.

he had warned his colleague against Laval. He had indeed recent and somewhat bitter experience at Geneva of his devious methods. Hoare replied that he need not worry: 'I shall not commit you to anything.'[1] Yet this was exactly what Hoare succeeded, consciously or unconsciously, in doing. On 7 December, two days after his successful but anodyne speech in the House, Hoare went for his skating holiday in Switzerland. He was in a poor state of health and in urgent need of rest. Unfortunately, he had agreed to break his journey in Paris for a discussion with Laval. He was joined by Vansittart, the Permanent Secretary at the Foreign Office. Vansittart was so obsessed by the fear of Germany that he was anxious to help the French and to prevent Italy lapsing finally into the German camp. By the afternoon of 8 December, Laval and Hoare had concocted a plan for a possible settlement of the Abyssinian problem. It conformed in broad outline to suggestions made in talks between Grandi and Vansittart on 3, 4, and 5 December. The plan in effect handed over two-thirds of Abyssinia to Italian control. The only advantage that Abyssinia was to receive in exchange was a corridor giving an outlet to the sea at Assab. But since it was not clear whether Abyssinia would be permitted even to build a railway along it, this proposal a few days later was blasted by *The Times*, with withering sarcasm, as a 'Corridor for Camels'. Unhappily, under strong pressure from Laval, Hoare not only agreed to, but initialled, the plan. This, Vansittart should never have allowed. At the same time Hoare agreed to a communiqué which stated explicitly that, although a formula had been agreed as a basis for a settlement, it could not be published because the British Government had not yet been informed of its terms. This was indeed a naïve expectation. As might have been assumed by anyone who had any experience of the normal procedure on such occasions, the story was leaked to the Press that same night. On the following morning, 9 December, the French newspapers carried accounts, broadly accurate, of the terms proposed. The official text did not reach Eden at the Foreign Office until the morning of the 9th, having been brought over from Paris by Maurice Peterson, who had for some weeks been discussing the possibilities of a settlement with his French counterpart, M. de

[1] The Earl of Avon, *The Eden Memoirs: Facing the Dictators*, p. 298.

St.-Quentin. Vansittart was still in Paris, trying to tie up any loose ends with Laval. Since he knew that the telephone was unsafe, he could say little to Eden. Hoare disappeared into the train *en route* for Switzerland and was incommunicado for many hours. The leakage in the French newspapers was of course at once taken up in the British Press. The evening papers had something of it and it was clear that in Tuesday's Press, 10 December, the whole story would hit the headlines.

The Cabinet, therefore, was in a serious quandary. It had to make a decision promptly. Hoare was unapproachable in his train; but before leaving he had telegraphed to his colleagues asking their approval for his plan. The Cabinet, therefore, had either to support their Foreign Secretary or disavow him. Yet he was not there to explain why he had acted in this way. The members of the Cabinet could hardly be blamed for presuming that he had some compelling reason for his action. Perhaps he had found Laval determined to retreat. Perhaps the French had refused to go on either with sanctions or with military support, if we found ourselves in difficulties in the Mediterranean. Perhaps Hoare felt that we had no choice unless we were to face war with Mussolini by ourselves. In any case, he was not there to explain and defend his decision. Such was Baldwin's kindness of heart and anxiety about Hoare's state of health that he did not summon him home. Baldwin felt afterwards that in this he had made a grave error.[1] But in any case, Hoare, who had arrived in Switzerland on the Monday, paid his first visit to the rink on Tuesday—the crucial day—only to fall on the ice and break his nose.[2] Even if Baldwin had recalled him, he would not have been allowed to travel for at least two days.[3] But I doubt whether his return would have made any difference. For once these proposals had been agreed with Laval, the real harm had been done. Laval had got his signature. He was not likely to let him or his colleagues off the hook. If we repudiated the plan, as we ultimately did, Laval could equally refuse to face the extension of sanctions, especially oil sanctions.

On Tuesday, 10 December, I was in the House of Commons at Question Time. The papers had carried sensational—and pretty

[1] A. W. Baldwin, *My Father: The True Story*, p. 290.
[2] The Earl of Avon, *The Eden Memoirs: Facing the Dictators*, p. 303.
[3] Viscount Templewood, *Nine Troubled Years*, p. 184.

accurate—accounts of the Hoare–Laval deal. Attlee, leading the Opposition, naturally asked a Private Notice question of the Prime Minister. Baldwin was in a most unhappy position. The Cabinet had heard for the first time of what Hoare had done on the previous day. The Cabinet meeting had taken place at 6 p.m. But little could be said to the House. Ministers had decided, under Eden's pressure, that the Hoare–Laval terms should at least be communicated immediately and simultaneously to Rome and Addis Ababa. But they could hardly throw over their Foreign Secretary in his absence. So Eden was instructed to 'recommend' the proposed agreement in both capitals. Hoare was not asked to return home and there seems to have been a vague hope that somehow the proposals, when reported to the League, might be improved.[1] None of this could the Prime Minister reveal. He therefore quite naturally took what refuge he could in saying that he had not examined the Press reports and no doubt there had been a leakage. He was very uneasy and showed it. (I can more readily sympathise with him now than then.) He was still imperfectly informed as to the proposed procedure regarding the Hoare–Laval plan, and the Cabinet had not reached a decision. After a number of questions from Attlee and Sinclair, Baldwin could only repeat that any plan must have the approval of the three parties: that is, the League, Italy, and Abyssinia. Since the Debate on the Address was not yet concluded, the Government was not able to avoid an immediate discussion. It had been agreed that the Liberal Amendment to the Address should be voted on about 7.30 p.m. that day. There followed at once a short but tense discussion upon the situation so far as it was now known. I sat through it all. I remember feeling a deep sympathy with Eden, who had to reply to the searching questions posed by Lees-Smith who opened for the Opposition. With great good humour and perfect self-possession, he managed in twenty minutes to do something to calm the growing excitement. But he could only repeat that France and Britain had been asked by the Council of the League to find a basis for negotiation, and that this had been done with the full knowledge and approval of all the members of the League. He said there were some inaccuracies, and important inaccuracies, in the

---

[1] The Earl of Avon, *The Eden Memoirs: Facing the Dictators*, p. 304.

version of the Hoare–Laval agreement published in the Press. He declared that the procedure as to what was to be done next had not been settled. He emphasised that the proposals did not necessarily represent the point of view of either the British or the French Governments, but were merely suggestions which might be helpful. He thus did his best to play down the whole affair. Looking back upon it, and knowing now the difficulties under which he laboured, it was an admirable performance. For in addition to the implications of the proposals themselves, which amounted to a complete sell-out to the aggressor, Laval was insisting that they should be communicated to Mussolini but not to the Emperor of Abyssinia. In other words, the criminal should be informed but not the victim. Laval tried to go further still. He was threatening that if we insisted on telling the Abyssinians, he would expect us to agree that any question of oil sanctions should be abandoned. Eden, who had to face all this pressure in Hoare's absence and with imperfect information of the language Hoare had used, made a robust answer. But he must have been shocked at the rapidity with which the blackmailer had begun to use the power that had been guilelessly put into his hands. All this, of course, was unknown to us. But it must have added to the burden which Eden was facing so gaily and so gallantly in public. After Eden, there were a number of speakers; but the House was so confused and puzzled that these were listened to with growing impatience. Everyone was waiting for the Prime Minister's reply. He rose at about a quarter to ten. Since it had been agreed that the debate should end at ten, he wisely left himself as little time as possible. The Opposition had announced that they would take the unusual course of voting against the Address. While disclaiming any discourtesy to His Majesty, it was the only means of entering a protest 'against the terrible crime that seems likely to be committed'.[1]

Baldwin did his best. 'My lips', he declared, 'are not yet unsealed. Were these troubles over I would make a case, and I guarantee that not a man would go into the Lobby against us.'[2] Nobody knew what

---

[1] *Hansard*, 10 December 1935.

[2] Ibid. Baldwin had used the phrase 'sealed lips' in another context in November 1933. Many will still remember the use that Low, the famous caricaturist, made of it—Baldwin was always represented with two pieces of sticking-plaster fixed across his mouth.

he meant then or later. Some thought that the mystery was the weakness of the British fleet. Some thought that Laval had fixed the whole plan with Mussolini in calculated betrayal of his British ally. According to Baldwin's son, he meant that he was morally sure that Laval had been bought by Mussolini, but could not very well say so.[1] For the rest of the time which he had somehow to fill, he could only philosophise in general about the difficulties of the League; the trickiness of the situation; the danger of war; and the weakness of human nature. We all had to learn our lesson from experience. Eden would be going to Geneva the next day and in due course we should find out more about all this. It was not very well done; but it was as well done as the circumstances allowed. He ended by saying—in the most matter-of-fact way—that he hoped the Division could be taken at once, so that the Government could conclude the Committee stage of the financial resolution on the Railway (Money) Bill and do this 'before we rise for Christmas, which we very much want to do'.[2] Baldwin's hopes were, in this respect, too sanguine. Before we rose for Christmas, the widespread revolt of the Government's supporters and the upsurge of public opinion on an unprecedented scale forced the Government to retreat, bag and baggage, and to abandon the Foreign Secretary in their hasty flight.

It was first decided that, in Hoare's absence, Eden should handle the situation as best he could. Laval continued to press his threat. He seemed confident that Mussolini would accept and that the Emperor would refuse the terms proposed. He therefore repeated his demand for an Anglo-French engagement that, if Abyssinia rejected the proposal, the oil sanctions would not be imposed. Eden was able to persuade the Cabinet that this was an impossible demand and the only thing to be done was to go to Geneva and take the line that the matter was entirely one for the League itself to settle. Although at first Baldwin had decided to face the storm, out of loyalty to his colleague, yet in the next few days the pressure was becoming irresistible. From all over the country there was mounting criticism. The Times led the attack with a series of caustic leading

[1] A. W. Baldwin, My Father: The True Story, p. 291.
[2] Hansard, 10 December 1935.

articles; and for Dawson to attack Baldwin was indeed like Brutus turning upon Caesar. Had the storm been confined to a vocal minority of Left-wing critics or fanatical supporters of the League, the Government no doubt could have ridden it out. But as the days passed, it became clear that the supporters of the Government, in and outside the House of Commons, were first puzzled, then indignant, and finally inflamed with genuine and searing anger. By the end of the week, Eden at Geneva had made it clear that the Government, without actually repudiating parentage, looked upon their child without affection and even with distaste. Over the weekend, including Monday, 16 December, when Hoare returned home, the inspired Press was taking the line that the Cabinet would meet the challenge and stand by the Foreign Secretary. Some of the younger members of the Cabinet—Walter Elliot, Oliver Stanley, Ormsby-Gore, and others (contemptuously called the 'Boys' Brigade' by Neville Chamberlain)—were pressing for Hoare's resignation. They appeared to be in close touch with *The Times*, and the agitation was fanned in the news, as well as in the views, columns of the paper. Up to Tuesday, 17 December, Baldwin had not finally made up his mind. But the revolt in the party had gone too far. There was a bitterness such as was afterwards only equalled in the weeks and months that followed Munich. Conservative Members whose views on politics were normally divergent came together in indignation. The Labour Party put down a motion, on which the debate was to take place, demanding the repudiation of the terms of the Hoare–Laval agreement. In reality, everybody agreed with the motion. But efforts were made on our side to find various alternative forms. The most popular was that in the name of General Spears and others, with which I was associated. It included among its first signatories Members of every different point of view. Yielding to a bad habit of those days, I wrote a letter to *The Times* from which I cannot forbear quoting certain passages:

Sir,—It must indeed be galling for the Prime Minister to reflect on the character of the limited support which his new foreign policy is receiving. In the House of Commons many members on the Government side are in open revolt; many more are anxious and distressed; the only whole-hearted supporters are to be found among the very men who for six years have been steadily engaged in fighting Mr. Baldwin's main policies and undermining his leadership. . . .

In this situation official and semi-official apologists are forecasting a debate in which the Prime Minister is to be given the ludicrous role of the Fat Boy in 'Pickwick', and to 'make our flesh creep' with all sorts of portentous prophecies of woe. It is to be hinted that our simple representatives have fallen victims to subtle Gallic wiles; that the French Government have refused to proceed with any further sanctions, especially the oil sanction, and have declined naval support in the event of this country and the League acting independently of France; finally, it is suggested that the Italian forces . . . might threaten with overwhelming disaster the whole embattled might of the British Empire.

. . . It may be true that we must face the failure or collapse of the League in its present form. That is no reason that we should help to undermine the very structure which a few weeks ago the nation authorized us to underpin.

I have never attended the funeral of a murdered man; but I take it that at such a ceremony some distinction is made between the mourners and the assassins.

This letter was published on 18 December, and widely reprinted or quoted in the rest of the Press, contrary to the ordinary custom.

The agitation continued to grow. Members supporting the Government could not reconcile themselves to so rapid a change of position so soon after the election. It is not cynical to say that, had this crisis risen three or four years later, Members might have found some justification in the changes in the situation during the interval. But their election speeches were still warm on their lips. They remembered the protestations of loyalty to the League and collective security, with which they had won the support of their constituents. Many of the most solid and respectable supporters of the Government felt outraged. They had been swindled; and if they were to toe the line now, they would feel guilty of having swindled those who voted for them.

The critical day was Tuesday the 17th, and the final blow was struck, as is so often the case, by the most respected Conservative back-bench Member—Austen Chamberlain, himself a former Foreign Secretary. Addressing a meeting of the Foreign Affairs Committee, which in effect was a meeting of almost all the back-bench Members of the party, he expressed the general view when he said that 'gentlemen do not behave in such a way'. That settled it. Hoare was forced to resign, and a few days later Eden was appointed in his place. Eden was not anxious to succeed him. He thought that the only way to restore the situation was that Austen Chamberlain should come back. He said this frankly to Baldwin. But Baldwin replied that Austen was too old and that he had told him so. Austen Chamberlain's own version of the conversation, which he told Eden the following day, was: 'He told me I was ga-ga.'[1] He may have been ga-ga. But he settled the fate of Hoare, and by his intervention convinced the Chief Whip that the game was up. Up to the day before the debate it was expected that Hoare would defend himself from the box as Foreign Secretary. Late on the night of Wednesday the 18th, his resignation was formally announced. Rightly or wrongly, the democratic processes in Parliament and outside had asserted themselves. It is rare for the public to intervene in a Parliamentary situation; but when it does, its force is generally decisive.

The announcement that the Government had made up their minds to jettison both the Foreign Secretary and presumably his policy naturally altered the whole character of the debate. Had they persisted, there is little doubt that they would have been faced with a degree of opposition in their own ranks which would have threatened their survival. Our able Chief Whip, David Margesson, who ruled the party by a combination of charm and military discipline, was under no illusion. With so large a majority, many risks can be taken. If the danger of abstention or a hostile vote had been confined to a few cranks like myself and some of my friends, he would have accepted it. But when anxiety and even anger spreads to the central body of the party, then there is nothing for it but to give in. The names on the various amendments, all demanding in one form or another the abandonment of the Hoare–Laval agreement, were conclusive in the Chief Whip's mind. Right, Centre, and Left of the party were equally disturbed. Only those few who were opponents of the whole concept of the League of Nations were triumphant. So poor Sam Hoare, who had returned to England but was still unable to leave his room owing to his accident and broken nose, had to be told that prudence, if not justice, required him to be the sacrifice. As

[1] The Earl of Avon, *The Eden Memoirs: Facing the Dictators*, p. 316.

always, Neville Chamberlain, whom Churchill had once described as the 'pack horse of the Government', was sent to do the job. The debate, although deprived of the excitement of an uncertain division at the conclusion, was not lacking in drama. In order to save the face of the Government, an 'unofficial' but inspired amendment to the Labour Party's motion of censure had been hastily concocted and put down in the name of Lord Winterton, who subsequently moved it in his own inimitable style. To this, it was clear that all the party would rally. Before the debate opened, Hoare made a personal explanation. It was generally agreed that he did this with dignity and success. He had rightly refused the proposal that he should apologise for his action and had insisted on resignation rather than recantation. Since the Cabinet would not stand by him, he was determined to make as an ex-Minister the defence which he would have made as a Minister. In this he was undoubtedly wise. He delivered a long speech, for nearly three-quarters of an hour, in unreserved and unrepentant justification of his actions. As a result, he cut the best figure of the day. He firmly refused to apologise or withdraw. He based his defence upon the danger of war and, above all, of a war in which Britain would find herself alone. He pointed out in an effective sentence that 'not a ship, not a machine, not a man has been moved by any other member State'.[1] This was in contrast to the military precautions which we had taken with the British fleet in the Mediterranean and the reinforcements in Egypt, Malta, and Aden. Yet in a sense he proved too much. His argument amounted to this. While sanctions were relatively ineffective, they were safe; as soon as they began to bite, they became too dangerous.

... up to the present this economic pressure has not brought us into the danger zone. Now that we are entering a new phase, I should not be candid with the House were I not to say that I believe we are entering upon a much more dangerous phase.[1]

Subsequent speakers were not slow to fasten upon the fundamental fallacy of this argument. Nor did Lord Winterton make it any better, when he came to speak, by declaring that 'if the imposition of oil sanctions led to armed resistance by Italy, it would not be

[1] *Hansard,* 19 December 1935.

in accord with the Government's election pledge'.[1] This was certainly not true. Hoare spoke firmly and effectively, but the logic of his argument was wholly contradictory to his speech at Geneva in September and the policy on which the Government had embarked with the enthusiastic support of the nation. He showed that in his heart he would have preferred the policy of satisfying the Italians, dividing Mussolini from Hitler and, if necessary, throwing Abyssinia to the wolves.

Hoare himself was a man who commanded at that time respect, if not affection. He had always proved an efficient Minister and, although his precise and rather mincing form of speech was uninspiring, his actual performances had been of a high Parliamentary order. In conducting the proposals for Indian reform over a long period—nearly four years—he had withstood the attacks both of the Right and of the Left. Faced with the formidable and persistent opposition of Churchill and his friends, he had nevertheless brought his measure to a successful conclusion, with infinite patience and considerable courage. At a later stage in the pre- and post-Munich period, he degenerated intellectually and morally, and became one of the worst and most sycophantic of Neville Chamberlain's advisers. But in December 1935 it seemed inconceivable how he had fallen into so grave an error of judgement and of tactics as to put his name to so dangerous a document. The true explanation is that he was following, consciously or unconsciously, a double policy—of the League on the one hand, and of appeasement of Italy on the other. Such a dualism was self-contradictory and bound to lead to disaster. He was certainly in a low state of health when he left for his holiday, and unfit for business—especially with so tricky a customer as Laval. His accident in Switzerland could not have been more unfortunately timed, for he was prevented from returning immediately the storm began to gather. Yet, since Hoare was a man of modest stature and a certain prim correctness of speech and behaviour, even his misfortunes had something ridiculous about them. Middle-aged Foreign Secretaries should not go skating; and there were naturally endless witticisms about the thinness of the ice on which he had chosen to practise his skill at this particular crisis.

[1] *Hansard*, 19 December 1935.

Nevertheless, with the generosity which Members always show to a fallen Minister, every speaker, however critical of his policies, showed a sympathy which was by no means merely conventional. I sat through the greater part of the debate and can still remember the impression that it made upon me. Attlee, who spoke after Hoare, had, in the circumstances, an easy task. He claimed with truth that practically the whole House was in support of the substance of his motion. He was quick to take up the point that the sanctions were beginning to have their effect and that was indeed their purpose. Why should they, therefore, be abandoned? They should be strengthened. If there were dangers, these should have been weighed before embarking upon the policy.

The Prime Minister spoke next. As usual, when in a difficulty, he displayed a remarkable power of 'evasive action'. First, he kept his speech short—about half an hour. Secondly, he made no attempt to defend what had happened. He began with a few generalisations and personal reminiscences, chiefly describing the cruel character of politics. He even recalled a Prime Minister, Lord Salisbury, whose friend, Lord Iddesleigh, suddenly fell down and died at his feet. He quoted a somewhat pedestrian observation which Lord Salisbury had made on that occasion in a letter to Lord Randolph Churchill, that 'politics was a cursed trade'. (I remember thinking this anecdote rather inappropriate and discouraging for Hoare.) He then went on frankly to admit dissatisfaction with his own conduct of this episode. He ought perhaps not to have allowed his friend to go to Paris for a difficult negotiation when he was in a low state of health. The liaison had broken down; he was not kept fully informed. In spite of his colleague's illness he ought immediately to have brought him back from Switzerland; this was an error of judgement on his part. He then proceeded to a number of reflections upon the disadvantages of the habit of personal discussions between Foreign Secretaries of different countries which had grown up since the war, instead of relying upon the old system of negotiation through Ambassadors. He went on to say that at no point had he or his colleagues felt any anxiety that they were not being true to the pledges given at the election. However, he admitted that these proposals had gone too far. He was not, therefore, surprised at the expression of feeling in the country; he was not expecting it, but it was a feeling based on grounds of conscience and honour.

The moment I am confronted with that I know that something has happened that has appealed to the deepest feelings of our countrymen, that some note has been struck that brings back from them a response from the depths. I examined again all that I had done, and I felt that with that feeling, which was perfectly obvious, there could not be the support in this country behind those proposals even as terms of negotiation. I felt that there could not be that volume of popular opinion which it is necessary to have in a democracy behind the Government in a matter so important as this.[1]

He added (since the House was becoming a little restive at this point):

It is perfectly obvious now that the proposals are absolutely and completely dead. This Government is certainly going to make no attempt to resurrect them. I might add this to what I have said about the feeling in the House and the country. If there arose a storm when I knew I was in the right I would let it break on me, and I would either survive it or break. If I felt after examination of myself that there was in that storm something which showed me that, however unconsciously, I had done something that was not wise or right, then I would bow to it.[1]

Once again, Baldwin followed his favourite technique. He 'owned up'. Once again, the House accepted this strange apologia. The rest of the debate, although of a high standard, was conducted in a fairly calm atmosphere. Austen Chamberlain, in the course of a fatherly contribution, pinned upon a sentence which Attlee had rather unwisely used in his attack on the Prime Minister. Attlee had said 'it is your honour which is at stake'. Austen Chamberlain replied that once this statement had been made, no Conservative would either abstain or vote against the Government. This is the kind of thing that worried supporters of a Government particularly welcome in a moment of anxiety.

It is unnecessary to recall, after so many years, all the arguments marshalled on that memorable day. Yet there was one emotion which was dominant, certainly on our side. In spite of Sir Austen's generous defence of his old colleague, it *was* a matter of honour. Harold

[1] *Hansard*, 19 December 1935.

Nicolson, who made a most effective speech, declared frankly that he had spent sleepless nights wondering whether in all honesty he could retain his seat. Those Members, he declared, who had only been returned by small majorities felt that they could not have succeeded, had any policy of this kind been announced at the time of the election. Had it not been for Hoare's resignation and Baldwin's frank confession, he would have felt it right to have returned his mandate to those who had voted for him by resigning his seat. This theme ran through the whole debate. But there was another which equally emerged, and which subsequently became more and more clear. In spite of the protestations of Ministers, in spite of the speeches of the Prime Minister and the Chancellor of the Exchequer, Neville Chamberlain, in winding up the debate, and in spite of the many uncertainties which remained, it seemed increasingly doubtful whether the League of Nations could survive the blow which had been dealt to its authority.

As the months passed, these doubts grew. Eden's appointment as Foreign Secretary in place of Hoare was well received, especially by the younger Members of the party. We had more confidence in him than in any other member of the Government. But the injury had been done. Although our honour as a nation had been saved by the successful revolt of the Conservative Party and of the public, our usefulness in the crisis was injured beyond repair. Eden did his best. But the policy of sanctions gradually faded. Oil sanctions were never in fact applied and, even if they had been, were probably by now too late. Within a few months, the Italian campaign was successful. At the beginning of May, the Emperor fled from Addis Ababa to a dignified exile in England. On 9 May 1936 Mussolini formally announced Italy's annexation of Abyssinia and the title of Emperor was transferred to the less impressive head of the King of Italy.

It is easier, thirty years later, to form a fair assessment of what seemed, at the time, an almost inexplicable change of front. It is now clear that Hoare, as indeed he says in his own reminiscences, was taken aback by the degree of enthusiasm excited by his Geneva speech in September 1935. Nor did he realise the effect throughout the world made by the immediate and impressive reinforcement of the Mediterranean fleet. Influenced, no doubt, by his anxieties about Germany and his determination, if at all possible, to separate Mussolini from Hitler, he regarded his speech and our military action partly as a bluff and partly as an incentive to the Duce to think hard about the offer which the Committee of Five were soon to make; an offer different in degree but not in kind from that contained in the Hoare–Laval proposals.[1]

Neville Chamberlain's part is not clear and the evidence is conflicting. But he seems to have been very much in line with Eden in November and early December, in pressing for the application of oil sanctions, partly to impress the Americans and Germans, and partly in the hope that the failure of one dictator would have its effect upon the other.

Eden was always in favour of going ahead at Geneva. He was not frightened by Mussolini's threats or of the alarms about a possible 'mad-dog' act upon Malta or on the British fleet. He did not believe that Mussolini would go to war if oil sanctions were imposed. He thought that he would be much more likely to find some method of withdrawing.

Baldwin felt that the great gain of the General Election was the mandate for rearmament. He was not going to risk anything which might involve war, for he knew as well as any man the weakness of our defences. He was not going to take a chance with Italy, any more than he was subsequently prepared to hazard a showdown over Hitler's remilitarisation of the Rhineland. He was no doubt impressed by the arguments that, in view of the dangers from Japan, we could not afford to risk the loss of any capital ships in the Mediterranean.

It is also clear that the Cabinet did not really consider the Hoare–Laval plan and had certainly not discussed it before Hoare left for Paris. Had they really been convinced by the views urged by Vansittart in private and Amery in public, they would not have been surprised and disgusted at the proposals when they first heard of them. At the same time, Ministers must have been aware of Laval's

[1] The Committee of Five had been appointed by the Council of the League early in September, to try to find a solution of the Abyssinian problem. Britain, France, Spain, Poland, and Turkey were the members. The Spanish representative, Señor de Madariaga, was elected to the chair.

hesitations. The secret staff conversations between France and Italy earlier in the year were also known. The enormous advantages to the military strength of France of a friendly Italy were fully appreciated. It is probable, therefore, that, as so often happens, the Cabinet fell between two stools. They would not go ahead and risk trouble with Mussolini and they were ashamed to go backwards and make a deal with him. The irony of it all was that it is almost certain that the Emperor would not have accepted the plan; it is not even clear whether Mussolini would have done so. Oil sanctions applied in the autumn might have been successful, but by the turn of the year the Italians had sufficient stocks to conduct at least a short campaign. The Germans naturally pursued an ambivalent policy. They made a significant denial of exports of raw materials to Italy and to this extent fell in with the sanctions policy. They were waiting to see, no doubt, which way the cat would jump. Had Mussolini suffered even a minor rebuff, still more, had he been forced to abandon the Abyssinian venture, it would no doubt have had a great effect on Hitler's mind. As the months passed, and the failure of British and French policy became apparent, Hitler was in touch with Rome and undoubtedly obtained Mussolini's acquiescence in the remilitarisation of the Rhineland, contrary to the Locarno Treaty which he had solemnly promised to observe.

It is perhaps worth recalling that both the British and French military assessments of the course of the Abyssinian war were wrong. It was thought that the Italians would not be able to conquer the country at least until the spring of 1937, by which time even comparatively mild sanctions would have had their effect on the Italian economy. If we had given sufficient arms to Abyssinia, this calculation might have been borne out. Even so, more devastating than guns or machine-guns was the use of gas. Since the Abyssinians normally fought barefoot, the gas caused them terrible sufferings and practically immobilised them as a result of burns. One whole army formation had to surrender in this condition. In any event, the moment of decision soon passed. By the time the Experts Committee reported on further sanctions, the remilitarisation of the Rhineland was imminent. Before reaching any decision about imposing oil sanctions on Italy, the French Government wanted to know what the British would do about sanctions on Germany. This major crisis nearer home, far more dangerous to the peace of the world, took, therefore, first place in the Government's mind. After the fall of Addis Ababa, it was thought best to bring the sorry story to an end as quickly as possible.

The situation to which Eden succeeded at the end of 1935 was certainly an unhappy one. All his efforts to galvanise the Committee of the League of Nations into effective action proved fruitless. At an earlier stage, he had fought strongly in the Cabinet for the imposition of oil sanctions and had set out his views in a Minute which he has since published. Had he been in authority then, a stronger policy might well have been followed. 'By early December, most member states of the League had said they would support the embargo if others did likewise, and President Roosevelt was trying to put pressure on the American oil companies not to increase their exports to Italy.'[1] Thirty years later, he has confirmed this opinion:

My own belief was, and remains, that a firm policy would have compelled Mussolini to negotiate for terms which the Emperor could have accepted, such as those proposed by the Committee of Five at Geneva. This would have immeasurably increased the League's authority, and have been a salutary warning to Hitler.[2]

How different might have been the unfolding of world events had this opportunity not been missed. In effect, the story of the Abyssinian débâcle is simply, as so often, a failure of will on the part of the Government of the day, combined with a vacillation between two opposing policies, either of which might have brought safety.

In the first months of 1936 Eden found himself confronted by Flandin, who had succeeded both to Laval's position and to his ambivalent policies. The situation was disintegrating rapidly, but even the final stages were marked with a singular lack of dignity. On 10 June Neville Chamberlain, addressing a Conservative political club, referred to the policy of continued or intensified sanctions as 'the very midsummer of madness. . . . Is it not apparent that the policy of sanctions involves, I do not say war, but a risk of war? . . .' Thus the Government's policy appeared to be announced not in the House

[1] The Earl of Avon, *The Eden Memoirs: Facing the Dictators*, p. 295.　[2] Ibid., p. 296.

of Commons by the Prime Minister or the Foreign Secretary, but by a speech of the Chancellor of the Exchequer at a party function. At the time, Chamberlain apologised to Eden for his lapse and Eden accepted his assurance with his customary courtesy and good humour. We now know from Chamberlain's diary that his action was deliberate. 'I did not consult Anthony Eden, because he would have been bound to beg me not to say what I proposed.'[1] The effect upon the House of Commons was, of course, explosive. The next day Attlee asked a Private Notice question about Chamberlain's declaration and the Prime Minister, who no doubt was as surprised as anybody else, had to wriggle out of it as best he could.

On 18 June a fierce debate took place. Eden did his best to defend the Government's decision and asked the House to face the fact that sanctions had failed to achieve the purpose for which they were imposed. Abyssinia had been conquered and resistance was practically at an end. Distasteful and indeed dangerous as was the situation, it must be faced. Other matters even more urgent called for the attention of all the peace-loving nations. This was followed by a memorable and indeed overwhelming attack by Lloyd George. He treated Eden more in sorrow than in anger, although he permitted himself a contrast with his predecessor who, he said, 'when his policy was thrown over, had the decency to resign'.[2] He then put in a biting sarcasm against Hoare who, after an adulatory speech about the Prime Minister a few weeks before, had been brought back into the Government as First Lord of the Admiralty, much to the distaste of many Government supporters. He said this:

It is true that he [Hoare] had a reassurance that he would be brought back after a period of quarantine, and when he comes back he finds the wind tempered to the bleating lamb.[2]

Lloyd George went on to say these terrible words in his most formidable tones:

I have been in this House very nearly half-a-century. . . . I have never before heard a British Minister, one holding the most important position in the Government next to the Prime Minister at the present moment, come down

[1] Keith Feiling, *Life of Neville Chamberlain*, p. 296.   [2] *Hansard*, 18 June 1936.

to the House of Commons and say that Britain was beaten, Britain and her Empire beaten, and that we must abandon an enterprise we had taken in hand.[1]

His most powerful blows were reserved for Baldwin. He quoted the Prime Minister's speech to the Peace Society: 'Let your aim be resolute and your footsteps firm and certain.' He went on to make devastating play with these words.

Here is the resolute aim; here is the certain footstep—running away ... this speech, which was delivered on the eve of the Election, was delivered to assure the world that we stand by our pledges. Only a few weeks after the Election was over, they were negotiating treachery to their pledges. Fifty nations ranged themselves behind that torch. They said, 'Here is the British Prime Minister, with the greatest Empire in the world marching; we will range ourselves behind him.' The Abyssinians believed it; the vast majority of the people of this country believed it. The Government had not been in for more than a few weeks before that torch was dimmed. To-night it is quenched—with a hiss; a hiss that will be re-echoed throughout the whole world.[1]

Nobody who heard it can ever forget the extraordinary power and scorn, enhanced by the Welsh intonation into which he always fell in moments of excitement, of the word 'hiss'. He ended by turning on Neville Chamberlain and quoted his election speech, and his words reflected on Chamberlain's recent assumption of the right to announce the Government's foreign policy.

The speech of the Chancellor of the Exchequer has been quoted. I am going to do myself the honour of reading a part of it again. The right hon. Gentleman is heir to the throne and recently he has been trying the crown on to see how it fits. I hope for his own sake that it does not. He has not merely tried the crown on. He has wielded the sceptre—which is just the sort of thing that heirs do when there are weak monarchs. The right hon. Gentleman said at the last election:

'The choice before us is whether we shall make a last effort at Geneva for peace and security or whether by a cowardly surrender we shall break all the promises we have made and hold ourselves up to the shame of our children and their children's children.'

To-night we have had the cowardly surrender, and *there* are the cowards.[1]

Churchill is on record as having described this speech as one of the greatest Parliamentary performances of all time. It certainly had a demoralising effect on the Treasury bench. On that day the Prime

[1] *Hansard*, 18 June 1936.

Minister seemed seriously shaken. But the practical arguments for abandoning this enterprise were now very strong, and when the formal vote of censure was moved on 23 June, the party as a whole was reconciled to the inevitable. Simon, to whom the main defence was entrusted, made a brilliant forensic reply, and incidentally seized upon an unlucky statement into which Lloyd George had been led, declaring that the people of this country would never be prepared to go to war in an Austrian quarrel. This dangerous, and wholly irrelevant, observation was symptomatic of a certain deterioration of Lloyd George and his grasp of the situation. His attitude on the Rhineland issue was weak. Only a few months later he was foolish enough to make a visit to Hitler and fell, temporarily at any rate, a victim to his fascination.

Nevertheless, whatever the logic of the case, I found myself personally in a very unhappy situation. I had fought the election, trusting to the Government's determination to stop Mussolini. While on home affairs I had stood upon my own programme, for which I claimed a full liberty of action and on which I had received the support of my constituents, on this foreign issue I had felt able to trust myself without hesitation to the Government's robust pledges. I did not now see how I could honourably go back upon those who had voted for me. Nor did one of my closest friends at this time, Vyvyan Adams. We therefore both took the serious step, not merely of abstaining on a motion of censure but voting in the Opposition lobby. To do this on such an occasion means that one must face at least a temporary disassociation from the official party machine. The Chief Whip, who always treated me with generous consideration, made no move. Indeed, it was intimated to me that there would be no attempt to deprive me of the Whip. I thought, however, that it was more honourable in the circumstances to take the decision myself. After some reflection, therefore, I wrote the following letter to the Prime Minister:

29th June, 1936.

Dear Prime Minister,

In view of my vote following upon the Foreign Affairs debate on Tuesday, June 23rd, I feel that some explanation is due to you, more especially because of the many kindnesses you have shown to me personally.

At the last General Election, I made it quite clear to my constituents that while I would give general support to the National Government, I would also pursue, by speech and vote, the special policies to which I was personally pledged.

Although I am still in favour of a National Government in these difficult times, and shall probably be found in the great majority of cases in the Government Lobby, there are some issues that have arisen or seem likely to arise, upon which I am unable to give the Government the support which it has, perhaps, the right to expect from those receiving the Government Whip. It occurs to me, therefore, that it would perhaps be more satisfactory if I was no longer regarded as being among the official supporters of the present administration.

> Yours sincerely,
> Harold Macmillan

to which I received the following formal reply:

> 7th July, 1936

My dear Macmillan,

I have received your letter telling me that you feel unable any longer to receive the National Government Whip. I regret this decision which you have thought it necessary to take.

> Yours sincerely,
> Stanley Baldwin

My constituents, however, did not show any marked dissatisfaction and rallied to my support. I held a meeting in my constituency which the local Press described as resulting in 'enthusiastic scenes, reminiscent of those which marked the announcement of his return to Parliament at the last election'. I did not in any way try to apologise for my action, nor to minimise the mounting dangers. In thanking the meeting for their support I said:

On the lead we give depends, in my view, not only the future of this country, but the whole future of civilised society, its religion, order, Christianity, progress, liberty, and all the things that all care for without distinction of creed or party, and things for which many of our comrades died, and for which many of us would be proud to give our lives now.

In the light of subsequent events these words do not appear to have been an overstatement.

I received a very large number of letters expressing sympathy and

approval and one is perhaps worth recalling. It was from Maynard
Keynes, who observed with characteristic sympathy:

I have been interested, but not surprised to hear that you are now refusing
the Government Whip. I wonder how that will end. If you go so far as that, it
probably means that under the surface you are feeling moved towards something
more considerable. I think that our states of mind towards politics may not be
dissimilar and I should like sometime to have a talk about it.

This was followed by many discussions, which proved very helpful
to me on the next stage of my journey—the preparation of an
ambitious book on the economic and political situation.

In order to make the story complete, I should perhaps add that in
1937, when Baldwin retired and Neville Chamberlain became Prime
Minister, I asked for the Whip again, which was readily granted to
me. Chamberlain took the occasion to write a friendly letter in the
following terms:

I was very glad to learn from your letter . . . that while you would wish to
preserve that latitude which has always been allowed to individual members of
the Conservative Party, you would like now again to receive the Government
Whip. I agree with you that you can render greater service to the cause we both
have at heart if you are enrolled in the ranks of the official supporters of the
Government, and I shall be very pleased to see you once more taking your place
among them.

From what I knew of him, I was persuaded that he would pursue a
more robust policy than his predecessor. Like many others, I was
doomed to disappointment.

Meanwhile, in the spring of 1936, a mortal blow was struck at
Western security and power. Hitler gave the order for the military
reoccupation, on 7 March, of the Rhineland territory. Although this
event did not cause any marked alarm in Britain, and gave rise to
little Parliamentary or political emotion, it had in reality a far
greater significance and far larger consequences than the Abyssinian
question, which was the subject of such prolonged and such bitter
disputes. It is difficult, perhaps, to realise today just what was
involved. Under Articles 42, 43, and 44 of the Versailles Treaty a
'demilitarised zone' had been set up, and it was laid down that
Germany should not have fortifications or military establishments or

military forces of any kind, either on the left bank of the Rhine or in a zone covering an area fifty kilometres from its right bank. In addition, in this zone no manœuvres should be held; nor should there be any facilities for military mobilisation. These provisions, of vital importance to France, did not, however, depend only on the now discredited Treaty of Versailles. Hitler could not claim them as part of the so-called *Diktat*. For they had been specifically confirmed and re-enacted by the Treaty of Locarno to which Germany had freely adhered. Hitler had declared over and over again that he would scrupulously respect treaties to which Germany had voluntarily acceded.

There was no doubt, therefore, that from the moral point of view the remilitarisation of the Rhineland was a flagrant breach of faith. Under the terms of the Locarno Treaty it was 'an unprovoked act of aggression', requiring immediate counteraction. Such a violation should be brought immediately before the League of Nations and the League was bound to advise the signatory Powers to give aid to the Power against whom the offence had been committed. For the results, both tactical and strategic, of Germany's action were formidable. So long as the Rhineland was unfortified, the reaction of the French against German aggression in any part of Europe could be swift and decisive; an attack could be launched at the very vitals of Germany. But once German troops had reoccupied and, still more important, refortified the Rhineland, the initiative passed from the Western Allies to the Nazi dictator. A new Hindenburg Line could be built, and indeed began to be built immediately. We had the bitter experience of the First War to remind us of the strength of such defences and the terrible cost in human life, as well as in time, necessary to overcome them.

Whatever may have been the British Government's private concern, it did not appear from their public statements that they had fully grasped the political and military significance of Hitler's coup. Public opinion was uncertain and confused. A popular view was that the Germans had a right to enter, in Lord Lothian's phrase, 'into their own back garden'. In the House of Commons, nearly all my friends, whether on the Right or on the Left of politics, seemed comparatively undisturbed. Lloyd George's 'Council of Action' passed a resolution comparing Hitler's breach of the Treaty of Versailles with the failure of the Allied Governments to disarm, thus altogether leaving out of account the breach of the subsequent Treaty of Locarno. I protested strongly against this. Indeed, except in very limited circles, there was no realisation of the fact that Hitler's action, if allowed to stand, would prove one of the turning-points in history. For it would face the Western Allies, within a very few years, with the grim alternative of surrender to aggression in many parts of Europe, or war under the worst possible conditions. In due course Germany would be able to threaten Central and Eastern Europe without fear of any effective French military measures. The countries which had been grouped under French leadership would be automatically cut off from France's support. As the 'barrier across Germany's front-door'[1] became increasingly fortified, the power of Britain and France to assist Austria and Czechoslovakia in 1938, or Poland in 1939, became correspondingly hampered and reduced. The advice, if any, given by the Chiefs of Staff has not yet been revealed. But there are detailed versions of the Rhineland crisis, written by two of the protagonists—Churchill, who as a private Member had neither authority nor responsibility, and Eden, the recently appointed Foreign Secretary. Broadly speaking, Eden explains and approves the inaction of the British Government; Churchill regards it as the final and fatal step which made war inevitable. According to Eden, the French, in spite of their pro-testations, had made no effective military plans to deal with the situation. Yet even without general mobilisation, the French Army should have been able to seize important points in the zone and in due course to have ejected any German troops and re-established a French occupation. As we now know, the German Army was in no condition to put up any prolonged resistance and, in the event of strong French pressure, the German generals would have forced Hitler to retreat. Unhappily, neither in the Government nor in the High Command did the will match the means. An alternative would have been a counter-occupation of the Saar; but Eden—probably rightly—believed that world opinion would be hostile—an important, but not a conclusive argument in a matter, as this was,

[1] Winston Churchill, *Hansard*, 26 March 1936.

of life and death. Eden is of course right in saying that British opinion would have viewed with disapproval and even alarm a French entry into the Rhineland to throw out the German forces. Such an operation, particularly 'if blood had flowed', might have fatally weakened the Anglo-French alliance. These are strong arguments. Nevertheless, I feel that if the French had acted rapidly and energetically, Britain would have been forced to follow. Eden no doubt is right in the final sentence of his summary:

What I now believe to be true is that the French and Belgian Governments did not at the time have sufficient support in their public opinions to allow them to use effective force and that, being democracies, they could not have acted without it, even if they had wished to do so.[1]

It is hard to see how this differs from the defence, two years later, of the Munich surrender. Yet military action, difficult and hazardous in 1938 after the building of Germany's defences in the Rhineland, would have been easy and successful in 1936.

In marked contrast to the discussions concerning Mussolini's venture in Abyssinia, the debates in the House of Commons were feeble and lifeless. Many Conservatives even objected to the one outcome of this tragic affair which Eden was able to secure—staff talks between France and Britain. It was known that some of the members of the Government, especially Simon (now Chancellor of the Exchequer) and Kingsley Wood (an important figure, particularly in the Methodist world), were averse to anything so reminiscent of the years before the Great War. Tom Jones records in his diary a meeting of leading personalities who revolved round the so-called 'Cliveden Group',[2] the conclusions of which were pitifully weak. Those gathered included Arnold Toynbee, who 'has just returned from a visit to Germany. . . . He had an interview with Hitler which lasted one-and-three-quarter hours. He is convinced of his sincerity in desiring peace in Europe and close friendship with England. . . .'[3] The Times leader, entitled 'A Chance to Rebuild', apparently accepting at its face value the new offer of a non-aggression pact—the normal accompaniment to the latest act of aggression—had a

[1] The Earl of Avon, The Eden Memoirs: Facing the Dictators, p. 354.
[2] Thomas Jones, A Diary with Letters, 1931–1950, pp. 179–80.   [3] Ibid., p. 181.

particularly depressing effect. If British opinion was confused, French views, as reflected in the French Cabinet, were hesitant and fumbling. Only four Cabinet Ministers were in favour of military action.[1] No plan of any kind existed. Mobilisation was thought politically impossible a few weeks before a General Election. These and other excuses were made by some of the French. Indeed, when Hitler made his decision, he found both the French and the British Governments already beginning to be mesmerised, partly by the consciousness of their own defective armaments and partly by the overwhelming desire for peace at almost any price by which both their countries were still dominated.

Hitler had chosen his moment well. As usual, the prelude to his aggression was one of studied calm. Relations between Great Britain, France, and Italy had been severely strained in recent months. Yet Hitler had made no move. Even the final ratification at the end of February of the Franco-Soviet Treaty caused no immediate reaction. In an interview with *Le Matin* at the end of this month, Hitler breathed friendship and conciliation.[2] So favourable seemed the mood that the French Ambassador in Berlin asked for a discussion of a general Franco-German *détente*. On 6 March Eden, as Foreign Secretary, made a proposal to the German Ambassador in London for an 'air Locarno'.[2] Yet on the very next day the German troops marched. Hitler had already learnt of the British and the growing French habit of stopping work from Friday to Monday. On this occasion, as so often later, he acted on Saturday. At the same time as he was guilty of this unblushing breach of international obligations, with his usual deviousness he proposed to the Western Ambassadors all kinds of mitigating plans for the future. These included a demilitarisation of an area on both sides of the Rhine (which, incidentally, would have dismantled all the elaborate French defences created at such immense cost). He also proposed a pact limiting air forces; and the usual non-aggression pacts with eastern and western neighbours. Most important of all, he offered to rejoin the League. This technique of covering hard and brutal deeds by soft and insinuating words was Hitler's favourite method. Even by

---

[1] The Earl of Avon, *The Eden Memoirs: Facing the Dictators*, p. 347.
[2] C. L. Mowat, *Britain Between the Wars, 1918–1940*, p. 564.

now we should have been suspicious. But right up to the end many worthy people fell for it, especially ecclesiastics and journalists. They had forgotten or never heard of the old Russian proverb: 'What you do speaks so loudly that I cannot hear what you say.'

It is unnecessary now to recall at length the various manœuvres in this affair: the hurrying of French Ministers to London; the formal appeal to the League and the complaints to the Council; the Council meetings in London and Paris; the condemnation of German action by the Council; and all the restless comings and goings of Ministers and diplomats which accompany an international crisis. All these have been faithfully and accurately described by Eden, who was busily engaged with these empty gestures. The Allied efforts ended in nothing. 'Staff talks' were the best that Eden could obtain and, so far as Britain was concerned, these proved somewhat perfunctory. Indeed, there was very little for the staffs to talk about except to deplore the futility of shutting the stable door after the horse had bolted. In the event, the remilitarisation of the Rhineland, which seemed to British opinion a minor, almost trivial, event, proved decisive. It was the stone which started the avalanche destined to engulf, in its devastating path, the whole world.

I should doubtless have shared the general complacency of public opinion had I not by now come to be more frequently in Churchill's company. Some of the reactions were certainly strange. Neville Chamberlain would have offered a colony to Germany to save peace. Lloyd George declared that there was 'provocation', which explained, if it did not altogether excuse, Hitler. Lord Snowden, the old Socialist leader, was impressed by Hitler's peace offer and begged that it should not be ignored. But Churchill saw the truth with unerring instinct. If the Germans were allowed to perfect great defences along the Rhine, they became free to commit aggression in Eastern and Central Europe to their heart's content. All Europe—certainly all Central and Eastern Europe—would fall into their hands. So it was to be. The same mistake as to the strategic importance of vital military positions was to be committed two years later at Munich, although on a smaller scale. Chamberlain did not seem to realise that the Czechs were not merely being asked to give up a few square miles of territory. They were being forced to abandon a well-fortified and defensible line, of great natural strength. Once this was gone they had lost everything, and Czechoslovakia was doomed. Tom Jones records a talk with Baldwin about this time:

'He had kept the country out of war' was a recurring thought. 'For three days I had terrible anxiety when Germany re-entered the demilitarized zone, and there were people clamouring that we should occupy the Rhineland.'[1]

Churchill did his best, in and out of Parliament. He has described how he tried to persuade Flandin, the French Foreign Minister, to stand firm.[2] Laval had fallen from office earlier in the year and Flandin had taken his place as Foreign Minister. I remember well meeting him on two occasions. The first was at a luncheon party arranged by General Spears. The second was at a dinner given by Churchill on the same night. At both gatherings Flandin certainly talked very big, and declared with apparent sincerity that if England would give the lead, all Europe would follow. Now was the last chance. If Germany was not stopped now, there would be no hope of holding her later. I was impressed by the man and his large and powerful figure. But I do remember even then a feeling that there was something wrong about him. He protested too much. He even tried a degree of blackmail, for he argued that if England would not now come out and stop Germany, France would be forced to adopt a pro-German policy. He hinted that he would not himself disapprove of this. Churchill wanted to believe in Flandin and did his best to stimulate him. But I had the feeling that he was slightly taken in by him. After all, it was for France to take the lead, and Britain would have had to follow. It is quite true that a British Government with more vision and determination would have encouraged the French. On reflection, I have a feeling that Flandin was not unwilling to escape by putting the blame on us. At any rate there was no sign that the French would act. Even at the Churchill dinner, when the discussion was frank and protracted, Flandin was appealing all the time for Britain to take the initiative. Nevertheless, these meetings and talks with Churchill affected me deeply. Unable to speak in the

[1] Thomas Jones, *A Diary with Letters, 1931–1950*, pp. 206–7.
[2] Winston Churchill, *The Second World War*, vol. i: *The Gathering Storm*, pp. 153–4.

debate, I contributed an article to a newspaper, which expressed my doubts and fears.

The nation as a whole has remained quite calm. In London, there have been 'rumours of war'; in the provinces, there has been a scarcely ruffled surface.

This is not altogether healthy. There is a tendency to exaggerate dangers in one part of the body politic; in another, there is a tendency to underrate them.

The national instinct, however, is the more correct, so far as the present crisis is concerned. There will be no war—now.

But will there be a comprehensive settlement which will establish Peace for a generation? Or will there be an armistice only—an interval of nervous and feverish competition in armaments, which must inevitably lead to war in two or three years' time? That is the real question which will be settled during the next few weeks. London is rightly nervous, if this great issue is paramount in our minds.

We have an uneasy conscience about Germany. We are not happy about the Treaty of Versailles. We are not happy about our policy since the Treaty.

Much as we abominate many aspects of Nazi mentality, we ask ourselves how far we are responsible.

We remember what we refused to Liberal Germany, and have been forced to allow to Totalitarian Germany. We remember the humiliations of Stresemann and Brüning; and we wonder how far we have been responsible for the triumphs of Hitler.

Nor can we shuffle off all this responsibility upon the French people or upon French Governments. It was difficult—perhaps impossible—for them to take the lead.

It was hard for them to make concessions. That duty lay upon us; and we have shirked it.

The main responsibility falls upon two men—and they cannot evade it. For nearly 13 years this country has been governed—either jointly or singly—by Mr. Baldwin and Mr. MacDonald. Just as they have shirked the social and economic problems—so that we find ourselves to-day almost at the top of an industrial boom with two million men unemployed and (according to Sir John Orr) nearly half our population undernourished—so they have shirked the foreign problem. They have drifted. They have thought things would 'settle themselves' if they were left alone. They have applied no strong and forceful direction to our policy.

They have elevated inactivity into a principle and feebleness into a virtue.

That is the tragic feature of the present crisis. There will be no war now.

But unless a settlement is made now—a settlement which can only be made by a vigorous lead from this country—there will be war in 1940 or 1941.

And unless there is a new European system built now—a system of peace, the acid test of which is the principle of declared armaments, internationally inspected and supervised, based upon agreements upon territorial and economic questions—we shall have a period of frantic re-armament, with intense jealousy and rivalry, which will inevitably lead to war.

This crisis is 'Agadir'; unless it is handled with immense courage and determination, 1914 will follow.

The country is calm. I fear it may be a false and deceptive mood.

For we must face these issues now. If Germany is sincere in her protestations about Peace, let us build the new Peace system now. If she refuses reasonable terms of an accommodation, and is proved to be insincere, let us coerce her now —while she is relatively weak—instead of waiting till 1940 or 1941, when she will be immensely strong.

Drift is fatal—and drift is the habit which these two statesmen—the Prime Minister and the Lord President—seem to have adopted as a policy—almost a creed.

Let us either settle with Germany now, or coerce her now. But don't let us purchase an uncertain peace at a terrible price to be paid later.[1]

I reproduce these words—written so long ago—not because of their intrinsic value, but because they represent what I (and some others) felt at the time. The sense of guilt about Versailles and our treatment of Germany is, of course, exaggerated. But it was almost universal. At any rate, the demand either to settle with Germany or to coerce her, to make peace or war, was practical. Failure to do either brought disaster.

Action taken at this moment might well have led to the fall of Hitler and prevented a second war. We have only to think of all that has flowed from that war to realise how tragic was the decision to be indecisive. With different men in charge—Barthou or Churchill—all this might have been averted. Yet perhaps this is to attribute too much influence to personalities. The mood of the people in Britain and throughout the Commonwealth was for peace at almost any cost. To some extent, this defeatism was mingled with true idealism; to some extent it was exhibitionism. We have seen the same symptoms repeat themselves after the Second War; young men and women

[1] *The Star*, 20 March 1936.

lying on the ground to protest against 'the Bomb'; university students debating their willingness to fight for their country. There is, alas, this difference. America's isolationism and persistent refusal to play any part in Europe; her abandonment of the League; the Johnson Act of 1934, followed by the neutrality legislation in 1935 —both destined to render more difficult the rearmament of the democratic States; the unwillingness to make any gesture to help: all these added to Britain's difficulties. Still, the decision lay then in our hands. Now that the American people have taken from us the main burden, we cannot but admire the thoroughness with which they have learnt the lesson of these years.

When the crisis was over, or rather postponed, Hitler proceeded to fortify the Rhineland with all possible speed, and at the same time to rearm on a prodigious scale. The British Government also took an important decision. Baldwin had at last yielded to the view that a single Minister should be made responsible for the co-ordination of defence. The appointment was the subject of wide speculation. Many names were put forward—Neville Chamberlain, Kingsley Wood, Swinton, Runciman, and others, including Hoare. An important debate on defence had taken place just before the Rhineland crisis. Hoare had spoken, from the back-benches; and, in the words of Chamberlain's diary, had made a curiously distasteful bid for office.

He began well but shocked the House at the end of his speech by an elaborate tribute to S.B. which sounded like an obvious and clumsy bid for power and created a thoroughly bad impression. . . .[1]

Prior to 7 March, there had been a strong and growing demand for Churchill. However, it appears that, as a result of Hitler's act of aggression, it was felt in Government circles that we must not do anything which would upset him. Neville Chamberlain's diary makes this clear.

The events of the weekend (occupation of the Rhineland by Hitler) afforded an excellent reason for discarding both Winston and Sam since both had European reputations which might make it dangerous to add them to the Cabinet at a critical moment. Inskip would create no jealousies. He would excite no enthusiasm but he would involve us in no fresh perplexities.[1]

[1] Iain Macleod, *Neville Chamberlain*, p. 193.

So, for this vital post, the choice fell upon Sir Thomas Inskip, the Solicitor-General. This gentleman was an adequate lawyer and an agreeable Parliamentary figure, popular and easy-going, but without military or administrative experience. Nor had he the slightest glimmer of that ruthless determination, by which alone such an office could have been made effective at such a time. Churchill describes the Prime Minister's choice as having been received 'with astonishment by Press and public'.[1] Astonishment is almost an understatement. Even the most defeatist and most adulatory of the Prime Minister's fans were aghast. The common phrase was that there had been nothing like it since Caligula made his horse Consul.

Meanwhile, under Eden's pressure, the Franco-British understanding drew somewhat nearer to a military alliance. Britain reaffirmed her obligations to France and Belgium under the Treaty of Locarno. Staff conversations were authorised. Formal letters were exchanged. It is perhaps the best comment on the value of these empty gestures that within a few months Belgium, at her own request, abandoned the Locarno protection and thought it more prudent to revert to the status of a neutral.

These critical months had a great effect upon me and my outlook. I determined to pursue with even greater effort my work for internal reforms, economic and social. Only, it seemed to me, by renewed attacks on the evils of unemployment and poverty, and the development of fairer economic conditions, could we find the strength and unity of purpose which the nation needed. At the same time, I was soon drawn more and more into the efforts which Churchill was making to unite Conservatives, trades unionists, Liberals—and indeed all those who believed in collective resistance—into a single movement.

The success of the two dictators, Mussolini in Abyssinia and Hitler in the Rhineland, added correspondingly to their prestige. Mussolini had audaciously flaunted the authority of the League—fifty nations led by one, as the British had boasted in their first enthusiasm following Hoare's dynamic lead in September 1935. As a result, an altogether fictitious estimate of the real power of Italy was current. It is true that for many years the Duce's diplomacy was

[1] Winston Churchill, *The Second World War*, vol. i: *The Gathering Storm*, p. 156.

assisted by maintaining an efficient spy system within the British Embassy. Telegrams and papers of all sorts, including a pessimistic military appreciation of the Far Eastern situation,[1] went straight from the Ambassador's desk or waste-paper basket to the Palazzo Chigi. At a later stage, the presence of Lady Chamberlain, Sir Austen's widow, as a visitor in Rome, was to add to the dangers of misunderstanding. Unlike her distinguished husband, Lady Chamberlain had fallen victim to the fascination of Fascism and held a firm belief in the benefit to the human race of Mussolini's work and character. After Eden's resignation as Foreign Secretary the Italian Government did not have to rely only on espionage. 'Appeasement' became more and more open. If Mussolini's position was largely bluff and, as was to be proved, unable to stand the harsh strains and stresses of war, the ground which Hitler had gained was substantial and growing daily firmer. The building of the defensive lines in the Rhineland area was pressed forward through the remainder of 1936 and 1937. By the spring of 1938, Hitler was ready to pounce again. In this perilous situation a number of unhappy distractions occupied public opinion at home and in France, which diverted the attention of Governments, Parliaments, and peoples from the true dangers with which they were menaced.

Among the most disruptive of these was the Spanish Civil War. For some three years, successive British and French Governments struggled with this problem. As was to be expected, the dictators sought only to advance their own interests, regardless of the sufferings of the Spanish people. Equally, the Russian Government, although they may have seen advantages in prolonging the conflict, felt committed to support their own side in an ideological war. Only the British and French Governments tried to mitigate the cruelties of the conflict and at least to confine the fighting to Spaniards. If the forces of the leading European nations were, without restraint, to use Spain as a convenient arena in which to fight out their own battles, general war in Europe seemed inevitable. From the point of view of British interests, therefore, Eden was right to support the policy of non-intervention when it was proposed to him by Léon Blum. It has

[1] Hugh Gibson (ed.), *The Ciano Diaries, 1939–43* (New York, 1946), p. 95, 8 June 1939.

been stated, but on rather slender authority, that Blum, the French Prime Minister, in the course of a visit to London in July 1936, tried to persuade the British Government to intervene on the side of the Republicans on two grounds: first, that they were the legitimate Government of Spain and, secondly, that they were friendly to Britain and France.[1] Blum never made this complaint himself, and Eden makes it clear that it is groundless.[2] Léon Blum and his Ministers in the Popular Front Government were well aware that any open intervention would be most dangerous for France. It would aggravate the division of the French people into two bitterly hostile sections and greatly impede the military preparations so urgently needed to meet the growing German danger. Moreover, open intervention by the European Powers, as opposed to covert assistance or the dispatch of volunteers, would make a general European war almost certain. The internal position of France was already precarious. The forces of the Right and of the Left glared at each other with growing hatred. Many Frenchmen of the Right nurtured for the French Left feelings of bitterness and loathing which they did not feel against the Germans. 'Better Hitler than Blum' was already a slogan of reaction. At the same time, the Popular Front, which was itself a coalition of parties, although sympathetic to the Spanish Republicans, would itself have been divided by any proposal for overt intervention. Eden, in the absence of Baldwin, who was more or less out of action through ill health during the autumn months of 1936, rightly decided to support the French Government in their 'non-intervention' policy and worked throughout in absolute loyalty with his friend Blum. There was another reason, perhaps more compelling but not so easily stated in public, for trying to stem any general flow of arms into Spain. If they were to be supplied to both sides, undoubtedly the Spanish rebels would do better than the legal Government. For by this time the arms production of Germany was on a formidable scale. Even Italy had quite a lot to spare. Anything given from French or British arsenals would have been to diminish still further their exiguous resources.

[1] John W. Wheeler-Bennett, *Munich: Prologue to Tragedy* (London, 1948), p. 260, gives this as a statement of M. Louis Lévy, described as an intimate of M. Blum.

[2] The Earl of Avon, *The Eden Memoirs: Facing the Dictators*, pp. 401 ff.

The avoidance of open intervention and thus almost certainly open war was clearly right. No issue could have been a worse one than this on which to challenge the dictators: both French and British opinion divided in sympathy; both largely unarmed and having recently consented, by their acceptance of the Rhineland coup, to a fearful enhancement of Germany's offensive and defensive strength. Eden also, as a student of history, was well aware that if the conflict could be circumscribed and if open intervention could be avoided, it was very unlikely that, even if Franco finally triumphed, he would feel himself under any particular obligation to Hitler or Mussolini for the assistance that they were able to give, either by arms or volunteers. He had not forgotten the Duke of Wellington's famous dictum after his experience in the Peninsular War. 'There is no country in Europe', the Duke had declared, 'in the affairs of which foreigners can interfere with so little advantage as Spain.' So fierce is the pride and so burning the patriotism of the Spanish people that even if one of their greatest benefactors were to claim any return at the expense of Spain's honour and integrity, the whole nation would at once unite in passionate resistance. Perhaps the most serious danger from the point of view of Britain and France was the possibility of some cessions of military strongpoints, at least temporarily, in the course of the conflict. The Balearic and the Canary Islands were the likely points of danger. Indeed, it looked as if the Italians would be able to entrench themselves, at least for a time, in the Balearics. But, as it turned out, Spanish sentiment would not allow the smallest concession.

Eden believed that except for the ideological satisfaction of having destroyed a Left-wing Government in Spain, neither Germany nor Italy would obtain any substantial advantage. In reaching this conclusion, he undoubtedly took a big risk. In view of the Prime Minister's almost complete detachment from foreign affairs at this time, he took it almost alone. There were of course to be some anxious moments later. Yet it is remarkable how accurate Eden's forecast proved. Even after the fall of France in 1940, an event which could not have been foreseen in 1936 and 1937, Franco resisted the temptations that were spread before him.

The policy of non-intervention was, therefore, clearly in the

interests both of France and of Britain. Unfortunately, the impossibility of making non-intervention effective during the long-
drawn-out war had a disastrous effect upon the public opinion and
the morale of both France and Britain. Bitterness in France grew to
a point hardly equalled in the history of the Republic. Blum and his
Government found it more and more difficult to maintain their
policy of closing the frontier to arms and volunteers and were unable
to resist the pressure to send some assistance to the Spanish Government. The Communist demands grew, and with them the corresponding anger of the Right. All this led to a steady deterioration of
the French economic situation, and a virtual standstill in the
rearmament programme. Nevertheless, it was alleged that without
any regard for the urgent needs of the French Air Force, with its
stock of increasingly obsolete or obsolescent machines, planes and
equipment were being secretly delivered to the Spanish Government. These accusations of the French Right played into the
dictators' hands, and provided Germany and Italy with an excuse
for sending their own matching supplies. Out of this exchange
Franco gained substantially, and France was weakened and divided.

In Britain, as the Civil War continued with unabated fury,
Left-wing opinion began to move away from its earlier support of
non-intervention. Strangely enough, the Labour and Left-wing
politicians, who for many years had violently opposed any form of
British rearmament, were now clamouring for the delivery of arms
to Spain. Many young men—by no means all with Socialist sympathies—joined the International Brigade to support the Spanish
Government, and fought heroically for their faith. Equally, some
Conservatives, especially Roman Catholics, were moved by the
appalling atrocities committed against priests, monks, and nuns to
join the rebels. Thus, something like a 'crisis of opinion'[1] was
produced in Britain. At a time when national unity was essential, the
Spanish Civil War was a cause of sharp division. Although many
Labour leaders inside and outside Parliament continued to feel that
the Government's policy was the only one practicable, yet a degree
of bitterness and class-consciousness developed to an extent of
which I certainly had no previous experience. Outside Parliament,

[1] C. L. Mowat, *Britain Between the Wars, 1918–1940*, p. 577.

divergent movements were organised to help one side or the other. A formidable campaign of propaganda and pamphleteering was begun. Yet in England, as in Spain, there were some strange contradictions. The Civil War was not, as many declared, the result of outside pressures, either Fascist or Communist. It was purely Spanish. Its roots lay deep in Spanish character and history. Yet the old regional and provincial divisions of Spain resulted in an extra-ordinary and often paradoxical confusion. For instance, the Basque Provinces—Catholic, Conservative, and highly nationalistic—sup-ported the Republicans whom they must have regarded as atheists or anarchists. Similarly, in our divisions at home, one of the most powerful pamphleteers and organisers for the Spanish Government was the Duchess of Atholl, who had recently held office in the Conservative Government and still sat in Parliament as a strong Unionist. Thus the Red Duchess matched the Red Dean.[1] All these emotions were violent and fierce at the time. Curiously enough, they have also proved lasting. Thirty years have passed. The Franco Government is stable and in full control. British people flock to Spain for their holidays in ever-increasing numbers. Yet it is still regarded as normal for Labour Governments to insult the Spanish Government in every possible way, regardless of the inconveniences and injuries which Spain can so easily inflict on a much-weakened Britain.

Thus, in these fateful years, not only was public opinion both in France and in Britain deeply divided, but the attention of Govern-ments, of Parliaments, Press, and the public was distracted from the real dangers immediately ahead. I remember Churchill talking to me with great fervour on this aspect of the Spanish question. He decided to declare himself neutral, for his eye was on the real enemy. In my small way, I took the same course. One further by-product followed soon. In spite of the blatant disregard for his obligations so recently shown by Mussolini, Eden had, under pressure from his colleagues, accepted the so-called 'Gentleman's Agreement' with Italy at the end of 1936.[2] He was soon to learn from the development of affairs in Spain that this declaration of amity and co-operation in

---

[1] The Dean of Canterbury, Hewlett Johnson, first became notorious at this time.
[2] The Earl of Avon, *The Eden Memoirs: Facing the Dictators*, bk. ii, ch. vi.

the Mediterranean was in fact valueless. Yet, if Eden's policy failed, in the sense that arms and volunteers were sent to both sides by Germany, Italy, and Russia, it had some temporary success which brought him great credit. In the autumn of 1937 the British and French asserted themselves against the open piracy being carried out by submarines of 'unknown' origin. At the Nyon Conference, summoned by the two Governments, they were able to enforce their plans for the patrolling of the sea by their navies. Mussolini did not like it, nor did Hitler; but by successful manœuvring, Eden forced both to fall into line. The result of Nyon was the one set-back that the dictators suffered. The spectacle of an Anglo-French fleet of eighty destroyers sweeping the Mediterranean, and of the Duce later asking to be allowed to join in hunting his own submarines, gave a good deal of pleasure to many individuals and countries who were heartily sick of continual retreats.

To sum up, Eden led the British Government to the right decision on the larger issue. With British and French deficiencies in armaments to be made up, especially in the air, involvement in the Spanish war would have been madness. His conviction that, even if Franco won, he would not be likely to show any great gratitude to the dictators, was to be proved well-founded. Mussolini no doubt regarded intervention as a matter of 'face' and, of course, with his jackal mind, hoped for some loot. Hitler, more far-seeing and more cunning, saw every advantage in keeping the Spanish cauldron on the boil. Too quick or too complete a victory for Franco was not his wish. If the tensions—internal and external—caused by the Spanish Civil War could be prolonged, France and Britain would certainly be weakened and perhaps ultimately embroiled. Germany could then act against Austria and Czechoslovakia in 1938. We now know that this argument was put by the Führer to his Foreign Secretary and Chiefs of Staff in November 1937.[1] In any event, France and Britain could be kept divided in temper and feeling. Their indignation could be turned inwards upon themselves, while the Führer was spinning fresh designs and hatching new plots for the mastery of the world.

If the Spanish Civil War served for nearly three years as a major

[1] *Documents on German Foreign Policy*, Series D, vol. i (London, 1949), pp. 29–39.

distraction from the imminent dangers which threatened the peace of Europe, another problem for a short but vital period occupied the minds of the Prime Minister and the Cabinet. This was caused by the desire of the King, Edward VIII, to embark upon a marriage which would be likely to provoke a grave constitutional crisis.

The whole of this sad story has been told at length by the Duke of Windsor himself and by other leading figures, or their biographers. I had known the Prince of Wales at Oxford; in the regiment; in Canada, where he made a splendidly successful visit when I was on the Governor-General's staff; and from occasional meetings in subsequent years. But mine was an acquaintance, not a friendship. Neither I nor my wife moved in his intimate circle. Thus I only knew by hearsay the rumours that began to spread in the summer and autumn of 1936. Before and after his accession to the throne, the King's clear sympathy for his suffering fellow-countrymen in the distressed areas had struck a responsive note in the hearts of many of his subjects. I personally rejoiced at his outspoken comments. For instance, in January 1929, he had openly shown his sincerity and depth of feeling during his visit to Durham as Prince of Wales. Shortly before the Abdication, during a tour of South Wales, on being greeted by the long lines of the unemployed miners, he had said, more than once and with marked emotion, 'Something must be done'. All this endeared him to a large section of his subjects; although, perhaps, it was not altogether popular in official circles. Nevertheless, when the crisis came, there was no doubt that the Prime Minister and the Government had the strong support of the country, as well as of the Governments and peoples of the Dominions, in insisting on the impossibility of the King's marriage with a woman who had two living husbands. The King himself recognised this. If such words are not patronising or impertinent, he behaved throughout correctly and honourably. At no point did he insist on any course which might be unacceptable to his peoples. The idea of morganatic marriage was at one moment proposed. When it was found not to be feasible, the King at once abandoned the project.

In later years I have had many meetings, both as Foreign Secretary and as Prime Minister, with the Duke of Windsor. His charm remains undiminished, as well as the affection which he commands from all who have known him. But at this stage in my story what I have to recall is some of the immediate and consequential effects of the royal crisis. For apart from the personal problems involved, grave injury was done to the public interest from a wider point of view. During many weeks—the whole of the late summer and autumn—the Prime Minister and his leading colleagues were almost exclusively concerned with this delicate and painful situation. Although the public crisis was very short, since the news of the King's intentions only broke on 2 December and the Abdication took place on 11 December, yet Ministers were occupied with the complications and distractions of this affair at a vital period. Baldwin, whose Parliamentary position had been gravely impaired by the defence debates in the spring, had been resting for some months. For this reason, he was of little use to Eden during the Spanish troubles. But his masterly handling of the King's affair wholly restored his prestige, in Parliament, in the country, and throughout the Commonwealth. Here, indeed, was a matter upon which his special talents and his lovable personality had their full play. The King's problem was, as it were, a supreme 'family' problem. Nobody could handle this kind of thing more skilfully or more sympathetically than Baldwin, or with a surer touch. When, after a few weeks' suspense, the matter was finally settled and the Duke of York had been proclaimed King as George VI, the monarchy, although shaken, was not seriously injured. The new King and Queen soon endeared themselves to all their peoples and won their respect and affection.

By an unlucky mischance, the Abdication crisis came to a head at a critical moment in our affairs at home. Churchill's movement, for 'a great drawing-together of men and women of all Parties . . . who saw the perils of the future, and were resolute upon practical measures to secure our safety and the cause of freedom', had been successfully launched. He had christened his policy 'Arms and the Covenant'. On 3 December a great meeting was held at the Albert Hall. It was attended by Conservatives of the Right (like Lord Lloyd), Conservatives of the Left (like myself), the leading figures in the League of Nations Union, the representatives of many trades unions, and Sir Archibald Sinclair, leader of the Liberal Party. Sir Walter Citrine, Secretary of the T.U.C., took the chair. This tremendous gathering might have proved a turning-point. All the forces which Churchill had called together might have succeeded in shaking the already weakened position of the Prime Minister. We might have been able to force a change of policy or of Government or of both. Alas! by a tragic coincidence, the meeting took place at the very moment when the Abdication crisis was upon us.[1] In the Albert Hall, Churchill said a few words of sympathy for the King. Subsequently, in the House of Commons, he pleaded for time and deliberation. He joined with others of the King's friends to see whether some way out could not be found, possibly by a morganatic marriage. He did not disguise his anxieties from the House. But his intervention was ill received. I well remember the universal hostility shown to him from every quarter—Conservatives, Socialists, and Liberals. It was known that the King, with the approval of the Prime Minister, had consulted Churchill, who remained in contact with him during those anxious days. Churchill himself was amazed and staggered by the opposition—even anger—which he aroused in the House of Commons. However, being Churchill, this only confirmed him in his determination. He continued to plead for 'patience and delay'.[2] But Parliament and the nation were against him. His personality, which was just emerging from a long period of shadow into the light of power, was once more darkened. Public confidence in his judgement was shaken. All the effect of the Albert Hall meeting was destroyed—first by the Abdication and secondly by the catastrophic fall in Churchill's prestige.

It was not possible to restore the situation. Baldwin's authority was immensely strengthened and Churchill's fallen almost to nothing. Baldwin remained in power until after the Coronation in May 1937, when he handed over to Neville Chamberlain. Six precious months were therefore wasted, while the man who was later to be the saviour of his country remained mistrusted and impotent. It was said at the time that Churchill's action was inspired

---

[1] The first news about the King's affair was published on 2 December. The Albert Hall meeting was on 3 December.

[2] Winston Churchill, *The Second World War*, vol. i: *The Gathering Storm*, p. 171.

by the hope that out of the confusion caused by the Royal troubles he might be able to overthrow the Baldwin Government and seize the power which he knew he alone could use to avert or, if necessary, to wage war. This was the common view, encouraged by Baldwin's friends and Churchill's enemies. It has since been repeated by many writers of memoirs and history. From what I knew of Churchill then, I did not believe it to be so. From what I was to learn about him during the next thirty years, I am certain that it is wholly false. What seemed to some a weakness, but to many the most attractive feature of Churchill's character, was his magnanimity. His heart went out, instinctively, to anyone in trouble. In the case of a King, this involved not merely deep respect for the Throne, but personal affection and loyalty to the Monarch, such as inspired the cavaliers of old days. To use his own words:

> I had known King Edward VIII since he was a child, and had in 1910 as Home Secretary read out to a wonderful assembly the Proclamation creating him Prince of Wales at Carnarvon Castle. I felt bound to place my personal loyalty to him upon the highest plane.[1]

This is a true description of the motives by which he was actuated during these anxious days. He was not thinking of a political intrigue to overthrow the administration. He was thinking of the duty which he felt a subject owed to his King—an obligation which the King's difficulties enhanced rather than diminished. Nevertheless, Churchill's motives were not understood in a less romantic age. The old prejudices against him were revived, and old suspicions were confirmed. All this was a deep injury to the State.

Thus the Abdication, apart from all the regrets and difficulties and perils involved, caused a fatal distraction of the Government from the main dangers ahead; confirmed an enfeebled Prime Minister in power for another five months; and undermined the reputation and political stature of the greatest and most prescient statesman then living.

[1] Winston Churchill, *The Second World War*, vol. i: *The Gathering Storm*, p. 171.

CHAPTER SIXTEEN

The Middle Way

THE year 1936 began sadly for me and my family. My father died at the end of March. Had he lived another few weeks he would have been eighty-three. Although the last few years of his life were clouded by serious illness, he remained almost to the end full of interest in the world and its doings. Two or three years before his death he began to lose his sight, becoming almost totally blind. All his life he had been a great reader. Yet he bore this hard deprivation of his chief pleasure very patiently. We were able to make arrangements for him to be read to during a great part of the day. When my children were at home for the holidays, he specially liked them to read aloud to him. My father was a great lover of Walter Scott, particularly the Scottish novels. Like many old men, he preferred to stick to what he knew to be good rather than experiment with the unknown. I think it would be true to say that he read his favourites through every year. We sometimes used to chaff him about this. One day when I went in to see him towards evening in his London house and inquired how he had spent the day, he made me this sad confession: 'I am bound to admit', he said, 'that parts of Scott read aloud sometimes seem rather prolix.' His death in the end came easily and quietly. But it was none the less a terrible shock to us all, the more so because of the loving and patient understanding and support, utterly reliable and completely unselfish, that he had so long given to his family. To my mother it was a shattering blow. Even her indomitable courage was quenched. She had almost lost the will to live. Less than eighteen months later she died in Sussex. I was in America, but hastened back when I heard that she had had a fall and was seriously ill. Happily, I got home in time to see her for the few unforgettable days that remained. My father and mother are both buried in the same grave in the quiet churchyard of our parish church, St. Giles, Horsted Keynes. My mother was in her eighty-second year.

To both my father and mother, in their different ways, I owe everything in my life. They were tolerant of follies and untiring in anything that could give their children pleasure or help in their advancement. Mine was the only family of grandchildren and my parents naturally took a special delight in the next generation. Although my father devoted all his life to business and private affairs, he encouraged my mother to take part in public activities of various kinds. Thus she was one of the founders and for many years honorary treasurer of the Victoria League. My father, although shy and reserved, was beloved by all who knew him. His judgement was sound, and his industry untiring. My mother, more impulsive, in a sense perhaps more ambitious, not for herself but for her children, retained till her death an almost passionate interest in the drama of life. Her own life, from her first decision to leave her small provincial home in Indiana in the 1870s, had been something of an adventure. My political career up to date must have been, in a sense, a disappointment to her, for the course that I had chosen to follow was not one likely to lead to office or preferment. Nevertheless, she fully sympathised with the general ideas which I was trying to promote. Although not wholly understanding the arguments and emotions by which I was swayed, she had a great faith, almost a superstitious faith, in my ultimate success. She was persuaded that it would all come right in the end. Her death deprived me of a rock-like, unshakeable support. Since neither of my brothers had any family, it was arranged that the Sussex house, after her death, should come to me. During my father and mother's lifetime, my wife and children spent a great part of the year there. It had become our true home. My mother's impress upon the house that she built and largely designed, the garden that she laid out, and the woods that she planted are all about me as I write. Some of the older employees are the boys she found and befriended. Although—or perhaps because—she had very exacting standards, she was always well served, and those who worked for her had not only respect but affection for her. Here, during the many years that have followed, I have often been conscious of her presence and, in times of difficulty or uncertainty, of her encouragement.

My father's death in March 1936 had been preceded, a few weeks before, by the death of George Macmillan, the son of my great-uncle Alexander, and one of the three partners of the second generation. Both he and my father had ceased to be actively concerned for the last two or three years, but up till that time had been continuously engaged in the publishing business. The third and senior partner was my uncle Sir Frederick Macmillan. He remained in perfect health until a few months before his death at the age of eighty-four. Unlike my father, he was what would now be called an extrovert. He loved friends and good company, gaiety, sport, and games. But he by no means neglected his business. He came every day; as the years grew on him, a little later in the morning, but always an hour or so before lunch, where he presided over the daily meeting of the partners. Although he gradually handed over the executive management to my brother Daniel and myself, he was able to devolve authority upon us, while retaining full knowledge of what was going on. Thus his advice, always wise, was readily available and welcome. He had an unrivalled knowledge of the book trade, in which he had worked for seventy years. His balanced and sensible judgement was of immense service to us and to the firm. Up to the end you would have thought him a man of sixty. Every morning he rode in the park before coming to the office. He would, I feel sure, have lived several years longer but for an accident which in those days was almost fatal. On the day that he was coming to Sussex for my father's funeral he slipped in his room and broke his hip. He rallied, and I was able to see him, still jaunty and full of interest in affairs. But he died in June, only two months after my father.

The death of the three senior partners and chief proprietors of our family business within a period of four months naturally threw a very heavy burden upon my brother and me. As regards day-to-day management, there was little difficulty, for we were already in active and effective control. But there were many complications such as necessarily follow the effect of death–duties on the transfer or purchase of shares. Even at the more modest rates of that time, my brother and I had many anxious discussions as to whether it would be possible to preserve a private and family concern. Naturally, when a business has been built up from nothing, without any outside capital, fed and sustained only by prudence and self-sacrifice—in other words, by continually reinvested profits—there are few liquid resources to meet the heavy taxation involved by the deaths of virtually all the owners. At that time, however, the duties were not completely punitive. After much thought, my brother and I decided that somehow or other we would be able to scrape together enough to pay the sums required, and retain the business in the family hands. Now, of course, a private business (or 'closed company' as it is called) has attracted the most unfavourable attention of the powers that be. What was once a virtue—to save and reinvest—is now penalised with special impositions.

I never regretted our decision. The chief burden, during the Second War and when I was in office, fell upon my devoted brother, Daniel, who was to me throughout his life a protecting and loving friend. Whenever I have been out of office I have tried to help. When I finally retired from politics in 1963, I came back, as soon as my health allowed, to give what assistance I could.

Much, therefore, of my time and energy in these years—1936 to 1938—was taken up with family and business affairs. Nevertheless, I stuck to my political work. My own children were beginning to grow up and had started their schooling. We lived largely in Sussex and after my mother's death in 1937 moved there altogether, giving up the London house where we had lived since our marriage. I was young then, and there always seemed to be time for everything. I had plenty of energy and enthusiasm. Great as were the pressures upon me for private obligations, I had then the strength to fulfil my public duties at Westminster and in the constituency, as well as the general political activities in which I was engaged.

There was much to be done at home. If war proved inevitable, we could still construct a society, neither Communist nor Fascist, united in its purpose, and with a sense of confidence in its ability to control at least a part of its destinies. For the next two and a half years, therefore, I devoted myself mainly, as in the previous Parliament, to economic and industrial questions. My friendship with Churchill kept me informed concerning developments in the field of defence and the growing German menace. Gradually, as I became persuaded that the foreign crisis was deepening and that we were drifting either to a shameful surrender, or to a war for which we were ill prepared, my interest in the internal reconstruction began to decline, except as an instrument for increasing our strength to meet external dangers. The turning-point, of course, was Munich. From that time all doubts ceased. Only one question then remained: under what circumstances and at what precise moment would the clash come.

All the time which I could spare from business was divided into three main activities. First, the continuation of work with other political groups with which I had become connected. Secondly, speeches in Parliament and talks in the country, together with newspaper articles and the like. Thirdly, my determination to write another and more ambitious book as a sequel to *Reconstruction*.

After much discussion, in the middle of February 1936 the Next Five Years Group was re-formed as a definite organisation, not as a new party but as a pressure group. In the Press announcement, it was made clear that it would be mainly concerned with the publication of further literature and other forms of propaganda. It was described as 'an association of persons belonging to all political parties and to none, who have found themselves in substantial agreement as to a practical programme of action for the immediate future'. In addition to occasional publications, the Group would undertake research, set up committees for consultation with other organisations, arrange meetings and lectures, and deputations to Ministers and local authorities. It was not intended to create a large rank-and-file membership to compete with existing parties or organisations, like the League of Nations Union. Lord Allen was the chairman; Mr. Barratt Brown, then Principal of Ruskin College, acted as honorary secretary. I was one of the joint honorary treasurers.

The working committee consisted chiefly of those who had been on the drafting committee of the original publication. There was much discussion amongst us as to whether we could produce a weekly or monthly periodical. In my experience there is nothing which causes so many difficulties and so much friction as when a number of amateurs try to enter in the exacting field of newspaper, periodical, or book publishing. We were not spared conflicts of opinion, and they were perhaps symptomatic of a divergence of view that was bound to develop among so varied a team. However, after many anxieties, a sufficient sum was collected for the publication of a monthly journal entitled *The New Outlook*. It was first issued in June 1936 and ran for something like a year. It was not a profitable undertaking, but it served its purpose. I do not regret all the time and labour devoted to it.

Meanwhile, differences began to develop as to the function of the Next Five Years Group. I became more and more anxious that the Group should make some practical contributions in view of the growing political dangers. Ours was not the only group in existence. There was still Lloyd George's organisation, the Council of Action, which had given support to many of my friends and myself at the recent election. There were also other bodies. Should we try to make some link with them and jointly exert effective pressure upon the Government? Lord Allen was doubtful of the wisdom of this course. He was particularly hostile to any question of collaboration with Lloyd George. Nevertheless, the success of the French Popular Front in the spring of 1936 did not go unnoticed in Britain. Should we not launch some kind of Popular Front, wide enough to embrace Progressive Conservatives, Radicals, Liberals, and those members of the Socialist Party who were prepared to work for a limited objective? Lord Allen, probably rightly, preferred to see the Next Five Years Group remain academic and educative. I wished it to enter the field of current politics, now so confused and almost desperate for leadership.

These problems might not have been at all serious had it not been for our success in launching *The New Outlook*. Since this was a journal, it had to have a view on what was now becoming an urgent political question. In the event, after long and amicable discussions, Lord Allen, Barratt Brown, Arthur Salter, and I were charged with devising a scheme of reorganisation. A plan was agreed by all; and *The New Outlook* was officially separated from the Next Five Years Group. Each was to pursue its own path, though many of our leading members supported both. *The New Outlook* suggested a five-point programme as follows: a clear policy of collective security; the abolition of the means test; strong action in the distressed areas; a willingness to reduce tariffs; considerable extension of public control over industry, extending in some cases to public ownership. In support of such a programme, we could see our way to rallying just the kind of people who had been sympathetic to the ideas embodied in *The Next Five Years*.

But as the months passed it became clear that the Next Five Years Group could not do much more along the old lines. It produced in February 1937 a booklet called *A Programme of Priorities*, which gave us a text for much speaking, pamphleteering, and formed the basis for articles and letters in the Press. Yet such groups and movements, in the continual changes of the political atmosphere, cannot live indefinitely. When they have served their purpose, they should not linger on. It was therefore thought best to wind up the Next Five Years Group, which was done formally on 25 November 1937.

Looking back on the work of the N.F.Y. Group, it is strange to read now proposals which seem today so commonplace and at that time appeared—to orthodox politicians on both flanks—so subversive. For instance, the compromise on the question of individualism and socialism was as follows:

The historic controversy between individualism and socialism—between the idea of a wholly competitive capitalistic system and one of State ownership, regulation and control—appears largely beside the mark, if regarded with a realistic appreciation of immediate needs. For it is clear that our actual system will in any case be a mixed one for many years to come; our economy will comprise, with great variety of degree and method, both direct State ownership and control, and management by public and semi-public concerns, and also a sphere in which private competitive enterprise will continue within a framework of appropriate public regulation.[1]

This 'middle way', which commended itself to such a divergent but

[1] *The Next Five Years*, p. 5.

distinguished body of men at that time, was equally shocking to official Conservative and Labour opinion. It seems, however, to have worked out pretty well.

I continued until the end of 1937 to work for combined political action. But the organisations available were not strong enough to carry to fruition any effective plan. The Council of Action began to fade out as Lloyd George realised that it could not succeed in overthrowing the Government or even in influencing it. In addition, many of us were dismayed by his visit to Hitler in September 1936–a strange and disturbing episode. Other bodies such as the Industrial Christian Fellowship were too vague for any political purpose. The People's Front Propaganda Committee was almost wholly Left-wing, and not very business-like. So, not unnaturally, by the end of 1937 these various movements, whether academic or political in a narrower sense, were nearing their end. Their multiplicity was a symptom of the growing sense of impotence and almost despair which pervaded the whole nation. Later on, Lord Allen himself seemed to be led into strange illusions about Germany. With his high idealism and undaunted courage, he was persuaded that he could mediate between our two countries. Thus, by 1938, we had drifted apart. His motives, like those of many others, were of the very highest; but it seemed to me that what he was trying to do was impracticable, and even dangerous. The idea of 'appeasement' began to dominate his mind. Like Chamberlain, he thought that some arrangement could be made by a four-Power conference to avoid war. To that effort he devoted the last months of his fragile life. His death early in 1939, after Munich but before the seizure of Prague, although it deprived the world of a selfless and noble spirit, at least spared him the torture of disillusionment.

As the years passed, the House of Commons became increasingly concerned with the claims of rearmament and European anxieties. Nevertheless, there was a continuing interest in economic, industrial, and social problems. Although there had been a marked recovery in trade in recent years, for which the Government was entitled to claim credit, the underlying weaknesses remained. Unemployment had fallen, but only to just below two million. Underemployment was widespread. The special areas showed some improvement, but were still in every sense of the word 'distressed'.

Poverty and, in many cases, undernourishment, although largely hidden, were well known to all social workers. If something had been accomplished, much remained to be done. The Chancellor of the Exchequer up till Baldwin's resignation in May 1937 was Neville Chamberlain, whose approach was more flexible than that of his successor, Simon, of whom it might be said that his logical mind, starting from false premises, arrived unerringly at the wrong conclusion. The writings of leading economists were now more generally studied by Members of Parliament, although they found difficulty in disentangling the essentials from the mass of complicated jargon which was more and more coming into fashion. There was even formed in the autumn of 1936, as a result of a movement of a number of Members, both of the Right and Left of the party, a powerful group to study monetary questions. It was therefore possible to deploy an argument, without losing the attention of the House, on lines which would have been hardly intelligible four or five years before.

During this period, however, I was chiefly engaged in trying to write a book in which I could develop the general theme which had occupied my mind for some years past. I therefore seldom attempted, until this was accomplished, to speak on these large questions of principle. I contented myself with intervening from time to time in the minor but important issues which arose. Nevertheless, as a kind of preliminary to the work in which I was mainly to be engaged, I spoke in May 1936 in the debate on the Finance Bill. In this speech I did my best to set out a kind of popular version of some of Keynes's ideas (to whom, of course, I paid full tribute), as well as some thoughts of my own. Having done this, not without some effect, I did not return to this theme until two years later when my book was finished. But I tried to keep my idea alive from time to time in various forms: by articles in serious journals; by addresses to many different organisations; by talks to Rotary Clubs or chambers of commerce, or, occasionally, by letters to the newspapers.

In the long discussions at this time as to the part that public works should play in stimulating the economy, insufficient attention was paid to the many months that it takes 'to turn the tap on', even should the need for some measure of reflation be recognised. All these kinds of schemes, whether local or national, require considerable preparation. They cannot be improvised. We were soon to learn this in respect of armaments—the long period between the decision to expand and the result. But 'the years that the locusts have eaten' apply equally to civil projects. I made, therefore, a continual plea that, apart from the view that might be taken as to the financial and economic justification for large policies on public works, at least plans should be ready so that we should not be caught unprepared. I developed this thought in a short speech on the Special Areas (Amendment) Bill in April 1937. I purposely put the point in an exaggerated but arresting form:

> What is the policy of the Government to take the place of armaments which themselves, perhaps, in our monetary expansion have taken the place of the housing boom of last year? Suppose the worst should happen. Suppose Herr Hitler, Signor Mussolini, my friend the Foreign Secretary and M. Blum make an agreement. Suppose the worst should happen and there is universal disarmament? Suppose this calamity of universal peace should descend upon the world. Germany goes back to 40 per cent. unemployed. Are our areas to go back to 30, 40, and 50 per cent. unemployed?[1]

To this plea the Government—not unnaturally—did not respond.

Meanwhile, the problem of the special areas remained unresolved even by the impulse given to some of the heavy industries by the gradual expansion of armaments. Their needs were therefore still a subject of continued pressure from those Members who represented them on both sides of the House. One of the major criticisms was the delimitation of areas which had arisen from the original investigation in the last Parliament. When the 1934 Act, the first to recognise the problem, was introduced, we were told that it was 'experimental' and that the areas omitted need have no grievance, for in any permanent legislation the question would be reconsidered. This was never done; and when, in 1936 and 1937, such legislation was introduced and amended, Members from all parts of the House, including Sir Robert Horne, an ex-Chancellor of the Exchequer and a leading industrialist, joined in their protests. The Minister of Labour throughout this period was Ernest

[1] *Hansard*, 6 April 1937.

Brown. He had political courage, but no kind of imagination or originality. Nevertheless it was impossible to get very angry with him, because he was a worthy man who had raised himself by his own efforts, first in the Regular Army and then in politics. He had started as a Liberal; he then became a Liberal National; and now was a devoted and highly orthodox supporter of the National Government. To use a phrase of Samuel Butler, he was a good man in the worst sense of the word.

As the months passed, feeling grew acute on this issue of the delimitation, by which many of the most deserving were excluded from the advantages which were to flow from the Government's legislation. Altogether, as many as forty Conservative Members in November 1936 joined together to press this question. Tee-side, in particular, felt a bitter grievance in being omitted from the list while Tyneside was included. I was to see the same kind of difficulty arise many years later when I was Prime Minister. Even in a period of full employment in the country as a whole, it was necessary to take some special steps to bring industry to certain parts of England and Scotland which were lagging behind. Remembering these old controversies, I was always on the side of meeting the claims even of borderline cases. By 1937, this question of location of industry was of considerable practical importance, with the creation of the new aircraft and other armament factories. Considerable indignation was caused by the decision of the Air Ministry to build a new aircraft factory at Maidenhead in the prosperous—or relatively prosperous—South. I protested against this in a letter to *The Times*, and many others joined me, including Lord Londonderry, the former Secretary of State. This was one of the few occasions upon which the absurdity of a Government plan was recognised and the decision revoked. This project, which *The Times* described as 'embodying almost every conceivable form of indiscretion', was quickly cancelled.

As a result of this incident, the whole question became more widely discussed, and a good deal of sympathy created for the pleas which my friends and I had long been making. Members of the Conservative Party, whether directly concerned or not, began to take an increasing interest. Our original committee was expanded and received support from such Members as Lord Wolmer, who became chairman of the Special Areas Group. Alan Lennox-Boyd and others, including Eustace Percy, joined us in this agitation. Among the latest recruits was Ronald Cartland. I well remember his maiden speech which deeply impressed the House by his clarity of exposition and deep sincerity. Poor Ronnie Cartland! He was one of the many young men in my lifetime who were cut off in their prime.[1] He had every quality—charm, ability, courage. I soon began to work closely with him. In 1938 we put forward a joint memorandum to the Royal Commission on the Distribution of Industrial Population, in which we suggested the wholesale destruction of the slums and mean quarters of our older towns, and the planning of new towns upon an imaginative basis. We also recommended the regulation of industrial development by licence, together with some suggestions about the equalisation of transport charges, in order to assist industry to move into the more distant areas. In these years, I found in Cartland a true and sympathetic friend. As the final crisis approached, even his enthusiasm began to be dimmed. His last speech in Parliament, just before the outbreak of war, was an outburst of anger and contempt for the failure of the Government to rise to the level of events, which was bitterly resented by Chamberlain and his friends. But it was the cry of a man who had the sense of impending doom.

What was exasperating for Members who felt with me was the attitude of the Treasury and of the Minister of Labour towards the whole of this problem. Though the Special Areas Reconstruction Act in 1936 certainly gave some help to a few areas, it was not in any way an imaginative or dramatic piece of work. The Government of the day (I suppose it may be true of other Governments before and after) took a line which was particularly irritating to us. Ministers continually declared that if anybody had any better ideas they would be glad to consider them. On this I could not help retorting:

The Government are apt to say—and I know it is the common feature of modern Government to say—that if anybody can think of a good plan, they will be prepared to consider it. But I would point out that the Government are

[1] He was killed in June 1940, in a rearguard action covering the retreat to Dunkirk.

not an examining body, like the Civil Service Commissioners, to say, 'You must write a good essay for us, and we will mark it and give you a scholarship if it is good.' They are the Government, and if they cannot govern, let them make way for somebody who can.[1]

Nearer home, in my own constituency, we did at least make some progress in a particular scheme for the alleviation of some of the hardships caused by long unemployment. Of these, perhaps the worst was the sense of uselessness, the days and weeks of waiting and the feeling that no one cared. With the help of various friends and institutions, we were able to purchase a derelict shipyard in the town. Using the offices and the surrounding space, we planned a social service centre where various forms of education and recreation would become available. The National Council for Social Service helped us with some of the capital and the London County Council Staff Association with some of the running costs. In memory of my father and grandfather, I made a substantial gift towards this project and I am happy to say that this good work was set in hand and proved of some use. Naturally, when the war came, the need disappeared. Nevertheless, our efforts were by no means wasted.

With so many preoccupations, the writing of the book took longer than I had hoped; it was not published until May 1938. By that time the minds of some of those in whose judgement I had most confidence, like Churchill and Eden, were becoming more and more occupied with the rapidly deteriorating state of Europe. Yet the mass of the public, unconscious of what awaited them, were not unreceptive of new ideas on the old questions of economic and social reform. My book–*The Middle Way*[2]–was well received by the Press, in spite of natural criticisms from the Left and from the Right. In looking through the reviews that I have preserved, I am struck by the large amount of space devoted to my work and the generous treatment. This was partly because it was a serious book–400 pages in length–and partly because it was very fully documented with tables and statistical information.

Its main theme followed the lines which I had been pursuing

[1] *Hansard*, 8 December 1936.
[2] Harold Macmillan, *The Middle Way* (London, 1938); reissued, with *The Middle Way: 20 Years After* (1966).

for many years; but it brought into a single whole all the complex arguments, considerations, thoughts, and hopes by which I had been absorbed. It began by setting out the needs of our modern society. It emphasised the twin evils of poverty and insecurity among the people as a whole. The evidence carefully collected by Seebohm Rowntree, Sir John Orr, and others proved that a considerable proportion of the population did not earn sufficient wages to enable them to buy the minimum of food, clothing, fuel, and shelter necessary for physical efficiency. Moreover, their income remained always precarious. It is worth perhaps noting that this analysis of the facts was not seriously challenged by any commentator. It was, alas, only too true about the Britain of my youth, and remained so almost to the outbreak of the Second World War.

Having set out the needs, I turned to the remedies. Broadly speaking, there were two schools of thought in Britain at that time. There were those who believed that private enterprise, left alone and allowed to operate untramelled, would in the long run produce wealth on a greater scale than any other system. It is true that the supporters of the *laissez-faire* view had been recently divided by the question of protective duties, and correspondingly weakened by the final triumph, after so many years of conflict, of protectionist policies. Moreover, all the interference with the free market that had grown up with the trade union system had largely destroyed the old classical position. Nevertheless, most Conservatives, having carried tariff reform, had not faced the logical consequences of their success. In any case, since many of them were originally Whigs or Liberals, they cherished their opinions like heirlooms. Their general view was 'the less interference the better; let private enterprise get on with it'. Of course, the alternative was beginning to be widely supported. But Socialism, although still the official doctrine of the Labour Party and still enshrined in its formal constitution, was hardly a practical programme. No one then (and I would judge few now) seriously proposed the nationalisation of all the means of production, distribution, and exchange.

What I tried to do in this volume was to set out a definite plan by which there could be reorganisation of industrial production and distribution, and new methods applied to import and export problems, as well as to finance and investment, so as to bring about the degree of central strategic planning necessary in modern society, while preserving the tactical independence of industry and commerce as a whole, and defending political and economic liberty. In this way, by an appropriate combination of methods, not merely could freedom be preserved, but the maximum and the most efficient production and distribution of wealth organised. In a sense, this was a plea for planned Capitalism.

I was naturally pleased with the interest shown in my book, not only by politicians and political writers, but by students and economists. Apart from the degree of approval or rejection of particular proposals, there was a very great deal of sympathy expressed with my purpose, and praise of the execution of my task. There was, I felt, a general desire to strike a medium between the intolerable restriction of a totalitarian State and the unfettered abuse of freedom under the old liberalism. From certain points of view, the growing international dangers seemed to emphasise the need for increasing the production of wealth, as well as developing the standards of well-being of the people as a whole.

Before passing finally from economic and social issues—the meat of politics in the twenty years between the Wars—it is perhaps right to add some general thoughts. The Second War, with its siege economy and vast claims upon the lives and wealth of the whole population, brought so great an extension of Government involvement in all economic affairs, that it is very difficult for those whose memories do not go back to the twenties and thirties to have any conception of the virulence with which the role of the State in a modern economy was contested. On the one side, any form of State intervention was believed to be necessarily incompetent, and the prelude to some form of dictatorship. Some of the most intelligent and most responsible leaders in many fields of national life had opposed tariffs on these grounds. They opposed industrial reorganisation; they opposed any attempt to deal with the almost hopeless difficulties of the coal industry; they would not allow the Government to interfere with the Central Bank or the economic health of the community, which depended on monetary policy. Special measures, by central planning, to deal with the special areas, were equally taboo. Everything was to be left to the operation of economic laws which were supposed 'in the long run' to produce maximum efficiency. But as Keynes observed, 'in the long run we shall all be dead'. All this set of doctrines, now largely obsolete, took no account of the difficulties and impediments to so-called automatic adjustment. These resulted, first, from humanitarian legislation such as the factory laws; secondly, from the growth of the power of the trade unions; thirdly, from the extremely complex structure of modern capitalism itself. On the other side were ranged the Labour and Socialist Parties who disclaimed all responsibility for all that was wrong, by repeating the parrot cry—'It is the fault of the system'. This was supposed to mean that there was nothing to be done except by revolutionary changes which would, paradoxically enough, have been singularly distasteful to most of those who recommended them. In theory, they were 'root and branch' men; in fact, they shrank in practice from the radical doctrines which they recommended in principle.

Nevertheless, much that I was advocating in those years has come about: a National Economic Development Council; a Government which controls the Central Bank, and assumes responsibility for the general level of economic activity through the bank rate and the Budget; extensions of the public utility principle in transport and fuel; even some welfare distribution of essential foods, such as the expanded school meals service and the orange-juice and cod-liver oil and milk for mothers and babies. The era of strict *laissez-faire* has passed into history, together with the derelict towns, the boarded-up shops, and the barefooted children, and—above all—the long rows of men and women outside the labour exchanges.

But the challenge to our intelligence remains, though the difficulties with which we must wrestle are almost precisely the reverse of those that beset us in the thirties. An overstrained economy with constant anxiety over the 'balance of payments', shortage of labour, and an inflation that has generated a new insecurity, replacing the poverty of unemployment by the distress of the old and the retired who cannot compete in the race to match rising prices with rising incomes—these are the problems with which contemporary statesmen must concern themselves. These were to trouble me later.

But, and we must be thankful for it, the 'great gulf' is bridged.

* * *

The year 1938 again brought us sorrow with the death of my wife's father. He lived almost in retirement and seemed to take his only pleasure in the presence of the large number of his grandchildren, for small children are not conscious of the failings of old age and treat them naturally. Yet his death, when it came, was a blow, and marked the end of an era in our lives. My son-in-law, Julian Amery, sent me recently a copy of a letter his father had received from the Prime Minister of Canada at this time. Leo Amery had sent him a copy of the Memorial Service for the old Duke. Mackenzie King wrote in reply as follows:

I was glad to receive the Order of the Memorial Service to our late friend, the Duke of Devonshire. Like you, I had a great admiration for the Duke's high sense of duty, his sound common sense, and his personal kindness; and, one might add, his great humility.

These are true words and sum up in a sentence the character of the man.

CHAPTER SEVENTEEN

Munich:
The Story of Appeasement

AT the end of May 1937, a few days after the coronation of the new King, Baldwin resigned his office. He was succeeded by Neville Chamberlain, his Chancellor of the Exchequer. In one form or another, either singly or jointly with MacDonald, Baldwin had held supreme power, with two short intervals, for some fourteen years. At various stages in this story I have recorded criticisms of what seemed to me at the time some of Baldwin's failings and weaknesses. I have tried to recall, as accurately and truthfully as possible, the impressions and emotions of a young back-bench Member, without any official position or authority, keenly and sincerely concerned with many large issues. Subsequent critics have been more harsh. If it is true that Baldwin misunderstood or neglected the signs of Germany's determination to seize the hegemony of Europe, he was not alone in this self-deception. He was not interested in the details of foreign affairs. He certainly left the day-to-day conduct of policy to the Foreign Secretary and the Foreign Office. Nor did he like foreigners or understand them. He seldom, if ever, visited any foreign capital. If he ever crossed the Channel, it was only on his annual pilgrimage to Aix-les-Bains, not in itself a notable observation-post from which to scan the changing moods of European countries. Nor was he well served by Simon and Hoare. If he equally neglected the fighting Services and only reluctantly set in motion tardy and insufficient measures of rearmament, it can fairly be argued that whatever his personal views had been, he could not have imposed them upon his Government, his party, the House of Commons, or the nation. That he did not try to do so was not merely weakness or political adroitness. He, above all statesmen, regarded politics as the art of the possible.

In any case, if these failings can certainly be marshalled against him on one side of the account, it should not be forgotten how real is the score on the other side. Baldwin was, for many years, the most powerful Prime Minister since Walpole, for whom he had a deep admiration. He had studied and understood the British people as accurately as his great predecessor had learnt to manage Parliament and the Court. He operated more by insight than by reason. The outstanding achievements of his political life were simple but, in his view, the true justification of his career. In 1922 he exercised, next to Bonar Law, the most effective influence in bringing down Lloyd George's Coalition Government. To the end of his life he regarded it as one of his main objects to prevent Lloyd George ever returning to office. He had been sickened by the least attractive characteristics of the Lloyd George régime, and shocked by what he regarded as a degradation of the tone of British politics. In this he made no allowance for the extraordinary conditions of the time, nor for the difficulties under which Lloyd George suffered by having no united political party at his command. He had therefore to use methods some of which Walpole would have sympathised with more readily than Baldwin. What Baldwin failed to understand was the genius of the greatest war leader that Britain had known since Chatham, only destined to be equalled and surpassed by Churchill. With Lloyd George's departure, a certain dynamic energy disappeared from Whitehall, which never returned until Churchill took control.

Similarly, Baldwin, who had no personal experience of the fighting Services, failed altogether to understand the character of modern armaments, even in the less sophisticated inter-war period. He was too old to fight in the First War; he had not been concerned with the making of munitions; and through his whole career he had never held office, either as a subordinate or as the chief Minister, in any of the Service Departments. So when a programme of rearmament was approved and he had obtained the national authority to proceed, it was a slow-motion affair. The appointment of Inskip as Minister for the 'Co-ordination of Defence' showed that he had no real understanding of the defence problem. Without a staff and with no clearly defined powers, no Minister could have succeeded. Indeed, it seems likely that the appointment was made as a result of strong agitation in the country and Parliament, without any clear picture of what was involved. When I went as Under-Secretary to the Ministry of Supply in 1940, I was to learn something of the immense complexity and the heart-rending delays in the design, development, and production of weapons. All this was outside the range of Baldwin's experience or imagination.

Nevertheless, in his main political objective–the destruction of the Lloyd George Coalition–he believed himself–apart from 'cleaning up public life'–to have this further justification. He had formed the view that sooner or later the Labour Party must develop from a small Opposition, still without the sense of responsibility that the holding or the expectation of office bring, to the position of one of the two main parties in the State. He realised that the bitter dispute caused by Lloyd George's ousting of Asquith at a vital moment of the First World War, brought about by methods no doubt justifiable in the circumstances, but rough and wounding, would lead to the disruption of the Liberal Party and its final dwindling into a mere Parliamentary group. He therefore deliberately destroyed the anti-Socialist Coalition of 1918–22, and was quite content to see the first Labour Government installed in 1924. In 1931 he accepted, rather than stimulated, the formation of the National Government.

His next purpose was so to conduct affairs as to bridge the dangerous division into which the nation had fallen in the years immediately following the First War. He therefore set out by studied moderation to win for himself a position almost above party. Baldwin wooed the Labour Members in the House of Commons and won their confidence. His whole philosophy led him to regard it as one of his main tasks to make the Labour Party safe for democracy, and to lead it away from revolutionary to constitutional methods. Moreover, he knew that the Conservative Party had no future unless it could win the support of that central body of electors, growing all the time in numbers since the franchise had been extended, which had no deep party allegiance. It should therefore be the Centre and Left of the Conservative Party which should dominate its policies, and not the Right. In this spirit and by such methods, class strife and crude ideologies would be gradually tamed. It was partly owing to his example and understanding that the terrible suffering and discontent, caused by large-scale unemployment, did not take the form of dangerous and subversive movements. Thus he carried on and extended the relief for the unemployed, which Lloyd George had begun in the first economic crisis of 1921, and which was contemptuously but foolishly described by Right-wing critics as 'the dole'. In this way, Baldwin presided over the beginnings of the social revolution which in the twenty years between the wars was deeper and more far-reaching than appeared to us at the time. Unable to understand or to remedy the malady which had caused the temporary breakdown of the capitalist system, he was equipped to deal with the worst symptoms of the disease. Even at moments of crisis, his calm temper, his obvious love of justice and fair play, his power to rise above petty or partisan recriminations, enabled him to do signal service. His handling of the General Strike in 1926 was a personal triumph. In the same way, he was able to sustain and eventually to disregard the persistent and violent attacks of the 'Press lords'. Indeed, the modern reader hardly knows the meaning of the term. There are today no Northcliffes, Rothermeres, and Beaverbrooks, demanding entrance into Downing Street, and forcing their views upon Ministers and party leaders by the authority of their circulations. Baldwin deserves the credit for this great victory for constitutional methods. It is true that he was helped by the coming of the radio. This, and the television, have now destroyed the Press monopoly. But in his time it was a fierce struggle, and Baldwin faced these magnates when their power was unchallenged and believed by many to be invincible.

His last great moment was the Abdication crisis. No man could have handled it more tenderly or with greater dignity. To him, therefore, both the Crown and the nation owe a lasting debt.

It is, unhappily, true that Baldwin and the Governments of which he was so long the head or the prop, by their confused handling of foreign affairs and their failure to back policy with military power, proved the unwilling and unconscious agents in promoting what Churchill has called 'the unnecessary war'. But that charge ought not to be levelled by many of those who have now found it convenient to frame it, sometimes out of malice and sometimes to serve partisan ends. The members of the Left, in and out of Parliament, were as blind and as culpable as those on whom they have since sought to place the whole blame. The Labour Party and even the small Liberal Party were bitter critics of rearmament when they must have known in their hearts that it was essential and already too long delayed. They lived on phrases, and neglected facts. Right up to the very edge of war they resisted national military service, essential in itself and the only gesture by which Britain could hope to encourage and inspire confidence in the democracies of the West. It has been my task to read in the course of preparing these chapters many books and pamphlets relating to this period. They are, of course, written with hindsight and long after the events they describe. Most of them are by no means free from bias. Churchill is one of the very few who has a right to criticise, for he rests on the authority that comes from his own record. Yet during all the formative years, Churchill was himself the subject of violent criticisms from the Left as well as from the Right, including many who subsequently posed as his supporters and as far-seeing patriots. Even in Churchill's own account,[1] there is some misunderstanding of Baldwin's difficulties and misinterpretation of his indiscretions. His son, with admirable filial piety, has put the case for the other side.[2]

Nevertheless, if, in the important task of preserving and fostering the underlying unity of the nation on which its ultimate strength depends, Baldwin succeeded, in the supreme duty of a Prime Minister—the preservation of honourable peace and the military posture to enable Britain to play in any period her appropriate role—he failed. He left to his successor, in terms of the foreign situation and the ability of Britain to meet the rapidly approaching dangers, a bleak and barren heritage, although he handed on, at any rate in terms of human feeling, a country where kindliness and decency still ruled, and men and women, when the test came, had the spirit to meet it worthily.

Baldwin's departure marked the end of an era. He had been the leader of the Conservative Party since I had first stood for Parliament fourteen years before. Grievous as had been my disappointment

[1] Winston Churchill, *The Second World War*, vol. i: *The Gathering Storm*.
[2] A. W. Baldwin, *My Father: The True Story*.

over what I felt to be his errors, both of omission and commission, I realised that mine might have been merely the judgement of youth and inexperience. Moreover, in spite of my disaffection, he had shown me both understanding and kindness. I therefore thought it would be right to send him some expression of sympathy, and wrote to him accordingly:

26th May, 1937

Dear Prime Minister,

I hope you will not think it impertinent of me if I venture to add to what must be an overwhelming correspondence.

It must be a great source of satisfaction to you to feel, on the eve of your retirement from high office, that you enjoy the respect and affection of the great mass of your fellow countrymen, quite regardless of their individual views on matters of public policy.

May I be allowed to wish you very many happy years in which to enjoy your well deserved rest.

Yours very sincerely,
Harold Macmillan

I received a characteristically friendly reply:

31st May, 1937

My dear Harold,

I am grateful for your letter which is one more proof of the amazing and generous kindness of known and unknown friends.

I thank you warmly for it.

Yours always sincerely,
Stanley Baldwin

Baldwin's resignation of the Premiership was accompanied by that of Ramsay MacDonald, who was Lord President in Baldwin's last Government. No authorised biography of MacDonald has yet been published. Here again was a man who has been harshly and even contemptuously treated by his critics. Although in his last years, as his health declined and his eyesight failed, he became a somewhat pathetic figure, he was a much more considerable man than it is now the fashion to admit. He was one of the creators, if not the chief architect, of the Labour Party. He brought it from a small membership in the House of Commons to a position in which it was able to hold office, not without credit, although in a minority, on two separate occasions—in 1924 and in 1929. His actions in 1931, by which he destroyed his own creation and doomed the Labour Party to a long eclipse, naturally caused intense bitterness among his old colleagues. But the formation of the National Government resulted from real devotion to what he sincerely believed to be the interests of the State. He was not an economist and had little knowledge of financial matters. He cannot be blamed for accepting what was the unequivocal view of almost all the leading experts as to what had to be done. Nor were the members of the Government who refused to follow him able to plead that their analysis of the situation was any different from that which he accepted. They believed as firmly as he and his advisers in the necessity for drastic and painful measures of economy. The only difference between MacDonald and those who deserted him is that he had the courage to follow the advice which he believed to be sound, while they shrank from the unpopularity of policies which they themselves admitted to be necessary. In the world of foreign affairs, MacDonald in the prime of his life moved easily, and with authority. He was respected and trusted abroad. If he lived to see the total failure of his efforts for the strengthening of the power of the League of Nations and for general disarmament, it can be pleaded in his justification that at least a possible chance of turning the League into an effective instrument for enforcing peace by its collective power may well have been the so-called Protocol, which MacDonald carried through at Geneva in the autumn of 1924. It was not formally agreed by his own Government and was rejected by the succeeding Government, partly because of Britain's instinctive recoil from the indefiniteness of the obligations and the weakness of the guarantees, and partly because of the strong objections of all the self-governing Dominions. If in his last years MacDonald sank into a woolly confusion of mind and language, the achievements of his life, taken as a whole, are by no means negligible.

The vacant positions were filled by familiar faces. Simon moved from the Home Office to Neville Chamberlain's place at the Exchequer. Hoare left the Admiralty for the Home Office, a transfer which Churchill greeted with incredulous contempt. It seemed strange to him that anyone should choose H.M. Prisons instead of H.M. Ships: 'The first man I've ever known to prefer

Jack Ketch to Jack Tar.'[1] He was replaced by Duff Cooper, soon to play a notable role in the Munich crisis. Inskip continued, in a feeble and futile manner, to 'co-ordinate defence'. Lord Swinton, whose work at the Air Ministry was the one outstanding achievement of the Government, was removed by Chamberlain in May 1938 because of Parliamentary pressure and succeeded by Kingsley Wood. Eden—the most popular member of the Government in the country generally—remained at the Foreign Office until his resignation nine months later, when he was succeeded by Halifax. All these were well-known and, in some cases, well-worn figures in the political scene. One remained outside. I had come by now to know Churchill well. He made no secret of the fact that Inskip's appointment by Baldwin in March 1936, when there was a general expectation that Churchill would be chosen, was a blow to him. He had then been out of office for seven years. He knew his powers, and to be excluded from any share in what were now admitted to be the necessary preparations for defence was almost an insult. I did not feel that he was much disappointed a year later. In his heart he believed that it was already too late; and that he was being reserved by destiny to take up the supreme burden when the time came.

The new Prime Minister, Neville Chamberlain, was a man of a very different stamp from his immediate predecessor. If he had none of Baldwin's lethargy, he had little of Baldwin's imagination. Baldwin had always been uncertain of himself; Chamberlain was only too sure that he was right on every question. Baldwin's attitude to problems was largely one of temperament and feeling; Chamberlain approached them with a clear, logical mind. The only trouble was that when he was wrong he was terribly wrong. Had Chamberlain retired or died in 1937, he would have gone down to history as a great social reformer and a great administrator. He would have been remembered above all by his tenure of the post of Minister of Health, which at that time included wide functions, including housing, which are now divided among several departments. Here he was both progressive and decisive, and left behind him an unequalled record of administrative and legislative achievement. In this office, as in the Treasury, he often showed willingness to con-

[1] The Earl of Avon, *The Eden Memoirs: Facing the Dictators*, p. 446.

sider novel and comprehensive remedies. This part of his character, like his father's, was in the old tradition of radical reform. Unlike Joseph Chamberlain, however, who developed into a second period of wide and audacious concepts, Neville's last phase was doomed to be unhappy for himself and disastrous for the country.

He was to be Prime Minister for just three years. After twenty-seven months of struggling against an increasingly menacing situation abroad, he was destined to see all his efforts fail and his country enter into the Second World War, which was to prove the most testing and perilous in its long history. It was then his misfortune, like the younger Pitt, to find himself cast in the role of War Minister, against which all his nature rebelled. Unhappily, he had neither the youth nor the resilience of Pitt. Beneath that cool and often harsh exterior, Chamberlain was shy and reserved, and easily offended. When his eyes were finally opened to Hitler's true character, he used expressions which seemed complaints that he had been deceived, rather than a clarion-call to a bewildered nation. After a few months of uncertainty, the fall of his Government was inevitable. For the instinct of the people, as so often, was sure. In the hour of supreme danger, they turned to the one man who through many years, without regard to misrepresentation and obloquy, had told them the truth.

It has been Neville Chamberlain's fate, as so often with statesmen, to be first obsequiously praised and then extravagantly abused. He must have taken, during the few months that remained of his life after his fall, a certain sardonic satisfaction in watching the rapid movements of the time-servers, so quick to abandon him and so anxious to attach themselves to the fortunes of his successor. Churchill, who treated Baldwin with exceptional kindness in his declining years, showed to Neville Chamberlain similar generosity and magnanimity. Today, when so many years have passed, it is right to recall Chamberlain's triumphs in the field of politics with which he was familiar, as well as his failures when he moved into spheres of which he had no knowledge. Unhappily for himself and his country, he seemed to regard himself as charged with an almost mystical mission to win peace by his own authority, disregarding all advice and all warnings until too late. He believed that you could do a bargain with Hitler which, once Germany's 'legitimate' demands were conceded, would be scrupulously respected. Having no understanding of the man with whom he tried to sup, he never provided himself with the necessary length of spoon.

The events of these two frantic years are well known and have been described in memoirs, biographies, and histories in great detail. I will not attempt to retell the whole story, but only emphasise some aspects of it which were unknown to my friends and myself at the time, but have now been revealed. I shall also recount the action taken, in our vain efforts to influence events, by those with whom I was associated. Perhaps it would first be convenient to recall the bare sequence of the drama as it was unfolded.

In July 1937 there began a new phase in Japan's aggression and conquest in China, followed by attacks on British and American warships. In February 1938 Eden, the Foreign Secretary, resigned from the Government and was replaced by Lord Halifax. In March 1938 Hitler achieved by violent means the absorption of Austria into the German Reich—the *Anschluss*. There followed immediately the pressure on Czechoslovakia. In May came Hitler's apparent climb-down in the face of French and British protests. When the pressure was resumed, Lord Runciman was sent at the end of July on his notorious but futile mission to Czechoslovakia, to 'mediate' between the Government of that country and the Sudeten Germans. In September 1938 came Chamberlain's visits to Hitler, three in number, culminating in the Munich Agreement, signed in the early hours of 30 September. On 15 March 1939 Hitler entered Prague and occupied what remained of Czechoslovakia. On 31 March the British guarantee to Poland was given. On 7 April Mussolini invaded and seized Albania. On 13 April British guarantees were given to Romania and Greece. In the course of July and August the German pressure on Danzig and the claims on Poland grew in intensity. On 22 August the Molotov–Ribbentrop Pact, assuring the neutrality of Russia, was published. On 1 September German forces invaded Poland. On 3 September Britain and France declared war on Germany.

Never in times of so-called peace have such a series of tremendous events taken place, both in the West and in the East. Never did our countrymen enter war with such foreboding or with such heavy hearts.

The Chamberlain régime began inauspiciously. Although the Coronation was an occasion which produced an impressive display of the Commonwealth's latent strength, the tone of the meetings at the conference of Prime Ministers was low and circumspect. The Dominions were very sensitive regarding their newly-won emancipation from London in matters of foreign policy. Australia and New Zealand, in spite of their traditional loyalty to the Crown and affection for the mother country, felt naturally more concern at Japanese than at German aggression. The South African Government could not but be conscious of the deep cleavage of feeling between the outward-looking and the inward-looking groups which divided that country. Canada, under the somewhat arid guidance of Mackenzie King, made it abundantly clear that she was by no means committed in advance to fight at Britain's side in another European war. Meanwhile, in the United States, there was certainly indignation at the growing Nazi brutality and Italy's flagrant annexation of Abyssinia. There was still deeper concern over Japan's expansion in China. But there was no sign of any serious movement away from the prevalent isolationism. Indeed, America's neutrality legislation tended to favour the dictatorships rather than the democracies.

Chamberlain realised, as no doubt did the whole Cabinet, the strategic difficulty of facing three potential enemies in widely separated theatres. After all, British Ministers could not but recall how only American help had turned the scales in the Great War. Germany, although for the moment quiescent, was clearly contemplating fresh moves. Mussolini was engaged in active intervention in Spain, and the practice of submarine piracy in the Mediterranean during 1937 was only suppressed by the strong measures on which Eden was able to get agreement at the Nyon Conference in the September of that year. In July, Japan attacked Shanghai, although the International Settlement was respected. Nanking and the lower Yangtse Valley were invaded and the Chinese Government, forced to evacuate their capital, were to appeal to the League in September. Faced with this world situation, what hope was there of keeping the peace and what methods should be set in motion? In view of the military unpreparedness of Britain and the political weakness of France, the traditional British policy of organising and leading an alliance seemed to Chamberlain and his Government impracticable, even if desirable. This old and established system of British foreign policy, carried on successfully century after century, must of course have taken new forms. The Dominions must be encouraged to realise the urgency of the approaching crisis. The United States must be wooed. The remaining members of the old League of Nations must be rallied to prepare the best resistance possible, by a combination of peace-loving peoples, to defend the principles on which the League was founded. This, broadly, was the programme which commended itself to Eden and which Churchill had now begun to preach with increasing intensity under the banner of 'Arms and the Covenant'. Such a policy would have involved rapid and large-scale rearmament in Britain, without too much regard to Treasury protests about the dislocation of industry and the risks to the economy. If there was as yet no need to adopt measures suitable to total war, the organisation of the production of munitions and the scale of the armed forces must be appropriate to the twilight between war and peace, which all men whose eyes were not self-blinded could now clearly recognise. It would have meant, equally, the recognition of the value of the League as the central pivot of a coalition against the dictators. It would have involved a Government of national concentration in Britain, embracing all men from the Right to the Left who had courage and vision. Such a lead by Britain might well have brought fresh energy and unity into France; it would have steadied Central and Eastern Europe and probably, in due course, brought Russia into a genuine partnership with the West. It would certainly have thrilled public opinion in the Dominions and perhaps galvanised their Governments into activity. It might, who knows, have succeeded in leading the American people at least some steps along the long road of international responsibility which they were destined within a few years to tread.

It was these ideas, however inchoately conceived or inadequately phrased, that began increasingly to occupy my mind. Parallel with my work on economic and social reform, I began now to speak in my constituency on these themes. In February 1937, for instance, I argued in favour of the historical role of England in the defence of freedom and the need for rapid and effective rearmament. The large amount of unemployed manpower and machine-power should facilitate this task. At the same time, I joined with many others, including Vyvyan Adams, George Barnes, a well-known trade union leader, Arthur Chamberlain, and Professor Temperley, in a letter to *The Times*, pleading for the restoration of the full authority of the League as an instrument, not only for its traditional function of conciliation, but for the effective enforcement of its decisions by an 'international police force of sufficient strength'. Indeed, this policy soon became embodied in an organisation called the New Commonwealth Society, which had Churchill's blessing and began to make rapid progress. In those days, as indeed now, nomenclature mattered a great deal. An international police force, operated by a League of Nations from which Germany, Italy, and Japan had resigned but round which all other nations might rally, was not so very different from the Grand Alliance which was destined, after many set-backs and six years of struggle, to save the freedom of mankind.

Chamberlain, however, after due reflection, decided to embark upon the opposite course. If the dictators could not be successfully opposed, they must be conciliated; and, in order to do so, the first step was surely to divide them. Faced with the menace of Germany, Italy, and Japan, the obvious course was to detach the weakest. This was clearly Italy. Accordingly, a few weeks after becoming Prime Minister, he set about this not uncongenial task with that confidence in the wisdom of his decisions and the probability of his success which so far had characterised all the main activities of his political life.

For Eden, as Foreign Secretary, the change of atmosphere in No. 10 Downing Street must have been striking. He had sometimes complained to his intimates of his concern that Baldwin took no interest in foreign affairs. At first, he welcomed the contrast. But if Baldwin had done too little, Chamberlain soon began to do too much. If Baldwin had been King Log, Chamberlain assumed with enthusiasm the role of King Stork.

As Churchill has emphasised, the Foreign Secretary 'has a special position in a British Cabinet'.[1] He and the Chancellor of the

[1] Winston Churchill, *The Second World War*, vol. i: *The Gathering Storm*, p. 187.

Exchequer hold the two most important posts in any administration next to the Prime Minister. Each of them must work in close harmony with the head of the Government and in complete confidence. Whereas the Treasury is not under any obligation to consult the Prime Minister except upon major questions of policy arising from time to time, foreign questions, from their very nature, have to be discussed almost day by day between the Foreign Office and No. 10. Moreover, unlike every other Department of the State, including even the Defence Ministries, the Foreign Office, so far as the Cabinet is concerned, except for matters of the highest secrecy, works completely in the open. All incoming and outgoing telegrams are circulated every day to Cabinet Ministers, as well as the record of interviews which the Foreign Secretary or other Foreign Office Ministers and officials may have with Ambassadors or Ministers of foreign countries. Thus the Foreign Secretary has not merely to consult his colleagues when a matter is ripe for decision, but every stage in the negotiation is available for their consideration and, if need be, criticism. A Prime Minister is, of course, responsible for the whole policy of his Government and must be in touch, either personally or through his Private Office, with all departments. Yet his relationship with the Foreign Secretary is of a unique character. Ideally, there should be a complete harmony of outlook on public affairs. But if, as may often be the case, there are differences of approach and temperament, that places a still greater obligation upon both that there should be no secrets between them. For a Prime Minister to communicate with the heads of foreign Governments or, indeed, to take any step in connection with foreign affairs, without informing the Foreign Secretary at every stage, is unpardonable. It is also bound to lead to disaster.

Unhappily, in Chamberlain's case there were many lapses. Accustomed to the full control of the departments over which he had presided, this conception of partnership was quite foreign to him. Even as Chancellor of the Exchequer he had erred in connection with the removal of sanctions on Italy by acting without reference to the Foreign Secretary. Now, as Prime Minister, he was guilty of a number of breaches, not merely of convention but of fair play, towards which Eden was almost too indulgent. In his anxiety to get on terms with Mussolini, he had written to him a personal letter in July 1937 which he did not show to the Foreign Secretary. Eden, when he discovered this fact through the Italian Ambassador, as he was bound to do, treated it as an unintentional slip. But he was too generous. Chamberlain wrote in his diary as follows:

> I did not show my letter to the Foreign Secretary for I had the feeling that he would object to it.[1]

Similarly, Chamberlain carried on through the post a correspondence with his sister-in-law Lady Chamberlain, who spent the autumn of 1937 in Rome. His letters were no doubt opened by the Italian Post Office and delivered to the Italian authorities. But in any event, Austen Chamberlain's widow, who had developed a curious admiration for Mussolini, was the worst possible confidante. Her advice was in every sense unreliable, and her indiscretions in her talks with Ciano embarrassing and dangerous. All this, when it was made known to him, added to Eden's anxieties. Finally, Chamberlain developed a certain contempt for the official methods of diplomacy and preferred advisers and intermediaries of his own. The most important of these was Sir Horace Wilson, Chief Industrial Adviser to the Government. Apart from the question of Wilson's qualifications in a field where he had no experience, he did little to ease the relations between No. 10 and the Foreign Office, at least during Eden's régime.[2]

Every Prime Minister has a right to choose intimate confidants, especially in times of stress. Churchill did not hesitate, for instance, to set up a statistical department in his office under 'the Prof.' (Lord Cherwell), whom he was known to consult on a wide variety of matters. But all this was open and above board; and although a certain amount of irritation was caused, there was nothing secret or hidden. In the same way, I used, with the full knowledge of my colleagues in the Cabinet, Lord Mills, who advised me on a number of economic and industrial questions beyond the range of his own department. In fact, other Ministers welcomed this arrangement, for they had great confidence in Lord Mills's experience and

[1] Keith Feiling, *Life of Neville Chamberlain*, p. 330.
[2] The Earl of Avon, *The Eden Memoirs: Facing the Dictators*, pp. 447 ff.

sagacity. Moreover, he was himself a Cabinet Minister. I also discussed the most secret and vital issues with Sir Norman Brook (later Lord Normanbrook), especially at the time of the Russian negotiations and in my meetings with President Eisenhower and President Kennedy. Sir Norman, as head of the Cabinet Secretariat, was known to all Ministers; all valued his advice and judgement; and he had both the delicacy and the wisdom to work in the closest co-operation with the professional heads of the Foreign Office and the other departments concerned. I never heard at any time, in spite of my great reliance upon him, the smallest criticism about his activities. On a lower level, it is perhaps worth noting that among the Private Secretaries at No. 10 there was, during Chamberlain's régime, no representative of the Foreign Office. This is very unusual and very unwise. Sir Philip de Zulueta, who filled this position on my staff throughout my Premiership, showed equal loyalty to me and to the Service of which he was a member. He would not hesitate to call my attention to any failure, in a moment of stress, to inform the Foreign Secretary and the appropriate departments of the Foreign Office of any action that I was taking or even contemplating. Without placing upon them too dark an interpretation, Sir Horace Wilson's activities, both in Whitehall and with foreign diplomats, were certainly not conducive to the confidence that should exist between No. 10 and the Foreign Office.

In spite of their friendly personal relations, the atmosphere between Chamberlain and Eden was clouded almost from the start. The prospect which these two Ministers had to face in the summer of 1937 was indeed grim. The League of Nations, with its attenuated membership, was clearly ineffective, and after its failures, both in Japan and in Abyssinia, incapable of fulfilling the obligations envisaged under the Covenant. As Mussolini is said to have observed with a certain sardonic humour, 'The trouble is that there are now more gangsters than policemen'. Public opinion was still hopeful of finding a solution without dividing the world into two opposing and rapidly arming groups menacing each other. For they feared that this would reproduce the conditions prior to 1914. Yet how, except by rallying the forces that stood for peace and honour, were Britain and France to act? We were faced by the great and

growing power of Germany, becoming daily more dominant in
Central Europe and increasingly protected, by the line of fortifications in the Rhineland which they were feverishly constructing,
from any effective Western intervention. Mussolini, having 'got
away with' his Abyssinian adventure, was maintaining large forces
in that territory, as well as in North Africa. He was beginning to
develop a dangerous hold upon the Mediterranean. In the Far East,
the Japanese aggression was extending its grip upon the mainland
of China, and menacing the vital interests of Britain and the United
States, both in China and in the adjoining territories. Yet Britain,
whose armaments were still hopelessly behind, and France, the
strength of whose Army in relation to that of Germany was bound
to diminish and whose country was torn by fierce internal dissension,
could scarcely alone contain the ambitions of these three countries
in the different parts of the world. It seemed therefore to many of
us at the time that the first and most urgent need of Britain was to
draw in as her allies in the cause of peace the two great nations in the
West and in the East—the United States and Russia. Unhappily,
Chamberlain was, by temperament, contemptuous of the one and
suspicious of the other.

During the comparatively peaceful months in Europe following
the seizure of the Rhineland, and in the intervals of his efforts to deal
with the Spanish problem, Eden turned his eyes towards the United
States with a prescience not shared by any of his colleagues. He had
realised that in the perils that lay before us, Britain, without the
assistance in one form or another of the United States, would be
greatly endangered. When Japanese operations in China took on a
new intensity, Eden saw his opportunity. The Americans were
angry; but not yet angry enough for any active retaliation. They had
to be content with apologies from the Japanese diplomats for the
actions which the Japanese military had taken on their own. Even
the sinking of the United States gunboat, *Panay*, did not lead to
more than stiff Notes from the State Department. Nevertheless,
Eden sensed that President Roosevelt would have liked to do more,
and was already trying to educate the people of the United States
out of their isolationism into an acceptance of their world responsibilities. This, of course, was bound to be a slow process. The

President was becoming more and more distressed by the deterioration of world conditions. He was looking about for something he could do to stop the rot. Eventually, in October, he made a speech—the famous 'quarantine' speech—which implied the possibility of some positive action by the United States. Although this caused a storm of criticism among isolationists, it at least showed the President's mood and aims. The next step was the summoning of the Brussels Conference—that is, of the Powers signatory to the Nine-Power Pact.[1] In this way, America could attend as a full member and not merely as an observer. Although the Conference ended in nothing but resolutions, yet the close contacts between Eden and Norman Davis, the American representative, were encouraging. Similarly, the visit in January 1938 of an American naval adviser, Captain R. E. Ingersoll, U.S.N., to hold staff conversations with the British naval staff, was a move of considerable significance.

Meanwhile, Chamberlain was determined to follow his own course. Undeterred by warnings of more experienced advisers, but with the full support of the inner circle of his Government, the Prime Minister appeared confident of his ability to reach some settlement first with Italy and then with Germany. This policy was soon to degenerate into 'appeasement' in the worst sense of the word. As regards Germany, Eden had unconsciously put into his hands an instrument which was later to be fatally used. He had appointed as Ambassador to Berlin, in succession to Sir Eric Phipps, Sir Nevile Henderson. Why he did so it is difficult to understand. Henderson had a respectable record and was at the time Ambassador in the Argentine. But Eden did not know him and had never seen him. Yet this was a key post. Henderson proved a complete disaster; hysterical, self-opinionated, and unreliable. Eden later realised what a terrible mistake he had made.[2]

Chamberlain's first effort in making contact with Germany took the form of the strange incident of the Halifax visit.[3] Here again, the Foreign Secretary made a grave error. By agreeing to it, he

[1] See above, p. 343.
[2] The Earl of Avon, *The Eden Memoirs: Facing the Dictators*, p. 504.
[3] Ibid., pp. 508–16. Lord Halifax was at this time Lord President.

weakened his own position and allowed quite a false impression of British ingenuousness to be created. The original invitation came from Marshal Göring. It was to attend a sports exhibition, where this distinguished Master of Foxhounds would be introduced into all the different methods by which foxes could be shot instead of hunted. Not only was Halifax's position awkward and undignified, for he was made to seek a meeting with Hitler, but the aims and significance of the mission were overplayed in the British Press, greatly to the annoyance of the Foreign Office. In the course of the great Viceroy's interview, he was told by Hitler that the proper way to deal with unrest in India was to shoot first Gandhi and then the leaders of the Congress. Halifax's sweet and Christian nature must have recoiled from this sort of barbarism; but he was too courteous to show his disgust. Unhappily, in the course of this long discussion, he did not reject with sufficient force Hitler's new thesis. This was that changes of territory and shifts of power in a changing world could come about only by one of two methods—either by war or by what he called the 'higher reason'. Hitler believed that the play of free forces—that is war—had to be replaced by the method of higher reason—that is bluff. In Eden's words, 'Would we be good enough to give what otherwise he would be compelled to take.'[1] Halifax should have rejected this argument with vigour. On the contrary, he referred to possible modifications which might come in due course over Danzig, Czechoslovakia, and Austria. All that England was interested in was to see that these changes should come about by peaceful evolution. This doctrine of peaceful evolution seemed dangerously near that of the higher reason. The Halifax visit did no good, and a great deal of potential harm.

After this futile and dangerous approach to Germany, Chamberlain then returned to his favourite plan of detaching Italy from her German alliance by cajolery or concessions.

But Eden, once bitten, was even more than twice shy. He had been tricked into the matter of the so-called 'Gentleman's Agreement' a year before, from which he had drawn no advantages, and he had learnt his lesson. It was useless in his view to negotiate a fresh agreement with Mussolini unless he first carried out the engagements

[1] The Earl of Avon, *The Eden Memoirs: Facing the Dictators*, p. 514.

into which he had already entered. A prolonged difference of opinion then took place between Chamberlain and his Foreign Secretary, which was not resolved until early 1938 by the latter's resignation. Chamberlain tried, by one means or another, to get a negotiation going. He was convinced that he could rescue Mussolini from Hitler's clutches. Eden, on the other hand, felt that to negotiate before Mussolini had given some sign of carrying out the promises he had already broken would give an impression of eagerness, which would encourage the appetites of the predatory Powers, and at the same time dismay and weaken actual or potential friends. In a word, Eden was not prepared to throw good money after bad.

This dispute was waged with growing acrimony on both sides of Downing Street and was still unresolved when an event took place which perhaps weighed more on Eden's mind than even his dislike of Chamberlain's pursuit of Mussolini. In the course of the autumn and winter months of 1937, Eden was not dissatisfied with the progress made in Anglo-American relations. It is true that nothing concrete had come out of the Brussels Conference except the presence in London of Captain Ingersoll. Nevertheless, a closer relationship was beginning to develop between the British Foreign Secretary and President Roosevelt, partly through Norman Davis, the American representative at Brussels, and partly through Robert Bingham, the American Ambassador in London. Eden was quick to realise, with his true instinct for the realities that lie behind diplomacy, the American picture. He was here greatly helped by the advice of Sir Ronald Lindsay, our Ambassador in Washington, who had himself been head of the Foreign Office. It was becoming evident that the President was pursuing his course of educating the American public, without undue political risks, with considerable skill. He was faced with the isolationist lobby, always jealous of British attempts to entangle the United States. These critics were particularly suspicious of any move to use our common interests in the Far East in order to embroil America in the outside world. This, after all, was not an unreasonable view, at any rate at that time. The population of the United States has its origins, broadly speaking, in peoples who decided, for one reason or another, to cast the dust of Europe from their feet. Many had been refugees from political or religious persecution; many the victims of a social system in their European homes which drove them to seek their fortune overseas. There seemed, therefore, no particular reason, either of sentiment or interest, for America to interfere in anything outside the American continent. There, whenever her interests were directly concerned, she would act firmly and even fiercely. It is true that towards the end of the First World War America was led to intervene, but scarcely of her own volition. Had it not been for the almost maniac policies involved in the unlimited submarine war, she might well have maintained her neutrality right to the end. Even in the Second World War, now approaching, it was not primarily to succour Europe that America was eventually drawn in, great as was her sympathy and vital as was the material aid which she gave. It was the treacherous blow at Pearl Harbour by the Japanese that proved the salvation of the British, then struggling alone in Western Europe.

Yet Eden knew that behind all this suspicion lay the strength of spiritual forces and the love of freedom which are the strongest motives in American life. When, therefore, in his absence the President made a proposal, strongly supported by the British Ambassador and communicated in advance to the Prime Minister, to which the President clearly attached the greatest importance, it seemed almost incredible that so promising a move should have received a rebuff on the Prime Minister's sole decision, contrary to the advice of Sir Alec Cadogan, the Permanent Under-Secretary of the Foreign Office. Eden was away for a short holiday in the south of France, but could easily have been summoned home, or at least consulted by special messenger. Chamberlain, filled with the one idea of getting conversations going, first with Mussolini and then with Hitler, decided to send a discouraging reply. Sumner Welles, the American Assistant Secretary of State, described it as 'a douche of cold water'.[1] Anyone who knew Chamberlain would realise that when he was in the mood he could indeed be icy.

The actual details of President Roosevelt's proposal are not now important. What he suggested was that he should call the whole

[1] The Earl of Avon, *The Eden Memoirs: Facing the Dictators*, p. 552.

diplomatic corps together on 22 January 1938, deplore the state of the world and its deteriorating standard of international life, and put before all the Governments the suggestion that they should agree 'on the essential principles to be observed in the conduct of international relations'. If the response was favourable, progress could be made. There were, as was to be expected, certain phrases in the President's draft, the terms of which were divulged only to Chamberlain, that might perhaps prove unsuitable or embarrassing. Nevertheless, as Sir Ronald Lindsay saw clearly, the President's plan, whatever its outcome, must have the effect of aligning American opinion with that of the democracies. The dictators would probably refuse the President's invitation. If they refused, more and more would the United States administration be able to rally American public opinion against them. It was a chance not to be missed. At the worst, it might cause Hitler and Mussolini to pause. Why then did Chamberlain send a reply so discouraging? Why did he take a course which the President never forgot and never forgave? Chamberlain was no fool, although at the moment under the influence of his somewhat mystical concept of himself as the peacemaker of the world. It was simply that he did not want to play the hand this way. He was afraid that an immediate acceptance by Britain, and no doubt by France, but a rejection by Germany and Italy, would be a further step in separating the world into two groups, and afford the pretext for a worsening of relations with Britain. Chamberlain sincerely believed that he could achieve a reconciliation between the democracies and the dictators. Moreover, he feared that Roosevelt's scheme would result in postponing the opening of the conversations with Italy and Germany on which he had set his heart. He knew, too, that the question of the *de jure* recognition of Italian sovereignty in Abyssinia, which he was ready to concede without any sufficient price in return, would prove an embarrassing obstacle.

On Eden's hurried return to England, he at once treated the Prime Minister with a dose of his own medicine. He sent telegrams on his own authority to the British Ambassador, urging him to try to restore the situation. Something was eventually done to soothe the President's wounded feelings, and friendly messages were interchanged between him and the Prime Minister. But it was too late. In the delicate relations that must always exist between the Heads of Government of two great Powers negotiating with each other at great distances, misunderstandings must often occur. Yet here, perhaps, there was no real misunderstanding. Chamberlain was obsessed with the idea of a private deal, first with Italy and then with Germany. His chilling reply to the President was not a lapse; it was carefully calculated. There will always be differences of opinion as to the likelihood of the President's proposal becoming fruitful. Hoare, in his own account, fully justifies Chamberlain's decision, and does so on the curious grounds that we had reason to doubt America; first, because of her breaking up the World Economic Conference in 1933, and secondly, because of the passing of the Johnson Act in 1934, prohibiting the raising of loans in the United States by foreign Governments not paying their full interest on the old war debt.[1] These criticisms, no doubt just, were totally irrelevant to the needs of the moment. In our grave situation we should have turned not to the past but to the future. We could look to no greater friend in our troubles than Roosevelt, and the right course would have been to cultivate that friendship. Churchill takes a different view. He regarded Chamberlain's rebuff of Roosevelt 'as the last frail chance to save the world from tyranny otherwise than by war'.[2] Certainly, 'Former Naval Person' would have sent a very different answer.[3] Whatever may be the final judgement of history, this episode, although patched up for the moment, must have made Eden feel that the break between himself and the Prime Minister could not long be delayed.

Chamberlain continued to insist on opening the negotiations with Mussolini. Eden demanded that Mussolini should at least make some gesture on his side. Would he accept the British formula for the withdrawal of Italian volunteers from Spain? This should be the test.

---

[1] Viscount Templewood, *Nine Troubled Years*, pp. 264–6.

[2] Winston Churchill, *The Second World War*, vol. i: *The Gathering Storm*, p. 199.

[3] 'Naval Person' was the title which Churchill adopted, as soon as he joined the Government as First Lord of the Admiralty after the outbreak of war, in his communications with President Roosevelt. When he became Prime Minister he changed it to 'Former Naval Person'.

Chamberlain's handling of this affair does not make a pretty story. He ignored the impudent refusal of Grandi, the Italian Ambassador, to come to the Foreign Office to see Eden on the ground that he was playing golf. He condoned this arrogance to the point of inviting him to come to No. 10, at which conference he required the Foreign Secretary's attendance. In this celebrated interview, the Foreign Secretary was placed in a humiliating, and Grandi in a triumphant, position. This meeting marks a low point indeed in Britain's honour and authority. Whether one accepts Grandi's version or not, the official record makes it clear that the Foreign Secretary's position had become impossible, and so he was now to feel.

This long conflict and these deep differences between the Prime Minister and his Foreign Secretary were unknown to the public at the time. The curtain has only gradually been drawn back since the end of the Second War. Nor were they appreciated by the Cabinet as a whole. Eden was scrupulous to keep his disagreement with the Prime Minister to himself and to his Foreign Office colleagues or officials. On his side there was no gossip. Chamberlain was equally discreet. His recent contacts with Grandi through Sir Joseph Ball[1] were successfully concealed. It was therefore a great shock to most Ministers when they were informed of the deadlock that had been reached. Even the more perspicacious of them, such as Duff Cooper, did not realise, when the decisive Cabinet meetings took place, that the Prime Minister had to go through the form of urging the Foreign Secretary to remain when he was, in fact, anxious to get rid of him as soon as possible.[2] If the dispute was a surprise to Ministers, the actual resignation, on 20 February 1938, was a violent shock, both to the party and to the country. In the House, the younger Members in particular had put their confidence in Eden and looked to him for a resolute line of foreign policy. So had large numbers of people throughout the nation, of all parties and of none. There was a feeling that Eden represented the generation that had fought in the War, of which he was one of the few survivors. He was known to possess that combination of idealism and realism on which alone

[1] Head of the Conservative Research Department.
[2] Duff Cooper, *Old Men Forget*, p. 215.

a successful foreign policy can be based. At the same time, it was not at all easy to understand exactly why he had resigned. Nor did his statement in the House and the subsequent debate make the immediate issue altogether clear. The main point, that negotiations with Mussolini should not take place until the plan for the withdrawal of volunteers had been agreed, seemed to have been met at the last moment by a mysterious message which had reached the Prime Minister through an intermediary whose name he would not reveal.[1] The truth is that it was impossible, or at any rate it would have done great injury to Britain's interests, for Eden to reveal the whole story. He could say nothing about the Roosevelt initiative and all that it implied. He could say nothing of the slow pace of rearmament about which he had repeatedly complained and his solemn warning to the Cabinet on this vital question. Nor could he reveal all the indignities to which he had been subjected. In particular, he could not complain of the unorthodox and discreditable methods which the Prime Minister had adopted in his blind pursuit of 'appeasement'.

It is indeed strange that Chamberlain, who shared with Baldwin a deep hatred for Lloyd George, should have imitated some of his less respectable methods. For instance, Press statements about foreign affairs were often in fact, though not in name, released from No. 10, without approval from the Foreign Office; Horace Wilson, working independently, had already become 'adviser' to the Prime Minister; the opinions of well-meaning amateurs were preferred to those of tried and experienced professionals. Similarly, by his daily communications with Hoare and his close reliance on Simon and Halifax, Chamberlain seemed determined to by-pass his own Foreign Secretary. Eden, at any rate, decided that he would not continue to show the same tolerance as Lord Curzon, who had suffered so long under Lloyd George.

When the resignation was announced, the sensation was immense. Yet because of the uncertainty and obscurity as to its real cause, the debate, when it came, turned out to be something of an anticlimax. Of course there was a considerable excitement in the

---

[1] The so-called volunteers amounted in fact to five divisions of the Italian Regular Army.

lobbies and meetings of different groups of Conservative Members. Eden's resignation speech, made from the traditional place—the corner of the third seat below the gangway—was delivered on 21 February and the debate on the Opposition vote of censure was continued throughout the next day. It was dignified and impressive, but still left Members somewhat uncertain as to what all the row was about. The speech of his Under-Secretary, Lord Cranborne, who resigned at the same time, was more pungent. Nevertheless, some Members were even disposed to credit the rumours that were freely circulated that Eden was suffering from a nervous breakdown. Naturally *The Times* did not fail to give publicity to this story, which was said to have been started by Simon.[1] Certainly it was a convenient explanation from the Government's point of view. I did not believe a word of it, in spite of the talk in the Press and the lobbies. I remembered Lord Melbourne's famous saying that he had generally found that nothing that was asserted was ever true, especially if it was 'on the best possible authority'. As a result, in spite of an anxious and sombre speech by Churchill, and a violent attack by Lloyd George (which rather missed fire), Chamberlain's position was not seriously shaken. Yet the party as a whole was much concerned and there were many who were beginning now to realise the terrible position into which we were drifting. Finally, as a result of consultation with Churchill, it was decided that the best course would be to abstain from voting. Vyvyan Adams felt so strongly that he insisted on voting against the Government. But the rest of us, numbering just under twenty, followed Churchill's advice. Our group included representatives of different wings of the parties supporting the Government. Harold Nicolson, Major Hills, General Spears, Anthony Crossley, Captain MacNamara, Ronnie Cartland, and I were habitual suspects. But the Whips must have been surprised to see us joined in this demonstration by such respectable figures as Sir Joseph Nall (a leading and rather Right-wing industrialist), Leonard Ropner, Robin Turton, and Dick Briscoe. Paul Emrys-Evans, who was soon to play a considerable role, and Hamilton Kerr also declined to vote. So, of course, did Churchill himself and Brendan Bracken. To 'abstain' is not perhaps a very

---

[1] The Earl of Avon, *The Eden Memoirs: Facing the Dictators*, p. 601.

courageous Parliamentary gesture. But it can be made into a real protest if it is made clear to all, including the Press, that absence from the voting lobby is not due to absence from the Chamber. This we took due care to ensure.

Churchill was almost in despair over the catastrophe. He already had a high regard for Eden and, characteristically, was much more concerned at the loss to the country by his departure than comforted by any consideration of the gain to the forces opposing the courses on which the Government seemed now to be set.

Eden was succeeded by Lord Halifax, who brought to the Government the benefit of his high reputation. Edward Halifax was a man of extraordinary charm, strong religious convictions, and long experience of public affairs. But he had not the strength to succeed where Eden failed. A Foreign Secretary in the House of Lords has some advantages. He has more time for his work and is not so distracted by the pressure of Parliamentary questions and debate, which are much more onerous in the Lower House. But the system demands a special relationship with the Prime Minister and complete confidence between the two holders of these great offices. Moreover, neither Halifax nor Chamberlain had any real experience or knowledge of foreign affairs. If Chamberlain approached them from a somewhat provincial point of view and believed almost to the end in the possibility of a 'business deal' with Hitler and Ribbentrop, Halifax, as a great gentleman and aristocrat, found it quite impossible to understand the minds of such men. He could hardly bring himself to accept that statesmen who were in charge of a great country could be so absolutely devoid of any sense of truth or honour. Eden had learnt this; but his successor, like the Prime Minister, continued to trust in the value of written undertakings and formal agreements. It seems curious that they did not remember the small importance attached to a 'scrap of paper' by a far more respectable figure than either of these gangsters.[1] Neither was Halifax spared the inconveniences caused by the Press and publicity activities of No. 10. He had continually to protest against the ill effects of the optimistic propaganda that was put out from the Prime Minister's office without consultation with the Foreign Office.

[1] Bethmann-Hollweg's famous description of the Belgian Treaty in 1914.

There were two further results of Halifax's appointment. First, the Prime Minister became more and more involved in the details of foreign affairs in the House of Commons. On every question, whether China, Spain, Italy, or Germany, the Prime Minister had to bear the brunt of the Opposition attacks.[1] Since his style of argument, although powerful, was never conciliatory, the result was an increasing bitterness at the very time when the largest degree of unity and understanding was desirable. The Labour and Liberal Members and some of the Conservatives began to feel something like a hatred for Chamberlain. It was this that made the formation of a truly national Government impossible until, in May 1940, his administration was brought down by what amounted to an adverse vote. The second result, partly because of Halifax's inexperience and modesty, was to throw the conduct of foreign affairs into the hands of what Hoare has described in his memoirs as the 'Big Four'.[2] This inner Cabinet consisted of Chamberlain, Halifax, Simon, and Hoare. It was this group that was in charge during the decisive conferences with French Ministers in April and September and continued in command until the end. It is difficult to imagine a more fatal team.

After Eden's resignation, the situation was one of sombre expectancy. We did not have to wait long for the next blow. Three weeks later, on 11 March 1938, came the rape of Austria.

Hitler did not like failure. In July 1934 he had arranged for the murder of Dollfuss, the Austrian Chancellor. This was accomplished by the local Nazis under German inspiration. However, the coup by which the absorption of Austria was to follow did not succeed. France and Italy drew together, and Mussolini felt himself strong enough to move several divisions to the Brenner Pass and so to induce Hitler to draw back. Now, nearly four years later, he was ready, and his anxieties about Italy were finally removed by Mussolini's acquiescence. Hitler showed an almost hysterical relief and, to be just, did not forget the debt he owed to his partner. For in the years immediately ahead, Italy proved almost more of an embarrassment than an advantage. In Greece; in North Africa, in Italy itself; German strength was drained away to try to redeem the failures of their Italian ally.

[1] Viscount Templewood, *Nine Troubled Years*, p. 281.   [2] Ibid., pp. 291, 301.

The final coup was well planned in what was to become common form for Nazi aggression. Schuschnigg, the Austrian Chancellor, was summoned to Berchtesgaden and submitted to a long day and night of threats, amounting almost to torture. As a result, he agreed to appoint a Nazi, Seyss-Inquart, as Minister of the Interior, with full control of the police. This was the decisive step. For during the next few weeks, demonstrations and disorders were staged, which threatened internal disintegration. Schuschnigg, however, made one last effort and announced, on 9 March, that there would be a referendum as to whether the people were for union with Germany or for an independent Austria. This courageous gesture was characterised by Nevile Henderson, who had long regarded the *Anschluss* as inevitable, as 'ill-conceived and ill-prepared folly'. Yet it seemed a not unreasonable reply to Hitler's demand to annex Austria to the Reich in the name of self-determination, to allow the Austrian people to make their own decision. At the time the view was widely held that Austria, deprived of the old Empire, was not a viable country, and that amalgamation with Germany was a natural and even healthy solution. Even so, it was one thing to join, of her free will, a liberal and democratic Reich and quite another to be forced by brutal methods into the Germany which Nazi tyranny had degraded and debased. In the event, Austria, after much travail, regained her position. I little thought, in 1938, that seventeen years later I should sign, in Vienna, as British Foreign Secretary, the instrument which restored her freedom and independence.

Chamberlain, speaking in the House of Commons on the day after the annexation, protested against Hitler's action with unusual vigour. He reminded us that Austria was a member of the League of Nations and that Great Britain, together with France and Italy, had a deep interest in her independence. Germany had committed an act of aggression and had even refused to accept the British protest, on the grounds that the question was a German family matter. Considering that the Prime Minister had only a few weeks before seemed to pour scorn on the security provisions of the Covenant of the League of Nations, many of us in the House who heard his statement were surprised and gratified. We felt that this new assertion of Britain's interest in Central Europe seemed to show a more robust attitude. Naturally, the occupation of Austria, when it was complete, would threaten the position of Czechoslovakia. The Prime Minister's statement, therefore, was very welcome to that Government. For Czechoslovakia was not only a member of the League, like Austria, but had a long-standing defensive alliance with France and Russia.[1]

The debate, however, was chiefly memorable for Churchill's remarkable speech. He was listened to with rapt attention, and many Members, at last beginning to face reality, were entranced by his picture of the gradual unfolding of what he called 'the programme of aggression nicely calculated and timed'. He asked how long we were to go on waiting upon events. How long was bluff to succeed until, behind the bluff, the forces which Germany was creating had become irresistible? He described the strategic importance of Vienna as a centre of communications with all the countries of the old Austrian Empire, by road, river, and rail; the new German ability to control the oil, minerals, and raw materials of south-eastern Europe; the danger to Czechoslovakia, whose flank was in some degree turned and whose trade might easily be strangled. He spoke with gravity and authority, but without bitterness or re-crimination. He displayed full command of his subject, based on his profound study of history and the art of war. I had just been reading the first three volumes of his splendid life of Marlborough and was looking forward to the publication of the last. This work, the finest in my judgement of all Churchill's writings, appeared suddenly almost topical. The spirit of his ancestor seemed to have descended on the biographer. He spoke as a man outside and above party, only for his country. This occasion moved me deeply. Three days later, I had to address a meeting of the women's branch of our Conservative Association in Stockton. This was an opportunity to say what was in my mind. I said:

I believe that it is not too late to avoid war. What has mainly shocked the world is not so much the combination of Germany with Austria but the methods by which it has been achieved, the disregard for world opinion shown, and the campaign of brutality and persecution which will of course be in-augurated in Austria as part of the movement.

[1] John W. Wheeler-Bennett, *Munich: Prologue to Tragedy*, p. 36.

We are in a situation not dissimilar to that of 1914. Many people have felt and many historians have felt that if Sir Edward Grey and the Liberal Government of 1914 had made it perfectly clear in July of that year that this country would support Belgium if attacked, there might never have been a war.

If we mean to make the invasion of Czechoslovakia a reason for going to war – I don't know whether we should do so or not but I do say if we mean to do so we had better say so now, that is if we mean to join with Russia and France; and not when it has happened.

At this time I should like to see a widening of the national basis of the Government by the introduction of some of the Liberals who left it before and some of the Labour leaders. I should also like to see the inclusion of a great outside figure like Mr. Winston Churchill, to demonstrate to the world that the party divisions which properly divide us in our internal affairs are subservient to the unity which we display when we are faced with threats from outside.[1]

This at least was something the Stockton ladies could understand. It was better than the economic lectures which they had sat through so patiently for so many years.

On 19 March the Russians, thoroughly alarmed, proposed a Four-Power conference to discuss measures to deal with the rapidly deteriorating conditions. Three days later, on 22 March, the Prime Minister and Foreign Secretary advised the Cabinet to reject this proposal. On 24 March, therefore, the Prime Minister made a further statement to which I also remember listening, which appeared to be somewhat of a retreat from what he had said under the first emotion of Hitler's arrogance. Sir John Wheeler-Bennett has described this statement as 'a masterpiece of obfuscation'.[2] It certainly left the world wondering what Britain would or would not do in various contingencies. Unhappily, the one definite statement affecting the country next on the list, Czechoslovakia, was almost an encouragement to Hitler, rather than a deterrent. He made it clear that the British Government was not willing now to declare their readiness to defend Czechoslovakia against unprovoked aggression, or take the lead in inviting other nations to do so. They could not be in a position where the decision between war and peace was automatic and not at the discretion of the Government of the day. At the

[1] *Northern Echo*, 18 March 1938.
[2] John W. Wheeler-Bennett, *Munich : Prologue to Tragedy*, p. 36.

same time, in a rather obscure conclusion, the Prime Minister
pointed out that, if war broke out over Czechoslovakia or some other
victim of aggression, it was unlikely to be confined to those countries
which had undertaken contractual obligations. Nobody could tell
where it would end. Other parties might be drawn in. This was
essentially true of Britain and France with their long friendship and
closely interwoven interests. The speech was somewhat oracular.
Some of us thought it conveyed at least a guarded warning to Hitler.
None of us could have dreamed that within a few months the Prime
Minister would be engaged in putting pressure on the French
Government to evade their treaty engagements to Czechoslovakia,
and thus release Britain from becoming involved.

There was one aspect, however, of the occupation of Austria
about which we now have full knowledge. Owing to the breakdown
of a large number of the tanks and a great part of the mechanised
transport, the triumphant entry into Vienna, the crowning moment
of Hitler's life when the Austrian corporal was to play the role of
another Caesar, threatened to become slightly ludicrous. Fortunately, these new instruments of war were successfully delivered to
Vienna in time for the parade, by being loaded on to railway trucks
and brought to their destination by the more conventional power of
steam.[1]

One question I have since asked myself is, what were the reports
given to the Government by the British military attachés and the
Secret Service? Having, for many years, seen something of the
remarkable accuracy of information reaching Whitehall, it seems
strange that the British Government were still so obsessed by their
own military weakness that they did not realise that the Germans
were suffering from similar troubles. It is quite clear that nothing
like the great mechanised onslaught which brought France to her
knees in 1940 would have been possible in 1938. Without the
advanced bases in occupied France, even Britain's inferiority in the
air would not have been so dangerous. This is one factor of importance which is seldom taken into account in discussing the gains or
losses of the Munich settlement from the military angle.

The House of Commons, dazed and confused, was now to have a

[1] Winston Churchill, *The Second World War*, vol. i: *The Gathering Storm*, p. 211.

certain measure of comfort from the seemingly more robust attitude
of the Government. After Austria, it was clear that Czechoslovakia
was next on the list of victims. The fact that after the Austrian
annexation Göring had given his word of honour to the Czecho-
slovakian Minister in Berlin that they 'had nothing to fear from the
Reich' should have put President Beneš on his guard. In addition,
Hitler had continued the arbitration treaty between the two countries
which dated from 1925. But Beneš, although perhaps insufficiently
distrustful at this time of German duplicity, naturally put his main
confidence in the treaties of mutual assistance which had been made
first with France and later with Russia.

Czechoslovakia, like many of the successor States, was certainly
composed of a number of different nationalities. There were 7
million Czechs, 3 million Germans, 2 million Slovaks, and small
numbers of Magyars, Ruthenians, and Poles. But the Germans had
never been included in Germany proper. To speak, as Hitler did
later, of their 'return' to Germany was historically false. For many
centuries they had been subjects of the Holy Roman Empire, and
from 1866 to 1918 of the Austrian Empire. No doubt the minorities
had certain grievances, although in none of the post-war States were
these minorities better treated than in Czechoslovakia. Within the
borders of the old kingdom of Bohemia there had grown up a
modern, efficient, well-governed, and democratic society. The
agitation of the Sudeten German Party, now fostered by Hitler, in
form demanded the redress of their grievances, including some
degree of local autonomy. But this was only a screen to conceal
Hitler's real aim. He was determined to destroy the Czech State
itself. For it occupied a strategic position in Central Europe of vital
significance. Its northern and north-western frontiers were composed
of natural features. In addition to the protection provided by the
mountain ranges, a powerful defensive system of fortifications had
been constructed, often compared with the French Maginot Line.[1]
It is true that the Austrian frontier, after the German occupation of
Austria, could scarcely have been defended for any length of time.
Nevertheless, the German generals, whose anxiety was real, were

---

[1] I have drawn for this summary upon C. L. Mowat, *Britain Between the Wars,
1918–1940*, pp. 604–5.

correspondingly relieved when the power of Czechoslovakia was destroyed without a blow.

The German propaganda campaign, with all its dirty ingenuity, was soon in full flow. It was believed in London, in the third week of May, that a German attack on Czechoslovakia was imminent. Sir Nevile Henderson was accordingly instructed to give a warning to Ribbentrop. Halifax spoke with equal firmness to the German Ambassador in London; and both France and Russia made similar protests. These warnings were thought to have had a considerable effect. Hitler, for whatever reason, seemed to hesitate. He was, perhaps, impressed by what seemed to be a strong Anglo-French and Russian combination. We now know that all Hitler's advisers, including the General Staff, strongly recommended retreat or at least delay. Hitler was furious, and all the more because of the exulting note that was sounded in the Press of the whole world. Perhaps a reason may be looked for as much in the failure of the tracks and engines of the tanks as in this last demonstration of Anglo-French firmness, supported by the Russian Government. In the existing state of German armaments and the known strength, both in equipment, defensive positions, and morale, of the Czech Army, Hitler could not face a war on two, and perhaps three, fronts. Nevertheless, we learn from the German records that Hitler only agreed to postpone his new venture till October. The generals must be ready by then, and France and England might repent of their sudden mood of determination.

If Hitler was angered by these events, Chamberlain was alarmed. It was only, it seems, with the greatest difficulty that he was persuaded in the talks with the French Prime Minister, Daladier, and the Foreign Secretary, Bonnet, at the end of April, to accept the formula which—or so it seemed—had caused Hitler to recoil. But how was another crisis to be avoided? The Czechs must be persuaded to agree to substantial concessions, and France must be dissuaded from too active support of Czechoslovakia. Effective negotiations must therefore be initiated in order to arrive at a 'peaceful settlement'. This term of art, which continually recurs through the long story of appeasement, in effect meant capitulation under duress. It meant that Germany was entitled to get anything she wanted by bluff, agitation, and pressure of all kinds, so long as these did not involve actual military operations. There was, of course, a long background to this defeatist mood. For many months, *The Times* newspaper, under Geoffrey Dawson's influence, had preached the need for an Anglo-German *entente* at the expense of Germany's neighbours. This was partly due to an exaggerated sense of Germany's grievances, and partly due to what might be called 'Imperialist Isolationism'. Britain should disengage from the Continent. It was a policy which might conceivably have been carried through by a cynical abandonment of all Europe to the German hegemony. Even so, it involved great risks. For once Europe had fallen, would Britain and the Empire stand? This policy had long been nurtured by careful doctoring of the news, and found many adherents, open or concealed. Tom Jones had pressed it strongly upon Baldwin and had therefore urged a meeting between Baldwin and Hitler in 1936. It was only from now on that the so-called 'Cliveden Set' began to become politically important as the centre of many distinguished sympathisers with this attitude. Jones significantly writes in his diary:

> He [Hitler] is therefore asking for an alliance with us to form a bulwark against the spread of Communism. . . . On foreign policy L.G. [Lloyd George] is nearer to S.B. [Baldwin] than he is to Winston.[1]

Lloyd George's visit to Hitler in 1936, described in full in Jones's diary,[2] gives a remarkable account of the discussions in which the great Radical and war-time Prime Minister seemed to disregard altogether the series of breaches of faith by Hitler, as well as the most discreditable aspects of the Nazi system, including the Jewish persecution. He was clearly at this time in favour of working with Germany against Russia, although after Munich he completely altered his view. Ribbentrop had also pressed for a meeting between Hitler and Baldwin, and it is possible that, except for Baldwin's temperamental dislike of any dramatic initiative and his unwillingness to go abroad except for his annual cure, he might have fallen for the idea.

The importance of all this lies in the fact that Chamberlain must

---

[1] Thomas Jones, *A Diary with Letters, 1931–1950*, p. 209.   [2] Ibid., pp. 241 ff.

have heard of these proposals, however vaguely, and may have been influenced at the critical moment in September. Curiously enough, Tom Jones had by now somewhat changed his opinion and writes in March 1938 that he would welcome Churchill in the Government at the Air Ministry. He goes on as follows:

He [Churchill] has commended himself to the Labour Party by his support of the League in his recent speeches and articles. Many would like a reconstruction of the Government on more national lines for this emergency, bringing in Bevin and Citrine, the two Trade Union leaders. Something must be done to remove the suspicion attaching to Neville of being too well disposed to the Fascists.[1]

All these defeatist activities had long continued and had their effect on the slow progress of rearmament. According to Eden, Halifax and Kingsley Wood were critical of anything in the rearmament field which would upset the Germans.[2] The famous White Paper of 1935 had been called by the *Economist* the 'Black Paper'. The Labour Party attacked the War Loans as 'borrowing for death' and opposed rearmament throughout. Any question of organising an army for operating on the Continent was, as late as 1938, described by Sir Archibald Sinclair, the leader of the Liberal Party, as 'a disastrous blunder'. It is a falsification of history to suggest that appeasement up to the time of Munich was not widely supported, either openly or by implication. It was only as the relentless march of events revealed the true character of the man who had seized control of Germany that opinion in Britain began to change. Eden's resignation had at least produced a pivot round which dissenting members of the Conservative Party could more readily form.

During this summer, therefore, the dissident Conservative groups began to take shape. The first was what might be called the 'Old Guard'—Churchill and his devoted supporters, four or five only in number, including Bracken, Sandys, and Boothby. The Eden Group—or the 'Glamour Boys'—numbering perhaps twenty in all, began to have regular meetings during the summer months as the new crisis was clearly approaching. These, presided over by Eden, took place in various houses; sometimes in that of J. P. L. Thomas

[1] Thomas Jones, *A Diary with Letters, 1931–1950*, p. 397.
[2] The Earl of Avon, *The Eden Memoirs: Facing the Dictators*, p. 501.

and sometimes at Mark Patrick's. The numbers rose gradually and after Munich reached thirty or more. Like all Parliamentary groups, the composition was fluid, but I remember, in particular, Paul Emrys-Evans, who acted as secretary, Cranborne, Amery, Wolmer, General Spears, Harold Nicolson, Ronald Tree, Sydney Herbert, Derrick Gunston, Crossley, and Ronald Cartland as the most active. I attached myself to the Eden Group but also kept in close contact with Churchill and acted in a sense as a link between the two bodies. Of course, Churchill was himself in constant consultation with Eden, but he agreed that it was wiser to keep himself and his immediate followers apart for the time being. Churchill had been so long in virtual opposition that Eden would be more likely to attract hitherto loyal supporters of the Government who were now beginning to doubt. Both Churchill and Eden were, of course, well informed from a great number of sources on what was going on, and I found myself, by my connection with both these groups, far better instructed in the inner significance of what was happening than ever before.

There now began a process of pressure both on Czechoslovakia and on France, which has been described with much wealth of detail by Sir John Wheeler-Bennett in his authoritative and well-documented history.[1] We, of course, although suspicious, could not know exactly what was going on. Meanwhile, the work of Parliament continued: the Finance Bill, the various processes of legislation, and the normal routine of Parliamentary life. But I remember those months as a time of anxious waiting—with a growing sense of impending disaster. In 1914, at any rate, the war had come to most people as a bolt from the blue. But now, for many months, war was openly discussed and regarded by many as almost inevitable. How terrible it was to feel that yet another generation might be doomed to undergo what we had suffered twenty-five years before. My only son was soon to leave school to go to the university. Was all that had happened to me and my contemporaries to be repeated with our children? Were all those horrors to return once again to a distracted world? Relying on the judgement of men like Churchill and Eden, and indeed on my own instinct, I was convinced that the only hope

[1] John W. Wheeler-Bennett, *Munich: Prologue to Tragedy.*

of avoiding war—either now or later—was a bold and powerful policy by which Hitler might perhaps be restrained. Yet I confess that the views of the great majority of my friends, in Parliament and outside, made me sometimes hesitate. Might Chamberlain after all be right? Was it possible to reach some settlement by negotiation? Or would we simply feed the appetite until we were forced to a position where we would fight with scarcely a friend? It is easy for the reader today, who has available the massive literature which has been published about this tragic period, to see the futility and danger of what the Government were trying to accomplish. Now we have all the German documents, including the minutes of Hitler's discussions and orders with his generals. These archives reveal a cynical but clearly thought-out plan for the gradual absorption of Europe, such as seems almost inconceivable for one man to have devised. The modern critic must remember that none of this was at the time more than surmise. We had to judge as best we could, partly by scraps of information, partly by instinct. We had not even the sources which the Government persisted in ignoring.

As the summer months passed and the pressure upon the unhappy Czechs increased day by day, our small Parliamentary band could only watch. We had no power to change the Government, even if we could have rallied at that time sufficient Members to bring about its fall. Nor was there much to encourage us in a Government that might follow. Liberals and Labour, all for 'standing up to the dictators' in principle, were still determined to reject the only practical means by which Britain's military power could be rapidly increased and her corresponding influence on France and other countries fortified. I had many contacts with the Opposition of that time. There were very few who did not seem hopelessly confused between these two opposing moods. One of those with whom I began to discuss these matters was Hugh Dalton. He was a fine, robust, and hearty fellow, who combined Socialism and patriotism in a good old-fashioned English way. He, at any rate, took a much more sensible view than many of his colleagues and, as we know from his memoirs, did his best to stimulate them into facing realities. He describes the Labour Party's line with some contempt. They seemed to regard collective security as something to which Britain should make little contribution except 'to sponge on the Red Army'.[1] They wanted the end but were not prepared to adopt the means.

The Government was known to be pressing Beneš, the Czech President, to adopt a 'conciliatory' policy and make continually widening concessions to the demands of the Sudeten Germans. All this, of course, was on the assumption that Henlein was a genuine local leader, seeking a compromise solution.[2] He was in fact a Nazi stooge, who never put forward a plan or took a decision without direct orders from Hitler. Hitler did not want a fair settlement to satisfy the German population of Czechoslovakia. He wanted a pretext for war. He was determined to liquidate this creation of the Versailles Treaty and thus remove the barrier to the east, still defended by the physical conformation of Czechoslovakia's frontiers and the strength of its Army, well organised and well equipped.

At the beginning of August, Chamberlain, seeing little progress, determined upon a move of his own. He decided to send out a British representative to intervene between the Czech Government and the Sudeten Germans. He chose for this purpose Lord Runciman. Somewhat disingenuously, he told the House of Commons on 24 July that this mission was to be sent 'in response to a request from the Government of Czechoslovakia'. He would act not as an arbitrator but 'as an investigator and mediator'. In fact, the Czech Government initiated no such request, and only after immense pressure and with the greatest reluctance agreed to issue what might be called a formal invitation. Nor could there be any effective negotiation with Henlein, whose orders were to refuse anything that might be offered. Chamberlain also told the House of Commons: 'we are not hustling the Czechs'.[3] Actually the British, and to some extent the French, had not ceased to 'hustle' the unhappy Czechs for many weeks and months. He added that in his view there was a

---

[1] Hugh Dalton, *Memoirs, 1931–1945: The Fateful Years* (London, 1957), p. 64.

[2] Konrad Henlein was the leader of the Sudeten German Party (S.D.P.). In fact, they by no means represented all the Germans in the Sudetenland. There were four other parties: the German Social Democratic Party; the German Agrarian Party; the German Christian Socialist Party; and the German Small-traders Party (John W. Wheeler-Bennett, *Munich: Prologue to Tragedy*, p. 82).

[3] *Hansard*, 26 July 1938.

relaxation of tension on the Continent as a whole. This was in spite of the news of Germany's military preparations of which he must have been aware. On the next day, Parliament adjourned in the normal way. Members dispersed for the holidays, most of them in a mood of modified optimism.

The Runciman Mission set out with considerable goodwill from the British Press and public, and began its work in Prague on 4 August. Of its usefulness, Churchill and Eden were sceptical. Nor were they impressed by the choice of the head of the mission or its composition. It included nobody with any knowledge of the subject, although happily, owing to the chance of there being a young gentleman in the Treasury who was on a bicycling holiday in the country, and had made some study of German minorities in Central Europe, they were able to add him to their number.[1] Runciman was a Liberal politician of considerable experience in home affairs, who had filled many positions in pre-war and post-war administrations with distinction. But he was not a commanding figure, nor did his method of carrying out his mission win the confidence of the Czech Government and people. Like many rich Liberals of middle-class origins and dissenting connections, he had a curious penchant towards the aristocracy. He therefore spent his weekends at the castles of members of the great Austrian nobility, survivors of the old Austrian Empire, who had never in their hearts accepted Czechoslovakia as their country. They showed their own feelings by guarding their estates with Henlein stormtroopers. It was as if today a mission was sent out to Eire to solve some difficult problem that had arisen and consorted only with the remnants of the Anglo-Irish landlords. Runciman was also subject during his labours to continuous pressure from London. In the event, when one plan after another had been put forward and refused, since Henlein was not really free to negotiate and the Czechs saw little reason to yield, it looked as if by the end of August the crisis would reach its peak. Beneš made one further concession. On 4 September, in the hope of reaching a settlement, he offered to accept the demands of the Sudeten Germans; that is to say, complete local autonomy. He only boggled at the impudent requirement that Czechoslovak foreign

[1] John W. Wheeler-Bennett, *Munich: Prologue to Tragedy*, p. 79.

policy should be entirely recast, by absorption into the German system.

This news seemed to most English people the prelude to a settlement. What more could Henlein ask? What indeed? Nobody was more aghast than Henlein at the acceptance of his demands. It was a repetition of the Austrian ultimatum to Serbia in 1914. Hitler was equally distressed. There came about this time two interventions by the British Press, both equally irresponsible. The *New Statesman*, representing the Left, declared that the strategical value of the Bohemian frontier should not be made an occasion for world war.[1] *The Times*, in its leading article on 7 September, with more authority, as a great national newspaper still regarded abroad as officially inspired, went still further:

If the Sudetens now ask for more than the Czech Government are ready to give in their latest set of proposals, it can only be inferred that the Germans are going beyond the mere removal of disabilities for those who do not find themselves at ease within the Czechoslovak Republic. In that case it might be worth while for the Czechoslovak Government to consider whether they should exclude altogether the project, which has found favour in some quarters, of making Czechoslovakia a more homogeneous state by the cession of that fringe of alien populations who are contiguous to the nation to which they are united by race.[2]

This roused even Halifax. The Foreign Office at once issued a statement repudiating any official authority for the statement by *The Times* and reaffirming Britain's determination to stand by France. But the harm was done, and could not be retrieved.

What would happen now? Hitler's speech at Nuremberg, due to take place on 12 September, would perhaps give us the answer.

My wife and I listened to the speech from our Sussex home. We were alone that day. But before it was due to start, the long, gaunt figure of Lord Cecil[3] appeared. He had walked over from Gale, his house in Ashdown Forest, a few hundred yards from our front gates.

Lord Cecil was a lifelong friend of our family. He had deeply

[1] *New Statesman*, 27 August 1938.   [2] *The Times*, 7 September 1938.
[3] Viscount Cecil of Chelwood.

impressed me as a child. My brothers and I greatly revered him, and stood in considerable awe of him. Above all, we envied him because he used to drive a primitive kind of motor-car, while we still had only a dog-cart or a pony and trap. It was operated by steam, and used frequently to burst into flames.

He was also a keen, if somewhat unorthodox, devotee of golf and tennis. I can see him now on the putting-green, stooping down almost to the level of the ground, and often displaying an ungainly but uncanny accuracy. At lawn tennis, of which he was very fond, he practised an artful 'cut' shot (drawn from real tennis) which on our grass court was always formidable and sometimes devastating.

We had in 1938 some kind of radio set, and he had none. So he came to listen to Hitler's speech. If I remember right, it was broadcast first in German, as delivered. This was followed by a translation and commentary.

I can see Lord Cecil now, lying at full length, almost flat, on the sofa in what had been my mother's and was now my wife's sitting-room, with his long, emaciated body, his splendid head, and the great beak nose—like a modern Savonarola. Neither he nor I spoke or understood German; but my wife had sufficient knowledge of the language, gathered from a succession of German governesses, to enable her to follow the general argument (such as it was) and to pick up particular phrases. But, whether German scholar or not, no listener could fail to grasp the import of the venomous insulting sentences hissed out by the orator—raucous, maniacal, almost inhuman—and of the roars of 'Sieg Heil!' from the frenzied audience, bawled out like the battle-cry of a horde of savages.

At the end, Lord Cecil, who had not moved throughout, slowly uncoiled himself from his recumbent position. He said, gravely and slowly, 'This means war'. But when next day the newspaper commentators began to analyse what Hitler had actually said, there seemed some doubt. In any case, as we now know, there was still a fortnight to go before the date fixed for 'Operation Green'—the invasion and conquest of Czechoslovakia. Nor did the speech, in spite of all its vulgar and low abuse of President Beneš, make any precise demand. It did not even ask for a plebiscite in Sudetenland or the transfer of territory. That was left for the Anglo-French plan to formulate. The speech was a threat, and a danger-signal–but, as yet, no more.

What then did the speech mean? To Henlein and the Nazi Party among the Sudeten Germans the message was clear. It meant rioting; the creation of 'incidents'; something like revolution. Unfortunately, to Hitler's intense annoyance, these demonstrations were easily controlled by the Czech police.

What did it mean to the French and British Governments? It meant, unhappily, the fascinated terror of the rabbit hypnotised by the stoat. Instead of a vigorous reply, in robust and ringing tones, not a squeak came from Paris or London. Indeed, the 'Anglo-French plan' was soon to be hatched, which involved giving Hitler something for which he had not yet asked–the partition of Czecho-slovakia and the cession of all the Sudeten territory to the Reich.

Parliament was in recess. No news could be had, no pressure exerted on the Government. It is true that the British fleet, in accordance with the usual routine, was moving to the appropriate stations for its annual exercises. At this time, also, French Regular troops, without any general mobilisation, took up their positions in the Maginot Line. But the French Government was torn by dissension. The majority were paralysed by fear. The minority, including Reynaud, were impotent. The British Ambassador reported that the French Cabinet could and would do nothing unless Britain took the lead. In effect, the French message to London was 'Make the best terms you can for us, but no threats and no crisis'. The British Government were immensely relieved. They had no intention of taking the lead. After all, France was Czechoslovakia's ally. It was for France to act. If she got into trouble, we would do what we could: the Navy; perhaps a couple of divisions. This was what Oliver Stanley called the plot–to frighten the French into ratting and then get out on their shoulders. Alas! with the exception of Duff Cooper, all the Ministers were only too willing to rat themselves. In any event, the reports from Paris gave Chamberlain the opportunity for which he had long been waiting. He would propose a personal talk with Hitler.

But the failure of Paris or London to react against the gross insults and provocations of the Nuremberg speech also gave Hitler the answer to his question, and that of his anxious advisers. Would France and Britain act? Hitler had been convinced that, in the end, they would yield. Chamberlain's willingness to visit him made him doubly sure.

It is difficult for a modern reader to realise the immense impression caused by the Prime Minister's decision. A flight from London to Germany does not seem particularly dramatic today. But thirty years ago, for an ageing statesman—nearly seventy—who had never undertaken any flight of any consequence, to set out on an air journey of seven hours in one of the primitive machines of the period, to be bumped about, probably to suffer from air-sickness, without heating or air-conditioning or any of the comforts now universal, was an act of high courage. Above all, it was 'sporting'; and was so hailed by the British public. It was indeed a proof of great physical endurance and gallantry. But it was a diplomatic tragedy. For it played straight into Hitler's hands.

The story of the three visits—to Berchtesgaden, Godesberg, and Munich—has often been told, in its strange and sinister detail. At the first encounter, Chamberlain's inexperience and Horace Wilson's advice led him into the trap of seeing Hitler alone, without any member of his own staff or even his own translator. Hitler's interpreter, the famous Dr. Schmidt, no doubt kept a record; but it was not given to Chamberlain, who had to reconstruct, as best he could, what he remembered of the conversation.

According to his own account, Chamberlain found Hitler so intransigent that he himself became a little nettled and reproached his host for having allowed him to undertake so long a journey to so little purpose. Hitler then played his winning card. Up to now there had been no question of cession of territory or a plebiscite in Sudetenland. He now boldly and impudently demanded of Chamberlain the acceptance of 'self-determination'. If Chamberlain could accept this as applying to the Sudeten area, it would stay his hand— at least for a few days. Otherwise, his armies must march. Chamberlain caught eagerly at this straw. He could not accept self-determination and all that this principle might imply without consultation with his colleagues. But he would return at once for this purpose. So, having set out to see Hitler on 15 September to discuss a compromise, he returned to England on the 16th, having only gained the point that Hitler would wait until he received a formal capitulation. Of course, since the operation was not to start anyway till 30 September–1 October, there was no concession at all, although Chamberlain could not know this.

In effect, the Munich settlement, for good or ill, was made on that day at Berchtesgaden. For in spite of the high drama of the Godesberg Conference on 22 September, and the final signature of the Munich Agreement in the early hours of 30 September, the only issue which arose after Chamberlain's first visit was not 'whether' but 'how' the dismemberment of Czechoslovakia should take place. On 19 September the British Labour leaders—Morrison, Dalton, and Citrine—made an appeal to Chamberlain to stand firm and tried in vain to persuade the French Socialists to bring similar pressure on Daladier. But both Governments were adamant for surrender. In the course of six days of cynical pressure on the Czechs after the Berchtesgaden meeting, the British and French Governments had decided to issue an ultimatum telling them to yield. This, after a vain attempt by President Beneš to seek Russian aid, for which he could not carry the agreement of all the Czech parties, was accepted by the Czech Government, in a mood of something like despair, on 22 September. As a result, after a few hectic days Chamberlain was empowered to return to Germany, with a full acceptance of Hitler's demands. He went off almost jauntily, thinking the crisis resolved. To his amazement and indignation, Hitler then insisted on the instant entry of his troops and refused point-blank the more respectable plan of betrayal, on which the French and British Governments were insistent. Although the main question in dispute—the cession of the Sudetenland to the Reich—had been agreed, the additional brutality of the German demand to march in their Army like victors instead of the orderly and 'peaceful' transference of territory by which Chamberlain and Daladier hoped to preserve a façade of 'negotiation', nearly led to war. On his return from Godesberg, with no concession except a 'delay' till 1 October (the date long fixed for 'Operation Green') and the usual protestations that Hitler had 'no further territorial demands in Europe', the indecency of the way in which the surrender was to be carried out caused mounting anger and dismay in London and Paris. In the following days some rapid preparations were made in the event of a final breakdown of negotiations. The A.R.P. organisation, still in a rudimentary form, was mobilised. A few anti-aircraft guns were mounted in London. Some pathetic trenches were hastily dug in the parks. The British people suddenly realised that war—so long dreaded and so long believed 'unthinkable'—was round the corner.

Among the precautions planned by the authorities was the evacuation of children from London and the great cities. Accordingly, some twenty-five children, belonging to the Rachel McMillan Nursery School in Deptford, came to us at Birch Grove House. We gave up to them a great part of the house, and these children, with their attendant teachers, became part of our lives for many weeks. For it proved, for some reason, much easier to get them out of London than to get them back. They actually stayed with us till after Christmas and the country air did them good. During the autumn, realising that war was inevitable sooner or later, I took the necessary steps. We were fortunately able to prepare a cottage for our own use, and in the following year, when war came, we gave up the whole house for a large nursery school, this time from Balham and under the direct control of the London County Council. These children, with additions or departures from time to time, stayed in our house till after the end of the war. They were followed by another school, and it was not until some fifteen years later that we returned to our old home.

In this mood of anger but resignation to the inevitable the House of Commons met on 28 September, expecting a speech from the Prime Minister which would repeat, in not dissimilar circumstances, Sir Edward Grey's famous declaration on 4 August 1914.[1] Although few of us had any clear picture of the precise differences between what Chamberlain had agreed at Berchtesgaden and what Hitler had demanded at Godesberg, there was no doubt, from the rumours in the clubs and the lobbies, that the Government had determined to resist any further concessions. I well remember the tense atmosphere when the Prime Minister rose, to be followed by the extraordinary scene when he announced that his last effort for peace—a Four-

[1] The day of the ultimatum following the German invasion of Belgium.

Power Conference—had been accepted by Mussolini and Hitler. In their relief from the almost intolerable strain, and their excitement at the manner in which the message from Hitler was brought to Chamberlain while he was speaking, all Members on both sides of the House stood up in honour of the Prime Minister, to wish him God-speed in his third journey to save the peace of Europe. My normal place was on one of the benches below the gangway, on the Opposition side of the House, into which our large Conservative membership overflowed. I stood up with the rest, sharing the general emotion. Then I saw one man silent and seated—with his head sunk on his shoulders, his whole demeanour depicting something between anger and despair. It was Churchill. Meanwhile, Eden just could not bear it; he got up and walked out of the Chamber. Another Member bravely sat still and refused to rise. It was Harold Nicolson.

This was the prelude to Munich. But the issue was really settled. Hitler had gained the Sudeten territory at his first meeting with Chamberlain. The Anglo-French plan had 'sold the Czechs down the river'. The rest was tragi-comedy. Hitler, it is true, was robbed of his immediate entry into Prague at the head of his armies. That had to be postponed for six months. But even Hitler, though angry at being deprived of the military triumph, which he expected but which involved some risks, must have realised that he was being given the fruits without the risks and trials of a campaign. When his generals saw the Czech defences, which were handed over without a blow, their relief and gratitude was only equalled by their amazement that the Führer's 'intuition' could have won this bloodless victory.

After Chamberlain's dramatic announcement, and a few words from the Opposition leaders, the House adjourned. But what had happened? What would be the outcome?

I learnt from Eden something of the contest that had gone on. In spite of the desire of the Foreign Office to bring in Russia, the Prime Minister and his immediate colleagues were determined to exclude any Soviet help. We learnt, too, that the Cabinet had been divided. Chamberlain, Hoare, and Simon would have accepted the Godesberg terms, and with some logic. For apart from the brutality of the execution, the essentials were not different from the Anglo-

French plan at Berchtesgaden. But Halifax, Duff Cooper, and the younger members of the Cabinet, like Oliver Stanley and Walter Elliot, had not been able to stomach the crudity of the surrender. So the Prime Minister had to find some way out, and hope that Hitler would help him. France could be relied on; the French Government, under Daladier and Bonnet, wanted nothing better than to shuffle off their responsibilities on to the British. The invitation to Mussolini was accepted by him after consultation with Hitler. The modification of the terms, which Hitler accepted at Munich and which Chamberlain claimed as important concessions, were prepared by Mussolini only after detailed discussion and argument between the two partners in crime.

Nevertheless, if so much was false in this whole episode, the feelings and emotions of the mass of British people were genuine. In the last few days of September—the five days that followed Chamberlain's return from Godesberg—they were grimly, but quietly and soberly, making up their minds to face war. They had been told that the devastation of air attack would be beyond all imagination. They had been led to expect civilian casualties on a colossal scale. They knew, in their hearts, that our military preparations were feeble and inadequate. They believed in the British Navy; but they took no comfort from any other source. Yet they faced their ordeal with calm and dignity.

When the Prime Minister left again on his peaceful mission, on 29 September, the whole nation waited with bated breath. Outside Government circles, people knew little of the issues involved. They had been told something of the complicated story by Chamberlain's broadcast on 27 September, when war seemed almost inevitable. They knew that their lives and futures were to be put in jeopardy 'because of a quarrel in a far-away country between people of whom we know nothing'. In this message to the nation, nothing was said of the sufferings of the Czech people, only sympathy with Hitler 'and his indignation that German grievances had not been dealt with before this', together with an offer to 'guarantee' that the Czech Government would 'carry out their promises'. It is true that Chamberlain stated that if he were 'convinced that any nation had made up its mind to dominate the world by fear of its force', he would 'feel that it must be resisted'. But it was clear that he did not regard Hitler's determination to seize the Sudeten territory, with the inevitable political and economic disintegration of Czechoslovakia, as a proof of his bid to dominate Europe. Churchill had grasped this truth at least three or four years before. Others of us, largely by his influence, had for some time been convinced. Within a few months it was to become clear to all the world.

Yet on that day and the next, hardly a man or woman throughout the land had any doubt. In the next day or two we should be at war—and a war of unparalleled horror and destruction.

The Prime Minister, supported by the goodwill of the House of Commons and the whole people, left London for his third and final visit on the morning of 29 September. At 2.30 a.m. on 30 September the Munich Agreement was signed by Hitler, Mussolini, Daladier, and Chamberlain. The Czech Government, although not members of the Conference, had been permitted, as a last-minute concession, to send two representatives to Munich but 'only to give information to the British and French delegations'. When they were finally summoned to the conference-room, in the early hours of the morning, Hitler and Mussolini had left. They were presented, in the absence of their enemies, with an ultimatum by their friends. Twelve hours later the Czech Government yielded.[1]

There was much discussion afterwards, in Parliament and outside, as to the difference between the Godesberg demands and the terms of the final Munich Agreement. On paper they were not without importance. Broadly they were twofold. There was to be a Czechoslovak representative at the International Commission in Berlin which was supposed to settle the new boundaries. In addition, 'in exceptional cases', there was the right—but not the duty—of the Commission to depart 'from the strict ethnical rule that all the predominantly German population areas of Czechoslovakia belonged automatically to Germany'.[2] In the event, both these modifications proved nugatory. The Germans simply ignored them.

Chamberlain returned to London on the afternoon of 30

[1] John W. Wheeler-Bennett, *Munich: Prologue to Tragedy*, pp. 173–5.
[2] Ibid., p. 177. Daladier hoped, in vain, that some kind of defensible frontier might be retained under this provision.

September, having secured what he regarded as a great personal success, not merely by the avoidance of immediate war, but in the shape of a declaration signed by Hitler and himself, pledging their two countries to a policy of mutual consultation in order to secure the peace of Europe. This bit of paper the Prime Minister had drawn up himself. He regarded it as of supreme importance. Hitler had signed it, without taking the trouble to do more than read it cursorily. It meant nothing.

Chamberlain came back in triumph, to a concentration of applause and even adulation hardly ever granted to any statesman in our history. It was perhaps a demonstration of relief, but it was genuine and almost universal. Unhappily, in the pardonable elation of the moment, he used some phrases in speaking to the enthusiastic crowd in Downing Street which he was soon to regret. He referred to 'Peace with honour. I believe it is peace for our time.' Alas ! the Peace of Munich was both dishonourable and short.

Yet from every part of the globe, congratulations poured in. All the Dominion Governments were enthusiastic. President Roosevelt sent a characteristic message of marked approval: 'Good man'. The whole world seemed united in gratitude to the man who had prevented war. No wonder the Prime Minister lived in an exalted, almost intoxicated, mood. To question his authority was treason; to deny his inspiration almost blasphemy.

I remember well the meetings of our various groups—Churchill's friends, and Eden's. Naturally, I had not escaped—indeed I shared— the general sense of relief. My son would stay at school and go to Oxford in the autumn. My home and children, like all the other homes throughout the country, would be spared—at least for the time. It was as if we had come to the edge of a precipice and then —by some miracle—been pulled back to safety.

Yet when we met to discuss the true situation and to hear the reflections of those whose judgement we trusted, we began to see beyond the fragile and insubstantial screen of complacency and self-deception, skilfully designed to delude a whole people and lull them into a fictitious sense of security. Churchill and Eden knew something, if not yet all, of the mean story of the betrayal of the Czechs and—still more discreditable than even the British Government's weakness—something of the much less pardonable story of France's collapse. They also understood the immense change in the whole strategic position of Central and Eastern Europe, resulting from the virtual destruction of the Czech power to resist German expansion. The West was correspondingly weakened and the French Army's relative strength reduced. For some forty Czech divisions, threatening Hitler's eastern front, were immobilised and disintegrated; vast fortifications were surrendered; huge arsenals and stores fell into German hands and France's elaborate structure of defensive alliances in the east was virtually undermined. At the same time, the new fortified lines being feverishly constructed in the Rhineland were each day increasingly protecting Germany from French pressure in the west. In a word, as Churchill explained to us, and as he was to declare to a dazed House, 'We are in the presence of a disaster of the first magnitude which has befallen Great Britain and France'.

In spite of these doubts, the debate was dominated by Chamberlain. He was the hero of the hour. Yet before he could open the discussion, he had first to listen to the personal explanation of the only Minister who in the end persevered with his resignation. This was Duff Cooper, a man of outstanding intellectual quality, strong character, and proved courage. I had always admired him and, from that day onwards, an ordinary friendship ripened into something deeper. We were later to work together as colleagues in the Churchill Government, and in the handling of the French problem during the war. After he became Ambassador in Paris, I saw him frequently. His widow, Lady Diana, is one of my closest friends. We were always proud of him; but never were we so proud of Duff as on that day, 3 October 1938. He had the rare power of speaking without a note and yet with complete fluency. I assumed that he had memorised his speech and could thus deliver it almost textually. It was beautifully phrased, and powerfully argued. The last sentences came like a hammer-blow to the House:

> I have given up the privilege of serving as lieutenant to a leader whom I still regard with the deepest admiration and affection. I have ruined, perhaps, my political career. But that is a little matter; I have retained something which is to me of great value—I can still walk about the world with my head erect.[1]

[1] Hansard, 3 October 1938.

Duff Cooper's resignation, contrary to the expectation of many of us, stood alone. There had been much talk of the younger members of the Cabinet, Walter Elliot, Oliver Stanley, Malcolm Mac-Donald, being likely to join him in their protest. Had they done so, I doubt whether the Chamberlain Government could have survived, at any rate for more than a few weeks. All these men were friends of mine for many years before and after. I realise now the great stress under which they had to make their decision and the divided loyalties by which they were distracted. At the time, so great was Chamberlain's dominance, resignation in protest against a policy of which they had already approved the objective, if not the method, may well have seemed illogical and useless. At any rate, Duff Cooper was the only one to go. He promptly joined our group of dissenters, in which he became a leading figure.

It is difficult, in reading through the columns of *Hansard*, to put oneself back into the atmosphere of those hectic days. Chamberlain in his opening speech gave a clear, although somewhat disingenuous, exposition of the sequence of events. The House and the country had, until a few days before, been living under the shadow of impending war. It was easy for Chamberlain to command general sympathy from both sides of the House for the frightful load of responsibility which he and his colleagues had lately carried. There was a genuine sense of gratitude for all his efforts. He naturally laid great emphasis on the difference between the demands made at Godesberg and the concessions obtained at Munich. Indeed, this was the main burden of his speech. In this way, the decisive surrender made at Berchtesgaden, to which even Duff Cooper had agreed, was obscured. That the occupation of the Sudeten territory was to be completed by stages between 1 October and 10 October, instead of by one operation on 1 October, was represented as a substantial gain. The international supervision of the final frontier, to be controlled by an International Commission on which Czechoslovakia was to be represented, was another important change. In addition, there were some further amendments which the Prime Minister had secured, to which he naturally attached great significance. Nevertheless, a more critical audience must have agreed with Churchill's summary:

The utmost he has been able to gain for Czechoslovakia and in the matters which were in dispute has been that the German dictator, instead of snatching his victuals from the table, has been content to have them served to him course by course.[1]

Yet even Churchill, in his famous account of the difference between the three meetings, understated his case. This is how he described Berchtesgaden, Godesberg, and Munich:

£1 was demanded at the pistol's point. When it was given, £2 were demanded at the pistol's point. Finally, the dictator consented to take £1 17s. 6d. and the rest in promises of good will for the future.[1]

Actually, the Berchtesgaden meeting was the occasion, and the Anglo-French plan the method, by which practically the full price was paid and the independence of Czechoslovakia undermined. But the House could not realise this at the time; and much unnecessary argument took place now and in the following months upon what were really secondary issues. In any event, even the concessions alleged to have been gained at Munich were soon to become nugatory. For instance, the International Commission to which Chamberlain attached such importance never allowed any Czechoslovak representative to take part. The Polish and Hungarian claims on Czechoslovakia were not referred, as Chamberlain claimed would happen, to a further meeting of the Four Powers. They were settled by Germany alone, and in such a way as to lead towards the final dissolution of the Czechoslovak State. This 'Vienna Award', although a flagrant breach of the Munich Agreement, was to be greeted by the British Government with relief rather than protest.

After paying some tribute to the Czech Government for their discipline and dignity which had saved the peace of Europe, the Prime Minister turned to the question of compensation. A loan of £30 million was to be raised in London, with Government guarantee. This led to some bitter gibes, inside and outside the House, about the inflated price of treachery today. What nearly two thousand years ago could be done for thirty pieces of silver now cost thirty millions sterling. Blows were exchanged over this quip, though not in the Chamber. Finally, the Prime Minister enlarged

[1] *Hansard*, 5 October 1938.

upon his personal relations with Hitler and the declaration for which he had obtained the Führer's signature in the early hours of that fatal morning.

Chamberlain obviously believed with the deepest conviction that this was a turning-point in the history of Europe, and that he would prove the saviour, not only of his country, but of all the world. The sacrifices demanded from Czechoslovakia were a pity. But they were necessary. For the Czechs were an obstacle to appeasement:

> The path which leads to appeasement is long and bristles with obstacles. The question of Czechoslovakia is the latest and perhaps the most dangerous. Now that we have got past it, I feel that it may be possible to make further progress along the road to sanity.[1]

As to the Chamberlain–Hitler pact, he used these words:

> I believe that there is sincerity and good will on both sides in this declaration. That is why to me its significance goes far beyond its actual words.[1]

These words ring true. Chamberlain still seemed to believe that if Russia could be kept at arm's length and if a practical approach could be taken towards Germany's ambitions in Central and Eastern Europe, with perhaps the transfer of a colony or two, a final settlement could be reached, and the peace of Europe secured. This concept so dominated his mind that, even when six months later Hitler broke his latest engagement in the most open and unscrupulous way by the occupation of Prague, Chamberlain was not easily dissuaded from the path that he had chosen. Indeed, he took the line that if Czechoslovakia had disappeared, so had the British guarantee of her integrity. It was the pressure exercised by Lord Halifax and by the Whip's office, now beginning to be alarmed, that made Chamberlain change his tune.[2] Indeed, some of his colleagues had a legitimate grievance over the suddenness of his conversion. Simon, for instance, like an old priest at some pagan altar, went on mumbling the obsolescent ritual of appeasement to a rapidly diminishing congregation.

Apart from the Prime Minister's two speeches—opening and

---

[1] *Hansard*, 3 October 1938.
[2] The Earl of Birkenhead, *The Life of Lord Halifax* (London, 1965), p. 432.

concluding the debate—there were two outstanding contributions in these three days. One, of course, was Churchill's, with its grand sweep and brilliant colouring; the other came from Dick Law, Bonar Law's youngest and only surviving son.[1] Dick was a recent rebel, and spoke with all a convert's traditional fervour. His intervention was brief but devastating. He poured scorn upon the exaggerated claims of Chamberlain's friends who asserted that he had won a personal victory and made Hitler recoil by the strength of his own personality. This proposition, which was reverently advanced by some of the more adulatory of those trusted Members whom the Whips put up to speak for the Government, was described by Law as altogether incredible, for it assumed

> that those men who have risen to power through violence and treachery, who have maintained themselves in power by violence and treachery, who have achieved their greatest triumph by violence and treachery, have suddenly been convinced by the magnetic eye of the Prime Minister (it can only have been by his eye, because it was done through an interpreter) that violence and treachery do not pay.[2]

For the rest, although many effective speeches were made and many arguments advanced, everyone knew that so great was the strength of the Government in the country that nothing could seriously shake them in Parliament. At our almost daily conferences with our friends, we had the gloomiest forebodings. The tide was, at present, too strong and it was flowing against us. There was a universal feeling of unbounded gratitude; Chamberlain was the saviour, above and beyond criticism.

Yet, as the historian of Munich has pointed out, it is a curious fact that, in a discussion on a policy based on 'Peace for our time', the only issue on which there was complete unanimity was the vital necessity for the rapid completion of Britain's preparation against war.[3] Even the Opposition now accepted the need for rearmament, and complained of the notorious deficiencies revealed at the moment of crisis. Nevertheless, Chamberlain did not appear convinced of the gravity of the position. He paid lip-service to rearmament, but what

[1] Later Lord Coleraine.   [2] *Hansard*, 3 October 1938.
[3] John W. Wheeler-Bennett, *Munich: Prologue to Tragedy*, p. 187.

he really believed in was the new era of universal peace which would follow his prodigious and unprecedented efforts.

So we embarked upon what has been called 'the golden age of appeasement'. The dream was to be rudely shattered six months later. On 15 March 1939 Hitler's proclamation to the German people contained this simple but dramatic sentence: 'Czechoslovakia has ceased to exist.' Six years later, after efforts unique in history, for a while alone and abandoned by her allies, but relying on that moral strength which never deserts her in the hour of need, Britain gave her answer to that proud boast. In the spring of 1945 Nazi Germany ceased to exist and, pray God, will never be restored.

*   *   *

During these anxious days, I had many discussions with the growing section of discontented Conservative Members. On 28 September, before the final and fatal decisions which led to Munich were reached, there was an important meeting at Churchill's house. There was much talk; but little effective action was open to us. When Duff's resignation became known, there was great jubilation in our ranks. I at once telegraphed to him:

Many congratulations on your inspiring lead to public opinion. Earnestly hope more of your colleagues will follow your example.

Alas! the second sentence was too optimistic.

But when the House met for that post-Munich debate, apart from the speeches to be made, two urgent questions arose: how should we vote and what could we do to prevent a snap election? The first would be largely settled by the form of words used. If the Opposition amendment were cast in terms neither too hostile nor too extravagant in their censure, the dissident Conservatives, including Churchill, Eden, Amery, and Duff Cooper, and now amounting to some twenty-five or thirty, might be ready to vote for it, or at least abstain. On this matter I got in touch, with Churchill's approval, with Dalton, who had made the last speech for the Opposition on the first day (3 October). I managed to see him about midnight; and I told him that there was a danger of an immediate General Election, in which the votes soon to be recorded would be treated as a test of policy. Those Conservatives or Liberals who voted for the Government would 'get the coupon'.[1] Those who opposed or abstained would be marked down for destruction and official candidates run against them. It would be another Maurice debate.[2] It was therefore vital to know what would be the terms of the official Opposition amendment. I persuaded Dalton, not without some difficulty, to come along to Brendan Bracken's house in Lord North Street for a talk. Here we found both Churchill and Eden, who explained to Dalton our hopes of organising a substantial Tory abstention, both on the Government's motion and on the amendment. Dalton has recorded an incident, which I, too, recall:

> Various drafts were suggested, centring round collective security. One draft which they pressed upon me spoke of 'national unity and strength'. I said to Churchill: 'That is not our jargon.' He replied: 'It is a jargon that we may all have to learn.'[3]

We also discussed the possibility of some co-operation between the dissident Conservatives and the Labour Party in the constituencies in the event of an early General Election. Dalton was not unsympathetic. He pointed out that there were obvious obstacles to be overcome, but that if anything like a coupon election were tried and the dissident Conservatives, led by Churchill, fought as Independents, there should not be great difficulty in seeing that they were given a clear run by the Socialists, at any rate in most places. This was encouraging. Although Dalton was careful to say that much further discussion would be needed and that he spoke without the authority of the leaders of the party, I felt that this somewhat unorthodox discussion had been worth while.

There was still a good deal of uncertainty as to how far some of Chamberlain's close friends and advisers were pressing on him the advantage of a General Election on the 1918 model, where he

---

[1] Asquith's contemptuous description of those Liberals who accepted support from Lloyd George and Bonar Law in the 1918 election.

[2] The debate on General Maurice's letter to *The Times*, attacking Lloyd George, which resulted in the great Liberal schism (May 1918). All those Liberals who voted against Lloyd George were opposed at the ensuing General Election.

[3] Hugh Dalton, *Memoirs, 1931–1945: The Fateful Years*, p. 199.

would be presented not as 'the man who won the War', but as 'the man who saved the Peace'. It was commonly believed that Kingsley Wood, one of his oldest adherents, was urging Chamberlain to exploit the position in this way. It was equally asserted that Halifax was working against it. The possibility, even the likelihood, of a dissolution was freely discussed in the lobbies during the debate. The threat was also being used as a deterrent to bring any hesitant Conservatives into line. Whether the plan was seriously considered or not by the Conservative managers, the idea was finally killed by one of those unexpected episodes which play so large a role in the life of the House of Commons. The plan—if there was a plan—or the plot—if there was a plot—was destroyed in less than twenty minutes by a speech by one of those figures, so influential inside the party, although almost unknown to the public, who at critical moments often exercise decisive authority.

Sidney Herbert, now in failing health, the result of severe wounds, and only able to walk with difficulty, would not normally have taken part in a debate of this kind. But he was moved by anger at the rumours going round the lobbies. He decided to speak, and was called at 7.30 p.m. on the second day, not a very good hour, when the House was empty. However, when his name went up on the boards, Members trooped in. Herbert had been for many years Parliamentary Secretary to Baldwin. He represented the Conservative tradition in its most loyal form. Rich, aristocratic, popular, he was also highly intelligent. He was, moreover, a man of courage and integrity; the sort of man to whom the rank and file look in moments of confusion. He did not mince his words. He made it clear that while everyone was grateful to the Prime Minister for what he had done, many would have reservations as to the policy pursued during recent years. He then referred to the loyalty which held the Conservative Party together but, he added, 'we can be led, not bullied'. He turned next to what was in everybody's mind. There could be no greater iniquity in the world than to force a General Election at this moment. After pointing out that from the national point of view nothing could be gained and much might be lost, and referring to the vastly more urgent question of rapid rearmament, he went on to say this:

There may be some tiny Tammany Hall ring who want such a solution but my solution would be quite different. I ask the Prime Minister here and now to do something quite different. I ask him to make his Government really national, to broaden its basis, to invite the Labour party into it, to invite, above all, the trade union leaders into it.[1]

The phrase 'Tammany Hall' went home. Perhaps as a result of our contacts with the Opposition leaders, an amendment was in fact put down on to paper, of a character which would allow us to abstain. In the event, therefore, we abstained in both divisions, that on the Government motion of approval and that on the Opposition amendment. Altogether, our number amounted to between twenty-five and thirty.

The Prime Minister's final speech was a little more robust than his opening exposition and more to the taste of the House. It may thus have got some doubters into the lobby. He received enthusiastic support from the party as a whole, and a good deal of sympathy from both the Liberal and the Labour benches. In the country, his position was overwhelmingly strong. One thing, at any rate, was gained. Yielding either to the view of his colleagues or to the central opinion of the party, or perhaps to his own better judgement, he made it clear that there would be no immediate General Election. Before the day ended, there was a small diversion. The adjournment of the short session had to be moved, and Churchill and his friends took the line that in the circumstances we ought not to separate for as long as four weeks. This led to a bitter dispute between the Prime Minister and Churchill. Knowing that I had little chance of speaking in the main debate, I took my opportunity on this adjournment motion on the morning of the last day. After a shaft directed at those Ministers who must be exhausted by the moral strain of resigning in the morning and withdrawing their resignations in the afternoon, I complained that:

We are being treated more and more as a kind of Reichstag to meet only to hear the orations and register the decrees of the government of the day.[2]

I ended by declaring my view that

... the situation with which we are faced to-day in this country, with which the world is faced, and with which freedom, justice and liberty are faced, is more

[1] *Hansard*, 4 October 1938.   [2] *Hansard*, 6 October 1938.

dangerous and more formidable, more terrible than at any time since the beginning of Christian civilisation.[1]

The first observation was an exaggeration; the second, alas, was not.

Thus ended, with the support of a great Parliamentary majority for Chamberlain and his Government, and amid the acclamations of the mass of the people, the first stage in the Munich controversy. There followed, and has continued ever since, strenuous debate as to the merits of the case. At the time, feeling was so strong as to create acute divisions, in every class of society, comparable only with the Irish issues of 1886 and 1914. For the first and for the last time in my recollection, there was one of those cleavages which divides friends and families and leaves behind them ineffaceable traces. No doubt in England, in the seventeenth century, there were families in which loyalties were divided between Roundhead and Cavalier; and so it was in America during the Civil War. Although the divisions caused by the Munich settlement were soon to be healed in common danger and suffering, yet the memories of this bitter dispute still remain. The Chamberlainites treated the rebels at first with contempt and then with growing apprehension. Those of their number, especially those in the inner circle, who were conscious of their own hesitations, were particularly sensitive. Meanwhile, every instrument of pressure and propaganda was brought into play. *The Times*, for instance, consistently misrepresented the truth, doctored the news, and generally displayed a temper which oscillated between deception and hysteria. The fatal leading article of 7 September, suggesting the handing over of the Sudetenland, had struck a cruel blow, which Halifax had deeply resented. On a lesser plane was an incident regarding Duff Cooper's resignation speech. *The Times* lobby correspondent, Anthony Winn, a young professional journalist, sent in an accurate report of the impact which the speech had made in the House and the way in which it had been received. The editor suppressed this, an action which was, I suppose, within his rights. But he went further and wrote a story of his own in which he described Duff Cooper's effort as 'a damp squib', and inserted this

[1] *Hansard*, 6 October 1938.

under a heading 'From Our Lobby Correspondent'. Young Winn instantly resigned. Two years later he was killed in action.[1]

Incidents like these added fuel to the flames. The hangers-on of Chamberlain became more and more servile and encouraged him in his blindness to realities. His opponents became more and more offensive in their turn. It now became the fashion among us to refer to the Prime Minister under the sobriquet 'the Coroner'. This nickname, I think, was invented by Brendan Bracken. It was at least not so brutal as the famous quotation of an American journalist describing Runciman's arrival in Prague: 'The hangman with his little bag came shuffling through the gloom.'[2]

In my own and my wife's family, feelings were divided. Lord Cranborne's resignation with Eden had already ranged the Cecils against the Government. The Cavendishes were slower to move. My brother Daniel increasingly shared my indignation. It was our custom every year, on 5 November, to have a fine bonfire at home and to crown it with a straw figure, wearing an old hat or cast-off suit. This was for the benefit of our children, and afterwards grandchildren, and all the children of the neighbourhood. This year we had a splendid representation of Chamberlain, and sacrificed for the purpose a black Homburg hat in quite good repair, as well as a rolled umbrella. Some of my relations were staying with us at the time and this caused a deep feud. What made the scene more dramatic was the presence of some forty or fifty Czech refugees to whom I had been able to give shelter and hospitality in various houses and cottages on our estate.

Munich in a sense, therefore, became the shibboleth. Although Churchill, who had no rancour in his nature, gave office or employment to many of the 'old gang', yet I do not think he ever gave any of them his real confidence. There have been many conflicts in my political life which at the time were fought with energy and even anger, but they were quickly forgotten. It is only in this case that the memory dies hard.

These were the conflicting emotions of the time, but the great question still remains to be argued for many years by historians—was Chamberlain right or wrong?

[1] Duff Cooper, *Old Men Forget*, p. 250.
[2] John W. Wheeler-Bennett, *Munich: Prologue to Tragedy*, p. 79.

The problem thus posed is really twofold. Was Chamberlain right in the actual decision taken at Berchtesgaden and afterwards endorsed in the formal agreement signed at Munich? Or would it have been both possible and wiser for Britain to have taken the lead in resistance, even at the risk of war? The second question is, how did all this come about? How did Baldwin and Chamberlain allow a situation to develop where the democratic countries were unable to put up a resistance to the now open German aggression?

The first and narrower point is no doubt finely balanced. Would it have been better to have fought then rather than a year later? Certainly the advice which the Prime Minister and his colleagues received from the Chiefs of Staff was that Britain in 1938 was not really in a position to resist. The chief reason was the unreadiness of the Air Force. It is true that if Churchill had been in power, every aspect of this advice would have been relentlessly examined and probed. Neither the Prime Minister nor any of his Ministers had either the knowledge or experience to undertake this task, even if they had had the will. It is clear that no proper appreciation was made of the importance of the Czech defences and the value which the Czech Army could have been in holding up any German attack. It was only when the German generals saw the strength of these defences that they realised the miracle of bluff which the Führer had performed. The second argument for delay was the feeling in the Dominions. It is certainly true that their attitude was by no means robust. But they had not received throughout the previous years and months the right kind of information or leadership. Moreover, Hitler skilfully made an appeal to the now widely accepted principle of self-determination. 'Oh self-determination, what crimes have been committed in thy name!' a lover of liberty might well exclaim. On the narrow ground of legal obligation, the French abandonment of their ally is far more reprehensible than the British hesitation. French leaders were only too glad to let Britain take the lead and shoulder the blame. But had the British Government taken a firmer view, they could no doubt have stimulated the French to honour their treaty commitments. Would it have been better to have faced war, assuming it to be inevitable, in 1938 rather than 1939? Undoubtedly, the majority of the Cabinet were impressed by the unreadiness of Britain for war, and the terrible responsibility of adopting a course of action which would lead to war. Among other deterrents, expert advice had indicated that bombing of London and the great cities would lead to casualties of the order of hundreds of thousands, or even millions, within a few weeks. We thought of air warfare in 1938 rather as people think of nuclear warfare today. Here again, Churchill would have pressed his inquiries on the actual possibilities of heavy bombing from the German airfields available before the conquest of France and the Low Countries. Nevertheless, if we are to condemn Chamberlain and his colleagues on the narrower issue, we must face the question squarely. In the circumstances of 1938, as they developed in that summer, would any of us have been ready to declare war on Germany? But of course the question is wider than this. How did we allow things to slide in the two or three years before the crisis? Why had we not made some real effort to bring Russia into active alliance? Why, if we saw our power drifting away to a position which would make further concessions necessary, did we not hurry on with rearmament, including National Service? Why did we not try to widen the basis of the Government? After all, we had plenty of warning from the remilitarisation of the Rhineland onwards. Perhaps the true answer is that we were all to blame. The British, after their prodigious efforts in the First War, seemed in the late twenties and thirties uncertain and bemused. They wanted to be a Great Power but would not pay the price. They were passionate for peace but lukewarm for the measures to maintain it. They were like the man who wants to win the lottery without buying a ticket.

How, then, did this all happen? How did the victorious Allies of 1918 suffer a reversal of fortune so swift and so startling that, within twenty years of victory, they were confronted by the fearful dilemma of moral defeat or, as it was thought, something like physical annihilation? The victorious War Alliance soon dissolved. Far the most decisive feature of this collapse was the retirement of the United States of America into isolation. During the whole of my life, the main problem confronting the Old World has been somehow or other to induce the New World to accept the responsibilities of its growing material and moral strength. The chief anxiety of far-seeing statesmen, like Eden or Churchill, has been to achieve this end. Chamberlain was too provincial and too self-centred to understand its importance. Now that at last we have seen the Americans accept the responsibilities of a world Power, it seems not merely ungracious but exceedingly foolish to criticise their use of their new authority. Some of my American friends are now distressed because their country, in spite of having distributed vast benefits in the shape of aid and defence from aggression throughout the globe, as it becomes more powerful becomes more unpopular. I keep reminding them that that is the inevitable reward for world-wide responsibilities. Britain guaranteed the freedom and maintained the peace of a great part of the world for at least a hundred years, besides bringing to her vast Empire a degree of progress and security hitherto unknown. Yet Britain was hated, reviled, and intrigued against in all the chancelleries of Europe and outside. Now the torch has passed largely into American hands. Now they in turn are reaping the same harvest. That is the 'price of admiralty'. However, in the period between the wars, the Americans evaded their responsibilities. At the same time, Japan was a dissatisfied country and ceased to co-operate with her war-time allies in the West. Similarly, Italy felt that she had been cheated of her full price for abandoning her long-standing alliance with Germany and Austria. Under Mussolini, territorial and colonial ambitions began to dominate the minds of her rulers. Britain and France, through all this period, were generally at loggerheads. When French policy was strong, British was weak. Alternatively, when the British seemed inclined to show a certain resolution, the French lapsed into internal dissension and defeatism.

The principal conditions, therefore, on which any world-wide collective security could be based were never fulfilled. Nor was there any group of like-minded Powers such as has now come together and for which Churchill, and others who thought with him, worked so hard in the last few years before the war. Moreover, in Britain and, above all, the United States, there were many delusions about the nature of international affairs. People's hopes were raised high by the institution of the League of Nations. It seemed to promise a perpetual peace merely by its existence; and even serious defections from its ranks did not altogether destroy this illusion. In Britain, the prospect of another war was regarded as 'unthinkable'. The unprecedented scale of casualties in the First War was a new experience for all the countries involved, but especially so in Britain, whose wars had been, on the whole, economically fought throughout her history. France perhaps knew more, but knew too much. The frightful losses of the French and the bloodbath from which she had suffered were accentuated by the decline in her population. Unilateral British disarmament had produced a classic example of a Power at once over-committed and under-armed. The partial paralysis from 1934 onwards resulted from the threat of facing three enemies in widely separated theatres—in Western Europe, in the Mediterranean, and in the Far East.

Finally, the very decency of ordinary men and women in Britain was a handicap. In our insularity, we neither read Hitler's gospel, *Mein Kampf*, nor understood the nature of his movement, or the scale of his ambitions. We shut our eyes to the character of his internal régime and comforted ourselves that if Germany had become a police State, it was no worse than Russia. We did not realise the difference. One country was slowly emerging from, the other relapsing into, barbarism. In any event, Germany was then the immediate threat to Britain and to Europe. Hitler had, or so it would appear, an almost mesmeric effect upon many of his visitors of very different types and backgrounds. Chamberlain was only the last of a long series of dupes who, having made the pilgrimage to Berchtesgaden, unexpectedly fell under his spell for varying periods of time. After his first meeting at Berchtesgaden, Chamberlain got the impression 'that here was a man who could be relied upon when he had given his word'.[1] All failed to realise his extraordinary methods as a negotiator; the depths of deceit which he would practise; and the infamies to which he would sink. Lloyd George is said to have remarked about Poincaré that having acquired a reputation for honesty, he could afford on occasion to be tricky. Hitler was notoriously guilty of dishonest breaches of faith time after time; yet, for some strange reason, he continued to be believed.

[1] Keith Feiling, *Life of Neville Chamberlain*, p. 367.

All these things together, including the universal aversion of the whole British people—Left, Right, and Centre—to war and even to preparations for war, were the cause of the apparent collapse of British authority in the world. The Left disguised their dislike of armaments by the parrot cry of 'Collective Security', to which apparently our contribution was to be rated very low. The Right distrusted the League and would have preferred a policy of semi-isolation, relying on the reserve power of the still potent Empire. But it refused to take the necessary military measures to secure such a policy. Certainly it is not true, as has sometimes been alleged, that the policy of appeasement, not in the right sense of pacification but for the purchase of time or comfort at others' expense, was a cleverly thought-out plan. No British Government was guilty of a Machiavellian plot to make, as it were, a Ribbentrop—Molotov pact in reverse. To conspire with Hitler, to let him dominate Central and Eastern Europe, if he would only let us alone, hoping that he would dissipate his strength in a Russian conflict—such a policy, cynical as it would have been, might have succeeded; although in the long run Hitler, like Napoleon, would never have been satisfied, and in the end would have turned on the Western democracies. There was no such plan. For the truth is, there was no plan at all.

Ought we to have fought at Munich? Or was the year of respite worth obtaining at almost any cost? The military aspects of this question, both tactical and strategic, will continue a subject of acute controversy as long as our history is studied and written. There are certainly great arguments to be deployed on both sides. At home, our own rearmament had made insufficient progress. The Army was small and still ill equipped, as was to be proved a year later. The Air Force, since the Spitfire had not yet come into service, relied upon obsolete or obsolescent machines; a bombing force scarcely existed. Only the Navy was in relatively good shape. The internal arrangements for air defence were primitive, but likely to gain substantially by delay. Overseas, the Dominions were hesitant and in no mood for another European war. The French Government and people were bitterly divided. Their Air Force was weak and in disarray. It was doubtful whether the French Army would do more in case of war than occupy the Maginot Line. Whatever the truth of the state

of the defences which the Germans were constructing in the Rhineland, the French were scarcely in the mood to attack them. Nor was
a British Expeditionary Force available to give them encouragement. Indeed, the principle of war on a basis of limited liability, that
is, of not sending British armies to the Continent, was the accepted
War Office doctrine up to March 1939. Neither we, therefore, nor
our Western Allies were in a good condition to fight. Russia was an
uncertain quantity. Might it not be that the Russians would decide
to remain neutral and watch the capitalist States destroy each other?
Against all this, we could hardly have been in so perilous a position
as that which we had to face in the summer of 1940. The armies of
France would have been intact. We should have had Germany
facing two fronts—a west and an east—with Czechoslovakia and
perhaps Poland to fight, and beyond them, Russia to fear. The
Czechoslovak Army was considerable and well armed. As regards
the air, in spite of our weakness, the German bombers would have
been at the disadvantage of having to attack from home stations—a
difference in mileage which was highly significant in relation to the
machines of that period. We might well have secured the support
of Russia, who regarded Munich as a sign of the moral and material
weakness of the West. The Dominions would doubtless have come
along in due course once the die was cast. Moreover, as we now
know, we might have stimulated the German generals to make a
serious attempt either to force Hitler to draw back or depose him
from power.

At the time, without of course having any access to any official
military appreciation, but relying on the opinions of Churchill and
others whose judgement I respected, I thought, as did many with
me, that we ought to have fought at Munich. Since then, after study
of much that has been written on both sides, I see no reason to
change this view.

Nevertheless, whatever may be the final judgement on the
Munich Agreement, Chamberlain was certainly guilty of myopic
self-satisfaction and self-delusion, both before and after. This is the
real ground for censure. He came back in an exalted mood. When
he used such phrases as 'Peace with honour' and 'good will on both
sides', he seemed quite unconscious of the shameful abandonment

of part of Czechoslovakia to the odious apparatus of Nazi rule. As the weeks passed, his defence of the Munich settlement raised more and more antipathy, not only in the Opposition but among his own party. He and his friends did not defend Munich, at any rate until much later, because it had given us a year's breathing-space. He defended it on its own merits and for the happy prospect of peaceful progress to which it pointed. Whatever some of his more sceptical colleagues may have thought, the policy of appeasement had one sincere exponent. Chamberlain believed in it. He thought that he could work with Hitler. He trusted in Hitler's professions. He saw himself as the author of a general pacification, as step by step the German claims became satisfied. Europe could then settle down to a long period of peace. It was only much later, after men's eyes were opened, that Chamberlain's friends claimed on his behalf that the peace of Munich was a truce, consciously entered into in spite of its disadvantages, to give us another year for military preparation. If after he had come back from Munich Chamberlain had told us frankly that he had accepted a disagreeable but inevitable rebuff, and that we must now get down to rearmament on a war scale, including National Service, much of the bitterness would have been mitigated and his reputation in history would have gained. But in fact it was not till the following spring or summer that the argument about 'gaining time' became fashionable. It would have been more convincing if the precious months had been used with greater vigour and resolution.

But Munich was only the end of a long and unhappy road. The wider and even more baffling question remains: how did all this come about? How did we drift into a position in which so terrible a dilemma confronted our Government and people? Here, certainly, the guilt does not lie with Chamberlain alone, or even with Baldwin and MacDonald. It must be shared by the whole nation. If a few of us can claim that we began to shed our illusions a little earlier than some others, we owe that to the privilege of our friendship with the one man whose instinctive grasp of world strategy and sense of history pointed the way.

Looking back upon these years, many people, especially readers of Churchill's *The Gathering Storm*, may find it incredible that the

British House of Commons remained apparently impervious to the steadily deteriorating position. The Government of the day neglected their duty. The Opposition encouraged them in that neglect; they even spent most of their time in blaming Ministers for the very small efforts that they belatedly made to remedy a rapidly worsening situation. How far these attacks were genuine and how far purely partisan it is hard now to assess. From 1931 onwards, a National Government, first under MacDonald, then under Baldwin, and finally under Chamberlain, had enjoyed an overwhelming majority in the House of Commons. There is no precedent in history for a Parliament allowing the country to concede one diplomatic defeat after another; suffering staggering strategic set-backs; and finally undergoing military defeats with so little protest. The only parallel is to be found in the Parliaments that supported Lord North's administration from 1776 to 1783 during the American Revolution. Yet Members were not corrupt; they were bemused.

The true causes of Britain's vacillations in the inter-war years are not to be found in Parliament alone. They lie far deeper. Nor are the emotions which led to our weakness wholly dishonourable. It is true that the pacifist movement in its narrowest sense could not of itself have influenced policy. The Quaker view, which was reinforced by Canon Sheppard and his movement, has always commanded respect in this country. But it has never had a sufficient number of genuinely conscientious supporters to affect national policy. What was much more dangerous and confusing was the large body of men, who although not pacifist in the sense of advocating complete non-resistance, believed with firm conviction that the 1914–18 war was the result of the building-up of alliances and armaments, and were determined—even when the facts proved intractable—to cling to their hopes of a better world. After all, had not the Great War been 'the war to end war'? All the enthusiasm of the idealist, backed by the practical experience of ordinary folk who had suffered, was ranged behind the world organisation which, it was believed, could guarantee perpetual peace. The support for the League of Nations was genuine and sincere. What our people failed to realise was the practical impossibility of enforcing the will of a body to which America had never acceded, from which one State after another—

Japan, Italy, Germany—had begun to secede and which degenerated into a rump. At a time when the rise of Hitler began to threaten the peace of Europe, Britain was still distracted by internal economic difficulties and the long period of coalition government tended to obscure the gravity of the international situation. The Left used 'collective security' as an escape from responsibility, rather than as a stimulus to build up any genuine collective force among the peace-loving nations. The voices of the Right, by nature more inclined to the classical motto 'If you wish for peace, prepare for war', were muted by the need to conform to the mood of the day. All this would perhaps have been impossible had it not been for the moral and psychological shock of the First War. It is difficult for anyone who did not live then, or in the years immediately following, to realise the extent to which the vast slaughter of this frightful contest affected almost every family in the land. Bravely as they stood up to the immediate blow, our people suffered a debilitating reaction. For the losses were indeed terrible. One has only to look at the memorials of that war, in churches or public squares, in small towns or great cities, in schools or universities, to get some picture of their scale. There are many hamlets and villages in the more remote areas of the island where the list of dead seems almost greater than the population could have supplied. That there not only *should* never be, but *could* never be, another war became an article of faith.

If, therefore, future generations should be inclined to pass upon their predecessors a severe criticism, they must not fall into the error of charging them with decadence. They were deluded, no doubt, by false visions. But when the awakening came and with it the great test, their response would be worthy of their ancestors. Whether in the fighting Services or among the civil population, subjected to novel and devastating forms of attack, there would be no wavering. Although the shame of Munich was the culmination of many years of a whole people's confusion and uncertainty, their finest hour was still to come.

CHAPTER EIGHTEEN

The Drift to War

WITHOUT waiting for the verdict of history, I, at any rate, had become a violent partisan. As soon as the House rose after its short session, I set to work. I began with meetings in my own constituency. In paying a tribute to the Czechs who had paid the immediate price, I declared my fear that the price would not prove to have been paid by them alone. We must now concentrate on one thing only—unity and strength. In the following week (19 October) I began to campaign in favour of National Service. It was now essential and it was bound to come.

We were soon given an opportunity of challenging the Government. A by-election was due to take place at Oxford City. This became something in the nature of a referendum on the Munich policy. Quintin Hogg, son of Lord Hailsham, stood as the official Conservative candidate and thus laid the foundations of a long and distinguished political career. With a view to forming a kind of Popular Front on this single issue, Dr. A. D. Lindsay, the Master of Balliol, was induced to stand as an Independent candidate. The Liberals withdrew their candidate and gave Lindsay their full support—a noble act. Most of my old friends of the Next Five Years Group also rallied to the support of Lindsay. Lord Cecil gave all the weight of his influence to the same end. Among several Conservative undergraduates who gave energetic support, one was conspicuous for skill and enthusiasm. His name was Edward Heath. I both spoke at a public meeting in support of the Independent candidate and sent him a message of goodwill. In my speech I declared that the election turned on the foreign policy which we had pursued and were still pursuing. It had so far been one of retreating before superior forces. I maintained that you could not always appease lions by throwing them Christians. If Dr. Lindsay were successful, this would mean the first sign of a move towards a truly National Government. I also wrote a letter in the following terms:

I feel myself in honour bound to say that if I were a voter in the Oxford constituency, I should unhesitatingly vote and work for your return to Parliament. The times are too grave and the issue is too vital for progressive Conservative opinion to allow itself to be influenced by Party loyalties or to tolerate the present uncertainty regarding the principles governing our foreign policy.

As a result of these activities, it was generally stated in the Press that the Whip would be withdrawn from me, and that at the next election in Stockton an official Conservative candidate would be put up against me. However, there were by this time a good number of Conservative Members who were equally causing trouble in one way or another. Although Hogg headed the poll, the result of the by-election was by no means satisfactory to the Government. Without so able a candidate as Quintin Hogg, the seat might easily have been lost. A majority of 6,645 in the General Election of 1935 dropped to one of 3,434. I was much amused to hear that the question of my ejection from the Carlton Club was being considered by the committee. It was apparently a rule of the Club that one member was not to oppose another in any election. However, I heard nothing, either from the Chief Whip or from the Club Secretary.

Meanwhile, in order to try to clarify my own mind and that of others, I prepared a pamphlet called *The Price of Peace*, which I circulated privately but widely.[1] It was a criticism of the policy that had been followed since the General Election and it set out the disastrous economic, political, and strategic consequences of the Peace of Munich. As for the future, it was a call not only for active rearmament but for the building-up of a powerful defence system, if possible within the structure of the League of Nations. The alliance should begin with Britain, France, and Russia. At the same time, I justified my Parliamentary record on these issues in the following words:

The action I have taken is in accordance with the mandate I sought from my constituency at the last election. It is not I who have to answer for a dereliction of duty.

[1] See Appendix 1.

I received, as a result, many appreciative letters, as well as some abusive ones. Lady Violet Bonham Carter (later Lady Asquith) wrote to me:

> I must thank you for sending me *The Price of Peace*—and say how deeply I feel the truth of every word in it.

She went on to refer to the Oxford election:

> The attitude of the Labour Party makes one despair—boycotting their own man at Oxford because Liberals and some Conservatives supported him—.... May I congratulate you on going and thank you for it? It *is* a lead to others in courage—and above all in realization of the issues at stake.
>
> I wasn't frightened before Munich—but since then I have felt our existence to be in the balance as well as honour gone.

At the same time, both in and out of Parliament, many efforts were being made to increase the pressure on the Government, or to find some different grouping of political forces. Active negotiations with Dalton continued, with Churchill's knowledge and approval. During the recess I tried to arrange for a meeting between Morrison, Dalton, and Churchill, with a view to some definite action. At first I was hopeful. But after preliminary discussion with Dalton, it was thought better to wait until things began to develop in the course of the winter. General Spears was also one of those who were strongly in favour of a combined effort to change the Government and bring Churchill in as Prime Minister. Amery refers to this in his diary at the end of September, as follows:

> ... the Spears conspirators ... I found some of these young men, particularly Harold Macmillan, very wild, clamouring for an immediate pogrom to get rid of Neville and make Winston Prime Minister before the House met. I poured cold water on that sort of talk. ...[1]

But events were moving rapidly. Not many months were to pass before Leo Amery was to be the leader in the attack on Chamberlain, in one of the most savage and devastating speeches ever delivered in Parliament.[2]

[1] From the Amery papers, unpublished.
[2] During the debate which led to fall of the Chamberlain Government, on 9 May 1940.

Towards the end of November, a by-election at Bridgwater struck an even more serious blow to the Government than at Oxford. Vernon Bartlett was elected as an Independent on a broad anti-Government platform by a majority of over 2,300—and this in a constituency which, at the General Election, had returned a Conservative by a majority of nearly 11,000. Here again the Liberals had withdrawn their candidate, and backed Bartlett. In addition, the Parliamentary agitation continued. A motion was put down in the names of 34 Conservative Members, demanding rearmament on a scale commensurate with the present requirements. This was followed by a remarkable debate on 18 November on the question of the creation of a Ministry of Supply. It was in this debate that Churchill astonished the House by his statement that the mechanised cavalry units had certainly not more than one-tenth of the establishment required and these, of course, were only light tanks. 'They have been mechanised for over three years—mechanised in the sense that their horses were taken away from them.' The proposal was one made by the Liberal and Labour Parties, but when it came to the division some of our people abstained. I voted for the motion and I was in good company. Two other Conservatives only voted in the same lobby, but one was Churchill, the other Bracken. Naturally, the various motions on the Paper critical of the Government called for a reply; and against our 35 or so there were 225 back-bench Members assuring the Prime Minister of their unqualified support of his successful efforts to preserve the peace.

So, through this dreary winter, a puzzled and worried House of Commons found itself unable to give a really firm lead to a more and more confused nation. Certainly, in the months immediately following Munich, the Prime Minister retained the sympathy and support of the Conservative Party, in and out of Parliament. Perhaps the most important event in opening the eyes of the ordinary people to the true character of the man on whose good faith we were called upon to rely was the appalling Jewish pogrom throughout Germany and German-controlled countries, which followed the shooting, by a young Polish Jew on 7 November, of Herr vom Rath, a junior member of the German Embassy in Paris. The indescribable brutalities ordered by Hitler horrified the whole

British people. Looking back on this strange period, I think that this had more effect in swinging opinion away from the rosy views of appeasement which were still being preached by Chamberlain and his supporters than any other event. The natural decency of the British people was deeply shocked. For the first time they began to see the truth about the gang who eventually expiated their crimes, either by suicide or on the gallows. Lord Baldwin was moved to leave his retirement to make an eloquent protest and an appeal to help the refugees. There was talk of breaking off relations with Berlin.

The refugee problem had become more and more acute; although something was done to assist, mostly by private charity. After much pressure on the Home Office, a small number of visas—three to four hundred—were issued to Czechs most in danger of persecution. This was a drop in the ocean. I took my full part in the Parliamentary Committee on Refugees and other organisations, but very little could be achieved. At my home in Sussex, partly from my own resources and partly with the help of generous neighbours, we were able to look after a group of some forty men and women, mostly Jews, who, by one means or another, had managed to reach this country after Munich. Some, especially those with some technical or professional qualifications, we were gradually able to place in jobs after the outbreak of war. Others reached America. This gave me my first insight into the terrible refugee problem, about to haunt the world for many years, and not yet finally resolved.

Although my talks with Dalton in October had proved abortive, towards the end of the year some of the Labour leaders were beginning to look more favourably on the possibility of co-operating with the Liberals and the dissident Conservatives. The National Executive of the Labour Party and the more conventional Members would not consider officially such a drastic move; but men like Greenwood, Dalton, Morrison, and A. V. Alexander, supported by Walter Citrine, Secretary of the T.U.C., were beginning to think seriously about the future. Undoubtedly, the Oxford and Bridgwater by-elections had their effect. There was a slow change of mood. The old suspicion and dislike of Churchill had begun to fade. Even his most determined opponents could not but admire his long

THE DRIFT TO WAR

and lonely fight. Nor could they avoid the conclusion that his predictions were being proved right and his criticisms well-founded. All this was to have its importance in May 1940. Even in that supreme crisis, nothing could have induced the Labour Party to serve in a Coalition Government under Chamberlain. Early in January 1939 Duncan Sandys called a meeting at the Caxton Hall 'with the object of forming a new political group'. This was another effort, not very successful in itself, but symptomatic. Meanwhile, it was freely rumoured that a number of the junior Ministers in the Government had got together to demand from the Prime Minister the resignation of some of the least efficient members of the Cabinet. All the time the anxiety about armaments continued. Nevertheless, in spite of everything, the discipline of the Conservative Party prevailed. The Parliamentary Correspondent of the *Spectator* wrote with truth:

Looking back on the last three months one cannot help being struck by the amazing solidarity of the Conservative Party. There have, of course, been acute differences of opinion within its ranks. A powerful minority was appalled by the Munich Agreement and by the diplomacy which preceded it. There have been – and still are – deep and widespread misgivings concerning the effectiveness of our rearmament.[1]

Yet nothing happened – at least nothing within our own control.

Before the end of the year, the ill-starred Anglo-Italian Agreement, which had led to Eden's resignation, was formally brought into force. It was indeed a ludicrous occasion. Even the Government could not show much enthusiasm. Once more, Churchill, Eden, Cranborne, and the rest of our friends thought the only thing to do was to abstain.

It was at the end of January 1939 that the nadir of appeasement was reached. Lord Perth, the British Ambassador in Rome, was instructed to show Ciano, for the approval of the Italian Government, the outline of the speech which the Prime Minister was to make to the House of Commons. According to Ciano, the Duce's comments were as follows:

I believe this is the first time that the head of the British Government sub-

[1] *Spectator*, 30 December 1938.

mits to a foreign Government the outline of one of his speeches. It is a bad sign for them.[1]

Nor did Chamberlain and Halifax, on their visit to Rome earlier in the same month, achieve any result except perhaps to add to Mussolini's conviction that Britain was no longer to be feared.

Meanwhile, I continued my activities as best I could. On 9 February I published a booklet on the economic aspects of defence.[2] In this, I set out the problem as I saw it: the degree of German preparation, the tasks that lay before Britain, and the need for urgency. It was now no longer a question of efficiency, but of survival. I also reprinted, as an appendix, the smaller pamphlet which I had circulated privately at the end of 1938 on the Munich settlement.[3] The little book was very favourably received and had a considerable sale. One journal went so far as to say that it 'compared with any of the great tracts in British political history'. In its compilation, especially in connection with the estimates of German military expenditure, I was fortunate in obtaining the expert assistance of Mr. T. Balogh and Dr. Paul Einzig.

Throughout all this period my constituents supported me nobly. There was naturally a certain amount of criticism, but on the whole I escaped more easily than some of those Conservative Members who had only lately ranged themselves more or less in opposition to the Government. At the end of February the Defence Loans Bill was brought in, which gave me the opportunity to deploy some of the points I had made in my last publication. The House seemed staggered to learn that in the five years from the coming of the Nazi régime to 1938, Germany had spent, on the best estimates available, £2,800 million on military expenditure alone. In the year 1937–8, their military expenditure amounted to £1,200 million, as against our £265 million. How then, I asked, could anyone object to the comparatively modest sum which the Government were now asking? What we are doing 'cannot be said by anybody to be too great, and if we regard it frankly, we must sometimes wonder whether the effort will be great enough'.[4] I could not help also calling attention

[1] Hugh Gibson (ed.), *The Ciano Diaries, 1939–43*, p. 17.
[2] Harold Macmillan, *Economic Aspects of Defence* (London, 1939); see Appendix 2.
[3] *The Price of Peace*; see Appendix 1.   [4] *Hansard*, 27 February 1939.

to the fact that Germany, during this period, had put 5 million unemployed into work and was now actually short of labour, while we still had nearly 2 million men standing idle.

Nevertheless, the Government had not yet abandoned the appeasement policy. They shut their eyes to Germany's continual breaches of the Munich Agreement, including the so-called 'Vienna Award', which handed over large parts of Czechoslovak territory to Poland and Hungary. When, as late as the beginning of March 1939, the German Government brusquely rejected an Anglo-French inquiry as to its intentions regarding the guarantee to be given to Czechoslovakia, by indicating that even to have made this *démarche* was an unwarranted and undesirable interference in a sphere of influence which was clearly recognised as being that of Germany,[1] the British and French Governments accepted this crushing snub without protest. A few days later, on 10 March, Chamberlain observed that all signs pointed to a tranquil political future and easing of the economic situation in Europe.[2] So matters drifted on, until Hitler was ready for his next blow. There was a growing sense of uncertainty and even of desperation. It seemed impossible to prevent the drift to war, and the distrust both of Government and of Parliament began to spread throughout the country. Yet, on 10 March, Chamberlain had told the Press correspondents in the House of Commons that Europe was 'settling down to a period of tranquillity'. On the same day, Hoare, in a speech of egregious folly, painted to his constituents a picture of a new age of peace and prosperity which the three dictators, Hitler, Mussolini, and Franco—the latter now finally victorious in Spain— could build in co-operation with the British and French Prime Ministers. The famous *Punch* cartoon entitled 'The Ides of March', depicting the nightmare of war escaping out of a window while John Bull was waking up from his bad dreams, was published on the very day that Hitler struck. Hitler, after encouraging Slovakia and Ruthenia to claim their independence under German suzerainty, forced the new President of Czechoslovakia to seek an interview

[1] John W. Wheeler-Bennett, *Munich: Prologue to Tragedy*, p. 318, based on the *French Yellow Book* (New York, 1940), pp. 61–65.

[2] John W. Wheeler-Bennett, *Munich: Prologue to Tragedy*, p. 318.

with him in Berlin. The unhappy Hácha was induced by methods amounting to torture to sign a treaty at 4.30 a.m. on 15 March, placing what remained of his country under German protection.[1] At 9 o'clock that same morning the German troops moved into Prague. Yet, as already described, even these events did not immediately shake the Prime Minister out of his complacency. At first, the Government maintained that, since the Czechoslovak State, whose frontiers we had proposed to guarantee, had dissolved by internal disruption, our obligation had consequently lapsed.

But Britain was now sick of appeasement. Almost overnight, the whole country turned with something like relief from the long period of drugged sleep to a new awakening. I can never forget the emotion in the House and throughout the country of the following days. Even when he was forced to protest against this new aggression, Chamberlain seemed to regard Hitler's actions more as a personal grievance than a public disaster:

> Surely, as a joint signatory of the Munich Agreement, I was entitled, if Herr Hitler thought it ought to be undone, to that consultation which is provided for.

Yet he now seemed to realise that, if Hitler was really attempting to dominate the world by force, 'Britain would do its best to meet such a challenge'. But what was to be done? The Russians proposed, on 18 March, a conference of the British, French, Russian, Polish, Roumanian, and Turkish Governments, 'to concert means of resisting aggression'.[2] Chamberlain rejected the Russian initiative as premature and the Poles, suspicious of Russia, would not agree to his alternative—a declaration by the three Great Powers, Britain, France and Russia, in which Poland should join.

Undeterred, however, by any diplomatic difficulties, Chamberlain now plunged into a headlong reversal of British policy. By the end of March he had issued a guarantee that, in the event of any action which threatened their independence, the British Government would give the Poles all the support in its power. This, indeed, was a rash, although perhaps an understandable, decision. For, as the event proved, we had no power to support Poland by any military operation. Its true meaning could only be that any further

[1] C. L. Mowat, *Britain Between the Wars, 1918–1940*, p. 637.   [2] Ibid., p. 638.

aggression would be the signal for general war. That the dictators were not impressed was proved by the fact that a week later, on 7 April, Mussolini invaded Albania. I was lunching with Churchill at Chartwell when the news came of the Italian landings. It was a scene that gave me my first picture of Churchill at work. Maps were brought out; secretaries were marshalled; telephones began to ring. 'Where was the British fleet?' That was the most urgent question. That considerable staff which, even as a private individual, Churchill always maintained to support his tremendous outflow of literary and political effort was at once brought into play. It turned out that the British fleet was scattered throughout the Mediterranean. Of the five great ships, one was at Gibralter, one in the Eastern Mediterranean, and the remaining three, in Churchill's words, 'lolling about inside or outside widely-separated Italian ports'.[1] A few days later he criticised these dispositions in a powerful speech in the House of Commons.

I shall always have a picture of that spring day and the sense of power and energy, the great flow of action, which came from Churchill, although he then held no public office. He alone seemed to be in command, when everyone else was dazed and hesitating. Lord Halifax's first reaction to Mussolini's blow was as characteristic as Churchill's. He is said to have exclaimed, when he heard of the sudden and treacherous attack: 'And on Good Friday too!' The British Ambassador was instructed to deliver a memorandum of which Ciano wrote in his diary that it 'might have been composed in our own offices'.[2] Italian policy was generally based on bluff and should certainly have been dealt with by determined action. As Bismarck—rather brutally—said of Italians, 'They have a big appetite and poor teeth'. It was certainly true of Mussolini.

The course of events is well known—the guarantee to Poland, followed by a guarantee to Roumania and Greece. The sudden change from appeasement to the widespread distribution of guarantees did not in itself carry conviction. It was too much like a death-bed repentance, which is all right if the sinner dies. Had the Government been re-formed on the basis proposed by Sidney

[1] Winston Churchill, *The Second World War*, vol. i: *The Gathering Storm*, p. 275.
[2] Hugh Gibson (ed.), *The Ciano Diaries, 1939–43*, p. 61.

Herbert in October, Hitler might have taken notice and Russia been correspondingly encouraged. As it was, a cynic was led to ask whether the Chamberlain Government were a greater menace as travellers in appeasement or as insurance brokers. They were indeed bankrupt. They should have resigned or at least re-formed and reconstituted the board, before trying to restart in business.

This feeling for a truly National Government, or at least the addition of powerful figures to it, now began to grow stronger. On 21 March, a few days after Hitler's coup, I wrote the following letter to *The Times*, which rather surprisingly printed it:

Sir,—It is surely clear that the present situation requires the immediate formation of a National Government on the broadest possible basis. This is essential for two purposes. First, it will demonstrate both to our potential friends and to our potential enemies our determination to abandon our former policy and to re-create a united front against agression. Secondly, it will enable us to carry through with the minimum of friction the stern measures now necessary to support a new foreign policy with adequate power.

Such a Government may eventually emerge after a prolonged period of hesitation and party controversy. On the other hand, it may be formed at once, without bitterness or useless recrimination, if the leading figures in all parties will rise to the occasion.

Fourteen months later, such a Government was formed, at a moment of our greatest danger since the sailing of the Armada. But then the long night of hesitation was over. Under the greatest of her leaders, Britain was at last to find 'national unity and strength'.

On 29 March I had joined with Churchill, Eden, and Duff Cooper in a motion demanding a stronger national policy, a National Government, and the fullest use of all our resources in men and money. This motion was signed by nearly thirty Members and new names began to be associated with us, who had not previously joined with us. Speaking in Stockton two days later, I declared that 'something must be done immediately if we are to avoid war and, worse even than war, defeat'. A National Government was an urgent necessity if Britain's latent strength was to be mobilised in time. Three weeks later, forty-six Members of Parliament, led by Leo Amery, signed a motion:

in favour of the immediate acceptance of the principle of the compulsory mobilisation of the man, munition, and money power of the nation.[1]

Our numbers were at last beginning to grow. Although no major change in the character of the Government took place, some changes of policy were made. At the end of April, the principle of National Service was at last accepted. Although it only involved an obligation on men of twenty and twenty-one years of age to serve for six months' training, it was at least a forward move. Even in this modified and restricted form it was bitterly opposed by the whole Labour Party in Parliament and most of the Liberals. Attlee denounced it with a singular mixture of pettiness and petulance. By some strange aberration, British Socialists still regarded the obligation of military service, applicable to the whole nation, as undemocratic. A Bill to enable the creation of a Ministry of Supply was introduced in June. But, as I pointed out in the debate, while rejoicing at the Government's tardy conversion on this important issue, even now the decision as to the pace at which the new Ministry should move and the field which it should cover was left undefined. As I was to find later when I became Parliamentary Secretary, there were serious weaknesses in the whole scheme. Moreover, the choice of the Minister, Dr. Burgin, was not very happy.

So the days and weeks dragged on. It was a period of waiting. The supporters of appeasement had now abandoned their policy, but not their positions. The 'Big Four', as Hoare called the new Cabal—Chamberlain, Halifax, Simon, and Hoare—remained in charge. Yet there was still hope. If Soviet Russia could be brought to join with the West, Hitler might even now be restrained.

If the British Government looked at Soviet Russia with suspicion, this was due to the history of some twenty years. Soviet propaganda and Communist subversion were rightly resented, not only at home where they were comparatively harmless, but throughout India and the Colonial Empire where they were more dangerous. Alliance with Bolshevist Russia may have been necessary, but it was distasteful. Moreover, the countries that we had so recently (and so suddenly) covered with our unilateral guarantees—Poland and Roumania—had already expressed their extreme reluctance—even

[1] *Yorkshire Post,* 19 April 1939.

their refusal—to receive Russian help, especially in the form of
Russian troops. They were quite as hostile to Russia as to Germany.
They feared (and, as it was to prove, with some justice) that the
Russians in your country were like the old music-hall joke about
mothers-in-law in your house: 'Once you let them in, you can never
get them out.' From this point of view, the almost overnight decision
to distribute guarantees to Poland and Roumania, without considering the Russian problem, was clumsy as well as rash. Nor need we
have troubled about the fear of 'provoking Germany into violent
action'. Hitler was always regarded by British politicians as if he
were a brilliant but temperamental genius, who could be soothed by
kindness or upset by hard words. It was this fearful misconception
about the nature of dictators that was the real reason for Eden's
quarrel with Chamberlain, and the root-cause of much that went
amiss in these tragic years.

If Britain had grounds for suspicion of Russia, the reverse was
also true. The hostility of the Western Powers after the First War;
the intervention in the Russian Civil War; the loss of territory
imposed on Russia: none of these were forgotten. More recently,
even after the rise of Nazism, German—Russian relations had been
good and even cordial. Hitler's violent and offensive anti-Communist
propaganda no doubt angered Stalin, but he was not a man to be
deterred by words from any action that he deemed advantageous.
Nevertheless, under Litvinov, Russian policy had been to seek
security through the League and by alliances with the Western
democracies. Munich was undoubtedly a great shock to the
Russians. Yet they held to this policy and, immediately after the
liquidation of Czechoslovakia, sought to underpin it by a formal
engagement.

This was the significance of the Russian offer of a Tripartite
Alliance—Britain, France, and Russia—on 16 April. This was
Litvinov's last chance. It was also ours.

Churchill's summary of the situation is no doubt correct. 'If, for
instance, Mr. Chamberlain on receipt of the Russian offer had
replied: "Yes. Let us three band together and break Hitler's neck",
or words to that effect, Parliament would have approved, Stalin
would have understood, and history might have taken a different

course.'[1] Unhappily, Chamberlain did not reply to the Russian offer in such robust and simple language. No pressure was put on Poland and Roumania to come into line. The British Government rejected the comprehensive Russian proposal, which included a military convention and a joint guarantee by France, Britain, and Russia to all the border States from the Baltic to the Black Sea. Instead, they proposed a unilateral guarantee by each of the countries. The Russian reply was not long delayed. On 3 May Litvinov, the protagonist of co-operation with the West and of collective security under the aegis of the League, was suddenly and even brutally dismissed. His place was taken by Molotov, destined to a long reign as Foreign Minister, first under Stalin and then under his successors. Molotov was ready to play any hand in any way that his master, Stalin, decided. He would, moreover, play it superbly well. He finally fell foul of Khrushchev, and was forced to resign. Under the more conventional régime which has happily developed in modern Russia, he lost his place but not his head. He now lives in retirement in Moscow.

Meanwhile, the pressure on Poland was growing. At the end of April, Hitler had demanded the return of Danzig to the Reich. At the same time, he denounced the German-Polish Non-Aggression Pact of 1934 and the Anglo-German Naval Treaty of 1935. Mussolini had not been altogether pleased by the German occupation of Czechoslovakia. Indeed, it is more than likely that the Italian seizure of Albania was something in the nature of a riposte to save his own face and restore his prestige in his own country. However, whatever his feelings of jealousy may have been, he was bound more closely than ever with his German partner in the 'Pact of Steel'. This was announced towards the end of May.[2]

There were other troublesome distractions which arose during these months. The Government's Palestine policy showed both confusion and indecision. There was much Parliamentary criticism and large abstentions or hostile votes by Conservative Members. There was a specially ugly by-product of Munich in respect of the

[1] Winston Churchill, *The Second World War*, vol. i: *The Gathering Storm*, p. 285.
[2] This was the name given to a formal military alliance between Germany and Italy signed on 22 May 1939.

handing over to the Germans of £6 million of Czechoslovak gold by the Bank of England. This took place at the end of March, that is after Hitler's seizure of Prague. It was defended by some technicality; but the affair led to bitter disputes and fierce debates in May and June. Simon, the Chancellor of the Exchequer, displayed a combination of legalism and cynicism which much disturbed the House. Even the Government's most loyal supporters could barely stomach so shocking and discreditable an affair. Churchill described this transaction as a public disaster. All this added to the distrust felt for the administration by growing sections of the Conservative Party.

Yet all the time through these summer months, one anxiety was dominant in all our minds—Russia. Naturally, we had little beyond rumour and hearsay to inform us. But Parliament did its best; and I recall the constant pressure, by question and debate, on a Government which seemed strangely hesitant and uncertain. Then, at any rate, it seemed to most of us that we ought to have acted with greater vigour and speed. Today, with the advantage of what has been written by eminent historians or by some of those actually concerned, the many difficulties and complications emerge.[1]

Perhaps the fundamental error of British policy during these critical months was the sincere desire not to divide the world into two hostile blocs, facing each other with ever-increasing military strength. This view was constantly reiterated by Lord Halifax and by *The Times*, under his friend Geoffrey Dawson's direction. It was based on the idea that in this rivalry between the Triple Alliance and the Triple Entente the First World War had its roots. It also continued into the post-Prague period a view of Hitler which might just have been tenable at Munich. By now it should surely have been clear that Hitler was a wild beast. He must be caged. He complained of encirclement. Then let Germany be encircled. But this is just what Chamberlain and Halifax had thought it wrong to do.

[1] The most authoritative and complete accounts are: L. B. Namier, *Diplomatic Prelude, 1938–1939* (London, 1948), pp. 143–210; John W. Wheeler-Bennett, *Munich: Prologue to Tragedy*, pp. 398–411, 430–2; Winston Churchill, *The Second World War*, vol. i: *The Gathering Storm*, chs. xx and xxi; Lord Strang, *Home and Abroad*.

These hesitations are clear from the aide-mémoire given on 29 April to the French Government, which defined the British aims. Our negotiators were to lose no chance of Soviet aid in the event of war; they were not to upset Poland and Roumania; they were not to give colour to German anti-Comintern propaganda; and lastly, not to provoke Germany into violent action.[1] These indeed were difficult and almost irreconcilable objectives, and they should in fairness be borne in mind when we judge the work of our diplomatists. They were partly legacies of the distant past, partly the result of more recent mistakes.

Parliament soon took up the running. Dalton proposed on 10 May that Halifax himself should go to Russia, which seemed reasonable enough. After all, Chamberlain had paid three visits to Hitler and one to Mussolini. Halifax had also made journeys to see both the Fascist dictators. In any case, Molotov was no less respectable than Ribbentrop or Ciano. Eden urged this course strongly upon Halifax, but Chamberlain did not approve.[2] Eden even offered to go himself—he was the one British Minister who had talked with Stalin. But this offer was not acceptable.[3] On 19 May there was a short but lively debate in Parliament. Both Lloyd George and Churchill spoke strongly in favour of the urgent need for a clear understanding and a firm alliance with Russia. Without it, our position was almost desperate. I remember particularly Lloyd George's impressive warnings. The atmosphere that day was like that of early 1918. Everyone knew that a great attack from Germany was impending. No one knew where it would fall. If it were to fall on Poland, what help could we give? Lloyd George complained, and with some justification, of the campaign of deprecation of Russia's power and value as an ally. Unfortunately this was true. British military opinion consistently overrated the strength of the Polish Army and underrated that of the Russians. Chamberlain, in reply,

[1] L. B. Namier, *Diplomatic Prelude, 1938–1939*, p. 157. The document, published by M. Gafencu, Roumanian Foreign Minister, is stated to have been communicated by Sir Eric Phipps to the French Foreign Minister.

[2] Halifax subsequently regretted that he had not made a warmer response to Russian overtures (The Earl of Birkenhead, *The Life of Lord Halifax*, p. 440).

[3] The Earl of Avon, *The Eden Memoirs: The Reckoning* (London, 1965), p. 55.

deprecated Lloyd George's pessimism. The situation was grave, but by no means desperate. He emphasised once more the danger of 'lining up opposing blocs of Powers in Europe, animated by hostile intentions towards one another'. This would prove 'an unstable policy'. He went on to hint at the difficulty caused by Polish anxieties about Soviet participation in any guarantee. Churchill replied by advocating the Tripartite Alliance. He could see nothing wrong in it. As for extending our guarantees to cover all the Baltic countries, well, 'You are up to the neck in it already'.

On 27 May formal discussions were started in Moscow, through the Ambassadors. In order to assist the Ambassador, an experienced and talented official, Sir William Strang, was sent out—but not a political Minister. Strang, who had treated me with such kindness during my visit to Russia, had also impressed me with his knowledge of Russian ways of thought. He would have been the first to realise the importance which revolutionaries attach to protocol. Why not a Minister? In his view,[1] given in a letter to Sir Orme Sargent, Deputy Under-Secretary at the Foreign Office, 'we could probably have got a better agreement by closing with the substance of the Soviet draft on the 2nd June than we shall get to-day'. Alas! we were to get none at all. By the end of July the British and French negotiators had met all or nearly all of the Russian proposals and a political agreement seemed in sight. The Russians then demanded that a military agreement should be discussed before the political agreement could be concluded.[2] But the military missions sent by Britain and France were slow in starting and of lower rank than they should have been. They travelled by boat and only reached Moscow on 11 August. By now, however, the Russians were already beginning to have second thoughts. At what date they took the final decision is not known. Their motives were simple. They did not now believe that even a Tripartite Alliance would deter Hitler, who was determined to crush Poland. They may also have over-estimated the Allied strength and reckoned that the war, if it came and was not avoided by a second Munich, would wear down the Germans. The gains from the policy of neutrality would be con-

[1] Lord Strang, *Home and Abroad*, p. 183.
[2] C. L. Mowat, *Britain Between the Wars, 1918–1940*, p. 643.

siderable. They would obtain time to reform their armies, which must have been to some extent demoralised by Stalin's 'purge', and complete their equipment. They were also to gain, under the secret clauses of their pact with Germany, large areas of territory—the Baltic States and half of Poland—by which their positions were extended to the west and the heart of Russia covered against a German attack, if and when it came. In Churchill's words, 'if their policy was cold-blooded, it was also at the moment realistic in a high degree'.[1]

Parliament dispersed before the blow fell. We were awaiting, with increasing impatience, news from Russia. On the motion for the adjournment, a sharp and disagreeable conflict arose. The strain was clearly telling on the Government, and the Prime Minister showed less than his usual skill in the management of the House. On 3 August the motion that the House should adjourn until 3 October was moved by him, in a speech which made it clear that he regarded it as little more than a formality. In view of the tense situation, the uncertainty about Russia, and the growing pressure on Poland, many of us deeply resented this long period of absence from the scene and asked for an assurance that in the event of any change in the situation the House should be recalled. In resisting the amendment, the Prime Minister went out of his way to refer to the speeches in a rather contemptuous way, and Churchill was much offended. As a result, a discussion which should have taken half an hour went on for five hours and a half. The only redeeming feature was the use that Churchill made of this opportunity. With all his powers of oratory, wit, and irony, he made a cruel contrast between Europe mobilised and Parliament going on a long holiday. It was odd, he said, 'that the Government should say to members at such a time, "Be off. Run away and play—and take your gas masks with you." ' Parliament, he declared—and this was a sentiment to which he proved his loyalty during the worst days of the war—however much it might be disparaged at home, counted throughout the world 'as the most formidable expression of the British national will and as an instrument of that will in resistance to aggression'.

One of the reasons that tempers were frayed was the renewed rumours of an immediate General Election. It seems difficult now

[1] Winston Churchill, *The Second World War*, vol. i: *The Gathering Storm*, p. 307.

to believe that, with the issues of peace and war trembling in the balance, such a plan was thought even worth consideration. But it was so. I have a letter from my friend, Dick Law, dated 20 August, which makes curious reading now:

In spite of appearances to the contrary, I still expect a general election rather than a war, or rather fancy that when the election does come it will be such that we shall find ourselves quite unable to support the Govt. even if we should wish to do so. Everyone is assuming that this time there will be no surrender. We underestimate the resourcefulness of our people. Besides, we never know when we're beaten. We didn't know it last September: we shan't know it this. I'm sure of this—that if there is an election we shall either have to submit to the yoke of Birmingham or we must fight it. There will be no safety, there will be no sense in a middle position. When we do get back to London we must concoct definite plans, those of us who don't want to conform. Otherwise the election will be on us and we shall all be scrambling back on the bandwagon without thought of dignity or honesty or anything else.

Members of the Eden Group, including its leader, were particularly disturbed about their position. They did not feel they could stand in support of the Government. Should they act as Independent Conservatives? Or should they try to create a new Independent party? What, above all, should be their relations with Churchill? I had no doubt, on my part, as to what I should do. I had stood on a very independent basis in the election of 1935 and had succeeded in getting elected. I could do the same again. As regards the question of a definite Independent party or group within the party, if it was to take formal shape, in my view there could be no leader now but Churchill himself.

On 22 August the news reached London that a German–Russian pact was imminent. I was on a short yachting holiday with my friend Wyndham Portal.[1] We had been cruising in the Channel and touched at various French ports. On the morning of 23 August we landed at Poole Harbour. As we were walking from the quay we bought all the papers and there for the first time heard the news which had shaken the world. For the Russo-German treaty meant either another easy victory for Hitler or war under the worst

[1] Afterwards Lord Portal, Minister of Works in the Churchill Government.

possible conditions, with Russia neutral, Czechoslovakia already overwhelmed, and France and Britain powerless to bring any effective aid to Poland, whose independence they had guaranteed. The Cabinet had met on 22 August and been informed that the Molotov–Ribbentrop pact was about to be signed. But now that the British Government had taken their stand, Chamberlain was in no mood for another surrender; Britain would stand by her obligations to Poland, come what may. In a communiqué issued that day, before Parliament could be recalled, this was made abundantly clear. When I got to London I heard that Parliament would meet on the 24th, for the purpose of passing the emergency legislation. Although the formal dismissal of the Allied staff missions to Moscow did not take place until 25 August, the die was cast. On the 24th the Emergency Powers Bill was passed, together with all the various formalities for calling up the reserves in the Army, Navy, and Air Force and for the alerting of the A.R.P. Chamberlain also sent, on that night, another personal letter to Hitler. But this time it was to warn him not to make the mistake which led to such 'tragic misunderstanding as in 1914'. He still felt that questions between Germany and Poland could be settled without the use of force. At the same time, he made it clear that the British Government were determined not to give way. On 25 August a treaty with Poland was approved, formalising the guarantees already given.

There followed an astonishing week. The House met again on 29 August. It was extremely difficult to discover what was really happening; but there appeared to be no sign of the British Government weakening. Chamberlain's speech in the House had been firm and he had received the full support of Greenwood, speaking for the Labour Party, and Sinclair for the Liberals. Eden had also spoken with great effect and it was clear that the country stood united and ready to fight. If they had no great enthusiasm for the Poles, they realised by now that it was the old question once more posed to the British people: 'Shall one man or one country be allowed to dominate Europe?' To this, there could only be one answer. There then followed a confused and even hectic period of official and unofficial diplomacy. Hitler postponed the date of the attack by a week, and it appears that he was hopeful of finding some method by which he could 'eliminate British intervention'.[1] He seems to have believed this still to be possible. That was the lesson which he had been taught at Munich. He could not bring himself to accept that Chamberlain, so malleable before, would prove so obstinate now. He put forward a 'large comprehensive offer' to settle all problems with Britain once and for all; to 'protect' the British Empire and to give us the support of Germany if it were ever threatened. All this was the usual deceptive talk. In view of the curious dualism of our policy, Hitler had perhaps some excuse for not understanding the new temper of the British Government and people. During July there had been conversations between the German trade representative and Rob Hudson, our Secretary for the Department of Overseas Trade, with hints of a loan for Germany. There had been discussions between Horace Wilson and the German Ambassador in London. According to the German Ambassador, these talks envisaged Britain gradually disembarrassing herself of her commitments towards Poland.[2] Whatever may be the truth about these discussions, Hitler certainly hoped to delude us once again.

But British opinion was steady. Indeed, the only fear in most people's minds was fear of another surrender. Had they known what awaited them in the six terrible years of war, I still do not think that they would have made any other choice. For they knew now in their hearts that one of the great testing moments of history had come. Whatever might be the fate that awaited us and whatever the end of the story, we had no choice.

Meanwhile, curious unofficial agencies were at work. A Swedish engineer, Dahlerus, supposed to be in the confidence of Göring and with a good number of business contacts, kept flying between London and Berlin. President Roosevelt and the King of the Belgians joined in with messages urging peace on both sides. Mussolini (but none of us knew this at the time) told Hitler that he could not fight. So, day after day, the contest of wills went on, while the House stood adjourned and we hung about the clubs waiting for news. The Eden Group met frequently. The pressure on Poland grew and the Polish Government, yielding to it, agreed to send a

[1] *The Trials of German Major War Criminals*, vol. ix (London, 1946), p. 480.
[2] L. B. Namier, *Europe in Decay, 1936–1940* (London, 1950), pp. 222–4.

representative to negotiate with Hitler, but at the same time they ordered total mobilisation of their armies. Through the last days of August the struggle went on, Sir Nevile Henderson trying up to the end to find some comfort in the German proposals. But finally, on 1 September, the game was played out. Hitler was too impatient and perhaps too sceptical. The invasion of Poland was launched.

Almost up to the end there were some of us who thought that Hitler would withdraw if we stood firm. Indeed, there was much pressure on him from Göring and others to do so. I had a letter from Cranborne[1] on 30 August, which is interesting:

The crisis you prophesied has come on us with a vengeance—Poor Neville! He has indeed reaped the whirlwind—I still feel that there is a faint gleam of hope that we shall escape war. . . . It looks as if the Russian—German Pact would go down to history as one of the classical examples of being too clever by half—Its only conceivable justification—and that an immoral one—would have been if it made resistance by France and us quite impossible. No doubt, this was Ribbentrop's calculation. He always was a second rate man—But now I can't see how they can help losing more than they have gained—They haven't got what they wanted without fighting, and they have been shown up, not only abroad but—what is for them far more disastrous—at home, as cynical opportunists. That is not the spirit in which to lead a nation into war. How they can extricate themselves from the position into which they have got, without a war I don't know—Perhaps they won't be able, and war we shall have—But I can't help feeling that it will be for them a desperate hopeless gamble. . . . In the meantime, I hope that we shall stand absolutely firm—It is the best hope of peace.

Although this prognostication did not prove to be true, it showed great acuteness. For it was the Russo-German Pact, which seemed so clever, for which, in the end, Germany paid a frightful forfeit.

As the days passed, the tension became almost unbearable, even for those of us who had no responsibilities. Telegrams and messages passed and re-passed. At 9.30 p.m. on the day of Germany's attack on Poland, the British Ambassador delivered a Note, declaring that we would stand by our obligations unless German forces were withdrawn. The French Government did the same.

The evacuation of the schoolchildren and mothers with young families began on 1 September. Parliament met on that day, and we

[1] Later Lord Salisbury.

were informed of the British ultimatum. I went home on Saturday—
2 September—to help my wife arrange for the arrival of a number of
evacuated children and their attendants. After the experience of the
previous year we had decided that if war came it would not be
possible for us to stay long in our own house, and that we would
move quite soon to a cottage which I had prepared for this purpose.
Actually, this move took several weeks to complete, partly because
the nursery school which was sent was not at full strength. In the
year between Munich and the outbreak of war, feeling certain that
war would come soon, I had taken the necessary steps. All the
furniture was to be stacked into one room; the mahogany doors
replaced; the chimney-pieces and surrounds protected by plywood
and various other devices to reduce the damage which even small
children normally inflict. By these means, scarcely any injury was
done in the course of these long years, although I suppose we
housed something between sixty and seventy children, together
with their teachers and nurses.

I came back to London on the afternoon of Saturday to find out
what was going on. There was great confusion, and some degree of
suspicion among our group. All that we were told was that we were
still waiting for a reply to our Note of 1 September. It seemed that
the Note was not in terms of an ultimatum, since there was no
time-limit fixed for a reply. The Opposition were particularly
disturbed and so were many of our supporters. Attlee was away ill
and Greenwood was acting as leader of the Labour Party. All that
the Prime Minister had told us was that Mussolini had put forward
a proposal for a Four-Power Conference. This was so like Munich
that a kind of shiver went through the House. But the Prime
Minister soon made it clear that Mussolini's plans could not be
entertained while Poland was invaded. He also said that we were
discussing with the French the time-limit that we should give to
allow the German forces to withdraw from Poland. In that case, a
discussion between the Polish and German Governments could take
place, on the understanding that Poland's interests were safeguarded
and guaranteed.[1] Since the unhappy Poles had been subjected to a

[1] L. S. Amery, *My Political Life*, vol. iii: *The Unforgiving Years, 1929–1940*, p.
323.

violent attack by ground and air for nearly two days, this seemed rather a weak statement. The memories of last year weighed down even the most loyal of the Government's supporters. When Greenwood rose to speak, there took place a scene which has often been recounted; it stands out vividly in my own memory. Amery called out 'Speak for England!', meaning that he should avoid a purely partisan speech. No doubt he realised that behind Chamberlain's rather halting words lay the difficulties with the French which it would have been unwise to divulge. Greenwood spoke with feeling and dignity. He insisted upon an answer as to where Britain stood. The Prime Minister thought it could be given at least by the next day. He then explained that the French Cabinet was in session and that he would know the result within a few hours.

After the House rose, Members hung about the lobbies and the smoking-room in a state of some confusion. Nobody could make out what lay behind Chamberlain's statement. We did not, of course, know of the last desperate efforts which Bonnet, the French Foreign Minister, was making behind Daladier's back to achieve yet another surrender. Ministers not 'in the know' insisted on a meeting of the Cabinet being held later that night, to clarify the position. The French were still making a plea for delay, giving as a reason the importance of completing mobilisation undisturbed by air attack and their being able to move without confusion into the Maginot Line. Daladier therefore asked for yet another forty-eight hours' delay. But the British Cabinet were now determined. Halifax told the French that the situation in Parliament could not be held unless, when the House met at noon on the next day, the Prime Minister was able to say that we were at war.

On Sunday the 3rd, the Eden Group met at Ronald Tree's house in Queen Anne's Gate. We were told that at 9 a.m. on this day a real ultimatum had been handed in to expire at 11 a.m. At a quarter past eleven we heard Chamberlain broadcast the news to the waiting people of the outbreak of the Second World War. His words expressed his deep emotion. They were dignified and sincere:

I cannot believe that there is anything more, or anything different, that I could have done.... It is evil things that we shall be fighting against, brute force, bad faith, injustice, oppression and persecution. And against them I am certain that the right will prevail.

After listening to the broadcast, we walked over to the House of Commons. When we got into New Palace Yard, there was a great blowing of whistles and hooting of sirens. I asked a policeman what it was all about. He said that, according to instructions, if it was a warbling note it meant an air-raid. I asked him if it was a warbling note. He replied: 'Well, sir, I don't know much about warbling, but it don't sound like warbling to me!' The House was not allowed to meet until this problem was resolved. Some effort was made to force Members into an air-raid shelter below the ground. This was too much for most of us. I remember going out on the terrace that fine Sunday morning with a number of my friends. One of the balloons was launched, apparently from County Hall, the L.C.C. building on the south bank of the river. This was greeted with cheers and the balloon immediately christened 'Herbert Morrison'. The warning, however, was soon found to be a mistake and we trooped back into the Chamber to hear the Prime Minister's formal announcement.

It was a sad speech. 'Everything that I have worked for,' he said, 'everything that I have hoped for, everything that I have believed in during my public life, has crashed in ruins.' He ended by these words: 'I cannot tell what part I may be allowed to play myself; I trust I may live to see the day when Hitlerism has been destroyed and a liberated Europe has been re-established.'

Alas, poor Chamberlain. He was to live only another year.

Hitlerism has been destroyed. But a liberated Europe has not been re-established. Vast forces once set loose cannot easily again be 'cabined, cribbed, confined'. Impoverished, partitioned, her relative power, moral and material, in the world gravely reduced, Europe has nevertheless emerged from her ordeal and faces the future with hope. But the winds of change were first to blow at gale force.

Appendixes

SUMMARY OF
The Price of Peace
(*Published 1938*)

The present Prime Minister, Mr. Neville Chamberlain, in his election address in 1935, stated:

'The preservation of the League is the keystone of our policy because the first object of that policy is the establishment of settled peace and the League alone can give us peace by the collective action of its members. We have, therefore, made it clear that, while we shall take no action apart from others, we intend to fulfil our obligations under the Covenant in common with our fellow-members. Only in this way can we make it plain to would-be aggressors that it does not pay to attack another nation in violation of engagements solemnly undertaken.'

Since then the Italians have conquered Abyssinia. Japan has invaded China. Germany has denounced the Locarno Treaty and reoccupied the demilitarised area of the Rhineland (March 1936), annexed Austria (March 1938), and, as a result of the threat of invasion, taken over a large part of the territory of Czechoslovakia (September 1938). It is beyond question also that, throughout the last two years, and in defiance of the non-intervention agreement, the Italians and Germans have supplied men, armaments, bombing planes, and other war material to the forces of General Franco in Spain.

The League of Nations has failed to prevent these violations of treaties and of international law. Its power and authority have been weakened by the withdrawal from membership of a number of countries.

On 28 May 1937 Mr. Chamberlain became Prime Minister. On 21 February 1938 Mr. Anthony Eden resigned his position as Foreign Secretary, owing to differences of opinion with Mr. Chamberlain regarding the course of British foreign policy, and Lord Cranborne resigned from his position of Under-Secretary for Foreign Affairs. Since then responsibility for the direction of foreign policy has rested mainly in the hands of Mr. Chamberlain. Following upon the announcement of the Munich agreement, we had the resignation of Mr. Duff Cooper from the Cabinet and a Parliamentary situation in which twenty Government supporters abstained from voting in favour of a motion approving the actions of the Government.

It is against this background of political history that the events of the recent crisis have to be considered. The differences of opinion concern not isolated incidents but the whole course and conception of foreign policy.

The Czechoslovak problem was not local; it was a matter of profound significance to the peace of the world and to the security of the British Empire. Arguments have been put forward in this country in defence of the British Government's handling of the situation which rest upon the assumption that what we were faced with was the rectification of an ordinary minorities problem. Critics of the Government's foreign policy have all along been pointing out that this was a complete misconception. If it had been a minorities problem, then it would have been solved on 5 September when the Czechoslovak Government produced a plan which in the opinion of Lord Runciman (the special mediator) embodied almost all the demands laid down by the Sudeten Germans. The fact that this solution was not accepted—was never even discussed—proved that it was not a minorities problem, but that the grievances of the Sudeten Germans were merely being used by the German Government as an excuse for territorial conquest and the achievement of economic and military objectives which would make them masters of Europe. These objectives have in fact been achieved.

Mr. Chamberlain and the Government agree that the new accession of economic and military strength to Germany makes it necessary for us to build up our armed forces and our defence organisation more rapidly and to greater strength than ever before contemplated. The threat against which we are arming can only be envisaged as coming from Germany and the Powers associated with her, and it is this potential enemy of Britain that has been enormously strengthened by the terms of the 'Peace'. What we have achieved is not peace but an armed truce for a temporary period with a prospect of war under conditions less favourable to us in the future.

We have two things to defend—the intangible things like peace, freedom, democracy, and cultural opportunity; and our economic position, without which the large population of these small islands could not be maintained. We shall be forced by economic necessity, if from no higher motive, to fight for our rightful place in the world, should it ever be menaced.

The Economic Consequences of the Peace

(a) For Czechoslovakia

The new boundaries of Czechoslovakia have been drawn without any reference whatsoever to economic considerations. The Munich agreement represents a complete capitulation to the racial principles of Nazi philosophy.

'The new line inflicts grievous injury upon the industrial scheme of the Czechoslovak State as originally constituted.'[1]

The balance of economic activity in Czechoslovakia was steadily poised between industrial production and food and forestry production. According to the 1930 census the employed population was almost evenly divided as follows:

Number engaged in Agriculture, Fishery, and Forestry 5,101,937
Number engaged in Industry 5,146,937

It would take up too much space to go into all the details of the economic difficulties that have been created for Czechoslovakia, but an impression of the drastic and ruinous unbalancing of the Czech economy is conveyed by the following estimate formulated in the *Economist* of 8 October:

'Many of her best industries will be lost to Germany and Poland. The extent of these losses can be estimated from the following figures, which are based on the official Census of 1930:

	Workers in German and Polish Areas	Proportion of Total (per cent)
Mines, etc.	58,240	48·1
Glass	39,226	61·8
Metals	93,783	24·0
Chemicals	14,373	34·6
Textiles	190,660	52·1
Paper	17,273	41·8
Woodwork	43,058	23·4
Musical instruments	5,992	79·0
Toys	1,911	68·1
Foodstuffs	62,103	25·4
Clothes and shoes	70,943	24·2
Other industries	164,959	27·6
Total Industry	762,521	33·3

The figures show the number of workers in these districts in the different industries and the proportion they bore to the total for the whole Republic. It must be emphasised that the districts to be ceded are almost certainly larger than those here included, and the proportions are therefore minima.

'These are appalling losses to a country that is largely dependent upon its industry.'

[1] *The Times*, leading article, 14 October 1938.

The transfer of territory tears away a large proportion of the industrial population and the industries in which they worked. The economic relations between the central agricultural plains of Bohemia and Moravia and the industrial districts will not be able to be maintained. Apart even from the fact that the exchange of goods would now have to surmount the new national frontier, there is the fact that the State-controlled economy of Germany will almost certainly distort the orientation of trade.

The frontier cuts through economic zones which were in the closest association. The lignite area of north Bohemia not only formed a raw-material basis for the industry located there, but supplied coal to the industrial regions east of Prague.

Semi-finished goods produced in the transferred areas were formerly finished by the industries in the interior. These economic lifelines are cut.

Electric power supplied to Prague came from the transferred areas; the industries of the interior must now be adapted to the fuel still remaining in the country, and this will have to be transported considerable distances, with the consequent increase in costs and prices, which may have incalculable effects upon the nation's foreign trade.

The heavy chemical industry which was built up on a lignite basis in the transferred areas will have to be built up afresh elsewhere if the light chemical industry of the interior is to continue in existence.

The printing and allied industries, including newspaper production, obtained their paper from works built up on the basis of the forests on the old Czech–German frontiers. All the industries exploiting timber must either move to the east or incur heavy transport charges.

In what remains of the textile industry the contact between weaving mills, spinning mills, and finishing works is broken by the new frontier.

The artificial-silk industry is partly cut off from its raw-material base (cellulose); what is left of it in the east of Czechoslovakia is not adequately equipped and will have to be fundamentally redeveloped.

As a result of this economic disruption, the new Czechoslovakia will be unable to survive as an independent State, unless substantial aid for capital reconstruction is forthcoming from Britain and France. In the absence of foreign aid, Czechoslovakia will become an economic and political vassal of the greater Germany.

(b) For Germany

What Czechoslovakia loses in raw-material resources and in industrial plant and equipment, Germany gains. The ceded areas are rich in mineral and other economic resources of immense value for war preparation. This is important.

But she also gets a new population of the most highly skilled workmen in Europe. The view has been blandly expressed that all Germany will gain is a 'depressed area'. It is quite true that under the 'free' economy of Czechoslovakia there was a high percentage of unemployment in the areas now ceded to Germany. But there will be no unemployment in the *controlled* economy into which the new population is now recruited. Germany's rigid control over all the factors in production—wages, hours of labour, the direction of investment —has been made possible by totalitarian methods which have involved drastic curtailment of the liberty of the subject.

The whole German economy has been, and is now, operated with a view to the maximum activity in war preparations—both military and economic. The new resources of the Sudetenland will be drawn into that system and the power of Germany correspondingly increased.

The Danubian States. Prior to the Czechoslovak crisis, Germany was already exercising great economic influence upon the Danubian countries. She occupied the leading place in regard to both the export and the import trades of Czechoslovakia, Bulgaria, Hungary, Roumania, and Yugoslavia. The extension of her frontiers over the natural barrier of the Sudeten Mountains and her acquisition of the predominantly industrial area of the former Czechoslovakia will increase her economic and political influence over the Danubian States still further. The vast resources of cereals, timber, and petroleum of these countries will now be placed increasingly at her disposal. In this way her power as a potential aggressor in the future is again increased. It is worth remembering also in this connection that the blockade was the determining factor in the last war. Access to the resources of the Danubian States makes Germany immune from the pressure of British naval power.

(c) For Britain

The industries taken over by Germany include a number which produce the same kind of goods as those which Britain sells in overseas markets. Under the German system of foreign trade, which enables them to sell without regard to costs of production, it is within her power to use the new supplies of coal, textiles, china, etc. etc., to undermine British trade and inflict serious economic losses upon us. The situation that may arise would be analogous to what happened some time ago as a result of the exports of cheap Russian timber by the Russian State export organisation. In that connection we remember the complaints of Canada. Soon *we* may be in the position that the depressed areas of Britain that are dependent upon coal and textile exports will be further menaced by the competition of products coming from Sudeten industries now acquired by Germany without capital cost and without compensation to the previous owners. If Germany sees fit to wage *economic* war on us, she is enormously strengthened to do so by the new industrial areas which she now controls.

The Political Consequences of the Peace

Czechoslovakia relied for her protection upon her treaty with France and Russia and upon the obligation undertaken by the League of Nations to protect the frontiers of member States against unprovoked aggression. It is no exaggeration to say that she has been regarded as a test case by all the other small Powers in Europe. She was encouraged to rely upon the big Powers for support and framed her foreign policy, as well as her internal affairs, upon that basis. Her desertion by the big Powers at the moment of crisis will be a signal to other Powers not to rely upon similar undertakings. The League system will be further disintegrated. It is not unlikely, also, that Russia, after having been studiously ignored in the negotiations about Czechoslovakia, will be disinclined to take any further interest in the Franco-Soviet pact. France will no longer be able to rely upon her treaty system with the States of Eastern Europe. She will find herself virtually isolated on the Continent, and her weakness will represent a constant invitation to the political domination of Germany, which will grow in might as the possible combination against her disintegrates.

*   *   *

In his broadcast of 27 September, after his return from Godesberg, Mr. Chamberlain said:

'If I were convinced that any nation had made up its mind to dominate the world by fear of its force, I should feel that it must be resisted.'

I was convinced that this is precisely what we were faced with long before we had succumbed to Hitler's intimidation by making the Franco-British proposals of 19 September. Mr. Chamberlain was convinced only after we had given away everything that was worth fighting for.

The Franco-British plan surrendered the natural mountain barrier to German aggression in the whole Danubian basin. It surrendered the Czech frontier line of defences which had cost about £100 millions to build. (Incidentally it was built and paid for by the Czechs, on the assumption that their allies and the League Powers would support them.) The Godesberg proposals of Herr Hitler differed only in detail and in respect of the time-table for German occupation. The full brutal, aggressive intention of Germany was, however, then openly expressed.

We had given Hitler all he demanded. We prepared to fight him on the question of the date when he should get it. The invitation to the conference at

Munich was greeted with relief. In fact the Munich conference merely acted as an executive for the carrying-out, under international approval, of the Godesberg programme that had been rejected a week earlier as intolerable. And this was greeted as a victory.

It is clear that if we had made up our minds months beforehand, when we knew the crisis was developing, (*a*) that Czechoslovakia was *not* to be defended against aggression, and (*b*) that the frontiers would have to be redrawn, then Czechoslovakia would certainly have negotiated a better settlement than has now resulted from the futile display of resistance which collapsed at the last moment.

The Future and Rearmament

The first thing for us to do is to make up our minds clearly and definitely whether there is anything in the world that we shall consider to be worth fighting to defend. If there is nothing, then let us disarm, and relinquish our position to the more virile Powers, with dignity and sense.

But, if there *are* things which we will fight to defend, then let us be quite clear *what* they are: let us make them clear to our potential enemies, and build up the forces of defence and attack that will enable us to sustain our case if it comes to war. By the method of clear, frank, and unmistakable determination, we should stand a chance of avoiding war altogether. If we are hesitant and weak, nothing will save us.

Do not let us be led into any false sense of security by greater rearmament in Britain. As a result of our foreign policy, Britain has been growing weaker instead of stronger during the period of rearmament. It is now almost certain that Hungary, as well as Czechoslovakia, has fallen irrevocably into the German orbit. The probabilities are that Poland will now adjust herself to the designs of German foreign policy. If our foreign policy continues to lose us friends, then let us be clear that no amount of British and French rearmament will ever compensate for the loss of Russia's power on our side and the neutralisation of the smaller States of Europe. Unless we are prepared *now* to end the drift of British foreign policy there will be little purpose in rearmament.

This contradiction between our foreign policy and our rearmament policy must be clearly stated. Our first step in the building-up of our defence system should be to re-create, as quickly as possible, the alliance of peace-loving Powers in the League of Nations. The door should be held open to all comers, but a beginning could be made with Britain, France, and Russia, together with the remaining League members in Europe, and with the approval and support of the Empire countries and the U.S.A.

In support of such a foreign policy, any sacrifice required from our people for the building-up of our armed strength would willingly be made. But the sacrifices needed will be greater if we go about the task in a half-hearted way. If we merely increase our expenditure without having regard to the efficient utilisation of our resources, the result will be a diversion of labour from the production of useful commodities to the production of armaments. The standard of life will fall. By a full utilisation of the labour power of those now unemployed, and by the elimination of the waste that now takes place because of competitive redundancy both in production and distribution, we could increase our production of armaments and of consumer goods as well. In this connection the reconstruction proposals in my book *The Middle Way* become more than ever relevant to the needs of our time.

SUMMARY OF
Economic Aspects of Defence
(*Published 1939*)

The capital resources and the manpower of the totalitarian States are already mobilised on a war footing. In modern conditions the strength of a nation is determined not only by the number of its soldiers, battleships, etc., but also by the degree of efficiency with which its economic resources can be organised in productive effort. Military power is a product of economic power. If our own defence is to be adequate and indomitable, the highest degree of economic efficiency is vital. We are challenged to prove that democracy has the will and the vigour to produce the results upon which its very existence now depends.

The economic power of a nation cannot be created overnight. The building-up of economic power for war purposes is therefore spread over a period when the nations are at peace with one another. The war starts on the economic front, and this preliminary war can be carried to even greater lengths today, for a nation may make other nations its enforced allies, by achieving first economic subjection and then, as a result of its economic stranglehold, political domination.

There are four main aspects of defence preparations which relate to economic organisation and, in the circumstances of our time, must be considered. They are:
(1) Overseas trade, and our general economic relations with other countries.
(2) The productive efficiency of our economic system as a whole.
(3) The accumulation of supplies of storable food-stuffs and raw material.
(4) The technical questions regarding the kind of war material to be produced, the location of the factories producing it, and the organisation of reserve productive capacity.

Germany Prepares

Germany is the nation most actively engaged in war preparations. By using her activities and achievements for purposes of comparison we may be able to estimate what *can* be done, and what *needs* to be done in Britain.

Germany's political policy does not arise out of her economic needs. On the contrary, the laws of the National Socialist State govern the economic order. The whole productive system is subordinated to the military ambitions and the power aspirations of her leaders. State-Secretary Rudolf Brinkmann of the German Ministry of Economics has admitted that

> 'the freedom of disposition of the entrepreneur in the sphere of commodity purchase is chained down by the system of supervisory boards and other regulations;
> 'the utilisation of labour is subject to various restrictions;
> 'the wage ceiling and prohibitions of price increases force a price level which in a liberal economy would be impossible;
> 'money intended for consumption is forcibly shifted to capital investment, and the entrepreneur sees himself forced under State interference to make capital investments which he would never have made if he been left to his own doing;
> 'money capital is enfeebled by the Law for the Compulsory Investment of Surplus Dividends and is forced, by the prohibition of private issues on the capital market, to offer itself at a cheap rate for purposes in which it is but little interested.'[1]

When the Nazi Party came to power in Germany there were 5 million unemployed. By March 1938 there were only half a million unemployed. The index of production which, taking 1929 as 100, had fallen to 69·2 in 1933, had risen by January 1939 to 146·0. The national income rose from 45·2 milliard RM. in 1932 to 76 milliard RM. in 1938. In 1937–8 about two-thirds of the German national income flowed through the hands of, and was redistributed by, the State.

The comprehensive planning of national production depends, of course, upon a complete control over foreign trade. The methods Germany employs are designed not for a normal competitive expansion of her sales but in order to achieve an economic stranglehold over certain countries with a view to their political as well as economic subjugation. In the process the British economic structure is weakened through our loss of foreign trade. By the use of export subsidies, by the offer of high prices for imports coupled with blocked marks which have to be expended upon such German goods as Germany dictates, Germany has very greatly increased her share of Balkan trade. A full development of the resources of south-east Europe would enable these countries to supply *all* Germany's requirements in cereals, timber, oil, tobacco, copper ore, skins and leather, livestock, meat, and fats, and a considerable proportion of her requirements in cotton and wool. Germany's economic aggression in other

[1] *Weekly Report of the German Institute for Business Research*, 2 November 1938.

areas has not been so successful, but her percentage share of some South American markets has increased. The dangers involved to the economic stability (and consequently the defensive strength) of this country are alarming.

The stranglehold that Germany is thus acquiring is at the expense of her own people, because it means raising the cost of living to her own people and, in fact, exporting goods at less than cost price.

The efforts made, however, have already been rewarded. No nation has ever gained more—in territory, in population, in prestige, and in economic and political influence—without resort to war. In 1935 the Saar was returned to Germany; in 1936 the Rhineland was reoccupied. In 1938 Austria was annexed, upon which the German Reich became the greatest of the European States (except for Soviet Russia) both in area and population. Six months later, by the annexation of the Sudetenland, Germany not only further increased both her area and her population, she also gained valuable economic assets and extended her political frontiers beyond the barrier of the mountains, greatly improving her strategic position. Dictatorship can certainly claim to have paid substantial dividends.

Britain's Task

Apart altogether from any threat of war, we must take action to defend the interests of our foreign trade. In addition, we must achieve greater strength and efficiency in our economic system generally if we are to be prepared for the possibility of war.

(1) Overseas Trade and our General Economic Relations with Other Countries

By subsidising her exports and by the manipulation of 'blocked marks', Germany ignores altogether the costs of production or the profits of trade. It is obviously impossible for the British exporter, acting invariably as a single individual or a single firm, to stand up to the competition of a State organisation which is not primarily interested in costs and prices. The Export Credits Bill, providing an additional £25 million for ordinary export credits and £10 million for extraordinary assistance where the political conditions demand it, is a welcome step. But Germany is not only subsidising her foreign trade, she is also mobilising her power as a buyer to enforce the sale of her goods. We must do the same. Nothing short of a *national* organisation of our export and import transactions will be adequate. We require a foreign-trade organisation which can either *fight* with whatever weapons others are using, or make peace on the basis of a fair division of world trade.

My proposals were published in detail in *The Middle Way*, published in May 1938. In brief, we require:

(*a*) the organisation of exporters in co-operative selling organisations;

(*b*) the organisation of importers to prevent competitive buying and to allocate the available funds for the purchase of imports in such order and quantities as correspond to the national interests;

(*c*) a single authoritative foreign-trade organisation, with representatives from the Import Duties Advisory Committee, the Exchange Equalisation Fund's experts, finance (to advise on foreign lending), and the exporters' and importers' organisations. This body would co-ordinate the different aspects of our overseas economic policy in the interests of the nation as a whole, taking strategic considerations into account.

(2) *Productive Efficiency*

Our economic and military strength depends in the last resort upon our ability to produce the maximum of goods with the minimum of men. All industrial efficiency is measured as an economy of labour. Competitive redundancy as well as unemployment is contributing to the present waste of labour in Britain.

(*a*) *Industrial reorganisation.* In almost every case in which the principles of industrial reconstruction have been embodied in proposed legislation, a narrowminded opposition has forced the measure to be withdrawn. Industry should be given the opportunity, under an Industrial Reorganisation (Enabling) Bill, to put its own house in order, and if it fails to do so, the Government should have the courage to step in and sweep aside every obstacle to the realisation of the plans essential for national defence and economic security.

(*b*) *The unemployed.* Under a national plan of defence preparations, either we should make use of all the available labour and, by increased production, maintain the standard of life, or we should leave part of our labour resources idle and, by diversion of other workers to armament production, allow the production of consumers' goods to decline and the standard of life to fall.

The easiest and most profitable way to employ idle workers is in their own industries. The most acute unemployment is in the export industries, and this could be mitigated by the foreign-trade proposals made above. The shipbuilding industry provides an example of the issues at stake. A strong Merchant Navy is vital to national and imperial defence, yet 'in 1914 we had 41·6 of the trading tonnage of the world, today approximately 26·4.... In personnel we have 60,000 fewer men at sea than in 1914.... Twenty years ago we had 312,000 men in the [shipbuilding] industry, today 171,920.... In 1929, to go back no farther, we built 50 per cent of world tonnage—at one time it was 80 per cent; today it is 33 per cent.'[1]

[1] Sir Charles M. Barrie, M.P., letter to *The Times,* 14 December 1938.

The facts quoted show the urgent need for a co-ordination of policy so that the question of assistance to British shipping and shipbuilding should be estimated in relation both to the amount of money we are now spending on the maintenance of unemployed workers in these trades, and to the vital needs of our defence policy.

(c) *Expansion*. A National Economic Council should be set up without delay to organise the direction of economic development including the direction of capital investment and labour resources. The whole cost of rearmament could easily be borne out of the increased activity that would result from an intelligent use of our idle, under-employed, and wrongly employed people.

(3) *Accumulation of Essential Commodities*

In war, as Mr. Keynes commented in speaking to the Economics Section of the British Association in August 1938, reserves of essential commodities would be 'better than a gold-mine'. He advocated the accumulation of £500 millions of essential commodities. The Government should offer storage in this country, free or at a nominal charge, to all Empire producers who had a surplus of specified raw materials. The Government would not become the owners, and owners would be free to dispose of the goods as and when they wished, but if international prospects appeared particularly threatening the Government could purchase the goods outright. The scheme would also be a means of preventing fluctuations in commodity prices. Home-produced pig-iron could also be stored, both for munitions and for smoothing out the trade-cycle. The cost would be about £20 million a year.

(4) *Technical Questions*

There is an urgent need for the creation of a Ministry of Supply. 'If we are to make arms on the requisite scale . . . priorities will have to be established. If they can be established voluntarily, a single Ministry can accomplish the task better than four; if they require compulsion, it will have to be forthcoming from a Ministry of Supply or elsewhere. . . . [There is also] the task of organising mass production, [which requires] a different kind of Ministry from those that are effective in peace-time.'[1]

Another reason for the establishment of such a Ministry is that some clear policy should be formulated with regard to the profits of the armament industries. Manufacturers who are asked to instal new plant, if left in uncertainty as to the extent to which the new plant will be utilised, are bound to seek recovery of their investment in the shortest possible time. But the question cannot be simplified to one of State ownership, since a wide range of concerns should be

[1] *Economist*, 5 November 1938.

so equipped as to enable them to switch over to armaments production if necessary.

A satisfactory policy would provide for a variety of methods, including State factories; the erection of State-owned plant in privately owned factories, in which case no question of the rate of depreciation would arise; and privately owned plant in factories normally concerned with peace-time production, in which case a Ministry of Supply should be able to arrange prices in relation to some guarantee of the orders to be placed.

Everyone who is not blinded by dangerous optimism realises that sooner or later a Ministry of Supply will have to be set up. Both patriotism and ordinary prudence demand that it should be done now.

Freedom

There are many who fear that freedom and democracy may be imperilled by the very measures initiated to defend them. The safeguard lies in the purpose and direction of our foreign policy. If we ally ourselves with the forces of freedom, progress, and enlightenment, the risk is not great. But if we are guided only by a desire to defend our material possessions, our defensive organisation might degenerate into tyranny.

Apart altogether from the urgency of our present special needs, economic reconstruction is essential to the liberation of the great mass of our people from the enslavement of poverty and economic insecurity. The freedom and liberty of the people cannot be safeguarded except upon the basis of a full exploitation of our resources.

Nationalism or Internationalism

We have been attempting for twenty years to achieve world peace through *political* agreement in the League of Nations. The League failed because political agreement cannot be based upon economic antagonism.

No amount of political and territorial 'appeasement' offered to the totalitarian States will provide either a solution of their own problems or a basis for world peace in the future. By weak concession we shall achieve nothing but our own destruction. By a determined resistance we could preserve for a time the economic integrity and cultural values of the democratic States, but we should have to continue to bear the strain of military preparedness.

While we prepare our resistance, we should at the same time be formulating a policy of international economic co-operation. Previous attempts to do so have failed because there was no organisational mechanism through which economic co-operation could be made practicable, and it was not within the power of Governments to direct international economic affairs. But we are now approaching a stage when the foreign trade, foreign lending, credit arrangements, and maintenance of merchant shipping will be organised in each country under a central control. It is true that these changes are being brought about under the compelling necessities of national or imperial policy. But once each country has thus overcome the conflict of interests among its own nationals, the way is prepared for international co-operation, as an alternative to the economic conflict between nations which will lead to war. If the principle of economic collaboration could once be established, and an international organisation of experts set up for constant supervision and review of current problems, the feet of the nations would be set upon the road which alone can lead to peace and prosperity.

We shall be forced sooner or later to create a national foreign-trade organisation, and build behind it an economic organisation conducted on rational lines for the full utilisation of our capital and labour resources. In doing so, we should be putting ourselves in a position to pursue a real policy of 'appeasement' by seeking to evolve a method of economic collaboration which would root out the causes of war.

Index